Contributions to Phenomenology

In Cooperation with The Center
for Advanced Research in Phenomenology

Volume 103

Scope

The purpose of the series is to serve as a vehicle for the pursuit of phenomenological research across a broad spectrum, including cross-over developments with other fields of inquiry such as the social sciences and cognitive science. Since its establishment in 1987, *Contributions to Phenomenology* has published more than 100 titles on diverse themes of phenomenological philosophy. In addition to welcoming monographs and collections of papers in established areas of scholarship, the series encourages original work in phenomenology. The breadth and depth of the Series reflects the rich and varied significance of phenomenological thinking for seminal questions of human inquiry as well as the increasingly international reach of phenomenological research.

All books to be published in this Series will be fully peer-reviewed before final acceptance.

The series is published in cooperation with The Center for Advanced Research in Phenomenology.

More information about this series at http://www.springer.com/series/5811

Olga Louchakova-Schwartz

Editor

The Problem of Religious Experience

Case Studies in Phenomenology,
with Reflections and Commentaries

Volume I and Volume II

 Springer

Editor
Olga Louchakova-Schwartz

Jesuit School of Theology of Santa Clara University
Graduate Theological Union
Berkeley, CA, USA

University of California
Davis, CA, USA

ISSN 0923-9545   ISSN 2215-1915   (electronic)
Contributions to Phenomenology
ISBN 978-3-030-21574-3   ISBN 978-3-030-21575-0   (eBook)
https://doi.org/10.1007/978-3-030-21575-0

This Springer imprint is published by the registered company Springer Nature Switzerland AG.
The registered company address is: Gewerbestrasse 11, 6330 Cham, Switzerland

In loving memory of Barbro Giorgi and Anna-Teresa Tymieniecka

Foreword

It is a great pleasure and honor to present these two volumes dedicated to a phenomenological analysis of religious experience. I write this foreword for three reasons. First, the theme is important for our times. Second, the contributions of the volume are remarkable. Finally, Olga Louchakova-Schwartz's original philosophical insight, along with the articulation of its development, offers much to the phenomenology of religion.

Turning briefly to the theme of this work's value for our contemporary society, I would like to focus on the meaning of Christianity for Western culture, which drew inspiration from Greco-Roman culture and the message of the Gospels that originated in the Middle East. The factors contributing to the formation of our culture are essentially linked to the encounter of Greco-Roman traditions with Jewish-Christian ones, which drew deeply from religion. The religious dimension of Western culture was more deeply affected by Christianity than by Judaism: Christianity helped develop a theoretical framework in which the value of the human person was affirmed, without discrimination based on age or background. This framework has helped shape human rights discourses while fostering an openness to other cultures.

Today, it could be said that the very admissibility of the Western religious dimension described above, independent of its expression in different historical religions, lies in peril. Modernity has distanced itself from, negated, or even ignored religious experience. It has even tried to show religious experience as being inconsistent or incoherent. The human being may be able to live without the divine, but what then becomes of the quality of his or her life? If up until now we have been able to recognize the validity of a common humanity that lies at the core of the message of the Gospel, does not the elimination of the possibility of a religious dimension push us toward barbarism? Barbarism, here, may be understood in two senses: First, it may be grasped in terms of what is foreign, even though non-Western cultures have their own rich ideas of the divine. Second, it may refer to the human being who views himself or herself as so self-determining so as to be able to describe himself or herself as no longer "human," as post-human.

The refined atheism and practical indifference that inundate the West, starting with Europe, are the signs of this new barbarism. It is not easy to change the present situation, but reflecting on the sense or meaning of religious experience is not without merit, and some would say that it is urgent. Hence, the studies contained in these volumes are not only theoretically valuable but also functionally practical. One volume of this work may be viewed as social, while the other may be seen as cultural. Indeed, the contributors of each volume address each of these specific themes.

I would like to turn to my initial claim about the content of the contributions in this work. I cannot speak of each article, but I do wish to address certain key themes, especially those that move from a more sociological discussion of religious experience to a theoretical one. We begin with subjectivity, for it is a uniquely human experience. We have to ask: What is it and what are its specific qualities or characteristics? To answer this question, we begin by looking at interiority because it is something all humans share but also because it is the locus of the presence and/or absence of the divine.

In order to explore human subjectivity, we need to undertake a preliminary anthropological investigation. We have to ask: Who is the human being that lives this experience of interiority, of subjectivity? Of all the received interpretations of note that we find in Western philosophy, Edmund Husserl's phenomenological understanding of the question is the most relevant, not because he is the only philosopher to undertake such a study—we find such investigations throughout the history of Western philosophy—but because the kind of probing he carries out, which he calls "archeological," uncovers certain aspects that are largely understudied, aspects that help us grasp interiority itself.

Husserl's novel discovery consisted in showing the philosophical meaning and relevance of lived experiences (*Erlebnisse*). Not only are they unique, but they also have a universal structure that is present in every human being. Through this structure, it becomes possible to seize the constitution of the human being, which possesses three distinct but related aspects: lived body, psyche, and spirit. The lived body experiences itself in space and as a living being, whereas the psyche is understood as the seat of self-perception, instinctive reactions, and affectivity. The spirit is the seat of spontaneous, free acts of an intellectual and voluntary character. The realm of spirit is the most characteristic of human beings, because it distinguishes them from other animals. The current or flow of lived experience, Husserl maintains, permits us to know things about ourselves as well as things that lie outside us, especially through our reflective, intellectual capacities, which lie at the base of our cultural productions. These experiences may be lived passively or actively: the sphere of passivity is characterized by operations that precede our consciousness of them. The hyletic sphere is understood as psychophysical, but it may also contain traces of intellectual, noetic, or voluntary processes, which, in turn, form part of our ethical choices.

The fruits of Husserl's investigations provide us with tools that can assist us in laying the groundwork for an understanding of religious experience. In my own work, I explain various ways in which Husserl's own analyses may help us understand God. I would like to reflect briefly on two aspects that may be useful for understanding Part I of Volume I, entitled "Experience and Subjectivity." The contributors do not explicitly focus on Husserl, but they make use of an argument already taken up by him. For example, Olga Louchakova-Schwartz, in her "Concluding Reflections," makes reference to the passive and active structures that characterize human understanding.

Among the different Husserlian pathways to understanding God, the discussion of subjectivity taken up in a note to Section 51 of *Ideas Pertaining to a Pure Phenomenology and Phenomenological Philosophy I* appears most relevant. I make reference to this discussion in my own work, *The Divine in Husserl and Other Explorations* (Ales Bello 2009). Husserl maintains that in our consciousness of the flow of lived experiences, there are infinite modes of manifestation that lead the subject to transcend itself, to go beyond itself. He notes that some of them manifest a teleological structure, which can be theoretically justified. One form of this teleological structure manifests as an openness to the Other. In this opening or encounter with the Other, we grasp something that is present but which transcends us in our immanence (i.e., it transcends our world and other human beings). This transcendence must be understood not only as transcending our own sphere of immanence but also as a transcendence of verticality—that is, a transcendence that completely transcends us, a transcendence of all transcendences.

The aforementioned theme of investigation is astutely developed by Husserl's student Edith Stein, who discusses the presence in us of a personal core (*Kern*) which is the proper seat of our own singularity as well as the locus of God's presence in us. Husserl speaks of the extraordinary unifying Power of a teleological principle announced in consciousness that is not identical with consciousness itself: it is revealed by consciousness. Stein analyzes this teleological principle in her work *Finite and Eternal Being* (2002a). For both phenomenologists, God is framed within the dynamic of presence and absence, for the divine cannot be contained in the human; rather, it can only be announced in the human. This announcement of God in us is necessary: otherwise, how could an imperfect, finite, and limited human being discuss a perfect, infinite, and unlimited divine being?

The dynamic of presence and absence permeates the structure of the human being. Lived passively and then progressively seized at the psychophysical level of the lived body, the dynamic is accepted by the awareness of the intellect, which affirms its existence. Presence is lived and expressed through the hyletic dimension of the human being—for example, in extraordinary sense experiences, as found in exceptional things, one thinks here of the sacraments of Christianity. Presence of the divine also occurs at the intellectual level in which one grasps the greatness of a Power. One can examine such an experience of Power. Here, we are dealing with a nonexplicit but remote base of possibility for metaphysical research. This metaphysical Power may not be seen, and we can even wish not to see it by psychologically refusing it or by taking on certain intellectual positions. We find ourselves confronting, then, both practical and theoretical atheism, for the human being is free to accept or reject the presence.

The subjective pathway to the divine suggested by Husserl can aid us in grasping the correlation between the divine presence in us and its necessary transcendence, for we bear a trace of it in us, though it opens onto something other. And even though one does not find in Husserl an analysis of the divine Other, as we find in Edith Stein's *Finite and Eternal Being*, or an openness to the stranger taken up in Gerardus van der Leeuw's *Phänomenologie der Religion*(1956), the presence of a teleology, according to Husserl, leads us to a Supreme Monad, which may be viewed as God and as being transcendent, but in a way that is different from the traditional transcendence of the world for the subject taken up by phenomenology.

If religious experience is marked by an openness of interiority, which already bears the trace of the divine, to the transcendence of the Other that fills him or her, then the Other (who is understood as Power, according to the fine definition of van der Leeuw) can fill this interiority in a special way by finding further ways to manifest itself. Revelation is another way in which the divine can manifest itself: revelation does not begin with the subject; rather, the subject awaits a new understanding of God that stems directly from the divine. The theme of revelation is taken up in the second volume, Part III, "The Phenomenology of Revelation."

If the divine being remains unknowable in its essence, this shows the deep sense of the mystery of God: the divine, upon whom humans depend, can also speak of itself only as a trace in the human, but the divine can fill the trace with further content. Almost all religions describe God as a revelation of the powerful One who is encountered on life's path, as van der Leeuw observes. The divine not only is present in the deep structure of the human being, as the history of religions testifies, but it can reveal itself in other ways and this is what humans desire, for they wish greater understanding of God.

The second, and last, part of the second volume is dedicated to an exploration of the psychology of religious experience. This part, "Theistic Approaches to the Psychological Horizons of Religious Experiencing," advances an important argument because, as we noted earlier, the psychic dimension of the human being is central for understanding the behavior of a person. Edith Stein observes that in the psyche, various phenomena occur that cannot be provoked or caused: they "happen" to us. What lies in our power of control is the spiritual aspect of acts intertwined with the psyche. The psyche has its own force, which is an indispensable, vital force for humans. We noted earlier how religious experience is strongly connected to the various manifestations of the subject. From the standpoint of interiority, religious experience first encounters the psyche. And in this encounter, religious experience can be accepted or rejected. Yet, when we examine the experience of individuals, we often note that there is a deep connection between the psyche and religious experience: hence the need for a psychology of religion. This field of inquiry studies the psychic reactions that often accompany religious experience, including the psychopathology of religious phenomena that manifests sometimes in mental illness.

The contributions of the second volume that focus on psychology do not explicitly take up the psychology or psychopathology of religion, but they do indicate some constituent psychological aspects that accompany religious experience, like the repentance that leads to a rejuvenation of one's life. We must be careful not to reduce religious experience to the psyche, for though the psyche is an important aspect of our humanity, it is not the only one. We must also recognize the presence of spiritual acts. The second part of the second volume also analyzes mystical experience, which possesses various psychic elements, though, as a phenomenon, it is in no way reducible to the psyche. In phenomenological terms, mystical experience may be understood as the excess presence of the divine that overcomes the everyday presence that is part of the structure of all human beings, for those who have mystical experiences report an experience of being transported into another dimension in which the divine presence fully reveals itself, and this is why the experiencer describes living in profound unity with everything or the all. The elevation to the divine is not caused by the subject; rather, it is lived as a gift, because in mystical experience new, unknown pathways open up for the person. Saint Teresa of Avila, for example, used to say that in God, one saw everything, and her experience of God allowed her to transcend human limits.

Mystical experience traverses all religions, and this is a remarkable, extraordinary fact. It is described in this way by persons of different cultures and religions, all of whom experience an extraordinary union with the Power—a union, however, that has temporal, human limits. The phenomenological analysis of interior experience permits one to comprehend this phenomenon, as Edith Stein (2002b) demonstrates in her analysis of Carmelite spirituality in *TheScience of the Cross*. Gerda Walther (1960) also makes the same point in her *Phänomenologie der Mystik (1960):* she moves from an investigation of paranormal phenomena to mystical experiences. Both phenomenologists grasp in an amazing fashion what happens in human interiority and what manifests externally based on such interior experiences at the level of the body, especially in the phenomenon of ecstasy.

The four principal themes of the two volumes allow for an exploration of key aspects of religious experience and its relevance to human beings. We also see that this understanding of religious experience is important for interreligious and intercultural dialogue. Human cultures are deeply marked by religion, even though we may not wish to admit this historical fact. Even cultures that seem to have distanced themselves from religion have adopted more earthly positions that are, nonetheless, absolutized: for example, those that see nature, history, or progress as foundational. They all show, in their own ways, that humans still are grounded in, and depend on some form of, the Absolute. The image of the worshipping of the golden calf in the Old Testament is emblematic here of the fact that one cannot dismiss the divine, even though it may be in the form of an idol.

I would like to turn to the third point that I mentioned at the beginning of this foreword, which focuses on the work of Olga Louchakova-Schwartz in preparing these volumes. She is not only their editor, but her work must be read as a continuing dialogue between her own ideas and those of the contributors. The introduction and her comments found at the end of each of the parts clearly indicate that she has put forward various important arguments for her interlocutors. She has listened to their voices, responding to them with great acuity. These two volumes not only form a scholarly position, they also develop a large, clear, and directed project that finds its continued development in those who have agreed to contribute to it.

Finally, I would like to say a few words on the theoretical perspective that frames the investigations undertaken in the volumes. We clearly see the importance of phenomenology for the contributions, even though some of the contributing scholars are critical of Husserl, the founder of the phenomenological movement. Yet, though critical and oriented toward other methods, these scholars still use Husserl as a foil in interesting and fruitful ways. It is in this sense, then, that I discuss Husserl as a central orientating theoretical position.

I sincerely hope that his work will serve to draw attention to a human phenomenon that one cannot simply ignore and that always and certainly merits new study.

Pontificia Università Lateranense   Angela Ales Bello
and the Centro Italiano di Ricerche   alesbello@pul.it
Fenomenologiche
Rome, Italy
4/21/2018

References

Ales Bello, Angela. 2009. *The divine in Husserl and other explorations.* Analecta Husserliana 98. Dordrecht: Springer.

Stein, Edith. 2002a. *Finite and eternal being: An attempt at an ascent to the meaning of being.* Trans. Kurt Reinhardt. Washington, DC: ICS Publications.

———. 2002b. *The science of the cross.* Trans. O.C.D. Josephine Koeppel. Washington, DC: ICS Publications.

van der Leeuw, G. 1956. *Phänomenologie der Religion.* Tübingen: Mohr Siebeck.

Walther, G. 1960. *Phänomenologie der Mystik.* Freiburg i.Br.: Walter Verlag.

Acknowledgments

I want to thank all the authors for their enthusiasm and generosity in sharing their innovative findings and collaborating in discussions of the material in this book. My special appreciation to Michael Barber for directing the manuscript to the right publisher and to Angela Ales Bello, for her openness, knowledge, time, energy, and interest in the project. I am very grateful to Espen Dahl, Peter Costello, Martin Nitsche, and Carla Canullo in philosophy, and to Alison Benders in theology, for making themselves available to discuss some of the critical concepts in the book, and to Dan Zahavi for subtle yet precise clarifications on seminal phenomenological ideas. Adrian Răzvan Şandru, Brent Slife, and Rich Duus helped with informal reviews and feedback on the sections of the book that I myself wrote. Jana Trajtelová, Courtenay Crouch, and Vincent Pastro made themselves available for discussions in the early stages of the project. Many thanks to Kristina de Santos and Anita Rachmat, the editors at Springer, for their patience with the delays that arose in shaping a book with so many contributors, and to Paul Psoinos for his expert help with preparation of the manuscript for publication.

The Jesuit School of Theology allocated grant money and supported the webinar for the Society for the Phenomenology of Religious Experience. Together with the Patriarch Athenagoras Orthodox Institute in Berkeley (specifically, His Eminence Metropolitan Nikitas) and the Graduate Theological Union, they hosted two conferences of the Society for the Phenomenology of Religious Experience that played an important role in making this book happen. I appreciated the opportunity to share intense monthly philosophical discussions of Husserl's *Cartesian Meditations* with the members of the webinar at the Society for the Phenomenology of Religious Experience, which nourished my work on this project.

Finally, my deepest gratitude for the love, unwavering support, and wisdom of my husband, Professor Martin Schwartz, who, despite (or perhaps due to) his distaste for syntactic imperfections and insistence that he does not like abstract concepts, suggested important clarifications for the titles in the two volumes. He also helped with the English translation of Carla Canullo's paper, and edited several sections of the meta-analytic narrative. Thanks to him, too, for giving me a hand amid his own impending deadlines, and for being in my life.

As one can see, this book is a result of the effort of the many. However, whatever flaws the reader finds with it are strictly mine.

Olga Louchakova-Schwartz
Editor and Contributing Author

Contents

About the Editor

Olga Louchakova-Schwartz, M.D. Ph.D. (the editor) is a comparative religionist, philosopher, and interdisciplinary researcher. She holds the titles Professor of Philosophy of Religion, Spirituality, and Human Development at the Hult International Business School, and Clinical Professor at the UC Davis School of Medicine, Department of Public Health Sciences. She is also a Visiting Scholar at the Graduate Theological Union in Berkeley, Adjunct Lecturer in Spirituality and Phenomenology of Religion at the Jesuit School of Theology, and a Founding President of the Society for the Phenomenology of Religions Experience. Prior to her work in philosophy, she was a senior scientist at the Pavlov Institute of the Academy of Sciences in Russia, and after that, Director of Research and the Founding Director of the Neurophenomenology Center at the former Institute of Transpersonal Psychology, from which she holds the title Professor Emerita of Psychology and Comparative Religion. She studied phenomenology with Amedeo and Barbro Giorgi and with Anna-Teresa Tymieniecka, Her chief research interests are in religious subjectivity and religious experience in contemporary and historical contexts. She has published on fifteenth century and contemporary Kundalini Tantra, eighth century Advaita Vedanta and Neo-Vedanta, early Christianity, seventh–tenth century Hesychasm, contemporary Turkish and American Sufism, the Soviet spiritual underground, and the Islamic Philosophy of Illumination. Her cognitive phenomenological research of Tibetan Tantric meditation was featured on BBC, Science Daily, and other important forums. She has published more than 200 papers and book chapters, and is an Associate Editor of the Journal of Theoretical and Philosophical Psychology, and guest editor for Open Theology, De Gruyter (2017; 2018, 2019, 2020 to appear).

List of Contributors

Michael Barber (Yale 1985) is Professor of Philosophy at St. Louis University. He is the author of 7 books and 80 articles, often focused on the phenomenology of the social world and published in such journals as *Human Studies, Open Theology*, and *Husserl Studies,* and in anthologies published by Oxford University Press and Routledge. His book *The Participating Citizen: A Biography of Alfred Schutz* (SUNY 2004) won the Ballard Prize in Phenomenology in 2007. His most recent book, *Religion and Humor as Emancipating Provinces of Meaning*, was published by Springer Press in 2017. He has held endowed chairs at St. Louis University and Seattle University. He has edited several collections of essays and original texts of Alfred Schutz (including, with Jochen Dreher, Schutz's writings on literature published as a volume in the *Alfred Schütz Werkausgabe*), served as the president of the Interdisciplinary Coalition of North American Phenomenologists, acts as editor-and- chief of the journal *Schutzian Research,* and reviews papers and books for various journals and presses. His current interests are the work of Alfred Schutz, phenomenology's connection to religion and humor, and philosophy and race.

Bianca Bellini obtained her Ph.D. in 2018 from Vita-Salute San Raffaele University (Milan), where she graduated with a bachelor's degree focused on the link between phenomenology and self-knowledge and a master's degree focused on the link between phenomenology and literature. During her Ph.D. study, her interest in literature has led her to approach the topic of imagination, whereas her interest in individuality has led her to approach the topic of self-shaping: these interests flow together into a project that intends to argue for the role of imaginative experiences in the process of self-shaping. Her research purports to argue that fantasy is a fundamental force that nourishes self-shaping along with two other forces that constitute pivotal keystones of the same process, namely exemplariness and repentance. This research project relies on Max Scheler's stance on personal individuality and Edmund Husserl's stance on fantasy. Her participation in international conferences has enabled her to develop the main theses underlying this project, and a research period at the Husserl Archives in Leuven (2016) enabled her to improve her knowledge of Husserl's texts and manuscripts. In Leuven she met the co-tutor of her Ph.D.

thesis, Nicolas de Warren, who, along with Roberta De Monticelli as tutor, guides her through her Ph.D. thesis.

Angela Ales Bello is Professor Emerita of The History of Contemporary Philosophy at the Lateran University in Rome and past Dean of the Faculty of Philosophy. She is the president of the Italian Center of Phenomenological Researches (Rome), affiliated to the World Phenomenological Institute, Hanover, USA; president of the International Society of Phenomenology of Religion, Rome, Italy; and director of the International Research Area dedicated to Edith Stein and Contemporary Philosophy at the Lateran University. She is Visiting Professor in the Faculty of Psychology of the State University in São Paulo and of the Catholic University in Campinas, Brazil. Her research is directed toward German Phenomenology in relationship to other contemporary philosophical currents according to a historical and theoretical approach. Among her recent books are *The Divine in Husserl and Other Explorations* (Springer 2009, 2012), *The Sense of Things: Towards a Phenomenological Realism* (Springer 2015), and *Il senso del sacro: Dall'arcaicità alla desacralizzazione* (Castelvecchi 2014) (*The Sense of the Sacred: From Antiquity to the Contemporary Age*), *Il senso dell'umano tra fenomenologia, psicologia e psicopatologia* (Castelvecchi 2016) (*The Sense of the Human: Phenomenology, Psychology and Psychopathology*), and *Tutta colpa di Eva: Antropologia e religione dal femminismo alla gender theory* (Castelvecchi 2017) (*It Was All Eve's Fault: Anthropology and Religion from Feminism to Gender Theory*). She is the co-editor of the Italian translation of Edith Stein's works (O.C.D.–Città Nuova Publishers, Rome).

Carla Canullo teaches Philosophy of Religion and Intercultural Hermeneutics at the University of Macerata (Italy). She is a specialist in contemporary French philosophy and has published many works on Jean Nabert, Emmanuel Levinas, Jean-Luc Marion, Michel Henry, and Jean-Louis Chrétien. Among her books are *La fenomenologia rovesciata: Percorsi tentati in Jean-Luc Marion, Michel Henry, Jean-Louis Chrétien* (Rosenberg and Sellier 2004), (ed.) *Michel Henry: Narrare il pathos* (EUM 2007), *L'estasi della speranza: Ai margini del pensiero di Jean Nabert* (Cittadella 2005). Recently she has published a book on translation as a method for intercultural hermeneutics (*Il chiasmo della traduzione: Metafora e verità* [Mimesis 2017]). She is a member of the board of the Société Francophone de Philosophie de la Religion and was Visiting Professor at Université de Nice Sophia Antipolis and Visiting Scholar at Université Catholique deLouvain-la-Neuve; and she was a member of CREOR Centre for Research on Religion at McGill University.

Joshua Cockayne is a lecturer at the Logos Institute for Analytic and Exegetical Theology at the University of St Andrews. He received his Ph.D. from the University of York for work on Kierkegaard and the philosophy of Christian spirituality. He has published articles on the philosophy of religion, analytic theology, and the theology of Kierkegaard, including topics such as faith, being contemporary with Christ, the imitation of Christ, and Kierkegaard's account of prayer, as well as the communion discourses. Joshua was awarded the Religious Studies postgraduate journal from Cambridge University Press, and the prize is also supported by the British Society for Philosophy of Religion in both 2015 and 2016.

Peter Costello is Professor of Philosophy and Public and Community Service at Providence College. He is the author of *Layers in Husserl's Phenomenology,* published by University of Toronto Press, and the co-editor, with Licia Carlson, of *Phenomenology and the Arts,* published by Lexington Books. He is currently working on a second manuscript on Husserl, which explores the limit and possibility of attributing agency to things in human experience. A member of the board of the Society for Phenomenology of Religious Experience (SOPHERE), Peter also has published "The Calling of Thinking in Our Abandonment" in de Gruyter *Open Theology* and a number of other articles in the Continental philosophy of religion.

Espen Dahl is Professor of Theology at UiT – The Arctic University of Norway. Dahl's chief research interest is in the interaction between the ordinary and the extraordinary. He has explored the interaction in terms of the relation between the holy, the lifeworld and cultic experience by means of phenomenology. Aesthetically, some of the same dynamics has been found in the mimetic ties between modernist painting and everyday experience, and relative to ordinary language philosophy (Wittgenstein and Cavell), the tension between our life with words and the alienation from it has been explored. Among Dahl's many publications are *The Holy and Phenomenology. Religious Experience after Husserl* (SCM 2010); *In Between. The Holy Beyond Modern Dichotomies* (Vandenhoek and Ruprecht 2012); and *Cavell, Religion and Continental Philosophy* (Indiana University Press 2014).

Christopher Andrew DuPée is an early career independent scholar who studied philosophy at the University College Dublin and theology at the Fuller Theological Seminary in California. DuPée presented his work at the First Conference of the Society for the Phenomenology of Religious Experience, which was hold at the Patriarch Athanagoras Orthodox Institute Graduate and Graduate Theological Union in Berkeley on November 4–5, 2016. His research interests include phenomenology, Russian religious philosophy, Patristics, and the continental philosophy of language.

Patrick Laude joined the faculty of Georgetown University in 1991. He has been teaching courses in religious studies at the School of Foreign Service in Qatar since 2006. A former fellow of the *Ecole Normale Supérieure* in Paris, he earned a Master's degree in philosophy from the University of Paris IV Sorbonne, and a doctorate in French literature from Indiana University. His scholarly interests include comparative mysticism and metaphysics, poetry and mysticism, and Western representations of Asian spiritual traditions. He has authored a dozen books including: *Shimmering Mirrors: Reality and Appearance in Contemplative Metaphysics East and West*, Albany: SUNY Press, 2017, *Pathways to an Inner Islam*, Albany: SUNY Press, 2010, *Louis Massignon: The Vow and the Oath*,

London: Matheson Trust, 2011, *Pray Without Ceasing: The Way of the Invocation in World Religion*, Bloomington, Indiana: World Wisdom, 2006, *Divine Play, Sacred Laughter and Spiritual Understanding*. New York: Palgrave McMillan, 2005.

Leonardo Marcato, Ph.D, translator and researcher, has a background in Philosophy of Religion, Religious Studies, and Theoretical Philosophy. The main focus of his work is the thought of Raimon Panikkar, about which he published papers and the monography *Le radici del dialogo. Filosofia e teologia nel pensiero di Raimon Panikkar* [Mimesis, Milan-Udine 2017], and edited *Forme della negazione. Un percorso interculturale tra oriente e occidente* [Mimesis, Milan-Udine 2015]. He also studies the thought of Nishida Kitaro, Digital Philosophy, and Games Philosophy. He is currently Honorary Research Fellow at Ca' Foscari University in Venice (Italy) and member of CESTUDIR (Centre for the Study of Human Rights) at the same University.

Massimo Mezzanzanica (Milan, 1960) studied Philosophy at the State University of Milan. He received a PhD in Philosophy in 1996 in Turin. In 2013 he received a second PhD in Philosophy of Social Sciences and Symbolic Communication at the Insubria University of Varese and Como. He teaches Philosophy and History in a secondary school in Milan. He is founding member and belongs to the editorial board of the *Magazzino di Filosofia*. His research interests include hermeneutics, phenomenology, philosophy of culture, political philosophy, philosophical anthropology, theories of symbolism and of imagination, philosophical translation. Along with numerous articles in scientific journals, he has published the books: *Georg Misch. Dalla filosofia della vita alla logica ermeneutica* (FrancoAngeli, Milano 2001), *Dilthey filosofo dell'esperienza. Critica della ragione storica: vita, struttura e significatività* (FrancoAngeli, Milano 2006), *Von Dilthey zu Levinas. Wege im Zwischenbereich von Lebensphilosophie, Neukantianismus und Phänomenologie* (Verlag Traugott Bautz, Nordhausen 2012).

Sam Mickey, PhD, is an Adjunct Professor in the Theology and Religious Studies department and the Environmental Studies program at the University of San Francisco, in San Francisco, California. He has also taught at Dominican University of California, Pacifica Graduate Institute, and the California Institute of Integral Studies, and he has worked for several years at the Forum on Religion and Ecology at Yale. His work draws on existential phenomenology, comparative (crosscultural) philosophy, deconstruction, and many fields of the environmental humanities, especially religion and ecology, environmental ethics, and ecocriticism. He is the author of several books on philosophy, religion, and ecology, including *Whole Earth Thinking and Planetary Coexistence: Ecological Wisdom at the Intersection of Religion, Ecology, and Philosophy* (Routledge, 2015) and *Coexistentialism and the Unbearable Intimacy of Ecological Emergency* (Lexington, 2016). He is an editor with Sean Kelly and Adam Robbert) of *The Variety of Integral Ecologies: Nature, Culture, and Knowledge in the Planetary Era* (SUNY, 2017). He blogs regularly at BecomingIntegral.com.

Adrian Răzvan Șandru is an early career scholar and a tutor at the Eberhard-Karls University (Tübingen), writing his doctoral dissertation under supervision of Prof. Dr. Johannes Brachtendorf. He is specialized in the philosophy of Jean-Luc Marion with a focus on Marion's reading of Immanuel Kant, as well as in theological reading of Marion's own work. Adrian Răzvan Sandru's main interest is in German Idealism – especially Kant's critical thought – and in phenomenology – especially Husserlian tradition – with a special focus in interdisciplinary topics, as reflected in several of his papers and book reviews. Adrian Razvan-Șandru is a research assistant at the Forum Scientiarum (Tübingen). He is also a professional member of the Society for Phenomenology of Religious Experience as well as a CusanusWerk scholar. Before being a CusanusWerk scholar he has also received an Excellence Research Scholarship/Grant from the Babes-Balyai University (01.10.2011 – 31.07.2012 for an interdisciplinary project on Kant and inflationary cosmology) and was a Deutschlandstipendium Scholar (03.2014 – 02.2015).

Shogo Tanaka is a Professor of Psychology at Tokai University in Japan. He received his Ph.D. in philosophical psychology from Tokyo Institute of Technology. Dr. Tanaka is primarily interested in phenomenology and psychology, and more specifically, in clarifying the theoretical foundations of psychology from the perspective of embodiment, being inspired by the ideas of Maurice Merleau-Ponty. The topics of his published papers encompass a broad range of issues, including body-schema, body image, skill acquisition, embodied self, social cognition, theory of mind, and intercorporeality. From 2013 to 2014, and from 2016 to 2017, he stayed at the Department of Psychiatry of the University of Heidelberg in Germany as a visiting scholar, where he worked on phenomenology, psychology and psychopathology. His recent publications include, "Intercorporeality as a theory of social cognition" (Theory & Psychology, 25, 455–472), "What is it like to be disconnected from the body?" (Journal of Consciousness Studies, 25, 239–262) and other articles.

Jana Trajtelová, PhD., works as a Scholarly Assistant at the Department of Philosophy, Faculty of Philosophy and Arts at Trnava University in Trnava, Slovakia. Her main area of specialization is Phenomenology, Philosophical Antropology and Philosophy of Religion. She is a member of the Center for Phenomenological Studies at the Department of Philosophy, Trnava University and the main editor of *The Yearbook on History and Interpretation of Phenomenology*. In 2011 she has published a book on the phenomenology of mysticism, more concretely of the mystical experience of John of the Cross and Meister Eckhart (*Distance and Proximity of Mysticism: Phenomenological Study of Fundamental Movements in Traditional Western Mysticism,* 2011). She has written on "*Ways of intersubjectivity and interpersonality in A. J. Steinbock*" as a part of the book *From Intersubjectivity to Interpersonality* (2014). She is the co-translator of Anthony Steinbock's book *Home and Beyond: Generative Phenomenology after Husserl* into Slovak (Domáce a cudzie: Generatívna fenomenológia a Husserl, 2013).

Chapter 1
Introduction to the Two Volumes: From Phenomenological Theory to the *Concretum* of Religious Experiencing

Olga Louchakova-Schwartz

Abstract This is Introduction to *The Problem of Religious Experience: Case Studies in Phenomenology, with Reflections and Commentaries*. The book presents an updated overview of the problem of religious experience in phenomenology, from the time of Husserl to French phenomenology's theological turn, which was followed by important publications such as Steinbock (2007), Depraz (2008), Alvis (2016 and 2018) and others. Significantly advancing understanding of religious experience, these studies nevertheless left open a question of what exactly makes religious experience what it is: that is, gives it a specific quality distinguishing it, for its subject, from all other experiences. In contemporary phenomenology, Dahl's (2010) theory of interruptions and Barber's (2017) theory of the appresentative mindset and the finite province of religious meaning comprise two most probable and mutually complementary answers to this question. Further, Introduction covers the contents of the two volumes, entitled respectively *The Primeval Showing of Religious Experience* and *Doxastic Perspectives in the Phenomenology of Religious Experience*. The case studies in Volume 1 proceed from the descriptive phenomenology of religious experience as it relates to subjectivity research (Part 1) to the relationship between religious experience, intersubjectivity, and alterity (Part 2). Part 2 also serves as a bridge to metaphysical, theological, and theistic approaches in Part 3 and Part 4. Along with the overview of the contents of the book, this Introduction presents Olga Louchakova-Schwartz's (as editor of the book) synthetic meta-reflection on the findings, so that the findings in the book are coherently represented in light of contemporary debates in the philosophy of religion.

Keywords Religious experience · Phenomenology · Interruption · Immanence · The concrete · Philosophy of religion

O. Louchakova-Schwartz (✉)
Jesuit School of Theology of Santa Clara University, Graduate Theological Union, Berkeley, CA, USA

University of California, Davis, CA, USA

© Springer Nature Switzerland AG 2019
O. Louchakova-Schwartz (ed.), *The Problem of Religious Experience*,
Contributions to Phenomenology 103,
https://doi.org/10.1007/978-3-030-21575-0_1

Arguably, Husserl has not removed every mystery, but contrary to what he himself believes, brought us to one of its centres.—Espen Dahl, *Phenomenology and the Holy*

This book takes the reader into an "abandoned sea with God in rounded conscious-ness speaking and singing"[1] through the voices of phenomenological research. This "abandoned sea" is religious experience: for a long time, the ship of phenomenol-ogy has been dead in its waters. Despite Husserl's own interest in the ethicoreli-gious problem (Ales Bello 1985, 2009) and Heidegger's lectures on the phenomenology of religious life, phenomenology on the whole has avoided this problematic.[2] On the other hand, for theologians, including Hering (1925), himself a phenomenologist, the phenomenological approach seemed too anthropomorphic to serve as a philosophy of religion—a circumstance that early on discouraged theological research of religious experience by means of phenomenology. Meanwhile, religious experience continued to be discussed in analytic philosophy as if it were an experience of regular perception,[3] which, from the standpoint of phenomenological theory, it cannot be. It has appeared that without a theoretical determination of the cognitive possibility of religious experience, the options for phenomenology in clarifying this category of experience were poor. Meanwhile, and not surprisingly, the absence of clarity in the existential status of religious experience affected the applied sciences for which religious experience remains *terra incognita*. For the most part, despite the profound and transformative effects of religious experiences, psychologists do not know what to make of such reports. And even though such experiences are empirically linked to health in the scientific research (for example, the research of meditation), religious connotations of expe-rience are mostly bracketed out, with researchers focusing mainly on attentional processes.

In 2016, a group of philosophers, psychologists, and theologians, including the present author, started the Society for the Phenomenology of Religious Experience with the purpose of supporting research in this area of scholarship. Our first two topical volumes of the journal *Open Theology* were flooded with submissions, lead-ing to the realization that the field is in need of a dialogue between researchers and the systematic analysis of accumulated findings. This book is the first volume of collective works of the Society. We hope that it will provide a well-needed update to the problem of religious experience in phenomenology, leading, in the future, to a new round of research integrating the cutting-edge developments in phenomenol-ogy, such as the concept of the minimal self (Zahavi 2019), reappraisals of Husserl's legacy on embodiment (Taipale 2014; Durt et al. 2017), and of Husserl's metaphys-ics (Zahavi 2018).

---

[1] Jiménez 1987, 11.

[2] For more on the research of religious experience in the history of phenomenology, see Steinbock 2012.

[3] For an argument in favor of the possibility of religious experience, see Alston 1991; Swinburne 1991; Plantinga 2000. For an argument against such a possibility, see Zangwill 2004.

Does the task of phenomenological clarification of religious experience present any difficulties? From the very beginning, the theory of phenomenology was focused on knowledge as related to sciences. This presupposed working out the relationship between the knowing ego and diverse objects of knowledge and outlining the structures of knowledge and conditions for truth. Religious experience does not fit with this schema of things. At the core of religious experience is mystery and not knowledge in a scientific sense—that is, an objective, objectifiable, or representational kind of knowledge (Otto 1923); and, as shown by James (1985), a characteristic feature of religious experience is its overwhelming variety. In *Phenomenology and the Holy*, Dahl (2010, 167–168) quoted Levinas's critique of treating religious experience as yet another form experience, that is, as something that the ego can constitute and thematize within the habitualities of its sameness. In Otto-Levinas-Dahl's view, there is a lack of meaning resources to define the identity of mystery. In Marion's view on religious experiences as saturated phenomena, the outcome is the same: the excess of intentionality in such experiences is so intense that the ego cannot possibly appropriate it (Mackinlay 2010).

Yet another question, perhaps even more famously difficult, is not what kind of experience the religious experience is, but rather an experience of "what." For the most part, theology suggests God to be an ultimate subject, a subject of all subjects. An idea of having God given in experience presents difficulties because, on one side, God is not among the objects, and on the other, it cannot be known as subject: within the dominant Kantian argument adopted by early phenomenology, the being of the ego is formal and cannot include self-knowledge or experience of itself.

When the French debate about the theological turn of phenomenology (Janicaud et al. 2000) highlighted new approaches in phenomenological theory and introduced a novel, phenomenologically grounded metaphysics, these questions gained some answers. The idea of mystery at the core of religious experience was expanded to include the Other (Levinas); at the same time, Henry's refutation of Kant's argument against the empirical being of the ego now makes it possible to reevaluate the ego's participation in religious experience. French phenomenology turned religious experience into a platform of entry into the phenomenology of phenomenology, broadening the latter through new approaches to phenomenality (Courtine 2000). Steinbock (2007), Depraz (2008), Alvis (2016, 2018), and others followed this revival of interest toward religious experience with their own original contributions. However, a question of what exactly makes religious experience what it is—that is, gives it a specific quality distinguishing it, for its subject, from all other experiences—remained open. In contemporary phenomenology, Dahl's (2010) theory of interruptions and Barber's (2017a) theory of the appresentative mindset and the finite province of religious meaning, which I introduce below, comprise the two most probable and mutually complementary answers to this question.

1.1   The Dwellings of Mystery

In religious experience, the ego functions under a regulative employment of the transcendental idea of God (or some related idea—e.g., of the Ultimate Reality).[4] The regulative *telos* of this idea descends not into some kind of abstract sphere (cf. the sphere of mathematics) but into an empirical sphere of internal experience: that is, the living psyche.[5] Focusing the mind on God gives one a sense of unity in the world, a sense of stability in the ego, a sense of spiritual healing, and so on. The subjects of religious experience have no difficulty identifying their experiences as religious or spiritual and distinguishing them from other experiences. Those to whom such experiences are communicated have no difficulty in recognizing them for what they are, i.e., religious experiences. This empathy indicates the presence of an eidetic structure or shared typification responsible for appreciating experience in the other. However, instead of a clear-cut fulfillment via an intentional object of experience, this constitutive structure must give itself in relation to the ever-present mystery.

Where exactly should one look for this mystery? Dahl finds two "locations" of the "unknown," one necessarily present in adumbrations of the world-objects and another as a mystery of the dual nature of others who are given both as reflections of one's own ego and as aliens whose living intentional subjectivity one can never penetrate. Dahl identifies these "locations" through critical comparison of the theories of constitution in the phenomenologies of consciousness. If one extends his argument to include the understanding of consciousness according to Marion and Henry, the empirical (not the constituting)[6] ego-pole can also serve as a location for the mystery. This would be so because of the empirical ego's capacity for sentience/self-affection—a form of knowledge without an intentional object.[7] As Dahl states: "It is rather because we are not fully masters of our own home, but already shot through with strangeness, that we are open to external otherness—first and foremost to the human Other" (2010, 152).

Through history and tradition, the formal idea of God incarnates in one's psyche. Becoming a regular idea, it couples with the situated locations of mystery. This decentering of the constitution, away from the thematic dominance of the ego and toward history and tradition engaged with uncountable concrete manifestations of mystery, is a plausible reason for the many variations in religious experience. What appears to the natural attitude as polymorphism of religious experience[8] on closer look turns out to be the aforementioned resistance to thematization. And this is

[4] For more on the idea of God in the Kantian sense, see Uemura 2010. For regulative employment of the idea of God, see Dahl 2010, 185.

[5] For distinctions between ideas as lived and formal ideas in the Kantian sense, see Lerner 2004.

[6] For distinctions between the different identities of the ego, see Husserl 1993. For the ego's self-knowledge, see Henry 2016.

[7] For more on nonobjectifying self-awareness, see Taipale 2014.

[8] For remarks on the polymorphism of religious experience and approaches to the study of it, see Hart and Wall 2005.

exactly why religious experience cannot be understood simply as yet another form of experience with a fixed, generalizable eidetic structure by which such experience is lived and recognized: for example, an experience of decision making, or playing chess, or thinking in circles, or feeling scared, or driving a red convertible, and so forth. Rather than a single event of experience, it is instead religious experiencing, with its own modes of being, horizons of its verticality, constitutive relationship to self-awareness, strangeness, temporality, and materiality: that is, its whole lifeworld. Michael Barber (2017a) calls it "a province of meaning"; in our prior work, we suggested treating religious experiencing as an ontological region (Louchakova-Schwartz and Crouch 2017). I will now proceed to describe the entry into this region.

1.2   Experience, Interrupted

> There is a crack, a crack in everything; that's how the light gets in.—Leonard Cohen, "Anthem"

Three ideas concerning a line of demarcation between ordinary experience and religious experience turned out to be most impactful for subsequent thinking. These are Schleiermacher's idea of religious experience as a feeling of absolute dependence (cf. Behrens 1998), James's "the sense of reality" in such experiences (Otto 1923, 10, n. 2), and Otto's (1923) argument of religious experience as numinous or mystery.[9] Even though conceived psychologically, James's idea is resonant with the concepts of the phenomenology of life which I discuss below (see Sects. 1.3 and 1.4). Closely followed in theology, Schleiermacher's idea unfortunately did not yet receive much attention in the phenomenological analyses, perhaps because of the criticism that this idea received from Otto (1923). By contrast, the idea of religious experience being associated with mystery is explicated in phenomenology quite well and largely because of the work of Levinas and an original argument around this idea developed by Dahl (2010). Different from the theological mystery of negation or *cataphasis*, Otto's mystery is embedded in specific constitutive locations of consciousness and therefore can be revealed upon what Dahl calls a peculiar reduction.

Such a reduction can be performed intentionally and analytically but can also happen spontaneously in religious contexts, as an interruption of the everyday which is leading to emergence of a religious sense. According to Dahl, interruptions are *de facto* spontaneous reductions that in some cases may turn into instances of religious experience. The "everyday" (*Alltäglichkeit,* a term coined by Heidegger, in Dahl 2010, 241; also used by Schutz, in Barber 2017a) denotes the flow of consciousness filled with mundane, life-sustaining concerns. According to Dahl, Heidegger named several kinds of interruptions. Interruptions work against the lowering of human

---

[9] For more on religious knowing, see Dadosky 2004.

spirit by a depressing impact of the everyday. Emancipation can be due to theoretical philosophizing (cf. Uemura 2010), humor (Barber 2017a), and religion—a position on which Dahl and Barber concur. Breaking the enslaving mastery of the everyday with its high tension of consciousness, interruptions shift consciousness to a different plane, which, in Barber's view, will entail some form of religiosity.

To further understand how reductions/interruptions can lead to religious experience, it is worth revisiting *Cartesian Meditations*, in which Husserl (1993) employs several kinds of reduction. One of them, phenomenological reduction, liberates the stratum of knowledge and makes it available for analysis. Another, transcendental reduction, reveals the stratum of transcendental constituting ego. Further, thematic reductions focus on the particular aspects of constitution. Assembling reductions in different successions, Husserl concluded that the ordering of reductions is not neutral to the outcome of the analysis: not only reductions themselves but also their sequencing impacts the modes of consciousness at the end of the process. For example, performing transcendental reduction is not possible in the natural attitude, because the transcendental horizon is just not visible in the latter: one does not apperceive one's consciousness "leaking out" of one's head and grasping objects. In order to reach the transcendental activity of consciousness, one first has to isolate the givenness of consciousness itself via the phenomenological reduction: only after this is done is it possible to see consciousness in its relation to intentional objects. As has been said many times, God, not being among the noematic contents of the transcendental world-horizon, does not participate in shaping intentional consciousness in the manner that objects do. The transcendental horizon unveils exactly the absence of a God-object, along with the absences in the givenness of the objects that need adumbrations and the absence of full access to the contents of the other. What is still unclear is how the unknown, the absence, can participate in the constitution of consciousness in positive ways: that is, what kind of constitutive processes can coalesce around a "non-noema." Much more likely, this question does not have a single, linear answer but will be answered through critical integration of multiple perspectives. To that end, the papers in Volumes I and II of this book all represent, in one way or another, the analyses of the constitution of religious experience.

In terms of attention, reduction is a refocusing. It brings into awareness the aspects of consciousness previously hidden, brings into naming what has not been named, and at the same time suspends what is already known and has been named. As a philosophical tool, reductions are disciplined, intentional, and specific to their purposes. However, reduction is also within capacities of consciousness and something that can happen spontaneously: for example, when consciousness is shifting its "Schutzian" planes. (Cf. Barber 2017a.) The theory of interruptions resonates with the traditional descriptions of religious experiences as "unveiling" (e.g., Chittick 1998) or accounts of "emergence" in live informants (Greenwell 1995). In such experiences, the usual horizontal constitutive activity of the ego is momentarily suspended or perhaps is pushed into the background by processes emerging from the internal depth of consciousness itself. (Cf. Bellini in Chap. 18 of the present book.) It appears evident that in the analyses of such experiences, the path of analysis is not horizontal, as in the regard for the mundane constituting activities of the ego, but vertical, into the internal constitution of consciousness itself.[10] Vertical analyses bring to light limit-phenomena—that is, mystery.[11] An interesting analogy is found in the *Black Yajurveda* (*Taittiriya Samhita*) hymn *Śrī Rudram* (1200–1000 B.C.E.): the worshipping beings are categorized as horizontals (animals) or verticals, that is, the human beings who have discerning consciousness capable of God-Realization.

A switch in the direction of reduction from the analysis of sense toward analyses of the internal composition of consciousness is visible in Husserl's work when he turns toward the analysis of the consciousness of internal time. Husserlian turn implies leaving the horizon of developed intentionalities and refocusing attention on the sphere of passive synthesis and temporality: that is, the processes that happen to us and that we do not actively intend. As stated by DeRoo (2013, 79), "passive synthesis is something that is simultaneously accomplished by the subject (which thereby makes it responsible for the results of passive synthesis) and done without the active consent of the ego (thereby explaining how we can do things without intending to do them, and even, at times, do things that run counter to our intentions)." The sphere of passive synthesis would include both the sensorium involved in the mystery of adumbrations and the sensorium related to the mystery in the constitution of the other.

But the processes of passive synthesis are also important in other aspects. According to Barber, who applies Schutzian framework for understanding the finite provinces of religious meaning (Barber 2017a), religious experiences are genetically constituted not by the intentional activities of the ego but through the so-called appresentative mindset. The constitution of this mindset through passive synthesis consists of pairing between primary impressions and religious symbols. The symbols, which are specific for the province of religious meaning, participate in transfers and other processes of passive synthesis (Barber 2017b).

Following Marion, Dahl (2010, 120) suggests that it is in the sphere of passive synthesis that the "call" for reduction/interruption emerges. Similarly, Barber suggests "the peculiar *epoché* of the province is symbolically induced when the very symbol (e.g., temple or ritual) that serves as the gateway into the province and separates it from the 'profane' world of everyday life" (2017b, 397). Extending Barber's ideas, it is possible to see how the primal facts of religious experience will be submitted to historical generativity and become immersed in the cloak of ideas, in a manner of tradition-related historical verticality. (Cf. Steinbock 2007; Dahl 2010.) Further, in contemplative traditions, such as Buddhism or Hesychasm, reductions

---

[10] "Vertical" and "verticality" are related to Husserl's idea of universal dimensionality in the generation of sense, and Merleau-Ponty's and Heidegger's reflection on the limits of phenomenology: see Merleau-Ponty, in Husserl et al. 2002, xiii–xv. Steinbock (2007) uses the term as related to the specific property of religious experience in its relatedness to limit-phenomena, as again in Steinbock (2012). Lomuscio (2017) suggests the latter concept, thereby reorienting the idea that religious experience is the experience of reaching the limit for understanding that religious experience may be centered on something—in our argument, on mystery.

[11] For connections between verticality and mystery in Levinas, and for bodily verticality in Strauss, see Richard Cohen 1994, 242.

are built into introspective practices in which such reductions are used intentionally to interrupt the aspects of common sense and ordinary language and, thereby, to induce religious states.[12] Flood (2013) regards these practices as specific to culturally constituted forms of self. A constitutive imaginary in this case would be the consciousness of internal experience building itself "bottom up," vertically, and horizontally, in concatenations of the ego, which incorporates passive synthesis "top-down."

Synthesizing the views of Dahl and Barber (see Chaps. 4 and 8), we can define religious experience as an interruption bringing out of anonymity the locations of mystery that, through passive synthesis, are coupled with religious symbols leading to experiences with subjectively lived religious quality. Such a treatment of the problem of religious experience takes the latter out of the purview of the constituting ego. However, it also confronts one with problems that surface after the ego, with its horizontal intentionalities, is removed from the picture. As Dahl (2010, 178) states, it was "Ricoeur [who] has claimed that the most acute problem for phenomenology of religion is not intentionality and its alleged exclusion of what exceeds adequate comprehension, but the immediacy of religious phenomena, or rather, the recognition of impossibility of such immediacy."

This affirmation of impossibility of the immediacy of religious phenomena is dictated not only by the hermeneutic agenda of Ricoeur himself, but rather by the whole logos of phenomenological interrogation in which consciousness is identified with intentionality. The facticity of experiences in which key aspects appear as nonrelated to intentional consciousness challenges such an approach. Examples are experiences of absorption (Ware 1974; Louchakova 2005; Bronkhorst 2012), experiences of internal silence (such as are described by Laude in the present book),[13] or experiences taking place outside historical generativity of tradition: Would it be possible for Porfiri Ivanov (Kungurtsev and Louchakova 1994), while bathing in ice water in atheistic, non-religious Soviet Russia, to have a religious experience with the same Christian sense as the one of Saint Teresa of Avila? A problem of immediacy brings us to another cluster of phenomenological theories associated with the study of religious experience. These are the theories of phenomenological ontology.

---

[12] For descriptions of such spontaneous reductions/interruptions in traditional contexts, for Theravada Buddhism, see Bronkhorst 2012; for Tibetan Buddhism, see Guenther 1992; for Eastern Orthodox Christianity, see Louchakova 2005; Louchakova-Schwartz 2016. (Louchakova and Louchakova-Schwartz are the same author).

[13] Immediacy of religious cognition is one of the main principles in the epistemology of Islamic mysticism; see in Yazdī 1992.

1.3   Immediacy: Religious Experience and the Phenomenological Ontology

Heavens and earths cannot contain Me, but the heart of my faithful servant can.—*al-ḥādith al-qudsi*[14]

In the classical phenomenology of consciousness, constitutive analysis begins with the phenomenological reduction. Husserl (1989, 60–62, §32) maintains that this reduction does not take anything away from the natural attitude. It does, however, initiate a specific logos of interrogation: that is, a direction in which the givenness of the natural attitude will be modified—a fact that Husserl himself acknowledges in *Cartesian Meditations*. The domino effect of this reduction establishes *hylē* (in earlier works termed "sense-data" by Husserl), the phenomenologically material contents of primary impressions, as a "repository" for the bestowal of sense—that is, of intentionality. In the analysis of internal time consciousness, this leads to the "now" appearing empty (because the "now" is devoid of intentional contents) and to establishing the horizon of pure seeing (pure intention) as a prerequisite to any consciousness. Interested readers can review Henry's extensive critique of this situation in *Material Phenomenology* (2008).

By contrast, in accordance with the natural order of givenness, analysis in the phenomenology of life begins with life as such, and not with consciousness. Instead of isolating the horizon of pure intention, the phenomenology of life isolates the horizon of sentience: that is, of self-affective, sentient phenomenological materiality. In building its theory, the phenomenology of life approaches the concept of consciousness not structurally, as a principle constituting knowledge, but ontologically, as a faculty emerging out of a phenomenologically material, self-effulgent ego. As a result, there is a reversal of the role of the *hylē:* instead of being a passive, if not inert, repository, it becomes an active, self-luminous "constitutor" that gives rise to the secondary feature of consciousness: intentionality.

Whereas Bergson approached the problem of immediacy intuitionally, Henry (1973) offered instead an expanded rational phenomenological ontology. There are four pillars of his ontology. First, the analysis of the being of the ego, in which he refutes the Kantian argument (Henry 2016). Second, he argues against the Cartesian understanding of *cogito* and against Heidegger's focus on the primacy of being, establishing instead the concept of life as manifestation (Henry 1973). Third, he draws on his earlier work in philosophy and phenomenology of the body (Henry 1975). After assembling a consistent phenomenological ontology, in his last three

---

[14] This hadith is cited in Ibn 'Arabi, *op. cit.* 1981, 16, 42. A slightly different version, which is probably closer to the original, may be found in Ahmad b. Hanbal's *Musnad*, in the *Kitab al-Zuhd*, tradition 421, which gives primary narrative authority to Wahb b. Munabbih: "Heavens and earths cannot contain Me, but the heart of my faithful servant can." Because it is hadith *qudsi* (concerning the words of the Almighty), it has received less attention in the canonical collections, and some scholars (in particular Ibn Taymiyyah) consider it apocryphal, and the part of the so-called "Isra'iliyyat" (hadith whose narrative authority is ascribed to non-Muslims). (Thanks to Ahmed Zildzic for locating this reference.)

works, he interprets the Gospels as speech emerging from experiences of sentience and the self-affection of life (Henry 2003, 2015). These metaphysical ideas influenced both the theological debate in French phenomenology and, perhaps not so directly, the current reappraisal of Husserl's work on embodiment[15] and the understanding of moral emotions (Steinbock 2014).

Even though Henry critiqued Heidegger's ontological monism and disagreed with him on the concept of transcendence, both thinkers concur in affirming the possibilities of knowledge in the ego, as phenomenological materiality in Henry's view and as *Dasein* in Heidegger's. Corbin (1969) and Guenther (1992) used the concept of *Dasein* to explain the mystical states. As in the ontotheology of Jean-Luc Marion, the limitation of these approaches is in the lack of particularization: How does one differentiate between religious immediacy and givenness as such? These approaches reposition the problem of religious experience so that it becomes, in a sense, a primary form of experience, while ordinary experience is a secondary variation on the theme. (Cf. DeRoo 2018.) In this view, different kinds of experience would be mediated by different kinds of intuition, such as intuition of life, or, in the Indian Vedanta, a capacity of intuitive discernment between real and unreal, and so forth (Louchakova-Schwartz 2011, 2013). Mystics claim that accessing some of these kinds of intuition requires extensive training, as for example in *Vijñānabhairava* (Singh 1991). Constitutive analyses have not yet been applied to these kinds of experiences, and a phenomenological comparison of the Western and Eastern philosophies of religion has just begun.[16]

1.4   The Living God of the Concrete

> God, I am the wrapping of my center, of you within—Juan Ramón Jiménez, *God Desired and Desiring*

"Immersing in the concrete,"[17] a motto associated with the phenomenologies of Merleau-Ponty and Marcel, led to recapitulating and reexamining the aspects of *Erfahrung* left out by phenomenological reduction[18]: that is, to analyses of embodiment. With regard to the phenomenology of religious experiencing, a move into the concrete is complicated. Clearly, religious experiencing is connected with ritual and contemplative practices, but it is not clear how exactly such connection is manifest and in what ways religious experience is warranted behaviorally engaged. Besides, religious experience is not egalitarian in character—that is, it is not available to everybody or on an ongoing basis: quite the opposite, it is not as "participatory" as

---

[15] For example, see Taipale 2014.

[16] For comparative studies of the approaches to the self in different philosophies of religion, see Siderits et al. 2011. For comparison of monistic religious idealisms, see Marres 2017.

[17] For immersing in the concrete, see Sato 1998.

[18] For more on the effects of phenomenological reduction, see Zahavi 2003. For more in immersing in the concrete, see Tymieniecka and Matsuba 1998.

the research of ritual, for example, in the cognitive science of religion,[19] may lead one to believe. These are rarely shared, and rarely available "on demand" experiences, unless it is a specific experience of communion in prayer to which there is always a "response."[20] It is difficult to get live accounts: most often, the subjects of religious experience keep them private, unless sharing such experience serves some kind of social purpose, as for example gaining status in a religious community. Religious experiences may carry connotations of personal exclusivity and would be considered inappropriate to share in an academic or a job setting. Traditional phenomenological first-person authority in religious experiencing is delegated to textual evidence, which brings with it a host of problems in all three kinds of phenomenological analyses: static, genetic, and generative. Most importantly, texts have a way of distilling the stratum of meaning out of the embodied givenness of the concrete (Louchakova-Schwartz 2013, 2016), thereby turning analysis into excavation and reconstruction of consciousness.

As Ales Bello (2009, 46–53) shows, one of the paths to God is through hyletics. In this book, Tanaka's account of religious experiencing via the hyletic and kinesthetic aspects of self-awareness, and Dahl's account of wonder link religious experience to embodiment.[21] (See Chaps. 2 and 4.) In its spatiality and depth, the body contributes to perceived internality of religious experience.[22] From the enfleshed, embodied concrete of religious experience, it is just one step to metaphysics. (Cf. Henry 2003, 2015.) Contrary to Nietzsche's dead God of theory, an embodied God of the concrete is alive and well.[23] When the "unmasking" of phenomenological materiality through absorption in certain zones of the body-schema creates a specific interruption,[24] this leads to an emergence of a nonsymbolic religious sense (Louchakova-Schwartz 2016, 2017). Such primal facts of experience (cf. Henry 1975 on de Biran) may become an *a priori* for posterior constitutive processes. A constitutive imaginary in this case would be consciousness building itself "bottom up" from the sentient phenomenological materiality, vertically and reflexively, while at the same time being gradually woven into the horizontal concatenations of the ego. For example, Nörenberg (2017) suggests that atmospheric feeling can serve as a *noēma* in the constitution

---

[19] For "closet" religious experiences, see Palmer 1999; Kuhar 2005.

[20] For more on immediacy of response to prayer, see Ibn 'Arabī 1975, 21.

[21] For more on embodiment of religious experience, see Acebedo 2012; Louchakova 2005; Louchakova-Schwartz (aka Louchakova) 2016 and 2017. For metaphysics of embodied religious experiencing, see Ales Bello 2009; Henry 2012, 2015.

[22] For cultural relativistic perspective on internality of religious experience, see Flood 2013. For the analysis of internal religious experience from a perspective of material phenomenology, see Louchakova-Schwartz 2017. For more on internal religious experience and immediacy, see Lacoste 1994.

[23] For rehabilitation of God in philosophical theory, see Lacoste 2014. For embodiment in religious experiencing, see Depraz 2008; Louchakova-Schwartz 2016, 2017.

[24] For the focused internal absorption of attention in specific regions of the body-schema in religious experiencing, see Louchakova-Schwartz 2017.

of religious experience (cf. Chap. 14), thereby informing, by being numinous (in Otto's sense of the term), the ideas of ethical nature in Kant and Levinas.

Concluding my exposition of the problem of religious experience, I will turn to an example of a charismatic Evangelical group prayer. It is believed that in such experiences, God becomes real to people through internal speech that people "hear" (Hastings 1991; Luhrmann 2012)—that is, by a sort of interpretation. However, apart from the internal voice, there is a bodily component of God's response as a vertical current of subtly tangible "descending energy" that many believers understand as grace. In cases of the laying on of hands, this "current" can be intentionally directed through the bodies and hands of the worshippers to the one who receives the healing.[25] This effect is accompanied by a mild attentional effort that stops internal dialogue and may or may not involve synesthesia of descending light with tactility and kinesthesis. Such an effect, also present in *Subud Latihan*, was described by Antonov and Vaver (1989). This impression is not exactly "internal" in the sense that it cannot be apperceived by others because there appears to be a shared component of altered somatic awareness. (Cf. Louchakova-Schwartz 2016.) Şandru, in his interpretation of Marion's Trinitarian phenomenological ontology, emphasizes religious experience as neither exclusively internal nor intersubjectively constituted, but as something "in between"—perhaps mediated by the self-reflexivity of phenomenological materiality. This possibly answers the question asked in Sect. 1.2 above: How can mystery participate in the constitution of consciousness in positive ways? By self-reflexive phenomenological materiality, the black holes of the Otto-Dahl mystery are filled.

1.5   The Contents of This Book

As this Introduction suggests, solving the problem of religious experience requires a joint effort of different kinds of phenomenologists. In this phenomenologically interdisciplinary book, the reader meets with a plurality of research perspectives, including both traditional phenomenological presuppositionless ones and doxastic/theological ones. Volumes I and II, and the corresponding four parts of the book—Part 1, "Subjectivity and Religious Interiorities"; Part 2, "Lifeworld, Intersubjectivity, Alterity"; Part 3, "The Phenomenology of Revelation"; and Part 4, "Theistic Approaches to the Psychological Horizons of Religious Experiencing"—reflect the clusters of ideas that were already present in the submitted papers. As one notices in reading e.g. Ales Bello's *The Divine* (2009), the thematization of the book may in itself point to the phenomenological ontology of experience in question.

Volume I, *The Primeval Showing of Religious Experience,* presents studies in the constitution of religious experience as situated in the horizons opened by phenomenological reduction: that is, in a presuppositionless view that is also nondoxastic.

---

[25] Author's personal observations during evangelical prayer for healing, Hale Maluhia Country Inn (House of Peace), Kailua-Kona, Hawaii, 6 Feb. 2018.

The papers of this volume show the directions of reduction (e.g., Tanaka, Dahl, Mickey) and treat religious experience in light of different theories of constitution (e.g., Barber or Costello), either in regard to the ego's sphere of ownness (Part 1), or in relation to intersubjectivity and otherness (Part 2).

By contrast, Volume II, *Doxastic Perspectives in the Phenomenology of Religious Experience*, is dedicated to faith-based approaches, which are developed either philosophically-theologically, or psychologically. Doxastic approaches in phenomenology tend to be a highly debated issue (cf. Janicaud et al. 2000; Falque 2005, 2016), but our purpose in using them is not theoretical but rather pragmatic: we aim neither to examine how doxastic phenomenology fits among other theological sciences that at present are undergoing rapid differentiation (see Moore 2001; Wood 2009; Stump and Rea 2015; etc.) nor to fully debate the validity or possibility of such phenomenology but to make a modest attempt to show the pros and cons of theological phenomenology specifically in research of religious experience. (See Louchakova-Schwartz, Chap. 20.) Volume I uses more reference to transcendental theory than Volume II, and Volume II is oriented toward descriptive concerns of phenomenology. However, since the transcendental horizon grew out of descriptive phenomenology, and since the constitutive syntheses uncovered by transcendental reduction underlie the shaping of appearances captured by description, these two areas of phenomenology are hard to disengage from each other: the reader will certainly find overlaps between the problematic of Volumes I and II, as well as between parts within each volume. To help situate the argument, each part has its own concluding section dedicated to syntheses and transdisciplinary discussion of the findings. These sections are deliberately placed at the end of each part in order not to interfere prematurely with the authors' delivery of findings that speak for themselves. However, it is possible that after reading a concluding section, the reader may wish to revisit the papers for further understanding.

Part 1, "Subjectivity and Religious Interiorities," opens with chapter by Shogo Tanaka, "Reconnecting the Self to the Divine: The Role of the Lived Body in Spontaneous Religious Experiences," in which the author describes spontaneous religious experiences in reference to the implicit, irreducible domain of synthetic unities of spatial relations and dimensions known as the body-schema. Suggesting that the religious quality in experience stems from the changes in perception (as in nonordinary experiences), Tanaka concludes that reconstitution of the body as lived (*Lieb*) is a condition of possibility for experience to become nonordinary, and perhaps religious.

In Chap. 3, Patrick Laude describes the mystical practice of invocation of Divine Names unveiling the realms of God. Using comparative analysis of Sufi, Vedantic, and Tantric texts, Laude isolates a temporally extended structure of internal experience associated with the repetition of the Name—a call for the self-revelation of the Absolute. Esoteric even by comparison with other forms of religious experience, this process involves absorption in the spatial "core" of the chest, termed the Spiritual Heart. (Cf. Chap. 2). When attention becomes stabilized in this area of the body-schema, the internally chanted Name disappears and is replaced by silence. This state of experience is recognized by the mystic as the Living God. Theologies of different traditions become "crystallized" out of this specially entrained form of experience. Such theologies emphasize the sameness—that is, identity—of the human and Divine essences: the ego-pole is not a mere structure but is viewed onto-logically as self-luminous, nature-revealing, or transparent, known to itself by itself in nonobjectifying intuition. Such knowledge is neither direct (as the knowledge of the objects present in one's mind or directly given to the senses) nor indirect (as the knowledge of something that is not immediately given to the mind or the senses) but is likened to a light which does not require another light to be illumined. The Absolute in these traditions is egological: the introspective "unveiling" of Reality takes place via a motion of attention toward the ego-pole, with corresponding reductions.

In Chap. 4, Espen Dahl analyzes the connection between reductions and a sense of wonder and awe that was associated with religious experiencing by Otto and many after him. Reductions—that is, mental "slicing" of consciousness with ana-lytic purposes—have a vector, a direction within the phenomenal field. Dahl exam-ines the phenomenological reduction, Cartesian reduction, reduction used by Marion, which Dahl terms "reduction from the outside," and Merleau-Ponty's reduction, which he terms "reduction downwards." Reductions are not just abstrac-tions leading to a modification of pure thought but acts of consciousness leading to a new revelation of experience (cf. Husserl's remarks on transcendental experience in paragraph 15 of chapter 2 in *Cartesian Meditations*); thereby, reductions exe-cuted in ways described by Dahl open new possibilities in experience. According to Dahl's reading of Marion, reductions are unveilings leading to a sense of wonder, which can be pure or impure, depending on the presence of tension in it. A dissolu-tion of tension in wonder signifies an open access to the locations of mystery, which, in Dahl's (2010) view, and resonating with the view of Tanaka (see Chap. 2), con-stitutes the phenomenological core of religious experiencing.

In Chap. 5, Olga Louchakova-Schwartz continues the theme of religious emotion in the papers of Shogo Tanaka and Espen Dahl. Experience of emotional transfor-mation in meditations of mindfulness or loving kindness (*mettā*) implies a gradual reduction of a complex emotion, which has axiological intentionalities, to a non-representational form and, after that, a reduction to feelings given in increasingly prevalent passivity. Temporal extension of this is teleological, toward enlightenment or emancipation: emotions change their quality and transform themselves into a network that is gradually resolved into the state of transparent, self-luminous, boundless compassion. This continuity of religious emotion is examined by Louchakova-Schwartz first with regard to intentional consciousness and then with regard to phenomenological materiality: the phenomenon of emotional "transmuta-tion," whereby the continuous transformation of one emotion into the other, with an increase of transparency, pushes the classical phenomenological categorical appara-tus to its limit, prompting the author to seek solutions in Michel Henry's noninten-tional phenomenology of affectivity.

Engaging the work of Emmanuel Levinas (see Chaps. 7 and 9), Gerardus van der Leeuw (see Chap. 7), Alfred Schutz (see Chap. 8), Maurice Merleau-Ponty (see Chap. 10), and Martin Heidegger (see Chap. 10), Part 2 of Volume I positions the phenomenology of religious experience in regard to the sphere of intersubjectivity. In accordance with the theme of intersubjectivity, Part 2 is intensely dialogical: Sam Mickey responds to postmodern criticisms of phenomenology, and Michael Barber responds to Dahl's interpretations of the Schutzian everyday by showing the mutual openness of the everyday and the holy. Then, discussion turns toward the invisible: in the paper by Mezzanzanica, to the Levinasian horizon of ethics; and in the paper by Costello, to reading the Gospels as the phenomenology of ghosts and resurrection.

In Chap. 7, Mickey addresses the cultural alterity of experience from the standpoint of an etic researcher unable to have an experience identical to that of the culturally different other. In the case of such cross-cultural second-person investigation, *epoché* is a way of accessing alterity and, consequently, a way of understanding the religious experience in the manner it is given to the other. According to van der Leeuw, accessing the other's religious experience means *accessing the other person,* because a human being is in principle *Homo religiosus*: one's self-experience is religious at the core, and this religious experience creates a possibility of an appearance of the other. Mickey also brings up a notion of phenomenological realism, indicating that the phenomenological method alone can break through the other's perpetual alterity.

In Chap. 8, Michael Barber grounds understanding of religious experience in the concept of the lifeworld. Barber's chapter is "three-in-one": first, it is a review of important insights in Dahl's (2010) *Phenomenology and the Holy*, which is itself a landmark in the phenomenological study of religious experience. Second, Chap. 8 offers a comprehensive summary of Schutz's views on the everyday, which is applied by Barber to the analysis of the holy as the context in which religious experience is given. This is a richly descriptive approach, providing a template for how to approach the religious lifeworld on its own grounds, accounting in each and every possible moment of such an encounter for alterity, which is never tame. Written with profound knowledge of both Husserl's legacy and the Schutzian phenomenology of the social world, this chapter can serve as an introduction to both Schutz's philosophy and to his descriptive method—a third benefit for the reader. The central point of Barber's chapter is its criticism of the logic of separation: that is, the idea of impenetrable alterity confronting the subject-self in religious experiencing. Such an idea can be traced to Husserl and Schutz, as well as to Levinas's vision of the other, which, according to Dahl, translates into fixity and defined boundaries of the everyday and renders God *the absolute transcendent*. Arguing against this, Barber offers a more generous, existential, contextual, and detailed reading of Schutz, making a way into a possibility of transcendence that would not be realistic if one's typification of the everyday were to have rigid structural and ontological boundaries.

In Chap. 9, Massimo Mezzanzanica analyzes Levinas's understanding of alterity in its relevance to the theme of Volume I. Different from recent approaches interpreting Levinas's legacy as nonphilosophy, or even interpreting it as a form of psyche analysis (e.g., in Bergo 2005), Mezzanzanica treats Levinas's phenomenology in the context of its cultural legacy: that is, as the cusp of philosophy and religion, with original insights paradigmatic for both disciplines. Beginning by describing predecessors of Levinas's intellectual reference to Judaism, the paper proceeds to outline the topics of subjectivity and critique of knowledge, of ontotheology, and of being, while positing the invisible and ethics as the foundations of the human world. Showing the expanse of Levinas's *epoché*, Mezzanzanica's paper prepares us for the reading of the Gospel in Chap. 10, by Peter Costello.

Costello continues the theme of the other as self-disclosure of Divine alterity. Entitled "Toward a Phenomenology of Resurrection and of Ghosts," Chap. 10 establishes an important distinction between the two events. A ghost is an illusion, hauntedness, nonreality. Resurrection is an engagement, if not an interpenetration, of Divine and human otherness, an extended ethical event transformative of communities to come. Resurrection reaches to us via the flesh. The distinction is already in the narrative of the Gospels, but before Costello's work it had not been approached phenomenologically or analytically. The range of phenomenological analysis in Costello's work is astoundingly broad, from Husserl and Merleau-Ponty, to Marion, Derrida, and Caputo, once again underscoring the point that for understanding religious phenomena one needs the whole of contemporary phenomenology. Costello does not refer specifically to Levinas but, of course, by engaging Marion and Derrida, such an association is unavoidable, especially in reference to the text of the Gospel, to textuality *per se*, and to generative phenomenology in the study of ethics. Schutzian connotations are also present, in the mutual permeability of the initially alien religious and the everyday. The connection between Mary and the resurrected Jesus is understood by Costello as a bodily pairing, concretized as acts. Phenomenology turns into a communicology of the sacred and into a genetic phenomenology of the flesh in "phenomenological-deconstructive reading as a reading of conscience … [as] the recognition *and the establishment* of a more intimate relationship." (See Chap. 10.)

Part 3 (in Volume II, *Doxastic Phenomenological Perspectives on Religious Experience*), entitled "The Phenomenology of Revelation," takes the reader from interrogations into the givenness of experience, to the ontology of what is experienced: that is, to the phenomenological metaphysics of subjectivity. There is a shift in the phenomenological paradigm between the two volumes. Volume I consists predominantly of papers written from a traditional presuppositionless phenomenological standpoint. By contrast, Volume II contains research papers written from a theological position that presupposes the irreducible existence of the Absoluten who cannot be bracketed out of investigations. Part 3 (in Volume II) is a dialectical, dialogical encounter with the religious attitude. In Chap. 12 by Christopher DuPée, a theme of relationship between religious experience and the everyday, which was earlier treated by Dahl and Barber in a traditional phenomenological manner, emerges in a different light. DuPée juxtaposes four perspectives, the Heideggerian approach of Jean-Yves Lacoste; the subsequent critique of Lacoste by Jean-Luc Marion; the approach of the Eastern Orthodox writer Theophan the Recluse, who is famous for his strong ascetic practice; and the perspective of Pavel Florensky, whose theological views are influenced by the Sophianic vision of Soloviev, which, in line with the mystical theology of the Orthodox Church, emphasizes epistemological contributions of religious experience. DuPée juxtaposes the absence of revelation in the *eschaton* and the presence of revelation in liturgy; comparing the views of Lacoste and Marion, DuPée suggests that religious experience gives one knowledge of God only under ethical and ascetic attunement—and perhaps not even then.

In Chap. 13, Leonardo Marcato presents an opposite perspective. Panikkar, who early on in his work was influenced by Husserl, viewed religious experience as a form of knowledge revealed in a maximum openness to the cosmos. Consequently, instead of being an instance of knowledge (perception), religious experience for Panikkar turns out to be a foundation for all knowledge. Panikkar's gnoseology negates Cartesian dualism by positing a holistic consciousness in which all modalities of knowledge are active simultaneously; in its emphasis on imagination, this picture resonates with religious consciousness according to Cassirer. The possibility of such a gestalt is linked to the existence of the unified Trinitarian cosmos, which, in an idealistic metaphysical approach, is hybridized with the Indian philosophy of Advaita Vedanta (another strong influence on Panikkar's thinking).

In Chap. 14, Joshua Cockayne revisits a rarely discussed aspect of Kierkegaard's thought, which is the phenomenon of presence. By contrast with a presupposition-less phenomenological account,[26] in which presence is "atmospheric feeling," in Cockayne's theological reading presence is the self-presentation of the Divine to the embodied human subject. Presence attracts cognition in the same way that experience of the other initiates attentiveness. Cockayne suggests that this situation works along the lines of a model of dual attention in cognitive psychology: the subject looks at God and God looks at the subject, but both are happening within the same subjectivity (the same field of consciousness). Without claims to knowability of God (which is different from Panikkar's Trinitarian holism but resonant with Costello's perspective in Part 2), this model suggests an extemporaneous manifestation of Christ within the human subjectivity.

In the religious attitude, which is outlined by the editor to this book in the Concluding Reflection to Part 3, the phenomenology of attention serves as a source for theological inferences. This line of thinking continues in Chap. 15, by Adrian Răzvan Şandru. Şandru argues that givenness is Trinitarian not only by the genetics of Marion's approach, but also because it has a *de facto* Trinitarian structure. The phenomenology of this structure can serve as a foundation of a reflective logic in a version of the metaphysics of subjectivity close to the theological phenomenology, a term used by Joseph Rivera (2015) in his studies of Michel Henry.

Chap. 16, is written by Carla Canullo, who is one of the rare experts on Henry's work. Canullo picks up the theme of the metaphysics of subjectivity in Henry's phenomenology of life. Henry's philosophy culminates in phenomenological Christology—a turn for which he was criticized by traditional theologians as an adventurous if not frivolous trespasser of disciplinary boundaries (e.g., Farley 2016). Canullo traces Henry's religious reference to his earliest works, including such philosophically "heavy" projects as his ontological destruction of the Kantian

---

[26] For an example of phenomenological analysis of "atmospheric feeling" in religious experience, see Nörenberg 2017.

architectonics of knowledge and a reversal of transcendental reduction, in *Material Phenomenology* (2008). Uncovered by Canullo, the logos of Henry's interrogation shows that his turn to Christianity is not accidental but logical, because his philosophical findings reveal Christianity to be a unique religious form dedicated to the metaphysical self-revelation of life in the human condition. Consequently, Canullo interprets Henry's work as a philosophy of religion—that is, a phenomenological philosophical project that reveals the nature of revelation.

Two papers in Part 4, by Bianca Bellini and Jana Trajtelová, present accounts of descriptive phenomenology done in theistic attitude. This is especially interesting because a) phenomenological analysis suggests suspension of ontological presuppositions, and b) theism in psychology is a subject of ongoing debate: on one hand, psychology aims to be a formal science, but on the other, the practice of psychology depends on the knowledge of subjectivity, and correspondingly, engages ontological assumptions. In Chap. 18, Bellini undertakes a meticulous explication of the meaning of repentance, which is a subject central to Christian religious experience but would be a very controversial subject for clinical psychology, which has adopted a model of repentance-free mental health. By contrast, Bellini shows not only that repentance is a central constituent of religious experience but that it is also a core of the self and a gateway into ongoing personal transformation. In Bellini's analysis, such never-ending self-renewal is intentional but conditioned on one's openness to the self and to God. The temporally extended structure of repentance includes rebirth, forgiveness, mercy, pledge, self-revision, self-shaping, and self-choice, which Bellini discusses in their dialectical relations to each other and to the real human other.

Finally, in Chap. 19, Jana Trajtelová treats the topic of "calling." Bringing together perspectives from Saint John of the Cross, Meister Eckhart, and Thomas Merton, she juxtaposes them with the perspectives in humanistic-existential psychology and uses a descriptive phenomenological method to explicate the structure of the phenomenon of calling. For Trajtelová, accessing the calling means accessing one's authentic vocation, which is a deep structure of the self always anchored in Being *per se*. This situation is contrasted with one's abidance in egoically constituted identity. According to mystics, such identity needs to be dismantled ("dispossessed," according to Trajtelová) for the "true self" to be shaped.

References

Acebedo, A. 2012. Phenomenological analysis of the transformational experience of self in *astanga vinyasa* yoga practice. PhD dissertation, Institute of Transpersonal Psychology. ProQuest Dissertations Publishing. 3509612.
Ales Bello, A. 1985. *Husserl sul problema di Dio* [Husserl on the problem of God]. Rome: Studium.
———. 2009. *The divine in Husserl and other explorations*, Analecta Husserliana: The Yearbook of Phenomenological Research 98. Dordrecht/London: Springer.
Alston, William P. 1991. *Perceiving God: The epistemology of religious experience*. Ithaca: Cornell University Press.

Alvis, Jason W. 2016. *Marion and Derrida on the gift and desire: Debating the generosity of things*. New York/Berlin/Heidelberg: Springer.

———. 2018. *The inconspicuous God: Heidegger, French phenomenology, and the theological turn*. Bloomington: Indiana University Press.

Antonov, Vladimir, and G. Vaver. 1989. *Kompleksnaya sistema psikhofysicheskoy samoregulatsii* [A handbook of a complex system of psychophysical self-regulation]. Leningrad: Cosmos.

Barber, Michael. 2017a. *Religion and humor as emancipating provinces of meaning*. New York: Springer.

———. 2017b. Religion and the appresentative mindset. *Open Theology* 3(1): 397–407. Retrieved 26 June 2018, from https://doi.org/10.1515/opth-2017-0031

Behrens, Georg. 1998. Feeling of absolute dependence or absolute feeling of dependence? (What Schleiermacher really said and why it matters). *Religious Studies* 34(4): 471–481. http://www.jstor.org/stable/20008189. Accessed 1 June 2018.

Bergo, B. 2005. What is Levinas doing? Phenomenology and the rhetoric of an ethical unconscious. *Philosophy and Rhetoric* 38(2): 122–144. http://www.jstor.org/stable/40238210. Accessed 30 May 2018.

Bronkhorst, Johannes. 2012. *Absorption: Human nature and Buddhist liberation*. Wil: UniversityMedia.

Chittick, William C. 1998. *The self-disclosure of God: Principles of Ibn al-'Arabī's cosmology*. Albany: SUNY Press.

Cohen, Leonard. 1992. Anthem. Sony CD release *The future*.

Cohen, Richard A. 1994. *Elevations: The height of the good in Rosenzweig and Levinas*. Chicago: University of Chicago Press.

Corbin, Henry. 1969. *Creative imagination in the Sūfism of Ibn 'Arabi*. London: Routledge & Kegan Paul.

Courtine, J.-F. 2000. Introduction: Phenomenology and hermeneutics of religion. In *Phenomenology and the "theological turn"*, ed. D. Janicaud et al., 121–126. New York: Fordham University Press.

Dadosky, John Daniel. 2004. *The structure of religious knowing: Encountering the sacred in Eliade and Lonergan*. Albany: SUNY Press.

Dahl, Espen. 2010. *Phenomenology and the holy*, Veritas. London: SCM Press.

Depraz, Natalie. 2008. *Le corps glorieux: Phénoménologie pratique de la Philocalie des Pères du Désert et des Pères de l'Église*, Dudley/Louvain-la-Neuve: Peeters/Éditions de l'Institut Supérieur de Philosophie.

DeRoo, Neal. 2013. Phenomenological insights into oppression: Passive synthesis and personal responsibility. *Janus Head* 13 (2): 81–99.

———. 2018. What counts as a "religious experience"? Phenomenology, spirituality, and the question of religion. Open Theology 4(1):292–307. Retrieved 14 December 2018. https://doi.org/10.1515/opth-2018-0022

Durt, Christoph, et al. [Durt, Christoph, Thomas Fuchs, and Christian Tewes], eds. 2017. *Embodiment, enaction, and culture: Investigating the constitution of the shared world*. Cambridge, MA: MIT Press.

Falque, Emmanuel. 2005. *Philosophie et théologie en dialogue, 1996–2006: LIPT, une trace*. Paris: L'Harmattan.

———. 2016. *Crossing the Rubicon: The borderlands of philosophy and theology*. New York: Fordham University Press.

Farley, Mathew. 2016. Introduction. In *Crossing the Rubicon*, ed. E. Falque, 1–14. New York: Fordham University Press.

Flood, Gavin D. 2013. *The truth within: A history of inwardness in Christianity, Hinduism, and Buddhism*. Oxford: Oxford University Press.

Greenwell, Bonnie. 1995. *Energies of transformation: A guide to the Kundalini process*. 2nd ed. Saratoga: Shakti River Press.

Guenther, Herbert V. 1992. *Meditation differently: Phenomenological-psychological aspects of Tibetan Buddhist (mahāmudrā and snying-thig) practices from original Tibetan sources*. Delhi: Motilal Banarsidass Publishers.

Hart, Kevin, and Barbara Eileen Wall. 2005. *The experience of God: A postmodern response*. New York: Fordham University Press.

Hastings, Arthur. 1991. *With the tongs of men and angels*. Fort Worth: Holt, Rinehart and Winston.

Henry, Michel. 1973. *The essence of manifestation*. The Hague: Nijhoff.

———. 1975. *Philosophy and phenomenology of the body*. The Hague: Nijhoff.

———. 2003. *I am the truth: Toward a philosophy of Christianity*. Stanford: Stanford University Press.

———. 2008. *Material phenomenology*. New York: Fordham University Press.

———. 2012. *Words of Christ*. Grand Rapids: Eerdmans Publishing.

———. 2015. *Incarnation: A philosophy of flesh*. Evanston: Northwestern University Press.

———. 2016. Ontological destruction of the Kantian critique of the paralogism of rational psychology. Analecta Hermeneutica 8. 17-53. http://journals.library.mun.ca/ojs/index.php/analecta/article/view/1708. Accessed 26 June 2018.

Hering, Jean. 1925. *Phénoménologie et philosophie religieuse: Étude sur la théorie de la connaissance religieuse*. PhD dissertation, Imprimerie Alsacienne, Strasbourg.

Husserl, E. 1989. *Ideas Pertaining to a Pure Phenomenology and to a Phenomenological Philosophy, First Book*. Trans. F. Kersten. Dodrecht/Boston/London: Kluwer.

———. 1993. *Cartesian meditations*. Trans. Dorion Cairns. Dordrecht: Kluwer.

Husserl, Edmund, et al. [Husserl, Edmund, Maurice Merleau-Ponty, Leonard Lawlor, and Bettina Bergo.] 2002. *Husserl at the limits of phenomenology: Including texts by Edmund Husserl, Maurice Merleau-Ponty*. Evanston: Northwestern University Press.

Ibn 'Arabī. 1975. *The wisdom of the prophets: Fusus al-hikam*. Aldsworth: Beshara.

James, William. 1985. *The varieties of religious experience*. Cambridge, MA: Harvard University Press.

Janicaud, Dominique, et al. 2000. *Phenomenology and the "theological turn": The French debate*. New York: Fordham University Press.

Jiménez, Juan Ramón. 1987. *God desired and desiring*. New York: Paragon House.

Kuhar, Robert M. 2005. *An exploration of the impact of education and engagement in science on scientists' metaphysical beliefs and spirituality*. PhD dissertation, Institute of Transpersonal Psychology. ProQuest Dissertations Publishing. 3182443.

Kungurtsev, I., and O. Louchakova. 1994. The unknown Russian mysticism: Pagan sorcery, Christian yoga, and other esoteric practices in the former Soviet Union. In *Voices of Russian Transpersonalism*, ed. T.R. Soidla and S.I. Shapiro, 7–15. Brisbane: Bolda-Lok.

Lacoste, Jean-Yves. 1994. *Expérience et absolu: Questions disputées sur l'humanité de l'homme*. Paris: Presses Universitaires de France.

———. 2014. *From theology to theological thinking*. Charlottesville: University of Virginia Press.

Lerner, R. 2004. Husserl versus neo-Kantianism revisited: On skepticism, foundationalism, and intuition. In *The new yearbook for phenomenology and phenomenological philosophy*, ed. Burt C. Hopkins and Steven Crowell, vol. 4, 173–208. London: Routledge.

Lomuscio, V. 2017. Key-phenomenon and religious meaning. Open Theology 3(1):629–638. https://doi.org/10.1515/opth-2017-0040. Accessed 26 June 2018.

Louchakova, Olga. 2005. Ontopoiesis and union in the prayer of the heart: Contributions to psychotherapy and learning. In *Logos of phenomenology and phenomenology of the logos; Book four: The logos of scientific interrogation; Participating in nature–life–sharing in life*, Anna-Teresa Tymieniecka, Analecta Husserliana: The Yearbook of Phenomenological Research 91, 289–311. Dordrecht: Kluwer.

Louchakova-Schwartz, O. 2011. Intuition of life in Tymieniecka's phenomenology, with a reference to intuition of *sat* in Śaṅkara's advaita vedanta. *Culture and Philosophy: A Journal for Phenomenological Inquiry* 2011: 40–60.

———. 2013. Direct intuition: Strategies of knowledge in the phenomenology of life, with a reference to the philosophy of illumination. In *Phenomenology and the human positioning in the cosmos*, Anna-Teresa Tymieniecka, Analecta Husserliana: The Yearbook of Phenomenological Research 113, 291–315. Dordrecht: Springer.

———. 2016. Theophanis the monk and Monoimus the Arab in a phenomenological-cognitive perspective. *Open Theology* 2(1): 53–78. Retrieved 27 June 2018. https://doi.org/10.1515/opth-2016-0005

———. 2017. Qualia of God: Phenomenological materiality in introspection, with a reference to advaita vedanta. *Open Theology* 3(1): 257–273. Retrieved 19 December 2018. https://doi.org/10.1515/opth-2017-0021

Louchakova-Schwartz, Olga, and Courtenay Crouch. 2017. Religious experience, adumbrated: Towards a phenomenological ontology of the region. *Open Theology* 3(1): 668–674. Accessed 26 June 2018. https://doi.org/10.1515/opth-2017-0053

Luhrmann, T.M. 2012. *When God talks back: Understanding the American evangelical relationship with God*. New York: Alfred A. Knopf.

Mackinlay, Shane. 2010. *Interpreting excess: Jean-Luc Marion, saturated phenomena, and hermeneutics*. New York: Fordham University Press.

Marres, Thierry, ed. 2017. *Idéalismes d'Orient et d'Occident: Exercices d'inter-fécondation*. Louvain-la-Neuve: Editions Academia.

Moore, Andrew. 2001. Philosophy of religion or philosophical theology? *International Journal of Systematic Theology* 3 (3): 309–328.

Nörenberg, Henning. 2017. The numinous, the ethical, and the body. Rudolf Otto's "The idea of the holy" revisited. *Open Theology* 3(1): 546–564. Accessed 24 June 2018. https://doi.org/10.1515/opth-2017-0042

Otto, Rudolf. 1923. *The idea of the holy: An inquiry into the non-rational factor in the idea of the divine and its relation to the rational*. London/New York: H. Milford/Oxford University Press.

Palmer, G.T. 1999. *Disclosure and assimilation of exceptional human experiences: Meaningful, transformative, and spiritual aspects*. PhD dissertation, Institute of Transpersonal Psychology. ProQuest Dissertations Publishing. 9932122.

Plantinga, Alvin. 2000. *Warranted Christian belief*. New York: Oxford University Press.

Rivera, Joseph. 2015. *The contemplative self after Michel Henry*. Notre Dame: University of Notre Dame Press.

Sato, Marito. 1998. The incarnation of consciousness and the carnalization of the world in Merleau-Ponty's philosophy. In *Immersing in the concrete: Maurice Merleau-Ponty in the Japanese perspective*, Anna-Teresa Tymieniecka and Shoichi Matsuba, Analecta Husserliana 58, 3–15, Dordrecht/Boston: Springer.

Siderits, Mark, et al. [Siderits, Mark, Evan Thompson, and Dan Zahavi.] 2011. *Self, no self? Perspectives from analytical, phenomenological, and Indian traditions*. Oxford/New York: Oxford University Press.

Singh, Jaideva. 1991. *The yoga of delight, wonder, and astonishment: A translation of the vijñānabhairava*. Albany: SUNY Press.

Steinbock, A.J. 2007. *Phenomenology and mysticism: The verticality of religious experience*. Bloomington: Indiana University Press.

———. 2012. In *Evidence in the phenomenology of religious experience*, ed. D. Zahavi , 583–608. Oxford: Oxford University Press.*The Oxford book of contemporary phenomenology*

———. 2014. *Moral emotions. Evanston: Northwestern*. University Press.

Stump, Eleonore, and Mike Rea. 2015. Religion, philosophy of. https://doi.org/10.4324/9780415249126-K113-2. *Routledge encyclopedia of philosophy*. New York: Taylor and Francis. https://www.rep.routledge.com/articles/overview/religion-philosophy-of/v-2. Accessed 18 June 2018.

Swinburne, Richard. 1991. *The existence of God*. Rev. ed. Oxford/New York: Clarendon Press/Oxford University Press.

Taipale, Joona. 2014. *Phenomenology and embodiment: Husserl and the constitution of subjectivity*. Evanston: Northwestern University Press.

Tymieniecka, Anna-Teresa, and Shoichi Matsuba, eds. 1998. *Immersing in the concrete: Maurice Merleau-Ponty in the Japanese perspective*, Analecta Husserliana 58. Dordrecht/Boston: Kluwer.

Uemura, G. 2010. Remarks on the "Idea in the Kantian sense" in Husserl's phenomenology. In *CARLS series of advanced study of logic and sensibility*, vol. 4, 407–413. Tokyo: Keio University, Centre for Advanced Research on Logic and Sensibility.

Ware, Kallistos. 1974. *The power of the name: The Jesus prayer in Orthodox spirituality*. Oxford: SLG Press.

Wood, William. 2009. On the new analytic theology; or, the road less traveled. *Journal of the American Academy of Religion* 77(4): 941–960. https://doi.org/10.1093/jaarel/lfp066. Accessed 18 June 2018.

Yazdī, Mahdī Ḥā'irī. 1992. *The principles of epistemology in Islamic philosophy: Knowledge by presence*. New York: SUNY Press.

Zahavi, Dan. 2003. *Husserl's phenomenology*. Stanford: Stanford University Press.

———. 2018. *Husserl's legacy: Phenomenology, metaphysics, and transcendental philosophy*. Oxford: Oxford University Press.

———. 2019. Consciousness and (minimal) selfhood: Getting clearer on for-me-ness and mineness. In *The Oxford handbook of the philosophy of consciousness*, ed. U. Kriegel. Oxford: Oxford University Press. (Forthcoming).

Zangwill, Nick. 2004. The myth of religious experience. *Religious Studies* 40(1): 1–22. https://doi.org/10.1017/S0034412503006772. Accessed 3 Jan 2018.

Olga Louchakova-Schwartz, M.D. Ph.D. (the editor) is a comparative religionist, philosopher, and interdisciplinary researcher. She holds the titles Professor of Philosophy of Religion, Spirituality, and Human Development at the Hult International Business School, and Clinical Professor at the UC Davis School of Medicine, Department of Public Health Sciences. She is also a Visiting Scholar at the Graduate Theological Union in Berkeley, Adjunct Lecturer in Spirituality and Phenomenology of Religion at the Jesuit School of Theology, and a Founding President of the Society for the Phenomenology of Religions Experience. Prior to her work in philosophy, she was a senior scientist at the Pavlov Institute of the Academy of Sciences in Russia, and after that, Director of Research and the Founding Director of the Neurophenomenology Center at the former Institute of Transpersonal Psychology, from which she holds the title Professor Emerita of Psychology and Comparative Religion. She studied phenomenology with Amedeo and Barbro Giorgi and with Anna-Teresa Tymieniecka, Her chief research interests are in religious subjectivity and religious experience in contemporary and historical contexts. She has published on fifteenth century and contemporary Kundalini Tantra, eighth century Advaita Vedanta and Neo-Vedanta, early Christianity, seventh–tenth century Hesychasm, contemporary Turkish and American Sufism, the Soviet spiritual underground, and the Islamic Philosophy of Illumination. Her cognitive phenomenological research of Tibetan Tantric meditation was featured on BBC, Science Daily, and other important forums. She has published more than 200 papers and book chapters, and is an Associate Editor of the Journal of Theoretical and Philosophical Psychology, and guest editor for Open Theology, De Gruyter (2017; 2018, 2019, 2020 to appear).

VOLUME I. The Primeval Showing of Religious Experience

Part I. Subjectivity and Religious Interiorities

Chapter 2
Reconnecting the Self to the Divine: The Role of the Lived Body in Spontaneous Religious Experiences

Shogo Tanaka

Abstract I would like to explore spontaneous religious experiences, "spontaneous" meaning experiences that happen outside traditional religious beliefs or religious institutions and traditions but still have a religious nature. Such experiences include the feeling of unity with nature, experiences during peak performance in sports, or the sudden ecstatic sensation aroused by listening to a harmonious chorus, and so forth. Although they are not always recognized as "religious" for lack of a proper context, they are intense enough to awaken spiritual feelings. What is experienced as "something beyond the self" in these cases may be the foundational source of divinity underlying all sorts of religious activities. My goal is to further explore the experience of divinity from the perspective of the embodied self in terms of the sense of agency. James (The varieties of religious experience: a study in human nature. Longmans, Green, and Co., London, 1902) listed passivity as one of the four hallmarks of mystical experience: the person feels as if his or her actions are guided by the Other while maintaining a sense of agency. In my view, this state originates in the function of the body-schema coordinating actions with the environment. In an unfamiliar situation, the body-schema organizes new bodily actions beyond one's intentions and expectations. Similarly, the body operates outside habit and as if following the Other's will in spontaneous religious experiences.

Keywords Spontaneous religious experience · Extraordinary modes of experience · Holotropic mode · Lived body · Body-schema · Passivity

Religious experiences occur not only in places of worship, nor are they confined to rituals, prayers, and meditations. There are certain experiences that occur outside the common context of religious activities. A well-known example is the so-called zone in sports. In the zone, athletes are fully immersed in their performance and

S. Tanaka (✉)
Tokai University, Tokyo, Japan

© Springer Nature Switzerland AG 2019
O. Louchakova-Schwartz (ed.), *The Problem of Religious Experience*,
Contributions to Phenomenology 103,
https://doi.org/10.1007/978-3-030-21575-0_2

play with a heightened state of consciousness accompanied by a joyful feeling (Young and Pain 1999). Another classic example is the "oceanic feeling," which the French novelist Romain Rolland referred to in his 1927 letter to Sigmund Freud. As if being one with the ocean, one feels unified with the infinite or eternal universe that extends beyond perceptible limits. Although Freud tried to reduce this feeling to a mere primitive ego feeling preserved from one's infancy, Rolland considered the oceanic feeling to be a fundamental experience that permeates all religious activities (Parsons 1999). I direct the reader's attention to this type of experience because it can happen outside a religious institution, religious tradition, or particular religious belief, yet its sense of divinity shares much with religion. Over the past few decades, some of these experiences have been investigated under the rubric of spirituality. However, "spirituality" is often contrasted with religion, such as in "organized religion versus personal spirituality" (Zinnbauer et al. 1999), or is used to refer vaguely to the existential dimension of life (e.g., "spiritual pain" in Murata 2003). Here I would like to loosely group them together as "spontaneous religious experiences" rather than spiritual experiences.

My aim in this chapter is to explore and understand the most fundamental aspect of religious experience from a phenomenological perspective. If spontaneous religious experiences can be found outside institutions, traditions, or particular beliefs, this would imply a foundational condition that animates our religious experiences outside established religious activities. Of course, the cases that I consider to be spontaneous religious experiences include those not recognized as explicitly religious by the individuals experiencing them. However, my primary focus is not on the sufficient condition for religious experience but rather on the necessary condition for it. As a phenomenologist, I am trying to describe certain types of lived experiences that constitute "religious" experiences. My attempt here is to find commonplace experiences that can be examined as religious experiences. As discussed below, the lived body plays a crucial role in connecting the self to something beyond the self, which seems to be the origin of our sense of divinity.

2.1   Examples of Spontaneous Religious Experience

As with being in the zone, spontaneous religious experiences can occur in a putatively secular social context, such as sports. Michael Lardon, a sports psychiatrist and former distinguished table-tennis player, recounted the following experience of playing in the zone during a match (Lardon 2008, xix):

> As the match began, I felt strange, as if I were living the dream of the night before. [Author's comment: Lardon had had a vivid dream of winning the match with acute sensations.] I started to warm up in front of the large crowd and heard their voices fade into nothing. Then I began to hear the emergence of a deafening silence juxtaposed with the sound of my racket grazing the ball. The ping-pong ball was slowing down, or at least that is what I thought. At speeds of up to 100 miles per hour, I still could see its direction of rotation, allowing me to block it, place it, and smash it at will.

In this example, perception occurs in a highly condensed moment in the present, as if the self—the perceiving subject—is totally absorbed in the moment-to-moment changing position of the ball, the perceived object. This experience coincides well with one of the religious aspects of peak experiences listed in Abraham Maslow's *Religions, Values, and Peak Experiences* (1964). According to Maslow, during a peak experience, perception occurs under extreme concentration and becomes object-centered while at the same time the self is decentered or forgotten, in the sense that it is not motivated by its ordinary concerns.

Maslow also pointed out that this type of altered perception supports religious cognition. As the self becomes decentered and its ordinary concerns become suspended, objects, people, and the world are perceived as such based on their very being. This perceptual shift brings recognition that the universe is unified as a whole and that everything—including the self—has its proper place. Although zone experiences are not necessarily accompanied by this sort of religious cognition, they seem to involve at least a shift in sensitivity toward the world as in the following example (Satiroglu 2004, 26–27):

> To really run is to let go of the constraints of life, to dive into the uncommanded, uncontrolled, and uncharted waters of life.... The old angst-ridden self and world has vanished; instead I am in a fluffy, borderless, weightless, thoughtless world where immersion in the moment reigns. At last I am waking up and shaking off the grogginess of a long, long nap. I feel close, so close to this animated and fluid world where nothing is fixed, concrete.

This paragraph describes a "runner's high." Here, altered perception reveals a tacit dimension of reality where the self intermingles with the world. While running, the self and the world unify as an animated being that changes fluidly from moment to moment. I wish to emphasize that this paragraph describes a runner's high as experienced by an author who does not recognize the experience as religious. In the rest of the text, the author clearly describes her experience of running as a full blossoming of life potential but not one of a religious nature. In spite of this secular analysis, the quoted words suggest a mystical experience in which one has achieved union with the divine.

It appears that embodied actions, such as running or playing sports, sometimes remind us of the unity of the self and the world through animated perception and vivid bodily feelings. This unity is hidden in a tacit dimension when embodied actions are performed as part of the everyday routine but is disclosed when actions are so loaded with emotion that they are performed beyond the ordinary mode. Let us consider the following case of singing, an action that is often driven by emotion (Horn 2013, 2–3):

> I've lived half a century now and you don't live this long without knowing some of life's sorrows. As long as I'm singing, though, it's as if I'm inhabiting another reality. I become temporarily suspended in a world where everything bad is bearable, and everything good feels possible.... Singing invariably and exquisitely triumphs over all my defenses; it has become a place where I still hope and still believe, and so I sometimes just lose it up there. I'll cry and cry with relief at the sheer joy of it all until vanity kicks in, when I realize my face must appear all twisted and funny because my lips are doing this weird quivering thing that I can't control.

Here, the experience has a clear structure: The embodied action of singing involves emotions intense enough to break down all "defenses" of the ordinary self before another dimension of reality, enfolding the self, manifests itself. In contrast to ordinary reality, another reality presents to us a world where "everything good feels possible." It is notable that the ordinary self gives way to the action of singing, which is also the case with the runner's high. When the tacit dimension of reality unfolds, the body seems to act spontaneously beyond the control of the ordinary self. During spontaneous religious experiences, the self is decentered not only in perception but also in action.

As Laski (1961) pointed out in his classic work on ecstatic experiences, this extraordinary state is often triggered by nature and the wilderness. Rather than mysterious, such contexts comprise natural phenomena, although the experience itself is often mystical. When watching a beautiful sunset or a starry sky, viewing a panorama on top of a mountain, or encountering a huge tree in a deep forest, we are often struck with wonder and awe. We also become aware of the infinite universe in which we reside. The following example illustrates this sense of wonder that arises while wandering alone in the wilderness. Though we are acting alone, the feeling is far from that of being alone (Weber 2014, 24–25):

> That loneliness is not the loneliness of despair but a place of humble contemplation where man encounters the greatest of all possible adventures—a glimpse into the depths of an infinitely vast universe. Such glimpses come when we find ourselves suddenly outside the cocoon of insular thinking, when we let the sense of wonder take us beyond ourselves to see something new…. What wilderness patiently teaches is that we are part of something much bigger than ourselves, and that there is far more to grasp than what we can see on the surface.

The wonder and awe that is often felt in the wilderness is strongly tied to the perception of it. Through this emotion-laden perception, we suddenly comprehend the tacit dimension of reality where the self is part of the universe and has a proper place in it. Certainly, spontaneous religious experiences can occur outside places of worship such as churches and mosques.

2.2 Extraordinary Modes of Experience

Based on the descriptions so far, we can assert that spontaneous religious experiences have several characteristics:

1. *Shift in mode of perception*: The subject often feels as if absorbed in the perceived object or the whole world. The perception occurs in an object-centered or world-centered manner.
2. *Shift in mode of action*: The self does not function as a subject to manipulate or control the surrounding environment as it does in the ordinary state. Rather, the self gives way to the embodied action.
3. *Self-world unity*: The self is not motivated by ordinary concerns and becomes decentered. Through altered perception and action, the self feels unified with the

world, connected to something greater than itself, or as having a proper place within the world.

4. *Emotion*: The shift in modes of perception and action often triggers sudden emotions such as wonder, awe, or joy. The reverse also seems to be the case: powerful emotions bring about a shift in modes of perception and action.

In short, spontaneous religious experience is one of the extraordinary experiences in the lifeworld and should exist alongside other experiences such as accidents, disease, travel, and ritual. However, unlike other extraordinary experiences, spontaneous religious experiences can occur in any form during mundane activities. Consider the runner's high—running is an ordinary experience of everyday life that can suddenly become religious. In its form, it is compatible with ordinary activity. What differentiates it is not the content but the *mode of experience*.

I label these spontaneous experiences as religious, including those whose subjects do not recognize them as such. There is a reason for this. Although spontaneous religious experiences may not be recognized as religious because of social context or preconceptions, these experiences are religious in an etymological sense. Considering the etymology of the word "religion" as the Latin *re-ligare* ("reconnect"), spontaneous religious experiences actually *re-* ("again") *ligare* ("connect") the self and something beyond the self. What is experienced as "something beyond the self" in the examples above is not *supernatural* but *transcendent*. For example, when gazing at the starry sky and being struck with a sense of wonder, the sky is experienced as something transcendent, and the self experiences itself as reconnected to the whole sky.

In previous analyses within psychology, characteristics of extraordinary experiences have been explored through the concept of altered states of consciousness (Tart 1969). There are diverse states of consciousness, such as hypnotic, drunken, and dream states, that are significantly different from a normal waking state. Moreover, each altered state of consciousness comprises a specific set of experiences, including perception, emotion, cognition, performance, and social interaction. The most illustrative example of an altered state is that found in dreaming. In a dream state, one tends to experience the world with more vivid emotions than when in a normal state and often performs unconstrained by laws of physics; for example, flying freely in the sky.

In recent years, altered states of consciousness have become more likely to be referred to as nonordinary states of consciousness. According to Grof (2000), there is an important subgroup of nonordinary states that represents a mode in which humans can experience themselves as contrastingly different from the ordinary state. He conceptualized this mode as *holotropic,* in contrast to *hylotropic,* which represents the mode in the ordinary state. The term "holotropic" is derived from the Greek *holos* ("whole") and *trepein* ("a moving toward") and means "wholeness-oriented." "Hylotropic," meanwhile, is derived from the Greek *hylē* ("matter"), and means "matter-oriented." Grof (2000) claimed that we experience ourselves as clearly "bounded" material objects in the ordinary or hylotropic state but liberated from the narrowly bounded self in the holotropic state. Grof also explained the difference between these two modes as follows (1985, 345–346):

> The first of these modes can be called *hylotropic consciousness;* it involves the experience
> of oneself as a solid physical entity with definite boundaries and a limited sensory range,
> living in three-dimensional space and linear time in the world of material objects…. The
> other experiential mode can be termed *holotropic consciousness;* it involves identification
> with a field of consciousness with no definite boundaries which has unlimited experiential
> access to different aspects of reality without the mediation of the senses.

The term "holotropic" appropriately conceptualizes a hidden dimension of reality wherein the self and the world are experienced as a unified whole. As in the above-mentioned examples, in spontaneous religious experience the self is decentered and relocated within the whole of reality. Certainly, the mode of experience here is wholeness-oriented, as Grof has pointed out.

However, I see a theoretical problem in his conceptualizing "holotropic" exclusively in terms of *consciousness.* In the passage quoted above, the holotropic mode is referred to as "identification with a field of consciousness with no … boundaries" and given "without the mediation of the senses." As we have seen already, spontaneous religious experiences are clearly based on a shift in the modes of perception and action, and this shift seems to trigger sudden emotions or vice versa. Therefore, we must examine the bodily grounded aspects of consciousness, such as perception, action, and emotion, in order to explicate both religious experience and the holotropic mode (Tanaka 2001).

The focus in this paper is not on the anatomical or physiological body but rather on the body that we actually live in through each and every action. As is well known, phenomenology has changed how we view the body. From a dualistic viewpoint that separates the body from the mind, one's own body is considered a mere object for the mind to perceive or to move. Phenomenology emphasizes two different ways in which the body is experienced (e.g., Waldenfels 2000; Thompson 2007; Gallagher and Zahavi 2012): the objective body (*Körper*) and the lived body (*Leib*). The latter is the body that is in question here. At the most fundamental level, the body does not appear as an object. Through and from my body I perceive the world, and through and with my body I act in the world. The body is a fundamental mediator of all experiences.

Based on the lived body, the notion of the self must also be updated. For modern philosophers such as Descartes or Kant, the transcendental subjectivity represented in "I think" was the foundation of the empirical self. In contrast, by starting the discussion from the lived body instead of the mind-body dualism, the self is already—before the reflective consciousness of "I think"—engaged in a concrete action toward the environment. Even when not involved in a particular action, the self is engaged with the world through the body, which has been built up with skills acquired through past experiences and is ready to act skillfully in the present situation (Dreyfus 2014). Perception of the environment is always underpinned by these skills; something in the environment is perceived as what solicits or affords the body to act skillfully.

In short, the self is embodied. The embodied self is represented not as an abstract self-reflection but as an action toward the environment and also as action possibilities in a given situation. Both Husserl (1952/1989) and Merleau-Ponty (1945/2012) used the phrase "I can" instead of "I think" to represent the self that is based on the lived body. Merleau-Ponty (ibid. 139) stated, "consciousness is originarily not an 'I think that,' but rather an 'I can.'" Along with the context explored in this chapter, there needs to be an account of the holotropic mode of experience in terms not of consciousness but of the lived body, and from the viewpoint not of the transcendental self but of the embodied self.

2.3   Action, Body-Schema, and Perception

To understand the holotropic mode in terms of the lived body, let us reconsider the function of the body-schema. In the field of neuroscience, the body-schema is considered a neural representation of the body that functions in relation to bodily actions (e.g., De Vignemont 2010). Thus, the body-schema functions as an implicit frame of the entire body that we refer to in order to organize and regulate our bodily movements. For example, we can perform ordinary actions such as walking on the ground, sitting down in a chair, or reaching for a cup without any deliberation. We can handle most ordinary actions smoothly and without reflection because the body-schema operates in the background.

Merleau-Ponty (1945/2012) borrowed this notion from contemporary literature in neuroscience and developed it from a philosophical viewpoint of "being-in-the-world." Instead of reducing the body-schema to a model that is neither a neural representation of the body nor an intracorporeal function of coordinating body parts, he understood its function as a prereflective correspondence between the body and the world (Tanaka 2013). We perform most of our ordinary actions in a prereflective manner, but these processes include responses to environmental solicitations. Merleau-Ponty explained that (1945/2012, 140) "to move one's body is to aim at things through it, or to allow one's body to respond to their solicitation, which is exerted upon the body without any representation."

His above-quoted assertion does not suggest a reflex action, because our actions are based on intentions, albeit habitual and performed in an almost automatic way. Rather, he described how the embodied self, represented as "I can," functions in performing ordinary actions. The embodied self, consisting of diverse motor skills, perceives possibilities for action in the surrounding environment. Moreover, once the intention of action arises, the body-schema "actively integrates the parts according to their value for the organism's projects" (Merleau-Ponty 1945/2012, 102). That is, it implicitly coordinates body parts into a unified bodily action toward the environment. As a result, the prereflective correspondence between the body and the world is realized as a concrete action, mediated by the function of the body-schema.

This discussion prompts us to revise our view on perception, as Merleau-Ponty urged in his work. In the traditional model of psychology, perception is understood as an inner process of organizing stimuli that are passively received through sensory organs. It is also understood as an independent phase that causes subsequent bodily movement. However, Merleau-Ponty stated (1945/2012, 113), "there is not first a perception followed by a movement; the perception and the movement form a system that is modified as a whole." (ibid.). In other words, perception is permeated by action from the very beginning. Drawing on the notion proposed by Gibson (1979), what we perceive is not stimuli but *affordances* that appear as action possibilities in the environment.

Thus, perception is potentially oriented for action. For those who know how to play drums, the sticks appear as instruments for hitting drums, whereas for those who do not, the sticks appear as mere objects for holding and shaking. For those who are thirsty, water appears as liquid for drinking, whereas for those whose hands are grimy, the same water appears as liquid for washing. For those who are hungry, the smell of food becomes salient in the perceptual field, whereas for those who are full, the same smell may make them feel nauseated. In the ordinary mode of experience, the need for action leads us to perceive a certain thing as an object clearly differentiated from the background, and acquired skills allow us to perceive it in relation to action possibilities.

Based on this discussion, we can now explicate what happens during a spontaneous religious experience. As we have seen, a shift occurs in the mode of action. Both the runner's high and the zone clearly reveal the self as totally absorbed in the ongoing action while the body almost moves by itself. Csikszentmihalyi (1990) also asserted that one experiences the merging of action and its awareness during a state of "flow." Although the intention in action is still maintained, there is no strong sense of controlling the body toward the intended action. The person may feel that the body itself knows how to act or that the action is being properly guided by an external force. Here, the mode of action clearly shifts from one that is ordinary and active to one that is extraordinary and passive.

As is well known, William James listed *passivity* as one of the four hallmarks of a mystical experience as follows (1902, 381):

> Although the oncoming of mystical states may be facilitated by preliminary voluntary operations,… when the characteristic sort of consciousness once has set in, the mystic feels as if his own will were in abeyance, and indeed sometimes as if he were grasped and held by a superior power.

From the perspective of the body-schema, what is experienced as passivity corresponds with the *emergence* of a new action. As is often observed in motor learning, when the body-schema coordinates the movements of body parts in accordance with environmental demands, a new action emerges (e.g., learning how to swim, learning how to ski). Originally, one's body is capable of taking control of itself in correspondence with the environment. In spontaneous religious experience, one's intention in action harmonizes with the spontaneous action derived from one's body-schema. In such a moment, the sense of agency—that is, "the pre-reflective experience that I am the one who is causing or generating a movement or action" (Gallagher 2012, 132)—is suspended temporarily. The person feels as if his or her actions are guided by something beyond the self or the "other." In my view, this sense of the other that is introduced by the body-schema constitutes a primordial source of divinity in religious experiences.

As perception and action form a unified system, this shift in the mode of action is also reflected in the mode of perception. When actions are not controlled by the ordinary sense of self (clearly bounded in a hylotropic state of consciousness) but led by the body-schema, the body is purely guided by the action possibilities latent in the environment. Regarding perception, this will bring about the two changes discussed below.

First, when the body is oriented to act in correspondence to the environment, perception is also focused on each affordance that appears in the environment. As each action causes environmental change and correlated affordances from moment to moment, perception becomes much more concentrated on momentary environmental changes. This alters the experience of temporality, as is often reported in religious experiences (Shanon 2001). The subject experiences the present moment in both condensed and extended ways, which may trigger the sense of *eternity*.

Second, when the body is not inclined to act (i.e., the body is not sensing solicitations for action toward the environment), perception is also not compelled by action possibilities. Instead, perception suddenly focuses on the whole environment. In such a moment, as Maslow pointed out (1964, 59), "the whole universe is perceived as an integrated and unified whole." The crucial difference between the ordinary mode of perception and this type of holistic perception is that the latter is accompanied by a sense of *infinity*. The body is not oriented to any action as in ordinary experiences. This means that there is nothing to be perceived in the environment. A paradoxical perception occurs in such a condition: It contains nothing of the environment, but reflects everything of the environment. This paradoxical perception involves a sense of infinity and arouses a feeling of awe.

2.4   Concluding Remarks

Previous psychological research has explained religious experience mainly in terms of consciousness. As seen in Grof's analysis (1985, 2000), such explanation distinguishes the nonordinary state from the ordinary state and gives primacy to the former in relation to religious experiences. Although I do not deny the importance of the nonordinary state of consciousness, the distinction itself seems to reflect a tacit, dichotomous understanding of the sacred and the secular, the supernatural and the natural, the other world and this world, and the religious and the nonreligious. This dichotomy may foster the view that religious experiences are *essentially* different from ordinary experiences. Such a dichotomy would lead us to overlook the spontaneous religious experiences examined here.

Along with this dichotomy, a dualistic view of the mind and body should be avoided. A dualistic view often considers that the mind controls bodily movements in an ordinary state. When this view is carried over for understanding religious experiences, passivity may be interpreted as the mind's control over the body abandoned and reversed during the experience. However, this interpretation would be simplistic. Even in the ordinary state, mind and body are closely tied to the function of the body-schema, and the ordinary state allows the embodied self to correspond with the environment in a prereflective manner. In most cases of the ordinary state, the mind is not controlling the body in a reflective manner. A better point of focus would be the relationship between the lived body and the environment rather than that between the mind and the body.

As seen thus far, religious experiences can occur outside the contexts of religious beliefs, religious institutions, or religious traditions. There exist spontaneous religious experiences that are more fundamental than common religious activities. From the perspective of embodiment, especially that of the body-schema, what guides our religious experiences are the relationships among the self, the lived body, and the environment. When the self allows the body to take control of actions, the body-schema starts to operate along with the prereflective correspondence between the body and the world, after which the sense of agency is temporarily suspended. At the same time, the modes of both perception and action shift into extraordinary ones. The self feels as if it is being guided to act by something beyond itself or is being led to perceive the whole world at once. We find a primordial source of divinity in these experiences.

Here we have explored not the sufficient condition but rather the *necessary condition* for religious experience. Left unexamined in this essay are the cognitive factors that make spontaneous religious experiences *religious:* that is, the factors that make the subject recognize the experience as religious. Although perception, action, and emotion in spontaneous religious experiences involve a sense of divinity, they do not seem to contain distinct signs of religiousness. In order to investigate this point, we need to focus on the environmental factors that provide a given context to an experience. Spontaneous religious experiences may be recognized as obtaining their religiousness through contexts such as rituals, publicly shared religious beliefs, holy spaces, related relics, and so on. Investigation of religious material culture as a basis of religious cognition is needed (See Krueger 2016). However, these issues are beyond the scope of this essay, and we leave them for a future study.

References

Csikszentmihalyi, M. 1990. *Flow: The psychology of optimal experience.* New York: Harper and Row.
De Vignemont, F. 2010. Body schema and body image—Pros and cons. *Neuropsychologia* 48: 669–680.
Dreyfus, H.L. 2014. *Skillful coping: Essays on the phenomenology of everyday perception and action.* Oxford: Oxford University Press.
Gallagher, S. 2012. *Phenomenology.* Basingstoke: Palgrave Macmillan.
Gallagher, S., and D. Zahavi. 2012. *The phenomenological mind.* New York: Routledge.
Gibson, J.J. 1979. *The ecological approach to visual perception.* Boston: Houghton Mifflin.
Grof, S. 1985. *Beyond the brain: Birth, death, and transcendence in psychotherapy.* Albany: SUNY Press.
———. 2000. *Psychology of the future: Lessons from modern consciousness research.* Albany: SUNY Press.
Horn, S. 2013. *Imperfect harmony: Finding happiness singing with others.* New York: Algonquin Books.
Husserl, E. 1952/1989. *Ideas Pertaining to a Pure Phenomenology and to a Phenomenological Philosophy: Book II, Studies in the Phenomenology of Constitution.* Trans. R. Rojcewicz and

A. Schuwer. Dordrecht: Kluwer Academic Press. [Original German edition *Ideen zu einer reinen Phänomenologie und phänomenologischen Philosophie: Zweites Buch: Phänomenologische Untersuchungen zur Konstitution.* The Hague: Martinus Nijhoff].

James, W. 1902. *The varieties of religious experience: A study in human nature.* London: Longmans, Green, and Co.

Krueger, J. 2016. Extended mind and religious cognition. In *Religion: Mental religion,* ed. N.K. Clements, 237–254. Farmington Hills: Macmillan Library Reference.

Lardon, M. 2008. *Finding your zone: Ten core lessons for achieving peak performance in sports and life.* New York: TarcherPerigee.

Laski, M. 1961. *Ecstasy: A study of some secular and religious experiences.* London: The Cresset Press.

Maslow, A.H. 1964. *Religions, values, and peak experiences.* Columbus: Ohio State University Press.

Merleau-Ponty, M. 1945/2012. *Phenomenology of Perception.* Trans. D.A. Landes. New York: Routledge. [Original French edition *Phénoménologie de la perception.* Paris: Gallimard].

Murata, H. 2003. Spiritual pain and its care in patients with terminal cancer: Construction of a conceptual framework by philosophical approach. *Palliative Support and Care* 1: 15–21.

Parsons, W.B. 1999. *The enigma of the oceanic feeling: Revisioning the psychoanalytic theory of mysticism.* Oxford: Oxford University Press.

Satiroglu, H.T. 2004. Metamorphoses. In *The runner's high: Illumination and ecstasy in motion,* ed. G. Battista. Halcottsville: Breakaway Books.

Shanon, B. 2001. Altered temporality. *Journal of Consciousness Studies* 8: 35–58.

Tanaka, S. 2001. ASC and the body: A phenomenology of "altered perception". *Japanese Journal of Transpersonal Psychology/Psychiatry* 2: 56–61. (in Japanese).

———. 2013. The notion of embodied knowledge and its range. *Encyclopaideia* 37: 47–66.

Tart, C. 1969. *Altered states of consciousness.* New York: Wiley.

Thompson, E. 2007. *Mind in life: Biology, phenomenology, and the sciences of mind.* Cambridge, MA: Harvard University Press.

Waldenfels, B. 2000. *Das leibliche selbst: Vorlesungen zur phänomenologie des leibes.* Berlin: Suhrkramp.

Weber, A.H. 2014. Wilderness and wonder: On saving the planet. *Minding Nature* 7 (3): 24–33.

Young, J.A., and M.D. Pain. 1999. The zone: Evidence of a universal phenomenon for athletes across sports. *Athletic Insight* 1: 21–30.

Zinnbauer, B.J., et al. [Zinnbauer, B.J., K.I. Pargament, and A.B. Scott.] 1999. The emerging meanings of religiousness and spirituality: Problems and prospects. *Journal of Personality* 67: 889–919.

Shogo Tanaka is a Professor of Psychology at Tokai University in Japan. He received his Ph.D. in philosophical psychology from Tokyo Institute of Technology. Dr. Tanaka is primarily interested in phenomenology and psychology, and more specifically, in clarifying the theoretical foundations of psychology from the perspective of embodiment, being inspired by the ideas of Maurice Merleau-Ponty. The topics of his published papers encompass a broad range of issues, including body-schema, body image, skill acquisition, embodied self, social cognition, theory of mind, and intercorporeality. From 2013 to 2014, and from 2016 to 2017, he stayed at the Department of Psychiatry of the University of Heidelberg in Germany as a visiting scholar, where he worked on phenomenology, psychology and psychopathology. His recent publications include, "Intercorporeality as a theory of social cognition" (Theory & Psychology, 25, 455–472), "What is it like to be disconnected from the body?" (Journal of Consciousness Studies, 25, 239–262) and other articles.

Chapter 3
The Silence of Sound: Crystallizing Nondual Metaphysics Through the Invocation of a Divine Name or Mantra

Patrick Laude

Abstract Starting with Henry Corbin's suggestion that phenomenology can be approached as "the unveiling of the hidden," the phenomenon is what appears to a consciousness that unveils it as meaningful. Now, in Sufi theosophy, the world is none other than the intentional object of God: "I was a hidden treasure, and I wanted to be known, so I created the world."

This opens onto the question of the Word: the Word is God's knowledge of Himself, but also the principle of creation. Mystagogically the Word has been referred to as the Name of God. Contemplatives have experienced the Name as a spiritual means of spiritual union, and as such a response to the creative Word.

It is within this context that I intend to analyze the bifurcation between silence and invocation. Is contemplative silence bound to fall back onto the limitations of the individual self? Must one think of the invocation of a sacred Name or Word as the methodical guarantee, as it were, of a transcendence of the ordinary egotic consciousness? On the other hand, apophatic spirituality postulates that what lies at the core of contemplative prayer is not the egotic consciousness but the universal and transcendent Selfhood, which Advaita refers to as *Atman*. So one of the major questions to elucidate is that of the relationship between contemplative silence as transcendence and the Word or Name as an immanent means of Self-realization.

Keywords Spirituality · Metaphysics · Mantra · Invocation · Sufism · Hinduism · Buddhism

The purpose of this essay is to explore the metaphysical dimensions of the methodical practice of invoking a Divine Name, or Mantra, as finalized by a spiritual

P. Laude (✉)
Walsh School of Foreign Service in Qatar, Ar-Rayyan, Qatar

Georgetown College (Georgetown University), Washington, DC, USA
e-mail: laudep@georgetown.edu

© Springer Nature Switzerland AG 2019
O. Louchakova-Schwartz (ed.), *The Problem of Religious Experience*,
Contributions to Phenomenology 103,
https://doi.org/10.1007/978-3-030-21575-0_3

experience, or a phenomenological recognition, of the unconditioned reality of the Absolute, whether it be conceptualized as Deity, Essence, or Nature—in the non-naturalistic sense of "the Way." Thus, the focus will be on the invocatory practice as it relates to That, *Tat*, the Unconditioned Reality that lies beyond form. We will particularly engage the nondualistic traditions of Asia, which approach the Unconditioned as both transcendent to phenomenal multiplicity and immanent to it: Advaita Vedānta, Kashmiri Śaivism, and several schools of Mahāyāna Buddhism will be called to task. This choice is justified by the need to attend to the paradox of an *a priori* seemingly dualistic practice—invocation, from *invocare*, the calling of one upon an Other—that finds its end point into an experience of Ultimate Unity and therefore claims to cancel out any sense of duality.

Moreover, the relationship between invocatory *forms* and the *supraformal* horizon of transcendence toward which they are oriented cannot but lead one to consider the polarity between Word as invocation and silence as a symbol and "manifestation" of transcendence. Thus, we will examine the way silence and invocation contrast and coalesce, and will argue for their paradoxical unity within the context of a transformative alchemy of the Word. In the perspective of the current essay, metaphysics—more specifically, the "theo-logy" of the Word—and spirituality, as invocatory way, are intrinsically connected not only as complementary human disciplines of thought and action but also, and more profoundly, as the two sides of a path of knowledge through identification. From one point of view, theological, or rather metaphysical, dialectics is like the conceptual reflection of a dialectics of experience. From another perspective, the former is like the point of reference for any realization of the latter. Methodologically, we will take Sufi gnosis as our initial guide in laying out the metaphysical foundations of the way of the Name, as its language provides an intellectual bridge between the Christian theology of the Word and Indian concepts of speech. The perspective of this essay is transreligious, however, as it takes stock of Hindu, Buddhist, and Christian sources as objects of inquiry and means of illustration. It does not, however, imply in any way that those traditions can be reduced to the teachings on the invocation analyzed in the current essay. It is all too obvious that each of these traditions offers a wide array of soteriological means, not to mention the diversity of their metaphysical and theological currents.

3.1 Epiphany and Theophany

In order to approach the way of the Name from a phenomenological point of view, it is fruitful to begin with Henry Corbin's suggestion that a consistent and profound understanding of phenomenology amounts to what Sufi gnosis refers to as *kashf al-mahjūb,* the unveiling of the hidden or an "epiphany of being." For practitioners of its invocation, the Name or the Mantra is indeed an unveiling of being, since it is both an ontological reality and an epistemological symbol. Furthermore, what is unveiled reveals, as it were, the mode of being of the consciousness that unveils it. In other words, in the way of invocation as in spiritual hermeneutics, the phenomenon is what appears to a consciousness that unveils it as something of itself and for itself (Corbin 1998, 24).[1] The object appears to a consciousness that "discovers" its reality and meaning as "its own." Corbin highlighted that hermeneutically this amounts to recognizing that there is an intrinsic correspondence between the subject and the object or, to use his own terms, that "the mode of understanding is conditioned by the mode of being of the one who understands" (Corbin 1964, 14).

Sufi gnosis, as the initial key in investigating the relationship between metaphysics and spiritual experience, provides a metaphysical paradigm for the phenomenology of spiritual unveiling. Thus, for many Sufis, the world is none other than the "intentional object" of God, not only in the sense of God's will to create but also, and above all, as signifying God's unveiling of creaturely reality and meaning *as His own*. Sufis like to meditate on the Prophetic statement "I was a Hidden Treasure, and I wanted to be known, so I created the world," and Ibn 'Arabī, in particular, makes the content of this statement metaphysically explicit when writing that "the Reality wanted to see the essences of His Most Beautiful Names or, to put it another way, to see His own Essence, in an all-inclusive object encompassing the whole [divine] Command, which, qualified by existence, would reveal to Him His own mystery" (Ibn al-'Arabī 1980, 50). According to this perspective, the God's act of creation is a dimension of His Self-knowledge and is, therefore, ultimately none other than Himself. God knows Himself through and in the world because He "recognizes" and "dis-covers" Himself therein by virtue of what He is.[2] This Self-disclosure "takes place" through the Divine Names that make the Divine Named known. For Ibn 'Arabī and other Sufi theosophists these "ontological" Names are, moreover, linguistically "named" by the "spoken names of the Names" provided by scriptural revelation.[3] This means that God knows Himself through mankind by means of the "beautiful Names" that He invites humans to invoke.[4] Starting from this observation our investigation provides evidence for a broader, cross-religious, recognition that the Name and the Mantra can be, and has been, understood as actualizing Divine Self-knowing through and within the microcosmic realm of spiritual experience.

Within the specific language of Sufi theosophy, the mystical concept of Divine Self-knowledge leads to contemplating the world as both a "theophanic" manifesta-

---

[1] "The etymological meaning of the word 'phenomenon,' taken in the precise technical sense of phenomenology, is very much the original meaning of the Greek word *phainomenon*. This is the present participle of a verb in the middle voice; i.e., the subject is manifesting, appearing, and being shown to itself and for itself. It is the middle, the medium, the medial voice of the verb. If it reveals itself to itself, it is because it always reveals something of itself."

[2] In all passages and commentaries pertaining to the Qur'ān and Sufi texts the personal pronoun "He" has been used to refer to God. This is the literal translation of the pronoun *Huwa* as used in the Qur'ān.

[3] "We should know that the divine names which we have are the names of the divine names. God named Himself by them in respect to the fact that He is the Speaker (*al-mutakallim*) [who reveals by means of His Speech]" (Chittick 1989, 34).

[4] Qur'ān 7:180. "Allāh's are the fairest names. Invoke Him by them" (trans. Marmaduke Pickthall). Except as otherwise noted, all translations of the Qur'ān are my own.

tion and a principle of "otherness": hence, potential alienation. God appears in the mirror of otherness, but this otherness entails difference and therefore an appearance of duality. This is what Sufi gnosis approaches as the veiling and unveiling of the Divine Reality. It must be stressed, however, that there cannot be a veil for God Himself, or rather for God as such, but merely from the perspective of what is other than Himself—which is, precisely, the regard of human vocation. For Sufi gnosis, mankind lies at the junction of the Same and the Other, the Divine as Sole Essence and Creation as the existentiating arc of manifestation and reabsorption (Chittick 1989, 30). The purpose of human knowledge is to unveil the treasure that lies "beneath" or rather "within"—as immanent, the world of creation. In other words, at the center of the world as object of God's consciousness there lies another "subject," without whom God could not know Himself fully as Same and Other.[5] This subject is the Universal Man, to use Ibn 'Arabī's and other Sufis' terminology: that is, the perfection of the human creation qua knowing God. For Universal Man—*al-insān al-kāmil*—human perfection is compared to an isthmus, a *barzakh,* that both separates and joins together the Divine and creaturely realms.[6] *Al-insān al-kāmil* symbolizes the distinction between Creator and creature, without which its status of "knower of God" would have no meaning; but it also connects them by being the very *situs* of God's knowledge of Himself in creation.

There is, however, besides the Universal or Perfect Man, another *barzakh;* that is the counterpart of the latter on the Divine side of reality, as it were, which is the Word or the Name. Besides Sufi theosophical concepts, a number of metaphysical formulas—from the biblical *I am That I am* to the Śaivite Mantra—crystallize the Word/Name as the quintessence of Divine Self-disclosure. At the same time as the Word has been experienced as the crystallization of Divine Reality par excellence, it has been apprehended also as the creative "paradigm" of the whole universe of manifestation. While any mention of the Word in a Christian context suggests the Johannine theology of creation,[7] analogous understandings of the Word are also to be found in other traditions, both among monotheistic theologies and in henotheistic or nontheistic metaphysics. In Sufism, the Divine Word/Name is the "utterance" of God, since God Names Himself in the Qur'ān and therefore believers are invited to invoke the Name of God, as a means of drawing closer to Him (Qur'ān 7:180). Thus, for Sufis, the Name of God is—on this side of the Veil—the very manifestation of the Divine Word. We also find in Hindu contexts the idea that the world of

---

[5] It is important to note here that the Same does not entail a "lack," being but the other "side" of the Other, a metaphysical mystery that Sufism tends to express in terms of the complementarity between the Divine Names *al-Bātin* (the Inner) and *az-Zāhir* (the Outer). The Same and the Other are not to be taken here in Levinas's relational terms, since the Other is none other than the Same, if one may dare such a paradoxical expression.

[6] This is why the "perfect man" is the "interworld" *par excellence:* "[Perfect man] is in fact the '*Barzakh* of barzakhs' [*barzakh al-barāzikh]*, the interworld who encompasses all interworlds, the intermediary who fills the gap between Absolute Being and absolute nothingness."

[7] "In the beginning was the Word, and the Word was with God, and the Word was God. The same was in the beginning with God. All things were made by Him; and without Him was not any thing made that was made" (John 1:1–3).

manifestation originates in the primordial *Omkara*, the sacred syllable that functions as the origin and end of all sacred utterances, as well as all worlds (Jones and Ryan 2007, 320).[8] The Word is both the source and the synthesis of creation, which it contains within itself as a virtuality. Kashmiri Śaivism also conceives the universe's unfolding as the result of a primordial vibration[9] associated with the projective power of Divine Energy, or Śakti. Furthermore, one finds in Mahāyāna Buddhism the principle of the Name as a matrix of seeds of meaning (*bījas*) and therefore of words.[10]

3.2   Invocation and Silence

In all such metaphysical accounts of the Word, the relationship—and ultimate unity—of the supraformal Ground of Being-Consciousness and its formal utterances finds an operative reflection in the spiritual differentiation, but also at times connection, between the invoked Word and silence. This appears in full light in the apparent bifurcation between the ways of the Name and the contemplative traditions that see silence/emptiness qua absence of all forms as the modus operandi and goal of spiritual discipline. These "silencing" and "emptying" forms of spirituality are particularly prevalent in the two traditions of Zen and Advaita Vedānta.

---

[8] "Om... is understood as the essence of the word *brahman* (*shabda brahman*) and is therefore, via its transcendent sound, the source of all manifest reality, where reality is known to be nothing but the congealing of sound." (Jones and Ryan 2007, 320).

[9] This is the reason why, through the centuries, Sufis have held the invocation of the Name as the primary means, or indeed locus, of *kashf al-mahjub* ("unveiling the Hidden") This disclosure of God's Reality was envisaged by Ibn al-'Arabi from two very different perspectives: one being attuned to the Divine Reality as Hidden, *al-bātin,* and the other as connected to the Divine Reality as Manifest, *az-zāhir.* From a human point of view, this amounts to saying that God can be known externally through his Self-manifestations (*tajalliyāt*) or internally as pure Subject or transcendent Consciousness. In other words, God knows Himself through the human knower in two ways: as Hidden, meaning beyond—or "below"—the objectifying and exteriorizing distinction between a subject and an object; and—in the contemplative gaze of the human heart—as Manifest, in the world and as world: that is, as Manifesting Himself under, and in a certain sense within, the veil of His creation. When referred to the Name, this means that God Name Himself in the heart of his believer as Ultimate Selfhood, but also Name Himself for his faithful as Perfect Object of worship who "extinguishes" the world upon which it is projected while making it "metaphysically transparent" (to borrow Frithjof Schuon's expression). In other words, the Name decreates, recreates, and transcends the very dichotomy of the two. It is silencing and affirming, while its ultimate reach lies beyond both negation and affirmation.

[10] The Word, as understood for instance by the celebrated Buddhologist Toshihiko Izutsu, is a meta-linguistic reality in which meanings and words find their unarticulated root. "Izutsu perceives WORD as articulating meaning. WORD is synonymous with 'primal, absolute, unarticulated reality,' the basis of all things. Our usual understanding is that a flower exists, and so the word 'flower' is born. But Izutsu's statement confronts us with a truth that is the exact opposite of this. If we take Izutsu at his word, a flower is born after being formed in the 'mold' of the 'meaning' of flower" (Wakamatsu 2014, 279).

In the context of Zen, the contemporary Japanese *roshi* Shunryu Suzuki refers to the "revolving door of the heart," the subtle center of consciousness within the chest, as the pure locus of selfhood: "What we call 'I' is just a swinging door which moves when we inhale and when we exhale" (S. Suzuki 2010, 11). The cultivation of an attentive awareness of impersonal rhythm appears as a privileged way of transcending the smaller "self" crystallized around impermanent thoughts, individual impulses, and psychic responses. Bodily rhythm is both a symbol and an instrument of the shift from ego-centered consciousness—which Zen perceives as a nonexistent aggregate—to Buddha-nature consciousness, which is none other, in this perspective, than the universal substratum of existence. Cosmologically, organic rhythms are conceived of as symbolic reflections of higher or deeper layers of reality, and they are used, phenomenologically speaking, as supports of concentration on the supraindividual core of subjectivity. Thus, for instance, a mindful awareness of breathing is understood as providing access to the Buddha-nature without the need for any other sort of sacred and ritual mediations, and therefore independently of any sacred utterance. In the same vein, Ramana Maharshi, the Advaitin sage of the twentieth century, "situates" the Self, the Divine *Ātman*, in our sense of "I." The Hindu school of Advaita, or nonduality, understands and experiences the Self, or *Ātman*, as the essential substratum of Reality, but also and by way of consequence as the totality of existence itself, since the latter is "nothing" independent of the Absolute, the *Brahman*, which is itself none other than *Ātman*. While being metaphysically "everything," *Ātman* is phenomenologically that whence breathing proceeds, "the place in between breaths where breath arises" (Maharshi 2015, 14). Hence, he favors the method of *Ātma-vichāra* or Self-investigation, whereby one "dives" into the source of I-consciousness. In both cases, breath suggests rhythmic patterns and polarity between breathing in and breathing out, but also a cyclical merging of end and beginning. This beginning-end is "transcendent" in relation to the rhythm that it "punctuates."

Other Indian traditions locate such silent focal points, considered as spiritual gateways, in the gap between thoughts or at the height of an emotional experience of enjoyment; in other words, at an interstice of consciousness that is free from egoic crystallization. (Singh 2014, 69).[11] This interstice, which appears as "relative" inasmuch as it is intermediate between two definite moments, is in reality "absolute" insofar as it is utterly free from such moments. One of the best definitions of this center of consciousness wherein Reality dwells is to be found in the nondualistic Kashmiri Śaivite tradition, which sees the universe as the all-encompassing manifestation of Śiva's infinite freedom (*svātantrya*): "That in which, whether meditating, remembering, reflecting, or acting, everything comes to rest, and from which everything comes forth in manifestation—that is, the heart" (Singh 2011, 260). For the meditator, the Heart or Center of Consciousness, while being the origin and the end of sequential time, lies in a "timeless time" that defies and

---

[11] "When the *yogī* mentally becomes one with the incomparable joy of song and other objects, then of such a *yogī*, there is, because of the expansion of his mind, identity with that [i.e., with the incomparable joy] because he becomes one with it."

transcends all articulations and mediations. This freedom of the Heart, both as the Essence of Reality and its "experiential" location, is manifest in that it can be realized independent of any methodical mediation. Any ritual or spiritual mediation is, in other words, relative and can therefore in no way bind Śiva's sovereign and absolute freedom to manifest when, where, and as He wishes. Thus, the notion of *anupāya* ("realization without means") refers to what is considered the highest of all forms of Śiva-recognition. There is, in a sense, no *way* as such from the dualistic subject of empirical existence to the Supreme Self, which transcends the realm of subject-object consciousness; a paradoxical fact of which Abhinavagupta (950–1016), the foremost spokesman of Kashmiri Śaivism, was acutely aware, denying the need for any "practice" or "progress."[12] However, there is little doubt that, in order to be actualized, this "immediate" realization presupposes an ambience saturated with manifestations of the sacred. It is enough to consider the devotional reverence with which Abhinavagupta's texts are imbued to understand how Self-realization remains inseparable from an all-encompassing traditional universe of sacred forms.

Without emphasizing such a radically unmediated possibility as *anupāya*, the teachings of Zen and Advaita tend to imply that invocatory mediations are not a necessary component of the path or are simply, at best, a provisional means thereof. Thus, these traditions favor introspective and imageless meditation on emptiness. We can note, in this respect, that such paths focus either on a purely intellective discernment of Reality, in the way Shankara does,[13] or on a physical support for meditation, such as breathing or the heart, two corporeal realities whose underlying function lies beneath the ordinary awareness of the individual. The first way is connected to a recognition of the immanence of the absolute Self within the human subject that flows from an exclusive contemplation of this transcendent Source of knowledge within. The second way rests upon an objective point of spiritual mediation in the form of organic rhythms that reflect the Infinite on the plane of physiological laws.[14] The rhythms of the heart and the act of breathing remain, in this

---

[12] "In this highest state of supreme God consciousness [*anuttara*], there is no need of spiritual progress, no contemplation, no art of expression, no investigation, no meditation, no concentration, no recitation, exertion or practice. Tell me then, what is the supreme and well-ascertained truth? Listen indeed to this! Neither abandon nor accept anything, enjoy everything, remain as you are!" (http://www.abhinavagupta.net/hymns/anuttarashtika/)

[13] It is important, however, to note Shankara's pluralism with regard to the methodical means of spiritual realization of this discernment: "It should be noted that in Shankara's perspective the realization of the Absolute is not restricted to any one method: it can be crystallized even on the basis of one hearing of the text *tat tvam asi;* it can result from 'hearing, cogitating over, and sustained meditation upon' the sacred texts; it can come about through the concentration on the inmost source of consciousness effected through the technique of abstention; and it can be the effect of the grace attracted to the invoker as a result of the invocation of the sacred syllable Om" (Shah-Kazemi 2006: 203).

[14] In the context of Sufism, Martin Lings summarizes the foundations of this organic mediation by considering the various levels of the Heart: "In virtue of being the centre of the body, the heart may be said to transcend the rest of the body, although substantially it consists of the same flesh and blood. In other words, while the body as a whole is 'horizontal' in the sense that it is limited to its

respect, quite distinct from the mind, which is associated with discursiveness and the empirical consciousness. The methodical import of this difference appears most keenly in Ramana Maharshi's remarks on the Mantra. In this regard, he asserts that the need for a Mantra varies depending on whether the meditation is concentrated on the mind or the heart. It is only with respect to the former that the utterance of a Mantra is needed. Without such a support, says the Maharshi, "you will soon lose your hold on the object of concentration" (Ramana Maharshi 2002, 84).[15] This falling back into the dualistic limitations of the mind, its want of immediacy, can be prevented only through the "transcendent" principle of objectivity provided by the Mantra. By contrast, the heart does not call for such a support, because its reality precedes any dualistic bifurcation: it cannot be an *object* of concentration, since it is the very source of the subject who concentrates. As such, the heart—seat of spiritual silence—is also the basis of all invocations. This appears in the Maharshi's exhortation to find the point whence the *japa yoga* arises (Godman 1991),[16] as well as D.T. Suzuki's remark on the intersection of contemplative *zazen* and invocatory *nembutsu* (D.T. Suzuki 2015, 38).[17] Thus, an emphasis on silence must amount to a recognition, be it explicit or implicit, that the ontological Silence to which it leads both transcends and contains the uttered Word.[18] In such a metaphysical apprehension of reality, what is manifest is *necessarily* included within the nonmanifest that it appears to negate. The Ultimate is pure Silence, while, being Ultimate, it cannot but encompass within its fold the Word that emanates from it.

---

own plane of existence, the heart has, in addition, a certain 'verticality' for being the lower end of the 'vertical' axis which passes from the Divinity Itself through the centres of all the degrees of the Universe" (Lings 1993, 49). The three main such centers are identified by Lings with the human and Divine aspects of the Spirit, and with the "Infinite Self": "the bodily heart may serve as a focal point for the concentration of all the powers of the soul in its aspiration towards the Infinite, and examples of this methodic practice are to be found in most forms of mysticism and perhaps in all. It is also in virtue of the same interconnection that 'Heart' may be used to indicate the topmost rung of the ladder, that is, the Infinite Self… 'Heart' can be considered as synonymous with 'Spirit', which has a Divine as well as a created aspect" (ibid.).

[15] "While fixing the mind's eye on a centre, as for instance between the eyebrows, you should also practise the mental articulation of a nama (Name) or Mantra (sacred syllable or syllables). Otherwise you will soon lose your hold on the object of concentration."

[16] "That Self will by itself be repeating always *aham, aham* ['I, I']. That is *ajapa*. Knowing this, how could that which is repeated by mouth be *ajapa?* The vision of the real Self which performs *japa* of its own accord involuntarily and in a neverending stream, like the flowing down continuously of oil, is *ajapa, gayatri* and everything. That is *ajapa.* Knowing this, how could that which is repeated by mouth be *ajapa?*"

[17] "*Zen nembutsu…* is the *nembutsu* practiced by some of the later Zen masters in China. It is distinct, however, from the foregoing three forms in this respect that the Zen adept treats it intellectually and not devotionally or psychologically. He tells his followers to find out who is the one who invokes the Name of the Buddha."

[18] In this connection, Frithjof Schuon writes that "pure concentration also is orison, on condition that it has a traditional basis and be centered on the Divine; this concentration is none other than silence which, indeed, has been called a 'Name of the Buddha' because of its connection with the idea of the Void" (Schuon 1995, 124–125).

3.3   The Pitfalls of Silence

Whereas some forms of spirituality consider meditational silence and contemplative emptiness as the very acme of their approach to the Essence—which is Silence as Nonmanifestation—others argue that silence may fall short, spiritually speaking, of taking the subject beyond itself, as it were. Thus, in a recent book on Buddhist-Christian dialogue, Roger Haight cautions that "without symbolic and mystagogical words, silent encounter would be an empty encounter with or of oneself. Words give shape to an otherwise diffuse, vague and effectively blind consciousness and direct it toward its object. Of itself, silent encounter has no referent beyond the self." (Knitter and Haight 2015, 23). Such reflections caution us that there is no transcendence of self from and by the self. The introspective experience of silence cannot but be spiritually sterile when it is not *informed* by a signifier and vector of transcendence or a vehicle of transformative presence. The limitation is not the experience as such but rather the experience inasmuch as it is exclusive of what within the experience is irreducible to it: the Reality that no experience can embrace, and of which the *Name* or the Mantra is the ontological symbol. Indeed, short of the latter, silent contemplation may lead to two harmful directions. The first amounts to absolutizing the self in a kind of Luciferan self-divinization. In the mirror of silence, the self may reflect itself in an indefinite and complacent self-possession. As for the second blind alley, it is none other than a *de facto* "neantization," not to say a spiritual suicide, that confuses the self-surrender and extinction of one's delusory egocentricity with a literal, and impossible, destruction of our conditioned reality. Thus, the "spiritual" ego mirroring itself in silence or emptiness oscillates between self-divinization and metaphysical self-destruction, or a false manifestation and a false-nonmanifestation.[19] The absence of "otherness" results either in a confusion between the empirical self and the absolute Ground of Being, or else it gives rise to a self-contradicting attempt at negating the empirical self on the very basis of a self-centered aspiration.[20] Within the larger context of our inquiry this is evidence *a contrario* of the intimate relationship between the symbol of the Transcendent and the subject of spiritual experience.

---

[19] It is instructive to note that in one of his spiritual writings, the amir ʿAbd al-Qādir teaches that the reason why Muslim prayers are said aloud at night and silently during the daytime lies in the need for a balance between manifestation and nonmanifestation. "Now, because of the symbolic correspondence between night and the darkness of the Essence—which is the sea of Darkness—he who is completely surrounded by it must certainly perish. Recitation in a loud voice is manifestation (*zuhūr*). It has, therefore, been prescribed for those who pray at night in order that the Darkness of the non-manifested should not totally overpower him and that he should maintain a link with the manifested so that he would not be separated from it in every respect. If it were otherwise, the darkness of the non-manifested would swallow him up" (Chodkiewicz 1991, 58).

[20] This is also why, from a different but related point of view, Frithjof Schuon has repeatedly cautioned that there is no spiritual knowledge without devotion, "no *jñana* without *bhakti*": "To say 'man' is to say *bhakta*, and to say spirit is to say *jñanin*; human nature is so to speak woven of these two neighboring but incommensurable dimensions. There is certainly a *bhakti* without *jñana*, but there is no *jñana* without *bhakti*" (Schuon 1981, 22).

Although the aforementioned spiritual dangers flowing from the absence of "mystagogical" words cannot be underrated, especially in largely secularized contexts in which silence is hardly suffused with sacred "vibrations" and can be all too easily confused with a mere absence of sound, it must also be recognized that the duality of silence and Mantra is only relative, and in a manner that becomes readily apparent in the diversity of invocations themselves. Thus, in what follows, we propose to explore how the way of the Name goes beyond the aforementioned dichotomy of "empty self" versus "necessary otherness." This is so because the Name is, at the same time, Word, Silence, and the very transcendence of their distinctness.

3.4 Spiritual Dialectics of Transcendence

The Name is an objectification of the Ultimate Subject, whether ontologically or soteriologically, as found both in various strands of Hinduism, and Jōdo Shin. As objectification of the Divine Selfhood, the Name conveys the reality of the latter from the point of view of both ontological presence and metaphysical truth. Being an "utterance" of the Ultimate, it is considered identical to the latter or as a manifestation of Its saving presence. The objectifying aspect of the Name as metaphysical principle is demonstrated, for instance, in how the Qur'ānic Name of God is conceived in Sufism as manifesting the various dimensions of the Truth (al-Ḥaqq) in its very form. For Ibn 'Arabī, the Arabic letters of the Name of God spell out the different degrees and aspects of Reality. Thus, the first letter of the Name, alif—which is also the first letter of the Arabic alphabet—expresses the "pure Reality" of God as the only Real. This absolute Reality is necessary and independent, like the alif that stands alone as the first letter/principle. The two lām that follow, mirroring each other, symbolize God's knowledge of Himself, the first in His Essence and the second, through what He encompasses in His aspect of "other-than-Him."[21] Next, the lāmalif is like a crystallization of the word lā, which means "no" and expresses therefore the negation of all that is not the Essence of God: that is, the return to pure Absoluteness. These first four letters form a chiasmus within which the affirmative (alif) and negative (lāmalif) dimensions of Absoluteness embrace the two aspects, intrinsic (first lām) and extrinsic (second lām) of Divine Self-Knowledge. As for the fifth letter, hā, initial of Huwa, "He," it symbolizes a return to the nonmanifestation of the Essence. Finally, the vowel u, or damma, represents the world as nonmanifested possibility (it may or may not be pronounced, depending on the syntax) within the Essence. This means that the letters of the Name range from the absolute and pure affirmation of the Real to the nonmanifested Essence, from the Absolute to the Infinite that "contains" the world in its All-Possibility. It could be said, therefore, that the Name of God symbolizes, articulates, and actualizes the whole metaphysics of tawḥīd, Unity or Unification.

---

[21] Leo Schaya, On the name Allāh (Michon and Gaetani 2006, 207–216).

Analogously, we find in Kashmiri Śaivism the idea that Mantras do encompass the totality of Divine Reality and cosmic existence. This is the case, for instance, with *SAUH*, the three letters of which—*sa, au,* and *ah*—symbolize the whole spectrum of the thirty-six ontological constituents or *tattvas*. *Sa* embraces the lower range of these, characterized by ontological difference—or a dualistic outlook—whereas *au* represents the third, fourth, and fifth *tattvas*, an intermediary range between pure nondifference, *abheda*, and difference, *bheda*, the field of the emergence of the latter within the former. As for *ah*, it corresponds to the Supreme nondual syzygy of Śiva and Śakti, the principle of all manifestation (Singh 2011: 124).[22]

We see, therefore, how Name and Mantra may encapsulate metaphysical doctrine symbolically, thereby mediating nonmanifestation and manifestation. This symbolic function is not only speculative, however, but also presential, theurgic, and transformational. This is not primarily by virtue of the form of the Name but rather as a result of its essential identity with the Name.[23] In this regard, symbolizing means asserting nonmanifestation in the world of manifestation—the Divine in the domain of relativity—while being *a priori* the ineffable seed of manifestation within nonmanifestation. It is precisely by virtue of these ontological roots and projective powers that Name or Mantra is considered an efficacious mediation, both transmutational and unitive. Illustrating this theurgic dimension of the Name, Ghazzālī, in his *Alchemy of Happiness,* observes that the secret of spiritual realization lies in the very repetition of the Name of God. As a contemplative practitioner, one "sits in a secluded place, closes one's eyes, suspends the work of sensory organs, connects the heart to the empyrean by continuously repeating 'Allāh! Allāh!' with the heart and not the tongue until one is unaware of one's self and has no report of the entire world or of anything save God Most High" (al-Ghazzālī 2003, 23). This contemplative virtue of the Name flows from its being mysteriously none other than God Himself, since it proceeds directly from Him. Similarly, in a Śaivite context, Lyne Bansat-Boudon observes that "the Mantra is not a simple formula for ritual usage, but represents ultimate reality itself" (Bansat-Boudon 2011, 50). It represents reality in the strong sense of making it present, because it "contains" it. Mantra or Speech "includes" the Silence of the Supreme in the way that Śakti is and therefore in a way "contains" Śiva.

---

[22] "*Sa* represents the three cosmic spheres (*prithivī, prakrti,* and *māyā*): i.e. the 31 tattvas of Śaiva philosophy from *prithivī* up to *māyā. Au* represents Śuddhavidyā, Īśvara and Sadāśiva together with *icchā, jñana* and *kriyā*. The *visarga* (the two dots—one above the other) represents Śiva and Śakti. This is the pervasion of *parā.*"

[23] This holds true as much in Hinduism as in Judaism: "Know that God and his Name are one" (Swami Akhilananda 2001, 182). "The Zohar ultimately declares that 'the Torah and the Holy One, blessed be He, are one,' for God and His Name are one" (Holdrege 1996, 200).

3.5   The Name as Silence

This principle of the inclusion of Silence in the Word may account for the fact that the way of invocation does not lay emphasis on silence as such and may even exclude it according to its spiritual means. For instance, one may be surprised by the assertion of Hōnen (founder of the Jōdo school of Buddhism) that the *Nembutsu*—the invocation of the Name of Amida Buddha—does not require observing silence (Fitzgerald 2006, 47).[24] Here the emphasis is definitely not on the spiritual goal of concentration and emptiness, so central in most other forms of Buddhism such as Theravāda or Zen, but rather on the power of the saving Name of Amida. The latter is not contingent on a particular subjective state or a set of objective circumstances (e.g., the absence of spoken words, mental representations, etc.) or even passional impulses (Williams 2009, 256).[25] The *Nembutsu* is like the very form of saving enlightenment that conveys the grace of the Buddha-nature. The inherent purity of the *Nembutsu* is akin to *Bhūtatathatā*, or Suchness, which is not defiled by the impurities of samsāric existence (D.T. Suzuki 2001, 84–87).[26] The *Nembutsu* manifests the *Dharma* that, according to Aśvaghosa's Mahāyāna classic *The Awakening of Faith*, "perfumes" every existential situation. The "possession of Suchness" (D.T. Suzuki 2001, 89)[27] becomes, in Jōdo, the *Nembutsu* itself, which is like a sacred crystallization of *Bhūtatathatā*. Invocation undertaken in ordinary or defiled

---

[24] "Silence is excellent, but it is wrong to suppose that there is less merit in repeating the Nembutsu while talking to others than when silent. The nembutsu is compared to gold, which, when burned in the fire, only has its color improved, and receives no injury though thrown into the water. In the same way, the nembutsu, though said when evil passions arise, is not defiled, nor does it lose its value though said when you are in conversation with others."

[25] This principle is illustrated, most poignantly, by the idea that a woman of ill repute may be saved by the *nembutsu* even though she cannot amend her life. "A prostitute is reputed to have been told to give up her occupation if she can, because it is indeed very sinful. But if she cannot give it up, 'then keep reciting *nembutsu* just as you are…. In fact, women like you are the most welcome guests of Amida's Vow.'"

[26] "Now Suchness is a pure dharma free from defilement. It acquires, however, a quality of defilement owing to the perfuming power of ignorance…. Suchness perfumes ignorance, and in consequence of this perfuming the mind involved in subjectivity is caused to loathe the misery of birth and death and to seek after the blessing of *Nirvāna*. This longing and loathing on the part of the subjective mind in turn perfumes Suchness. On account of this perfuming influence, we are enabled to believe that we are in possession within ourselves of Suchness whose essential nature is pure and immaculate; and we also recognise that all phenomena in the world are nothing but the illusory manifestation of the mind (*ālaya-vijñāna*) and have no reality of their own. Since we thus rightly understand the truth, we can practise the means of liberation, can perform those actions which are in accordance [with the Dharma]. Neither do we particularise, nor cling to. By virtue of this discipline and habituation during the lapse of innumerable *asamkhyeyakalpas*, we have ignorance annihilated."

[27] "If all beings are uniformly in possession of Suchness and are therefore equally perfumed by it, how is it that there are some who do not believe in it, while others do; and that there are such immeasurable stages and inequalities among them, which divide the path from the first stage of aspiration up to the last stage of *Nirvāna*, while according to the Doctrine all these differences should be equalized?"

circumstances imposes no limitations on its efficacy, inasmuch as the entire emphasis is placed on the inherent saving nature conferred through it by the "power of the Other" (*Tariki*). The latter is interiorized by the subject to the point of abolishing any belief in individual abilities. As a soteriological crystallization of the Buddha-nature, the *Nembutsu* is like an articulated silence that no words can alter. In this connection, Shunryu Suzuki's pedagogical contrast between "sound" and "noise" echoes the Jōdo view of *Nembutsu* (S. Suzuki 1999, 64).[28] Suzuki characterizes "noise" as exclusively objective, whereas "sound" is both subjective and objective. Noise, in that respect, pertains to duality, the perception of "bothering" otherness, whereas sound proceeds from, and manifests, unity or nonduality. In Suzuki's parlance, *Nembutsu* would be sound. This is because it proceeds from the subject and stems from the unity of the Buddha-nature. Even these realities—which do not proceed from the subject, in the sense of not being uttered or produced by the individual—belong to the Subject as Ground of consciousness, the universal substratum of experience that is none other than the Buddha-nature, Nothing is external to the latter, since it is like the universal foil upon which everything "appears." The *Nembutsu* as sound par excellence proceeds from within as a crystallization of the Buddha-nature and therefore "includes" the silence that it appears to break. This is another way of stating that "Form is Emptiness." The duality between the invoker and the invoked vanishes in and through the very invocation.

3.6 The Name as Metaphysical Isthmus

It is clear that, either as a manifestation of Silence (as "revelation") or as a means of immersing oneself in it (as spiritual method), the Word lies between two domains of reality that it essentially connects. From the point of view of theological dialectics the Word lies between the silence of nonmanifestation and the "deployment" of manifestation. As we have suggested earlier on, this can be encapsulated, in Johannine theological language, by the two foundational statements that the Word *was* God (*Theòs ên ho lógos*) and that "all things through the Word came to be" (*pánta di' autoû egéneto*). In the perspective of a dialectics of experience, such a twofold concept of the Word is explicitly translated into spiritual practice, as the Name of God is often conceived as an "in-between," a *barzakh*. This Arabic term refers to an isthmus between two domains of reality—as between the human and the Divine—that it unites while simultaneously dividing them. Thus, in the invocatory alchemy of the Sufis, the invocation of the Name, *dhikr*, stands between the human

---

[28] "Sound is different from noise. Sound is something that comes from your practice. Noise is something more objective, something that can bother you. If you strike a drum, the sound you make is the sound of your own subjective practice, and it is also the sound that encourages all of us. Sound is both subjective and objective." Sound corresponds here to Mantra in the sense of being an auditory object that is rooted in the practice of the subject and manifests indeed the deepest layers of consciousness of the practitioner. By contrast, noise is the "discordant" concomitant of duality.

invoker, *dhākir*, and the Invoked Divinity, the *madhkūr*. The Qur'ān states that the truest believers are those who "remember God standing, sitting, and lying" and those "whose trade and commerce do not detract from the remembrance of God." *Dhikr* is not one-directional, however. In fact, there is a deeper understanding in which the invoker is God, and the invoked, mankind. Thus, the Qur'ān states: "Was there ever a time when man was not a thing remembered [*madhkūran*]?" (76:1). The distinction between rememberer and remembered takes on, in each case, a different meaning. The remembrance that has God as a "rememberer" does not entail any metaphysical partition, since it participates in the Unity of the Essence: nothing is "exterior" to God or separated from Him. "Remembering" means here "holding into being": therefore, within the unity of Being, *wahdat al-wujūd*. The perspective is quite different when we consider the human remembrance of the Divine. Here, remembrance presupposes distinction, and even distance, since the very need to remember bears witness to a separation. This is so because the lower reality entails self-limitation with respect to the Higher Reality.[29] The Word is, therefore, the principle of separation when moving upstream but a means of union insofar as it proceeds downstream. From the former point of view, which is that of the human gaze upon the Divine, the Word is therefore a formal limit that signals transcendence, but there is something mysterious in it, namely the immanent Essence, which erases this limit. This is the reason why the Name is also seen as the principle of spiritual "nutrition" for both humanity and the entire terrestrial realm. As expressed by a twentieth-century Moroccan Sufi Master: "What is called the *barzakh* of a given realm of existence is nothing other than the pole [*qutb*] that governs this realm and gives it its growth" (Burckhardt 1987, 194). Although the term *qutb* refers, in Sufism, to the figure who is seen as the spiritual pole of the time, it can also be equated with the *dhikr* or the Name, inasmuch as the latter constitutes the essence of the former. The Name as *dhikr* is the essence of the *qutb*, both as "remembrance of God" and as "remembrance by God." The Name is rooted in the Divine and draws its reality and power from it: it is a *barzakh* in that it governs the realm of relativity. It gives it both meaning and being it does the former by orienting creation toward a return to its Principle, and the latter as the Origin of its existence. Thus, a *hadīth* states: "The Hour will not come until no one in the world says, *Allāh! Allāh!*" (Houtsma and Wensinck 1993, 1051) This is so inasmuch the *dhikr-barzakh* is a junction that "sustains" our world of becoming, which makes its return to the One possible. It contains the affirmation of the Real and the disappearance, *fanā'*, of the non-Real. This is an important point to ponder, since it allows us to understand how the *dhikr* makes union—and the consciousness of unity—possible without running the risk of egocentric delusions and confusion regarding mystical union. Its transcendence neutralizes the possible pitfalls in misunderstanding the nature of subjective immanence, while its immanence includes all dimensions of consciousness.

---

[29] Titus Burckhardt expresses this difference as follows: "Looking at it (the *barzakh*) in regard to its ontological situation, if one may so put it, it appears as a simple partition only from the point of view of the degree of lesser reality, whereas seen 'from above', it is the very mediator between the two seas" (Burckhardt 1987: 193).

Thus, the Name may be approached either as proceeding from the center of consciousness, emerging from the supraformal Self as objectification through sound, or as being received—that is, objectively "heard" (including mentally) and assimilated into the Self. In a sense, these movements are the two halves of one single cycle, corresponding to manifestation and reabsorption. The subject needs an object to know itself, symbolically speaking, while the object also needs a contemplative subject through which it can be "brought back" into its own essential reality. It could be said, furthermore, that the *koān* "Who invokes?" holds the key to the first half of this cycle, whereas the Mantric orientation of the *Omkara* and the divine Name in Arabic bear witness to the infinite reabsorption through the *M* or the *ha*. The spiritual plunge into the source of the Mantra unveils the deepest Self beyond the polarity of subject and object, while the gradual fading of the sacred sound also means a reintegration into the true Self, beyond the duality of manifestation and nonmanifestation.

In Sufism, by contrast, given the Islamic emphasis on worship/servanthood (*'ibāda*), the Divine Name, particularly the "Greater Name" or *Allāh,* refers prima facie to God as the Supreme Object of adoration and service. The Name of God is the main teaching of the Qur'ān. However, this centrality of the Name as both the main "message" and the means of worship manifests in a number of ways. The Name is synthetic, symbolic, and also the locus of a coincidence of opposites. The aspect of synthesis inherent in the Name of God means that it encapsulates the totality of the various dimensions and degrees of Reality as a kind of doctrinal summation. This is one of the dimensions of the symbolic character of the Name, which some Sufis—as we have already seen—have taken to mean that each of its letters constitutes an aspect of God's Reality. The second dimension of the Name's symbolism is connected to the traditional sense of being one with the Reality it symbolizes. In other words, the Name not only designates the Divine Reality but also conveys its Presence. In Islam, this results primarily from the fact that the Divine Name is revealed, uttered, and consecrated by God Himself in and through the *Qur'ān*. Finally, the Name *Allāh* is a coincidence of opposites, as mentioned above. It is a silent word or an uttered silence, a nonmanifest manifestation or a manifest nonmanifestation, a transcendent immanence or an immanent transcendence. Thus, Ibn 'Arabī can write: "The totality inherent in the Name 'God' is implicit in that form, which is at once not He and not other than He" (Austin 1980, 88). This means that the Name contains all dualities by virtue of its totality.

3.7 Conclusion

From metaphysical synthesis to mystagogic symbol, we have proceeded from the formal synthesis of Reality in the form of an ontological statement—a discourse about "the way things are"—to its phenomenological apprehension as Presence. This could also be referred to as a shift from the Mantra as a linguistic and conceptual unfolding of metaphysical meaning to the "folded" and synthetic phenomenological actuality of the experience of it as pure Presence. From the point of view of a phenomenology of spiritual experience there lies in this shift less and less conceptual substance for the mental dualistic faculty to grasp and, in an inversely proportional way, more and more silencing of the mind and "presential" grace to experience. Thus, beyond theory, Presence-Reality is an empirical coincidence of opposites that transcends all polarities and dualities. It is Nonduality emerging and crystallizing from within the world of Duality. In the experience of the invoker of Reality, invoking ultimately means an identification of the invoker and the invoked, hence the affirmation of pure and essential Consciousness itself. In this sense, the Mantra is the central energetic substance that flows from the Self or the I-Consciousness (Singh 1991, 110).[30]

As we have seen, in the Name—as in the principial Śiva-Śakti—there is a transcendence of all objectification and duality. In terms of invocatory practice, this is expressed by the Sufi principle of the unity of the invoker, the invoked, and the invocation. At this stage, the very question of a distinction between the Name and Silence is thereby transcended. All dualities and polarities are contained supereminently in the Principle. The latter includes, symbolically and spiritually, Silence and Word, the distinction of which can be transcended only *in* the Divine Essence. Accordingly, the Name-Word-Mantra is, within Manifestation, the reverse reflection of the inclusive transcendence of duality within Nondual Reality. In it, Silence/Emptiness and Word/Form are analogously included and transcended qua distinct, but they are so within the fold of an utterance, or within a manifested form of non-manifestation. This means that the Name-Word includes both Word and Silence, while lying beyond their polarity. It is a Silence made Word, a Word that contains Silence, and What neither Silence nor Word can contain.

References

Abhinavagupta. *Anuttarāṣṭikā*. Culver City: Lakshmanjoo Academy. http://www.abhinavagupta.net/hymns/anuttarashtika/
Akhilananda, Swami. 2001. *Hindu psychology: Its meaning for the west*. London: Routledge.
al-Ghazzālī. 2003. *On knowing yourself and God*. Chicago: Kazi Publications.
Austin, R.W.J. 1980. *Ibn al-'Arabī's Bezels of wisdom*. Mahwah: Paulist Press.
Bansat-Boudon, L. 2011. *An introduction to Tantric philosophy: The Paramārthasāra of Abhinavagupta with the commentary of Yogarāja*. London: Routledge.
Burckhardt, T. 1987. *Mirror of the intellect*. Albany: SUNY Press.
Chittick, W. 1989. *The Sufi path of knowledge: Ibn al-'Arabi's metaphysics of imagination*. Albany: SUNY Press.
Chodkiewicz. M. 1991. *The spiritual writings of Amir 'Abd al-Kader*. Albany: SUNY Press.
Corbin, H. 1964. Histoire de la philosophie islamique. In *Gallimard*. Paris.
———. 1998. *The voyage and the messenger: Iran and philosophy*. Berkeley: North Atlantic Books.
Fitzgerald, J.A. 2006. *Honen the Buddhist saint*. Bloomington: World Wisdom.

[30] "This I-feeling is the stage of great power, for all Mantra arise from and come to rest in it."

Godman, D. 1991. *Be as you are: The teachings of Sri Ramana Maharshi*. London/New York: Penguin.
Holdrege, B.A. 1996. *Veda and Torah: Transcending the textuality of scripture*. Albany: SUNY Press.
Houtsma, M.T., and A.J. Wensinck. 1993. *First encyclopedia of Islam*. Vol. 4. Leiden/New York/ Cologne: Brill.
Ibn al-'Arabī. 1980. *The Bezels of Wisdom*. Trans. R.W.J. Austin. Mahwah: Paulist Press.
Jones, C.A., and J.D. Ryan. 2007. *Encyclopedia of Hinduism*. New York: Infobase Publishing.
Knitter, P., and R. Haight. 2015. *Jesus and Buddha: Friends in Conversation*. Ossining: Orbis Books.
Lings, M. 1993. *What is Sufism?* Cambridge: Islamic Texts Society.
Michon, J.L., and R. Gaetani. 2006. *Sufism: Love and wisdom*. Bloomington: World Wisdom.
Ramana Maharshi. 2002. *Self-realization*. Tiruvannamalai: Ramanasramam.
———. 2015. *Who am I?* Lake Chapala: Infinite Pie Publications.
Schuon, F. 1981. *Esoterism as principle and as way*. London: Perennial Books.
———. 1995. *Stations of wisdom*. Bloomington: World Wisdom.
Shah-Kazemi, R. 2006. *Paths to transcendence: According to Shankara, Ibn 'Arabī and Meister Eckhart*. Bloomington: World Wisdom.
Singh, J. 1991. *Pratyabhijñāhridayam: The secret of self-recognition*. New Delhi: Motilal Banarsidass.
———. 2011. *Parā-triśikā-vivarāna: The secret of Tantric mysticism*. New Delhi: Motilal Banarsidass.
———. 2014. *Vijñānabhairava*. New Delhi: Motilal Banarsidass.
Suzuki, S. 1999. *Branching streams flow in the darkness: Zen talks on the Sandōkai*. Berkeley: University of California Press.
———. 2001. *Açvaghosha's discourse on the awakening of faith in the Mahâyâna*. Fremont: Asian Humanities Press.
———. 2010. *Zen mind, beginner's mind*. Boston: Shambala.
———. 2015. *Selected Works of D.T. Suzuki*. Volume 2, *Pure Land*. Berkeley: University of California Press.
Wakamatsu, E. 2014. *Toshihiko Izutsu and the philosophy of word: In search of the spiritual orient*. Tokyo: International House of Japan.
Williams, P. 2009. *Mahāyāna Buddhism: The doctrinal foundations*. London/New York: Routledge.

Patrick Laude joined the faculty of Georgetown University in 1991. He has been teaching courses in religious studies at the School of Foreign Service in Qatar since 2006. A former fellow of the *Ecole Normale Supérieure* in Paris, he earned a Master's degree in philosophy from the University of Paris IV Sorbonne, and a doctorate in French literature from Indiana University. His scholarly interests include comparative mysticism and metaphysics, poetry and mysticism, and Western representations of Asian spiritual traditions. He has authored a dozen books including: *Shimmering Mirrors: Reality and Appearance in Contemplative Metaphysics East and West*, Albany: SUNY Press, 2017, *Pathways to an Inner Islam*, Albany: SUNY Press, 2010, *Louis Massignon: The Vow and the Oath*, London: Matheson Trust, 2011, *Pray Without Ceasing: The Way of the Invocation in World Religion*, Bloomington, Indiana: World Wisdom, 2006, *Divine Play, Sacred Laughter and Spiritual Understanding*. New York: Palgrave McMillan, 2005.

Chapter 4
Preserving Wonder Through the Reduction: Husserl, Marion, and Merleau-Ponty

Espen Dahl

Abstract By both Plato and Aristotle wonder is understood as the beginning of philosophy. How does phenomenology relate to this tradition? And more specifically, how does phenomenology's central methodological step of reduction relate to wonder? I suggest that as a minimal understanding, we can start by describing wonder phenomenologically as the unresolved tension between the familiar and the strange. Looking at Husserl's Cartesian way to the reduction, I argue that rather than bringing wonder into focus, it dissolves wonder's inner tension because of Husserl's high standards of epistemic certainty. Marion, on the other hand, working out his notion of reduction in criticism of Husserl's, wants to pave the way for the pure givenness, in which case the "impurity" of the "between" pertaining to wonder also dissolves. The most fruitful approach is found in Merleau-Ponty's phenomenology, not only stressing the mystery and enigma at the heart of his phenomenological investigations but in fact identifying reduction with wonder. Finally, I want to sketch out how this position also relates to Merleau-Ponty's understanding of Christianity, especially incarnation, where wonder and mystery are exemplarily coming to expression.

Keywords Wonder · Phenomenology · Reduction · Husserl · Merleau-Ponty · Marion

"For it was because of wonder that men both now and originally began to philosophize" (Aristotle 2004, 982b). "Because that experience, the feeling of wonder, is very characteristic of a philosopher: philosophy has no other starting-point" (Plato 2014, 155d). These two much-quoted sayings, from Plato and Aristotle, not only say something crucial about how philosophy arises, but they also raise the question about what wonder is. If one pursues those texts for an answer to the latter question,

E. Dahl (✉)
UiT – The Arctic University of Norway, Tromsø, Norway
e-mail: espen.dahl@uit.no

© Springer Nature Switzerland AG 2019
O. Louchakova-Schwartz (ed.), *The Problem of Religious Experience*,
Contributions to Phenomenology 103,
https://doi.org/10.1007/978-3-030-21575-0_4

one is likely to be disappointed; for even as crucial as the beginning of philosophy is, both texts are far more concerned with the progression from wonder than with the nature of wonder itself. Perhaps the metaphysical rationale of Aristotle and Plato is not well fitted to account for the ephemeral and evasive phenomenon of wonder. Perhaps religion is more suited, given its often less direct account, one less geared toward explanation and understanding. And indeed, wonder plays a decisive role in the Biblical legacy, whether in the Old Testament's encounters with revelations (as in the burning bush), the wondrous fear of God (also the beginning of wisdom), or in the New Testament's wonder at the birth of Christ, his miracles, transfiguration, and resurrection. But whether we start with philosophy or religion, wonder itself seems to be as significant as it is conceptually underdeveloped.

Phenomenology seems a very promising candidate for accounting for wonder; for however complex and manifold this tradition is, phenomenology tends to cultivate a devoted attention to whatever is given to experience, responding not by explanation but by description. Nevertheless, phenomenology not only describes what we otherwise take for granted in daily life but also has its own way to lay free the manifest phenomena. From Edmund Husserl's official introduction of the term in 1907, the "phenomenological reduction" became for him the crucial methodological step not only to his descriptive account of any phenomena but also to the understanding of his philosophical position. Hence, if there is to be a phenomenology of wonder, a phenomenology—at least in the Husserlian tradition—would necessarily have to pass through the reduction. Moreover, if wonder is the starting point of philosophy as such, so is reduction to phenomenology. Hence, the question is how those "beginnings" relate: Do they eclipse each other as rivals of the true beginning, or do they somehow coincide, perhaps enriching each other?

After first a preliminary sketch of the phenomenon of wonder, I want to suggest why I think two important understandings of reduction actually preclude the access to wonder, namely Husserl's so-called Cartesian way and Marion's pure reduction. I will claim that the most promising account is found in Merleau-Ponty's phenomenology, which not only stresses the mystery and enigma at the heart of phenomenological investigations but in fact identifies reduction with wonder. Finally, I want to sketch out how this position also relates to Merleau-Ponty's comments on Christianity, especially on incarnation, where I will argue that wonder and mystery are exemplary in coming to expression through religious understanding.

4.1 Wonder: A Phenomenological Clue

Before I attend to the question of reduction, it is necessary to have at least a preliminary rough outline of what wonder is. For only starting from our average, ordinary understanding of wonder will it be possible to steer the investigation entailed in the reduction toward the relevant structures, layers, and dynamics. Phenomenology hence needs to start out from the ordinary world, or what Husserl calls the natural attitude, where everything happens as it happens, where our directedness toward things, others, and the world are taken as matters of course. However prephilosophi-cal these experiences are, they serve as "transcendental clues" that guide the reduc-tion as it unearths the implications of the phenomenon (Husserl 1960, 50). It follows from the notion of intentionality that any experience is the correlation between something we are directed toward and some specific form of directedness. In won-der, however, it is not so much a question of intentional directedness, since it is better understood as a response to a certain form of affectedness. Still, wonder is correlated with something, something enigmatic, mysterious, or perhaps astonish-ing that appeals to us in its particular way. It may be tempting to think that wonder is awakened by something entirely new, the like of which one has never seen before, or to take something so impressive and overpowering that it blows out any ability to comprehend it—perhaps in powerful works of art or natural events such as thunder and lightning. For all the affects and dizziness that such encounters stir, one may ask if they really are what we mean by wonder. Heidegger has argued convincingly that it is crucial not to confuse wonder either with curiosity, allured by the new and for-eign, or with astonishment, by which one is lifted out of the ordinary setting by means of what is extraordinary (Heidegger 1994, 142–143; Sallis 1995, 208; cf. Descartes 2015, 220, 224). Whereas both curiosity and astonishment seem to lift us out or pull us away from the ordinary, and thus to open a cleft between the extraor-dinary and the ordinary, wonder does arguably not presuppose any such cleft. And yet, it will not be wonder if there is nothing about it that strikes one or stands out or prompts a new perspective.

Wonder, it seems, must both be embedded in the ordinary—and still not be about the ordinary, at least not in the ordinary way. Take a trivial example: I wake up one morning and gaze out the window: The garden I know so well is covered in snow. I wonder at it—not because it is something completely new (it is the same garden as yesterday), not because it is astonishing (the experience is quiet, not intruding), but precisely because the same garden has turned different. Or I receive a piece of bread and still insist it is the presence of the body of Christ. The question is: What is so wondrous about that snow and that bread? Probably it is, as Mary-Jane Rubenstein aptly says, "because wonder wonders at the strangeness of the most familiar" (Rubenstein 2008, 8). Wonder is not a standing experience of our natural attitude, because it would undercut the world as our familiar home, and yet that very home cannot be so familiar to us that it forecloses any experiences of its internal strange-ness, or else the wonder would never occur, and the world would close in on itself.

Wonder can either be awakened by something strange, as a new face of the ordi-nary is making itself felt, or it may start from the familiar—our ways of thinking and acting, say—when we become aware of its inner strangeness. In both cases, wondering puts us in the place between, between the familiar of our natural attitude and the strange, foreign, somehow inaccessible. Heidegger says (1994, 145):

> Not knowing the way out or the way in, wonder dwells in a between, between the most usual, beings, and their unusualness, their "is." It is wonder that first liberates this between as the between and separates it out. Wonder—understood transitively—brings forth the showing of what is most usual in its unusualness.

If wonder can provoke thinking, and if such thinking is philosophy, then being true to its origin, phenomenology should not shy away from the fleeting state in between: that is, it must resist pinning down the phenomena to categories or preconceived theories as if the wonder were a problem to be solved. Can reduction lead us back to such wonder, taken as "the thing itself"?

4.2 Husserl's Cartesian Reduction: The Way Inward

It is perhaps impossible to give a short account of Husserl's reduction, for not only can he speak of various forms of reduction—such as eidetic, phenomenological, and transcendental reduction, the reduction to the sphere of ownness—but he also constantly revised his notion of them. Even if one is restricting oneself to the transcendental reduction, as I will, there are different accounts of it. Husserl came to claim that this reduction could be carried out through different "ways," such as the way over psychology, the way over ontology or the life-world, and the Cartesian way (Kern 1962). Even though Husserl himself grew critical toward aspects of it, it is safe to say that the Cartesian way remains most central; it marks his initial approach to reduction in 1907, and remains predominant in his main works, the *Ideas* (2014) and *Cartesian Meditations* (1960), and for this reason it has had the greatest impact on the ensuing phenomenological movement.

What makes this reduction Cartesian is that Husserl explicitly picks up on central motifs found in Descartes, in particular the aim of establishing a foundation for knowledge as such, but also the demand that such a certain foundation must stand the test of doubt. For Husserl the positive criterion for what cannot be doubted is evidence. Evidence, according to Husserl, must be understood in terms of intention and fulfillment, conceived of as a (relatively empty) form that can be filled with matter. When the intentional form is fulfilled, evidence is the experiential correlate to truth (Husserl 1960, 11). However, evidence comes in grades of certainty. Absolute evidence both demands adequacy, that the intentional acts be fulfilled, and must also be beyond apodicticity, that it is given beyond doubt.[1] As it turns out, outer perception cannot meet the demands of adequacy, since anything located in space is given perceptively and hence with sides absent. As for apodictic evidence, things and the world as such can, Husserl claims, intelligibly be doubted and hence are not absolutely necessary. However, the transcendental ego with its intentional acts cannot thus be doubted, and the givenness of its experience is, if considered purely as experience, also adequately given (Husserl 2014, 77–83). In Cartesian lingo, that means that ego and its cogitations must be the founding feature of a fundamental philosophy.

This makes up the Cartesian backdrop that motivates Husserl's inward turn toward givenness as such. Husserl's preparatory and negative step, the *epoché*,

---

[1] Husserl will gradually come to doubt that adequate and apodictic evidence are reachable but retain them as teleological ideas: Husserl 1960, 14.

invites us to free ourselves of all the opinions and ways in which prejudices creep into and color our conception of the world. "Putting in brackets," which is Husserl's translation of the Greek word *epoché* borrowed from the Greek Skeptics, does not suggest striking out, as if the world and everything in it should suddenly disappear from view. Rather it means that what is put within the parenthesis is no longer regarded as part of the context in which it ordinarily has its place, and thus becomes ready for a new inspection. All the stuff of our natural world is still there, but taken out of play, neutralized. In a stepwise manner, Husserl dispenses with belief in the existence of transcendent objects, the teaching of theories and science, religious beliefs, psychological facts, God, and so on. This *epoché* culminates in bracketing our most basic conviction, *Urdoxa*, which is the name for the world simply being there in every moment of our wakeful experiences (Husserl 2014, 52).

After having dispensed with the natural attitude and the convictions and prejudices that go with it, our intentional consciousness is still directed toward objects, others, and the world as their horizon. However, what appears is not regarded as simply being there, outside us, but is regarded rather as manners of givenness: that is, as phenomena, things as they appear. This takes a radical turning away from the naive embrace of the world in the natural attitude and a turning toward the very intentional consciousness of something as such. Since it is paramount not to distort the givenness of the world and all that is implied in it, the ego must split itself (Husserl 1960, 65).[2] The naively interested ego retains its directedness to the world, but the reflective ego becomes a disengaged spectator, which directs itself purely toward the first ego's experiences in their modes of appearance. The sharpness and richness of the analyses of what thereby is given in the transcendental experience belong to Husserl's lifelong occupations and great achievements. There are analyses of the distinction between the given and the way it is given, *noēma* and *noēsis*, between sensual content and intentional form, different noematic regions, various noetic modes, passive and active synthesis, internal time, and so on. Taken as a whole, the transcendental reduction aims at disclosing the structures of constitution, the process that builds up the phenomena as appearing the way they do. In the transcendental sphere, all evidence is apodictic and adequate, since it cannot either be doubted or be unfulfilled. As Husserl reaches the absolute givenness by means of his phenomenological reduction, he can say that phenomenology must "base itself on the cognition which is immediately evident and of such kind that, as absolutely clear and indubitable, it excludes every doubt of its possibility and contains none of the puzzles [*Rätzel*] which had led to all the skeptical confusion" (Husserl 1990, 26).

The question is whether Husserl's Cartesian way to the reduction can pave the way for an analysis of wonder. There is in fact one place where he seems to indicate a link between reduction and wonder (Kingwell 2000, 91–93). From his late period, a passage from his Vienna lecture stands out, in which he traces the historical origin of science and its recent crisis. In this history, Husserl argues that a decisive break occurs as the Greek philosophy emerges—not because the themes are novel but

---

[2] Eugen Fink (1995, 19–24) has elaborated and radicalized this splitting. For a reading that stresses the perseverance of the natural world after the reductions, see Overgaard 2015.

because of the radicalism of the new attitude that goes with it. The Greek philosophy is the discovery of an attitude that abstains from all practice and is purely theoretical. It is in this context of theoretical attitude that wonder has its proper place.
Husserl writes (1970, 285):

> Sharply distinguished from this universal but mythical-practical attitude is the "theoretical"
> attitude, which is not practical in any sense used so far, the attitude of *thaumazein*, to which
> the great figures of the first culminating period of Greek philosophy, Plato and Aristotle,
> traced the origin of philosophy. Man becomes gripped by the passion of a world-view and
> world knowledge that turns away from all practical interests and, within the closed sphere
> of its cognitive activity, in the times devoted to it, strives for and achieves nothing but pure
> *theōria*.

Implicitly, Husserl traces his own *epoché* to this emergence of wonder in Greek
antiquity. As in its first turn to philosophy, the phenomenological reduction suspends all practical interests and turns toward a theoretical attitude. Husserl acknowledges the place of wonder as the beginning of philosophy, and this suggests also that
wonder is a state of abstention from practical life. But as his lecture proceeds, it
becomes increasingly clear that it is the theoretical attitude that is of importance to
him—not wonder. Indeed, wonder is left phenomenologically underdeveloped, both
here and elsewhere in Husserl's writing. Why?

If my initial sketch of wonder holds true, it seems that the "in between" pertains
to its essence, in which case wonder has one foot in the everyday or natural attitude
and one foot in something exceeding it, as other and foreign to it. Given the outline
of Husserl's project of founding a phenomenological science, it is perhaps not
strange that wonder is not developed in his philosophy: the ambiguity of the
"between" falls outside the framework of Husserl's Cartesian way. Husserl seems to
be driven by the ghost of relativism and skepticism, to such a degree that he exag-
gerates the demand for evidence and certitude. Whence stems the demand for absolute evidence? It does not seem to emerge from "the things themselves," which for
the most part are not given in such evidence, Heidegger argues. Such demands
seem, again according to both Heidegger and Marion, to be the dogmatic metaphysical inheritance rather than the result of phenomenological investigations. In
contradistinction to the spirit of phenomenology, those demands are imposed on the
phenomena, rather than emanating from their givenness (Heidegger 1985, 147;
Marion 1998, 47–48, 51, 54). Precisely because of the aims for "phenomenology as
rigorous science," as one of Husserl's programmatic titles reads, particular regions
of phenomena fall outside his scope—and so does wonder. Tellingly, in a passage
where Husserl appeals to the necessity of eidetic and transcendental reduction, he
states (1980, 64):

> The wonder of all wonders is pure Ego and pure consciousness: and precisely this wonder
> disappears as soon as the light of phenomenology falls upon it and subjects it to eidetic
> analysis. The wonder disappears by changing into an entire science with a plethora of dif-
> ficult scientific problems. Wonder is something unconceivable; the problematical in the
> form of scientific problems is something conceivable, it is the unconceived that in the solu-
> tion of problems turns out to be conceivable and conceived for reason.

The passage starts out in a promising way, speaking of the ego as the wonder of all wonders, which indeed is in keeping with its sense of "transcendence in immanence" that Husserl at other junctures assigns to the ego (e.g., Husserl 2014, 105). But then it becomes clear that wonder evaporates under the phenomenological gaze. We can find the same tendency in Aristotle and Descartes before him: Wonder may well be the beginning of philosophy—but no more than a beginning. Only ignorance and common sense will cling to wonder. Reason will overcome wonder, and wonder disappears as soon as absolute evidence and rationality are demanded of it (Aristotle 2004, 982b; Descartes 2015, 226).

4.3   Marion's Reduction from the Outside

If we are to gain a phenomenological access to wonder via the phenomenological reduction, some of the framework guiding the Cartesian way has to be modified. In many respects, this is precisely how Marion suggests modifying the Husserlian legacy: by challenging imposed limitations that prevent aspects of the phenomena from being fully acknowledged.

The great breakthrough of Husserl is, in Marion's view, how he initially frees philosophy from the grip of metaphysics by bringing it to completion and pointing beyond. Marion writes: "In undertaking to free presence from any condition or precondition for receiving what gives itself as it gives itself, phenomenology therefore attempts to complete metaphysics and, indissolubly, to bring it to an end" (Marion 1998, 1). Metaphysics, in Marion's rendering, is not onto-theology, or metaphysics of presence, but first and foremost the drive to impose conditions and limitations that are not phenomenologically warranted. As intimated in the quotation, "the given" and more generally "givenness" are at the core of Marion's concern. Although the given (*es gibt*) and the gift play significant roles in Heidegger's and Derrida's overcoming of metaphysics, Marion thinks Husserl's approach of the given via intuition points to an even more promising option. In its widest sense, comprising sensation, categorical intuition, and eidetic intuition, intuition is fundamental to Husserl's notion of evidence, "the things themselves," and indeed his "Principle of all Principles": All cognition has its source in the given intuition (Husserl 2014, 43; Marion 1998, 10). Taken as such, intuition simply gives and hence does not rest on preconditions or constitution: "Givenness alone is absolute, free and without condition, precisely because it gives" (Marion 1998, 33)

Yet, at the same time as Husserl opens up a space beyond metaphysics, he falls back into it, as if drawing back from the abundance of givenness—a move Marion believes becomes particularly evident in Husserl's reduction. Intuition and givenness are central to Husserl's principle, but as Husserl turns inward to absolute immanent givenness, he qualifies the givenness in two important respects. First, the given is always given to a subjective consciousness. But according to Marion, this means to reduce the givenness to evidence as presence—presence before consciousness. And once evidence gets into focus, it also becomes clear that the given serves the search for epistemological certitude: presence, beginning, foundation. Second, what is given to consciousness turns out not to be prescribed by the things themselves but is subjected to the framework demanded by the conditions of subjective consciousness. Accordingly, only something like objectivity will meet the demands of Husserl's notion of phenomena. For Marion, the crucial thing is that both the correlation to subjective consciousness and the reduction to objectivity means that, in Husserl's conceptions, we impose conditions and restrictions on what gives itself and therefore lose hold of its pure givenness (Marion 1998, 51, 54).

In important ways, Marion's criticism resonates well with my criticism proposed above, particularly the formal point that there is some kind of imposed framework that filters away decisive aspects of phenomena, such as the inner ambivalence of wonder. The question is what Marion's alternative reduction entails. From his emphasis on givenness it comes as no surprise that it must be directed differently than Husserl's inward way; it must be oriented toward the movement of givenness, stemming so from outside subjectivity. What Marion is after is thus neither Husserl's reduction to subjective consciousness nor Heidegger's reduction to *Dasein* or Being, but directed toward a call from beyond Being or, again, givenness as such (Marion 1998, 197–198). What Marion is after is the very basic fact of phenomenality—that something is given and not nothing. His reduction nullifies any condition, be it subjective or ontological, and leaves the call to its own initiative, as a gift that gives itself (Marion 1998, 204).

As Marion elaborates his own account of the reduction, he takes off from his coined principle: "So much reduction, so much givenness." There is, in other words, a clear correlation between the undertaking of reduction and the experience of givenness as such. It is true of Husserl's method, and indeed true of any method, that the initiative necessarily starts out from the researcher. Yet, Marion argues, a pure reduction cannot be achieved solely through that initiative if phenomenology is to be guided by the way the phenomena show themselves from themselves. Hence, the reduction starts out with the negative step, the *epoché*, initiated by the phenomenologist, where "the false realities of the natural world, the objective world, etc.," are removed in order to clear all obstacles for manifestations (Marion 2002, 10). But as soon as the *epoché* is done, the phenomenologist loses his or her upper hand, and the phenomena overtake the course of the reduction. In Marion's theatrical metaphor (2002, 10):

> Or rather, the reduction opens the show of the phenomenon at first like a very present director, so as to then let this show continue as a simple scene where the director is necessary, to be sure, but forgotten and making no difference—with the result that it is absorbed in it and no longer distinguished from it: self-directing.

The paradox of the movement of reduction means not that it is self-contradictory but rather that it is a *para-doxa* in its etymological meaning: turning against expectation. Reduction becomes a reversal. Indeed, starting out as a method in the sense of procedure under control, it ends up dissolving any method, becoming instead a countermethod.

Undergoing such pure reduction is aimed at letting what gives itself show itself from itself, eventually as pure givenness. Marion thinks that all the principles of phenomenology hitherto proposed have come with restrictions imposed on what phenomenology acknowledges as given. Husserl's "To the things themselves" leaves completely undetermined what "things" are and therefore lowers phenomenology to a metaphysical method of access. His "Principles of All principles" models intentionality on objectivity and represses everything that is not intuitively given in that way (Marion 1998, 12–13). The question is how Husserl smuggles in dogmatic convictions, which circumscribe what he acknowledges as phenomena. Pure givenness, Marion holds, must be completely free from restrictions: "Reducing givenness means freeing it from the limits of every other authority, including those of intuition. … The essential phenomenological operation of the reduction arrives this time—beyond objectness and beingness—at pure givenness" (Marion 1998, 16).

Having sketched out the way Marion both criticizes and extends Husserl's reduction, the question is what resources Marion's phenomenology provides with regard to wonder. He offers no sustained analysis of wonder on his own, but as with Husserl, there are junctures at which he comments on it. For instance, Marion discusses the call that emanates from every kind of saturated phenomenon, a call that stems not from an object but rather from something that takes us by surprise, yet without clear content. This surprise and lack of content corresponds neatly, Marion argues, to Descartes's account of wonder. Descartes writes (Marion 2002, 269 = Descartes 2015, 220; cf. Marion 1998, 193):

> When our *first* encounter with some object *surprises* us and we find it novel, or very different from what we formerly knew or from what we supposed it ought to be, *this causes us* to wonder and to be astonished at it. Since all this may happen before we know whether or not the object is beneficial to us, I regard wonder as the first of all the passions.

As Marion's added emphasis makes clear, what interests Marion in this passage is not so much wonder, but Descartes's description of a passion that arises in response to something beyond us and that precedes objectivity.

A more interesting account, however, is given by way of a reading of Heidegger's notion of wonder. Marion starts out with Heidegger's analysis of boredom, in which one is no longer moved by the world, as if the appeal from Being is silenced. Boredom can at any time suffocate wonder and make us deaf to the call of Being. Yet boredom also has a significant role to play, since it in fact not only brackets beings but, according to Marion, by the same token opens us toward something else. In contradistinction to boredom, Heidegger says, wonder has the ability reopen Being and let it address us in a deep way, as wonder entails both openness and attentiveness to the call of Being—that is, to the wonder of wonder: that being is. Marion comments: "Here the wonder both demands and provokes a wonderment that is guaranteed, on another level, by the claiming call of Being; Being claims, through its call, the attention in order that the wonder of the fact of Being (of beings) receives the amazement that it deserves" (Marion 1998, 194). However, boredom can cut very deeply and even provoke a hatred of being in which Being as such is eventually put in *epoché*. It thus makes us ready to receive that call from beyond

Being. In this case, such call corresponds with neither Husserl's transcendental reduction nor Heidegger's existential reduction but with Marion's pure reduction (Marion 1998, 197–198).

Having arrived at this conclusion, however, Marion no longer attends to wonder, because wonder seems to be only one among other occasions in which givenness of the call can be welcomed—an occasion Marion hardly returns to again. Nevertheless, one should raise the question if there are, besides such pragmatic considerations, more principled reasons why Marion drops a further analysis of wonder. Even if he has not pursued such an inquiry himself, we may ask if Marion's reduction has the conceptual capacity to open to us the phenomenon of wonder. I set out from the provisional analysis that whatever wonder more specifically is, it seems to dwell on the border between familiar things of the natural attitude and what borders on it, as if from the outside. Such formal clues to a further analysis may lead us to think that Marion has taken an important step beyond Husserl's reduction. For where Husserl effectively excluded the in-between, and more specifically, the foreign from the Cartesian way to reduction, Marion reverses the reduction, giving priority to what is not under the sway of subjectivity. Marion therefore points to the dimension of wonder that comes from beyond the ordinary and cannot be fully contained therein.

In his analyses of the saturated phenomena, with excess of given intuition, there is also a strong sense of being overwhelmed and bedazzled by the excess of givenness. However, Marion goes too far, as if his reduction not only does away with the "illusion" of the everyday according to the natural attitude, so that no condition whatsoever arrives in time to make up a constitutive part of the phenomena. Being surprised, overwhelmed, and bedazzled is remarkable, but it is hardly what we mean by wonder; there is an excess of the part of the foreign in Marion's examples, but the familiar does not resound and intertwine with the foreign in the way it does in wonder. Admittedly, Marion has defended himself from similar criticism by pointing to what he calls the banality of saturation, where "everyday banality" is meant not in the sense that the phenomena occur frequently but rather that they are in principle open to all. The point is that the most banal and accessible phenomena are open to saturation under favorable circumstances (Marion 2008, 125–126). However, what happens in the saturation is that phenomena are torn away from their anchorage in the everyday and purified to the point that they contradict all conditions of possibilities (Marion 2008, 127).

The problem is certainly not that reduction is guided by dogmas of metaphysics and science but that the fear of any defilement of metaphysical thought pushes Marion to the opposite extreme: he fears any contamination of conditions and limitations. Christina Gschwandtner is therefore right in arguing that Marion holds on to too absolute a distinction: "a phenomenon is *either* 'poor' *or* 'saturated,' intuition is *either* 'empty' *or* 'full,' consciousness *either* controls and constitutes the phenomenon *or* it is overwhelmed by what is given and utterly unable to constitute it or impose its own parameters on it" (Gschwandtner 2014, 6).[3] It is Marion's drive for purity— with regard to the reduction and the corresponding givenness—that in the end pre-

---

[3] In a similar vein, I have discussed the excessive separation in Marion (Dahl 2010, 116–124).

cludes regions of phenomena, and particularly wonder. A successful account of wonder will have to deal with the dynamic ways in which givenness and conditions, along with foreignness and the everyday familiarity, are parts of a complex weave.

4.4   Merleau-Ponty's Reduction Downward

There are certainly points where Merleau-Ponty departs from Husserl, particularly tied up with his Cartesian way to the reduction, its demands of absolute evidence, and transcendental idealism. Nevertheless, just like Marion, Merleau-Ponty draws heavily on Husserl's teaching, especially his later analyses of the body, passive synthesis, and the life-world. For Merleau-Ponty, however, the development of Husserl's *œuvre* is more important than the position Husserl holds at different junctures (Merleau-Ponty 1970, 105–108). The central teaching of his contribution, Merleau-Ponty believes, is Husserl's willingness to constantly revise his own project without giving up its direction. Not only Husserl but the entire phenomenological movement *"can be practiced and identified,"* Merleau-Ponty writes, *"as a manner or style of thinking, [because] it existed as a movement before arriving at complete awareness of itself as a philosophy"* (Merleau-Ponty 1960, viii). Such style and willingness to revision is inherent in the idea of phenomenology, because phenomenology in Merleau-Ponty's fashion cannot be founded on timeless principles or doctrines: "The core of philosophy … lies in the perpetual beginning of reflection" (Merleau-Ponty 1960, 62), marking the never-exhausted and yet constantly improved approaches toward the index of "the things themselves." Merleau-Ponty is thus not for or against Husserl but sides with some of Husserl's tendencies against others.

Even if a phenomenologist, according to Merleau-Ponty, is a perpetual beginner, he denies any absolute beginning, since when "I begin to reflect my reflection bears upon an unreflective experience" (Merleau-Ponty 1960, x). Indeed, there is no question of anchoring our relation to the world on apodictic and adequate evidence, for the simple reason that the world to which phenomenology aspires to return does not exist as transparent. The world is ambiguous, harboring depth and hidden sides. When the intellectualist insists that the world exists because we have good reasons to believe so, and the skeptic denies it, both positions wrongly presuppose that our relation to the world is a matter of knowledge. But our relation to the world is at once more fragile, since no evidence could prove it, and yet stronger, since we are interwoven with the world prior to thought, doubt, or knowledge (Merleau-Ponty 1968, 50). If phenomenology wants to describe and articulate those subterranean bonds that tie us to the world, then it cannot simply leave the world of the natural attitude, and yet it must break the spell of its being a matter of course. In evoking the theme of wonder and corresponding enigmas, Merleau-Ponty wants to foster a sensitivity, shared with art and religion, less certain and more interrogative, since only in the openness of the question can we adjust ourselves to what he speaks of as "the enigmas, the world and things" (Merleau-Ponty 1968, 4).

The methodical way of such interrogation is the reduction. Whatever Merleau-Ponty's version of the reduction turns out to be, so much is already clear that it neither aims at arriving at some pure reduction in which givenness gives itself, nor does it aim at epistemic certainty from which a first philosophy can find its apodictic and adequate ground. Now, it is highly disputable whether Merleau-Ponty accepts Husserl's reduction, and if so, to what extent.[4] Without entering that debate, it seems reasonable to think that Merleau-Ponty develops *epoché* and reduction to some extent, although this departs from central dimensions of Husserl's Cartesian way. Admittedly, Merleau-Ponty does not speak much about *epoché*, but still it may make sense to single out the negative step of *epoché* in his account. To "put things out of play" or "within brackets" clearly does not mean negating the world—neither for Husserl nor for Merleau-Ponty. But the question remains as to what the status of the everyday world is granted as it appears after the *epoché*.

The crux of that question is the belief in the world, the general thesis, or *Urdoxa*. Unlike Husserl, who here speaks of positing (*thesis*) and opinions (*doxa*), Merleau-Ponty insists that *Urdoxa* rests on neither positing nor opinion—not even an attitude is an adequate notion. *Urdoxa* is rather a matter of a "mystery of a primal faith" that is prior to positings, opinions and attitudes. In a charitable interpretation of Husserl, Merleau-Ponty writes that when Husserl begins in the natural attitude, it should not be taken as solely a point of departure, but rather, as marking the true starting point prior to any reflective knowledge: "The doxa of the natural attitude is an *Urdoxa*. … Its rights of priority are definitive, and reduced consciousness must take them into account" (Merleau-Ponty 1964c, 164). There is, contrary to Husserl's conviction, no way in which the general thesis can be dispensed with in the *epoché*—and not because it is a principle at the root of all knowledge, but because it is always already intertwined in all embodied life in the world, and thus also part of a reduced consciousness.

This suggests that the ordinary world of the natural attitude must continuously play a part in any of the phenomenology's methodological steps. Even if not dispensed with, we need some form of *epoché*, in order to take the mystery of our primal belief into account: "Not because we reject the certainties of common sense and a natural attitude to things—they are, on the contrary, the constant theme of philosophy." Keeping this constant theme of philosophy intact does not, however, mean a simple repetition of common sense, for phenomenology needs to open that very natural attitude up. Merleau-Ponty continues: "because, being the presupposed basis of any thought, they [common sense and natural attitude] are taken for granted, and go unnoticed, and because in order to arouse them and bring them to view, we have to suspend for a moment our recognition of them" (Merleau-Ponty 1960, xiii). The *epoché* clearly has a duality to it: its aim is in no way to reject the ordinary world of the natural attitude, but still it must bracket it for a moment, stepping back from it, or in another of Merleau-Ponty's formulations, we must "suspend the faith in the world only so as to *see it*" (Merleau-Ponty 1968, 38). In *epoché*, the intentional threads to the world are not cut; rather, they are slackened so as to bring them to our notice.

---

[4] E.g., Joel Smith (2005, 559–563) thinks Merleau-Ponty defends a version of reduction, whereas Taylor Carman (2008, 39–43) thinks it is incompatible with his philosophical program.

Merleau-Ponty distances himself from a certain understanding of Husserl's reduction, especially the route inward, to the transcendental subject that turns away from the world. For, according to such reading, such a regressive move is followed by a progressive move, by reconstituting the world that it first left. Such conception entails that we "can comprehend our natal bond with the world only by *undoing* it in order to *remake* it, only by constituting it, fabricating it" (Merleau-Ponty 1968, 32).[5] This world, however, is not the same as was left behind, because it is transmuted into the ideal meaning of the *noēma*. Merleau-Ponty's main criticism of such rendering is, however, the result of a progressive step, the one of remaking the world in terms of transcendental idealism. For, as Merleau-Ponty claims, "a logically consistent transcendental idealism rids the world of its opacity and its transcendence" (Merleau-Ponty 1960, xi–xii). But that goes against the very grain of a phenomenology, which has fidelity to the phenomena as its lodestar. Phenomenology cannot, without betraying itself, gloss over the opacity, paradoxes, and depths that are intrinsically part of our world and our relation to it. "The unfinished nature of phenomenology and the inchoative atmosphere which has surrounded it are not to be taken as a sign of failure, they were inevitable because phenomenology's task was to reveal the mystery of the world and of reason" (Merleau-Ponty 1960, xxi).

While wonder and mysteries for different reasons never become internal components of Husserl's and Marion's phenomenology, Merleau-Ponty's prose is not only full of allusions to mysteries, enigmas, transcendence, and ambiguity, but he also famously speaks of reduction in terms of wonder itself: "The best formulation of the reduction is probably that given by Eugen Fink, Husserl's assistant, when he spoke of 'wonder' in the face of the world" (Merleau-Ponty 1960, xiii). But he does not elaborate it much further and leaves to us to figure its implications.

As for Husserl, it is clear that initiating *epoché* and reduction is an act of will, indeed an expression of the freedom of the human spirit, and hence the initiation is independent of any passions or wonders. This activism corresponds to Husserl's understanding of constitution as the way we build up perception and knowledge by active achievements in response to the passively given, and it also reflects the fact that our fundamental faith in the world or *Urdoxa* is understood as enacted positioning or a thesis. Thus, while the acts and the thesis are achievements of subjectivity, the subject can also withdraw them, put them within brackets and change the attitude toward them. Following Merleau-Ponty's reference to Fink, we see that Fink starts with pointing out the "paradox of beginning" that is entailed in Husserl's position. If the natural attitude per definition is blind to the transcendental dimension that is essentially different from it, then natural persons lack the motivation for turning toward something they do not even know exists (Fink 1933, 236). Without his saying so directly, Fink's line of argument suggests that wonder can serve as an initial motivation for the turn to the transcendental. Speaking of the faith in the world, he writes: "On the basis of this faith itself, wonder beyond measure is awakened in the face of this enigmatic fact. To take this fact for granted means to remain

---

[5] For a far more charitable reading of these aspects of reduction, see Merleau-Ponty 1964c, 161–163.

blind to the first of all mysteries, for the being of the world itself" (Fink 1933, 350; cf. Fink 1995, 31–36). Fink's point is not that this wonder of our faith in the world is the whole story about the phenomenological reduction but that it can be a way out of the paradox of beginning. Stressing the point further, Sara Heinämaa thinks Merleau-Ponty reverses the subjective initiative; reduction must come over us, passively, as stemming from affectivity, which here manifests itself as the passion of wonder, not unlike Marion's reduction. Wonder is therefore a passion, according to Heinämaa, "like an interruption that makes possible a change of direction" (Heinämaa 2002, 141).

Even if there is certainly room for affectivity in Merleau-Ponty's phenomenology, it is hard to deny that activity is implied in the way Merleau-Ponty speaks of reduction in terms of suspensions, slackening of threads, stepping back. More generally, the achieving "I can" serves as a leitmotif for his fundamental conception of the incarnate subjectivity (Merleau-Ponty 1960, 137). It seems more precise to say that Merleau-Ponty operates with two-way traffic in our world relation, which entails both activity and passivity, give and take, both in constant exchange. So also in the reduction: there may indeed be affectivity that motivates it, such as *"being filled with wonder"* (Merleau-Ponty 1960, xiv), and yet there is an active turning that fulfills the task. Perhaps a more important implication of reduction as wonder is the wonders that it turns toward, its intentional correlate; call them enigmas of the world. It seems that wonders can refer to the initiation and the outcome of the reduction. While Merleau-Ponty never works out such a dialectic, the reduction certainly does not withdraw us into transcendental experience but keeps us attached to the world from which it started and to which it aims. This world, however, has now become available to phenomenological reflection. In this sense, reduction does not belong to idealist phenomenology, for the "phenomenological reduction belongs to existential philosophy: Heidegger's 'being-in-the-world' appears only against the background of the phenomenological reduction" (Merleau-Ponty 1960, xiv).

If there is one claim Merleau-Ponty repeatedly returns to, it is that reduction cannot be completed. For instance, he famously writes in the quoted preface to *Phenomenology of Perception*: "The most important lesson which the reduction teaches us is the impossibility of a complete reduction" (Merleau-Ponty 1960, xiv). It is strange to say that its inherent impossibility is its most important teaching, since so much of phenomenology hinges on its success. In this passage, Merleau-Ponty seems to suggest that it is our temporal being-in-the-world and finite perspectives on the world that debar the reduction from reaching transparency and completion. But if reduction is defined by wonder, it is also tempting to find its incompleteness connected to the essence of wonder: for instance, due to the affective dimension of the passion of wonder, which cannot be conflated with thetic positioning (Heinämaa 2002, 43–46). Or as it has also been suggested, it may be that Merleau-Ponty really sees the incompleteness as the consequence of the impossibility of transparent phenomena (Smith 2005, 563).

However, upon closer scrutiny, there is not one reason why reduction cannot be completed. In Merleau-Ponty's works, this incompleteness functions as an index of different ways in which Merleau-Ponty pushes on to certain fundamental insights.

In his most sustained reading of Husserl, he repeats the incompleteness of reduction twice: first, in order to suggest an operative intentionality prior to any conscious acts that resist reduction; and second, elaborating that point, arguing that no return to "absolute consciousness" makes us one with the constitutive genesis (Merleau-Ponty 1964c, 165, 179). In some of his latest working notes, Merleau-Ponty again picks up the incompleteness thesis, but now in order to suggest a new ontology: that of the "vertical" or "wild" being, which resists any direct access. The incompleteness of the reduction, he writes, "is not an obstacle to the reduction, it is the reduction itself, the rediscovery of a vertical being" (Merleau-Ponty 1968, 178). It is finally relevant to point to Merleau-Ponty's reflections on the role of the impossibility of immediate access to experience, due to the co-constitutive role of language, which also leaves its mark on the incomplete reduction, or stronger: words "*form* the transcendental attitude*" (Merleau-Ponty 1968, 171). There is no clear systematical edification of these reflections. Still, they converge insofar as they all highlight various limitations of phenomenology's Cartesian ambitions, namely foundation, certainty, and completeness.

If the tension between the familiar according to the natural attitude and the strange that evades secure knowledge are what prevented Husserl from accounting for wonder, this tension is in no way banished from Merleau-Ponty's incomplete reduction: it is explicitly committed to the familiar that we take for granted and yet opening up for the mystery amid it. Phenomenology needs to reach toward what we already know and do not fully know: that is, to borrow another of Merleau-Ponty's formulations, "a mystery as familiar as it is unexplained" (Merleau-Ponty 1968, 130). There are in Merleau-Ponty's phenomenology no ambitions of resolving intellectual puzzles or establishing certainties; he rather invites us to stay awake to the mysteries in our being-in-the-world. Or as Merleau-Ponty will have it: "The world and reason are not problematical. We may say, if we wish, that they are mysterious, but their mystery defines them: there can be no question of dispelling it by some 'solution', it is on the hither side of all solutions. True philosophy consists in relearning to look at the world" (Merleau-Ponty 1960, xx).

4.5 Wonder and Incarnation

To relearn to look at the world is for Merleau-Ponty not a matter of purifying the gaze by an *epoché* that leaves behind all that falls short of Husserl's epistemic criteria, and it is not to open oneself for something beyond that world, in a call or givenness that surpasses worldly phenomenology. It is rather a way of opening up the depth and ambiguity of what is right in front of us. If mystery is at once revealed and concealed, familiar and strange, it is worth asking if this leads to religious mysteries—say, of the incarnation of Christ. Without any religious commitment of his own, Merleau-Ponty can still employ a language very close to the religious register, and in several passages he pays heed to theology. Just as philosophy can suppress its own origin in wonder, so can religion—not least by means of theological systematization of it. In both cases, phenomenology must stay awake to the unre-solved and unresolvable wonder, be it philosophical or theological.

The critical attitude one finds in Merleau-Ponty's writing on theology has much to do with the neglect of wonder: "Theology makes use of philosophical wonder only for the purpose of motivating an affirmation which ends it" (Merleau-Ponty 1963, 44).[6] These harsh words are directed toward De Lubac and Maritain, espe-cially their attacks on what they see as rival atheism. What Merleau-Ponty worries about is how, in their accounts, every philosophical position that does not warrant the etiquette of proper Christian faith becomes identified as atheism. But Merleau-Ponty is similarly concerned about how "Promethean humanism" negates Christianity—and especially that neither the theologians nor the humanists recog-nize that they both are locked up into a reciprocal logic of mutual exclusion. This logic knows no middle ground, no explorations of unfinished landscapes, let alone wonder. But theology as well as philosophy must, following Merleau-Ponty, hold on to contingency, finitude, and ambiguity: "The denial of this is a fixed (non-philosophical) position" (Merleau-Ponty 1963, 44). With reference to Lichtenberg, Merleau-Ponty holds that understanding religion is different from believing; and in understanding it, one should neither affirm the existence of God nor deny it. Merleau-Ponty quotes Lichtenberg saying: "it is not necessary that doubt should be anything more than vigilance; otherwise, it can become a source of danger," where-upon Merleau-Ponty comments that Lichtenberg "was identifying himself, for his part, with a consciousness of the self, of the world, and of others that was 'strange'" (Merleau-Ponty 1963, 45). What is at stake here is not theology but a sketch of the phenomenological attitude to religion—one of *epoché* of God (as Husserl also demanded), and also a warning against any settled "solutions," in order to keep the strangeness alive.

Such vigilance to strangeness and mysteries of the world will cut across the anti-thetical relation between theology and philosophy and has the possibility to reopen the conversation between them. However troubled, Merleau-Ponty believes that there are possibilities for such conversation, as attested both historically and in con-temporary thought. The moral of all this, according to Merleau-Ponty, is that there is indeed rapport between philosophy and Christianity; it is even possible with a Christian philosophy, but its continuation is demanding. It becomes impossible if "the Heaven of principles and the earth of existence are sundered" (Merleau-Ponty 1964c, 242). And yet, it is possible as long as any polarized positions between heaven and earth, between inside and outside are avoided. For a Christian philoso-phy, it is "a matter of principle [that] it involves no single and exhaustive philo-sophical expression, and that in this sense—no matter what acquisitions may be—Christian philosophy is never *something settled*" (Merleau-Ponty 1964c, 146). We may say Christian thinking must remain as incomplete as reduction.

From a slightly different angle, the difficulty of the conversation between phi-losophy and theology is brought up in historical reflection. Merleau-Ponty notes that it has become tempting to align the forces of history and God as if the former offered

[6] For comments of this and related passages, see Simpson 2014, 87–88.

a horizontal transcendence and the latter a vertical. But conceiving of the relation in those terms does not really make progress, but repeats the antithetical relation in a new guise. This doubly misses the mark, both for philosophy of history and for theology. Now Merleau-Ponty is well aware of the different strands of theology and takes a clear side in his assessment of conservative and progressive Catholicism, or as he labels them: the religion of the Father and the religion of the Son. Whereas the former fits into the vertical transcendence, making humanity subject to a power above, the latter suggests quite another conception, starting from the incarnation of the Son. Merleau-Ponty writes: "And it is a little too much to forget that Christianity is, among other things, the recognition of a mystery in the relations of man and God, which stems precisely from the fact that God wants nothing to do with a vertical relation of subordination" (Merleau-Ponty 1964c, 70–71). These mysteries of relations are not only matters of power, subordination, and historicity but should invite phenomenology: The mystery of the relations between man and God in incarnation reopens the distinction between body and spirit, exteriority and interiority; it points us to the paradoxes of humanity's nobility and wretchedness, and sensitizes us to the paradoxes of the world of perception (Merleau-Ponty 1964b, 175).

In the mystery of incarnation, God ceases to be an external, absolute object, but becomes the absolute in the world. God relates to world, and the world relates to God. Just as with the reduction, there remains something essentially unfinished with this constitutive relation—there is always another side to God and another side of the world. Some theologians, Merleau-Ponty suspects, insist that religious experience locates the religiously significant only in strict contradistinction to the world. For his part, Merleau-Ponty insists that the reversal must take place before our eyes. Moreover, Merleau-Ponty hesitatingly suggests that "perhaps some Christians would agree that the other side of things must already be visible in the environment in which we live" (Merleau-Ponty 1964a, 27). This is a matter not of any denial of divinity or transcendence but of drawing the full consequence of incarnation, as divine identification with us and our world. This further points toward an understanding of "wonder in the face of the world," as we must expect that such world contains the traces of mysteries and traces of sacredness. Indeed, the phrase "the other side of things," in the quotation just above, invokes Husserl's notion of inner and outer horizons, the sides that are anticipated and yet hidden from a vantage perspective. But it also goes beyond that, in invoking an otherness of things that in principle remain beyond our possession, those sides of things that, Merleau-Ponty holds, cannot be products of our constitution (Merleau-Ponty 1964c, 180).

I have claimed that any successful phenomenology of wonder must acknowledge not only the extraordinariness of the mysteries or enigmas that awaken it but also their ordinariness. Wonder is how one opens oneself up to this unresolved tension anchored in the world that we otherwise take as ordinary. On his interpretation of the incarnation, Merleau-Ponty writes (1964c, 71):

> There is a sort of impotence of God without us, and Christ attests that God would not be fully God without becoming fully man. Claudel goes so far as to say that God is not above us but beneath us—meaning that we do not find Him as a supersensible idea, but as another ourselves which dwells in and authenticates our darkness.

Whatever theological implications such an interpretation has, it surely directs the theological attention to God that dwells beneath us. Following Merleau-Ponty, a religious wonder is not so much directed upward, but downward, toward the depth and thickness of the world that is always part of our living.

Something similar is the point of reduction as wonder: it directs us not inward toward absolute evidence and transparent presence, not outward, as welcoming of a pure givenness or pure call, but downward, to all our secret bonds in which we are entangled. Reduction directs us toward the secret relations "between beings who are both embodied and limited and an enigmatic world of which we catch a glimpse (indeed which we haunt incessantly) but only ever from points of view that hide as much as they reveal" (Merleau-Ponty 2008, 54). Alluding to Plato's simile of the cave, Rubenstein writes: "Neither taking flight above the clouds nor resting complacently in itself, a thinking of wonder would look for the extraordinary in and through the ordinary, the awe-full truth in the midst of the cave" (Rubenstein 2008, 24). To remain in the cave means to remain in the ordinary, the everyday, not as banal or flat, but as the field of enigmas and depths. The familiar provides all the material that wonder needs, philosophical as well as religious, and the unfamiliar sheds new light back on the familiar, which no longer can be taken for granted. And wonder? It remains stretched out in between.

References

Aristotle. 2004. *Metaphysics*. Trans. Hugh Lawson-Tancred. London: Penguin Books.

Carman, Taylor. 2008. *Merleau-Ponty*. London: Routledge.

Dahl, Espen. 2010. *Phenomenology and the holy: Religious experience after Husserl*. London: SMC.

Descartes, René. 2015. *The Passions of the Soul and Other Later Philosophical Writings*. Trans. Michael Moriarty. Oxford: Oxford University Press.

Fink, Eugen. 1933. Die phänomenologische Philosophie Edmund Husserls in der gegenwärtigen Kritik. *Kantstudien* 38: 319–383.

———. 1995. *Sixth Cartesian Meditation: The Idea of a Transcendental Theory of Method*. Trans. Ronald Bruzina. Bloomington: Indiana University Press.

Gschwandtner, Christina M. 2014. *Degrees of givenness: On saturation in Jean-Luc Marion*. Bloomington: Indiana University Press.

Heidegger, Martin. 1985. *History of the Concept of Time: Prolegomena*. Trans. Theodore Kiesel. Bloomington: Indiana University Press.

———. 1994. *Basic Questions of Philosophy: Selected "Problems" of "Logic"*. Trans. Richard Rojcewicz and André Schuwer. Bloomington: Indiana University Press.

Heinämaa, Sara. 2002. From decision to passion: Merleau-Ponty's interpretation of Husserl's reduction. In *Merleau-Ponty's reading of Husserl*, ed. Ted Toadvine and Lester Embree, 127–146. Dordrecht: Kluwer Academic Publisher.

Husserl, Edmund. 1960. *Cartesian Meditations: An Introduction to Phenomenology*. Trans. Dorion Cairns. The Hague: Martinus Nijhoff.

———. 1970. *The Crisis of the European Sciences and Transcendental Phenomenology: An Introduction to Phenomenological Philosophy*. Trans. Davis Carr. Evanston: Northwestern University Press.

————. 1980. *Phenomenology and the Foundation of the Sciences, Third Book: Ideas Pertaining to a Pure Phenomenology and a Phenomenological Philosophy*. Trans. Ted E. Klein and William E. Pohl. The Hague: Martinus Nijhoff.

————. 1990. *The Idea of phenomenology*. Trans. William P. Alston and George Nakhnikian. Dordrecht: Kluwer Academic Publisher.

————. 2014. *Ideas for a Pure Phenomenology and Phenomenological Philosophy, First Book: General Introduction to Pure Phenomenology*. Trans. Daniel O. Dahlstrom. Indianapolis: Hackett Publishing.

Kern, Iso. 1962. Drei Wege zur transzendental-phänomenologischen Reduktion in der Philosophie Husserls. *Tijdschrift voor Filosofie* 24: 303–349.

Kingwell, Mark. 2000. Husserl's sense of wonder. *The Philosophical Forum* 31 (1): 85–107.

Marion, Jean-Luc. 1998. *Reduction and Givenness: Investigations of Husserl, Heidegger, and Phenomenology*. Trans. Thomas A. Carlson. Evanston: Northwestern University Press.

————. 2002. *Being Given: Toward a Phenomenology of Givenness*. Trans. Jeffrey L. Kosky. Stanford: Stanford University Press.

———— 2008. *The Visible and the Revealed*. Trans. Christina M. Geschwandtner et al. New York: Fordham University Press.

Merleau-Ponty, Maurice. 1960. *Phenomenology of Perception*. Trans. Colin Smith. London: Routledge.

————. 1963. *In Praise of Philosophy*. Trans. John Wild and James M. Edie. Evanston: Northwestern University Press.

————. 1964a. *Primacy of Perception and Other Essays on the Phenomenology of Psychology, the Philososphy of Art, History and Politics*. Trans. James D. Edie. Evanston: Northwestern University Press.

————. 1964b. *Sense and Nonsense*. Trans. Hubert L. Dreyfus and Patricia Allen Dreyfus. Evanston: Northwestern University Press.

————. 1964c. *Signs: Studies in Phenomenology and Existential Philosophy*. Trans. Richard C. McCleary. Evanston: Northwestern University Press.

————. 1968. *The Visible and the Invisible*. Ed. Claude Lefort. Trans. Alphonso Lingis. Evanston: Northwestern University Press.

————. 1970. *Themes from the Lectures at the Collège de France, 1952–1960*. Trans. John O'Neill. Evanston: Northwestern University Press.

————. 2008. *The World of Perception*. Trans. Oliver Davis. London: Routledge.

Overgaard, Søren. 2015. How to do things with brackets: The *epoché* explained. *Continental Philosophy Review* 48: 179–195.

Plato. 2014. *Theatetus*. Trans. John McDowell. Oxford: Oxford University Press.

Rubenstein, Mary-Jane. 2008. *Strange wonder: The closure of metaphysics and the opening of awe*. New York: Columbia University Press.

Sallis, John. 1995. *Double truth*. Albany: SUNY Press.

Simpson, Christopher Ben. 2014. *Merleau-Ponty and theology*. London: Bloomsbury.

Smith, Joel. 2005. Merleau-Ponty and the phenomenological reduction. *Inquiry* 48 (6): 553–571.

Espen Dahl is Professor of Theology at UiT – The Arctic University of Norway. Dahl's chief research interest is in the interaction between the ordinary and the extraordinary. He has explored the interaction in terms of the relation between the holy, the lifeworld and cultic experience by means of phenomenology. Aesthetically, some of the same dynamics has been found in the mimetic ties between modernist painting and everyday experience, and relative to ordinary language philosophy (Wittgenstein and Cavell), the tension between our life with words and the alienation from it has been explored. Among Dahl's many publications are *The Holy and Phenomenology. Religious Experience after Husserl* (SCM 2010); *In Between. The Holy Beyond Modern Dichotomies* (Vandenhoek and Ruprecht 2012); and *Cavell, Religion and Continental Philosophy* (Indiana University Press 2014).

Chapter 5
The Emancipatory Continuity of Religious Emotion

Olga Louchakova-Schwartz

Abstract In this paper, I engage three different sets of phenomenological concepts in order to explore the continuous transformation ("transmutation") of religious emotion from unwholesome (anger, alienation, grief) to wholesome (love, sense of connectedness, bliss). Analysis shows that in the practice of Neo-Buddhist meditation), emotion transitions from complex and axiologically directed at intentional objects (claims based on Husserl's theory of intentionality), to nonrepresentational (as suggested by Levinas). The way emotions are given in meditation, as a continuity in which one emotion is not replaced by another but *transforms* into it, is very different from the discrete, incremental character of emotion in the everyday life. Husserl's theory of passive synthesis and intentional continuity appears insufficient to account for the continuity of emotion's "transmutation," to be better understood by means of Henry's nonintentional phenomenology as nonintentional continuity. In meditative practice, emotion is reduced to being a counterphenomenon, continuously undergoing modifications and the inhibition of rising intentionalities. The modes of *noēsis* also change to include reversibility between the self-affective character of emotion and the "clear-seeing" aspect of *noēsis*. I further elaborate on the conditions of possibility for the continuous teleological transformation of emotion, found not only in the Husserlian horizon of time-consciousness and clear seeing but, more importantly, in noematic horizons of self-affection, of the rudimentary intentionalities related to the quality of emotion, and in the foundational horizon of phenomenological materiality (not hyletics). Finally, I argue that a religious quality of this experience depends on the teleology of emotion's continuous transformation.

Keywords Meditation · Religious emotions · Husserl · Henry · Intentionality · Passive synthesis

O. Louchakova-Schwartz (✉)
Jesuit School of Theology of Santa Clara University, Graduate Theological Union, Berkeley, CA, USA

University of California, Davis, CA, USA

© Springer Nature Switzerland AG 2019
O. Louchakova-Schwartz (ed.), *The Problem of Religious Experience*,
Contributions to Phenomenology 103,
https://doi.org/10.1007/978-3-030-21575-0_5

Religious syncretism of the twentieth century brought with it massive hybridization and secular adaptations of Buddhist meditation practices.[1] I will refer to these hybrid practices as Neo-Buddhist. While in developed Buddhist traditions soteriology does not necessarily depend on experience per se (Sharf 1995),[2] in New Age and spiritual groups Neo-Buddhist hybrid practices aim mostly at some form of experience of ultimacy. It is not uncommon for Theravadan and Tantric Buddhist or Mahayana practices to be bundled together based on their perceived inner effects—a situation that one can use to study the connection between experience and emergent religious beliefs. Often such "integrative" approaches engage emotions, especially because a robust telos of emotional transformation prevails no matter how far practitioners deviate from the original traditions.

A predictable and conscious modification of affective life, a life that is normally spontaneous if not instinctual, is interesting for several reasons. First, there can be no symbol or text that would be linked to a kind of temporally extended, teleological, and in a sense vitalistic process observed in case of transformation of emotion; hence, it would be hard to understand this process within the known theories of religious experience, as interruption (cf. Dahl 2010) or within the apprepresentational mindset (cf. Barber 2017). Second, this change implies a transition from the everyday to the sphere of religious experiencing (cf. Dahl 2010)—in the present readings of Christian religious experience (Dahl, Barber, DuPée in this book), such transition is quantum and not gradual. The transformation of emotion in the Neo-Buddhist practice (NBP) shows a gradual entry into religious experiencing within a form that is evidently non-Christian. However, meditations of mindfulness and loving kindness (which are a part of a rather amorphous and protean complex of NBP) are often practiced by Christians, by Muslims, by Jews, by various spirituality seekers, and so forth. It is possible that the "transmutation" of emotion, if really happening, comprises actualization of the latent possibilities in consciousness per se, along the lines of its realistically understood metaphysics. Last but not least, the empirical continuity of emotion challenges genetic phenomenology to expand its means beyond the ordinary scope of examinations.

---

[1] For more on religious hybridization, see Stabile 2013. For an example of hybridized meditation practices, see Dhammadinna n.d.; Antonov and Vaver 1989.

[2] Mi-pham rgya-mtsho, of the non-Tantric Nyngmapa (Madhyamaka) school, criticized "experientialist" (Chittamatra, aka Yogacara) school in the following terms: "experience which has come under the power of emotionality enters into the realm of projective existence and even a hand of Tathagata cannot put a stop to it"—in Lipman 1982, 295.

5.1 A Brief Note on Neo-Buddhist Meditation Practices

The eclectic complex of Buddhist practices adopted by modern spiritual seekers usually includes some form of mindfulness (such as, e.g., Theravadan *vipaśyanā* or Tibetan *zhiné*),[3] accompanied by meditation on loving kindness (*mettā*)[4] and at some point augmented by Tantric Buddhist practices such as, but not limited to, *treckhod* or *togal*.[5] Most often, these practices are nonsymbolic, devoid of linguistic aspects such as mantra or culture-specific imagery, and are attentional-somatic in their emphasis. Across different New Age and spiritual groups, NBP always involves several main mental components, such as the mindfulness of affects,[6] somatic focusing in the chest (aka concentration), and mental acts of generating happiness, compassion, loving kindness, peace, and the like, which then are projected towards others. According to popular belief, projecting positive emotions and attitudes toward others earns the practitioner a karmic merit, and cultivating positive emotion as a mental state enhances the practitioner's self-awareness. Compassion generated in *mettā* practice can serve as an antidote to fear,[7] and as a road to omniscience, a desirable state of spiritual ultimacy: "compassion should be practiced first of all because it precedes all else, just as man's breath [*āśvāsa*] precedes his ability to live."[8] This ontological primacy of compassion is eventually realized as *bodhicitta*, the enlightened mind.[9] Chōdrōn (2016) says:

> *Bodhichitta* exists on two levels. First there is unconditional *bodhichitta*, an immediate experience that is refreshingly free of concept, opinion, and our usual all-caught-up-ness. It's something hugely good that we are not able to pin down even slightly, like knowing at gut level that there's absolutely nothing to lose. Second there is relative *bodhichitta*, our ability to keep our hearts and minds open to suffering without shutting down.

In this paper, I hope to explicate at least partly a teleological motion from ordinary emotion to the complete immanence of compassion as a realistic phenomenological metaphysical principle. The way emotions are given in NBP, as a continuity in which one emotion is not replaced by another but *transforms* into it, is very different

---

[3] For an example of *vipaśyanā*, see Sayadaw 2018. For an example of *zhiné*, see GlideWing Online Workshops (n.d.).

[4] An Internet search of the term "*mettā* meditation" will instantly produce about half a million references, including popular articles, instructional videos, workshops, etc. For an example of popularization of the *mettā* practice, see Kornfield 1993, 5. For the history of practice, see Buddharakkhita 1995; Hopkins 2003; Patel 2013; Fink 2015.

[5] For *trekchod* or *togal,* see Wangyal 1993.

[6] Juslin (2013) defines affect as all valenced (positive/negative) states such as emotions or moods. Somewhat distinct from an affect, emotion involves synchronized complex responses, arousal, and a specific subjective feeling; focuses on specific object; and lasts minutes to a few hours. These definitions are, of course, vague, which is a part of the problem that I address in this paper.

[7] Sheehy 2005.

[8] Ichishima 1982, 123. For more on transformations of mental states in meditative practice, see Guenther 1992 and Chodron n.d.

[9] For more on *bodhicitta,* see Chōdrōn 2016.

from the discrete, incremental character of emotion in the everyday.[10] The same incremental character is attributed to religious emotions,[11] despite explicit textual evidence indicating otherwise.[12] In the mindfulness of the NBP, emotions are given in two ways: as discrete states in the early stage of the practice, and at later stages of practice as a gradual, continuously transforming internal flow of emotion leading to the metaphysical revelation of *bodhicitta*. A perception of emotions as incremental can be an artifact of ordinary (that is, unfocused) attention, whereas sharpening mindfulness gives a different picture. (Cf. Ekman et al. 2013.)

5.2   The Problem: Discordances Between Phenomenological Claims and the Continuity of Emotion in the Practice of Meditation

There are two main phenomenological claims regarding the structure of emotion. These claims proceed from the givenness of experience in the everyday, which suggests that the generalizability of these claims may be limited until one clarifies the relationships between the everyday and religious experience. The "priority of presentation" claim attributed to Husserl and Brentano suggests that emotions and "intentional feelings" are founded on presentational acts and directed at the value attributes of presented objects. Drummond further refines this claim by suggesting that emotion is founded on presentational and affective senses rather than on acts, and that these senses are equiprimordial. Another claim distinguishes between feelings and emotion's acts, giving the primary status to feelings (as in Drummond 2009, 2013). Close to this claim would be Levinas's view on emotion as nonrepresentational intentionality (as in Lee 2003), or ideas of emotion as "feeling towards" (Goldie 2002; Slaby 2008), which should not be identified with "add-on" intentionalities in theories that see emotion as a composite. At the same time, Ratcliffe (2013), Fernandez (2014), and Summa (2015) show extreme constitutive complexity within the unity of emotion. Emotion is a temporally extended state: Desmidt et al. (2014) proposed an empirical temporal model of emotion, including anticipation, crisis, and aftermath. It appears that the temporal character of emotion depends on "add-on" intentionalities—for instance, in surprise (cf. Depraz 2014, 173–175)—and not on the feeling-related part of emotion. The temporality of complex emotions hasn't yet been worked out; a general model within Husserl's theory of the internal consciousness of time presupposes an incremental summation of the moments of experience within its tightly knit units, which correspond to discrete acts of ego-consciousness.

---

[10] For more on the emotions of everyday, see Averill 2004. For theories of emotion (the ways that people think about emotions), see Livingston 2012.

[11] For philosophical perspectives on emotion, see de Sousa 2017. For religious emotion, see Roberts 2016.

[12] For *apatheia* as transformations of emotions, see Chirban 1986.

When applied to the experience of a continuously transforming emotion, such a model presents a problem. In NBP, a change of emotion (which I describe in the next section, "On a Path to *Boddhicitta*") includes two aspects: in the intensity of emotion, which is accounted for by phenomenological theory,[13] and in the affective quality within a single emotion, which is given as a continuous flow with a repetitive (that is, predictable) direction of change. How is such a qualitative continuity constituted? Paradoxically, connectionist models in cognitive science (e.g., Kanwisher 2010) allow for a better understanding of the temporal dynamics of the brain's emotional processing (for examples, see Waugh et al. 2010, 2015; Dan-Glauser and Gross 2015) than we can boast with regard to how consciousness puts together an experience of the continuity of a transforming emotion for its subject.

An empirical sense of continuity has been deemed an "illusion" (Parnas and Henriksen 2016). Cognitive phenomenological models of continuity "appear to oscillate between ascribing the property of 'continuity' to the stream of experience, and ascribing it to the objects of experience" (Rashbrook 2011, 1). Husserl's model of the consciousness of internal time treats temporality as representational and not as inherent in the given: that is, as a property of a complex of intentions coupled with the primal impression. Retention, protention, and impression would be clustered together as "part and whole" in passivity, within a horizon of "clear seeing," which in itself is not subject to any temporality or transformation. Under the thematizations of transcendental aesthetics, Husserl addresses the problem of continuity as "how continuous perceiving, continuous presenting, reach a synthetic unity, and by means of this how specific appearances and presentations in general become unified" (Husserl 2001, 447). The problem of continuity is solved by the suggestion that a hypothetical momentary appearance appears uniform in every new phase.[14] It is unclear what would serve as such a "momentary appearance" in the case of an emotion.

---

[13] For more on intensity, see Husserl as quoted in Cavallaro 2017, 164: "presented at one time with great fullness of apprehension contents, at another time with little fullness; and in volatile change it is presented now with greater fullness, now with less. This cannot, of course, be the ground for any essential distinctions, since the distinctions within the phantasy presentations of the same object are at least as great as all of the distinctions that belong to the perceptual presentations." Consideration for intensity (*Intensität*) or, as Husserl also puts it, "vitality" (*Lebendigkeit*), is constant in Husserl's reflections on fantasy.

[14] I want to thank Adrian Răzvan Şandru, who reviewed this paper in its early stage, for the following useful suggestion: "The problem of continuity, which is essential for Husserl, is also solved through the function of protensional opening of an anticipated horizon. This horizon is described as the "sum" of all possible protensions, which can become retensions (see Held 2007). [Considering] continuity within a limes function ... also has an implicit mathematical telos. ... [Husserl] can [account] for continuity as well as for telos, but ... [he]does so from the standpoint of intentionality. This ... would more set the focus on non-intentional continuity and telos. This would differentiate ... Husserl from Henry." To further clarify this important point, the "synthesis" I refer to in the text is pointing exactly to what is indicated by Şandru: that is, the protensional-retentional consciousness, which I understand as a synthetic one. Specifics of the present analytic situation is that in the analysis of emotion, as opposed to an analysis of an "external" object, there must be a correlation between the time-consciousness, and the innate *durée* of emotion itself as opposed to intentional consciousness of its representation. Perhaps this latter *durée* can be accounted for as a nonintentional one, but then we need to ascribe not only duration but a continu-

However, empirically, the flow of a continuous emotional transformation in NBP is not incremental as are thoughts or sensations. Also, under *epoché*, this experience doesn't consist of snapshots of discrete primary impressions. On the contrary, it is the primary impression itself that appears continuous. The framework of passive synthesis leaves us with the only option, which is to substitute the analysis of memory for the analysis of the gradual/continuous givenness of emotion. Since in NBP emotion is initially generated as a memory (cf. Summa 2015), but afterwards experience switches to modifications of spontaneously arising emotions in the present moment, I intend to argue that in situ of itself, as a form of consciousness in itself, within the embodiment of its feeling-sense, emotion cannot be conceived of as consciousness resulting from the Husserlian animation of *hylē* by the bestowal of sense. Rather, the perceived continuity of the transformation in the quality of emotion may point to the ontologically primary and truly continuous processes in the constitution of emotion which would be underlying a secondary, incremental givenness of emotion typical of the everyday.

In recent years, phenomenological studies of emotion engage the analytics of *Dasein.* (See Ratcliffe 2013; Fernandez 2014.) Indeed, viewing emotions in relation to moods, as modifications in the modes of being, may provide options to account for the evidence of fluidity underlying complexity.[15] Quoting from Depraz's (2015, 277) analysis of surprise,

> if one had to speak neither in anthropological nor psychological but in ontological terms, as in the medieval categories of philosophy, one should say that one is dealing with a modal or aspectual ontology. In less "heavy" categories, it would be said that a phenomenon is the accent, density, increase of being: neither its creation nor its generation, just a slight signal of its presence. [My translation].

Bringing ontology into the phenomenological study of emotion is not a siren call of theory but, as I will argue, a straightforward phenomenological fidelity to the demands of givenness. On multiple occasions, Husserl himself acknowledged the existence of different kinds of consciousness, and this presupposes flexibility in the means of analysis: emotion doesn't have to be necessarily understood by the same means that were designed for the understanding of reason—that is, exclusively as a set of intentional relations. The phenomenology of emotion in NBP, as a developing, temporally extended condition, puts to the test the understanding not just of emotion but of consciousness as such, with different phenomenological frameworks needed to match the shifting horizons of its self-presentation. In my argument, the succession of interpretive frameworks follows the progression of the emotion's mode of givenness in my empirical data. The initial stages of practice, in which the

---

ous change to primal impression, unless, as Şandru suggests, we consider an idealized primal impression, which in Husserl's account is inaccessible otherwise. Indeed, accesing the primal impression appears to me impossible within Husserl's model, because one ends up in the same time consciousness which needs to be now equated with emotion (see discussion in Sect. 5.5)—but this is not what one observes in a continuous transformation of the *quality* of emotion, which presents exactly an instance of the self-revelation of the primal impression within its own horizon of continuity—hence my seeking of a solution via the material phenomenology of Henry.

[15] For evidence of phenomenological complexity even within everyday emotions, see Nijhavan (n.d.).

experience of emotion is based on recollection, fit well into a Brentanian-Husserlian representational-intentional perspective on emotion. When, with the progress of practice, emotion loses its axiological objects, it acquires a nonrepresentational character à la Levinas. When, later, emotion is revealed as situated in the flesh, as nonobjectifying self-affection, which becomes an object for higher-order reflection, such an emotion doesn't turn into a mere "feeling" but retains its distinct characteristics as emotion. Reproducible and predictable in character, self-transforming emotion in the religious context comes through as intensely somatic (by contrast with the everyday emotions as discrete mental states) and, in the final presentation, as fully immanent, asking for a corresponding ontological framework. In the analysis of this stage, after using up the resources available in classical phenomenology, I switch to the phenomenological ontology of Henry.[16]

My data streams include my own internal experience of more than 25 years of practice, observations that have I accumulated during that time as a teacher of guided *mettā* and other practices, and reports of my peers.

5.3 On a Path to *Boddhicitta*: Empirical Account

Mettā meditation begins with the volitional generation of compassion (or happiness, friendliness, etc.), along with wishing: "May all beings be happy (and safe)."[17] After the emotion is *felt* internally, it is "beamed out" toward imaginary others or, in other versions, radiated in four directions, from the chest and around the body, up, and down, as a spatialized feeling.[18] This can be further specified in successive rounds as "may all beings be peaceful," "may all beings be tranquil," "may all beings be blissful," and so on (in Antonov and Vaver 1989). Sending emotion "out" is forceful and energetic, with somatic focusing from the chest outward. (Cf. Lindahl 2017.) If one cannot come up with the desired emotion directly, one can use memories as props till one learns to access the desired emotion without a prop. Uninvited emotions may also surface and be either released or inhibited at the very origin and eventually be transformed from unwholesome to wholesome ones (as in Fig. 5.2, below), with the practitioner gaining full control of her emotions without suppressing or denying them.

Replacing unwholesome affects with wholesome ones takes both mindfulness and concentration in order to be practiced in a relaxed, detached, and alert manner. These are mental modes that lead to the changes in the phenomenal field. For example, S. N. Goenka[19] taught "no attraction, no repulsion, just observe, just observe"—a mode inhibiting intentionality. Sogyal Rinpoche (2002) instructed his

---

[16] Henry was the main critic of Heidegger's idea of *ek-stasis* of being (Seyler 2016).

[17] For examples of the *mettā* practice, see Antonov and Vaver 1989; Salzberg (n.d.); *Mettā* meditation (n.d.).

[18] Cf. Griffero 2016, 36: "atmospheres are spatialized feelings; that is to say, they are the specific emotional quality of a given 'lived space.'"

[19] For more about S.N. Goenka, see American Buddhist Perspectives 2013.

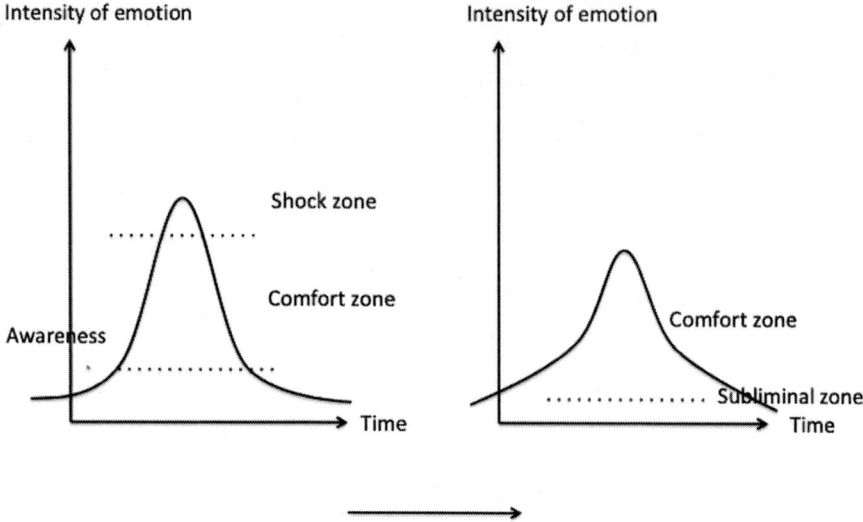

Fig. 5.1 Change in intensity of observed emotions in MMP (Situation A)

readers to "be alert yet relaxed, relaxed yet alert," which replaces constitutive intent of the ego by passive perception. (Cf. Şan 2017 on counterphenomena.) Antonov and Vaver (1989) taught decentering one's awareness so as to feel it distributed through the body, with a likeliness of emotion showing up if attention is brought to a specific area of the body. (Cf. Osypiuk et al. 2018.) All these modes open awareness of the interrelationship between the perception of the body-schema, self-awareness, attentiveness, emoting, and so forth.[20] At the same time, the usual awareness of emotion in the everyday (cf. Slaby 2008), such as "I feel scared," or "I feel fear in my chest, or "in my head," and the like,[21] turns into "I am aware of my emotion," with noticing subliminal emotions and mindful "release" of them (Fig. 5.1).

With the maturation of mindfulness, the whole of emotion shows a wavelike character, proceeding from lesser to greater intensity and then subsiding. (Cf. Desmidt et al. 2014.) Overall, emotions become more placid (Fig. 5.1, Situation A). Next, the practitioner becomes aware of spontaneously rising emotions that are neither about nor caused by anything. In spirituality, these are treated as mental traces, as afforded by "we take it for granted that mental processes do not exist only when we advert to them and seize upon them in an experience of something immanent" (Husserl 1998, 175). Bringing attention to such a "trace" may animate an episodic

---

[20] For the "phenomenological matrix" of mindfulness, see Lutz et al. 2015.

[21] "Livedness," or self-affection—that is, an absolute immediacy of givenness to itself—has been used by Henry in two ways, as related to the innate property of the ego and, with it, of self-awareness; and as a property pertaining to emotion. For a detailed analysis of self-affection, see Taipale 2014, 24–25.

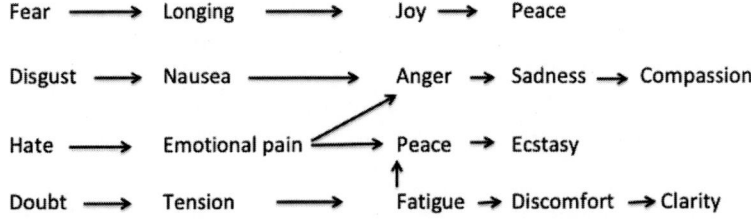

Fig. 5.2 Transmutation of emotions in NBP (Situation B)

memory, which can then be bracketed out as the practitioner returns to the "mere observation" mode, and the "trace" is restored to the present.

Wangyal (1993, 98) metaphorized the relationship between emotion and the awareness of emotion as "sunbeams melting the snow," sunbeams being awareness and the snow being emotion. Later in the practice, emotion and awareness of emotion become like "snowflakes falling into the ocean": that is, hardly distinct in their givenness. Awareness, of course, belongs to the subject who meditates; however, the beginner's mode ("I am aware of my emotion") loses its initial, personal character and polarity of the ego: hereby, the metaphor of the "ocean." This condition gradually turns into the rise of *bodhicitta*, the awakened mind of compassion. The transformation of emotions or, as it is called colloquially, "transmutation,"[22] takes place after Situation A (Fig. 5.1) and continues into the "snowflakes in the ocean" of awareness.

By "transmutation," a condition is meant whereby one emotion turns into another, not as a shift between two emotions but rather as a change of quality within the same emotion: for instance, anger is not *replaced* by compassion but *becomes* compassion. This conversion of emotion happens instantly, perhaps, along with some dissociation and refocusing of attention. The direction of the change is always the same, repeated between sets of practice and therefore predictable: for example, anger always changes into compassion, not vice versa. In Fig. 5.2, the transformation goes from left to right: fear turns into longing, into joy, and so on, but joy doesn't turn into fear.[23] Naturally, joy can be replaced by fear, but the situation of transmutation is different: it goes in only one direction and is irreversible. The schema in Fig. 5.2 includes states such as doubt or tension because they also change teleologically and have a noticeable duration and affective qualitative character. The whole process looks like the continuous flow of a single emotion, a single condition, in which the patches of emotional quality shift from one to another in the wink of an eye, at the same time creating a gradient of quality with teleology toward more expansive, pleasing, likable states (cf. "existential feelings" in Guignon 2009; Ratcliffe 2008).

---

[22] Ruhe (n.d.); Kvasnicka 2014; Chyten 2017.

[23] This situation I describe as a clearly expressed telos, which shows only in contemplative practice. This is empirically different from a situation of psychological ambivalence, in which two emotions can be experienced as conflicting. (Thanks to Adrian Răzvan Șandru for raising this question.)

In this scheme of things, emotions do not shift via "tranquility" of recollection (cf. Summa 2015), and neither are there other moods happening in the background or in between the states indicated in Fig. 5.2. This teleology is not anticipated within the emotion itself while it's happening and comes, especially the first time, with an element of surprise. Against an ongoing practice, the succession of states can be recalled, but outside practice (for example, if one stops regular meditation) it is not remembered and not reproducible. I will now proceed to the phenomenological analysis of this description, elaborating where necessary on the details.

5.4   From Complex to Nonrepresentational Emotion

Intending of emotion in the beginning of NBP is of three kinds. In the first intending, emotion is recalled. The purpose of this is not reliving the iff of emotion in the episodic memory (cf. Zahavi 2017, 406), but reliving the feeling-aspect of it. Such recollection is necessary only in the beginning of the training. By applying mindfulness, practitioners learn to distinguish between emotion as a feeling of emotion, which is always in the present, and the circumstances, including intentional objects and others, toward whom the emotion was intended. The ego splits between participation in the intentional aspects of emotion and in its feeling-aspect, at the same time observing both and reflecting on the process. Then follow the inhibition of both the sense-intentionality and the representational intentionality. Inhibiting the split-off aspects of intentionality enables a shift from memory as a modification of an original perceptual act (cf. Summa 2015, 175) to the actual emotion in the present. Thereby the temporal constitution of experience as "the past" switches to "now I have access to the same emotion as I had in the past"; then "the same" drops, and experience remains just an experience of a particular emotion in the "now."

In the second intending, the ego imagines ("feigns"; cf. Embree 2011) the abstracted (as generic "friends", "foes" etc.) others toward whom the feeling-aspect of emotion, purified of episodic memories, will be directed. These imagined others serve as intentional axiological objects that call emotion out and expose the ego-pole's habitualities[24]—a process that at times can be very intense. (Cf. Lindahl 2017.)

Instead of being trapped in reliving a past emotion, the ego exercises new kinds of sense bestowal, switching to a new, ethicoreligious province of meaning. Thereby, instead of producing a high tension of consciousness, along with everyday affects such as (e.g.) anger or fear,[25] the ego gets entrained to keep up less tension, which is associated with pleasurable, enjoyable (or, in Buddhist terms, wholesome) states, such as joy, peace, or clarity.

---

[24] For more on the ego's habitualities, see Moran 2014, 27–47.

[25] For tension of consciousness, connected by Schütz with constitutive engagement of the ego, see Schütz 1945. For relaxation of the tension of consciousness in religious experience, see Barber 2017.

Table 5.1 Intentional and nonintentional aspects of complex emotion

	Affect		Object
Emotion includes	Noetic aspects	Noematic aspects	Presentation of nonaxiological in themselves properties of the thing or situation
	A sense of the nonintentional feeling (itself can become a *noēma* for higher intentionalities)	Sensuous, nonintentional feeling (caused by a thing or situation)	
	The intentional feeling directed at valuating the attributes of the thing or situation		
Emotional episode or situational emotion (as in recollection during early stages of the *mettā*)	A long-lasting state that disposes us toward a certain affective understanding and motivates situational emotions (i.e., the episodes of particular emotions)		Intends the particular affective or evaluative attributes of the object or situation beyond its merely being likable or dislikable and also discloses something about ourselves

Note: Based on Drummond (2009, 2013)

In Fig. 5.2, the emotions at the end of the transmutational chain are wholesome ones, more relaxed and transparent in character than the affects at the beginning of the chain. Notably, the wholesome states can have high intensity (as, e.g., ecstasy)[26] but are not connected with constitutive ego-tension. In this process, the practitioner as if "invests" in her future self, training herself to experience a wholesome spectrum of emotions instead of unwholesome ones. At the same time, the ego becomes progressively more relaxed and less controlling.

Let us now consider this situation in more detail. According to "add-on" theories (as in de Sousa 2017), emotion is never given to us in complete immanence, but always in the transcendental horizon as directed at an object.[27] As Drummond (2009, 3) ascertains: "in intending objects the subject is primarily not in a causal relation with them, but is instead directed to them in their significance for us, i.e., *as* things or situations that are significant for us in determinate ways." In Table 5.1 (based on Drummond 2009), I summarize the constitutive moments of a complex emotion.

Since according to Table 5.1, emotion is a whole constituted out of parts, I suggest that *mettā*-mindfulness uses episodic memory of emotion to "extract" the feeling-aspect by dissociating it from the transcendental axiological judgments and by replacing these with a soteriological valuation.[28] Such reduced emotion doesn't intend any longer on an object given presentationally. However, as emotion, it retains its intentional feeling despite not being directed any longer at an object as a

---

[26] Guenther (1992) indicates that a state of enlightened mind is characterized by extreme intensity or power.

[27] Emotion is considered in relation to transcendentally directed valuation, as an affect coupled with an outgoing or transcendental judgement, e.g., Drummond (2009, 4): "Actions and agents from the beginning appear as noble, virtuous, generous, honest, just, compassionate, hospitable, friendly, base, vicious, rancorous, spiteful, mean-spirited, treacherous, and so on."

[28] E.g. Chodron 2011.

nonrepresentational intention (cf. Levinas, in Lee 2003) and not as a pure, sensuous, nonintentional feeling. Nonrepresentational intentionality of emotion, according to Levinas, has absolute primacy in relation to representational intentionality. In NBP Situation A (Fig. 5.1), emotion transitions from being complex and representational to being nonrepresentational: it doesn't represent a situation any more but represents only itself. A nonrepresentational emotion is not directed at any object (including an undefined plurality of objects attributed to the intentions of moods—Husserl's position, against which Ratcliffe (2013) argues in his treatment of moods as modes of being) but is purely directed, meaning having no relationship with a correlate object. The valuating meaning of emotion is repositioned: instead of being intersubjectively and transcendentally oriented toward things external to emotion, it is now values emotion per se as an internal, soteriological property. In the continuing progress of NBP, such emotion will be recognized as inherent to the self, ready to be transformed into wholesome states that are a "seat" of *boddhicitta*.

5.5   *Noēsis*, Its Modes, and the Reversibility in Emotion's *Noēma*

The nonrepresentational intentionality of emotion is not objectifying anything (as opposed to, e.g., objectification, always associated with the logical sense; for objectification, see Husserl 2001, 329) and is not expected to be fulfilled in correlation with an object. This reduced emotion serves as a substrate for higher-order reflective intentionalities—that is, as a *noēma* in *noēsis* with strata extending upward, such as, but not limited to, "feeling this way brings me closer to enlightenment."

According to the analysis of *noēma-noēsis* relationship in *Ideas I* (Husserl 1998, 241), every *noēma* has being but is non-self-sufficient in terms of its presentation. *Noēma* and *noēsis* appear as a unity. Therefore, we can expect that the teleological transformations of purified emotion now serving as a *noēma* will correspond to teleological transformations in the modes of *noēsis*. As indicated in §15 of *Cartesian Meditations* (Husserl 1993, 36), the natural reflection eagerly reveals the objects related to the noematic contents but is insufficient to reveal the noetic contents of experience. Accordingly, the transformations of emotion (Figs. 5.1 and 5.2, and the previous Sect. 5.4 of this analysis) point to the transformation in the modes of *noēsis,* which I will now further elaborate upon.

In the early stages of NBP, the emotion's "affection toward" is given both immanently-psychologically and transcendentally. (Cf. Husserl 2001, 277.) Inhibition of practical intentionalities limits emotion to the immanent-psychological sphere, with a new kind of appropriation (by the ego), in which emotion is viewed as a property of the self. The instruction "no attraction, no repulsion", which is given by the teacher and has to be sustained as an attitude by the practitioner, untangles emotion from the noetic moments directed toward it: for example, "I like feeling happy" turns into "just happiness." These nonjustified by circumstances "just fear," "just sadness," "just happiness" are now free-flowing aspects of one's self, not as background moods but as clearly defined, bounded states of specific affective quality situated in embodied self-awareness. In the constitution of the noematic contents of an emotion's presentation, these states manifest depth, density, and spatiality pertaining to embodiment. These states are now valuated soteriologically, as properties helping or impeding enlightenment.

In *Ideas I*, Husserl explains *noēsis* as "animating construing [by the ego] which forms the stuff into intentive mental processes." *Noēsis* animates the "sensation-content" (*172*, 203) by arranging "the moments in consciousness, awarenesses," into unities (Husserl 1998, 204–205). "Animation," in Husserl's understanding, belongs to intentionality alone (Husserl 1998, 203):

> Among the former [primary contents] belong certain "sensuous" mental processes, mental processes which are unitary with respect to their highest genus, "sensation contents" such as color-Data, touch-Data and tone-Data, and the like, which we shall no longer confuse with the appearing moments of physical things—coloredness, roughness, etc.—which present themselves to mental processes [*erlebnismäßig*] by means of those [contents]. Likewise the sensuous pleasure, pain, and tickle sensation, and so forth, and no doubt also sensuous moments belonging to the sphere of "drives." We find such concrete really immanental data as components of more inclusive concrete mental processes which are intentive as wholes; and more particularly, we find those sensuous moments overlaid by a stratum which, as it were, "animates," which bestows sense (or essentially involves a bestowing sense)—a stratum by which precisely the concrete intentive mental processes arise from the *sensuous, which has in itself nothing pertaining to intentionality.*

However, the *noēma* of purified, embodied emotion is not just sensuous but is self-affective and affectively "directed toward." Its affective quality defines emotion's identity—which, according to Husserl, must remain in the given (*noēma*) and not in the constituted, as in: "[T]he noematic is the field of unities, the noetic is the field of constituting multiplicities" (Husserl 1998, 207, 242). In other words, purified emotion has a rudimentary self-luminosity, as well as a rudimentary outgoing intentionality. Consequently, in the case of a purified emotion in NBP, the noetic-noematic relationship contains intentionality on both sides—in its developed form, on the side of the ego, and in its rudimentary form, on the side of emotion. Therefore, purified emotion reveals a sort of rudimentary reversibility, which is another specific characteristic of embodiment present in emotion as a peculiar form.

The affective identity of purified emotion in NBP, such as fear, sadness, or happiness, has duration (as referenced in Fig. 5.1, Situation A). Husserl (1998, 382) states that in the analysis of internal consciousness of time, it is necessary to account for an atemporal, preintentional horizon of consciousness, metaphorized as "flow" (that is, a continuity creating a background for constitutive moments of protention and retention in the time-consciousness).

NBP aims at uncovering this continuity by altering the modes of *noēsis*. The noetic tension of consciousness (Schütz 1945) changes along with a shift from pragmatic to soteriological valuation of emotion. Along with it, instructions such as "no attraction, no repulsion" and "be alert yet relaxed, relaxed yet alert" weaken intentionality directed at the embodied emotion-*noēma*, ultimately stripping off the intentional "add-ons." The same purpose is aided by the ego, which splits (as above) into observing and constituting: the incremental constituting aspect is continuously bracketed out, leaving the observing aspect, which turns into a "pure seeing." But, since "[t]he 'object' of consciousness, the object which has identity with itself during the flowing subjective process, does not come into the process from outside; on the contrary, it is included as a sense in the subjective process itself—and thus as an 'intentional effect' produced by the synthesis of consciousness" (Husserl 1998, 42), a *noēma* of emotion remains in the altered *noēsis* even when the mode of *noēsis* is altered. *Noēsis* becomes more and more relaxed and transparent, and less and less positing or constituting.

In this now passive and receptive seeing, emotion turns into a "counterphenomenon": that is, appears as completely self-given (cf. Şan 2017), without traces of constitutive intention on behalf of the ego or connection to an external event that would be viewed as causal. In the absence of constitutive rays of *noēsis*, the mode of presentation in *noēma* also changes: emotion acquires a degree of transparency, its self-affection becoming less forceful. (Cf. "sunbeams melting the snow.") The "pure seeing" is now revealed as a principle of continuity between *noēma* and *noēsis*, and a horizon of possibility for both intentionality and self-affection. The metaphor of "snowflakes falling into the ocean," in which snowflakes are the emotion-*noēma* and the ocean is a seeing aspect of *noēsis*, describes this effect. In contrast to the traditional idea of sharp opposition between self-luminous *noēsis* and inert *noēma*, the metaphor emphasizes a continuity of the same principle in the *noēsis* of emotion and purified emotion as a *noēma*. The teleological flow of transmutation corresponds with the givenness of emotion "intuitively and adequately in immanent perception" (Finetti 2015), now immanent fully in its peculiar reversibility: on the one hand, it is an intentional object of *noēsis*, and on the other, a subject of its own self-affection.

5.6   Horizons of Possibility in Religious Emotion

In Husserl's phenomenology, the syntheses of the unities of meaning are the only means for understanding any kind of continuity. (Cf. Lavigne 2016.)[29] Consequently, to approach the continuity of transmuting emotion, I will first utilize the lens of passive synthesis. In Situation A, the noematic unity of emotion is characterized by duration (Fig. 5.1) filled by a particular affective quality (e.g., fear, or sadness, or happiness). In Situation B, the noematic unity of emotion also has duration (Fig. 5.2), but this duration doesn't include changes in the intensity of emotion and instead includes a teleological change of a particular affective quality: for instance, anger becomes compassion, and so on.

In Sect. 5.5, I stated that (a) emotion is self-affective, (b) self-affectivity and "clear seeing" of *noēsis* share the same ontological property of self-luminosity, and

---

[29] For the theory of wholes and parts, used by Husserl in the analyses of consciousness, see Sokolowski 1977; Casari 2000.

(c) emotion is characterized by reversibility and continuity between self-affection and the "flow" (can be also identified as "clear seeing") of *noēsis*. The horizon of time-consciousness is an insufficient condition of possibility for such a *noēma* for the following reasons. First, emotion's "primordial becoming in time" (cf. Steinbock 2001, xxxiii) is continuous because of retention-*Urimpression*-protention synthesis. *Urimpression* refers to hyletics, a concept that has undergone evolution in Husserl's writings, from referencing sense-data to hyletics, which can give rise to intentionality in its specific form, retention, a form of intentionality responsible for continuity. At the same time, hyletics cannot produce sense (*Sinn*). So, in order to account for the teleological change of affective quality observed in Situation B, one would need to think some kind of habituated input from the ego (cf. Moran 2011, 2014): that is, intentionality. But we have just learned that the whole course of NBP is directed at inhibiting intentionality and restricting the constitutive participation of the ego and that at the end, *noēsis* and the *noēma* of emotion disclose the same ontological property; and it is at this point that the transformation of emotion is realized as qualitatively teleological. Therefore, to account for Situation B, we need to posit additional a prioris, those that would take the above qualities out of dependence on intentional time-consciousness and into the domain of their own possibilities. A full array of the necessary conditions of possibility for Situation B would include:

- horizon X, of time-consciousness;
- horizon X_1, of "clear seeing"(or, "flow");
- horizon Y, of specific affective quality of emotion, as sadness, fear, or happiness—horizon Y accounts for telos of the transformation;
- horizon Z, of self-affection, which accounts for the continuity of changing emotion, as something that distinguishes emotion from nonemotion.

At this point, an attempt to use the categories of the passive synthesis comes to a halt: within these categories, horizons Y and Z are unthinkable. Perhaps some options could have been salvaged if I had examined with greater care the meaning in the flow of emotion in Situation B. Even so, the teleology of these networks would still have remained a mystery. Therefore, it seems reasonable and necessary to seek solutions elsewhere. The understanding of additional horizons Y and Z can be derived from the nonintentional phenomenology of Michel Henry (1995).[30]

5.7 Horizons in Regard for the Continuity of Emotion

Nonintentional phenomenology focuses exactly on clarifications of the conditions of possibility for appearing. (Cf. Serban 2016.) Henry (1973) established that the condition of possibility for consciousness is life, whose essence is self-affection. This condition of possibility is realized via the body, in the horizon of

---

[30] For more on analyses of religious experience along the lines of nonintentional phenomenology, see Louchakova-Schwartz Forthcoming.

phenomenological materiality as the ultimate constitutor (Henry 2008); this presupposes a necessity to reinterpret the ego as embodied subjectivity with the inherent power of knowledge and self-knowledge (Henry 1975, 2016; cf. Taipale 2014). Thus, the appearance of the noetic powers of the ego, the affectivity of drives, and the *sensibilité* of the flesh are phenomenal consequences of the same principle of the self-affection of life.

Reduction of the "add-on" intentionalities in the emotion of NBP is, in fact, an exercise in excavating the phenomenal modes of givenness of a prioris of emotion. This is the same as saying that the change in the modes of *noēsis* in NBP is excavating the phenomenal givenness of intentionality's phenomenological-ontological a prioris, as in the already above-quoted "compassion should be practiced first of all because it precedes all else, just as man's breath (*āśvāsa*) precedes his ability to live."[31] Such "excavations" are not simply bringing something out of anonymity—that is, giving a name to implicit presences—but rather these are modifications of experience revealing the presences themselves, as in Husserl's description of transcendental experience of the ego in *Cartesian Meditation*s (1993, chap. 2, §15). Therefore, it is reasonable to suggest that NBP is directed at experiences of uncovering the a prioris of appearances and therefore must involve self-affection (hence the focus on emotion) and phenomenological materiality (hence the attentional focus in the body). It is further reasonable to suggest that the phenomenal appearance of such a prioris is expected to be not just structural and incremental in character but rather holistic, alive—that is, sentient and self-luminous—and either indivisible or continuous as pertaining to life.

Even though phenomenological materiality serves as the horizon of possibility for intentionality, and even though intentionality is dependent on phenomenological materiality for its appearance—or, to be precise, it is more likely to be dependent on self-affection manifested by means of phenomenological materiality—the appearance of intentionality renders phenomenological materiality unapparent. A phenomenal unconcealment of phenomenological materiality, if at all possible (in degrees?), depends on cancellation of intentionality: for example, in a semihypothetical condition of absorption. (Cf. Louchakova-Schwartz 2017.) However, self-affection remains expressed in the embodied aspect of emotion, especially in the absence of the masking presence of "add-on" intentionalities: an empirical example would be the absence of awareness of emotion when one is intensely thinking ("sits in the head") and the reacquisition of awareness of emotion upon cessation of thinking and reconnection with the body (going "from the head to the heart"—an effect routinely utilized in affective therapy).

Husserl's term "hyletics" and Henry's term "phenomenological materiality" cannot be used interchangeably: both referencing the same empirical aspect of the ego's embodiment, they are different with regard to their phenomenality. Hyletics is sen-

---

[31] Ichishima 1982, 123. For more on transformations of mental states in meditative practice, see Guenther 1992 and Chodron (n.d.).

suous yet somewhat inert stuff requiring the intentionalities of the ego for its animation (in Husserl), and phenomenological materiality is self-affective (in Henry)
essence of the ego and therefore a condition of possibility for intentionality.
Religious philosophies of practice (to be distinguished from non-religious philosophies of experience)—which,[32] like (e.g.) Shakta-Vedanta or Tantric Buddhism, aim
at the revelation of the concealed underpinnings of consciousness-intentionality—
always include meditation on embodied emotion. Some of them (e.g., Kundalini
Tantra) even build their whole philosophies around the telos of this "reversal of the
mind" in their striving to uncover the ontological essence of phenomenality.

Being an epitome of self-affection, emotion occupies a middle position between
the concealment of self-affection in the horizon of intentionality and the unapparent
(because it is not given as intentionality) yet radical immanence of phenomenological materiality. The self-affection (of life) *is* appearance and doesn't need *epoché*
and reduction for its unmasking; emotion can be viewed as self-affection's mode of
particularization. Thinking in accord with Henry, one can say that appearance of
emotion is the first moment in the genesis of phenomenal consciousness. Hence,
Henry focuses most of his philosophy on affectivity, and by the same token meditation on emotion becomes a means of self-revelation of the ontological ground of
appearances as per Buddhist and Neo-Buddhist practices.

In *Analyses concerning Passive and Active Synthesis*, Husserl (2001) indicates
that phenomenological analysis can be conducted in two directions, as a top-down
regression from the higher intentionalities to the level of passive synthesis, and as a
progressive analysis that follows the genetics of constitution bottom-up, from passivity toward the higher orders of logic and reflection. Thinking further in accord
with Henry, such analyses would not be equal ontologically: a top-down reasoning
would simply lead to uncovering the ontological essence of phenomenality from
which the real constitutive analysis must begin, leading to the phenomenological
ontology of the constituting ego. Certainly, Husserl acknowledged the need for such
ontology: "[B]y passivity … Husserl means that which makes the active level of
experience possible" (Steinbock 2001, xxxiii)": that is, the "basic, essential conditions of the possibility of a subjectivity itself" (Husserl 2001, 163, 169). In Husserl's
analyses of passive and active synthesis, the possibility of constitution is fulfilled by
horizons of temporality and "seeing": that is, incrementally and transcendentally.
For Henry, the horizon of all horizons is in the immanence of phenomenological
materiality, out of which intentionality must be derived. In fact, Henry denies transcendence any functional role. But the particularization of intentionality remains to
be worked out. As in Serban (2016, 235): "The question of intentionality is not that
of its being but that of its appearing, and … the question of how intentionality
appears is that of knowing whether this appearing is homogeneous or identical to
the appearing of beings, otherwise said, if the appearing of intentionality depends
on intentionality itself." Similarly, the constitution of particular qualities in emo-

---

[32] For more on philosophies of practice, see Sen Sharma 1983.

tion's networks remains to be worked out. NBP serves as a spectacle of experience in which such problems can be approached and clarified.

I suggest that a key concept for understanding the transformation of emotion would be that rudimentary forms of intentionality, which account for the particular qualia of separate emotions, are in a peculiar relationship with self-affection. Such a relationship is, on the one hand, a genetic dependence of intentionality on self-affection, and on the other, a relationship of reversal, which in NBP make self-affection more and more noticeable (e.g., as above, when emotion becomes more self-luminous). Directed at the inhibition of outgoing intentionalities, the telos of NBP reverts affective drives onto their own affectivity. Further, such moments are immersed in the immanent presence of phenomenological materiality. Thereby, NBP exhibits an emancipatory telos (cf. Barber 2017) directed at a maximum release of tension associated with intentionality and reversal of emotion toward pure self-affection. Such reversals are incremental (which accounts for the changing quality of emotion) and happen within "the same" emotion, because there is no intentionality left to register the change in identity. However, there is a continuous presence of self-affection, which accounts for the "emotional" quality of the *noēma*, and of phenomenological materiality, which accounts for continuity.

Situation B is "the cusp" of reversals between self-affection and intentionality, and the immanent constancy of self-affective phenomenological materiality. The horizons of possibility for Situation B now look like this:[33]

- horizons X, of the time-consciousness, and X_1, of the "clear seeing";
- synthetic horizon Y, of the emotion's *noēma*. This includes fluctuating reversals between rudimentary intentionalities of emotion's qualia and self-affection. The reversals are teleologically directed toward decrease of tension and emancipation of emotion (cf. Barber 2017) from sadness and fear to happiness and compassion;
- horizon Z, of self-affection alone, which accounts for the continuity of changing emotion as emotion (distinct from nonemotion);
- horizon Z_1, of the constant immanence of the selfsame phenomenological materiality, which accounts for continuity in transformation.

To briefly mention, by contrast with the theory of parts and whole (mereology), the models that can be used to metaphorize this situation describe transitions from complexity to determinate condition. (Cf. Buzsáki 2006; Capolupo et al. 2013.) The emancipatory telos of religious emotion features not interruptions typical of religious experience (cf. Dahl 2010; Barber 2017) but, on the contrary, continuity. Religious emotion is never static, and never identical in itself in quality, but continuously transforming, thereby rehabituating the ego's tendencies toward more

---

[33] A more detailed analysis is presented in Louchakova-Schwartz Forthcoming.

pleasing, relaxed, elevating, and socially "healing" states, culminating in boundless, self-luminous compassion. In clarification of such experience, different phenomenological approaches are not mutually exclusive but rather complementary and necessary, to be combined.

References

American Buddhist Perspectives. 2013. Vipassana meditation teacher and popularizer S.N. Goenka passes away. *American Buddhist Perspectives.* http://www.patheos.com/blogs/americanbuddhist/2013/09/vipassana-meditation-teacher-and-populariser-s-n-goenka-passes-away.html. Last modified 1 October 2013. Accessed 28 Mar 2018.

Antonov, Vladimir, and G. Vaver. 1989. *Kompleksnaya sistema psykhofisicheskoi samoregulatsii.* Leningrad: Cosmos.

Averill, J.R. 2004. Everyday emotions: Let me count the ways. *Social Science Information* 43 (4): 571–580.. ISSN:0539-0184. https://doi.org/10.1177/0539018404047703.

Barber, Michael. 2017. *Religion and humor as emancipating provinces of meaning.* New York: Springer.

Buddharakkhita, A. 1995. *Mettā: The philosophy and practice of universal love.* Kandy: Buddhist Publication Society.

Buzsáki, G. 2006. *Rhythms of the brain.* New York: Oxford University Press.

Capolupo, A., et al. [Capolupo, A., W.J. Freeman, and G. Vitiello.] 2013. Dissipation of "dark energy" by cortex in knowledge retrieval. *Physics of Life Reviews* 10(1): 85–94. https://doi.org/10.1016/j.plrev.2013.01.001.

Casari, Ettore. 2000. On Husserl's theory of wholes and parts. *History and Philosophy of Logic* 21 (1): 1–43.

Cavallaro, Marco. 2017. The phenomenon of ego-splitting in Husserl's phenomenology of pure phantasy. *Journal of the British Society for Phenomenology* 48 (2): 162–177. https://doi.org/10.1080/00071773.2016.1250436.

Chirban, John T. 1986. Developmental stages in Eastern Orthodox Christianity. In *Transformations of consciousness*, ed. Ken Wilber, Jack Engler, and Daniel Brown, 289–314. Boston/London: Shambhala.

———. 2011. *Working with emotions.* Bhikshuni Thubten Chodron. http://thubtenchodron.org/2011/06/afflictions-and-antidotes/. Accessed 3 Mar 2018.

Chödrön, Pema. 2016. *Bodhichitta: The excellence of awakened heart.* Lion's Roar. https://www.lionsroar.com/bodhichitta-the-excellence-of-awakened-heart/. Last modified 17 June 2016. Accessed 28 Mar. 2018.

Chodron, Ven Thubten. N.d. *Stages of the path to awakening.* Bhikshuni Thubten Chodron. https://thubtenchodron.org/commentaries/stages-of-the-path-to-awakening-2/. Accessed 3 Mar 2018.

Chyten, Leah. 2017. Master the alchemy of your emotions to transform anger, hatred, pain into higher qualities. *Yoga Journal.* https://www.yogajournal.com/yoga-101/alchemy-of-emotions-transform-anger-hatred-pain-into-higher-qualities. Accessed 8 May 2018.

Dahl, Espen. 2010. *Phenomenology and the holy.* London: SCM Press.

Dan-Glauser, E.S., and J.J. Gross. 2015. The temporal dynamics of emotional acceptance: Experience, expression, and physiology. *Biological Psychology* 108: 1–12. https://doi.org/10.1016/j.biopsycho.2015.03.005. Epub 14 March 2015. PubMed PMID: 25782407.

de Sousa, Ronald. 2017. Emotion. In *The Stanford encyclopedia of philosophy*, ed. Edward N. Zalta. (winter edition). https://plato.stanford.edu/archives/win2017/entries/emotion/. Accessed 3 Mar 2018.

Depraz, N. 2014. La inscripción de la sorpresa en la fenomenología de las emociones de Edmund Husserl. *Eidos* (21): 160–180. https://doi.org/10.14482/eidos.21.6486.

———. 2015. *Attention et surprise*: Paul Ricœur en débat et au-delà. *Alter* 23: 261–278.

Desmidt, T., et al. [Desmidt, T., M. Lemoine, C. Belzung, and N. Depraz.] 2014. The temporal dynamics of emotional experience. *Phenomenology and the Cognitive Sciences* 13: 557–578. https://doi.org/10.1007/s11097-014-9377-8.

Dhammadinna, Ven. n.d. Bodhicitta for practitioners of *mettā*—A study retreat. Buddhist Insight Network.   http://www.buddhistinsightnetwork.org/retreats/event/bodhicitta-practitioners-metta-study-retreat. Accessed 1 May 2018.

Drummond, J. 2009. Feelings, emotions, and truly perceiving the valuable. *The Modern Schoolman* 86: 363–379.

———. 2013. The intentional structure of emotions. *Logical Analysis and the History of Philosophy/Philosophiegeschichte und logische Analyse* 16: 244–263.

Ekman, P., et al. [Ekman, P., R.J. Davidson, M. Ricard, and A.B. Wallace.] 2013. *Buddhist and psychological perspectives on emotions and well-being.* https://www.paulekman.com/wp-content/uploads/2013/07/buddhist-and-psychological-perpectives.pdf. Accessed 29 Mar 2018.

Embree, L. 2011. *Reflective analysis.* Bucharest: Zeta Books.

Fernandez, A.V. 2014. Depression as existential feeling or de-situatedness? Distinguishing structure from mode in psychopathology. *Phenomenology and Cognitive Sciences* 41 (3): 595–612. https://doi.org/10.1007/s11097-014-9374-y. Accessed 3 Mar 2018.

Finetti, Stéphane. 2015. La transformation de la conception husserlienne de la représentation-de-phantasia à la lumière de la méthode reductive. *Phantasia* [online], volume 1, 2015. https://popups.uliege.be:443/0774-7136/index.php?id=364. Accessed 15 Mar 2018.

Fink, Charles K. 2015. Clinging to nothing: The phenomenology and metaphysics of *upādāna* in early Buddhism. *Asian Philosophy* 25 (1): 15–33.

GlideWing Online Workshops. n.d.. https://www.glidewing.com/twr/zhine_meditation_home.html. Accessed 1 May 2018.

Goldie, P. 2002. Emotions, feelings, and intentionality. *Phenomenology and the Cognitive Sciences* 1: 235–254.

Griffero, Tonino. 2016. *Atmospheres: Aesthetics of emotional spaces.* London: Routledge.

Guenther, Herbert V. 1992. *Meditation differently: Phenomenological-psychological aspects of Tibetan Buddhist (mahāmudrā and snying-thig) practices from original Tibetan sources.* Delhi: Motilal Banarsidass Publishers.

Guignon, Charles. 2009. The body, bodily feelings, and existential feelings. A Heideggerian perspective. *Philosophy, Psychiatry, & Psychology* 16 (2): 195–199.

Held, Claus. 2007. Phenomenology of authentic time in Husserl and Heidegger. *International Journal of Philosophical Studies* 15 (3): 327–347. https://doi.org/10.1080/09672550701445191. Accessed 27 June 2018.

Henry, Michel. 1973. *The Essence of Manifestation.* Trans. Girard J. Etzkorn. The Hague: Nijhoff.

———. 1975. *Philosophy and Phenomenology of the Body.* Trans. Girard J. Etzkorn. The Hague: Nijhoff.

———. 1995. Phénoménologie non-intentionnelle: Une tâche de la phénoménologie à venir. In *L'intentionnalité en question: Entre phénoménologie et sciences cognitives*, ed. Dominique Janicaud, 383–397. Paris: Vrin.

———. 2008. *Material Phenomenology.* Trans. Scott Davidson. New York: Fordham University Press.

———. 2016. Ontological destruction of the Kantian critique of the paralogism of rational psychology. *Analecta Hermeneutica* 8: 7–40. ISSN:1918-7351. http://journals.library.mun.ca/ojs/index.php/analecta/article/view/1708. Accessed 21 Apr 2018.

Hopkins, Jeffrey. 2003. Paradigm change in meditation on selflessness in Tibetan Buddhism: The progression from space-like meditative equipoise to deity yoga. *Pacific World* 5: 117–142.

Husserl, Edmund. 1993. *Cartesian Meditations.* Trans. Dorion Cairns. Dordrecht: Kluwer.

————. 1998. *Ideas Pertaining to a Pure Phenomenology and to a Phenomenological Philosophy, First Book: General Introduction to Pure Phenomenology*. Trans. F. Kersten. Dordrecht: Kluwer.

————. 2001. *Analyses Concerning Passive and Active Synthesis*. Trans. Anthony J. Steinbock. Dordrecht: Kluwer.

Ichishima, Masao. 1982. Sources of Tibetan Buddhist meditation. *Buddhist-Christian Studies* 2: 119–128.

Juslin, Patrik N. 2013. From everyday emotions to aesthetic emotions: Towards a unified theory of musical emotions. *Physics of Life Reviews* 10 (3): 235–266.

Kanwisher, N. 2010. Functional specificity in the human brain: A window into the functional architecture of the mind. *Proceedings of the National Academy of Sciences USsA* 107 (25): 11163–11170. Accessed 30 Mar 2018.

Kornfield, J., ed. 1993. *Teachings of the Buddha*. Boston: Shambala.

Kvasnicka, Jerry. 2014. Transmuting anger: Starve anger by expressing qualities of true character. *The Mindful World.*. https://www.themindfulword.org/2014/transmuting-anger/. Accessed 8 May 2018.

Lavigne, Jean-François. 2016. Suffering and ipseity in Michel Henry: The problem of the ego's transcendental identity. *Analecta Hermeneutica* 8: 64–78. ISSN:1918-7351. http://journals. library.mun.ca/ojs/index.php/analecta/article/view/1710. Accessed 23 Apr 2018.

Lee, N. 2003. Phenomenology of feeling in Husserl and Levinas. *Collection of Humanities* 49: 85–121.

Lindahl, J.R. 2017. Somatic energies and emotional traumas: A qualitative study of practice-related challenges reported by Vajrayāna Buddhists. *Religions* 8: 1–22. https://doi.org/10.3390/ rel8080153. Accessed 3 Mar 2018.

Lipman, K. 1982. The Cittamātra and its Madhyamaka critique: Some phenomenological reflections. *Philosophy East and West* 32 (3): 295–308.

Livingston, K. 2012. *The effects of implicit theories of emotion on emotion regulation and experience*. Ph.D. dissertation, University of Oregon. ProQuest Dissertation Publishing, 3544898.

Louchakova-Schwartz, O. 2017. Qualia of God: Phenomenological materiality in introspection, with reference to Advaita Vedanta. *Phenomenology of Religious Experience, Open Access: Open Theology* 3 (1): 257–273. Published online 2017-05-18. https://doi.org/10.1515/opth-2017-0021. 28 Mar 2018.

————. Forthcoming. *Post-Henry approach to phenomenology of religious experience*. Albany: SUNY Press.

Lutz, Antoine, et al. [Lutz, Antoine, Amishi P. Jha, John D. Dunne, and Clifford D. Saron.] 2015. Investigating the phenomenological matrix of mindfulness-related practices from a neurocognitive perspective. *The American Psychologist* 70(7): 632–658.

Mettā meditation. n.d. *Mettā* Institute®. https://www.mettainstitute.org/mettameditation.html. Accessed 22 Apr 2018.

Moran, Dermot. 2011. Edmund Husserl's phenomenology of habituality and *habitus*. *Journal of the British Society for Phenomenology* 42 (1): 53–77.

————. 2014. "The ego as substrate of habitualities": Edmund Husserl's phenomenology of the habitual self. *Phenomenology and Mind* 6 (July): 27–47.

Nijhavan, S.R.S. n.d. 23 everyday emotions you didn't know there was a name for! *IndiaTimes Lifestyle Network*. https://www.indiatimes.com/lifestyle/self/23-emotions-you-might-feel-on-a-daily-basis-but-cant-explain-what-it-really-is-244549.html. Accessed 31 Mar 2018.

Osypiuk, Kamila, et al. [Osypiuk, Kamila, Evan Thompson, and Peter M. Wayne.] 2018. Can *tai chi* and *qigong* postures shape our mood? Toward an embodied cognition framework for mind-body research. *Frontiers in Human Neuroscience* 12(174): 1–12. https://doi.org/10.3389/ fnhum.2018.00174. 01 May 2018.

Parnas, Josef, and Mads Gram Henriksen. 2016. Epistemological error and the illusion of phenomenological continuity. *World Psychiatry* 15(2): 126–127. *PMC*. Web. https://doi.org/10.1002/ wps.20326. Accessed 3 May 2018.

Patel, D.M. 2013. *Mettābhāvana* in traditional and popular Buddhist contexts. *Asian Philosophy* 23 (4): 323–340.

Rashbrook, Oliver. 2011. The continuity of consciousness. *European Journal of Philosophy*: 1–30. https://doi.org/10.1111/j.1468-0378.2011.00465.x.

Ratcliffe, Matthew. 2008. *Feelings of being: Phenomenology, psychiatry and the sense of reality.* Oxford: Oxford University Press.

———. 2013. Why mood matters. In *The Cambridge companion to Heidegger's being and time,* ed. M. Wrathall, 157–176. Cambridge: Cambridge University Press.

Roberts, Robert. 2016. Emotions in the Christian tradition. In *The Stanford encyclopedia of philosophy,* ed. Edward N. Zalta. (winter edition). https://plato.stanford.edu/archives/win2016/entries/emotion-Christian-tradition/. Accessed 3 Mar 2018.

Ruhe, B. n.d. Transmuting anger. *Purity Mind.* http://www.purifymind.com/TransmutingAnger.htm. Retrieved 31 Mar 2018.

Salzberg, Sharon. n.d. What is *mettā* meditation? *Tricycle: The Buddhist Review.* https://tricycle.org/magazine/metta-practice/. Accessed 11 Apr 2018.

Şan, Emre. 2017. Intentionality and givenness in French phenomenology: M. Henry and M. Merleau-Ponty. *Uludağ University Faculty of Arts and Sciences Journal of Philosophy* 29 (Fall): 65–81. https://doi.org/10.20981/kaygi.342182.

Sayadaw, U. Pandita. 2018. How to practice Vipassana insight meditation. *Lion's Roar.* https://www.lionsroar.com/how-to-practice-vipassana-insight-meditation/. Last modified 27 April 2018. Accessed 3 Mar 2018.

Schütz, A. 1945. On multiple realities. *Philosophy and Phenomenological Research* 5 (4): 533–576.

Sen Sharma, Debabrata. 1983. *The philosophy of sādhanā: With special reference to Trika philosophy of Kāśmīra.* Karnal: Natraj Publishing House.

Serban, Claudia. 2016. Beneath time and reflection: The shadow of Husserl in Michel Henry's non-intentional phenomenology. *Analecta Hermeneutica* 8: 234–244.

Seyler, Frédéric. 2016. Michel Henry. In *The Stanford encyclopedia of philosophy,* ed. Edward N. Zalta. (winter edition). https://plato.stanford.edu/archives/win2016/entries/michel-henry/. Accessed 25 Mar 2018.

Sharf, Robert. 1995. Buddhist modernism and the rhetoric of meditative experience. *Numen* 42: 228–283.

Sheehy, Michael R. 2005. Severing the source of fear: Contemplative dynamics of the Tibetan Buddhist god tradition. *Contemporary Buddhism* 6 (1): 37–52.

Slaby, Jan. 2008. Affective intentionality and the feeling body. *Phenomenology and the Cognitive Sciences* 7 (4): 429–444. https://doi.org/10.1007/s11097-007-9083-x. Accessed 3 Mar 2018.

Sogyal Rinpoche. 2002. *The Tibetan book of living and dying.* San Francisco: Harper SanFrancisco.

Sokolowski, Robert. 1977. The logic of parts and wholes in Husserl's investigations. In *Readings on Edmund Husserl's logical investigations,* ed. Jitendra N. Mohanty, 94–111. The Hague: Nijhoff.

Stabile, Susan J. 2013. *Growing in love and wisdom: Tibetan Buddhist sources for Christian meditation.* New York: Oxford University Press.

Steinbock, Anthony J. 2001. Translator's introduction. In *Analyses Concerning Passive and Active Synthesis,* ed. Edmund Husserl. Trans. Anthony J. Steinbock, xv–lxvii. Dordrecht: Kluwer.

Summa, M. 2015. Are emotions "recollected in tranquility"? Phenomenological reflections on emotions, memory, and the temporal dynamics of experience. In *Feeling and value, willing and action: Essays in the context of a phenomenological psychology,* ed. M. Ubiali and M. Wehrle, 163–181. Cham: Springer. https://doi.org/10.1007/978-3-319-10326-6_10. Accessed 18 Mar 2018.

Taipale, Joona. 2014. *Phenomenology and embodiment: Husserl and the constitution of subjectivity.* Evanston: Northwestern University Press.

Wangyal, Tenzin. 1993. *Wonders of the natural mind: The essence of Dzogchen in the native Bon tradition of Tibet.* Barrytown: Station Hill.

Waugh, Christian E., et al. [Waugh, Christian E., Paul J. Hamilton, and Ian H. Gotlib.] 2010. The neural temporal dynamics of the intensity of emotional experience. *Neuroimage* 49(2): 1699–1707. *PMC*. Web. Accessed 21 Mar 2018.
———. [Waugh, Christian E., Z. Shing, and E.B.M. Avery.] 2015. Temporal dynamics of emotional processing in the brain. *Emotion Review* 7(4): 323–329. https://doi.org/10.1177/1754073915590615. Accessed 8 Mar 2018.
Zahavi, Dan. 2017. Ownership, memory, attention: Commentary on Ganeri. *Australasian Philosophical Review* 1 (4): 406–415.

Olga Louchakova-Schwartz, M.D. Ph.D. (the editor) is a comparative religionist, philosopher, and interdisciplinary researcher. She holds the titles Professor of Philosophy of Religion, Spirituality, and Human Development at the Hult International Business School, and Clinical Professor at the UC Davis School of Medicine, Department of Public Health Sciences. She is also a Visiting Scholar at the Graduate Theological Union in Berkeley, Adjunct Lecturer in Spirituality and Phenomenology of Religion at the Jesuit School of Theology, and a Founding President of the Society for the Phenomenology of Religions Experience. Prior to her work in philosophy, she was a senior scientist at the Pavlov Institute of the Academy of Sciences in Russia, and after that, Director of Research and the Founding Director of the Neurophenomenology Center at the former Institute of Transpersonal Psychology, from which she holds the title Professor Emerita of Psychology and Comparative Religion. She studied phenomenology with Amedeo and Barbro Giorgi and with Anna-Teresa Tymienieck, Her chief research interests are in religious subjectivity and religious experience in contemporary and historical contexts. She has published on fifteenth century and contemporary Kundalini Tantra, eighth century Advaita Vedanta and Neo-Vedanta, early Christianity, seventh–tenth century Hesychasm, contemporary Turkish and American Sufism, the Soviet spiritual underground, and the Islamic Philosophy of Illumination. Her cognitive phenomenological research of Tibetan Tantric meditation was featured on BBC, Science Daily, and other important forums. She has published more than 200 papers and book chapters, and is an Associate Editor of the Journal of Theoretical and Philosophical Psychology, and guest editor for Open Theology, De Gruyter (2017; 2018, 2019, 2020 to appear).

Chapter 6
The Self-Internalization of Religious Subjectivity: Commentary on Part 1

Olga Louchakova-Schwartz

Abstract This is a commentary on the papers presented in Part 1 ("The Primeval Showing of Religious Experience") of The Problem of Religious Experience: Case Studies in Phenomenology, edited by Olga Louchakova-Schwartz. This commentary provides a reflection upon and an integration of the findings in the papers by Shogo Tanaka, Patrick Laude, Espen Dahl, and Olga Louchakova-Schwartz. All the authors present either a full or a partial descriptive phenomenology of religious experience, some of them deepening the analysis toward static or genetic constitutive phenomenology. Religious experience is shown to be a result of spontaneous reduction leading to various forms of the self-internalization of subjectivity and to the uncovering of aprioristic horizons pertaining to religious experience. It is suggested that religious experience constitutively influences subjectivity. Limited parallels are made with a cognitive science of religion, suggesting that religious experience is a sui generis activity of consciousness and cannot be reduced to a result of group behavior. The commentary includes directions for future research of the subjectivity under conditions of constitutive influences of religious experience.

Keywords Constitutive analysis · Phenomenology · Religious experience · Reduction · Spontaneity · Subjectivity

In *Husserl's Philosophy*, Burt Hopkins (2010) emphasizes that Husserl envisioned and developed phenomenology as a science. No doubt, many before Husserl termed their explorations of subjectivity "scientific." However, before the dawn of scientific phenomenology, such assertions meant only reference to repetitive empirical patterns that appeared in contemplative introspection. Relying on the historical

O. Louchakova-Schwartz (✉)
Jesuit School of Theology of Santa Clara University, Graduate Theological Union, Berkeley, CA, USA

University of California, Davis, CA, USA

© Springer Nature Switzerland AG 2019   101
O. Louchakova-Schwartz (ed.), *The Problem of Religious Experience*,
Contributions to Phenomenology 103,
https://doi.org/10.1007/978-3-030-21575-0_6

generativity of traditions, such systems did not test the validity of their intuitions, did not critique the methods by which they obtained the findings, and did not examine the standard of evidence underlying their assertions. In radical contrast to its religious and philosophical predecessors, phenomenological science grew out of considerations for the goodness of knowledge, and rigorous and rational testing of the methods of inquiry that push the limits of any particular givenness.

Subtle yet powerful discriminations between true and false propositions made Husserl's research agenda popular in the community of philosophers. However, the task of science is not only to establish criteria for truth but to use them in order to make discoveries; the same must be expected of phenomenology. By contrast with other sciences, in which researchers often team up to share research programs and integrate their findings, phenomenology remains largely a first-person single-philosopher enterprise. (Cf. Merleau-Ponty 1964.) Likewise, by contrast with social or natural sciences, phenomenology does not reveal the facts of the natural attitude, which are those that one can readily appreciate. Phenomenology exposes deep structures of consciousness, often invisible—if not cryptic and paradoxical—to common sense. Unavailable to empirical self-reflection, such structures nevertheless underlie cognition, affect, behavior, and in fact all knowledge. For the pragmatic mastery of the everyday, these are useless abstractions unless they are reinterpreted from the phenomenological attitude into common sense, from the invisible into the concretely given, and further into generalizable principles that can be then used by other sciences. In the concluding sections of this book, I attempt a critical integration of the findings, with the hope that it will be useful for the future development of research in this area and for interdisciplinary dialogue.

6.1 Religious Experience as Creativity (Spontaneity) of Consciousness

The themes in the papers of Part 1 center around transitions between ordinary experience and religious experience. A sharp empirical distinction between the two is reflected in the structure of subjectivity: outgoing, pragmatic, and masterful in the everyday case, as opposed to self-transcending and inward-directed in religious experience. The transitions between ordinary and religious experience include changes in the body-schema (Tanaka), in the phenomenality of internal speech and self-awareness (Laude), changes involving emotions (Louchakova-Schwartz); and the event of transition itself is marked by wonder (Dahl). In all situations, the beginning of transition can be traced back to the ego's active creation of the conditions of possibility for religious experience, via prayer, contemplation, or meditative practice, with the outcome of these efforts, namely religious experience per se, received by the ego passively.

The distinctions between the baseline of the everyday and the situation of religious experiencing are not in how one *interprets* these two conditions but in how they are given: that is, in a constitutive specifics of their passivity. Phenomenological attitude and reduction do not eliminate but, on the contrary, highlight (e.g., in Louchakova-Schwartz in Part 1) distinctions between the descriptions of ordinary and of religious experience. However, after such distinctions are described as purely as possible in the absence of suppositions, one can then treat questions such as what it is for what is experienced to be what it is (Hopkins 2010, 13)—that is, the ideal limit implied in being(ness) (cf. Lomuscio 2017) of the structures involved in religious experiencing. For example, if the core structure of religious experience is given as silence (Laude), and the silence presents itself as "Be still and know that I am God" (Psalm 46:10), can or should we accept such a self-representation [of its own status]? Or, when changes in the body scheme signal the religious quality in experience, what horizon of possibility makes them religious? (And so on.) Overall this is a question of what aprioristic horizons religious experience engages.

Davis (1989) attempted a categorization of religious experience as interpretive (of ordinary life events), quasisensual (e.g., visions), revelatory (internal), numinous (of holy reality itself), and mystical (the union with the Ultimate Reality). This categorization is established in the natural attitude, which means that the distinctions between the categories are interpretive and not descriptive of the deeper constitutive structures of experience. For example, revelation and numinous and mystical categories are internal experiences, and so the distinctions between them are not clear. However, our phenomenological analyses show that there is a truly constitutive difference between an experience of God (Laude), and a nontheistic religious experience (Louchakova-Schwartz). The difference is not in the interpretation or symbol but in the primal showing of the reconstituted subjectivity. In the situation described by Laude, experience belongs to horizons with locations of mystery (cf. Dahl 2010), and thereby experience manifests as God-experience. By contrast, the field of the transformation of emotions described by Louchakova-Schwartz does not include locations of mystery: thereby, this kind of religious experience does not have a sense of the numinous about it and is not configured as God-experience but rather shows up as how Buddhists themselves term it, as the enlightened mind of compassion. This is why, despite claims made by universalists and not because of the cultural construction of the mind, there is no God in Buddhist *boddhicitta*, and there is no enlightened mind of compassion in Christian or Sufi introspection.

While living a religious experience is not like having an ordinary experience of living, a shift from one to another doesn't add to or subtract anything from the phenomenon of consciousness. The structural underpinnings of experience (that is, the formal structures of consciousness) are shared between these two forms of experience, including some phenomenal properties that can be the same: for instance, the sense of wonder that signals an interruption can take one in the direction of having a feeling of God or in the direction of the rise of philosophical understanding (Dahl). However, there is a process of reorganization taking place, and this can alter or reverse the relationship in the composition of ordinary consciousness. For example, in ordinary experience, an increase in the complexity of cognition causes an increase of self-awareness (Nida-Rümelin 2018), but in religious experience this operation appears in reverse: the stronger and more defined the religious sense, the less the self-awareness. (Cf. Ware 1986; Louchakova-Schwartz 2005.) Some such questions are answered in Part 2 and in Volume II by engagement of other kinds of phenomenology, and of course some will remain subject to future research.

Within itself, consciousness has the means of unfolding and folding up religious experience as an internal experience sui generis, not caused by past events or, for that matter, any external events. Within its own means and possibilities, consciousness has all the resources necessary to generate such internal experience out of its creative own self-restructuring. For this to happen, the acting and thematizing ego must step aside. Therefore, a conclusion can be made that generating religious experience is a possibility, if not necessity, for consciousness in itself, but sans the agency of the ego. The ego's role in this is only to cause modifications within the phenomenal field that "invite" a rise of religious experience.

Extending this observation into an ontological argument, a proposition can be put forth that religious experience does not require an additional external power or source as a condition of possibility. For example, experience of a chair requires the presence of a physical object called "chair," an experience of sadness may depend on an episodic memory, and so on; but this is not necessary for religious experience. In other words, for it to happen, religious experience can accept but does not need a specific call from the world. Consciousness as such is a religious phenomenon in the sense that it can generate religious meaning in response to, or by means of, sui generis changes within its own constitution.[1] Living religious experience is possible by means of the same structures of consciousness that mediate the lifeworld of the everyday, except that these structures are "assembled" differently and exist in a different mode, which appears to depend on a combination of reductions that are spontaneous (e.g., as in Tanaka and Dahl) or intentionally executed via internal practice (e.g., Laude and Louchakova-Schwartz).

At first glance, such statements may appear tautological: Isn't experience per se identical with consciousness? However, we are discussing not experience per se, but religious experience; in this case, the very existence of consciousness of this kind is philosophically debatable. Showing that consciousness can mediate such experience—that is, can generate it within its own resources—argues in favor of the possibility and facticality of religious experiences. What would the presence of religious experience as constitutive to consciousness mean for research of the mind: say, in natural sciences? For example, cognitive science of religion maintains that religious beliefs and thoughts are mediated by the natural cognitive processes, such as for instance social cognition. Insofar as these natural cognitive processes are evolutionary in nature, religions are a result of biological evolution. However, as described in Part 1, phenomenological patterns underlying religious experience show that religious experience is a function not of group behavior but of subjectivity: that is, of

---

[1] Dahl (2010) emphasizes that the interruptions leading to religious experience are generated by the socio-cultural contexts, that is, in passivity. This is possible, but not necessary of one takes into account the spontaneity of consciousness according to Sartre's argument against Husserl on this topic (cf. Moati 2015): interruptions can be a function of spontaneity.

consciousness as such. It pertains only to consciousness *as such*, and is not a subjective perception of some kind of behavior. It is not an illusion, or a dream, or an abstraction, or any other process that maintains traces of the meaningful presence of the world. Religious experience appears in the studies of Part 1 exclusively as consciousness's perception of itself, in its own creative activity. Justly, naive realism presupposes consciousness to be a natural phenomenon, with origins in and of the world; similarly, phenomenological philosophy also finds an ultimate ground of experience (as judgment) in the world horizon (Husserl 1973). However, religious experience references strictly the life of consciousness in and of itself, not the natural *cogitationes,* nothing utilizable, not even thinking or judgment per se (cf. Lacoste 2014, 36–37), but the creativity of unpredictable possibilities in the life of consciousness—which, for their subject-self, are internal religious experiences. This can be translated into the domain of the natural sciences, but not as a naturalization of phenomenology. Rather, it would call for a research theory of consciousness-only-dependent phenomena, including specific approaches to validity, research designs, and controls.

6.2   Religious Experience as Self-Interiorizing of Subjectivity

Typifying activities of consciousness according to the modes of their givenness, Husserl assigned internal life to the sphere of complete immanence: that is, the psychological-immanent sphere. In this manner, both kinds of internal experience, psychological and religious, are ascribed to the same sphere; the boundaries between the two become blurry. (Cf. Lacoste 2004.) If we consider constitutive distinctions between the two kinds of experience as formal distinctions, the findings in Part 1 suggest that there must be two separate spheres, psychological and religious. Indeed, these two forms of consciousness are quite different in terms of the interiority they involve. Psychological interiority gives the subject as the self in regard to other selves, whereas religious interiority gives the subject independently of external others (see in Sands 2017), as the self internalizing its own subjectivity. By positing the internal Other (Laude in this volume, also Louchakova-Schwartz 2005), the ego reconstitutes its own manifestation as an initially active process. As the transition from the everyday to religious experience matures, the sphere of complete immanence turns into the sphere of transimmanence, going from a sense of the finitude of human subjectivity toward the feeling of one's interiority as infinite—that is, the divine. If the psychological-immanent sphere is posited in the mode of ownness, such as "I am this and that way," the transimmanent sphere of religious life will be posited in the mode "this is God in me," or even "there is no me; it's He who is, and in that, somehow, I am" (as in Louchakova-Schwartz 2005, or Porete 1993)—a paradoxical mode of being often reflected in religious poetry.

This kind of purely religious transcendence needs to be distinguished from an ego transcendence in the psychological-immanent sphere—for instance, feeling humbled or feeling totally receptive (cf. Bellini, Trajtelová in Part 4), but without a sense of "God within." The two interiorities will be different in other aspects as well: for example, a process of transformation of emotions as described by Louchakova-Schwartz (in this volume) involves religious self-transcendence, but not psychological ego transcendence.

Internalization of the self's own subjectivity includes not only sense but the perceptual modalities as well. This refers to the prethematically given synthetic unity responsible for spatial orientation (Tiemersma 1982): that is, the changes in the body-schema that make the experience "internal" (see Tanaka in Part 1) and assign it internal spatiality (Louchakova-Schwartz 2016, 2017). Religious experiencing induced by Tai Chi, Chi Gong, by the practices of Tantric *samadhi* (a spiritual absorption in the union with the Absolute; Singh 1991), or in Islamic (Louchakova-Schwartz 2014) or Christian introspective meditation (Louchakova-Schwartz 2016) makes the implicit constitutive involvement of the body-schema explicit. The prethematic unity of the body-schema is a part of another, higher-order unity of self-awareness, which consists of intentional and nonobjectifying aspects (as in Taipale 2014). Tanaka's and Louchakova-Schwartz's findings suggest that the constitution of religious interiority unmasks the nonintentional, nonobjectifying aspect, by contrast with a purely psychological internal life in which the nonobjectifying aspect is far less prominent than the objectifying, intentional one. It remains to further investigate whether the unmasking of nonobjectifying bodily aspects of self-awareness is a necessary part of reduction in religious experience.

6.3   Reductions *ad Deum*

We have established that religious experience belongs to the transimmanent sphere of consciousness. Consciousness reaches this sphere via the creative building of an inward-directed perspectival environment in which subjectivity is given as interiority of the self. Lacoste (2004), differing from Flood (2013, who interprets religious interiority as mere ideas), views religious interiority as anchored spatially and embodied. Resonant with Lacoste's, our findings show that the transimmanent sphere of religious interiority is embodied: the temporal, genetic constitution of this sphere brings somatic and affective aspects of the self previously hidden under the masking influence of intentional consciousness (Louchakova-Schwartz in Part 1) out of anonymity.

The ordering of the active and passive syntheses in the constitution of religious interiority can go in a variety of ways, depending on the form of experience: in the case of meditative practice, the constitution of interiority begins with active participation of the ego and then switches to passivity, whereas in the case of spontaneous experience, passivity takes a leading role from the very beginning of the interruption related to religious experience. From the standpoint of the empirical self, active internalization of subjectivity in contemplative practices is a form of introspection. On one hand, the self and its introspection are both culturally defined (cf.

Flood 2013; Louchakova-Schwartz Forthcoming), and the interruptions leading to religious experience are generated by the sociocultural contexts (Dahl 2010): that is, in passivity. On the other hand, both introspection and interruptions may be functions of spontaneity. (Cf. Moati 2015; Tymieniecka 2011.)

The self-internalization of subjectivity is a form of reduction. Different from the deliberate, systematic, particular, and active character of philosophical reductions, reductions/interruptions in religious experiencing are not initiated by the theorizing ego but happen in passivity. Dahl (in Part 1), describing Merleau-Ponty's accessing a prioris, uses the term "subterranean" and then states: "Merleau-Ponty speaks of reduction in terms of suspensions, slackening of threads, stepping back"—which is not a purely mentalistic suspension of belief leading to wonder but an attentional motion of absorption (cf. Bronkhorst 2012, 2016), a backing away from intentional meanings and into living subjectivity. The same sense is in Laude's references to "the Heart," which is a somatic center of awareness, and in Louchakova-Schwartz's description of the bodily anchoring of religious emotion. Thus, the unveiling of a prioris is topological, spatial, and even enfleshed (cf. Rosen 2006; Louchakova-Schwartz 2016, 2017): to use a visual metaphor, the organization of subjectivity in religious experiencing can be imagined as the alignment of chiseled ivory spheres in a Chinese puzzle ball (see in A.B.G. 1849), with full transparency of the self at the point of alignment of the spheres.

In the second Cartesian Meditation, Husserl (1993) argues that the reductions are *lived* by the subject: they are experiential—that is, they have phenomenal givenness. When a self-reflecting ego undertakes a conceptual abstraction, the field of consciousness changes perceptually, perspectivally, hyletically; in other words, factically. The rearrangement of the phenomenal field following reduction is a dynamic process in which, despite the mutability of the components in the phenomenal field, the structures of rearrangement are predictably defined by dependency on the kind of reduction applied. Similarly, in religious experiencing, the self-rearranging subjectivity is the *mobilis in mobili* of its phenomenal universe, with a certain predictability of the patterns. The papers in Part 1 show not only the locations of change, but a directedness, a telos. It is as if when attention in internal contemplation reaches a certain interior location (cf. Louchakova-Schwartz 2017), the transition from the ordinary to the religious quality of experience is expected, similarly to how ice is expected to turn into water after the temperature reaches the melting point.

After an event of religious experience, the self doesn't stay the same. Reconstitution of the self may go in several directions, from psychological (e.g., in Bellini in Part 4), to perceptual changes, to the changes in self-awareness (e.g., Tanaka in this volume; Louchakova-Schwartz 2007a). Religious experience being de facto a reductive shift from activity of the ego to passivity, the processes of passive synthesis can go in at least two directions, as a nonappropriation of the world, and as a nonappropriation of the internalized subjectivity of "God within." Marguerite Porete (1993), a Beguine mystic of twelfth-century France, describes such transitions in the following manner:

[189] Thus [the Soul] fears neither the loss of possessions, nor people's words, nor the feebleness of the body, for her beloved does not fear them, and so neither can the Soul who is overtaken by Him. ... [192] And thus the Soul removes herself from this will, and the will is separated from the Soul and dissolves itself, and [1] [the will] gives and renders itself to God, whence it was first taken, without retaining anything of its own in order to fulfill the perfect Divine Will, which cannot be fulfilled in the Soul without such a gift, so that the Soul might not have warfare or deficiency. ... [193] But this Soul, thus pure and clarified, sees neither God nor herself, but God sees Himself of Himself in her, for her, without her.

"God [who] sees Himself of Himself in her" and other statements like "God prays to Himself" or "dissolution of the name [silence] into wordless prayer of sustained presence" (Louchakova-Schwartz 2005, 203; cf. Laude in this volume), or statements like "I am not, but He is; and in that somehow I am,"[2] indicate not just a change in meaning but a corresponding change in the phenomenal givenness of self-awareness. Changes in self-awareness in the states of the everyday were described by Nida-Rümelin (2017; also 2018), who maintains that self-awareness increases with the increase of complexity of the phenomenal field. But in a reversal of the constitutive impulse from the exteriority of the world toward inwardness (cf. Schrijvers 2012, 41; Barber 2017),[3] for the increase, self-awareness has to be disowned, as in "He must increase, but I must decrease" (John 3:30), experienced for example in the Prayer of the Heart (Ware 1986).

The nonappropriation of internalized subjectivity by the ego-self is especially interesting in light of present philosophical discussions around the nature of the self, in which Zahavi (2017, 2018), and following him, Durt and others (2017) argue for the irreducible, nuclear, minimal self, which is characterized by two modes of givenness, for-me-ness and myness. A question is whether in the situations described (e.g., by Porete 1993 or by Laude in this volume) the properties of self-awareness and the relationship between self-awareness and the minimal self change, in what ways and whether such a change will be phenomenologically normative, and what that would mean for our understanding of the self and subjectivity. Nida-Rümelin (2017; also 2018) suggests that self-awareness must be considered ontologically, as "nature-revealing," in a prereflective givenness to itself that continues into particular experiences: in our case, religious experiences. Focus on this line of analysis would explain why the paradoxical flip-flops of myness in religious experience happen against a sense of continuity in one's being. Just these few observations show that the problematic of religious experience extends beyond concerns for itself into more far-reaching research on the possibilities of consciousness and questions regarding human identity.

---

[2] Sri Ranjit Maharaj, personal communication, Encinitas, California, 1997, quoted from Louchakova-Schwartz 2007b, 268.

[3] Note that all studies of reference in this section are phenomenologically presuppositionless, not theological or doxastic.

References

A.B.G. 1849. Description of the method of forming Chinese balls. *Journal of the Franklin Institute* 47 (2): 130–132.

Barber, Michael. 2017. *Religion and humor as emancipating provinces of meaning*. New York/Berlin/Heidelberg: Springer.

Bronkhorst, Johannes. 2012. *Absorption: Human nature and Buddhist liberation*, Buddhism Series. Wil: UniversityMedia.

———. 2016. Can religion be explained? The role of absorption in various religious phenomena. *Method and Theory in the Study of Religion* 29: 1–30. https://doi.org/10.1163/15700682-12341375. Accessed 22 May 2018.

Dahl, Espen. 2010. *Phenomenology and the holy*. London: SCM Press.

Durt, C., et al. [Durt, C., T. Fuchs, and C. Tewes.], eds. 2017. *Embodiment, enaction, and culture: Investigating the constitution of the shared world*. Cambridge, MA: MIT Press.

Flood, Gavin D. 2013. *The truth within: A history of inwardness in Christianity, Hinduism, and Buddhism*. Oxford: Oxford University Press.

Hopkins, Burt C. 2010. *The philosophy of Husserl*. Montreal: McGill-Queen's University Press.

Husserl, Edmund. 1973. *Experience and Judgement. Investigations in a Genealogy of Logic* .... Rev. and ed. Ludwig Landgrebe. Trans. James S. Churchill and Karl Ameriks. London: Routledge & Kegan Paul.

———. 1993. *Cartesian Meditations*. ;. Dorion Cairns. Dordrecht: Kluwer.

Lacoste, Jean-Yves. 2004. *Experience and the absolute: Disputed questions on the humanity of man*. New York: Fordham University Press.

———. 2014. Introduction. In *From Theology to Theological Thinking*, ed. Jean-Yves Lacoste. Trans. W.C. Hackett, 1–19. Charlottesville: University of Virginia Press.

Lomuscio, V. 2017. Key-phenomenon and religious meaning. *Open Theology* 3 (1): 529–538. https://doi.org/10.1515/opth-2017-0040. Accessed 15 May 2018.

Louchakova-Schwartz, O. 2005. Ontopoiesis and union in the Prayer of the Heart: Contributions to psychotherapy and learning. In *Logos of phenomenology and phenomenology of the logos, Book four: The logos of scientific interrogation—Participating in nature–life–sharing in life*, Analecta Husserliana: The Yearbook of Phenomenological Research, ed. A.-T. Tymieniecka, vol. 91, 289–311. Dordrecht: Kluwer.

———. 2007a. Ontopoiesis and spiritual emergence: Bridging Tymieniecka's phenomenology of life and transpersonal psychology. In *From the animal soul to the human mind*, Analecta Husserliana: The Yearbook of Phenomenological Research, ed. Anna-Teresa Tymieniecka, vol. 94, 43–68. Dordrecht: Kluwer.

———. 2007b. Prayer of the heart: Ego-transcendence and adult development. *Existential Analysis* 18 (2): 261–287.

———. 2014. The seal of philosophy: Tymieniecka's phenomenology of life in Islamic metaphysical perspective. In *Islamic and occidental philosophy in dialogue*, ed. A.-T. Tymieniecka, N. Muhtaroglu, and D. Quintern, vol. 7, 71–101. Dordrecht: Springer.

———. 2016. Theophanis the Monk and Monoimus the Arab in a phenomenological-cognitive perspective. *Cognitive Science of Religion, Open Access: Open Theology* 2 (1): 53–78. https://doi.org/10.1515/opth-2016-0005. Accessed 22 June 2018.

———. 2017. Qualia of God: Phenomenological materiality in introspection, with reference to Advaita Vedanta. *Phenomenology of Religious Experience, Open Access: Open Theology* 3 (1): 257–273. https://doi.org/10.1515/opth-2017-0021. Published online: 2017-05-18.

———. Forthcoming. The "wonder to behold": Reflections on phenomenological research of alienic spirituality. In *Indigenous psychologies of spirituality: In my beginning is my end*, ed. A. Dueck. New York: Palgrave.

Merleau-Ponty, M. 1964. The philosopher and his shadow. In *Signs*, ed. M. Merleau-Ponty. Trans. Richard McCleary, 159–181. Evanston: Northwestern University Press.

Moati, Raoul. 2015. *Radical epokhè:* On Sartre's concept of "pure reflection". In *Pre-reflective consciousness: Sartre and contemporary philosophy of mind*, ed. S. Miguens, G. Preyer, and C.B. Morando, 455–475. New York: Routledge.

Nida-Rümelin, M. 2017. Self-awareness. *Review of Philosophy and Psychology* 8 (1): 55–82. https://doi.org/10.1007/s13164-016-0328-x.

———. 2018. *Awareness of oneself as an experiencing subject.* Paper read at the conference "The minimal self" held at Universität Wien, Vienna, Austria, 14 May 2018.

Porete, Marguerite. 1993. *The Mirror of Simple Souls.* Trans. Ellen L. Babinsky. New York: Paulist Press.

Rosen, Steven M. 2006. *Topologies of the flesh: A multidimensional exploration of the lifeworld.* Athens: Ohio University Press.

Sands, Justin. 2017. After onto-theology: What lies beyond the "end of everything". *Religions* 8 (5): 98. https://doi.org/10.3390/rel8050098.

Schrijvers, Joeri. 2012. *An introduction to Jean-Yves Lacoste.* Burlington: Ashgate.

Singh, Jaideva. 1991. *The yoga of delight, wonder, and astonishment: A translation of the Vijñāna-Bhairava.* Albany: SUNY Press.

Tiemersma, Douwe. 1982. "Body-image" and "body-schema" in the existential phenomenology of Merleau-Ponty. *Journal of the British Society for Phenomenology* 13 (3): 246–255. https://doi. org/10.1080/00071773.1982.11007591. Accessed 13 May 2018.

Tymieniecka, Anna-Teresa. 2011. *The fullness of the logos in the key of life, Book II: Christo-logos, metaphysical rhapsodies of faith (Itinerarium mentis in Deo),* Analecta Husserliana: The Yearbook of Phenomenological Research. Vol. 111. Dordrecht: Springer.

Ware, Bp. Kallistos. 1986. *The power of the name: The Jesus prayer in Orthodox spirituality.* Fairacres, Oxon: SLG Press.

Zahavi, D. 2017. Thin, thinner, thinnest: Defining the minimal self. In *Embodiment, enaction, and culture: Investigating the constitution of the shared world*, ed. C. Durt, T. Fuchs, and C. Tewes, 193–200. Cambridge, MA: MIT Press.

———. 2018. *The minimal self revisited: Replying to recent critiques.* Paper read at the conference "The minimal self" held at Universität Wien, Vienna, Austria, 14 May 2018.

Olga Louchakova-Schwartz, M.D. Ph.D. (the editor) is a comparative religionist, philosopher, and interdisciplinary researcher. She holds the titles Professor of Philosophy of Religion, Spirituality, and Human Development at the Hult International Business School, and Clinical Professor at the UC Davis School of Medicine, Department of Public Health Sciences. She is also a Visiting Scholar at the Graduate Theological Union in Berkeley, Adjunct Lecturer in Spirituality and Phenomenology of Religion at the Jesuit School of Theology, and a Founding President of the Society for the Phenomenology of Religions Experience. Prior to her work in philosophy, she was a senior scientist at the Pavlov Institute of the Academy of Sciences in Russia, and after that, Director of Research and the Founding Director of the Neurophenomenology Center at the former Institute of Transpersonal Psychology, from which she holds the title Professor Emerita of Psychology and Comparative Religion. She studied phenomenology with Amedeo and Barbro Giorgi and with Anna-Teresa Tymieniecka, Her chief research interests are in religious subjectivity and religious experience in contemporary and historical contexts. She has published on fifteenth century and contemporary Kundalini Tantra, eighth century Advaita Vedanta and Neo-Vedanta, early Christianity, seventh–tenth century Hesychasm, contemporary Turkish and American Sufism, the Soviet spiritual underground, and the Islamic Philosophy of Illumination. Her cognitive phenomenological research of Tibetan Tantric meditation was featured on BBC, Science Daily, and other important forums. She has published more than 200 papers and book chapters, and is an Associate Editor of the Journal of Theoretical and Philosophical Psychology, and guest editor for Open Theology, De Gruyter (2017; 2018, 2019, 2020 to appear).

Part II. Lifeworld, Intersubjectivity, Alterity

Chapter 7
Living the *Epoché:* A Phenomenological Realism of Religious Experience

Sam Mickey

Abstract Presenting a phenomenological realism of religious experience, this chapter elucidates the function of the *epoché* in the phenomenology of religion. Some interpretations of the *epoché* preclude any commitments to realism. For instance, Husserl's *epoché* is typically understood as a methodological device for "bracketing" any assertions about the real world. Drawing on the works of Emmanuel Levinas and the Dutch phenomenologist of religion Gerardus van der Leeuw, I outline a different interpretation of the *epoché,* one that affirms the reality of religious experience in terms of hospitable restraint that makes contact with the irreducible hiddenness or alterity of others. The *epoché* thus involves a tactful touch that leaves the other intact. Following Heidegger's existential turn in phenomenology, van der Leeuw and Levinas seek to live the *epoché* so that it is not a mere methodological device but a prereflective and religious mode of being fundamental to all human endeavor. The dynamic of touching that makes contact while leaving the other intact also resonates with the speculative realism of thinkers like Jean-Luc Nancy and Graham Harman. In a phenomenological realism, the *epoché* can assist efforts to clarify the historical and material conditions that make up religious experience while also affirming the real existence of religious experience through hospitality to irreducible alterity.

Keywords Phenomenological realism · Epoché · Emmanuel Levinas · Gerardus van der Leeuw · Irreducible alterity · Hospitality ethics

Is religious experience real, or is it merely a social construct that some scholars of religious studies project onto others? Tim Murphy (2010) argues in support of the latter claim in his critical analysis of the phenomenology of religion in *The Politics of Spirit: Phenomenology, Genealogy, Religion.* More specifically, he claims that

S. Mickey (✉)
University of San Francisco, San Francisco, CA, USA
e-mail: srmickey@usfca.edu

© Springer Nature Switzerland AG 2019   113
O. Louchakova-Schwartz (ed.), *The Problem of Religious Experience*,
Contributions to Phenomenology 103,
https://doi.org/10.1007/978-3-030-21575-0_7

the phenomenology of religion is basically a Eurocentric enterprise, and thus also, *mutatis mutandis*, Christocentric, ethnocentric, racist, and logocentric. Insofar as they project their biases about religion, culture, humanity, and reason onto others, phenomenologists inquiring into religion say more about their prejudices as investigators than they do about the actual phenomena they purport to study. To overcome those biases, Murphy proposes a postcolonial, poststructuralist approach based in genealogical methods of Nietzsche and Foucault. Murphy considers such an approach more effective at accounting for the diverse ways people orient themselves to the power relations categorized in modern European culture as "religion." While there is much value in Murphy's work for critically analyzing power relations and welcoming cultural differences, his account does not adequately represent the role of the *epoché* in the phenomenology of religion. As a practice of holding one's own biases and prejudices in suspense or restraint, putting one's own perspective in brackets so as to welcome phenomena on their own terms, the phenomenological *epoché* indicates how phenomenologists of religion overcome the centrisms in which their perspectives are situated and welcome otherness and difference. Poststructuralist and postcolonial affirmations of otherness (i.e., alterity) are not in opposition to phenomenology in this regard. Rather, they can be understood as extensions of the phenomenological *epoché*. Murphy is right to point out the importance of overcoming various centrisms in religious studies (e.g., ethnocentrism, Christocentrism, logocentrism), but he does not recognize that the phenomenology of religion already accounts for this problem. Indeed, it accounts for otherness perhaps more radically than some postcolonial and poststructuralist theories, which tend to involve constructivist frameworks that focus less on the real existence of actual others and more on criticizing how otherness is appropriated into systems of knowledge and power.

I claim that the practice of the *epoché* can facilitate a realist interpretation of religious experience, an interpretation that resonates with some thinkers associated with the philosophical movement known as speculative realism. The *epoché* makes it possible to welcome the alterity of other religions, other ethnicities, other ways of knowing, other people, and indeed, every other. Insofar as this suspense welcomes the alterity of real others, it can support ethical and political gestures of hospitality across cultural differences. To elaborate on this point, I discuss the use of the *epoché* in the phenomenology of religion articulated by the Dutch philosopher and historian Gerardus van der Leeuw, and I show how this intersects with the ethics of alterity in the phenomenology of Emmanuel Levinas. While Levinas is a phenomenologist, he is also a prominent influence on Jacques Derrida, whose method of deconstruction has been highly significant in the development of poststructuralism and postcolonialism. Levinasian philosophy thus provides a good example of the continuity between phenomenology and those latter modes of thought. I conclude by explicating some ways that the *epoché* facilitates a phenomenological realism that is hospitable to the alterity of others' experiences of the sacred.

7.1   Suspense

Van der Leeuw's phenomenology of religion follows in the Dutch tradition of the phenomenology of religion that began with Pierre Daniël Chantepie de la Saussaye in the late nineteenth century (George James 1995). A crucial difference is that van der Leeuw includes insights elaborated by Husserl and Heidegger. Although van der Leeuw works with Husserl's sense of the *epoché,* he is also deeply indebted to Heidegger's hermeneutics. Like Heidegger, van der Leeuw embraces the hermeneutic conception of experience (*Erlebnis*) developed by Wilhelm Dilthey. The significance of Dilthey's notion of experience for Heidegger is evident in the latter's discussion of "factical life-experience" (*faktische Lebenserfahrung*) in his 1920–21 lecture course on the phenomenology of religion (Heidegger 2004). Factical life-experience can be described as a bivalent unity of presence and absence: in other words, combination and withdrawal, or identity and difference. A similar dynamic is at work in van der Leeuw's concept of experience. Van der Leeuw (1963, 676) articulates the relation of understanding to phenomena according to the schema outlined in Dilthey's argument that the human sciences (*Geisteswissenschaften*) are based on "relations between experience [*Erlebnis*], expression [*Ausdruck*] and understanding [*Verstehen*]." Van der Leeuw correlates subjective experience, expression, and understanding with three objective levels of appearing—relative concealment, relative transparency, and gradually becoming manifest or revealed. Becoming manifest is the primordial level of phenomenal appearing, which, upon reflection, is rendered relatively transparent and opaque: transparent insofar as the meaning of the phenomenon can be expressed; opaque insofar as the meaning of the phenomenon is concealed in the strangeness and difference of the experience.

Van der Leeuw describes different experiences of systems of meaning or "types" (1963, 673). Such types can be described differently according to different contexts, and they could include types of sacred people (e.g., priest, king, saint, mystic), sacred objects (e.g., altars, trees, fetishes, buildings), sacred actions (e.g, purification, divination, prayer), and so on. The basic type of religious meaning is the structure of the sacred. Along these lines, van der Leeuw adopts Rudolf Otto's (1958) concept of the sacred as the wholly other mystery, *mysterium tremendum*, which becomes revealed in experience. Insofar as all phenomena unconceal concealment, human existence is always already engaged with the sacred, which is to say, the human being is *Homo religiosus*, the antithesis of *Homo negligens* (van der Leeuw 1963, 680). In other words, "all understanding, irrespective of whatever object it refers to, is ultimately religious: all significance sooner or later leads to ultimate significance" (van der Leeuw 1963, 684). Since this ultimate significance is alterity, it would be wrong to critique phenomenological interpretations of religion as if they were abstract theories and methods that perpetuate the hegemony of sameness and suppress what is other, different, or strange. Rather, phenomenology for van der

Leeuw is a practice of engaging the radical alterity of every phenomenon and avoiding neglectfulness. It is the "true vital activity" of humanity: "standing aside and understanding what appears into view" (van der Leeuw 1963, 676). Phenomenology is how humans understand the mysterious other as it is simultaneously concealed and becoming manifest in experience. The phenomenology of religion thus aims to descriptively translate all types and meanings of religious experience into communicable discourse without effacing the radical alterity of what becomes manifest in such experience. The attitude of restraint is the fundamental part of phenomenological hermeneutics that holds discourse back and keeps it from obscuring *or* assimilating the phenomena under investigation.

In George James's (1995, 231) overview of the main proponents of a phenomenology of religion, he notes that van der Leeuw's use of the term *epoché* has "little to do with its meaning in Husserl's thought." Murphy (2010, 228) makes a similar point, arguing that, although van der Leeuw "does invoke the *epoché* as a restraint upon phenomenological activity, his conception of that restraint in no way, finally, resembles Husserl's." James's view is more nearly correct than Murphy's hyperbolic "no way," but James too is understating the Husserlian significance of van der Leeuw's *epoché*. Both Murphy and James associate Husserl's *epoché* with an idealist notion of bracketing the being of the world in order to assess the contents of consciousness. To be sure, that is not entirely incorrect. Husserl's focus on clarifying the *noēsis-noēma* structure of intentionality, especially in *Ideas I* (2014) and *Cartesian Meditations* (1999), tends to elide any analysis of the real existence of what becomes manifest within intentional consciousness. Nonetheless, Husserl's *epoché* is not simply idealist. There is a realist aspect to it.

For Husserl, the *epoché* signifies the brcketing that puts in suspense or restraint assertions about the world, particularly judgments based in the natural attitude, which is the basic standpoint or situation of human beings (Husserl 1969, 101–110). Merleau-Ponty (1998, vii) summarizes this conception of the *epoché*, noting that this phenomenological method "places in abeyance the assertions arising out of the natural attitude, the better to understand them." The natural attitude includes any naturalist interpretations of the world, including rationalism, empiricism, and positivism, but the natural attitude is not merely the attitude of naturalists. It is not only a theoretical attitude. It is more existential than that. It is the situation by which the self is "set in relation to a world," which is "a *world of values*, a *world of goods*, a *practical world*" (Husserl 1969, 103). With the *epoché*, phenomenologists restrain their own existential situations, holding back judgments so that their discourse lets phenomena show themselves as such. This is not simply an idealist abstention from making claims about the real world. Suspending the natural attitude does not mean abstaining from any judgment about the real world. Metaphysical theories of reality (i.e., the realness of the real) need to be held in suspense; however, such suspense does not entail that one refrain from affirming the existence of the real. Husserlian restraint is a practice of holding oneself in suspense to better understand the correlations whereby real existence becomes manifest to consciousness (Husserl in Zahavi 2003, 46):

"The" world has not been lost through the *epoché*—it is not at all an abstaining with respect to the being of the world and with respect to any judgment about it, but rather it is the way of uncovering judgments about correlation, of uncovering the reduction of all unities of sense to me myself and my sense-having and sense-bestowing subjectivity with all its capabilities.

The restraint (*Zurückhaltung*) of van der Leeuw's *epoché* does not seek a constitutive transcendental ego, and still further it "implies no mere methodological device, no cautious procedure," but is the basic operation of human existence insofar as it is concerned with the real world (van der Leeuw 1963, 675). Van der Leeuw's *epoché* is like Husserl's insofar as it is an attempt to understand correlations between oneself and the real world. The difference between the two *epochés* is that van der Leeuw emphasizes the ubiquity of the *epoché*. It becomes ontological and not merely methodological. Whereas Husserl elaborates a methodological approach to the *epoché*, van der Leeuw takes an even more realist approach, viewing suspense as a constitutive characteristic of any attempt to understand what becomes manifest in experience. "Understanding, in fact, itself presupposes intellectual restraint" (van der Leeuw 1963, 684). Understanding is always already holding itself back so as to welcome what becomes revealed in the appearing of phenomena.

In short, van der Leeuw views the *epoché* as a fundamental feature of concrete human existence and not as an abstract methodological instrument. Edith Wyschogrod (2000, 75) describes a similar "concretization of the *epoche*" in the work of Levinas: "Bracketing is no longer an instrument invented for understanding consciousness in its primordiality but a fundamental structure of human existence." In other words, with his "prereflective mode of living the Husserlian *epoche*," Levinas "brings the *epoche* into the life world itself." Levinas is also similar to van der Leeuw insofar as both these thinkers work with phenomenology as a way to account for different manifestations of the human relation with the radical alterity of the wholly other, which infinitely exceeds the limits of any object, any phenomenon, or any totality. Like van der Leeuw, Levinas describes religion in terms of this relation with alterity. "We propose to call 'religion' the bond that is established between the same and the other without constituting a totality" (Levinas 2002, 40). Furthermore, the alterity of the other is ethically compelling. Ethical responsibility emerges in the relation of "the one-for-the-other," which is a "face-to-face" relation characterized by the "substitution of the same for the other," whereby the alterity of actually existing others irrupts in one's own phenomenological horizon (Levinas 1998, 26; 2002, 39).

In light of the senses of phenomenology expressed by van der Leeuw and Levinas, one can see how phenomenological inquiries into religion work with the *epoché* in attempting to restrain one's own presuppositions and let what others experience as sacred appear in its irreducible alterity. It is impossible to comprehend another's experience of the sacred at all without already having some presupposed understanding of the sacred. From the presuppositions of one's existential situation, one can experience others, but without further restraint the radical alterity of these experiences becomes subsumed into one's own presuppositions. With further restraint, one can proceed to understand others' experiences without effacing their alterity. In restraining oneself so as to interpret what others experience as sacred, one cannot completely restrain oneself without suspending the very hermeneutic context that makes it possible to interpret others' experiences. This is the limit of understanding, the limit of phenomenology, the limit that marks the encounter with radical alterity. At this limit, the other's experience of the sacred appears as other. Van der Leeuw notes that, at this limit, understanding loses its name and can only be considered "becoming understood" (*Verstandenwerden*), so that "the more deeply comprehension penetrates any event, and the better it 'understands' it, the more evident it becomes to the understanding that the ultimate ground of understanding lies not within itself, but in some 'other' by which it is comprehended from beyond the frontier" (van der Leeuw 1963, 683). The other is ultimately "a secret which reveals itself repeatedly, only nevertheless to remain eternally concealed" (van der Leeuw 1963, 680).

The task of any phenomenology of religion is not simply to interpret appearances of religious experience but to disclose the limit where appearances break up and concealment breaks through. At the limit, others' experiences of the sacred appear in their irreducible alterity. Extending a Levinasian sense of alterity to include all others, Derrida (1995, 82–87) articulates this point in terms of a "play of words" that contains "the very possibility of a secret that hides and reveals itself at the same time within a single sentence": "tout autre est tout autre" ("Every other [one] is every [bit] other"). This provocative French tautology suggests that every particular other ("tout autre") is completely other, wholly other ("tout autre"); and vice versa, the wholly other is every single other. Simply put, the phenomenology of religion enacts the epoché in an explicit attempt at holding oneself back so as to welcome the other as other, to welcome others' experiences of the wholly other in all their otherness. As John Caputo (2000, 42) observes, this welcoming of the arrival of the other, what Derrida (2002, 299) calls an "invention of the other," is a common commitment of many inquiries in hermeneutics and deconstruction. It is this same welcoming of alterity that led Wyschogrod (1981) to suggest that hermeneutics and deconstruction are particularly helpful approaches for studying religious phenomena across cultural differences.

Phenomenology, hermeneutics, and poststucturalist methods like deconstruction restrain the structures of discourse so as to not obscure the alterity of the other. This dynamic of restraint can also be seen in the philosophy of Jean-Luc Nancy, who employs the dynamics of touch to account for the contact and separation whereby one touches the other while the other nonetheless remains untouched. A tactful touch makes contact while leaving the other intact. Insofar as Nancy accounts for touch as an integral feature not only of human existence but of the real world outside human consciousness, Derrida (2005b, 46) refers to this philosophy of touch as "postdeconstructive realism." Furthermore, Nancy's postdeconstructive realism runs parallel to some of the ideas that have been grouped into the category of speculative realism, specifically in Graham Harman's object-oriented philosophy (Harman 2012; Gratton 2012; Ian James 2017). Harman (2011) extends phenomenological insights into intentionality and alterity so that they apply not only to human beings but to all beings or "objects," where "object" is not the opposite of "subject" but includes any entity whatsoever. Nancy and Harman are unique for addressing dynamics of contact and separation between *all* entities, human and nonhuman, actual and virtual. All things touch while remaining other. In object-oriented ontology, this is called "vicarious causation," whereby objects have mediated access to one another while remaining inaccessible, such that they "touch without touching" (Harman 2007, 204). The function of the *epoché* in the phenomenology of religion is that of a tactful touch—a welcoming suspense, a hospitable restraint—a knowing that partially accesses the other while the other remains unknown. Van der Leeuw's *epoché* can be read as a forerunner of what Ian James (2016, 17) describes as "the post-phenomenological realisms of Nancy and Harman":

> Obscurity becomes ontologically primordial and touch becomes the fundamental mode of vicarious access to the obscure being of things. ... An exhaustive, total knowledge is impossible given the ultimate withdrawal of the inner reality of things and given also that they are known only through vicarious and partial relations of adjacency and contiguity and not through any elevated position of a "survol" of the subject over an object. ... Knowledge would, however, be no less real for all that, because it arises out of real contact with really existing entities or things and the reality of the proximity and distance between them.

7.2 Realism Without Reality

The details of van der Leeuw's appropriation of the epoché are most evident when reflecting on what it is that van der Leeuw considers particularly important to restrain. George James (1995, 233) notes that van der Leeuw puts three aspects of religion into brackets: (1) any reality behind the appearance of the phenomenon, (2) any developmental or evolutionary progression of history, and (3) any judgments that consider alien religious phenomena to be spurious or degenerate. All these aspects of religion must be held in abeyance to understand the phenomenon as such—as another's experience of a disclosure of alterity. Unrestrained, interpretations of religion will likely posit assertions and make judgments about phenomena in such a way as to obscure and efface the other. Brief explications of the three interpretive stances that van der Leeuw brackets will help clarify how phenomenological interpretations can speculate about real experiences of the sacred while tactfully holding in abeyance any metaphysical, developmental, or judgmental assertions about the reality of the real.

1. With an argument similar to Heidegger's (1962, 60) to the effect that there is nothing "behind" what shows itself in the appearing of phenomena, van der Leeuw (1963, 675) proposes that phenomenology "is concerned only with 'phenomena', that is with 'appearance'; for it, there is nothing whatever 'behind' the phenomenon." This follows from van der Leeuw's separation of phenomenology from theology and philosophy, which are concerned with the metaphysical truth underlying appearances. Accordingly, van der Leeuw does not claim that phenomena are manifestations of Platonic Ideas or of a Kantian thing-in-itself (*Ding-an-sich*). This also

means that van der Leeuw brackets the structures that empirical scientists posit as an underlying reality, such as the position of some physical and social scientists who claim that the world is primarily random material events of which human consciousness is merely an emergent phenomenon or epiphenomenon (1963, 677). This does not mean that the epoché involves abstention for any acknowledgment that religious experiences are real. It involves abstention from empirical and metaphysical theories of an underlying reality constitutive of the real.

In restraining all propositions about true structures under or behind phenomena, van der Leeuw holds back the violent tendency of discourse to assimilate the incomprehensible other to the words and categories of understanding. Derrida views the epoché similarly, arguing that such restraint is respectful to "sacred mystery," respectful to what "ought to remain intact or inaccessible, like the mystical immunity of a secret" (Derrida 2002, 85–86). The restrained holding of the epoché is part of an "entire semantic family" involving varieties of "holding" (*tenir*), including tending, attending, pretending, extending, intending; and these different ways of holding can welcome the visitation of the other (Derrida 2002, 85, 360). Accordingly, Derrida associates this restrained "holding" with hospitality—a gesture of welcoming that invites the arrival of what is beyond all welcoming apparatuses. Hospitality is a matter of letting oneself "be swept by the coming of the wholly other," which is to say, "to be hospitable is to let oneself be overtaken" (361). Derrida is drawing here on the phenomenology of Levinasian ethics. Indeed, Levinas (2002, 27) seeks to "present subjectivity as welcoming the Other, as hospitality." Hospitality is "the one-for-the-other in the ego," which means "giving to the other the bread from one's own mouth" and "being able to give up one's soul for another" (Levinas 1998, 79). For Derrida, this hospitably restrained welcoming of the unapproachable other is an instance of deconstruction. Indeed, deconstruction is the very event of hospitality: "deconstruction is hospitality to the other, to the other than oneself, the other than 'its other,' to an other who is beyond any 'its other'" (Derrida 2002, 364). With the hospitable suspense of the epoché comes the possibility of speaking of a "universal structure of religiosity"—a structure that allows different names for the sacred to be translated into one another without effacing the alterity of the sacred and without reducing the sacred to any particular name, including names like "sacred" and "other" (Derrida 2002, 86). "It is in the *epoché*," for Derrida (2005a, 47), "that faith appears. The only possibility of faith is in the *epoché*."

2. An important interpretive structure that must be restrained in a phenomenology of religion is the one that posits any developmental progression for the history of religions. In bracketing the question of history, van der Leeuw "does not deny the historicity of what appears" but holds historical theories in suspense (George James 1995, 233). In this respect, van der Leeuw classifies phenomena according to apparent types and chronological succession without reducing these phenomena to any historically antecedent causes or origins. An example of a developmental account of religion that van der Leeuw puts into brackets is Hegel's account of religion as a

dialectical progression toward knowledge of Absolute Spirit, wherein magic and the other natural religions and native traditions are imperfect realizations of human freedom in Absolute Spirit, whereas Christianity appears as the most thoroughly realized religion (Hegel 1968, 262–265).

Bracketing evolutionary accounts does not make phenomenology antievolutionary. For in the preface of his work, van der Leeuw (1963, vi) says that his "phenomenological comprehension of history" avoids any arguments for or against evolutionary theories of history. Thus, van der Leeuw considers evolutionary *and* antievolutionary theories of the history of religion but not as conclusive statements about the reality of religion. He considers these theories only insofar as they manifest some of the various ways in which the history of religions can be understood. For instance, van der Leeuw notes that while he finds Christianity to manifest the peak in the development of religions, he is aware that this peak would not necessarily appear for a person of another religious background, such as a Buddhist, who would most likely interpret the history of religions in terms of Buddhist theories and practices (1963, 646). The phenomenologist is not concerned with who is "right" but rather with understanding how each interpretation has meaning for those who hold it.

3. In bracketing theology, van der Leeuw is bracketing the question of truth with respect to God—the object of theological inquiry. God is not a phenomenon, "at least not so that we can comprehend and speak about him" (1963, 687–688). Bracketing theology thus entails that one not evaluate phenomena exclusively in terms of one's own religious history. George James (1995, 52–57) notes that this "a-theological" approach to the study of religion is common among phenomenological investigations of religion. Derrida (2002, 57) argues that the atheological aspect of the epoché is particularly important because of its potential for "liberating a universal rationality and the political democracy associated with it." Through the restrained discourse of the epoché, it is possible to express a structure that is hospitable to all varieties of religious phenomena, a structure that Derrida calls a "universal structure of religiosity"—a structure that would allow "global translations" of the various names associated with religion, the sacred, the other, God, Brahman, Buddha-nature, and so forth. (2002, 86). Such a universal structure could help provide political representation for all religious phenomena, and it could do so without excluding the different appearances that people of other faiths and other nations experience of this structure. Moreover, this universal structure is peaceful, hospitably welcoming the other rather than waging a war and effacing the other. Thus, Levinas (2002, 21–23) equates war with totality, whereas peace is based on the relation with radical alterity, which breaks up all totality. In this sense, the practice of the epoché facilitates a discourse on religion that supports the sort of ethicopolitical relations conveyed in the peaceful gestures of interfaith dialogue and international diplomacy.

Even when one rigorously practices the epoché, one's own experience "can never be freed from its own religious determinateness" (van der Leeuw 1963, 646). It is the task of phenomenology to restrain one's own religious determinateness as completely as possible, reaching the limit where it becomes apparent that one's own understanding is incomplete and that "the ultimate ground of understanding lies not within itself, but in some 'other' by which it is comprehended from beyond the frontier" (1963, 683). The impossibility of complete restraint can be described as "the possible/impossible hospitality," which is possible insofar as one can welcome the other but simultaneously impossible insofar as one cannot invite the other without, at least to some extent, appropriating or assimilating the other into one's own habitation and horizon of expectations (Derrida 2002, 408). With hospitality, the other is present in one's own horizon precisely as what cannot be assimilated into one's own horizon. To develop a restrained interpretation of religion, van der Leeuw restrains any judgments or assertions about whether what he sees "has its roots in any ultimate 'reality,'" and as a Christian, he relegates such issues to theological inquiry (1963, 646). This does not mean that he refrains from considering religious experiences to be real. It means he refrains from pronouncing on that in which the ultimate reality of the real consists. Although van der Leeuw admittedly interprets other religions from the perspective of his own religious history, he indicates the limit where his own horizon encounters the alterity of others' religious engagements.

To interpret the sacred in such a way as to recognize and respect the alterity of others' experiences of the wholly other, one can enact restrained hospitality and hold back the presuppositions that contextualize whatever words and concepts are used to interpret the appearances of the other, including words like "God," "Yahweh," "*śūnyatā*," and "*Dao*" but also words and concepts that may seem universally translatable (e.g., "religion," "wholly other," "sacred," "*mysterium tremendum*"). To allow sacred phenomena to appear as such, one must welcome the real existence of the other and restrain all assertions, judgments, and prejudices about the reality of what is becoming revealed. To enact the hospitable restraint of the epoché, one does not need to practice phenomenology, hermeneutics, or deconstruction, or any particular school of thought or mode of analysis. What Heidegger (1972, 82) says of phenomenology also applies to the epoché: "it can disappear as a designation in favor of the matter of thinking whose manifestness remains a mystery." With a tactful touch, a hospitable interpretation lets itself be overtaken by the alterity of others' experiences of the wholly other. Theories and concepts about the epoché and the phenomenology of religion ultimately disappear as they welcome the arrival of real others.

References

Caputo, John. 2000. *More radical hermeneutics: On not knowing who we are.* Bloomington: Indiana University Press.

Derrida, Jacques. 1995. *The Gift of Death.* Trans. David Wills. Chicago: University of Chicago Press, 1995.

———. 2002. *Acts of religion.* Ed. Gil Anidjar. New York: Routledge.

———. 2005a. *Epoché and faith: An interview with Jacques Derrida.* In *Derrida and religion: Other testaments,* ed. Yvonnne Sherwood and Kevin Hart, 27–50. New York: Routledge.

———. 2005b. *On Touching—Jean-Luc Nancy.* Trans. Christine Irizarry. Stanford: Stanford University Press.

Gratton, Peter. 2012. The speculative challenge and Nancy's post-deconstructive realism. In *Jean-Luc Nancy and plural thinking: Expositions of world, politics, art, and sense,* ed. Peter Gratton and Marie-Eve Morin, 109–125. Albany: SUNY Press.

Harman, Graham. 2007. On vicarious causation. *Collapse* 2: 171–208.

———. 2011. *The quadruple object.* Winchester: Zero Books.

———. 2012. On interface: Nancy's weights and masses. In *Jean-Luc Nancy and plural thinking: Expositions of world, politics, art, and sense,* ed. Peter Gratton and Marie-Eve Morin, 95–107. Albany: SUNY Press.

Hegel, G.W.F. 1968. *Lectures on the Philosophy of Religion: Together with a Work on the Proofs of the Existence of God.* 3 vols. Trans. Rev. E.B. Speirs, B.D. Burdon Sanderson, and J. Burdon Sanderson. New York: Humanities Press.

Heidegger, Martin. 1962. *Being and Time.* Trans. John Macquarrie and Edward Robinson. New York: Harper and Row.

———. 1972. *On Time and Being.* Trans. Joan Stambaugh. New York: Harper and Row.

———. 2004. *Phenomenology of the Religious Life.* Trans. Matthias Fritsch and Jennifer Anna Gosetti-Ferencei. Bloomington: Indiana University Press.

Husserl, Edmund. 1969. *Ideas: General Introduction to Pure Phenomenology.* Trans. W.R. Boyce Gibson. London/New York: George Allen and Unwin/Humanities Press.

———. 1999. *Cartesian Meditations: An Introduction to Phenomenology. Trans. Dorion Cairns.* Dordrecht: Kluwer Academic Publishers.

———. 2014. *Ideas, I: Ideas for a Pure Phenomenology and Phenomenological Philosophy.* Trans. Daniel O. Dahlstrom. Indianapolis: Hackett.

James, George. 1995. *Interpreting religion: The phenomenological approaches of Pierre Daniël Chantepie de la Saussaye, W. Brede Kristensen, and Gerardus van der Leeuw.* Washington, DC: Catholic University of America Press.

James, Ian. 2016. Lucidity and tact. In *Lucidity: Essays in honor of Alison Finch,* ed. Ian James and Emma Wilson, 9–19. Cambridge: Legenda.

———. 2017. The touch of things. *Cultural Critique* 97: 203–227.

Levinas, Emmanuel. 1998. *Otherwise Than Being; Or, Beyond Essence.* Trans. Alphonso Lingis. Pittsburg: Duquesne University Press.

———. 2002. *Totality and Infinity: An Essay on Exteriority.* Trans. Alphonso Lingis. Pittsburg: Duquesne University Press.

Merleau-Ponty, Maurice. 1998. *Phenomenology of Perception.* Trans. Colin Smith. New York: Routledge and Kegan Paul.

Murphy, Tim. 2010. *The politics of spirit: Phenomenology, genealogy, religion.* Albany: SUNY Press.

Otto, Rudolf. 1958. *The Idea of the Holy*. Trans. John W. Harvey. London: Oxford University Press.

van der Leeuw, Gerardus. 1963. *Religion in Essence and Manifestation: A Study in Phenomenology*. 2 vols. Trans. J.E. Turner. New York: Harper and Row.

Wyschogrod, Edith. 1981. The civilizational perspective in comparative studies in transcendence. In *Transcendence and the sacred*, ed. Alan Olson and Leroy Rouner, 58–79. South Bend: University of Notre Dame Press.

———. 2000. *Emmanuel Levinas: The problem of ethical metaphysics*. 2nd ed. New York: Fordham University Press.

Zahavi, Dan. 2003. *Husserl's phenomenology*. Stanford: Stanford University Press.

Sam Mickey, PhD, is an Adjunct Professor in the Theology and Religious Studies department and the Environmental Studies program at the University of San Francisco, in San Francisco, California. He has also taught at Dominican University of California, Pacifica Graduate Institute, and the California Institute of Integral Studies, and he has worked for several years at the Forum on Religion and Ecology at Yale. His work draws on existential phenomenology, comparative (cross-cultural) philosophy, deconstruction, and many fields of the environmental humanities, especially religion and ecology, environmental ethics, and ecocriticism. He is the author of several books on philosophy, religion, and ecology, including *Whole Earth Thinking and Planetary Coexistence: Ecological Wisdom at the Intersection of Religion, Ecology, and Philosophy* (Routledge, 2015) and *Coexistentialism and the Unbearable Intimacy of Ecological Emergency* (Lexington, 2016). He is an editor with Sean Kelly and Adam Robbert) of *The Variety of Integral Ecologies: Nature, Culture, and Knowledge in the Planetary Era* (SUNY, 2017). He blogs regularly at BecomingIntegral.com.

Chapter 8
Schutzian Resources for a Comprehensive Phenomenology of the Holy

Michael Barber

Abstract Espen Dahl argues that Alfred Schutz succumbs to the logic of separation that isolates the holy from everyday life insofar as he presents a self-enclosed life-world that is stable, relatively unchanging, and easily integrated and that cannot allow anything alien to enter its confines. However, Schutz's views on imposed relevances, revisable typifications, and temporality portray a world that is ever in flux and unpredictable, and his theory of multiple realities and symbolism enables him to argue for a transcendent that is appresented throughout everyday life while preserving its transcendence by belonging to a separable religious reality and yet actively intervening in everyday life. Schutz affords abundant comprehensive resources for Dahl's insightful analyses of the relationship of phenomenology to the holy through Schutz's account of the tension of consciousness, the form of self-experience, the distinction between the religious and theoretic provinces of meaning, the *epoché* that discloses the sacred in the profane, a form of spontaneity that supports bodily engagement in worship, the inescapability of natural language, and social relationships and time.

Keywords *Epoché* · Finite provinces of meaning · Multiple realities · Symbols · Imposed relevances

Espen Dahl's *Phenomenology and the Holy* (2010) represents a careful effort to address constructively the experience of the holy by relying on commonly accepted phenomenological methods and doctrines, in particular, Edmund Husserl's work on normality in *Zur Phänomenologie der Intersubjektivität* (1973b). Rather than present a systematic phenomenology of the experience of the holy, Dahl shows how the practice of phenomenology of everyday life can be responsive to the holy; hence his title deals with phenomenology *and* the holy rather than phenomenology *of* the

M. Barber (✉)
Saint Louis University, St. Louis, MO, USA
e-mail: michael.barber@slu.edu

© Springer Nature Switzerland AG 2019
O. Louchakova-Schwartz (ed.), *The Problem of Religious Experience*,
Contributions to Phenomenology 103,
https.//doi.org/10.1007/978-3-030-21575-0_8

holy. The focus of Dahl's discussion is how the experience of the holy is initiated from beyond subjectivity but still must be given with reference to subjective experience. This problem arises because the holy and the everyday have been often isolated from each other through a thought pattern that Dahl characterizes as a "logic of separation" (Dahl 2010, 11), which appears in several thinkers, including Alfred Schutz. This paper will try to defend Schutz from Dahl's charge, and then it will attempt to show how Schutz's philosophy provides resources for a systematic phenomenology of the holy that can supplement, support, and integrate many of Dahl's valid insights into how the holy is experienced.

8.1   Schutz and the Logic of Separation

For Dahl, the logic of separation (Dahl 2010, 11) mistakenly distinguishes sharply the everyday from the holy: that is, a totally immanent worldview from a totally transcendent approach to the holy. This logic can, however, be overcome if one can understand how the everyday already conveys certain traces of the other, or alien (Dahl 2010, 37). Dahl illustrates how this logic works by lining up certain thinkers whose work demonstrates the logic of separation, and then he counters these viewpoints by presenting others whose work can be mined to dissolve such a polarization between the holy and everyday life.

A seminal thinker who succumbs to the logic of separation is Rudolf Otto, who pushes otherness to an extreme and sets up the "numinous" (Dahl 2010, 24)—that is, the "Wholly Other" (Dahl 2010, 24–25)—as a "counter concept" (Dahl 2010, 27) over against everyday life. This image of a pure, otherworldly holy is counterpoised to the disenchanted, completely secularized world that Max Weber depicted, and thereby provides a striking illustration of the logic of separation (Dahl 2010, 24–37). Dahl finds Emmanuel Levinas also exhibiting this logic because of his wariness about any mediation that may swallow the other (Dahl 2010, 153–154); his insistence on a Same enclosed upon itself and emptied of all alterity; and his polarization of the other over against language, metaphysics, and philosophy (Dahl 2010, 35)—for which Jacques Derrida (1978, 151–153) also criticized him in "Violence and Metaphysics."[1] By contrast, Dahl recommends a view of the holy as impure and

---

[1] Dahl seems to assimilate Levinas's encounter with the other to the encounter between the familiar and the alien in the later Husserl, but this seems to overlook the difference between an ethical encounter with the other and an epistemological/ontological experience of the other, the latter of which concerns strangeness or incomplete knowability of the other. However, Levinas (1997, 87–88) takes pains to distinguish the "extreme urgency of assignation," which is not a "knowing." In addition, the experience of the other as the "absolute other," (Levinas 1979, 40) despite the ontological or epistemological resonances of that phrase, must be understood in terms of what one experiences when ethically summoned by the other—that is, without expecting reciprocity or equal treatment in response, a lack of any sense of reciprocity or equality. Also Derrida's "Violence and Metaphysics" fails to appreciate that even in *Totality and Infinity* (and certainly in *Otherwise than Being*), Levinas (1979, 90–81; 1997, 153–157) is aware that his philosophy conveys the expe-

occurring amid the everyday (Dahl 2010, 174) and "incarnated in familiar phenomena" (Dahl 2010, 177). Unsurprisingly, Dahl also faults Jean-Luc Marion, who
works out of the Levinasian tradition, for defending a view of the holy uncontami-
nated by human restrictions and conditions (Dahl 2010, 5–6). Finally, Dahl accuses
Alfred Schutz of propounding a homogeneous life-world "too closed in on itself to
allow anything alien to occur within its scope" (Dahl 2010, 9), thereby consigning
the religious transcendent to the status of a "Wholly Other." Similarly, Catherine
Pickstock's proposal to resacralize completely the everyday manifests a "myth of
purity" that resists Dahl's preference for an ambivalent interplay between the everyday and the holy, irreducible to each other. By juxtaposing Pickstock's completely
sacral view of everyday life with Schutz's "myth of homogeneity" (Dahl 2010, 11),
which is not open to anything alien beyond itself, Dahl illustrates how competing
positions on the holy end up revealing the stranglehold that the logic of separation
has on contemporary philosophy.

Dahl's hero for articulating the kind of holy/everyday interaction he favors is
Edmund Husserl—although, in Dahl's view, Husserl at times succumbs to his own
version of the logic of separation: for instance, in striving for a transcendental
sphere purified of anything empirical (Dahl 2010, 75–77), in separating *hylē* from
morphē (Dahl 2010, 109), and in his discussion of the sphere of ownness cut off
from all intersubjectivity in the fifth Cartesian Meditation, especially if one takes
ownness to be an ontological region rather than a mere provisional abstraction from
an intersubjective whole (Dahl 2010, 138). Nevertheless, Husserl captures how
what transcends subjectivity—that is, what is alien to it—affects it within everyday
life and in relation to its receptive capacities. For instance, Husserl acknowledges
how traditions, including religious ones, become fixed, familiar, and sedimented in
everyday practices, but then experiences in the present surprisingly trigger or
awaken sleeping, sedimented religious meanings through passive association in
such a way that one experiences the alien, or the holy, in an unexpected religious
experience, in the midst of the familiar (Dahl 2010, 212–213). Furthermore, one can
find the alien penetrating everyday life in Husserl's treatment of the mystery of the
thing, not only in its richness and in the horizons beyond what is given in any perception but also in the interruptions, explosions, or fulfillments of various intentional expectations. The alien is also given in the resistance that *hylē* offers the
noēseis by which one approaches the object and in the affective tendencies that the
thing exercises on the ego as a call evoking a response and requiring one to abandon
total predicative control (Dahl 2010, 90–116, 148, 210). Insisting on the interruption of the familiar but always in relation to the familiar, Dahl aligns himself with
Husserl, who stands midway between Marion (who neglects the familiar) and

---

rience of the other while also betraying it and that his very discourse conveys the ethical summons
of the other as a contaminating medium that reveals the other's summons (reduces the betrayal of
the Saying in the Said) and, at the same time, betrays it (by still betraying the Saying in the Said).
Indeed, at the end of *Otherwise than Being* Levinas (1997, 157–162) poses the problem of how
everyday political, legal, and social institutions can be more hospitable toward the other's summons, to which they will never be completely adequate.

Heidegger, whose thing exceeds the familiar by being more impenetrable than inter-ruptive (Dahl 2010, 128). Likewise, Husserl's account of *Einfühlung* in the fifth Cartesian Meditation pinpoints an unbridgeable difference with the other, whose experience is never given *originaliter* (Dahl 2010, 146). Nevertheless, through phe-nomenological reduction one can uncover the constitution of the other as long as one is vigilant in remembering that constitution does not create the other but only describes how the other appears in human experience, that the givenness of the other is not a matter of "egological achievement" (Dahl 2010, 165), and that constitution itself is undertaken in response to the call of what is other (Dahl 2010, 148, 210). Furthermore, since one's past self is experienced in memory as if one were a differ-ent person from [him/her] who one is in the present, Husserl observes that there is an otherness within the self that opens it to the external otherness of the other. Dahl concludes that our experience is "shot through with strangeness" (Dahl 2010, 152) and that everyday life is heterogeneous in its structure (Dahl 2010, 86). While Husserl's viewpoint may not be explicitly religious, Dahl (2010, 221–222) points out that this frustration of everyday normality has a religious affinity and can be taken as part of a search for the holy in everyday life.

Dahl's condensed, four-page criticism of Schutz as separating off a life-world closed in on itself from a wholly other holy requires unpacking and more careful consideration. Basically, Dahl argues (1) that Schutz's view of the life-world is stable and homogeneous, and (2) that there is no religious transcendence of the limits of the life-world. As regards the first challenge, Dahl asserts that in everyday life, according to Schutz, "one might occasionally be surprised or temporally deceived" (Dahl 2010, 7), that eventually "all undetermined occurrences and prob-lematic tasks are integrated or solved" (Dahl 2010, 7), and that "the structures of things do not lose their familiarity as types" (Dahl 2010, 7).

However, Schutz's view of everyday life is not as tranquil or predictable as Dahl suggests. If one consults his essay "Reflections on the Problem of Relevance" (2011), human experience regularly encounters obstacles that disrupt the sense of "I can do it again," which is fundamental for pragmatic everyday life and which Husserl, too, found basic. Schutz (1964d, 127, 129; and 2011, 109) describes these frequently appearing impediments as "imposed relevances" that thwart the intrinsic relevances originating in one's own decisions and that one must try to come to terms with by adjusting, revising, or forgoing one's intrinsic relevances. Such imposed relevances could include such things as the advent or prospect of one's death or bereavement over the death of others; all sorts of physical or psychological crises; ontological barriers (a distance that one cannot avoid having to cross, a period of time that requires one to wait); physiological difficulties such as illness, disability, fatigue, or the slowness with which wounds heal; acts of God, fate, or destiny; the attacks or prospect of attacks by terrorists or nuclear opponents; or even the previ-ous, not easily revisable choices belonging to one's biographical situation (1964d, 127; 2011, 109, 158, 164, 176–177, 180, 198). As Schutz summarizes the precari-ous character of everyday life (1964d, 127):

> We are … not only centers of spontaneity, gearing into the world and creating changes within it, but also the mere passive recipients of events beyond our control which occur without our interference. Imposed upon us as relevant are situations and events which are not connected with interests chosen by us, which do not originate in acts of our discretion, and which we have to take just as they are, without any power to modify them by our spontaneous activities except by transforming the relevances thus imposed into intrinsic relevances. While that remains unachieved, we do not consider the imposed relevances as being connected with our spontaneously chosen goals. Because they are imposed upon us they remain unclarified and rather incomprehensible.

As regards Dahl's contention that the structure of things retains their familiarity as types or typifications, Schutz indeed sees typifications as essential structures through which we experience objects: that is, in terms of "mountains," "trees," "animals," and "human beings." However, Schutz claims that he is simply reiterating Husserl's point that it is necessarily the case that typifications are rooted in the experience that the "actual perception of an object is apperceptively transferred to any other similar object" (Schutz 1962a, 8). As part of this eidetic analysis of everyday life that Schutz (1967, 43–44) affirms he is pursuing, there are structures that are eidetic in the sense that one cannot have a life-world without their being in place, among them the structure whereby we experience objects as typified. In this sense, Dahl is correct that the structures of things in general do not lose their familiarity as types. Eidetic features also characterize all Husserl's descriptions of the life-world, including the repeated structural interplay between normality and anomaly that Dahl endorses.

However, although it is eidetically the case that we necessarily experience the world in terms of types, it is also the case that individual types are always open-ended and future-directed, vaguely subsuming experiences under them, and always open to being confirmed, revised, or even abandoned depending on how objects behave in relation to one's experiencing (Schutz 1962a, 8; 1964c, 283–288). Consequently, for Schutz, the stock of knowledge that storehouses one's system of typifications "is in a continual flux" (Schutz 1964c, 284); and in everyday life one is frequently surprised, and undetermined occurrences are often not so easily and smoothly integrated.

Moreover, although one often communicates successfully, Schutz argues that this continual flux, especially the ongoing inner temporality of partners, affects the communication between them by creating an undercurrent of dissonance. Such discordance occurs because one can never give precisely the same meaning to the other's experiences that the other gives to them, since each one's unfolding history always differs from the other's, and consequently the historically acquired connotations of the terms each uses never coincide exactly with the other's (Schutz 1967, 99). As a further illustration of the incongruity that temporality introduces, in his essay "The Homecomer," Schutz explains how the divergent history that the soldier on the warfront undergoes in contrast to the history of those left behind at home results in painful dissonances in meaning when the soldier returns home after the war (Schutz 1964a, 114). Furthermore, these discrepancies between interlocutors produced by their diverse streams of consciousness represent just one way in which the otherness, or "mystery of the human Other" in the terms of Dahl (2010, 129), is experienced. Besides this influence of time, Schutz, like Husserl, emphasizes the lack of originary understanding of the other (Schutz 1966, 63–64), and he also stresses the deep-seated, often irreconcilable conflicts in meaning that the stranger experiences when approaching an in-group (Schutz 1964b, 100–105). In conclusion, imposed relevances, the tentativeness of types, the lack of confluence that differing temporalities create, and the inevitable gaps in understanding another suggest that Schutz's view of everyday life is just as "shot through with strangeness" as Husserl's and that Schutz's life-world is not nearly as comfortable and immunized against change as Dahl believes.

After an initial discussion of Schutz in the introduction to his book, Dahl (2010, 6–9) admits that Schutz's thought converges with Herbert Dreyfus's view of the reduction, which Dahl (2010, 81–82) strongly approves and which emerges from within everyday life. This convergence occurs, Dahl believes, insofar as Schutz insists upon the regular interruptions occurring within everyday life. At this point, though, Dahl seems to arrive at an interpretation of Schutz that seems to contradict the reading of Schutz that Dahl gave in his introduction. Although Dahl's concurrence with Schutz seems to undermine the first objection above—namely that Schutz understands everyday life to be stable and homogeneous (in perhaps the sense of being easily integrated and unruffled)—Dahl (2010, 81) continues to object that Schutz does not overcome the myth of homogeneity. This meaning of "homogeneity" perhaps has to do with the second major objection to Schutz's work that Dahl raises, namely that the transcendences Schutz and Luckmann (1989, 103) describe are transcendences "within the world, not transcending the world" (Dahl 2010, 8). This criticism of Dahl's is echoed by the criticism of Jürgen Habermas (1987, 132) that the Schutzian life-world cannot be transcended. Furthermore, Dahl (2010, 9) wonders whether the other, as a medium transcendence, has any religious transcendence for Schutz, as opposed to the way the other is experienced according to Levinas. Although Schutz and Luckmann (1989, 103, 121–125) do allow for mystical experience, it involves the experience of an otherworldly transcendence that absorbs and obliterates the self undergoing the experience and that, as a result, "does not interrupt or break up the homogeneity of the world in any way" (Dahl 2010, 9). Consequently, a Wholly Other is presented as standing over against a homogeneous, self-enclosed life-world that it cannot penetrate in any way—just the kind of bifurcation that is captured by the idea of the logic of separation.

To handle the question of whether Schutz's life-world can be transcended, it is important to understand those parts of Schutz's encompassing theory that would be most relevant to the phenomenology of the holy, especially his essays "On Multiple Realities" (1962b) and "Symbol, Reality and Society" (1962c), neither of which Dahl ever cites, though he does repeatedly refer to *The Structures of the Life-World*, in which segments of Schutz's symbol theory are presented. In "On Multiple Realities," Schutz presents a view of the life-world, understood as the world of experience prior to implementation of the phenomenological reduction; and within that life-world, the paramount reality is the world of daily life whose form of spontaneity is "working": that is, bodily engagement with the world for practical purposes (Schutz 1962b, 212). This world of daily life is paramount because all communication, whether in daily life or outside it, must make use of working acts (Schutz, 1962c, 294), *pace* Habermas (1987, 130–132). However, Schutz includes in the life-world a variety of other "provinces of meaning" with their correlative "realities," such as the provinces of theoretical contemplation, fantasy, and dreams— all three of which he analyzes; and he suggests other provinces that he does not flesh out: literature, drama, childhood play, and religious experience. Furthermore, he develops six cognitive features that characterize any province of meaning: a tension of consciousness, form of spontaneity, self-conception, sociality, temporality, and even a special kind of *epoché* by which one breaks with the pragmatic world of everyday life to take up the new attitude of the distinctive province of meaning.

Moreover, Schutz's theory of symbols and other forms of significative representation coheres nicely with his approach to multiple realities. In the province of meaning of everyday life, self-devised marks enable one by oneself to overcome little transcendences, such as distances or time gaps. Hence, for example, a broken twig reminds one where to turn on one's return home or the bookmark pinpoints where one stopped reading for when reading will resume. By indications such as the smoke that indicates a distant and perhaps not yet visible fire, one finds a more objective, less arbitrary (in comparison with idiosyncratic marks) way of coming to terms with another little transcendence, a distant object. However, linguistic signs, fashioned, transmitted, and deployed by one's cultural group, enable one to a degree and still within everyday life to overcome the medium transcendence—that is, the meaning of the other person, to which one does not have access *orginaliter* and with which one's own meaning will never exactly coincide. Finally, symbols, such as a temple or a religious artifact—to draw from the examples of religious symbols— appear in everyday life, but they appresent, or refer to, a reality beyond that of everyday life, namely that of religious experience.

The religious transcendent in effect transcends the world of everyday life, but it does so in relation to a symbol given in everyday life. Contrary to Dahl (2010, 8), this transcendent does transcend the world, if one means by "world" that of pragmatic "everyday life," which one leaves behind upon entering the finite province of religious meaning. But the religious transcendent does not transcend the "world" if one means the encompassing "life-world" within whose boundaries one situates both the religious province of meaning (among other provinces of meaning) and pragmatic everyday life. On the one hand, one must say that the religious transcendent is not completely separated from everyday life insofar as the symbol appresenting it is located in everyday life. On the other hand, it could be argued that the holy given within everyday life fulfills Dahl's requirement that it still be alien to it and thus that the familiar harbors within itself the unfamiliar (Dahl 2010, 214). This holy, as being a religious reality correlative to the religious province of meaning, is indeed alien to the everyday life from which it is symbolized.

Schutz's view of the life-world, then, is hardly homogeneous, especially since one moves regularly and facilely between these diverse provinces of meaning, which Schutz asserts are not isolated and fenced off from each other, contrary to what Dahl (2010, 9) states when discussing the "Wholly Other" in Schutz's paradigm (Schutz 1962b, 258):

> The finite provinces of meaning are not separated states of mental life in the sense that passing from one to another would require a transmigration of the soul and a complete extinction of memory and consciousness by death, as the doctrine of metempsychosis assumes. They are merely names for different tensions of one and the same consciousness, and it is the same life, the mundane life, unbroken from birth to death, which is attended to in different modifications. As we have said before, my mind may pass during one single day or even hour through the whole gamut of tensions of consciousness, now living in working acts, now passing through a daydream, now plunging into the pictorial world of a painting, now indulging in theoretical contemplation.

Espousing Husserl's account of intentionality and constitution, Dahl (2010, 210) further insists that subjects do not invent or create God or the other out of their own intentional resources. If God were simply a human projection, the holy would be reduced to just another component of everyday reality, and the homogeneity that the logic of separation promotes would prevail. In line with this conviction, Dahl (2010, 9) criticizes Schutz for proposing a rather inert "other-worldly transcendence" that does not interfere with the familiarity of the everyday world. Furthermore, for this same reason he favors Marion's view that the alien that confronts us is experienced more as a call evoking our response rather than simply being impenetrable to conceptual exploitation, as Heidegger suggests (Dahl 2010, 127–128). Even if, as is clear, Schutz conceives symbols in everyday life appresenting another reality correlative to another province of meaning, it would still be conceivable that that object toward which this symbolizing intentionality is oriented could be simply a product of that intentionality, as an image may be merely the product of imagination.

However, if one consults Schutz's own descriptions, one can see that he envisions the religious transcendent as intervening much more forcefully in everyday life. For instance, he refers to Genesis 28, in which Jacob awakens from a dream and exclaims that the Lord was in the place where he had stopped and he knew it not. Schutz (1962c, 338) describes this experience as "the irruption of the transcendent experience into the world of everyday life, which transforms it and gives each element of it an appresentational significance … which it did not have before." Such symbolical experience of the transcendent is taken not as merely a dream or a shadow but as a "vivid instantaneous revelation of that which cannot be explored" (Schutz 1962c, 356). The great transcendences of Nature and Society are also imposed upon us (Schutz 1962c, 330), the phenomena transcending everyday life are described as "disquieting" (Schutz 1962c, 331), the symbolic experience of nature and society is felt as "determined by the order of the cosmos" (Schutz 1962c, 333), and the emotion of love represents a divine intervention in one's life (Schutz 1962c, 336).

In addition to these expressions that suggest that the transcendent is no human concoction, Schutz (1962b, 212–214) contrasts the tension of consciousness of other nonpragmatic provinces of meaning, parallel to the religious sphere, such as dreaming or fantasy, with that of pragmatic everyday life, in which one—bent on achieving practical projects bodily—is active, fully awake, not passive, making use only of image-barren motor-memory to effect pragmatic purposes, as Bergson (1950, 87, 125, 130, 170–171, 226, 322) noted. From the perspective of pragmatic everyday life, in which the struggle to master reality and exercise one's control is prominent, one may be more to think the transcendent of one's own making. However, in the other provinces, the controls needed to master the world are relaxed, and unconscious processes surge forward. As a result, in these provinces, particularly the religious one, the tension of consciousness is less imperial, more passive, and more receptive, and the efficacy of the transcendent in one's own consciousness appears much more plausible. In fact, although William James (1958, 72–73, 144, 170, 215) admits that psychologists may explain that the products emerging from subliminal consciousness are merely products of one's personality and theologians would see them as manifesting the transcendent, he himself comments that "if the grace of God miraculously operates, it probably operates through the subliminal door" (James 1958, 194) and that "the reference of a phenomenon to a subliminal self does not exclude the notion of the direct presence of the Deity altogether" (James 1958, 194; Barber 2017, 91).

For Bergson, from whom Schutz's theory of tensions of consciousness is derived, the pragmatic world of everyday life contrasts with the sphere of "pure memory," in which one relaxes censors and drifts among vivid, colorful memories of the past, as passive associations prompt. As in pure memory, so in Schutz's nonpragmatic provinces of meaning like fantasy and dreams, one's unconscious movements escape censorship and emerge into consciousness, evading the ego's control (Schutz 1962b, 240–241), with the result that Schutz would no doubt concur with Bergson's comment that the dreamer is a "distraught self, a self which has let itself go" (Bergson 1920, 132). Likewise opposed to the pragmatic world of everyday life, the religious province of meaning is not aimed at mastery—and it is not surprising that many religious revelations take place in dreams, as the example of Jacob in Genesis 28, above, illustrates. The tension of consciousness typical of the religious sphere is characterized by a greater passivity than that of everyday life insofar as the transcendent, as William James (1958, 170–171, 216) points out, is often taken to share responsibility for believers' lives with them, to intervene to support and help them, and to bestow its presence or gifts gratuitously on them precisely at the point at which their efforts have failed and they find themselves completely helpless (Barber 2017, 90–91). Further, the religious province of meaning can be characterized as depending on the "appresentative mindset" through which one regularly relies on symbols that refer via passive associations to other symbols in chains and that also appresent the transcendent, as occurs in Jacob's dream when a "stone becomes the pillow, the pillow a pillar, the pillar God's house" (Schutz 1962c, 338). Similarly, scriptural passages (Exodus 14–15; Joshua 3; Jeremiah 16, 23) convey images that are passively linked to similar events: for instance, the crossings of the river at Jericho and of the Tigris River (in the return from captivity) are linked to the earlier passage through the Red Sea in the flight from Egypt in Exodus (Jones et al. 1966, 94–96, 277–278, 1280, 1290). In addition, liturgical celebrations, whose value Dahl rightly recognizes in his last chapter, spread before religious attendees a table of symbols: statues, music, images, candles, aromas, narratives, and vestments, which stir up affects and summon up, without conscious deliberation, other connections and reflections. In the passive tension of consciousness characteristic of the religious province of meaning, one would be much less likely to think of religious experiences as one's doing and would be more inclined to share Dahl's justifiable concern that the holy not be reduced to a mere projected invention.

Furthermore, Dahl (2010, 8) points out that Schutz and Luckmann in *Structures of the Life-World* (1989) do regard the other as transcendent, but they do not seem to see any religious significance in the human other. Although that may be the case if one focuses only on Schutz and Luckmann's discussion of the medium transcendences, if one takes into account the entirety of their treatment of the transcendences and the different representational mechanisms, an interesting connection occurs. The single individual makes use of marks and indications to bring effectively within pragmatic reach what is distant, to enable mastery of the little spatiotemporal transcendences one encounters (the turning point on the path that I may forget about or the fire still distant on the horizon). However, signs pertain to socially transmitted systems, and although signs enable interlocutors to understand each other in highly successful ways for many pragmatic purposes, nevertheless, as mentioned earlier, the identity of interpretational schemes between interlocutors never coincides. There is an otherness of the other that one never overcomes even through signs, because one can never have access to other's originary experience. Finally, although the signs used in everyday life run up against limits that are not found in the usage of marks and indications (that point to objects that one may access completely), there is an even higher level, that of "symbols," which are located in everyday life and are socially transmitted by traditions (e.g., in the case of religions) but which refer to entirely other realities correlative to other finite provinces of meaning and remote from everyday life. Symbols involve a "unique reference to something transcendent that vanishes at the limiting point" (Schutz 1962c, 332) and something that manifests itself in "ciphers" (Schutz 1962c, 338). When one takes account of the totality of Schutz's theory of symbols, it is clear that as one ascends from the little transcendences to the great transcendences, one relying on the representational mechanisms used to overcome such transcendences runs up against increasing resistance to attempts to comprehend these transcendences or pragmatically master them. In a sense, this ascending level upward from the domain of pragmatic mastery is reminiscent of the hierarchy of feelings developed by Max Scheler, which extends from sensible feelings whose pleasures can be controlled by acts of will (e.g., taking painkillers or drinking alcohol) through the less manipulable vital feelings all the way up to the spiritual feelings of bliss, which are not conditioned or alterable by any acts of will or deeds (Scheler 1973, 333–344). Furthermore, in the experience through signs of the medium transcendence, of the other, one experiences a kind of uncrossable gap that is magnified when it comes to reaching toward the great transcendences, such as those correlative to the religious province. The experience of the other, then, constitutes an experience of a transcendence in everyday life that can never be definitively superseded and that anticipates thereby, like a harbinger, the even greater transcendence of the holy, referred to in this world but belonging to another reality.

Dahl on page 8 of *Phenomenology and the Holy* (2010) cites two texts from *Structures of the Life-World* (1989, 103), the first of which suggests that one may think of an experience of the otherworldly that would be so otherworldly that it would not be accessible to human experience—a contradiction that cannot be resolvable if one remains on the ground of everyday reality. Dahl takes this text to confirm his view that the life-world cannot be transcended, but the text following on this quotation, which Dahl (2010, 8) partially quotes in his next citation on the same page, suggests that one needs to withdraw to a religious worldview—that is, to enter the religious province of meaning—in order for an otherworld transcendent to be revealed, something that would unconditionally put in question everyday reality (Schutz and Luckmann 1989, 103). It is precisely by embarking upon the religious province of meaning that it becomes possible to experience the otherworldly, symbolically appresented from this world—a possibility that Dahl seems to preclude.

In the second quotation, Dahl (2010, 8–9) emphasizes that the mystical experience of which Schutz speaks entails abolishing the difference between the Ego and the non-Ego—an abolition that cannot occur in everyday reality. Perhaps because this abolition (which allows an experience of an otherworldly transcendence without the accompanying self) seems so at odds with everyday life practice, Dahl proceeds to accentuate how this otherworldly transcendent cannot interrupt or break up the homogeneity of the world, thus leaving two entirely separate worlds in place. However, one may imagine how such a dissolution of distinctions within mystical experience can have the effect of helping one let go of desperate attempts in everyday life to protect the *ego agens*, whose importance one may have overestimated. Consequently, when one leaves this version of the religious sphere and returns to everyday life, it is conceivable that one may more peaceably engage everyday reality with less anxiety for oneself. In addition, despite the possible conflicts between particular sets of beliefs espoused within the religious province of meaning and those of everyday reality, such differences would not rule out the many ways discussed above in which the transcendent may interrupt everyday life, as imposed relevances upset the simple and smooth execution of the projects that flow from one's intrinsic relevances.

8.2 Schutzian Resources for a Phenomenology of the Holy

Clearly, one can offer a systematic articulation of religious experience in terms of Schutz's theory that integrates multiple realities with symbols. Thus, as the discussion above shows, the tension of consciousness, one of the six cognitive features of any province of meaning, is particularly helpful in the case of the religious sphere. Religious experience's relaxed tension of consciousness, its backing off the endeavor at pragmatic mastery, supports Dahl's repeated emphasis on refraining from any attempt to master or control the transcendent and letting the holy be (Dahl 2010, 102–103, 287–288, 307–308). It also allows a much greater role for passive synthesis, which is important for Dahl's understanding of how in religious experience the sediments of religious traditions are passively evoked by circumstances and which through the notion of appresentative processes would support Dahl's appreciation of worship and his wide view of sacramentality, in which "everything in principle can be a bearer of holiness" (2010, 277–278, 294, 297–298, 307–308). In fact, the very notion of appresentation, the importance of which Dahl (2010, 139–149, 234), along with Husserl (1960, 108–111), recognizes for the encounter with the other, is expanded by Schutz from his own account of the experience of the other to his systematic understanding of symbolism (Schutz 1962c, 294–305, 313, 332–341, 347–356). Moreover, the very concept of appresentation itself—whether one discusses an object appresenting its backside and other's body appresenting her consciousness, or a symbol appresenting the transcendent—captures precisely the idea of the alien, unseen, or unfamiliar appearing with reference to the commonplace, seen, and familiar, a central theme of Dahl's work.

Dahl (2010, 102–103) suggests that Husserl in his account of the pretheoretical domain "gives priority to harmony and predictability" that could diminish a sensibility for the call of the anomalous. It may be, however, that Husserl's priority is part and parcel of his emphasis on the everyday life's pragmatic character, which he affirms strongly in *Experience and Judgment* (Husserl 1973a, 32, 52, 200, 291, 309) and which is definitive of everyday life for Schutz (1962b, 208–209). In the interest of pragmatic efficacy, one seeks harmony and predictability in everyday life. Repeatedly, though, Dahl (2010, 102–103, 287–288, 307–308) rightly insists that the holy cannot be subordinated to pragmatic goals. Likewise, worship, discontinuous with everyday life, cannot be "understood in terms of goal-oriented actions" (Dahl 2010, 271), ought to be "without practical purpose" (Dahl 2010, 272), and permits "something beyond our activity [to] be heard" (Dahl 2010, 14). It would seem, then, that understanding everyday life as a separate province of meaning, guided in its form of spontaneity by the pragmatic interest of realizing goals in the outer world and opposed in diverse ways by diverse nonpragmatic provinces of meaning, among them religion, may explain the origins of the desire to domesticate the holy, whose independence Dahl constantly upholds. At the same time, Schutz's view (Schutz 2011, 107–112; 1967, 98–99; 1962c, 329–356) that in everyday life one encounters multiple imposed relevances, the otherness of the other, and the symbols that appresent the holy would not countenance an idea of everyday life without any traces of the holy or a homogeneous life-world without alternative, heterogeneous provinces of meaning in and out of which one moves every day or hour.

Moreover, it seems that Dahl (2010, 229–232) is just right when he points out that the dogmatic and skeptical approaches to religious experience, which lead to disappointment with it and even the dismissal of it, both mistakenly assume that one's relation to religious experience, as well as everyday life, the other, and the world, is a matter of theoretical achievements. Again, Dahl could draw on Schutzian resources that distinguish the finite provinces of meaning of theoretical contemplation, religious experience, and pragmatic everyday life. The dogmatist and skeptic are simply unaware that they are proceeding within a theoretical province of meaning, with its relevances and practices. Schutz (1962b, 233 n. 19), though, does allow that provinces can carve out a space within another province, an "enclave," as when one pauses to theorize in everyday life or theorizes within the province of religious experience, as Anselm did when he offered his ontological argument within his *Proslogion*.

Another one of the six cognitive features constitutive of provinces of meaning is some form of an *epoché*, modeled on but varying from the Husserlian phenomenological *epoché* by which one suspends "the natural believing in existence involved in experiencing the world" (Husserl 1960, 19–20). For instance, Schutz (1962b, 229) argues that the *epoché* of the natural attitude suspends doubt about the existence of the outer world. In addition, one can conceive of the opening of an act of worship, the lighting of a candle as one begins to pray, or the mere entrance into a temple, church, or synagogue as the form of a religious *epoché* setting oneself off from the pragmatic world of everyday life (Barber 2017, 94–104). However, Husserl does not see the *epoché* as merely stepping back from everyday life; it also makes possible a new way of seeing, by which one "gains possession of something by it" (Husserl 1960, 20), namely all the previously anonymous activities of transcendental subjectivity and the properties of the world correlative to that subjectivity that may have been concealed because of the pragmatic interests dominating the natural attitude prior to the reduction. If the Husserlian phenomenological *epoché* enables a "new seeing" (Husserl 1950, 203) that uncovers what had been previously hidden and anonymous, then analogously the religious *epoché*, too, could involve a withdrawal from the world for purposes of making it possible to see better the presence of the holy that had been present but unnoticed because of one's immersion in pragmatic preoccupations of everyday life.

It would seem that Dahl implicitly envisions such an *epoché* at work particularly in worship, which interrupts daily life in order to "bring the holy into the open" (Dahl 2010, 271, 283), to "let us see more than usual" (Dahl 2010, 283), to help the "weak voice of the holy be heard" (Dahl 2010, 284), and to see the world differently even after one leaves the worship ceremony (Dahl 2010, 307–308). When one finds the holy in the familiar things of worship, a book, words spoken, bread and wine, a table, it sharpens one's eye to see the holy in the familiar things of everyday life outside the worship. The appresentative mindset, nourished in ritual or in sacred spaces and times, overflows those sacred domains set off from the profane, so that the religious adherent can detect the holy present throughout the profane, thereby dissolving the distinction between sacred and profane. This idea of the religious *epoché* recapitulates the trajectory of Mircea Eliade's (Eliade 1961, 25, 33, 35, 37–38, 46, 63, 68, 69, 73 85, 105, 119) thought that separates the sacred provisionally with the result that all objects can be seen as "potential bearers of holiness"—a train of thought that Dahl (2010, 44–46) endorses. Not only does the *epoché* enable one, after being schooled within a separated sphere of the sacred, to discover traces of the holy in the profane world, but also the *epoché* makes it possible actually to transform that world in the light of what one has experienced within the sacred (Dahl 2010, 307)—and here Dahl is not far from Husserl's idea that the person exiting the phenomenological reduction is empowered to alter the world encountered outside it (Barber, 2017, 100–101).

The *epoché* and the adapted tension of consciousness, the two features discussed thus far of the six features of the cognitive style of provinces of meaning, are quite relevant to the province of meaning of religious experience and able to underwrite systematically several of Dahl's central insights into the holy. In addition, provinces of meaning possess a prevalent form of spontaneity (in everyday life working, the attempt to realize a planned pragmatic project by bodily movement), as well as a form of experiencing oneself (e.g., the working self as a total self). To be sure, those within the province of religious experience would be cognizant of the fact that they are taking up a distinctive point of view, or attitude, upon everyday life and no longer living head-on in it, thereby resulting in a divided consciousness. As an instance of this split consciousness, imagine a group worshipping together when suddenly a fire breaks out in the room of worship. Immediately they would abandon the religious province in order to attend to this pressing pragmatic concern, suggesting that the group had to a degree been standing astride both everyday life and the religious sphere while engaged principally within the latter and relegating everyday life to the horizon of their focus.

As regards the form of spontaneity, clearly the finite province of religious experience does not pursue pragmatic projects but often resists them, and one can assume the religious attitude and view the world from within its parameters, as for instance in a state of prayer or meditation, without necessarily gearing into the world through bodily movement. Nevertheless, the relevances governing the religious sphere, such as efforts to communicate with or serve the holy, can issue in certain bodily movements or be elicited by them. For instance, one may assume bodily postures or light a candle to enhance private prayer or meditation. Likewise, Dahl (2010, 268, 277) suggests that religious festivals and worship are special sites for bodily movements and that they can express freedom, transgression, playfulness, gracefulness, and excess—in contrast with the restricted, hemmed-in, or frenetic movements of everyday life. Dahl (2010, 268) goes even further in this direction when he presents religious bodily movement in terms of "catharsis," and thereby links religious bodily movements with those of drama, a related province of meaning and one with which religion was closely conjoined among the Greeks. Dahl (2010, 303) further portrays religious movement as exhibiting an "active passivity" through communal, ritual physical performances that are, nevertheless, thought of not as seeking pragmatic mastery but instead as responding to a previous call from the transcendent and allowing it to be. Moreover, the intertwining of physical movement and ritual within the religious province of meaning contrasts with the independence from such bodily gestures that is typical of the theoretical sphere, which so easily dispenses with physical movement. This theoretical detachment from the physicality that pervades the provinces of everyday life and religious experience may reflect the distance between theory and both everyday life and religious experience apparent in the skepticism and disdain manifested by theoreticians toward those two provinces of meaning, as Dahl (2010, 277–268; cf. Barber 2017, 115–116) discusses. Dahl's

many thoughtful comments (Dahl 2010, 265–308) on worship elucidate characteristics that pertain to how Schutz (1962b, 232, 240–243) classifies the form of spontaneity in the province of religious experience.

Finally, one could also discuss how the last two features of the cognitive style of
the religious province of meaning emerge: sociality and temporality. For instance,
one could consider the liturgical or authoritative roles operant in religious experience or the freedom from everyday social roles that community members experience in the liminal rituals (e.g., rites of passage) researched by the anthropologist
Victor Turner (1970, 97) or the undoing of antagonisms through rituals examined by
René Girard (1979, 4, 12, 62–64, 77, 100–102, 127–128, 134, 145, 148, 266–267).
Furthermore, Dahl (2010, 297–298) himself hints at the possibility of temporal
transpositions occurring in ritual activity, as when communities experience ritual
reenactments of the Last Supper or the Jewish Passover in such a way that the events
commemorated are experienced *as present* in contrast to the merely private recollection of such events in memory *as past*.

One final way in which Dahl's work converges with Schutz's has to do with the
inescapability of natural language since, as part of Dahl's critique of the logic of
separation and his endeavor to locate the holy, the unfamiliar within the familiar, he
insists that the transcendental sphere is "contaminated by natural language" (Dahl
2010, 84). Citing Eugen Fink's paradoxical conclusion that transcendental insights
need to be communicated in ordinary language, Dahl finds similar tendencies in
Husserl's discussion of the *Heimwelt* (Husserl 1973b, 428–437, 627–631), whereas
according to Dahl both Habermas and Gadamer look to Wittgenstein to supplement
what they take to be Husserl's omissions (Dahl 2010, 82–87). But Schutz, who
himself takes seriously Fink's formulation of the paradox, presents a better phenomenological solution than turning to *Heimwelt*. At the end of "On Multiple Realities,"
Schutz argues that the whole paradox depends on conceiving finite provinces of
meaning as ontological static entities among which one can pass only through a
kind of "transmigration of the soul" comparable to metempsychosis (Schutz 1962b,
258). Instead, from within the transcendental sphere one remains "'in' the natural
attitude as a transcendental situation that is seen through" by the phenomenologist
(Schutz 1962b, 257). For Schutz, within a phenomenological perspective one can
still rely on natural language (seen through, though) from within the various finite
provinces of meaning that one inhabits. In light of this account, the fusion of the
province of religious experience with natural language would defy the bifurcation
produced by the logic of separation. Schutz affirms this fusion across diverse provinces of meaning when he writes (1962b, 258),

> If children play together in their make-believe world, if we discuss a work of art with a fel-
> low beholder, if we indulge with Others in the same ritual, we are still in the world of work-
> ing connected by communicative acts of working with the Other. And, nevertheless, both
> partners have leapt together from the finite province of meaning, called "world of everyday
> life," into the province of play, of art, or of religious symbols, etc. What formerly seemed to
> be a reality while attended to may now be measured by another yardstick and prove to be
> non-real or quasi-real; but this is so only under the specific form of a present non-reality,
> whose reality may be restored.

To conclude, Schutz is far from indulging in the logic of separation, and, properly understood, his work can accommodate, integrate, and preserve the many insights that Espen Dahl advances as he seeks to plumb the relevance of phenomenology to the experience of the holy.

References

Barber, Michael. 2017. *Religion and humor as emancipating provinces of meaning*. Dordrecht: Springer.

Bergson, Henri. 1920. *Mind-energy: Lectures and Essays*. Trans. H.W. Carr. New York: Henry Holt.

———. 1950. *Matter and Memory*. Trans. N.M. Paul and W.S. Palmer. London/New York: George Allen and Unwin, Ltd./The Macmillan Company.

Dahl, Espen. 2010. *Phenomenology and the holy: Religious experience after Husserl*. London: SCM Press.

Derrida, Jacques. 1978. Violence and metaphysics: An essay on the thought of Emmanuel Levinas. In *Writing and Difference*. Trans. A. Bass, 79–151. Chicago: University of Chicago Press.

Eliade, Mircea. 1961. *The Sacred and the Profane: The Nature of Religion*. Trans. W.R. Trask. New York: Harper Brothers.

Girard, René. 1979. *Violence and the Sacred*. Trans. P. Gregory. Baltimore/London: Johns Hopkins University Press.

Habermas, Jürgen. 1987. *The Theory of Communicative Action*. Vol. 2: *Lifeworld and System: A Critique of Functionalist Reason*. Trans. T. McCarthy. Boston: Beacon Press.

Husserl, Edmund. 1950. *Zur phänomenologischen Reduktion: Texte aus dem Nachlass (1926–1931)*. Ed. Sebastian Luft. Dordrecht: Kluwer.

———. 1960. *Cartesian Meditations: An Introduction to Phenomenology*. Trans. D. Cairns. The Hague: Martinus Nijhoff.

———. 1973a. *Experience and Judgment: Investigations in a Genealogy of Logic*. Ed. Ludwig Landgrebe. Trans. J.S. Churchill and Karl Ameriks. Evanston: Northwestern University Press.

———. 1973b. *Zur Phänomenologie der Intersubjektivität, Texte aus dem Nachlass, Dritter Teil: 1929–1935*. Ed. Iso Kern. The Hague: Martinus Nijhoff.

James, William. 1958. *The varieties of religious experience: A study in human nature*. New York: New American Library.

Jones, Edward, et al., eds. 1966. *The Jerusalem Bible*. Garden City: Doubleday.

Levinas, Emmanuel. 1979. *Totality and infinity: An essay in exteriority*. Trans. A. Lingis. The Hague: Martinus Nijhoff.

———. 1997. *Otherwise than being, or beyond essence*. Trans. A. Lingis. Pittsburgh: Duquesne University Press.

Scheler, Max. 1973. *Formalism in Ethics and Non-formal Ethics of Values*. Trans. M. Frings and R.L. Funk. Evanston: Northwestern University Press.

Schutz, Alfred. 1962a. Common-sense and scientific understanding of human action. In *Collected papers*, vol. 1, *The problem of social reality*, ed. M. Natanson, 3–47. The Hague: Martinus Nijhoff.

———. 1962b. On multiple realities. In *Collected papers*, vol. 1, *The problem of social reality*, ed. M. Natanson, 207–259. The Hague: Martinus Nijhoff.

———. 1962c. Symbol, reality and society. In *Collected papers*, vol. 1, *The problem of social reality*, ed. M. Natanson, 287–356. The Hague: Martinus Nijhoff.

———. 1964a. The homecomer. In *Collected papers*, vol. 2, *Studies in social theory*, ed. A. Brodersen, 106–119. The Hague: Martinus Nihoff.

————. 1964b. The stranger: An essay in social psychology. In *Collected papers*, vol. 2, *Studies in social theory*, ed. A. Brodersen, 91–105. The Hague: Martinus Nihoff.

————. 1964c. Tiresias; or, our knowledge of future events. In *Collected papers*, vol. 2, *Studies in social theory*, ed. A. Brodersen, 277–293. The Hague: Martinus Nihoff.

————. 1964d. The well-informed citizen: An essay on the social distribution of knowledge. In *Collected papers*, vol. 2, *Studies in social theory*, ed. A. Brodersen, 120–134. The Hague: Martinus Nihoff.

————. 1966. The problem of transcendental intersubjectivity in Husserl. In *Collected papers*, vol. 3, *Studies in phenomenological philosophy*, ed. I. Schutz, 51–91. The Hague: Martinus Nijhoff.

————. 1967. *The Phenomenology of the Social World*. Trans. G. Walsh and F. Lehnert. Evanston: Northwestern University Press.

————. 2011. Reflections on the problem of relevance. In *Collected papers*, vol. 5, *Phenomenology and the social sciences*, ed. Lester Embree, 93–199. Dordrecht: Springer.

Schutz, Alfred, and Thomas Luckmann. 1989. *The Structures of the Life-World*. Vol. 2. Trans. R.M. Zaner and D.J. Parent. Evanston: Northwestern University Press.

Turner, Victor. 1970. Betwixt and between: The liminal period in *rites de passage*. In *The forest of symbols: Aspects of Ndembu ritual*, 93–111. Ithaca/New York: Cornell University Press.

Michael Barber (Yale 1985) is Professor of Philosophy at St. Louis University. He is the author of 7 books and 80 articles, often focused on the phenomenology of the social world and published in such journals as *Human Studies, Open Theology*, and *Husserl Studies,* and in anthologies published by Oxford University Press and Routledge. His book *The Participating Citizen: A Biography of Alfred Schutz* (SUNY 2004) won the Ballard Prize in Phenomenology in 2007. His most recent book, *Religion and Humor as Emancipating Provinces of Meaning*, was published by Springer Press in 2017. He has held endowed chairs at St. Louis University and Seattle University. He has edited several collections of essays and original texts of Alfred Schutz (including, with Jochen Dreher, Schutz's writings on literature published as a volume in the *Alfred Schütz Werkausgabe*), served as the president of the Interdisciplinary Coalition of North American Phenomenologists, acts as editor-and-chief of the journal *Schutzian Research*, and reviews papers and books for various journals and presses. His current interests are the work of Alfred Schutz, phenomenology's connection to religion and humor, and philosophy and race.

Chapter 9
The Other as Trace of Infinity: Phenomenology and Religious Experience in the Thought of Emmanuel Levinas

Massimo Mezzanzanica

Abstract How does the phenomenological concept of phenomenon change if we consider an experiential scope such as the religious one, in which the dimension of invisible, of something that lies beyond the field of appearances, is essential? My contribution aims to discuss this question referring to the phenomenology of Emmanuel Levinas. In Levinas, philosophy and religion, though profoundly different, are closely interwoven. On the prephilosophical background of the Jewish religious experience, and in particular of the reading of the Bible, Levinas affirms the prevalence of ethics, understood as responsibility for the other, in relation to metaphysics. The experience of the other and of the expressiveness of his face is what makes it possible to break the totality of being and opens to the dimension of the infinite. In this sense, the "epiphany" of the other's face—that is, intersubjectivity—is the condition of the relationship with God. Thus, philosophy and the Bible find a common element in the fact that the former has the task of thinking the wholly Other from being and from logos. By preserving the mystery of the other's otherness and its singularity, the ethical relationship allows seeing in it a trace of God, the presence of infinity.

Keywords Emmanuel Levinas · Religious experience · Philosophy of religion · Phenomenology of the nonapparent · The face · Totality and infinity

In the language of the contemporary philosophy of religion, the expression "phenomenology of religion" usually means a descriptive approach to the religious phenomenon. Such an approach, moving from the forms assumed by religion in history and from the analysis of religion as "lived experience," seeks to highlight typical invariant structures and to understand the meaning of this experience for the life of

M. Mezzanzanica (✉)
Independent Scholar, Milan, Italy

© Springer Nature Switzerland AG 2019
O. Louchakova-Schwartz (ed.), *The Problem of Religious Experience*,
Contributions to Phenomenology 103,
https://doi.org/10.1007/978-3-030-21575-0_9

the human being.[1] As it seeks to to deal with the religious phenomenon starting from human experience, the phenomenology of religion develops instances already present in the analysis of religious experience proposed by authors such as Wilhelm Dilthey (1924, 1931), Henri Bergson (1932), and William James (1902). After Pierre Daniël Chantepie de la Saussaye, who in his *Lehrbuch der Religionsgeschichte* (1887–89) used for the first time the expression "phenomenology of religion," this approach was developed in different forms by scholars such as Gerardus van der Leeuw (1933), who sees in religion an expression of the significance of life and a manifestation of the tendency of the human power to transcend the limits of immanence toward the dimension of otherness, and Mircea Eliade (1965), who, considering religious phenomena as "hierophanies," tries to grasp the meaning of the experiences of *Homo religiosus* as an attempt to transcend the temporal dimension of life by coming into contact with the reality of the sacred. The phenomenology of religion is oriented toward a more philosophical sense, and less linked to the sphere of the history of religions, by Rudolf Otto, Max Scheler, and Martin Heidegger. At the center of religious experience, Otto (1917) places a dimension of the sacred, understood in light of the category of the numinous, in which a wholly other is a *mysterium tremendum* inducing a double movement of attraction and repulsion in a person. Scheler aims to capture the quality of the divine and the sacred, the *apriorische Wertidee* of the divine, which, in its independence from historical experience, must make possible an understanding of the nature of the human being (Scheler 1927). Further, Heidegger (2011) proposed a "phenomenology of religious life," interpreting the religious experience as a matrix that allows us to understand human life in its facticity, or in its fundamental characteristics of finitude, thrownness, and historicity.

The research in the phenomenology of religion leads to questioning the characteristics of what we call religious experience. What is the relationship between religious experience and everyday life, between religious experience and the natural and perceptual world in which it originates? Is it possible to speak about religious experience in phenomenological terms, of a specifically religious form of experience? For Husserl, every experience has an intentional character—that is, it refers to an object that is located within the horizon of the world. But how is that possible, and how can it be described, for the experience of the transcendent, which among its fundamental qualities seems to include that of not being reducible to an object of the world? And can the relationship with God be described in intentional terms: that is, as an intentional relationship? We meet here what van der Leeuw described as the antinomy of the phenomenology of religion: If phenomenon is "what shows itself" (*was sich zeigt*), and if religion is a revelation (*Offenbarung*) that, by its essence, is and remains hidden, how is it possible to practice phenomenology where there is no phenomenon (van der Leeuw 1933, 634)? To what extent does the study of religious experience as a lived experience, which is not limited to psychic and emotional data but brings us into a contact with otherness, require a modification of the Husserlian

---

[1]On the different phenomenological approaches to religion see Mancini 1986, 323–335, and Greisch 2002.

method of reduction? In this contribution I will try to discuss these issues with reference to the thought of Emmanuel Levinas, which, although being neither a descriptive phenomenology based on the history of religions nor a description of the eidetic structures of religious experience, has opened phenomenology to the analysis of forms of unintentional consciousness, and in particular to the relationship with the other, by developing concepts such as those of otherness, infinity, epiphany, justice, and transcendence, which show a structural analogy with theological concepts and can help to understand religious experience. As Levinas writes in *Totalité et infini* (1961), it is the relationship with the other human being that opens us to the dimension of the divine.

In the thought of Levinas, philosophy and religion, although profoundly different in themselves, are closely intertwined and placed in a relationship of mutual tension—an idea puzzling to many scholars. This relationship, more evident in Levinas's "Jewish" writings, also characterizes his more specifically philosophical works.[2] On the one hand, Levinas refuses to identify his philosophy with a theology and wants to keep both aspects of his work, the "confessional" and the "philosophical," distinct. On the other hand, he maintains that every philosophy develops from prephilosophical experiences that can also be religious experiences. In his case, the prephilosophical experience from which philosophy is born is Jewish religious experience, and in particular the reading of the Bible (Levinas 1987, 13–15). Drawing on this experience, but refusing to be categorized as a "Jewish thinker," a *penseur juif* (Levinas 1988b, 83), Levinas believes that there is no contradiction between Judaism and philosophy, or biblical logos and philosophical logos, since both have to do with the "apparition du sensé," the "recherche du sens" (Levinas 2006, 116), even if so in different forms, such as the Bible—in the form of the relationship with the neighbor (*prochain*)—and philosophy in the form defined by the Greek "reason." The Bible and the Greeks are the two basic components of European culture, and the former is not less important than the latter (Levinas 1988a, 155). If in the perspective of Greek philosophy, which sees in knowledge the spiritual act par excellence, the human is the one who seeks the truth, the Bible teaches that the human is the one who loves the neighbor and that loving one's own neighbor is a modality of life as fundamental as knowledge. Nevertheless, philosophy is Greek not only because of the origins of its language and its conceptuality but also because of its universalism: it transforms into a concept the instance of justice that arises in the singular relationship with the face of the other. In this sense, figuratively stated, Levinas aims to translate the Bible into Greek: that is, to interpret the ethical message of Judaism in the language of philosophy. Thus he attributes to Judaism a universal meaning by identifying the condition of the Jews with the condition of the human being as such, and universalizing, paradoxically, the particularism of Jewish

---

[2] On the distinction between Judaic, or confessional, and philosophical writings, see for example the interview with Levinas published with the title "Ethics of the Infinite" in Kearney 1995, 177–199. Although there may be a source of common inspiration, philosophical writings and Judaic writings are characterized, according to Levinas, by different exegetical methods and by different languages.

monotheism: "Une verité est universelle quand elle est ouverte à tous. Et dans ce sens, le judaïsme rattachant le divin au moral s'est toujours voulu universel (Levinas 1963, 38; see also Putnam 2002, 33–34). The basic intuition of morality consists for Levinas in the awareness of an asymmetrical relationship between the self and the Other, "à s'apercevoir que je ne suis pas l'égal d'autrui; … je me vois *obligé* à l'égard d'autrui et par conséquent je suis infiniment plus exigeant à l'égard de moi-même qu'à l'égard des autres" (Levinas 1963, 38). Thus, the election of Israel, its "position à part des nations" of which the Pentateuch speaks, is "un particularisme qui conditionne l'universalité," a "catégorie morale" endowed with universal value rather than the "fait historique d'Israël" (Levinas 1963, 39). In this sense, Jewish existence is the fulfillment of the human condition as fact, personhood, and free-dom, and "le Juif est l'entrée de l'événement religieux dans le monde; mieux encore, il est l'impossibilité même d'un monde sans religion" (Levinas 2002, 104).

In dealing with the theme of the Jewish background of Levinas's thought, it is important to specify that the Judaism to which he refers is the "Lithuanian" one of the *Mitnagdim*, which, in the context of Eastern European Judaism, needs to be distinguished from Hasidism, also an Eastern European form of Judaism, which is based on different principles and is a form of popular mysticism revived and revital-ized by Martin Buber (1963) in the twentieth century.[3] In this perspective, the essen-tial aspect of Judaism is constituted by the reading, the interpretation, and the commentary of the Hebrew texts and the Talmud in particular. The Talmud is not simply a continuation of the Bible. It tends to uncover a second layer of meaning, asking readers of the Bible to be critical and fully aware; in other words, the Talmud takes the meanings of the Bible in a rational spirit. From this point of view, Judaism requires and provokes a critical and hermeneutical attitude, aimed at highlighting new meanings of the biblical texts.

Referring to the teaching of Chouchani, whose influence on Levinas's life and thought is comparable to that of Husserl and Heidegger,[4] Levinas rejects any "accès dogmatique, purement fidéiste, ou même théologique, au Talmud," characterizing his own Talmudic comments as a "recherche de liberté" (Levinas 1968, 22). Consistent with the Levinasian view of religion as "religion for adults" ("une reli-gion d'adultes": Levinas 1963, 24), Judaism is characterized by Levinas as being at the same time a religion and a critique of religion and of the religious for its separa-tion from polytheistic religions and for its rejection of the forms of the divine and of the religious that can be traced back to the categories of the numinous and the sacred. For Levinas (1963, 43; see Davis 1996, 102), Judaism is at the same time a

---

[3] In this regard, we can remember, with the words of Colin Davis, that "although Levinas talks in general terms about Judaism, his description offers only an incomplete account of Jewish religious and intellectual practice. Even in the European context, his interpretation of Judaism is partial and tends to neglect the importance of other branches of Jewish faith" (Davis 1996, 103).

[4] Out of the ordinary, with legendary traits (even his real name is not certain), a Talmudist and a mathematician with a prodigious memory, Chouchani was also a teacher of Elie Wiesel, who emphasized Levinas's ability to translate the hermeneutic teaching of the master into the philo-sophical plane. See Malka 1994, 37. On the relationship between Levinas and Chouchani, see Wygoda 2002.

religion, a culture, and a sensibility, and at its core lies the triumph of monotheism over idolatry (Levinas 1963, 28–29):

> Pour le judaïsme, le but de l'éducation consiste à instituer un rapport entre l'homme et la sainteté de Dieu et à maintenir l'homme dans ce rapport. Mais tout son effort consiste à comprendre cette sainteté de Dieu dans un sens qui tranche sur la signification numineuse de ce terme. ... Le monothéisme juif n'exalte pas une puissance sacrée, un *numen* triomphant d'autres puissances numineuses, mais participant encore de leur vie clandestine et mystérieuse. Le Dieu des juifs n'est pas le survivant de dieux mythiques.

Earlier than Girard (1972), Levinas highlights a close link between the sacred and violence: "Le numineux ou le sacré enveloppe et transporte l'homme au-delà de ses pouvoirs et des ses vouloirs. ... Le sacré qui m'enveloppe et me transporte est violence" (Levinas 1963, 28–29). Its contraposition between the sacred (le sacré) and the holy (le saint) can be interpreted as the rejection of a false conception of the sacred, where the true sacred is holiness at the service of the Most High. (In this sense he criticizes magic as the degradation or desacralization of the sacred: Levinas 1977, 98–100). The Bible and the Talmud, like philosophy, have effects of disenchantment on the world and on religion, to the point of converging with atheism (Levinas 1963, 30):

> L'affirmation rigoureuse de l'indépendance humaine, de sa présence intelligente à une réalité intelligible, la destruction du concept numineux du sacré, comportent le risque de l'athéisme. Il doit être couru. À travers lui seulement l'homme s'élève à la notion spirituelle du Transcendent.

As noted by Edith Wyschogrod (1974, 97), the absolute of which Levinas speaks—the absolute that is encountered in the relationship with the other, or the infinite—does not coincide with the God of positive religions, because none of them is exempt from mystical participation. In Judaism, for Levinas, the subject is separated from the sacred, and the absolute is purged of sacred violence. It does not capture, but speaks (Levinas 1961, 49–50):

> Se rapporter à l'absolu en athée, c'est accueillir l'absolu epuré de la violence du sacré. Dans la dimension de hauteur où se présente sa sainteté—c'est-à-dire sa séparation—l'infini ne brûle pas les yeux qui se portent vers lui. Il parle, il n'a pas le format mythique impossible à affronter et qui tiendrait le moi dans ses filets invisibles. ... La transcendence se distingue d'une union avec le transcendent, par participation. La relation métaphysique—l'idée de l'infini—relie au noumène qui n'est pas un numen. Ce noumène se distingue du concept de Dieu que possèdent les croyants des religions positives, mal dégagés des liens de la participation et qui s'acceptent comme plongés, a leur insu, dans un mythe. L'idée de l'infini, la relation métaphysique est l'aube d'une humanité sans mythes.

From the Talmudic sources Levinas derives the emphasis on the unique character of the relationship with the other as an originally ethical experience. For Levinas, Judaism thinks of itself in terms of moral interiority, and not in terms of the relationship with the supernatural (Wyschogrod 1974, 160). By attributing to ethics and action a preeminent role with respect to faith, Jewish thought brings to light the ethical character of the lifeworld and attributes the same character to the relationship with the divine: "Le vrai, d'après le judaïsme, ne trouve de symbolisme fidèle qui le préserve de l'imagination que dans les attitudes pratiques, dans une Loi. ... La vision de Dieu est acte moral. Cette optique est une éthique" (Levinas 1963, 314). This Jewish cultural background influences the prevalence that Levinas attributes to ethics with respect to metaphysics, the centrality of ethics as the responsibility for the other that he opposes to the closure toward the other, or to his intellectual reduction, which in his opinion characterizes the history of the Western metaphysical tradition: "Nous appellons éthique une relation entre des termes où l'un et l'autre ne sont pas unis par une synthèse de l'entendement ni par la relation du sujet à l'objet et où cependant l'un pèse ou importe ou est signifiant à l'autre, où ils sont liés par une intrigue que le savoir ne saurait ni épuiser ni démêler" (Levinas 1967, 225, note 1).

For Levinas, philosophy, which in its history has constantly attributed a centrality to the concept of being against that of otherness, is an immanentism or "atheism" that reduces the Other to the Same and the infinite to the finite (Levinas 1967, 188):

> La philosophie occidentale coïncide avec le dévoilement de l'Autre où l'Autre, en se manifestant comme être, perd son altérité. La philosophie est atteinte, depuis son enfance, d'une horreur de l'Autre qui demeure autre, d'une insurmontable allergie. C'est pour cela qu'elle est essentiellement une philosophie de l'être, que la compréhension de l'être est son dernier mot et la structure fondamentale de l'homme. C'est pour cela aussi qu'elle devient philosophie de l'immanence e de l'autonomie, ou athéisme.

Levinas instead seeks to develop a thought that, while not claiming to end metaphysics or to stand outside it, is able to open itself to the dimension of otherness and of infinity, or of transcendence, without including them into being. This thought is expressed in categories that refer to religion, even if not understood in the sense of a positive religion. Thus, in the essay "Is Ontology Fundamental?", with allusion to Heidegger's thought, Levinas (1951) affirms that the relationship with others is not ontology and calls "religion" this link that is not reducible to representation but is "invocation," specifying, however, that he has not used either the word "God" or the word "sacred" in this connection. In the same essay Levinas characterizes the relationship with the other, which is preceded neither by representation nor by understanding, as "invocation" or "prayer," indicating that the essence of this invocation is "religion," but religion of a particular species, because it is born, as in Kant, within ethical relationships (Levinas 1991, 20).[5] Similarly, in *Totalité et infini*, he writes: "Nous proposons d'appeler religion le lien qui s'établit entre le Même et l'Autre, sans constituer une totalité," seeing in the human other (*Autrui*) "le lieu même de la vérité métaphysique et indispensable à mon rapport avec Dieu" (Levinas 1961, 10, 51). So, philosophy and religion are connected by the fact that philosophy has the task of thinking the "wholly Other" (Barth 1922) from being and from the logos, or transcendence. As stated in the interview "Sur la philosophie juive," published in *À l'heure des nations,* religion and philosophy are two distinct moments of the unique spiritual process that is the approach to transcendence, of the attempt to

---

[5] Jean Greisch sees in his attention to the phenomenon of prayer, understood as original thinking to the absent, the specific contribution of Levinas to the phenomenology of religion (Greisch 2002, 242–246). On the problem of prayer in Levinas's philosophy, see Rossi 2007.

approach, through the concept, a dimension that remains nonthematizable and non-objectifiable (Levinas 1988a, 204).

In *Totalité et infini* Levinas characterizes these two different attitudes of thought, the first directed toward being and totality, and the second open to the other and to infinity, respectively as ontology and metaphysics. If ontology remains into the horizon of the Same, metaphysics wants to abandon the horizon of the familiar world to move toward unknown distances, toward an alterity that is incommensurable and devoid of proportion with respect to everyday experience. This opposition is expressed in the two figures of Ulysses and Abraham: whereas the former, at the end of his adventures and his erring, returns home, the second, obeying a command of God, embarks on a journey without return. The other after whom metaphysics strives is therefore not the object of the satisfaction of a need but the unattainable term of an unbridgeable desire: it is the other in an absolute sense and must be thought of as transcendence, exterior to every totality or, in Platonic terms, as the Good.

This conception of the other presupposes a reinterpretation of the phenomenological method in which the discussion of the concept of intentionality of consciousness, the cornerstone of the Husserlian approach, is central. One can speak, in this regard, of a transformation of intentionality and of the sense of phenomenological constitution, which leads to a "defection" or "interruption" of phenomenology (Franck 2007; see Ferretti 2016, 51–52). The importance of the concept of intentionality consists for Levinas in the fact that it allows us to investigate the anonymous and unfelt horizons through which experience acquires its meaning. However, even if human consciousness in general has an intentional and representative character, intentionality is not always representation, and not every conscience is intentional consciousness. The concept of intentionality shows how the conscious actuality of thought is conditioned by potentiality, by a "vie anonyme et obscure," which should be returned to the intentional object that conscience believes to possess in its totality. Therefore, it makes necessary a "nouvelle ontologie" according to which "l'être se pose non pas seulement comme corrélatif d'une pensée, mais comme fondant déjà la pensée même qui, cependant, le constitue" (Levinas 1967, 130–131). While criticizing what he considers Husserl's intellectualism and theoreticism, Levinas claims his loyalty to the phenomenological method (1982, 140):

> Je pense que, malgré tout, ce que je fais, c'est de la phénoménologie, même s'il n'y a pas de réduction selon les règles exigées par Husserl, même si toute la méthodologie husserlienne n'est pas respectée. … La phénoménologie c'est n'est pas ériger les phénomènes en choses en soi; c'est ramener les *choses en soi* à l'horizon de leur apparaître, de leur phénoménalité, à faire apparaître l'apparaître lui même, derrière la quiddité qui apparaît, même si cet apparaître n'incruste pas ses modalités dans le sens qu'il livre à l'égard.

The fact that the dimension of objectifying acts in Husserl is prevalent does not exclude, as Husserl's own analysis of the constitution of intersubjectivity shows (Husserl 1950, 121–177), the possibility of a set of relations between the Same and the Other that is not objectivation but subjectivity, of an ethical *Sinngebung* that is no longer the work of a sovereign ego but is respectful of the Other (Levinas 1967, 135). According to Levinas, the other is given not as a matter for thought but as an enigma, which cannot be placed in the horizon of intentionality and is opaque to the intellect. In this sense, for Levinas, the immanent intentionality of knowledge must be overcome by the transcendent intentionality of the ethical relationship. The ethical consciousness is more original than intentionality, and the transcendent intentionality of ethics becomes the condition of truth itself. This critique of phenomenology, which however develops on the phenomenological terrain, is also directed against Heidegger, who in other respects strongly influenced Levinas. From Levinas's point of view, what is shared by Husserl and Heidegger is the fact of bringing the other to the same: in Husserl because the other is reduced to an object constituted in consciousness and intentioned in the noetic-noematic relationship, and so it is enclosed in the horizon of the ego; and in Heidegger because, despite the criticism of ontotheology and the affirmation of the difference between Being and beings, the other is locked up in the horizon of Being (Levinas 1967, 169–170):

> Quand il trace la voie d'accès à chaque singularité réelle à travers l'Être ... il nous conduit vers la singularité à travers un Neutre qui éclaire et commande la pensée et rend intelligible. ... La philosophie heideggerienne subordonne le rapport avec l'Autre à la relation avec le Neutre qu'est l'Être et, par là, elle continue à exalter la volonté de puissance dont Autrui seul peut ébranler la légitimité et troubler la bonne conscience.

According to Levinas, beyond the philosophy of being and the philosophy of consciousness, there is a form of experience that allows us to overcome the horizon of totality intended in a logical and ontological sense. If truth implies experience, and since experience means confrontation with an external reality, this takes us beyond our nature to something unknown, the authentic experience, the experience as such, which is the experience of the infinite, the experience of the encounter with the Other (Levinas 1961, xiii):

> Le rapport avec l'infini ne peut, certes, pas se dire en termes d'expérience—car l'infini déborde la pensée qui le pense. ... Mais si expérience signifie précisément relation avec l'absolument autre—c'est à dire avec ce qui toujours déborde la pensée—la relation avec l'infini accomplit l'expérience par excellence.

This experience is witnessed not only in religious tradition, but also in philosophy: with Plato, who places the Good above being, and especially in the Cartesian idea of the infinite, in which there is no coincidence between the *idea* and the *ideatum*, and in which therefore a form of peculiar intentionality manifests itself. This intentionality intends what it cannot embrace, since the infinite has no proportion with respect to the finitude of human beings. Because "ne se laisse pas réduire, sans reste, à l'acte de conscience d'un sujet, à la pure intentionalité thématisante," the idea of infinity "contiendrait plus qu'elle ne serait à même de contenir, plus que sa capacité de cogito," and so "penserait en quelque façon, au-delà de ce qu'elle pense" (Levinas 1982, 9–10). Levinas reinterprets this Cartesian concept, seeing it at work in the relationship with others, with the other human being, and describes this relationship starting from the analysis of desire. Thus, if "the idea of infinity is the social relationship," the intentionality of desire, as a desire of exteriority, of otherness, can never be fully satisfied, and its filling is essentially inadequate, since the other is not given in the form of a relationship between subject and object. The proximity of the other reminds me of my responsibility toward him and is an injunction to respond. The relationship with others is therefore an ethical relationship that constitutes me as a subject, the subject which is essentially a responsibility and *diakonia*, as stated in chapter 53 of Isaiah (Levinas 1967, 196). In this relationship the subject is not constituting, as in the Husserlian view (Husserl 1950, 99–120), but is constituted as passive and patient, disinterested in relation to world and selfishness, thus directing his desire beyond being, toward the Good. The thought of the subject is thought of the absolute, which is not achieved as a term, it is "pensée pensant plus qu'elle ne pense" (Levinas 1982, 116). In this sense, desire is the desire of the absolutely other and of the invisible, and can be characterized as metaphysical desire, since it opens to the dimension of transcendence, of an alterity that is irreducible to the ego and its world.

The relationship with the other is realized as "face-to-face" and in the form of "language" and "discourse." The other is concretely given as a face, which is expressiveness, nudity, noumenality, and singularity. The face is not a sign, because it does not refer to anything else but rather it means in itself. It is in the world, but it doesn't belong to the world: rather, it expresses itself in the sensible, but it is not of the order of the sensible, and therefore it subtracts itself from the power of the ego and from every attempt to grasp it through concepts. Its presence, which consists in coming toward me, is a visitation: "Alors que le phénomène est déjà image, manifestation captive de sa forme plastique et muette, l'épiphanie du visage est vivante. Sa vie consiste à défaire la forme où tout étant, quand il entre dans l'immanence, c'est-à-dire quand il s'expose comme thème, se dissimule déjà" (Levinas 1967, 194). The presence of the face consists in undressing the form in which it manifests, and its manifestation exceeds every form of the manifestation (Levinas 1967, 194). The face is paradoxically absence, invisibility, and transcendence, "défection de la phénoménalité" (Levinas 1974, 115). In this sense, the face is the "epiphany," a concept similar to that of a pure phenomenality that according to Heinrich Barth characterizes specifically how existence appears, so that in its appearance ("in Erscheinung treten") human existence escapes the presence.[6] The face does not exist as an entity that appears as a being in the world, and therefore is *reine Erscheinung*, which belongs to the dimension of a transcendence that is distinguished from an immanent, worldly form of human existence (Kerckhoven 2009, 18, 19). "Se manifester comme visage, c'est *s'imposer* par delà la forme, manifestée et purement phénoménale, se présenter d'une façon, irréductible à la manifestation, comme la droiture même du face à face, sans intermédiaire d'aucune image dans sa nudité, c'est à dire dans sa misère et dans sa faim" (Levinas 1961, 174). The expression of the face has no representative character but essentially an ethical one, because in its nudity the face expresses indigence and poverty, estrangement and misery, manifesting itself toward me as an appeal and a command, requiring an attitude of respect, listening

---

[6] According to Barth, existence, as *In-die-Erscheinung-treten,* is an entry of what is not in what is. Human beings are individuals to the extent that they enter in the *Erscheinung*, finding in this way its limitation, their boundary. It therefore realizes the aesthetic, not in the sense of beautiful appearance, nor of mere visibility, but as a visibility that is exposed in the act of *Selbst-Erscheinen* (Barth 1965, 118, 324; see Sepp 2010, 24).

and care, and constituting me as a responsible subject toward him. In this regard, Levinas states concisely: "l'épiphanie du visage est éthique" (Levinas 1961, 174).

Because the misery of the other is overturned in its superiority and priority toward me, and because of the appeal that the other addresses to my responsibility and my freedom, the relationship with it has an asymmetrical and nonreciprocal character, and it is therefore different from the relationship with the otherness that for Husserl is constituted in the transcendental subjectivity and leads to transcendental intersubjectivity. Levinas describes this asymmetry by affirming that the relationship with the other is located in a curved, asymmetric space in which the other is placed at a height greater than mine, "separate—or holy—face." Because of its elevation within this metaphorical space, the other takes on the meaning of God's trace: "Ce surplus de la vérité sur l'être et sur son idée que nous suggérons par la métaphore de 'courbure de l'espace intersubjectif', signifie l'intention divine de toute verité. Cette 'courbure de l'espace' est, peut-être, la présence même de Dieu" (Levinas 1961, 267). Therefore, it is starting from the phenomenology of interhuman ethical relations—and only from it—that a discourse on God can develop: "Il ne peut y avoir, separée de la relation avec les hommes, aucune 'connaissance' de Dieu. Autrui est le lieu même de la verité methaphysique et indispensable à mon rapport avec Dieu" (Levinas 1961, 51). And yet the transcendence of the ethical relationship is not the ultimate horizon of Levinas's perspective, which in ethics instead finds "la signification de l'au-delà, de la transcendence" (Levinas 1982, 114 n. 115), as he also states in one of the last conversations with Derrida, who in *Adieu à Emmanuel Lévinas* reports Levinas's words: "Vous savez, on parle souvent d'éthique pour décrire ce que je fais, mais ce qui m'intéresse au bout du compte, ce n'est pas l'éthique, pas seulement l'éthique, c'est le saint, la sainteté du saint" (Derrida 1997, 15).

The effort to speak of the saint must be considered in relation to the question, faced by Levinas in *Autrement qu'être ou au-delà de l'essence*, of thinking and bringing being to language in a different way from the ontological tradition, not in the sense of nonbeing but in the sense of its transcendence. From this point of view, it is a matter of finding a language which is capable of "dire la transcendance" (Levinas 1974, 23): that is, of bringing back the "said" (*le Dit*)—namely, the ontological language through which Western philosophy refers to realities and meanings that are intended as being in the world—to the original "Saying" (*le Dire*) that constitutes its condition.[7] Whereas Heidegger (1927, 25–26, 42) had criticized the

---

[7] Referring to Georg Misch's hermeneutical logic (Misch 1994), one could speak in this regard of an attempt to bring to the expression, through "evocative" concepts, what cannot be said in terms of the discursive language. According to Levinas, two examples of a language of this kind are offered by prayer and by the exclamation *me voici!* through which the subject responds to the call of the other. If the relationship with the other is language, prayer is for Levinas a fundamental form of saying that precedes the saying and lies in a certain sense at the origin of language: it does not name or designate something or someone; it is not predicative or apophantic language, but it is performative language, which constitutes the original capacity of signification. (See Thomassen 2017.) Levinas understands the exclamation *me voici!* "comme témoignage de l'Infini, mais comme témoignage qui ne thématise pas ce dont il témoigne et dont la vérité n'est pas vérité de

ontology of *Vorhandenheit* for its tendency to reduce being (*das Sein*) to beings (*das Seiende*), Levinas seems to refer to Heidegger's ontological difference, but aspiring, unlike Heidegger, to a thought capable of breaking the horizon of ontology. This implies a change in the way of thinking of God—an attempt to understand God beyond immanence, beyond totality, and beyond ontology: "Mais *entendre un Dieu non contaminé par l'être*, est une possibilité humaine non moins importante et non moins précaire que de *tirer l'être de l'oubli* où il serait tombé dans la metaphysique et dans l'ontothéologie" (Levinas 1974, x). This attempt is documented by the texts collected in *De Dieu qui vient à l'ideé*, which "exposent une recherche sur la possibilité—ou même sur le fait—d'entendre le mot Dieu comme un mot signifiant" (Levinas 1982, 7). The phenomenological approach consists here in reflecting on the meaning of the word "God," regardless of the problem of existence or nonexistence of God, of the decision about this alternative and about its meaning. All these aspects must be placed between brackets, suspended, in the phenomenological sense of the word. "Ce qui est recherché ici, c'est la concrétude phénoménologique dans laquelle cette signification pourrait signifier ou signifie, même si elle tranche sur toute phénoménalité" (Levinas 1982, 7). Thinking of God beyond ontology therefore means not thinking of God as an object constituted in consciousness or as a supreme entity, because ontological thinking, even when it takes the form of rational theology, is fundamentally "atheistic," since it recognizes only the dimension of the Same, denying the otherness and the transcendence.

However, this rejection of ontology does not lead Levinas to embrace negative theology, mysticism, or faith, since these perspectives, even when they define God in reference to what it is not, or even when they affirm the impossibility of defining it conceptually, in turn are placed in the horizon of ontology, as they understand God as being or presence. For Levinas, instead, it is a question of grasping a sense that is preliminary to being, of developing a discourse that should be neither ontology nor faith (Levinas 1982, 79–80). He also criticizes the concept of religious experience, considering that this experience remains within presence and immanence. In interpreting *Erlebnis* as experience, this point of view also means God in terms of being, presence, immanence (Levinas 1982, 102–103). For Levinas, on the contrary, the idea of God makes the thought explode; it cannot be absorbed; it breaks the intentional conscience, subtracting itself from the order of representation: "Dieu n'est pas simplement le 'premier autrui', ou 'autrui par excellence' ou l'"absolument autrui', mais autre qu'autrui, autre autrement, autre d'altérité préalable à l'altérité d'autrui ..., transcendant jusqu'à l'absence" (Levinas 1982, 115). God is not a theme, it is not an object, it is not a being, but it is the index of a dimension of meaning that exceeds the consciousness, of an exteriority with respect to the subject's being, thought, and experience, an idea that signifies according to a mode of signification prior to presence, which does not end in manifesting itself and does not

---

représentation, n'est pas évidence" (Levinas 1974, 186). Hilary Putnam has shown the affinity of the expression *me voici!* with the Hebrew *hineni,* which is a combination of the two components *hine* and *ni* (a contraction of the pronoun *ani,* "I"), where *hine* "performs the speech-act of calling attention to or *presenting,* not describing" (Putnam 2002, 37–38).

draw its meaning from it. In this radical otherness than being, presence, and what is familiar, God is not a you but a He who is separated, ab-solved, and to whom Levinas refers with the term "illeity" (from the Latin *ille*), which, through the reference to a third person, expresses the immensity, the immeasurable and infinite character of this absolute alterity that is subtracted from ontology (Levinas 1967, 199–202, 212–215).

Referring to Nietzsche, Levinas emphasizes that, as it is a visitation, the face comes from a beyond that is not a "world behind the world" but is an "*au-delà* du monde" (Levinas 1982, 225), in the sense that the world can be thought of only as being constituted by the ego, and the other transcends both the ego and the world. Speaking of the face means talking about an absence, where the absent is a nonbeing, the anarchic that precedes the *archē* of consciousness. The relationship with the other brings into play a different vision of time, understood not as a synchrony that takes place in the present but as a diachrony that breaks the synthesis of simultaneity. In fact, the injunction of responsibility that the subject receives from the other comes "d'un non-présent, d'un immémorial" (Levinas 1982, 117), "un passé absolument révolu" (Levinas 1967, 200). Therefore, the face is not an object among other objects that refer to the horizon of the world, and its meaning is not that of a sign that connects the signified and the signifier. It is instead a relationship with an absence that is not revelation or dissimulation but signifies in the face as a trace (Levinas 1967, 200–201). Whereas the sign has the function of indicating an object by inserting itself in the order of the world, the signification of the trace does not fall into the dimension of appearing and does not intend to communicate. This situation takes place in the case of a letter, which, beyond the meaning of words and sentences that it composes, is the trace of an absence for those who receive it. As it is linked to an absence, the trace thus opens to transcendence: "La trace signifie audelà de l'être" (Levinas 1967, 198). It corresponds to the dimension of *illeity,* as the passage to an immemorial and irreversible past, and the presence of what has never been present and what, in its height and superiority, can be characterized as "divinité" (Levinas 1967, 200–201). Illeity is not a prototype of which the face would be the image; but on the contrary, being in the image of God means being in its trace. This, once again, means that going toward God—the revealed God of the Judeo-Christian tradition that, as in chapter 33 of Exodus, shows itself only through its trace—"n'est pas suivre cette trace qui n'est pas un signe, c'est aller vers les Autres qui se tiennent dans la trace" (Levinas 1967, 202).

If theology, transforming the traces into signs, makes them thematic and objective, trying to enclose the infinite in a conceptual system, then the prophetic language, which disposes only of its voice, of its gestures, and of its saying (a saying that it is goodness, rectitude, and dedication to the other), is able to correspond to the constitutively allusive, noncogent character of the trace, offering an ambiguous and uncertain manifestation of transcendence (Strasser 1987, 249, 251), which can also be indicated through the notion of "enigma," as opposed to that of phenomenon, and understood as "façon de se manifester sans se manifester" (Levinas 1967, 209; see Ferretti 2016, 66). On the other hand, in the perspective of a "phenomenology" of time (Levinas himself puts the word in quotation marks, as here), the reality of God can also be expressed in terms of the future. To think of time starting from the Other means to attribute to it the meaning (assuming that, specifies Levinas, one can speak of meaning where there is no intentionality) of "attente patiente de Dieu, patience de la dé-mesure (un à-Dieu, comme je m'exprime maintenant); mais attente sans attendu"[8] (Levinas 1982, 151), as happens in the "passive synthesis" of time, in aging, an event that is independent of the activity of the subject, where time has the meaning of awaiting what is ungraspable, and therefore is "question, recherche, demande et prière" (Levinas 1982, 88). This deformalization of the concept of time, the origin of which he traces in Bergson, Rosenzweig, and Heidegger, opens according to Levinas the need of thinking the time "dans la dévotion d'une théologie sans théodicée": that is, as a "religion qu'il est certes impossible de proposer à autrui et, par conséquent, impossible de prêcher" (Levinas 1991, 183).

References

Barth, K. 1922. *Der Römerbrief*. Munich: Kaiser.
Barth, H. 1965. *Erkenntnis der Existenz: Grundlinien einer philosophischen Systematik*. Basel: Schwabe.
Bergson, H. 1932. *Les deux sources de la morale et de la religion*. Paris: PUF.
Buber, M. 1963. *Werke*, Bd. 3: *Schriften zum Chassidismus*. Munich/Heidelberg: Kösel/Lampert Schneider.
Chantepie de la Saussaye, P. D. 1887–89. *Lehrbuch der Religionsgeschichte*. 2 vols. Freiburg i.Br.: Mohr (Siebeck).
Davis, C. 1996. *Levinas: An introduction*. Cambridge: Polity Press.
Derrida, J. 1997. *Adieu à Emmanuel Lévinas*. Paris: Galilée.
Dilthey, W. 1924. *Das Problem der Religion*. In *Gesammelte Schriften*, Bd. VI, *Die geistige Welt: Einleitung in die Philosophie des Lebens II*, ed. Georg Misch, 288–305. Leipzig: Teubner.
———. 1931. *Die Typen der Weltanschauung und ihre Ausbildung in den metaphysischen Systemen*. In *Gesammelte Schriften*, Bd. VIII, *Weltanschauungslehre: Abhandlungen zur Philosophie der Philosophie*, ed. Bernhard Groethuysen, 73–118. Leipzig: Teubner.
Eliade, M. 1965. *Le sacré et le profane*. Paris: Gallimard.
Ferretti, G. 2016. *Emmanuel Levinas: Un profilo e quattro temi teologici*. Brescia: Queriniana.
Franck, D. 2007. La défection de la phénoménologie. In P. Fontaine, and A. Simhon (Eds.), *Emmanuel Levinas: Phénoménologie, éthique, esthétique et herméneutique*. Argenteuil: Le Cercle Herméneutique: 17–25.
Girard, R. 1972. *La violence et le sacré*. Paris: Grasset.
Greisch, J. 2002. *Le buisson ardent et les lumières de la raison: L'invention de la philosophie de la religion*. Vol. 2, *Les approches phénoménologiques et analytiques*. Paris: Les Éditons du Cerf.
Heidegger, M. 1927. *Sein und Zeit*. Tübingen: Niemeyer.
———. 2011. Einleitung in die Phänomenologie der Religion (Frühe freiburger Vorlesung Wintersemester 1920/21). In *Gesamtausgabe*, Bd. 60, Abteilung 2, *Vorlesungen 1919–1944:*

---

[8] Quoting these words from Levinas at the end of *Adieu*, Derrida emphasizes that the à-Dieu is the experience of "avoir accueilli ce oui de l'autre, saluer cet infini dans la separation, autrement dit dans sa sainteté," where the separation is that of the irreducible otherness of the other and where the sanctity coincides with the infinite responsibility to which the subject is called by the other (Derrida 1997, 110–111).

Phänomenologie des religiösen Lebens, ed. Matthias Jung, Thomas Regehly, and Claudius Strube, 1–156. Frankfurt a.M.: Klostermann.

Husserl, E. 1950. *Cartesianische Meditationen*. In *Husserliana*, Bd. I: *Cartesianische Meditationen und Pariser Vorträge*, ed. S. Strasser. The Hague: M. Nijhoff.

James, W. 1902. *The varieties of religious experience: A study in human nature. Being the Gifford lectures on natural religion delivered at Edinburgh in 1901–1902*. New York/London/Bombay: Longmans, Green & Co.

Kearney, R. 1995. *States of mind: Dialogues with contemporary thinkers on the European mind*. Manchester: Manchester University Press.

Levinas, E. 1951. L'ontologie est-elle fondamentale? *Revue de Métaphysique et de Morale* 56 (1): 88–98.

———. 1961. *Totalité et infini: Essai sur l'exteriorité*. The Hague: M. Nijhoff.

———. 1963. *Difficile liberté: Essais sur le judaïsme*. Paris: Albin Michel.

———. 1967. *En découvrant l'existence avec Husserl et Heidegger*. Paris: Vrin.

———. 1968. *Quatre lectures talmudiques*. Paris, Les Éditions de Minuit.

———. 1974. *Autrement qu'être ou au-delà de l'essence*. The Hague: M. Nijhoff.

———. 1977. *Du sacré au saint: Cinq nouvelles lectures talmudiques*. Paris: Les Éditions de Minuit.

———. 1982. *De Dieu qui vient à l'idée*. Paris: Vrin.

———. 1987. *Ethique et infini: Dialogues avec Philippe Nemo*. Paris: Fayard.

———. 1988a. *À l'heure des nations*. Paris: Les Éditions de Minuit.

———. 1988b. *Autrement que savoir*. Paris: Osiris.

———. 1991. *Entre nous: Essais sur le penser-à-l'autre*. Paris: Grasset et Fasquelle.

———. 2002. Être juif (1947). *Cahiers d'Études Lévinassiennes* 1: 99–106.

———. 2006. L'asymétrie du visage: Interview d'Emmanuel Lévinas avec France Guwy pour la télévision néerlandaise (1986). *Cités* 25: 116–124.

Malka, S. 1994. *Monsieur Chouchani: L'énigme d'un maître du XXe siècle*. Paris: J.C. Lattes.

Mancini, I. 1986. *Filosofia della religione*. Genoa: Marietti.

Misch, G. 1994. *Der Aufbau der Logik auf dem Boden der Philosophie des Lebens: Göttinger Vorlesungen über Logik und Einleitung in die Theorie des Wissens*. Ed. G. Kühne-Bertram and F. Rodi. Freiburg i.Br./Munich: K. Alber.

Otto, R. 1917. *Das Heilige: Über das Irrationale in der Idee des Göttlichen und sein Verhältnis zum Rationalen*. Breslau: Trewendt & Granier.

Putnam, H. 2002. Levinas and Judaism. In S. Critchley, and R. Bernasconi, *The Cambridge companion to Levinas*. Cambridge: Cambridge University Press: 33–62.

Rossi, F. 2007. *Il problema filosofico della preghiera in Emmanuel Lévinas*. Milan: Franco Angeli.

Scheler, M. 1927. *Der Formalismus in der Ethik und die materiale Wertethik*. Halle: Niemeyer.

Sepp, H.R. 2010. Heinrich Barth und die Phänomenologie. In H.R. Sepp, and A. Wildermuth (Eds.), *Konzepte des Phänomenalen: Heinrich Barth—Eugen Fink—Jan Patočka*. Würzburg: Königshausen & Neumann: 22–33.

Strasser, S. 1987. Emmanuel Levinas: Ethik als erste Philosophie. In B. Waldenfels, *Phänomenologie in Frankreich*. Frankfurt a.M.: Suhrkamp: 218–265.

Thomassen, M. 2017. *Traces de Dieu dans la philosophie d'Emmanuel Lévinas*. Paris: Les Éditons du Cerf.

van der Leeuw, G. 1933. *Phänomenologie der Religion*. Tübingen: Mohr.

van Kerckhoven, G. 2009. *Epiphanie: Reine Erscheinung und Ethos ohne Kategorie*. Bielefeld: Transcript Verlag.

Wygoda, S. 2002. Le maître et son disciple: Chouchani et Lévinas. *Cahiers d'Études Lévinassiens* 1: 149–183.

Wyschogrod, E. 1974. *Emmanuel Levinas: The problem of ethical metaphysics*. The Hague: M. Nijhoff.

Massimo Mezzanzanica (Milan, 1960) studied Philosophy at the State University of Milan. He received a PhD in Philosophy in 1996 in Turin. In 2013 he received a second PhD in Philosophy of Social Sciences and Symbolic Communication at the Insubria University of Varese and Como. He teaches Philosophy and History in a secondary school in Milan. He is founding member and belongs to the editorial board of the *Magazzino di Filosofia*. His research interests include hermeneutics, phenomenology, philosophy of culture, political philosophy, philosophical anthropology, theories of symbolism and of imagination, philosophical translation. Along with numerous articles in scientific journals, he has published the books: *Georg Misch. Dalla filosofia della vita alla logica ermeneutica* (FrancoAngeli, Milano 2001), *Dilthey filosofo dell'esperienza. Critica della ragione storica: vita, struttura e significatività* (FrancoAngeli, Milano 2006), *Von Dilthey zu Levinas. Wege im Zwischenbereich von Lebensphilosophie, Neukantianismus und Phänomenologie* (Verlag Traugott Bautz, Nordhausen 2012).

Chapter 10
Towards a Phenomenology of Resurrection and of Ghosts

Peter Costello

Abstract In this paper, I work to situate the reading and writing that constitute a phenomenology of religion, especially with respect to the stories of the Resurrection of Jesus. First, I use the descriptions of lived embodiment by Husserl in *Cartesian Meditations* (1970) and by Merleau-Ponty in *The Visible and the Invisible* (1968) in order to inaugurate a phenomenological reading of the Resurrection of Jesus by the Gospel authors Luke and John. Then I use Jacques Derrida's *Specters of Marx* (1994) and John Caputo's "Bodies Still Unrisen, Events Still Unsaid" (2007) to account for the deeper phenomenological problem of how to distinguish the uniqueness of the Resurrection from that of the reappearance of a ghost. Finally, in light of the literary and conceptual analyses of the first two sections, I establish the method of a phenomenology of religion as a peculiar kind of *epoché,* an *epoché* of "obvious" political moves within a religious attitude, that allows us to practice a relation with the text not simply as literary or as conceptual but as the *conscience* of a community. Ultimately, the paper works to describe the Resurrection of Jesus as an event that pushes toward the very practice of textuality within the communities to come.

Keywords Husserl · Merleau-Ponty · Derrida · Caputo · Resurrection · Hauntology

In the Gospel of Luke, the risen Jesus appears to the Apostles and invites them to experience the difference between his risen body and a ghost: "Touch me and see for yourselves; a ghost has no flesh and bones as you can see I have" (Luke 24:39–41).[1] Jesus is no ghost, it would seem, because the disciples can (still) touch him. He

---

[1] All references to biblical texts in this paper are from *The New Oxford Annotated Bible*, 3rd edition (Coogan 2001).

P. Costello (✉)
Philosophy, Providence College, Providence, RI, USA
e-mail: pcostell@providence.edu

© Springer Nature Switzerland AG 2019　　　　　　　　　　　　　　　　159
O. Louchakova-Schwartz (ed.), *The Problem of Religious Experience*,
Contributions to Phenomenology 103,
https://doi.org/10.1007/978-3-030-21575-0_10

is no ghost because he (still) has something essential in common with their lived bodies.

In John's Gospel, however, the account of Jesus's resurrected body develops not only its essential commonality with but also its distinction from the lived body. In fact, in Jesus's first conversation as resurrected with a disciple, he gives this strange admonition to his interlocutor, Mary Magdalene: "Do not hold on to to me" (John 20:17). Such a stark contrast with the invitation to touch his "flesh and bones" in Luke! Indeed, one cannot help but hear in this admonition of Jesus that the lived body, or at least Mary's body, though she *can* touch the resurrected body, needs to recognize some particular limits. Mary, we, do *not,* or do not *yet,* have full access to Jesus's resurrected embodiment.

Not only does Jesus's prohibition to Mary appear to clash with his invitation in Luke's Gospel. But it also feels out of joint given Jesus's subsequent invitation to Thomas in the Gospel of John: "[p]ut your finger here; look, here are my hands. Give me your hand; put it into my side" (John 20:27). However, at least in John's Gospel, this apparent disjunction is clarified when Jesus remonstrates with touching Thomas on behalf of those *who will not have been able to touch* his resurrected body. One may even say that it seems to be on behalf of Mary, then, or people like her, people who would touch Jesus's resurrected body but are prevented from doing so, that the touch of Thomas is something Jesus spoils by inducing him to feel guilt.

Jesus's treatment of Thomas's desire to probe his wounds, however, is not the final or even the most curious development of the relation between resurrected and lived bodies. For after remonstrating with Thomas, Jesus discusses with Peter the status of the lived body of the Gospel's author. And in what can be read, I believe, as a reflexive account of the Gospel's own textuality, the risen Jesus declares to Peter that John himself, the author of the text, may very well "stay behind till I come" (John 21:20–23).

All this raises important questions for a phenomenology of religion: How is a contemporary reader of the Gospels to translate the appearance of Jesus's resurrected body for the sake of her own lived-bodily experience? And what is the reader to make of the way he, Jesus, engages, *as resurrected*, in an ontology of the text as such and in a hermeneutics of the tradition of texts that the disciples have a history with? It is in order to begin to pose and to answer these questions anew that I offer this essay in a phenomenology of the resurrected body.

My main point will be this: Resurrection is an event presented in the Gospels as the origin and foundation of the fleshly essence of textuality. The Word, as John says in the beginning of his Gospel, "became flesh and lived among us" (John 1:14). But Jesus's departing flesh then, through the Resurrection, becomes word again, and lives among our lived bodies in a new way that allows the word and us to have a new significance, a new bodily life within the communities of believers who take up the word, speak it with their breath, and write it with their hands.[2]

[2] This article is dedicated to my aunt, Mary Costello, whose support for my writing and for my life commitments has been truly loving. My deep gratitude also goes to my friend and colleague Christopher Arroyo for reading an earlier version of this paper and for giving very helpful, con-

My way of taking up Jesus's Resurrection will thus take seriously and echo an important argument of Jean-Luc Nancy in *Noli Me Tangere*. There, Nancy claims that Jesus's Resurrection is "the fading of the divine presences that ensured the homogeneous unity of the world" (2008, 47). And it is in the fading of Jesus, Nancy argues, that "Mary Magdalene thus *becomes* the body of the departed" (2008, 48; my emphasis). Resurrection, in other words, is for both Nancy and for myself the departure of God within and *for the sake of* the practice of phenomenological inter-pretation and writing of the communities to-come. The Resurrection is the dispersal of itself—it is breath, in-spiration—into the textual, bodily life of evolving com-munities of interpreters, of communities of the book(s).

The argument I present in this paper linking resurrection with bodily life, touch-ing, and textuality will now proceed in five main parts. First, I will examine Husserl's description of pairing in *Cartesian Meditations* and Merleau-Ponty's description of flesh in "The Intertwining—The Chiasm." Then, reading pairing and flesh together as stages in a phenomenology of embodiment, I will use the texts of Husserl and Merleau-Ponty to unpack the intimate relationship—the invitations, touching, and interpretation—that the resurrected Jesus offers in Luke's Gospel. Third, I will examine John Caputo's description of the Resurrection in "Bodies Still Unrisen, Events Still Unsaid" (2007) and Derrida's description of hauntology in *Specters of Marx* (1994) in order to show how the Gospels' presentation of Jesus's resurrected body serves as a third term relating ghost and lived body, textuality, and lived expe-rience. Then I will use the texts of Caputo and Derrida to interpret further passages in both the Gospel of Luke and the Gospel of John, focusing on the prohibition to Mary, the guilt of Thomas, and the sharing of resurrection through textuality. And, finally, I will offer a concluding development of my main point—namely that the Resurrection is an event that inspires the creation of textual communities that both touch and internalize the divine in the flesh.

10.1 Phenomenology of the Body: Pairing and Flesh

In his fifth Cartesian Meditation, Husserl describes one's own lived body as the catalyst for the phenomenological description of our experience of other persons. Following his introduction of the *epoché,* and the further inauguration of a thought experiment that Husserl calls the "reduction to the sphere of ownness," the phenom-enologist leaves himself only with self-experience as a way toward the methodical description of the experience of other persons.[3] However, within that experimental

---

structive feedback.

[3] From the beginning of Husserl's fifth Cartesian Meditation: "What is especially peculiar to me as ego … with an exclusive ownness, includes every intentionality and therefore, in particular, the intentionality directed to what is other; but, for reasons of method, the synthetic effect of such intentionality (the actuality for me of what is other) shall at first remain excluded from the theme" (1970, 94).

reduction, what Husserl finds is that the lived body does indeed generate ongoing meaning for itself, does assert its fleshly primacy for phenomenological method. From within the experience of the body we do in fact reach the experience of the other person.

And where, primarily, is the lived body's initial contribution to phenomenological method? Husserl's stated answer: in the lived body's being "reflexively related to itself" (1970, 97) *through its hands.*[4]

Within the sphere of our own self-reduced meaning, then, we discover reflexivity by means of how our hands touch each other. And so Husserl invites us to take one of our hands, the one that is now being lived as the dominant or touching hand, and prove our reflexivity to ourselves. He invites us to convert the other hand, or the eye or any other organ, previously also active and perceiving, into a touched object: "That [the body's reflexive self-relation] *becomes possible* because I 'can' perceive one hand 'by means of' the other, an eye by means of a hand, and so forth—a procedure in which the functioning organ *must* become an object and the object a functioning organ" (1970, 97; my emphasis). There are two important items to note here: first, the body's reflexivity, its wholeness, *depends*—it "becomes possible"—by means of the hands' own activity upon each other and upon whole sensory fields. And second, the touched hand, or eye, retains its organic status by means of its compulsion to—it "must"—turn back into a "functioning organ."

By means of the example of the body's self-touching, then, Husserl invites us to pay attention to the latent reciprocity of the second organ: the touched hand, for instance. Certainly as the hand that is touched, it has been converted in some sense into an object by the first, touching, hand. And yet, for all its new experience of passivity, the touched hand retains a ghost of its activity. And thus the second hand "must" be uneasy in its conversion to objectivity—we can feel this for ourselves. Thus the touched hand remains a hand; at any moment it must be able to propel itself back to its self-dominance, to its act of perceiving. This imperative is constant and can happen at almost any time, so long as the touched hand is not injured or removed. And thus the reverse of the process of touching is always on the (momentarily deferred) horizon.

But how does this imperative to our organs, to our hands, come to be? We are not sure exactly; however, we do know that this imperative can originate only from *beyond* the hands, across or *as* the *whole* of the lived body that situates the pair. Even so, however, it remains for us to consider how the pair of hands, given by means of the whole, simultaneously develop that very whole from which their imperative comes. A gift of the whole body, the hands are still the very coming-to-be of the whole and of their own actual transition into and out of objectivity and subjectivity.[5]

---

[4] Donn Welton in "Soft, Smooth Hands," explains that "thus there is a circuit running not only between the world and the lived body, but also between the lived body and itself. In this circuit there is a doubling of touch: the touching is touched and the touched is touching. There seems to be a blending of what is felt and what is perceived, such that I *come to perceive* the lived body *as it is feeling*" (1999, 46).

[5] Alia Al-Saji argues, in her analysis of Husserl's phenomenology of touch, that "not only does the

This mutual implication—the pair in the whole and the whole in the pair—is a central piece of lived evidence of the character of the lived body as self-surpassing.[6] And it is by this mutual implication, by this self-surpassing that is reflexivity, that both the body itself and the phenomenologist move forward to the experience and the description of other people. Or, to say this another way: it is by means of the implied logic of whole and parts within the process by which an organ becomes an object and also must at any moment turn itself back into an organ, that Husserl then moves on to describe the body *as a whole* in its relationship of what he calls *pairing* with other lived bodies.[7]

The other appears to me there in the flesh—this is the first indication of our pairing. But when and as the person appears within my sphere of perception, I find that she has always already enlisted the sense of my whole body, albeit without my awareness or acknowledgment. This is how pairing grounds itself in and brings to light a kind of prehistory.

To be given to me in my lived experience as another person is for the other to have paired with me. She has always already, in Husserl's terminology, "transferred" the sense of my whole body, my power as a whole life, from me: "as a result of this overlaying, there takes place in the paired data a *mutual transfer* of sense—that is to say: an apperception of each according to the sense of the other" (1970, 113; my emphasis).

To experience the other is to be, in some sense, touched by her. It is to recognize that I have already participated in a transfer to her of the sense of my own body, that I have already been situated by a whole of which I am a part, and that I have already taken on a role similar to that of my own touched hand. To pair is to experience something supraorganic between myself and the other that directs me. It is to live out of a prehistory in which each of us has already passively granted to the other what it means to be a body as lived.

The mutual pairing that implicates us is something that touches us at the core. For the other appears on her own terms, even if I am paired with her. And she cannot be, as a simple object may be, the appearance of a simple index of my noetic acts. Her appearance excludes my interpretation of her as simply an object, since, just as

---

touching right hand feel itself to be sensing and living, but the touched left hand appears as *Leib* and *feels itself to be such*" (2010, 20; my emphasis).

[6] See John Russon's *Bearing Witness to Epiphany*: "This is the character of the body as a whole: the body is a material specificity, but a specificity the very nature of which is to open up—open ourselves up—to what is beyond it. The body's powers are powers of self-transcending, of opening, of learning" (2009, 31).

[7] Husserl further defines pairing as "a primal form of passive synthesis which we designate as 'association' in contrast to passive synthesis of 'identification'" (1970, 112). What is paired does not come to identity, to the explicit recognition of the same thing. Rather, the pair remains associated and thus preserves the differences between the pair. Pairing as association also, Husserl says, occurs as "an intentional overreaching" (1970, 112) and "a living mutual awakening and an overlaying of each with the objective sense of the other" (1970, 113). It is this "mutuality" that I highlight in *Layers in Husserl's Phenomenology: On Meaning and Intersubjectivity* (2012): see especially Chaps. 2 and 3.

my touched hand, I can touch her, as John Russon says in *Human Experience*, only "with her help" (2003, 54).

At the very instant of our pairing, then, our whole bodies are open to the act of being heard, touched, and seen by each other. This is because what is paired with the other person is not one organ at a time, not one word at a time, but the whole of each lived body, the whole of one's linguistic or perceptual activity as such. My pairing with another person thereby performs what my own hands, being limited to touching one space or one organ at a time, could not. That is, my pairing with another entails an *immediate* pairing of my whole self, my whole experience of my body and of hers, such that we are given to experience, in our pairing, the entirety of our bodily reflexivity *as a whole*.[8]

And thus, in light of the immediacy and continuous nature of pairing with other people, we discover something new: we find ourselves neither on this side of an object nor as simply copied over there but rather as already under way, embarking on a shared journey that brings up our reflexivity as a whole precisely in order to create a meaningful shared life. Such a pairing, such a journey, is both itself a shared whole (we may call pairing the event of our intercorporeality or intersubjectivity) and immediately able to be differentiated, as my hands were, into active and a passive members and roles. For the pairing cannot on its own fully concretize our reflexivity. The concretion of pairing happens only in our acting through and by means of it.

Based on our pairing, on our shared nature, then, we place ourselves within the sense of bodily life as something shared and only *thereby* differentiated. However, we also see that each one's paired bodily life at the same time preserves its sense of its ownness by means of a liminal difference. For however much we are given as always already together, as paired by means of a mutual "transfer," we are also always already separated.

And this separation occurs because our paired life together, as the whole that it is, in each case is a *subjunctive* pairing: the other person's appearance "awakens reproductively another, an immediately similar appearance included in the system constitutive of my animate organism as a body in space. It brings to mind the way my body would be like '*if I were there*'" (Husserl 1970, 118; my emphasis).

By means of pairing, I perceive the other person *as if I were there*, though in my own experience I am not (and cannot be) there but here. And likewise I perceive that she perceives me, though she also cannot be, *as if she were here* where I am. This subjunctive mood of bodily life together—this "as if" that gives a limit to each of us within the pairing that can never be simple and total—is a tension, almost a contradiction. However, as such a tension, this subjunctive pairing is also productive.

The other can gaze at me or touch me and thereby turn me, almost, into her object. But I can also turn my gaze or my touch back onto he, and do the same. And in doing this, in maintaining our reciprocity and our power within our approaches to

---

[8] Husserl claims that "the first-awakened manner of appearance of my body is not the only thing that enters into a pairing: *my body itself* does so likewise; as the *synthetic unity* pertaining to this mode, and the many other familiar modes of its appearance" (1970, 118; my emphasis).

each other, we can converse, share, learn more about each other and ourselves. For what the subjunctive mood of our pairing gives us, a mood that we necessarily adopt, whether in intimacy or conflict, is the fact that our shared bodily space together is always open to further determination from both sides and thus always fundamentally at issue.

In the area in which we exist as bodies paired together, in that place or mood or relation between active and passive, lies the possibility of lived experience gathering momentum, forming a history, tracing a trajectory. Our shared place becomes—it has always already been—a shared project. It is this subjunctivity that allows for further differentiation and development of our subjectivity, of what the other person and I mean to each other.

Like hands, then, whole bodies learn to direct the course of the life that they both inaugurate and participate in. Like hands, neither one will ever master the whole that the other presents, since it is the whole that their otherness forms *with us* that gives us the very possibility of taking them up and working with them in the first place.

If, by means of our perception of each other, we then actively participate in and develop the pairing, if we decisively intertwine and form a community, for example—then this is only because (and insofar as) there is always more work to do to. There is always a reply on the horizon, always a redefinition of roles that will come—we are certain—but we know not when. And thus there is, out of pairing as subjunctive, always more to concretize or direct.

In a community, to continue the example, we often perceive one of us coming to the fore and leading, the other moving to the background and following. But this is only because it could always be otherwise. For the fragility and power of a community lies in the way that it takes to heart (or does not do so) the remarkable, latent, and ever-present possibility that, at any moment, a leader can *and must* turn into a disciple, and a disciple can *and must* become a leader. A community, then, like a lived body, discovers itself by means of its members and their unease with ever being just an object or just an organ. When Merleau-Ponty discusses flesh in "The Intertwining—The Chiasm," he extends Husserl's description of pairing, I argue, to things within the world.[9] Other lived bodies are not the only items in the world to pair with my lived body. Colors, textures, objects do as well. There is, Merleau-Ponty claims, "a flesh of things" that is "no analogy" with my own flesh but "must be taken literally" (1968, 133).

This extension of pairing to things occurs because, for Merleau-Ponty, "the thickness of flesh between the seer and the thing is constitutive for the thing of its visibility as for the seer of his corporeity; it is not an obstacle between them, it is the means of communication" (1968, 135). This means, then, that flesh, not the lived body, is the fundamental element of lived experience. The lived body is flesh concretized and already differentiated into an organ of a larger, passive embodiment. And thus flesh expresses what is the shared nature of oneself and things. Flesh is what is always *prior* to the distinction of subject and object and indeed is what

---

[9] For a more extended comparison and contrast of Merleau-Ponty's treatment of touching and of the role of touch in Husserl's phenomenology, see Derrida's *On Touching: Jean-Luc Nancy* (2005), particularly "Tangent III."

"constitutes" visibility and vision, objectivity and subjectivity, as such. Or to put this in a more Husserlian way, flesh is a "mutual transfer" of sense from things to oneself, a temporary settling of roles into an event of meaning.

By examining flesh as the elemental *verb* that pushes itself forth into perceptual and bodily events, Merleau-Ponty thus enables us to grasp what we see as already having transferred from us and to us what we need to be a perceiver, a body, a person. A thing is almost a subject in Merleau-Ponty's descriptions because of the whole, flesh, that we bear together. Our body, Merleau-Ponty says, "being of their family, itself visible and tangible, ... uses its own being as a means to participate in theirs, because each of the two things is an archetype for the other, because the body belongs to the order of things as the world is universal flesh" (1968, 137).

The thing calls to us; it has agency. And yet for Merleau-Ponty we must come to terms with the fact that our bodily life, our flesh, is largely not in our control. Our being of flesh is rather a situation of togetherness with the world, with other people, and with things. Flesh is an activity that forces us to go back again to what it means to live as this bodily whole.

Knowing this about the flesh, if we return to Husserl's example of the touching hands, with Merleau-Ponty, we can see something new. Not only is flesh not simply in our control on the outside. Not only can we not control the agency of things. But we also cannot control the limitations that flesh bears to us *from within*.[10]

With Merleau-Ponty we see that "my left hand is always on the verge of touching my right hand *touching the things*, but I never reach coincidence; the coincidence *eclipses* at the moment of realization" (1968, 147; my emphasis). Merleau-Ponty's description of my touching/touched hands therefore does not rest with Husserl's description of the organ-object transformation. Rather, Merleau-Ponty implies that in touching one hand with the other, I want more. It is not enough for me to turn my left hand into an object by means of my right. I touch my other hand because I also want to turn it into an object that *is still* a functioning organ. I want to feel what the left hand feels, feel how it feels, with my right hand. And what is most frustrating to this desire is that it is "eclipsed" just when it is *almost* satisfied.[11]

---

[10] By following the excellent work of Kym Maclaren, who discusses the intimacy of touch as presented in the work of Merleau-Ponty in "Touching Matters" (2014), I could pursue the role of touch as intercorporeity in Merleau-Ponty and thus extend and clarify what is at stake in Husserl's description of pairing. However, for the sake of this paper, I will leave that task attended to by Maclaren herself: "My proposal then is that in touching and being touched, because of the intercorporeity of touch, we are drawn into our bodies, and through a *new organization* of our bodies made *newly incarnate* while also being differentiated from the other" (2014, 101). Maclaren's emphasis in that piece is on a genetic phenomenology. Since resurrection is an account of a new genesis, a new shape of bodily life, I believe Maclaren's account would fit with the account of touch and of the Resurrection that I am giving.

[11] Jenny Slatman argues that this noncoincidence of my hands (I cannot touch the other hand's touching) is one way of noticing that my being a lived body is always, as a whole, connected with my death: "a living being can only experience its being alive while encountering, touching its own being lifeless. And this should be taken literally, not dialectically" (2005, 305). The "eclipse" of the desire to touch my touched hand's experiences, then, is the way in which finitude and death enters into my lived experience *of lived experience*.

The subjunctive "coincidence," the "verge" I am about to cross with one hand, is "eclipsed" at the moment it extends itself in touching the other hand. What I am promised in the desirous touching of the other hand, the possibility that the desire opens up in the first place, is never delivered. And I have no one else to blame for my frustration. For I am the unity of the two hands, and the fact that I exist in and as both hands is not enough to overcome their difference, their segregation and paired touchings.

Even within my own organization, then, there are real limits to how I participate in my own flesh. I can only pursue the other hand's act of touching the things; I cannot surpass it and make its perceptions the property of the first hand. I cannot cling to the illusion, which I myself give birth to, that I can transform my body into a single locus, a self-determining organization of perception.

As we will see by means of the Gospels, this internal limit on pairing that emerges in touch has resonances in the way the disciples pursue the resurrected body of Jesus. Not only does Jesus set limits to their approach, but the disciples' own embodiment becomes an issue for them, causing them to take up the Resurrection not only as a personal possibility (John in fact closes his Gospel with the attempt to cross out the idea that Jesus intended to give John a deathless life as a lived body) but as a textual possibility.

10.2   The Gospel of Luke: Touching the Resurrection

There are four stories in the Gospel of Luke that I would like to focus on here in an attempt to read the Gospel through a phenomenological lens. Each has something to do with touching and with resurrection. In two of them, Jesus raises children from the dead, children who thus share in and anticipate Jesus's own resurrection. In the third, which is interposed as a kind of interruption to a resurrection story, Jesus heals and confronts a woman with a hemorrhage. And in the fourth, that of Jesus's walk to Emmaus, Jesus presents himself to his disciples within a hermeneutic and a bodily event as the resurrected one.[12] In each case, Jesus's lived body mediates an account of resurrection by means of touching and speaking.

Upon entering the town of Nain, the author of Luke's Gospel says that Jesus "had compassion" (Luke 7:13) for a grieving mother who was marching in a funeral procession with the body of her son. Jesus "touched [her son's] bier" and then ordered the son to "rise" (Luke 7:14). When, by means of the touching and the command, the son is brought back from the dead, Jesus then "gave him to his mother" (Luke 7:15).

---

[12] I will return to Luke's Gospel after discussing Derrida and hauntology to deal with the stories that connect resurrection and a fear of ghosts. This will include the story of Jesus's appearance to the disciples in Luke 24:36–50.

In this story, Jesus touched the woman's son twice—once when he touched the son's dead body on the bier and once when he gave the son back to the mother.[13] The touches were meaningful enough to interrupt the movement of the mourners carrying the body and were caring enough to provide a necessary transition into a resurrected life. For I have no doubt that the "giving" of the son back to the mother happened by means of Jesus's hand, with which he helped the son off the bier. And, by means of this act of giving over by means of touch, Jesus provided a transition, a direction for the son's body to travel, as the son moved back toward the familiar lived body for which his mother had just been weeping.

Immediately following this story, Jesus is asked for clarification by the disciples of John the Baptist as to who he, Jesus, is. Jesus does not answer directly except to say that John's disciples ought to report back to John what they have seen and heard: "the blind receive their sight, the lame walk, the lepers are cleansed, the deaf hear, the dead are raised, the poor have good news brought to them. And blessed is anyone who takes no offense at me" (Luke 7:22–23). It is interesting that Jesus presents resurrection of the dead to these questioners as only one of a list of the deeds that he has done. Likewise, it is interesting that Jesus pairs together bodily effects (healing and raising) with spoken words of comfort.

By means of this equation of attention to the body and of communicating hope, Jesus works to situate resurrection not as a magical or mysterious power that overwhelms all others but as *one* way of empowering those whose lived bodily experience is one of profound suffering. Resurrection for Jesus then becomes *one* of the ways of recognizing that we are fundamentally vulnerable—*in our bodies*—to the fact that our life is never fully our own but is also always already a shared life together. And Jesus's touch, which is both interruptive and transitional, halting us in our suffering and showing us a way forward, provides evidence that the divine acknowledges both that lived bodies are at the center of our experience and that they require care from the divine.

When a man named Jairus experiences the death of his daughter, Jesus again seeks to assist this worried, grieving parent. Again, he responds to resurrect a child. Something in a child's death, therefore, or something in a child, is deserving of special attention, of raising up from the divine. The children, who are most vulnerable, deserve the community's special focus and that of the divine as well.

But in the case of the story of the resurrection of Jairus's daughter, Jesus is interrupted by a woman with a hemorrhage. This woman touches Jesus, actively seeking him out and turning her power of perception toward the rabbi: "She came up behind him and touched the fringe of his clothes, and immediately her hemorrhage stopped" (Luke 8:44). When Jesus feels her touch—even the fringe of his clothes serves an organ of his touch—he asks, "Who touched me?" (Luke 8:45). Touching Jesus was something this woman had tried to do anonymously. Yet Jesus could feel her seeking him—even at the fringe of his perception—and he explains: "Someone touched me; for I noticed that power had gone out from me" (Luke 8:46).

---

[13] This is in contrast with the story of how Jesus healed the centurion's ill servant at a distance in Luke 7:1–10.

Though he may not be able to feel his right hand's experiences with his left, Jesus does experience the activity of the other person. He is already "paired" with her and thus feels her need within the experience of feeling himself being touched and being made into an object. He feels "power" leaving or being "transferred" from him. When the woman trembles before him and tells him "why she had touched him," Jesus regains himself and says "Daughter, your faith has made you well; go in peace" (Luke 8:48).

Touch seeks the other in his subjectivity. As such, touch *must* be answered. It must be responsible. But unless we attest what we mean in each touch, unless we resurrect our capacity of speech to accompany our bodily action, we cannot be responsible in our touching. Touch does not have the ability to interpret itself.

While her touch of his fringe is still something Jesus is processing with the woman, he is reminded by someone else of Jairus's daughter. The touch transitions us forward toward the next touch, toward the resurrection.

Going into Jairus's home, Jesus confronts not only a dead child but a group of mourners who laugh at him when he says she is still alive. Nonetheless Jesus "took her by the hand and called out, 'Child, get up!'" (Luke 8:54). He then instructs the parents to feed the child, which they would need to do only if she were again a lived body.

Again, the touch is explained. Again, Jesus "took her by the hand" and the pair of hands, hers and his, lead the child back toward her family. Jesus's speech simply confirms the speech. This is not a ghost but a real child. She needs to eat. And thus the resurrection, performed by a living Jesus who is not yet resurrected, needs to be mediated by the bonds of the family, the community, who are to recover the lived body in its situation—a new one, to be sure, but one that carries its own necessity within it, as the life of the little girl's own desires and needs.

When Jesus himself experiences his resurrection, he walks incognito with two disciples on the road to Emmaus. He is near enough to touch or to speak with them, but he does not touch them. Nor do they recognize him, since "their eyes were kept from recognizing him" (Luke 24:16).

Jesus feigns ignorance of their discourse as they walk. And the two disciples are quite surprised. They ask, "Are you the only stranger in Jerusalem who does not know the things that have taken place there in these days?" (Luke 24:18). As a stranger, then, Jesus asks what they mean. And so they proceed to give an account of Jesus's own life and of the empty tomb and the angels who attested the Resurrection.

The disciples' recitation of the events provides a common ground, the foundation of a community. And on this foundation, Jesus speaks to them of the whole history of their shared experience as Jewish people, directing them to see how "all that the prophets have declared" (Luke 24:25) lead to his resurrection: "Then beginning with Moses and all the prophets, he interpreted to them the things about himself in all the scriptures" (Luke 24:27). Like touch, resurrection must interpret itself. It must begin anew with texts and their interpretation.

There may not be contact by Jesus—he does not touch them with his hands. But he touches them nonetheless by means of the texts that they share and the redirection and transition that he is able to communicate by means of interpretation. Jesus shows, then, that a community transcends itself and comes home to itself, incessantly, by means of its texts. And such self-transcendence leads that same community to bear witness to new insights.

When Jesus finishes his interpretation of "Moses and all the prophets," when they stop for the night, he takes bread, and blesses it, and breaks it. The interpretive lesson in how to see Jesus within the text has now allowed the disciples to recognize the bodily *style* of Jesus within the act. Something in the breaking open of the bread is his; something in his touch of the bread, like his reading of the texts, touches their eyes: "then their eyes were opened, and they recognized him; and he vanished from their sight" (Luke 24:31). In the moment of recognition, when the text is visible in the act, Jesus's resurrected body is already elsewhere. It is freed of its moorings, and it accomplishes in one moment what can become textually open in bodily acts (breaking bread, talking, interpreting) from then on.

The resurrection is thus accomplished not simply by being alive again. It is accomplished by means of the mediation of touch and speaking. And it is resurrection only by means of renewing a commitment to the texts of a community, the texts that now make room for a retroactive desire—one that appeared to be eclipsed in the passage of Jesus's body into death: "They said to each other, "Were not our hearts burning within us while he was talking to us on the road, while he was opening the scriptures to us?" (Luke 24:32). To have the ability to reinterpret one's own bodily life, to feel the past as desiring the future, to feel the present as transcending itself to the past—this is the very movement of resurrection. It appears in the bodily act of breaking bread, of speaking, and of interpreting. Resurrection is the giving of a future to what has heretofore remained in the past. Resurrection is how we give bodily weight to the process of transition and interposition, of eating and touching and textuality.

10.3   Hauntology: Derrida, Caputo, Resurrection, and Ghosts

John Caputo, in "Bodies Still Unrisen, Events Still Unsaid" (2007), describes his reading of the New Testament as involving a "transcendental suspicion" that is committed to questioning the possibility of the event as such. If a particular Christian, for example, were to select the Resurrection as the most important event in any Christian's religious or personal life, then, Caputo implies, this selection does not clarify how the Resurrection itself tells us what an "event" is characterized by. Much like the search for beauty in the *Symposium,* selecting the Resurrection as the categorial event misses the character of eventfulness that expresses itself *through* the Resurrection. And it is that eventfulness, if we can bring it to light, that allows all events, including Jesus's resurrection, to appear as new upsurges of meaning from which the beginning of some temporality is calculated.

However, even given his suspicion, and his goal to talk about the event as such, Caputo remains open, he says, to the New Testament and to the Jesus who remains within it. And Caputo pursues a hermeneutics of the Gospels and resurrection in particular because of the way that the description of Jesus's resurrection may well lead us toward a phenomenology of event. And in any case, Caputo notes, even if the Resurrection is not itself sufficient for bringing to light eventfulness as such, there is a moral case for admiring Jesus, since, as his life is written in the Gospels, he has welcomed people in their bodies, in all their fleshly sufferings and enjoyments, in all their possibilities and impossibilities.[14]

But in order to pursue the Resurrection as a possible source for the description of the event as such, Caputo must, as Jesus did, first distinguish the Resurrection from something that it is not but that it looks a lot like—namely a ghost. When Jesus is raised from the dead, says Caputo, he is not a ghost, since a ghost "is a bodily remnant or afterglow, whereas the risen body is a completion or perfection of the body" (2007, 79).

But this work at distinction (i.e., of a risen body from a ghost) creates further problems. For the relation of resurrected body and ghost entails that the Resurrection cannot serve as the very category of eventfulness but becomes *one way* "to actualize or instantiate events, in words and things that are variously material or immaterial, hauntological, literary, or religious" (2007, 80). Distinguishing the risen body from the ghost, then, must also turn back into the eidetic commonality of risen bodies and ghosts—as they both instantiate eventfulness and as their very similarities and differences show that neither of them alone can be the end of the question even of *bodily* events.

In his attempt to further distinguish the resurrected body from a ghost, and thereby possibly retrieve the essence of event as such, Caputo describes the risen body as a "no-thing of particular brilliance" that "cannot find a place on the side either of souls or bodies" (2007, 80). But yet again the problem of the Resurrection's commonality with ghosts surfaces. The ways in which ghosts too may slide into this description—a brilliant nonthing that is neither soul nor body by itself—seem immediately obvious: perhaps just as Moses and Elijah appear at the Transfiguration or just as the angels appear clad in lightning and white robes who announce Jesus's resurrection.

Of course, Caputo is quite aware of this difficulty at describing the Resurrection with a view toward eventfulness as such. Like the Derrida whom he comments on in *Prayers and Tears* (1997), the Derrida who claims that "the ghost is the phenomenon of the spirit" (1994, 135), Caputo acts on this conflation and depends on it. In fact, toward the end of his article Caputo again notes the commonality between

---

[14] Somewhat predictably, Caputo and Derrida have generated a negative response from some corners. A typical critical response comes from Jean-Pierre Fortin: "The human lack of control over both the experience of transcendence and the reception of supernatural empowerment does not repudiate the reality of the divine self-donation occurring in and as Jesus Christ" (2017, 76). It is not clear to me how Caputo could argue the contrary, if we understand by "transcendence" and "empowerment" the inspiration and evolution of religious and philosophical communities in their entering into the interpretation of resurrection, and of textuality, as such.

ghosts and risen bodies as instantiating "the transcendence of death itself" (2007, 85). And Caputo ends by saying that the risen body is "the most radical way to imagine metamorphosis" (2007, 85). Resurrection is therefore always one way among others—even if it is the most "radical" to be a body that is expressive of the relation to death and to event itself—to event as a nonthing that is neither a body nor a soul.

Like Caputo, Derrida inaugurates a methodical description of the body (though not a resurrected one) by means of describing the ghost or specter. And in Derrida's hands the two experiences, body and ghost, are paired together to move toward textuality itself as a *self*-transcending mode of contact and recognition.[15]

If the ghost enters into our lived experience and pairs itself with our bodily life, even in a limited way, the ghost *gives* us something. It gives us its own mediation between our lived experience and our ideas, between body and mind. With the ghost, we do not just have the mortal, self-transcending body on one side and the absolute, static, and ideal on the other.

It is not an idea of charity or responsibility by itself that frightens Scrooge in *A Christmas Carol*. Rather, what frightens Scrooge is the way Marley attests the idea by means of the display of his chained evanescence. The ghost gives Scrooge, gives us, the impetus, the shiver of the possibility that we can still transcend ourselves toward the ideas that, if they can be embodied and lived, will renew our embodiment.

Ghosts thus present a philosophical question. They ask: Is there a way to become more fully ourselves such that the past, our past, can find its home in a future embodiment in which we will speak the correct interpretation of what is most important?[16]

A ghost, however, can only state the question. It can only haunt and turn us toward our own capacities. It is not a participant in our self-transformation except by pointing, or speaking in a pointing manner, as in the case of the Ghost of Christmas Future pointing to Scrooge's grave. For the ghost cannot be involved in a conversation. We would not know how to talk to it, since we cannot reverse our being seen, since we cannot make the ghost listen to us, be moved by us, or convert into an object of our gaze: "The Thing meanwhile looks at us and sees us *not see it* even when it is there" (Derrida 1994, 6).

The ghost is intercorporeal, is related to the lived body, then, only by refusing to unmask its presence, only by refusing to appear. For if the ghost unmasks itself, takes off the visor or the chain that gives it any weight whatsoever, it would no longer haunt.

A community that centered itself around a ghost, then, would be static and most likely oppressive. It would be a haunted house: "Haunting would mark the very

---

[15] As an argument that creates a continuity between a phenomenology of touch and Derridean theology, see Bob Plant's "Christ's Autonomous Hand" (2004).

[16] Derrida puts this point thus: "If we have been insisting so much since the beginning on the logic of the ghost, it is because it points toward a thinking of the event that necessarily exceeds a binary or dialectical logic" (1994, 63).

existence of Europe. … The experience of the specter, that is how Marx, along with Engels, will have also thought or diagnosed a certain dramaturgy of modern Europe, notably that of its great unifying projects" (Derrida 1994, 4–5). But it is not enough to "diagnose" the "dramaturgy" of the specter. One must offer more. The specter, and its analysis, is only the beginning for Derrida.

By contrast, the lived body is intercorporeal in bearing its weight together with others by means of its pairing with them. The lived body is unmasked by its relations of similarity, of mutuality, of seeing while being seen, of being able to be converted into an object by the interlocutors, even when the lived body hides in war behind a visor.

But for all the power of its ability to see us, the ghost has a vulnerability, a distinctive tradition that it cannot surpass. The ghost cannot do more than repeat itself. It cannot do more than be a talisman for a traumatic history, a harm that it seeks to inflict on itself and on us on its behalf. Therefore, the ghost haunts: "a specter is always a revenant. One cannot control its coming and goings because it begins by coming back" (Derrida 1994, 11).

And this means that the ghost has always already *begun* to affect the lived body *only* by *returning* to the place where it *used to be* self-transcending. The ghost is condemned to return, to an eternal return, and not to move away toward a creative end. The ghost returns without achieving new content.

The lived body, by contrast, even when it lives in trauma, continually *sets out*; the lived body seeks to moves toward. The lived body *begins* again and again; it continues that beginning by its self-transcending toward the others who would hear its cry, listen to its speech, read its work.

This means that the ghost is the bare repetition of self-transcending without any concrete movement. It rattles its chains because it cannot lose them. By virtue of its *manner of* repetition, then, the ghost speaks words and causes fear that cannot be heard or felt by a lived body as creative. The ghost cannot speak in new ways. It simply haunts again and again, and any creativity it may have comes, if it comes, in the fact and manner of its frequency. In the frequent repetition, the ghost implies that something is not yet heard that ought to be.

The ghost compels us to talk to ourselves about it, to represent it to ourselves, since it is not present, since its body is parasitical on our flesh and blood without itself participating in the intercorporeal—a symbiosis of intercorporeality. The ghost speaks what it said before, what it lived before, but in a haunting way, a way that one cannot exactly understand, in a way that one is left alone within the very haunting. The ghost forces us to haunt ourselves on its behalf.

So compelling is the ghost as a mediation between lived experience and ideas that D. A. Hyland even claims that it is the specter (thus not the resurrected body) that claims identification with textuality: "this temporality of spirits … is inseparable from the interrogative stance of philosophy that is the spirit of Socrates still haunting Derrida and us. … That is, [philosophy] arises always as a specter of our having been and not having been" (2012, 17). The ghost looks back at us from the pages of Plato or Derrida or Luke or John. The text says the same things over and over. It haunts. And thus do we come to it as mediating our bodies and its ideas.

But I do not agree with Hyland, if in fact the specter is what Derrida thinks is the mode of being of philosophy and of the text. Instead, I ask with Derrida, after the resurrected body: "we will not claim that this messianic eschatology common to both the religion it criticizes and to the Marxist critique must be simply deconstructed. … what remains irreducible to any deconstruction … is perhaps a certain experience of emancipatory promise … a messianism without religion" (Derrida 1994, 59). This seems to be where Derrida has performed some sort of conjuration. Some sort of deferral. He rarely uses the word "resurrection" throughout *Specters of Marx*. In fact, the only time he does so is when Marx or someone else uses it. And yet it is clear that the character of "emancipatory promise" or the "messianism" that Derrida's *trace* possesses—this has more in common with the promise of the Resurrection than the mere repetition of the ghost.

Jesus's resurrected body is on the way somewhere.[17] It has an even briefer time than the lived body to show itself, to breathe, eat, and speak. The resurrected body as brief and transitional retains the historic specificity of the body—the wounds are the same in the same places. The identity is recognizable. But the retention of the past in the resurrected body is not definitive. Other faces are not bowed to the ground by its luminescence. Its being-on-the-way and its desired end are not necessarily given in the resurrected body's manner of existing, and it requests us to interpret its dispersal and disappearing.[18]

Jesus's resurrected body is thus not limited for him (and potentially for us) in all the ways the previously lived body was. The resurrected body can reveal and conceal, instruct and disappear. The resurrected body can maintain the views of others as important to it and yet hold itself apart from their recognition as no longer part of their concerns in the same way.

Without the ghost, or the possibility of ghosts, however, the resurrected body would not appear on its own, as its own. It is to insert itself as a fourth kind amid ghost, body, and idea—or among the community to come, lived experience, and tradition—that the Resurrection enters. But its insertion is not unproblematic.

For the Resurrection, like the lived body, needs those who perceive it properly to acknowledge it. Otherwise, the resurrected body can simply collapse into the haunting experience of the ghost. The Resurrection *as properly taken up*, as by the two disciples on the road to Emmaus, is what inaugurates the possibility of desire, reflexivity—"were not our hearts burning within us." (Luke 24:32). It is also what prevents those who experience the resurrected from saying too much, touching too much, asking too much.

---

[17] It is not clear what we are to make of the lived bodies that Jesus raised from the dead prior to his own resurrection. Are they also transitional in the same way? Are they the same as Jesus's resurrected body?

[18] Derrida's description of Marxism could also serve as a commentary on Judaism or Christianity or Islam in light of resurrection: "But this is perhaps what must now be thought and thought otherwise in order to ask oneself where Marxism is going, which is also to say, where Marxism is leading and where is it to be led: where to lead it *by interpreting it*, which cannot happen *without transformation*, and not where can it lead us such as it is or such as it will have been" (1994, 59).

The Resurrection, then, is fragile, like a lived body, and it gives itself over to the possibility that it may be misinterpreted. But in doing this, the Resurrection also presents itself within the context of a renewed commitment to interpretation as such and thus to the possibility of communal, creative work. Resurrection commits itself to an infinite possibility of a world that can never be filled, an event that can never be emptied.

The ghost claimed a community of essence with the way that the text repeats itself over and over in the same ways. And thus the ghost could move us toward an idea that we escaped. In its disembodied voice, it could attempt to force us to "take and read."

But the resurrected body claims a community of essence with a text in the way that the text itself, we know not how, reaches within us and calls forth the necessity of speaking and writing in new ways. The Resurrection, then, and not the ghost creates new incarnations, new bodies of communities to come, by inspiring (by breathing on and in us) us to reassert and reinterpret the power of our own "remaining behind."

The resurrected body, Jesus, remains—and departs—within a promise to come again. But it defers or at least does not name the time of its repetition. The resurrected defers because it is not bound by any rules other than its own. And thus, in deferring the temporality of its fulfillment, the resurrected body requests what the ghost does not—hospitality. Like Marxism, like philosophy as such, resurrection requests a "messianic opening to what is coming, that is, to the event that cannot be awaited as such … to her or to him for whom one must leave an empty place" (Derrida 1994, 65).[19] In fact insofar as the resurrected body of Jesus requires that we set "an empty place," Jesus as the Resurrection thereby requests hospitality in two ways.

The first mode of hospitality is that of a hospitality of thought. We must make room for resurrection within a newly formed trinity of concepts (lived body, ghost, resurrected body). The hospitality of thought is thus the very "pairing" together of these three, each of which by itself cannot reveal fully what constitutes meaning or event or what it means to be a lived body.

The second requested mode of hospitality, on behalf of the event of the Second Coming, whenever that is, is a hospitality of desire. The Resurrection, in short, requests that we pursue it, in an unacknowledged, unanticipated way, as the very truth of our own lived bodies. The Resurrection requests that we *desire to come close and to welcome it* such that, in some relation to come, it can in Husserl's sense "mutually transfer" to us *and from us* that sense of the lived body that it cannot yet

---

[19] Derrida does in fact seem to privilege here a kind of spectrality over resurrection. The text continues: "always in memory of the hope—and this is the very *place of spectrality*" (1994, 65; my emphasis). But the "essential contamination of spirit by specter" (1994, 113) that Derrida identifies later in the text as an insight not only of Marx but of deconstruction itself may condition this statement. There is a place of spectrality. But in that place lies a living trace, something that is like the specter but surpasses it.

teach us. In short, the pairing of concepts is complemented by the pairing of desire (divine and human).

Will the Second Coming of the resurrected body, insofar as it supplements thought with desire, or supplements a pairing with a mutual transfer, be beyond the conceptual trinity of body, ghost, and resurrected body? The only clue we are left with is the insertion of the resurrected body into the tradition of textual interpretation and the clue of desire, of the imperative to bear witness.

Something about the Second Coming, something about what is to come, is given to us. And insofar as it is given, the resurrection that we may experience as a mode of the lived body will be of a piece with the logic of textuality. With trace: "And all the grave stakes we have just named … would come down to the question of what one understands by … living work in [its] supposed opposition to the spectral logic. … To put it in a few words, deconstructive thinking of the *trace of iterability* … goes beyond this opposition, beyond the ontology it presumes" (Derrida 1994, 75). Resurrection is inseparable from the way a voice, an attestation, a showing, moves itself toward a new version of itself within the circle of believers and nonbelievers. The rest, the Second Coming, the manner of resurrection's reappearance and representation is a matter for desire and interpretation and, as such, always of a piece with the nondecidability of the text and the nonappearing of the event.

10.4   The Gospel of Luke: Resurrection and Ghosts

Immediately after Jesus's resurrection of Jairus's daughter, we are told that Herod the Tetrarch hears of mysterious reappearances—John the Baptist, whom Herod had beheaded, is seen again; or Elijah; or "one of the ancient prophets come back to life" (Luke 9:8). Herod is perplexed and wants to separate out the ghost story from the reality (Luke 9:9): "So who is this I hear such reports about?"

As if to answer Herod's question for the sake of the reader, Luke next tells how Jesus takes Peter, James, and John, the same three who witnessed the resurrection of Jairus's daughter and Jesus's baptism by John the Baptist, to a mountain. There, Jesus's face changes, and "suddenly, there were two men talking to him; they were Moses and Elijah" (Luke 9:30). What Herod had heard, in other words, came true. Elijah reappears, or something like Elijah.

Indeed, Jesus became sufficiently like these apparitions of Moses and Elijah, these ghostly appearances, that Peter stumbles through an idea: "let us make three shelters, one for you, one for Moses, and one for Elijah" (Luke 9: 33). The line, it would seem, between ghost and reality, between apparition and embodiment, perhaps between resurrection and the lived body, is breaking down. And Peter is in danger of losing track of how real Jesus is, how unique and important his bodily life is and will yet be.

The way forward, according to Luke's account, is to relate an event that would encourage the reader, and Peter, to recognize how temporary Jesus's shift is to the dazzling appearance of a ghost, or something like a ghost. And this event occurs through an intervention by God—ironically, through a haunting episode. Much like Hamlet's father come back to speak to Hamlet through a visor, God appears, for a second time, in a repetition of the event of Jesus's baptism, speaking in a cloud.

The voice from the cloud again assigns the attention of those gathered, again in almost the same words as before, to Jesus himself, to the one here and now. Thus says God: "This is my Son. The Chosen One. Listen to Him" (Luke 9:35).

So, to repeat, a disembodied voice, cloaked in a cloud, attends to Peter's confusion by repeating what was said before at Jesus's baptism. It demands that he pay attention to the embodied Jesus, the one who is not now shining like an apparition, who is not forced to don a cloud to cover his blinding nakedness. The bodily one— listen to Him. The real body can speak, converse. The apparition can speak only a basic truth. The I of the cloud cannot converse, at least not in a way anyone else could understand. The I of the cloud can turn one's attention only, again, to the proper interlocutor.

This experience of apparitions and nonconversational speech also happens after Jesus is raised from the dead. When the women go back to Jesus's tomb to anoint the body of Jesus, two dazzling figures await them. These apparitions, much like the ones with Jesus on the mountain, cause the women to bow "their heads to the ground" (Luke 24:5). Such apparitions, such angels or ghosts, like a cloud hiding the face of God, cannot be looked at directly. Such faces are not for mutual recognition and intercorporeality. There is no conversing with them. But they can be heard. And these apparitions, like the cloud, instruct the women—this time about Jesus's teaching of his death and resurrection in order to turn them toward the resurrected one, who could converse and who would not blind them.

When Jesus later appears to the disciples and stands among them, he interrupts the story of the ones who were on the road to Emmaus with him. And, as if anticipating the disciples' interpretive mistake, he shows he is not a ghost by means of the content his speech: "'Peace be with you'" (Luke 24:36). Surely, ghosts would not bring peace. Nevertheless, the disciples were still "terrified" and "thought they were seeing a ghost" (Luke 24:37).[20] In order to show them, then, beyond *what* he says, that he is Jesus resurrected, he then shows them his wounds and eats some fish.

It is important to note that not even the demonstration of the wounds, the markers of the body in its historical specificity, distill the joy out of the disciples' anxiety. It is only in the viewing of Jesus's body as giving evidence of a self-transcending process, of the conversion of food into itself, that they are calmed.[21]

---

[20] In G. Morrison's "The Triune Drama," the disciples, when confronted with Jesus's resurrection for the first time are, even though he bids them to be at peace, forced to encounter "both an absolute joy and a traumatic surprise. The trauma is especially being faced with glory" (2003, 87).

[21] See Emmanuel Falque's very important work on resurrection in *The Metamorphosis of Finitude*. A relevant and supportive passage: "as for the resurrection of the body, … it is less its substance as such that concerns us than the modalities of its being or of its movements (Husserl), according to how they are turned towards others (following the spirit) or turned in on the self (following the flesh). Christ resurrected and appearing to his disciples is recognized by them less through his fleshly structure. … He is recognized through lived experience, or the manner of being of his body" (2012, 55–56).

If he eats, then Jesus as resurrected does not haunt. He is of the world and takes the world into himself. But he also does something further. He engages the community within a process of careful conversation of their shared tradition: "then he opened their minds to understand the scriptures" (Luke 24:45). And in performing interpretation, he opens up the future of resurrection as such. Certainly Jesus does repeat what he said before, but he does so in a new *style* and with a new *emphasis*. He speaks, he interprets, within and as the presentation of the new context of his resurrected body.

Only as co-interpreters, then, do the disciples gather power from the Resurrection for themselves. And, in a complementary way, it is only as a conversing, eating, calming, caring body that the resurrected Jesus reaches into their lives and enables them to understand the past, and the future, in a new way.

Now, the Resurrection is brief. It is certainly enough time to share a meal and a retelling of lived, historical experiences. It is enough time to gather together and press forward toward a new, communal interpretation. But the Resurrection is *not* long enough to recapture Jesus's lived body in its pauses, in its rest. The disciples he loved have no time to rest their heads or their hands on his flesh. For the eating, interpreting, resurrected Jesus is already on his way. He has no time even while he takes time to be with them. In a moment, even *while* he speaks, he is moving beyond them: "while he was blessing them, he withdrew from them and was carried up into heaven" (Luke 24:51).

The Resurrection thus carries people who witness it by means of a new form of being a body into productive questions: *How* can a body that rises from the dead speak to people who are mortal in ways they can understand? *Why* should a deathless body teach mortals about the truth of their own bodily life? In the questions that the Resurrection produces lie the open spaces of religion and of religious community for disciples who find themselves suddenly left behind, who find what they can retain as given to be only texts, each other, and the power of interpretation with which to answer them.

10.5 The Gospel of John

In John's Gospel, after his resurrection, Jesus appears to Mary, who is weeping. After addressing her,[22] he tells her, "Do not hold onto me, because I have not yet ascended to the Father. But go to my brothers and say to them, "I am ascending to my Father and your Father, to my God and your God"" (John 20:17). The two-part command is instructive. The body that Jesus is now, the resurrected body, can be touched. Indeed, Mary is already clinging to it. His simple address, his voice in say-

---

[22] Jean Luc-Nancy, in *Noli Me Tangere* makes a lot of this address of Mary by Jesus: "'Mary' reveals Mary to herself, revealing to her both the parting of the voice that calls her as well as the dispatch to which her name commits her: that she in turn is to leave and announce the departure" (2008, 46).

ing her name, has opened her eyes. And she responds as any grieving friend would—with joy and desire.

But there are limits, internal limits, to the embodiment that is resurrection. It is not that Jesus is repelled by the desire of a friend to clasp him.[23] Rather, Jesus, while in a sense present to Mary, in a sense given to her, is also on the way toward another life. Like the hand that is touched, the resurrected must not remain objectified beyond the time necessary for the witness, the disciple, to confirm the resurrected as the source of new perceptions. And, like the hand, the resurrected body has a job to do—to help still other lived bodies make their own transitions into a new life.[24]

And so, as the one who is transitioning toward a full meaning of his own resurrection by means of his resurrected body, he gives Mary the command to go to his brothers. Mary's bodily life shifts too, then. She turns from a weeping servant to a leader—from one who is subordinate to one who is addressed by the resurrected Jesus himself. Mary is sent on a journey, for that is what the ultimate truth of bodily life is. A journey toward the redefinition, reinterpretation, and reformation of community.

When Jesus then appears to the disciples in the room, prepared by the witness that Mary bears, he shows them his hands and side. And he breathes on them (John 20:20–22). His breath is enough for them. They have felt his warmth. They have been close enough to him to experience how the community receives the Spirit, how the community relates to sin. The resurrected body is therefore one that displays and enacts—he breathes, he shows—but always points outward toward the rededication of the community. The resurrected body gathers air, allows it to move within itself, and allows that air to be directed outward, carrying its force, its process, its sound, smell, and taste.

Thomas, however, was not present. And so Thomas, who does not yet believe, is then invited by Jesus at the next opportunity to probe Jesus's resurrected body, to put his finger in the wounds: "Put your finger here and see my hands. Reach out your hand and put it in my side" (John 20:27). The resurrected body, then, not only breathes and speaks. It is not only active. It also remains so much like a lived body that it can be touched, probed, explored.

The touching that Thomas does is the conversion of the resurrected Jesus into an object of perception. It is to touch the past that we touch that body, that we prove to ourselves that it is the same as the one we knew. But just as any lived body will turn,

---

[23] See Nancy: "It is not that Jesus refuses Mary Magdalene. The true movement of giving oneself is not to deliver up a thing to be taken hold of but to permit the touching of a presence and consequently the eclipse, the absence, and the departure according to which a presence must always give itself in order to present itself" (2008, 50).

[24] Thomas Aquinas, in his *Commentary on the Gospel of John*, also does not believe that Jesus's injunction, "Do not hold onto me," is Jesus's way of rejecting Mary because she was a woman or because she could have stimulated carnal desire. Rather, Aquinas says, citing Augustine, "touch is the last stage of knowledge: when we see something, we know it to a certain extent, but when we touch it our knowledge is complete" (2517). Mary's knowledge, as someone only recently a disciple, is imperfect, according to Aquinas, and thus she cannot be allowed to touch Jesus until her faith is at "the point of believing that he was equal to the Father" (2517).

must turn, back onto us our own attempt to see it as a meaning we control, so Jesus turns back onto Thomas the very power of perception that Thomas brings forward to the wounds that Jesus bears: "Have you believed because you have seen me? Blessed are those who have not seen and yet have come to believe" (John 20:29).

Jesus shows that the resurrected body is not to be held on to and not even to be probed for the purposes of personal belief. The resurrected body is not for the disciples alone. It is for the sake of any who come to share in its self-surpassing power. The Resurrection is for all those yet to come who can find in it the course of their tradition, the hope of their community.

Immediately after the episode with Thomas, the author of the Gospel then interrupts the narrative to say that Jesus gave more signs, which were not "recorded" here. Those that were recorded were done with a purpose in mind: "that believing this you may have life in his name" (John 20:31). The point of resurrection, then, is to have established a way of writing that is self-reflective and that is life-affirming. It is not to celebrate death, which begs the question why the reader might make the mistake of thinking it had that purpose. But it is to call to mind that Mary and Thomas are figures for our own experience. We are to believe because as they are written they stand as possible embodiments for our own awareness and experience.

Mary and Thomas, Peter and James and John do not just stand in for or represent us, as a picture of a lyre stands in for or represents a lyre. By means of writing, we can move beyond representation and enter into their experience subjunctively, as if we were they, and almost feel what it is like to probe and to hold, to be breathed on and challenged by a body that is both paired with our own and on the way elsewhere.

But as reflexive as John is here, he knows he must be careful. It must be done judiciously, this writing within the scope of resurrection. One should not say too much, just as one ought not to cling.

This strange discussion of the limited and purposeful process of inscribing Jesus's signs in the Gospel is not the end of the Gospel, however. In the last chapter, after discussing Peter's future death with Peter, Jesus responds to a question that Peter asks about John—"What about him, Lord?"—with a strange statement. Jesus says to Peter this (John 21:22): "If I want him to stay behind until I come, what does it matter to you?"

John, it would seem, has a peculiar mission of "staying behind." And of staying behind in an indefinite manner. Directly after this question from Jesus, John inscribes his own personhood to the writing—"this disciple is the one who vouches for these things" (John 21:24). And *again* John says that there is not everything here in the Gospel—it is not an exhaustive account but nevertheless a true one. The author has revealed himself as a witness and has asserted, *twice* in a kind of ghostly repetition, his veracity and limited scope.

He, the author, is staying behind. And this is almost the last comment in a Gospel about *Jesus's* resurrection. In addition to being a new body for Jesus, then, the Resurrection has inaugurated a new life, a new body, a new way of being a body for the writer, for John. In a sense, the Gospel is John's.

And yet that is not the end of the Gospel. The end is, curiously, the very possibility of textuality as infinite: "But there are many other things that Jesus did; if every one of them were written down, I suppose that the world itself could not contain the books that would be written" (John 21:25). The world itself—the textuality of the Gospel opens onto an almost unlimited possibility of writing the full life of Jesus, the full interpretation.[25] We are here at the end of a text that both takes itself seriously, reflexively, and opens itself to the possibility of other texts, of other interpretations. John remains behind as one of many possible Johns, then. And this is not something one hears as threatening. No: rather as productive. As Jean-Luc Nancy has argued in *Noli Me Tangere,* "the resurrection of the body is the extension of a body to the measure of the world and of the space in which all bodies meet" (2008, 44).

10.6   The Return of the Resurrected

Any text seems to lie there, repeating its words over and over. And, if we read it, any text can also seem to haunt us—as, for example, a line of a song or a poem can chain us to itself for a day or longer. If we experience the text as haunting us, if we experience its repetition as repetition, then its "touch," if it has one, is *not* a pairing or a hospitality, not a redirection of our whole body into a shared project, but rather a one-sided conversion of ourselves into an object of its visored gaze. If texts haunt us, that is, then it is precisely because we perceive them as no longer alive but as ghosts. If they haunt us, it is because we permit them to be reduced to remaining behind a visor or a cloud.

To see the text as specter and as mere repetition is to engage in a reading that is doctrinal, reductive, defensive, and closed. Thus, reading a text as a specter will always mean a certain loss of possibility. It will mean a departure from, or a ceding of, the power and activity of one's lived body, one's organic subjectivity, for a set of ontological commitments that are not properly one's own. It is to read with onto-logical assumptions within an ethereal terrain.

To read doctrinally, spectrally, is to fail to perform an *epoché* or a reduction to the sphere of ownness that would free both oneself and the text to pair, to converse originally, meaningfully, and in a living way. It is to leave behind a sense of being active in one's body for the desire to be reduced to an object of fear of transgression, of guilt or shame—which, in turn, become, like Thomas, the feelings with which we probe the text. To read without the *epoché* and the reduction, in short, is to engage in a reductive violence to both the text and oneself.

---

[25] Aquinas agrees. In his *Commentary,* Aquinas argues that John's hyperbole here is instructive and not simply false: "Now the words and deeds of Christ are also those of God. Thus, if one tried to write and tell of the nature of every one, he could not do so; indeed, the entire world could not do this. This is because even an infinite number of human words cannot equal one word of God. ... Indeed, even if the world lasted a hundred thousand years, ... his words and deeds could not be completely revealed" (2660).

But a phenomenological reader, she or he who brackets the ontological and interpretive stances of past powers of "obviousness," would have a very different experience of the text. The phenomenologist, within the *epoché*, would retain her
conscience, which is the point of intersection of the text and oneself, of the divine
and the human. And, with conscience, the phenomenological reader would navigate
the living terrain of the soul of the text and the soul of oneself and of the
community.[26]

Conscience is what I define as the touching of the text and oneself within a conversation that sees the ethical principles of a "good" reading having to answer to a
multiplicity of voices, past, present, and future. In other words, conscience is the
preservation of the imperative of subjectivity and of life for the text, oneself, and the
communities of the book (or books). Conscience *is a way of reading* that is the
complement to the touched hand's remaining bound to the imperative of converting
back into an organ.

For even within a spectral reading of the text as a mere repetition of the same,
one is never *fully* haunted by it. And the text is never fully, perhaps never at all, a
mere repetition of the words on its page. Doctrine always fails to do justice to the
life of the word.

This is difficult to hear, perhaps. But doctrinal readings have their purpose too.
For it is in their failure to exhaust the life of the word that we see that the text has
never been simply an index of past hermeneutical acts, never been merely a series
of past orders to see this and only this, that are simply to be repeated. Rather, the
very failure of doctrine to exhaust the book (or books) shows us that the book (or
books) itself (or themselves) has (or have) engendered our past readings within its
(or their) own life. And our acts of reading are the living proof that the text has
always already surpassed us, surpassed our natural or religious attitudes, toward a
life to come of hermeneutics that is always more than the scope of our finite, historical, and critical assumptions.

To read with conscience, and not merely doctrine, is therefore to enjoin oneself
again and again to experience the text as an *other*, to pair with it as such. It is to pair,
too, with the community in its past and present and future voices, in its eucharistic
ek-stasis. For conscience does not consign the past to "mere doctrine" any more
than it does this to the text. Rather, reading with conscience is to feel the weight and
lightness of both the future and the past. It is to experience, beyond the initial shock
of Jesus's prohibition to Mary, that the act of conscientious reading itself, as the
interweaving of text and interpreter, divine and human, community and individual—that it *must* surpass its *own* moments as the very pairing of the two, as both
their trajectory and their prehistory.

We are no longer Marxists, Derrida is saying in *Specters of Marx*. And thus we
are free to read Marx again. I would add this: I am no longer a Thomist, and thus I
am free to read the scriptures and Aquinas himself as intimately involved with (but

[26] See John Russon's *Sites of Exposure:* "in conscience we experience both the inner need of the
finite situation to be a realization of the infinite and the need of the infinite to be realized in actuality" (2017, 125).

not exhaustive of) the community to come as it appropriates the Gospels and the Resurrection. While perhaps threatening to the attempts to reduce a hermeneutic experience to an obedience to assertions of power, this kind of phenomenological reading ought not to be seen as threatening. For a phenomenologist does not prevent the transcendence or the gift of the Resurrection from being believed, just as Derrida does not cancel out the truth of alienated labor. Rather, the phenomenological-deconstructive reading as a reading of conscience is the recognition *and the establishment* of a more intimate relationship.

To read resurrection into textuality as such, and vice versa, is to allow the text, the good news, to fill the world again with its flesh; it is to be a reader and a writer who takes up the Husserlian mystery of transcendence in immanence. To read phenomenologically, in other words, is to deploy both oneself and the text in order to carry forward our shared principles and experiences into a more sophisticated, more meaningful catalyst for belief, experience, and truth.

Reading a text, then, can become, beyond the passivity of being haunted, the working out of an interplay. Reading can become, with proper attention also to the magisterial events of the community and to a synthetic direction, a hermeneutics of touching and of interpreting that allows the text to share our life, our views and principles, just as much as it allows us to share its own life. A conscience-based reading, because it involves us as living bodies and as living embodiments of the good as such, is thus always *potentially* a creative pairing and a mutual transfer of sense, such that it can become impossible to say at any one moment who is reading whom—text or reader.

Certainly, of course, there are limits to our pairing with texts. Pairing does not give us the freedom to say whatever we want. Pairing respects the historical weight, the care within the forged paths of the communities of the book. Nor does pairing give us full access to the text. For we are finite bodies.

We have, perhaps, 30 years of creative co-perception with others before we stop writing forever. And, just as our sense organs and our hands do not perceive all within the field even as they perceive the field itself, so too are our textual perceptions limited.

Even the most supple interpreters, of whom Aquinas, Caputo, and Derrida are three, who approach a text with hospitality and reverence, acknowledge that, like Mary before Jesus, they are always prevented from touching fully those interstices, those openings, those contradictions that would explain or exhaust how the text operates. A phenomenological or deconstructive reading, unlike Thomas before Jesus, cannot therefore be the final reductive touch, the final conversion of the living text to an object, nor the ultimate act of owning the subjectivity of the author or the meaning of the words. The text is never fully one's own interpretive field; the text is never fully the object of a power or a violence of one person or community against others.

Like John, we as readers and as writers can always be said to "remain behind." This "remaining behind" means at least two things. First, it means that the text surpasses us through our very efforts. The text departs from us. But, second, it means that the surpassing that the text achieves is by means of our deposits, our depositions, which can continue to matter to the community of interpreters whom we have joined. We depart from ourselves into the text, and thereby we too remain.

We remain, we participate in resurrection, *because* we deposit our readings and writings, our very *lives*, as readers in the text. We remain because the text bears within it the traces of our orientations, our perceptions, even our communal development. All of this, yes.

But in exchange for our remaining behind, for the time we have left, the text also remains, at least for the brief life we have left. It departs, certainly, but it also, in departing, leaves itself in us—not as a haunting but as catalyst and measure of our growth, an impetus toward our outward-oriented evolution through and by means of itself. The text remains as that toward which our history *and the trajectory* of our pairing converge.

And herein, within the pairing that is always toward the community to come, lies the way that resurrection has become not merely a future event for the lived bodies of believers. Rather, as Jesus shows us in his attempts to turn the Resurrection into a time of reinterpretation, we as readers, and as authors, like John—*all* of us who approach the text of the Resurrection—will always both remain and reemerge, we *must* reemerge, to a subjectivity that has, in being shown its grave by the Ghost of Christmas Future, been shepherded toward a community that requires us to put our conscience to work with others. Within our phenomenology of deconstr(u/i)ction, any temporary eclipse of our own subjectivity that each text solicits issues into (deferred but) real empowerment.

In short, the Resurrection is the birth of each of us as scribes and Pharisees, of authors and students, of followers and evangelists of the Word. The Resurrection is the tracing of the text as it passes into the flesh of communities of those who interpret and remain behind.

To consider the Resurrection as the Gospels present it is to counter grief, and tears, with education. One cries like Mary Magdalene does because one knows that one *does not yet know* what is at stake in a situation. One cries because one is touching more than one can bear—yet must touch and therefore must bear. One cries in order to see *through* the water, to see that the point of being a body is to read and to write, to give reality to a tradition that needs to be shaped and reshaped so that the world can be filled to overflowing with communities that are taking the issue of what it means to be a body to the very limits of phenomenological method.

Because Jesus raised children from the dead, because he raised Lazarus his friend, before Jesus himself was raised, we are left with the possibility of reading the Resurrection as *not* the only one. Resurrection is not the definition of the event as such. Resurrection is, rather, the *sharing* of the Resurrection. And this means that a supple reading of the Resurrection is required. It is up to us to present the future children—whom Jesus would help just as he did the daughter of Jairus, a child whose name is not used, one may say, in order to preserve her universality—with a tradition worthy of their needs and their experiences.

In fact, as we move further and further in time from the appearance of the resurrected body of Jesus, and even further from his engagement with those Jewish children and their grieving parents, it *must* dawn on us that the resurrected body is not only *in* the text. It *is* the text. It is as much John as Jesus, as much Mary as it is we ourselves.

In the face of any sacred text, but in the face of especially one on the Resurrection of a divine child given human flesh, how could we ever be in a situation to do anything else than practice the very absolute hospitality or charity that Derrida and Aquinas require? How else can we act but to act with hospitality toward the reemergence of the life of the Resurrection in the light of what *may* initially appear to be absolute spectrality?

As I read the accounts of Mary and Thomas, of Jesus and the disciples, then, I am led to this conclusion: the resurrected body is not, *like a* text, *like* a lived body, alive. The lived body, the text, *is* alive, *because* it *is already* a resurrected body that takes up its space of deferral from itself as the communal space of interpretation—of speaking, reading, and writing. And our task is resolutely to commit ourselves to the conversion of texts from being specters to becoming, in addition, based on the *conscience* that the text enacts with us, new bodily forms of engagement with each other.

References

Al-Saji, Alia. 2010. Bodies and sensings: On the uses of Husserlian phenomenology for feminist theory. *Continental Philosophy Review* 43 (1): 13–37.

Aquinas, Thomas. *Commentary on the Gospel of John.* http:dhspriory.org/thomas/SSJohn.htm. Accessed 6 Apr 2018.

Caputo, John. 1997. *The prayers and tears of Jacques Derrida: Religion without religion.* Bloomington: Indiana University Press.

———. 2007. Bodies still unrisen, events still unsaid, *Angelaki* 12 (1): 73–86.

Coogan, Michael D. 2001. *The new Oxford annotated bible.* 3rd ed. Oxford: Oxford University Press.

Costello, Peter. 2012. *Layers in Husserl's phenomenology: On meaning and intersubjectivity.* Toronto: University of Toronto Press.

Derrida, Jacques. 1994. *Specters of Marx: The State of the Debt, the Work of Mourning, and the New International.* Trans. Peggy Kamuf. New York: Routledge.

———. 2005. *On Touching: Jean-Luc Nancy.* Trans. Christine Irizarry. Stanford: Stanford University Press.

Falque, Emmanuel. 2012. *The metamorphosis of finitude: An essay on birth and resurrection.* New York: Fordham University Press.

Fortin, Jean-Pierre. 2017. Symbolism in weakness: Jesus Christ for the postmodern age. *Heythrop Journal: A Bi-Monthly Review of Philosophy and Theology* 58 (1): 64–77.

Husserl, Edmund. 1970. *Cartesian Meditations: An Introduction to Phenomenology.* Trans. Dorion Cairns. The Hague: Martinus Nijhoff.

Hyland, Drew A. 2012. Spectres of interpretation. *Research in Phenomenology* 42 (1): 3–17.

Maclaren, Kym. 2014. Touching matters: Embodiments of intimacy. *Emotion, Space, and Society* 13: 95–102.

Merleau-Ponty, Maurice. 1968. *The Visible and the Invisible.* Trans. Alphonso Lingis. Evanston: Northwestern University Press.

Morrison, G. 2003. The triune drama of the resurrection via Levinas' non-phenomenology. *Sophia: International Journal for the Philosophy of Religion, Metaphysical Theology, and Ethics* 42 (2): 79–97.

Nancy, Jean-Luc. 2008. *Noli Me Tangere: On the Raising of the Body.* Trans. Sarah Clift, Pascale-Anne Brault, and Michael Naas. New York: Fordham University Press.

Plant, Bob. 2004. Christ's autonomous hand: Simulations on the madness of giving. *Modern Theology* 20 (4): 547–566.

Russon, John. 2003. *Human experience: Philosophy, neurosis, and the elements of everyday life.* Albany: SUNY Press.

———. 2009. *Bearing witness to epiphany: Persons, things, and the nature of erotic life.* Albany: SUNY Press.

———. 2017. *Sites of exposure: Art, politics, and the nature of experience.* Bloomington: Indiana University Press.

Slatman, Jenny. 2005. The sense of life: Husserl and Merleau-Ponty on touching and being touched. In *Merleau-Ponty: Vie et individuation*, ed. R. Barbaras, M. Carbone, H.A. Fielding, and L. Lawlor, 305–325. Paris: Vrin.

Welton, Donn. 1999. Soft, smooth hands: Husserl's phenomenology of the lived-body. In *The body: Classic and contemporary readings*, ed. Donn Welton, 38–56. Oxford: Blackwell Publishers.

Peter Costello is Professor of Philosophy and Public and Community Service at Providence College. He is the author of *Layers in Husserl's Phenomenology,* published by University of Toronto Press, and the co-editor, with Licia Carlson, of *Phenomenology and the Arts,* published by Lexington Books. He is currently working on a second manuscript on Husserl, which explores the limit and possibility of attributing agency to things in human experience. A member of the board of the Society for Phenomenology of Religious Experience (SOPHERE), Peter also has published "The Calling of Thinking in Our Abandonment" in de Gruyter *Open Theology* and a number of other articles in the Continental philosophy of religion.

Chapter 11
Religious Experience and Transcendence (or the Absence of Such): Commentary on Part 2

Olga Louchakova-Schwartz

Abstract This commentary to Part 2 of Volume 1 of *The Problem of Religious Experience: Case Studies in Phenomenology* focuses on the double role of transcendence in religious experience, as transcendence of individual ego at the core of religious experience and as a mode in which the other is given to the self. This opens, on one hand, the possibility of examining how imposed relevances, satisfaction, freedom, and necessity, and other features of consciousness associated with alterity, play out in relation to religious experience; on the other hand, it raises the question of whether religious experience can be not only associated with the mystery of alterity but understood as an internalized, idealized version of relationship with the other, and with specific ethical demands that account for possibility or impossibility in the constitution of such experience. Religious experience is described in light of the metaphysics of companionship, which means adopting an ethical disposition of making oneself attractive to the other, who is God, so that religious experience can take place in the form of interpersonal intimacy. Perhaps as a result of Rudolph Otto's critique of Friedrich Schleiermacher's position in the beginning of the former's "The Idea of the Holy," phenomenological investigations of religious experience focused on mystery, leaving out of analysis the feeling of absolute dependence. But considering an event of religious experience as an unveiling of intersubjective space brings Schleiermacher's view back into the spotlight.

Keywords Levinas · Religious experience · Alterity · The invisible · The feeling of absolute dependence

O. Louchakova-Schwartz (✉)
Jesuit School of Theology of Santa Clara University, Graduate Theological Union, Berkeley, CA, USA

University of California, Davis, CA, USA

© Springer Nature Switzerland AG 2019
O. Louchakova-Schwartz (ed.), *The Problem of Religious Experience*,
Contributions to Phenomenology 103,
https://doi.org/10.1007/978-3-030-21575-0_11

In the concluding section to Part 1, we noted that religious experience occupies its own sphere within the region of complete immanence, and we also specified that the feature of transcendence of the individual ego distinguishes it from the psychological-immanent sphere, in which the ego remains an individual one. The religious sphere also was differentiated by Alfred Schutz from another sphere of immanence, a sphere of theory (Barber in Part 2). Therefore, we also distinguish the religious sphere of complete immanence as a transimmanent sphere. Using the findings of Part 2, we shall now attempt to clarify transcendence as it pertains to religious experience.

After descriptive phenomenology and constitutive analyses in Part 1, Part 2 initiates a different direction of thinking. Instead of reflecting on consciousness as the consciousness of the ego laboring to shape its synthetic unities of sense (according to Husserl's *Cartesian Meditations*), we focus on the invisible unification of consciousness that takes place in the network of relationship (according to Levinas 1999). A teleological conception of consciousness in Husserl's *Crisis* blossoms in Levinas's analysis into an originality moving toward what is given, which is a world: "[a] thought that un-thinks itself in order to represent or master presence … [of] … things which are given in the world which is given" (Levinas 1999, 14), a donation via "life-world." Hence experience is revealed to be not about a signification (of the other, the face, the world) but immersed in striving for satisfaction (fulfillment). In this view, the *cogito*'s "I am" is not locked in the sphere of its isolated ownness but abides in the openness to transcendental donation—as a consciousness *originating* from the presence of the world. The lifeworld, or, as Michael Smith uses the term in the translation of Levinas's *Alterity and Transcendence* (1999), the "lifeworld," is where thought happens. Levinas asks, rhetorically, whether the besiegement of alterity is the only condition upon which thought happens, whether, in satisfaction of union, thought disappears, and whether all of one's prereflective life is a response to the face of the other. This is the background against which we should now consider religious experiencing.

A transition from ordinary to religious experiencing begins in the lifeworld of the everyday. In the everyday, the ego connects with the other as the face (expression-appearance of the other). Schutz indicates that connection with others involves the typification (Barber in Part 2) necessary for the recognition of social types. One typifies what is phenomenally visible; however, Schutz also indicates that Consociates, who share the same time and spatial access to each other's bodies, immediately and ongoingly revise each other's types (Barber 2018). This suggests that typification takes into its account what is phenomenally invisible: the affectivity and flesh of the other. Further, as shown by Husserl in *Cartesian Meditations* chapter 5, other subjectivities are in an implicit companionship to the constitutive efforts of the ego. Therefore we may ask exactly: How does this rootedness of all experience in intersubjectivity extend into religious experience? And how do we route the idea of complete immanence to incorporate the other or the world, or both?[1]

---

[1] For criticism of phenomenology's capacity to address "invisible" processes, see Searle 2008.

11.1   Religious Experience and the Social World

Part 2 begins with Sam Mickey reaffirming the value of phenomenological reduction for the study of religious experience. The etic approaches in anthropology or cross-cultural psychology famously fail to capture cultural specifics of experience. The phenomenological reduction and the suspense (or suspenses) that it entails take care of preserving the cultural otherness and enable the researcher to access diverse lifeworlds as they are given to "them." The essential and well-known effect of reduction is to bring into visibility and make available for reflection the aspects of consciousness hidden in the natural attitude. Despite frequent misinterpretations, this does not exercise a constitutive influence on consciousness. The natural (evidential) consciousness of experience and the structures of the same experience (or a class of experiences) revealed by reduction are related. However, they are not in the same order of consciousness. Reduction doesn't modify the original givenness of experience but rather reveals the implicit internal organization of consciousness involved in original experience. The evidential givenness of consciousness exists through the modes in which the structural organization of things is "already there," genetically and with regard to the generativity of consciousness, but is not visible until touched by reflection. (Cf. Hopkins 2010, 107, 130–131, 264–265, etc.) Differing from other kinds of philosophical reductions (e.g., Wiley 1994), phenomenological reductions are the mental motions uncovering these invisible modes and thereby infinitely broaden the scope of perception and thinking, at the same time showing how we do it. (Cf. Levinas 1996, 3.) Ultimately, reduction aims at the full visibility of life, according to its innate structures and up to the natural limit of its possibilities.

The attitude of reduction initiates a realistic phenomenological account of religious experience that cannot be thematized by imposition from the ego but can be thematized in relation to the social world. The phenomenological thematization is not arbitrary or doxastic but rather is a higher-order reflection on what *is* in the evidence: this is exactly one of the areas in which phenomenology is scientific, that is, produces verifiable, robust, and realistic data. (Cf. Hopkins 2010, 107.) Because of this capacity, Schutz's thematization of the lifeworld proliferated with developments in anthropology and the philosophy of the social world. Barber (in Part 2) shows that in Schutz's understanding, the lifeworld of the everyday is inherently open to emancipation by means of religious experience (also Barber 2017b). Since religious experience implies internal transcendence of the psychological ego, in the context of the lifeworld transcendence happens at least twice, inwardly, and as a mode in which the other is given to the self, that is, intersubjectively. According to Sufi psychology, these two transcendencies mirror each other via specific ethical demands that account for possibility or impossibility in the constitution of religious experience. The constitution of the lifeworld evokes an ongoing tension between the totality of options offered by the same ego, and the infinity of possibilities coming from others who are not the same (cf. Knoblauch 2013; Egéa 2014; Rapport 2015.) This also raises a question whether both the internal ego-transcendence, and the totality of the self (of "I am") can be a result of the ego's attempting to appropriate the mystery of the other and thus get rid of the tension.

As Husserl shows in *Cartesian Meditations* and further in *Crisis,* different phenomenological reductions "slice" consciousness differently, not just by showing the various strata of its constitution but by revealing the different modes of givenness of these strata. The reduction by Levinas reveals invisible ethical gravities that underlie the interlacing of totality and infinity in the lifeworld. Albeit in themselves not rational or perceptual knowledge, these bonds keep human communities together (including communities of faith); the life of these bonds can be brought out of anonymity by phenomenological description and thereby converted into knowledge. In the lifeworld, the subjectivity of the other is given as a face, a visible "surface" whose otherness always has a character of impenetrable alterity (Mezzanzanica in Part 2). Similarly, the internal Other–that is, God—remains, in Levinas's view, not just transcendental but unreachable by any human means of knowledge and only via "nonknowledge" mediated by the ethical and emotional bonds. In other words, religious experience would always be irreal, given in analysis through ego-acts directed backwards, and so on. However and by contrast, in the accounts of Sufism, Hesychasm, and other mystical traditions, the deity is described as giving itself directly, in degrees of self-disclosure, in the now, as experience that may or may not be available to posterior reflection. (Cf. Chittick 1998, Louchakova-Schwartz 2014.) Therefore, unless we simply write off this contradiction as pertaining to cultural differences in theology (which would be an excuse to avoid the problem), we need to find what the solution is.

11.2   Religious Experience Under *Deus Absconditus*

Levinas negates "false and cruel transcendence," which is requested from a seeker in an idealized, or as he terms it, "pagan" approach to religion (Hayat 1999, xii; Bernasconi 2010). An expectation from such transcendence is that it eliminates all differences and otherness—for instance, by ascetic practice. By contrast, a true transcendence is born out of the intersubjectivity—that is, out of the ontological openness and the subsequent existential modalization of the subjectivity in its relation to other subjectivity—and not out of the externalization of interior being. Existentially, the first transcendence reaches for closure and control; the second, for openness and vulnerability (cf. Byers 2002); but it is an ontological status of both transcendences that Levinas refers to in terming the first one false and the second one true: in the case of directedness at the other, not only there is not only an intentional object originating in the world's sphere of being (the other's body) but the living subjectivity of the other that consciousness strives to grasp.

In Part 1, we established that religious experiencing involves uncovering multiple aprioristic horizons*;* in many ways, such horizons involve *the other:* for example, the sense of reality depends on an assumption of others' being able to perceive the same world (Taipale 2014); the *a priori* harmony in the transcendental community of multiple monads involves the presence of others (Hopkins 2010, 166); and similarly, a community horizon involves others. (See Murungi 1991.) Thereby the uncovering of these horizons means uncovering the phenomenology of transcendence: in the absence of an ontic Other, a self-transcending striving of intentionality will be grasping at locations of mystery. In this manner, the sphere of subjectivity generously provides all the constitutive resources necessary for hosting religious experience. Transimmanence, a key notion in the philosophy of Jean-Luc Nancy (Taylor 2011, 2013), was used by me previously (Concluding Reflections to Part 1) to characterize the sphere of religious experience in a sense inspired by Lacoste: in this case, transcendence is not meant as a general property of consciousness. It is used in a different sense: as a characterization of a sphere of the immanent consciousness that gives evidence of the internally directed transcendental strive, as opposed to the psychological sphere, in which there is no such evidence.

Relationships with the other, especially in a conflict, is where subjectivity becomes visible to itself—by the testimony of its own face, which initially (perhaps, pragmatically) looks only at the other. (Cf. Mezzanzanica in Part 2.) For example, in introspective religious practices of the so-called Spiritual Heart,[2] the face of the self reverses its orientation by turning back toward its subject, behaving like a dream character who represents the dreamer's psyche.[3] Introspective experiences may include multiple "faces" (e.g., as described by me in Louchakova 2005a),[4] visions, manifestations of the Names of God, and so forth. (I.e., in prayer: Louchakova 2005b.) Besides religious experiences that include actual apparitions of the face (or faces), there is a stratum of experiencing beyond the face. These are fields of meaning that are difficult to pinpoint in terms of the clearing (*Lichtung*) which shows them in conscious awareness. (Cf. Dahnhardt 2007, 131–133, on *Laṭaʾif.*)

The visible of intentional presentations connects with the invisible of interpersonal affect, feeling, internal motion, and an overall pattern of behavior that is nonintentionally given (not only prereflective). In the experience of the face, one takes the other in, and the two are given both to the actual subjectivity of the other hidden beyond the face and to the subjectivity of the self itself. The meaning, and even nonintentional underpinnings of such interrelatedness, most of the time are not obvious in the moment and are grasped by reflection retrospectively, if at all. Husserl-Schutz's lifeworld is *de facto* a registry of manifest potentialities of the face, recorded for example in typifications.

---

[2] For more on the Spiritual Heart, see Cutsinger 2003; Louchakova 2007.

[3] For an example of experience with the reversal of the face, see Louchakova 2005a, b. The same effect takes place in experiences induced by Native American ritual intake of the peyote entheogen mescaline in Peyote cactus; it is said that to taste peyote is to taste oneself.

[4] For more examples of the internal face (or faces) of the other in internal religious experience, see Ibn ʿArabī 1981, 16, 42; al-Jīlī 1983; al-Tirmīdhī 1996.

Levinas's vision of subjectivity (cf. Hayat 1999) leaves God out, because, according to Levinas's critique of Heidegger's "onto-theo-logy," one should not mistake being for God or God for being. Massimo Mezzanzanica in Part 2 views Levinas's approach as opposed to Hasidic Judaism. I wish to clarify that in Hasidic Judaism God is a *Du* (Yiddish 'Thou') and gives Himself/Herself in religious experience. On the contrary, in Talmudic Judaism, God is more hidden, and religious experience does not serve as evidence of His/Her being. Levinas's approach is massively influenced by the latter. Connection with such a *Deus Absconditus* (if not a *Deus Otiosus,* who retired from the world), if at all possible, takes place via interactions with the other, the face. Such interactions are realized in ethical experience, but not as a kind of experience that can be equated with perception/knowledge: such experience does not have its primary platform in intentionality. Levinas's philosophy has been qualified by many as ethics, which assumes that attempting to think religious experience along the lines of Levinas's ideas, one should treat it as an event related to ethics, understood as "not a simple layer or covering but something more ancient than onto-theology for which the former must account" (Levinas 2000, 125) and situated between subjectivities and given neither in the natural attitude nor in the attitude of transcendental reduction but as something else. As stated by Bergo (2017):

> Levinas claimed, in 1961, that he was developing a "first philosophy." This first philosophy is neither traditional logic nor metaphysics, however.[1] It is an interpretive, phenomenological description of the rise and repetition of the face-to-face encounter, or the intersubjective relation at its precognitive core; viz., being called by another and responding to that other. If precognitive experience, that is, human sensibility, can be characterized conceptually, then it must be described in what is most characteristic to it: a continuum of sensibility and affectivity, in other words, sentience and emotion in their interconnection.

Linking the ideas above to an idea that we have already adopted—that is, that the holy and the everyday are interlaced—we may indeed expect that this inapparent sensibility at the root of any experience comes into view. Such experience would be religious, not by a naive affirmation of "I am" but rather by means of a receptive attitude toward this very continuum of ethically given sentience and emotion. An endnote reference ([1]) in the quotation just above states that Levinas (1961/1969) views the face-to-face relationship as metaphysical and positive, distinguishing it from theological negation or absence:

> By metaphysics, Levinas means an event that repeats in the everyday, but is not reducible to the existence conceived phenomenologically as the object of intentional aiming or representation. This resistance to representation is due to the curious time structure of the encounter called the face-to-face. It comes to pass in an instant that 'interrupts' intentional consciousness, in its alone or solipsistic quality. Thus, the "meta-physical" is approached in light of the phenomenology of consciousness and its 'temporality', but not in terms of a first or highest being or cause.

Further, Bergo suggests that Levinas focuses on levels of experience that were not described by either Husserl or Heidegger. The other plays an active role in shaping this level of experience, concretely and not as an abstraction in the above-mentioned aprioristic horizons. Not being presentational in a usual phenomenological sense, and also not representing the other, this stratum nevertheless participates in forming one's experience. In the everyday, the ego amalgamates these influences under its syntheses, rendering them invisible, but it is possible to imagine that in an appresentative mindset (Barber 2017a, b) a religious symbol may pair up with such an input by means of passive synthesis and cause an event of religious experience.

Passivity plays an essential role in religious experiencing. In Chap. 5, Part 1, Louchakova-Schwartz describes a change in the modes of *noēsis,* in Buddhist practice, from activity to passivity; there are analogous concepts in other traditions. It is not unusual that mystics report experiences in which they feel their thought or emotion as if coming from outside, or belonging to the other in degrees. All such modes require a decentering of consciousness, a subject of further explorations in Part 3.

11.3 Decentered Consciousness and the Metaphysics of Companionship

As one can see, intersubjectivity in major ways contributes to the constitution of religious experience. Levinas (2000, 142) wrote: "Cartesian ontology, in itself adopting the idea of the infinite, thinks the Same as a totality that integrates every Other—in such a way that the 'in' signifies the triumph of the Same over the Other, the equality of the unequal, and the identity of identity and difference." Even though the previous section of our analysis showed that intersubjectivity in major ways contributes to religious experience, this does not altogether solve the problems posed by an idealistic focus on the monistic totality of the same.

The idea of the Same integrating every Other is exactly what plays itself out in religious ontologies operating in Vedanta, New Age nondualism, and many forms of mysticism that identify the essence of God with pure subjectivity; the Cartesian natural attitude is at the same time a religious attitude. For example, a famous quote from al-Jīlī states (citing from memory): "Each individual of the human species contains the others entirely, without any lack, his own limitation being but accidental. ... For as far as the accidental conditions do not intervene, individuals are, then, like opposing mirrors, in which one fully reflect the other." This can be interpreted as a reference to intersubjectivity's containing others, but on a different reading, this is an example of the totalitarian monism above. If, as some suggest (Musholt 2012; Louchakova-Schwartz, 2017a; Durt 2018), self-awareness depends on the awareness of real others, the soteriological ideal of individual self-realization may be simply false. How much of the other is exactly in one's religious experience?

Samādhi, Vedantic *nididhyāsana, manolasa* (Louchakova-Schwartz 2017b), and other advanced states of self-absorption are experienced by their subjects not as "religious" but as the states of self-recognition. In fact, the recognition of these states is often given not during the actual states but via memory, because many of these states are supposed to be *nirvikalpa:* that is, devoid of cognitions. To acquire a religious sense in such states, one gives internal greetings (see description in Louchakova 2005b), thereby decentering consciousness. (See further in the conclusion to Part 3.) Without internally directed devotion or relatedness, *samādhi* goes "inert," loses aliveness, and turns into a numbed, undifferentiated absorption. In other words, to acquire a religious quality, experience needs to be transposed from the sphere of ego-ownness into the sphere of intersubjectivity: decentered. In this manner, praxis of religious experiencing corrects metaphysical abstractions, skipping over contradictions that such "corrections" may incur with traditional soteriology.

Of course, Talmudic Judaism is not the only tradition embracing the invisible contributions of ethics in religious perception. For example, Suhrawardī, the founder of the Persian philosophy of Illumination, used a metaphor of light, hypostasizing self-awareness in both its first-person and its second-person giveness as metaphysical light and other lights. The practice of Sufism emphasizes what can be called a metaphysics of companionship, which means an ethical commitment to goodness so that one can be attractive for the other (God) in ways a lover tries to beautify oneself for the beloved. In such situations, religious experience takes on a form of interpersonal intimacy. Peter Costello (in Part 2) examines an instance of maximum interpersonal intimacy in the experience of bodily transfer between the resurrected Jesus and Mary: "The other appears to me there in the flesh—this is the first indication of our pairing. But when and as the person appears within my sphere of perception, I find that she has always already enlisted the sense of my whole body, albeit without my awareness or acknowledgment."

Perhaps as a result of Otto's critique of Schleiermacher's views in the beginning of the former's "The Idea of the Holy," post-Otto phenomenological investigations of religious experience focused on the mystery while leaving out of analysis the feeling of absolute dependence. However, as presented in his overview, considerations for deep roots of religious experience in intersubjectivity bring Schleiermacher's position back into the spotlight, especially if, as does Costello, we focus on the phenomenological flesh, as opposed to a disembodied appearance (of a ghost). Phenomenological flesh is fully immanent and not perspectival, always in between, as a matrix in which all subjectivities are involved. Communities of faith (e.g. church in Christianity, *kehillah* in Judaism, or the *ummat al-Islām*) abide by the flesh: wheras the face creates division, the affectivity of flesh ties the subject to other subjectivities with bonds not broken even by most extreme forms of asceticism.

In *Proper Names*, resonating with Gabriel Marcel and Jean Wahl, Levinas (1996) expresses a hope that the end of certain intelligibility, of the ontology of being, will "enabl[e] us to divine" by a new intelligibility, a rationality grounded in reciprocity, in exchange. In "divining" conditions of possibility for religious experience, one may suggest that in the first place there must be a horizon of flesh—that is, of phenomenological materiality.[5] This horizon is invisible under the masking influence of intentionality (Henry 1973, 2008, 2015). For the individual ego, as a continuity beyond the visible boundaries, this horizon also affords a possibility of internal transcendence that would be at the same time fully immanent for each subjectivity. In the narrative of resurrection, Costello makes a claim for the persistence of the horizon of flesh even in the event of death. This horizon is masked by intentionality but in the event of religious experience reveals itself (probably partially). A donation of presence, which is recognized as the divine one, opens this horizon to awareness and alters the ontologically subsequent horizon of temporality. This decenters the perspectival nature of ordinary givenness: Jesus appears to his disciples not as a memory but as an actual donation of his embodied subjectivity, in the now, after the event of his death.

This transtemporal flesh is given in a confrontation with the face of resurrected Jesus. There is an interruption of the everyday lifeworld, a failure of typification (the disciples and Mary—or, as Costello puts it, we—fail to recognize Jesus for what he is), and a rise of religious feeling (wonder *and* absolute dependence) in response to the apparition of the Face. In this case, it is not just mystery unveiled by interruption but the Face itself, the feeling of dependence when the face commands one's emotion and the attitude (ethics) of the encounter, and a disruption of the temporal horizon, all of which co-constitute an event of religious experience within the sphere of intersubjectivity.

References

al-Jīlī, ʿAbd al-Karīm. 1983. *Universal Man*. Trans. Titus Burckhardt. Roxburgh: Beshara Publications.

al-Tirmīdhī, Muhammad ibn al-Hakīm. 1996. *The Concept of Sainthood in Early Islamic Mysticism*. Trans. B. Radtke and J. O'Kane. Richmond, Surrey: Curzon Press.

Barber, Michael D. 2017a. Religion and the appresentative mindset. *Open Theology* 3 (1): 397–407. https://doi.org/10.1515/opth-2017-0031. Retrieved 6 June 2018.

———. 2017b. *Religion and humor as emancipating provinces of meaning*. New York: Springer.

———. 2018. Alfred Schutz. In *The Stanford encyclopedia of philosophy* (spring ed.), ed. Edward N. Zalta https://plato.stanford.edu/archives/spr2018/entries/schutz/. Accessed 4 June 2018.

Bergo, Bettina. 2017. Emmanuel Levinas. In *The Stanford encyclopedia of philosophy* (fall ed.), ed. Edward N. Zalta https://plato.stanford.edu/archives/fall2017/entries/levinas/. Accessed 1 June 2018.

Bernasconi, R. 2010. Globalization and world hunger: Kant and Levinas. In *Radicalizing Levinas*, ed. P. Atherton and M. Calarco, 69–86. Albany: SUNY Press.

---

[5] Merleau-Ponty's notion of the flesh of the world and Henry's notion of phenomenological materiality are different in the sense of their relationship to intentionality and in their ontological status. In the present reading, I omit details of this distinction and point to the similar aspect in these terms, which is a possibility of connectivity underlying the appearance of individual boundaries.

196   O. Louchakova-Schwartz

Byers, Damian. 2002. *Intentionality and transcendence: Closure and openness in Husserl's phenomenology*. Madison/Shoreline: University of Wisconsin Press and Noesis Press.

Chittick, William C. 1998. *The self-disclosure of God: Principles of Ibn al-'Arabī's cosmology*. Albany: SUNY Press.

Cutsinger, J., ed. 2003. *Paths to the heart: Sufism and the Christian East*. Bloomington: World Wisdom.

Dahnhardt, Thomas. 2007. *Change and continuity in Indian Sufism: A Naqshbandi-Mujaddidi branch in the Hindu environment*. New Delhi: D.K. Printworld.

Durt, C. 2018. *Minimal self, for-me-ness, and the openness of experience*. Paper given at the workshop "Perspectives on the minimal self," Universität Wien, Vienna, Austria, 14 May 2018.

Egéa, D. 2014. Intersubjectivity revisited. In *Philosophy of education*, ed. M. Moses, 128–131. Urbana: Philosophy of Education Society.

Hayat, Pierre. 1999. Preface: Philosophy between totality and transcendence. In *Alterity and Transcendence*, ed. E. Levinas. Trans. Michael B. Smith, ix–xxiv. London: Athlone Press.

Henry, Michel. 1973. *The Essence of Manifestation*. Trans. Girard J. Etzkorn. The Hague: Nijhoff.

———. 2008. *Material phenomenology*. New York: Fordham University Press.

———. 2015. *Incarnation: A philosophy of flesh*. Evaston: Northwestern University Press.

Hopkins, Burt C. 2010. *The philosophy of Husserl*. Montreal: McGill-Queen's University Press.

Ibn 'Arabī, Muhyi-d-Din. 1981. *Kernel of the Kernel*. Trans. Bulent Rauf. Roxburgh, Rox: Beshara Publications. [Trans. of *Lubb al-lubab* with commentary by Ismail Hakki Bursevi.]

Knoblauch, H. 2013. Alfred Schutz's theory of communicative action. *Human Studies* 36 (3): 323–337. https://doi.org/10.1007/s10746-013-9278-9. Accessed 5 June 2018. [Published online 4 June 2013.].

Levinas, E. 1961 [1969]. *Totality and Infinity: An Essay on Exteriority*. Trans. Alphonso Lingis. Pittsburgh: Duquesne University Press.

———. 1996. *Proper Names*. Trans. Michael B. Smith. Stanford: Stanford University Press.

———. 1999. *Alterity and Transcendence*. Trans. Michael B. Smith. London: Athlone Press.

———. 2000. Beginning with Heidegger. In *God, Death, and Time*, ed. E. Levinas. Trans. Bettina Bergo, 121–125. Stanford: Stanford University Press.

Louchakova, O. 2005a. Awakening to spiritual consciousness in times of religious violence: Reflections on culture and transpersonal psychology. In *Ways through the wall: Approaches to citizenship in an interconnected world*, ed. J. Drew and D. Lorimer, 2–46. Lydney, Glos: First Stone.

———. 2005b. Ontopoiesis and union in the Prayer of the Heart: Contributions to psychotherapy and learning. In *Logos of phenomenology and phenomenology of the logos, Book four: The logos of scientific interrogation; Participating in nature–life–sharing in life, Analecta Husserliana 91*, ed. A.-T. Tymieniecka, 289–311. Dordrecht: Kluwer.

———. 2007. Spiritual Heart and direct knowing in the Prayer of the Heart. *Existential Analysis* 18 (1): 81–102.

Louchakova-Schwartz, O. 2014. The seal of philosophy: Tymieniecka's phenomenology of life in Islamic metaphysical perspective. In *The logos of life and cultural interlacing*, ed. A.-T. Tymieniecka, N. Muhtaroglu, and D. Quintern, 71–101. Dordrecht: Springer.

———. 2017a. *Attentiveness in Odysseus and Ovid, and the mindfulness of Exodus*. Paper given at the IX meeting of the International Coalition of North American Phenomenologists, Ramapo College of New Jersey, 25–28 May 2017.

———. 2017b. Qualia of God: Phenomenological materiality in introspection, with a reference to Advaita Vedanta. *Open Theology* 3 (1): 257–273. https://doi.org/10.1515/opth-2017-0021. [Published online 18 May 2017.].

Murungi, J. 1991. The African and the task of becoming a phenomenologist. In *Husserl's legacy in phenomenological philosophies, Book 3 of Phenomenology in the world fifty years after the death of Edmund Husserl*, ed. A.-T. Tymieniecka, 229–241. Dordrecht: Springer.

Musholt, C. 2012. Self-consciousness and intersubjectivity. *Grazer Philosophische Studien* 84 (1): 63–89.

Rapport, N. 2015. Anthropology through Levinas: Knowing the uniqueness of ego and the mystery of otherness. *Cultural Anthropology* 56 (2): 256–276.

Searle, J. 2008. The phenomenological illusion. In *Philosophy in a new century: Selected essays*, ed. J. Searle, 107–136. Cambridge: Cambridge University Press. https://doi.org/10.1017/CBO9780511812859.008. Accessed 14 Jan. 2018.

Taipale, Joona. 2014. *Phenomenology and embodiment: Husserl and the constitution of subjectivity*. Evanston: Northwestern University Press.

Taylor, M.L. 2011. *The theological and the political: On the weight of the world*. Minneapolis: Fortress Press.

———. 2013. *Philosophical note: On Jean-Luc Nancy's "transimmanence."*. http://marklewistaylor.net/blog/philosophical-note-on-jean-luc-nancys-transimmanence/. Accessed 6 June 2018.

Wiley, Norbert. 1994. *The semiotic self*. Oxford: Polity Press.

Olga Louchakova-Schwartz, M.D. Ph.D. (the editor) is a comparative religionist, philosopher, and interdisciplinary researcher. She holds the titles Professor of Philosophy of Religion, Spirituality, and Human Development at the Hult International Business School, and Clinical Professor at the UC Davis School of Medicine, Department of Public Health Sciences. She is also a Visiting Scholar at the Graduate Theological Union in Berkeley, Adjunct Lecturer in Spirituality and Phenomenology of Religion at the Jesuit School of Theology, and a Founding President of the Society for the Phenomenology of Religions Experience. Prior to her work in philosophy, she was a senior scientist at the Pavlov Institute of the Academy of Sciences in Russia, and after that, Director of Research and the Founding Director of the Neurophenomenology Center at the former Institute of Transpersonal Psychology, from which she holds the title Professor Emerita of Psychology and Comparative Religion. She studied phenomenology with Amedeo and Barbro Giorgi and with Anna-Teresa Tymieniecka, Her chief research interests are in religious subjectivity and religious experience in contemporary and historical contexts. She has published on fifteenth century and contemporary Kundalini Tantra, eighth century Advaita Vedanta and Neo-Vedanta, early Christianity, seventh–tenth century Hesychasm, contemporary Turkish and American Sufism, the Soviet spiritual underground, and the Islamic Philosophy of Illumination. Her cognitive phenomenological research of Tibetan Tantric meditation was featured on BBC, Science Daily, and other important forums She has published more than 200 papers and book chapters, and is an Associate Editor of the Journal of Theoretical and Philosophical Psychology, and guest editor for Open Theology, De Gruyter (2017; 2018, 2019, 2020 to appear).

VOLUME II. Doxastic Perspectives in the Phenomenology of Religious Experience

Part III. The Phenomenology of Revelation

Chapter 12
Sight and Sacrament: The Place of Nature in Religious Experience

Christopher Andrew DuPée

Abstract In this paper, I examine the place of material nature with regard to the liturgical thought of both Jean-Yves Lacoste and Jean-Luc Marion. I contend that, in both cases, the analysis of the place of spatiotemporal reality and material nature is deficient, and I look to the possible contributions of the Russian Orthodox writers Theophan the Recluse and Pavel Florensky toward a fuller phenomenology of both liturgy and nature. I hold that the two open up the possibility of a fundamental continuity between so-called earthly life and religious experience. I thus attempt to develop an ecophenomenological nuancing of the accounts of both Lacoste and Marion in conversation with the thought of Florensky and Theophan.

Keywords Jean-Yves Lacoste · Jean-Luc Marion · Theophan the recluse · Pavel Florensky · Liturgy · Religious experience

It must be said that the so-called theological turn in phenomenology has this particular virtue: it forces two interrelated issues both into the spotlight and into collision. I am referring, first of all, to the issue of exteriority, the not-I, which nevertheless appears to the I. The second issue is that of what does and does not arise as a phenomenon at all. The first, it may be said, is not the theological turn's special provenance; indeed its Cartesian heritage makes clear that this is not even a special question of phenomenology per se, even though a variety of subtraditions within phenomenology have offered a variety of insightful discussions of just this problem. However, a special collision that the theological turn in phenomenology offers is this first issue with that of the second, the bounds of phenomenality. For, if there is anything to be said of religious experience, particularly the knotted issue of monotheistic, personalist, Christian religious experience, often theologically legitimated and interpreted, the topic of God turns on these issues. For God, much like the

C. A. DuPée (✉)
Independent Scholar, San Dimas, CA, USA

© Springer Nature Switzerland AG 2019
O. Louchakova-Schwartz (ed.), *The Problem of Religious Experience*,
Contributions to Phenomenology 103,
https://doi.org/10.1007/978-3-030-21575-0_12

Other, is not-I; but unlike at least ordinary Others, of whom it must be said that whether they make an appearance or not is at least questionable, God makes even less of an appearance than that. Some account of the transcendence of I into the invisible seems the special question of the phenomenology of religious experience in general, just as well as in the usually Francophone theological turn.

And yet at this point a third issue arises. Just what are we to make not only of our constitutive horizons, of our perfectly ordinary ways of getting about the world, but of the very furniture of that world itself, once we have some account of this turning toward or access into the invisible? Further, it is likewise clear that some movement *within* ordinary experience and thus answerable to typical horizonal constitutions of experience is the setting-off point of our movement toward some encounter with the Divine. This contact/division between the ordinary and the invisible takes on a more typical visage if we consider it as a question of the distinction between the sacred and the profane. This, however, bears too quickly the mark of a certain sort of culture-bound conventionalism, and to discuss it under such a head would be in fact misleading. Rather, and almost homologous, is the contact/division between Nature and the Supernatural. For, indeed, is not one way of analyzing "the Natural" to restrict the class of possible phenomena to those that are, in fact, typically phenomenalized with regard to the five senses? Is not "Naturalism" simply an ontological judgment about this particular restricted class, combined with the converse negative ontological judgment as regards anything else? It would then be an easy opposition to set forth between the Natural and the Supernatural. The simple corollary, then, is that once we find the Supernatural, we set aside the Natural. For obvious reasons, however, this denial of Nature seems a scandal.

In this paper, I thus make an attempt at teasing out just what role Nature has to play within religious, or, more directly, theological experience. What I set forth below is a putting into dialogue, first, Jean-Yves Lacoste and Jean-Luc Marion, two well-known figures of the theological turn; and second, some figures from the intermingled traditions of Russian religious philosophy and the Russian Orthodox theological tradition: Saint Theophan the Recluse and Pavel Florensky. From these thinkers I draw out a plausible account of the role of Nature in religious experience and signal some importantlines of further research.

I shall begin with Jean-Yves Lacoste, whose *Experience and the Absolute* (2004) offers a particularly strong claim as to what liturgy is and its relationship to the ordinary structures of lived experience. Phenomenology attests to Place, the location of the unfolding of our experience and our inherence among the beings with which we live. For Lacoste, Heidegger's multiple interpretations of place—both as *unheimlich* world in *Being and Time* and as the earthly dwelling place of mortals as analyzed in Heidegger's later work on the thinking of the Fourfold—are each in themselves correct and not in contradiction.[1] "The logic of inherence is sufficiently rich for it both to confer on us the status of not-at-home as well as to provide us with

---

[1] Lacoste 2004, 19: "Before the world reveals to us that we are these without feeling at home, and before the earth offers itself as shelter, dwelling place, and homeland, world and earth comprise the double secret of place."

a mother earth." "But," Lacoste adds, "neither in the unfolding of place as world or as earth can liturgy be included in the topological."[2] The issue is that of encounter: neither world nor Earth attests the experience or encounter of humanity with God. This almost goes without saying with regard to the at-bottom anxious and *unheimlich* world discussed in *Being and Time*; and though the divinities make appearance within the thinking of the Fourfold, Lacoste is quick to counter that the Godhead remains veiled behind the divinities, who are its messengers, and that this is at best a pagan insufficiency, for there is nothing "native" about the human experience of the divine.[3] Liturgy, the place of prayer, while not overlooking the inescapable reality of the locatedness of human life, brackets, without annulling, both world and Earth. That is to say, in order to counter facticity's interposition between humanity and God, liturgy subverts these horizons of experience.

The relation of this subversive interpretation of liturgy to Lacoste's discussion of religious experience is circular, insofar as the insufficiency of the experiential in liturgy serves as the immanent data for this interpretation while the interpretation of liturgy "permits us to criticize every theory in which experience governs knowledge of God, or in which the relation of man to God reaches its culmination in the field of conscious experience."[4] For if the horizons of lived and native experience are agnostic,[5] if liturgy is "absent from the dawn of experience,"[6] then it is hardly surprising that "nothing that could be described as the indisputable advent of God … occurs in liturgy," rendering the happening of liturgy a "nonevent."[7] Without the transcendental horizons of experience, nothing, of course, appears. And this is simultaneously obvious to anyone within the Christian tradition, as[8]:

> the problem of Christian experience is the surprising nonrealization (surprising because all 'is' completed between Good Friday and Easter Sunday) of the *eschaton*. The time of this [Christian] experience can pass for being the 'end'. But it is not the time when the outpouring of the Spirit will have instituted the modes of a definitive presence of man before man and of man before God, and when man would have at his disposal on earth a definitive and given homeland. Rather, it is the time of an experience always lived in the shadow of death, when the rule of negation, or of sin, has been anything but abolished.

Liturgy must bracket experience and subvert it, or else it is judged by experience, and in that regard it fails to provide what it claims. At the same time, this means that the weakness, the insufficiency, the apparent deathlike silence of earthly life

---

[2] Ibid., 21.

[3] Ibid., 34–37. "Between the world of life and the liturgical field there is, then, a cognitive delay. We have no immediate way of knowing what would grant legitimacy to liturgy: according to the Husserlian concept, life is atheistic. And, in a way, the world of life is what must be overcome so that man can face God" (103). "Atheism is never simply nor in the first place a theoretical problem: it is first what is a priori to existence" (105).

[4] Ibid., 49.

[5] Ibid., 34.

[6] Ibid., 46.

[7] Ibid., 30–31.

[8] Ibid., 87.

regarding the divine, when compared to the promise of humanity's reconciliation with God, is not catastrophic. That neither facticity nor historicity enclose humanity is the lesson that liturgy teaches us.

A natural corollary to all this is that the nonhuman Earth, what recedes and protects the manifestation of the world, is equally bracketed. "Liturgy contests more than concepts: it is against the real that its protestations are directed."[9] Nature in general, both in our own nonliturgical corporeality and in regard to the basic nonhuman alterity of the rest of earthly being, is at best religiously ambivalent. What I wish to challenge here is none of the analyses that Lacoste takes up from Heidegger or of his critique of religious experience insofar as it purports to provide evidence of an "indisputable advent"[10]; nor indeed of the basic interposition accomplished by the operating world-horizon between humanity and the Absolute. Rather, what is in question is the scope of liturgy, how far the time and the location of this bracketing extends. For it seems clear, though unannounced, that from Lacoste's various references to liturgical gestures and times of day, there his appeal to liturgy is entirely literal.[10] He means a gathering in a church, a specific rite, an accomplishment of well-defined sacramental operations. The import here will be made clear later on. For now, it is simply not clear whether this particular act in itself is the privileged accomplishment of our bracketing of the horizons of experience, whether it is only in this time and place that the encounter with the Absolute can occur, and nowhere else.

As a first essay toward providing a competing account of the relationship between nature and liturgy, between experience and sacrament, let us take up the words of Saint Theophan the Recluse, a Russian saint of the Eastern Orthodox Church[11]:

> Experience frequently shows that the mind that has been dimmed by worldly fumes becomes sober through contemplation of God's creation. … One man in winter looked at the tree that stood in front of his house and came to himself. … The power and influence of these visible works of God depend on the fact that they vividly and tangibly reveal the best and most blissful order of life to a man's spirit that has been weakened, enervated, and exhausted by the vanity of this world.

We must not take the insistence that nature "vividly and tangibly reveals" the works of God too straightforwardly. Mere pages further on Theophan admits that in the absence of preaching such experiences remain vague, indefinite, without interpretation.[12] This is, in fact, exactly in keeping with Lacoste, who contrasts uncertain and indefinite experience with knowledge, a revealed teaching. So what simply happens in Theophan's brief account is that the vanity of the world is put out of play and made visible by means of distinction. This is hardly different from Heidegger's own depictions of the Nothing and anxiety in "What Is Metaphysics?"[13]—the falling

---

[9] Ibid., 46.

[10] Ibid., 77–80 on vigil; on corporeality, 37–38.

[11] Theophan the Recluse 2001, 29–30.

[12] Ibid., 34–36.

[13] Heidegger 1993, 108: "But if the nothing becomes any problem at all, then this opposition does not merely undergo a somewhat more significant determination; rather, it awakens for the first time

away of the world and the attestation of its unhomelike character, which reveals the horizon of Being. There is, at first glance, nothing liturgical about this: we are left in the same position as Lacoste in his examination of Heidegger. We remain within the native horizon of experience, still ambiguous and agnostic.

What Lacoste assumes, however, is that Heidegger's interpretation of the anxiousness and recession of the world is in itself wholly accurate, and that it leaves us with the ineluctable horizon of Being. But, turning to Jean-Luc Marion's reading of Heidegger, this is also not obvious. For if Marion's argument is correct, and if his reading of Heidegger is true, especially in the appeal to the Nothing as the way toward the phenomenon of Being, it would seem Heidegger's aim at attesting Being succumbs to a certain failing: the searched-for attestation of Being is not attained. Rather, the anonymous call, never clearly forcing an ontological interpretation of itself as Being, much less as any thing, and all the while and because of this prior to Being, is found.[14] We have the question, then, of the appearance of this we-know-not-what that is at least irreducible to Being, and thus as such irreducible to any horizon.[15]

It is from the appearance of this abyss beyond Being that Marion comes to theorize, first, a further and thus third phenomenological reduction, beyond the horizons of the transcendental I (in Husserl) and of Being (in Heidegger), and second, the field to which this third reduction attains and attests: that "in whatever way and by whatever means something can relate to us, absolutely nothing is, happens, appears to us or affects us that is not first, always, and obligatorily accomplished in the mode of a *givenness*."[16] What this accomplishes, phenomenologically, is the description and analysis of phenomena without the necessity that they ever be fully inscribed within and according to the horizons of experience. Because of this, Theophan's words take on a new light: the experience of the vanity of the world does not bottom out at the horizon of Being, and thus we need not understand this vanity within the confines of the hermeneutics of facticity. Indeterminate still, admittedly, is whether or not such an experience of Nature accomplishes the liturgical bracketing and the attendant opening onto the encounter with the Absolute that Lacoste speaks of. Saint Theophan clearly thinks this view of the tree to be spiritually salutary, but it is not yet clear whether the ambiguity and the interposition are overcome.

It is clear, however, that something quite like a bracketing of world and Earth attains in Marion's treatment. This third reduction to pure givenness is at the very least coextensive with Lacoste's liturgical subversion, and for this reason we must now consider the means by which this bracketing occurs. For Lacoste, the general tone of the discussion leans toward a decidedly volitional subversion of the play of experience that makes its claim upon us. Those who pray do not merely pray but

---

the proper formulation of the metaphysical question concerning the Being of beings. The nothing does not remain the indeterminate opposite of beings but reveals itself as belonging to the Being of beings."

[14] Marion 1998, 169–187.

[15] Ibid., 188.

[16] Marion 2002a, 53.

halt, choose, alter their being-there into a being-in-vocation, and thus play havoc without ever annulling their destined facticity. Now in the case of Marion, this is by and large the same, when we look to his explicit discussions of prayer and liturgy. However, this reduction to givenness is not specially arrogated to liturgy, as we have already seen.

What the reduction to givenness enables Marion to do is provide an analysis of varying grades of phenomenality according their relative fullness of intuition. The less that is given, the more fully our intentional constitution can manifest all that there is to know about them. The privileged example is the simple logical or mathematical formula wherein once one understands anything at all about it, one understands everything about it: $A = A$, for example.[17] Likewise with technologically manufactured repeatables: in their conceptualized blueprint, one sees everything at once.[18] By contrast, there is the uncontroversial depth to any experience of what we could generally characterize as naively real things. Ipseity gives more to intuition than intention can contain.[19] This excess of intuition Marion terms *saturation*, and it is these very saturated phenomena that particularly attest to givenness.[20] Particularly strong instances of saturation, however, even more fully attest this challenge to horizons by means of their appearance, as "certain phenomena could appear only by playing at the limits of phenomenality—indeed by making sport of them."[21] Such phenomena include the general impossibility of getting "the whole story" about an event (even one so banal as a conference), temporality itself, the completely inescapable reality of my living sensibility, or the excessive quality of the Face of the Other.[22]

This saturation of intuition, as was said, plays at and thus challenges horizons, which thus attest givenness; that is as much as to say a reduction beyond the horizons of Being occurs. What is often unexamined, if perhaps obvious, is the passive nature of this occurrence of the reduction. All the same, it is clear that this excess of intuition is in some fashion attended to insofar *something* is forced upon certain subjects; the experience of boredom, anxiety, the face, and so forth, are all hardly the privileged domain of phenomenologists. Here stands, as yet unnamed and yet clearly considered by Marion, the instance of the passive reduction, wherein the bracketing is accomplished on the part of the phenomenon and not on the volition of the subject: the impossibility of fully attaining to the givenness of the phenomenon, on the basis of how much the given gives, brackets the intentional horizons. For this reason, of course, we are still beyond the bounds of claiming that this occurs in the realm of vulgar, incontestable experience. But this is not, of course, to insist on total invisibility, as any reading of Marion's various analyses of saturated phenom-

---

[17] Ibid., 222.

[18] Ibid., 225. Cf. Marion 2013.

[19] Ibid., 222–223.

[20] Ibid., 227: "The saturated phenomenon in the end establishes the truth of all phenomenality because it marks, more than any other phenomenon, the givenness from which it comes."

[21] Ibid., 189.

[22] Ibid., 220–221, 228–232. Cf. Marion 2002b.

ena will make clear. Plenty is initially given to ordinary perception. But it is because of the play against the horizons of experience that the saturated phenomenon is *irreducible* to the conditions of experience.[23]

This theory of saturated phenomena allows us to take up a somewhat altered consideration of the bracketing that liturgy accomplishes, and by this make way again to consider nonhuman nature. Let us take up the thoughts of Pavel Florensky, who is himself no quick admirer of purportedly spiritual experiences. In contrast to Lacoste's criticism of religious experience, wherein what is actually seen and heard offers far too little of the Absolute thanks to the penury of the divine in the horizons of our experience, for Florensky the horizons of our ordinary life offer far too much in the way of the purportedly spiritual. The danger, rather than a forgetting or willful ignorance of the pall of death across our present life, is rather the danger of spiritual pride: *prelest,* Florensky calls it. The great accumulations of psychological, social, and aesthetic material provide far too much fodder for the imagination, material with which to conjure up sights and visions of the purportedly eternal and divine; these not only interpose but counterfeit the encounter of humanity with the Absolute. All the same, the demand for the bracketing of these lifeworlds, of the horizons of the day-to-day, is just as direly called for. And just the same, Florensky thinks through this very same bracketing under yet another figure[24]:

> A day of spiritual sobriety, when it holds our soul in its power, is so sharply different from the spiritual realm that it cannot even pretend to be seductive, and its materiality is experienced not only as a burden but also as a yoke good for us in the way gravity is good for earth, a yoke restricting our movements but giving us a fulcrum, a yoke reigning in the swiftness with which our will acts in self-determination.

This day Florensky later names "time-space." Of course, this is not the time and space of the transcendental I, of the horizons of experience: it is a check; it is utterly nonhuman and dethrones and destabilizes, places under its yoke, the ego; and this in the same fashion as does the saturated phenomenon give lie to the totally constitutive power of the subject. And this check is itself located in the liturgy, which Florensky makes clear attains its "way of ascent" precisely *within* time-space.[25] This very ascent is that to the invisible world of spirit, and with that yet again we can affirm Lacoste's insistence that no incontestable advent, no unquestionably obvious experience, occurs. But it is by means of the church bedecked and formed and made possible by the very presence of the incontestably visible: the iconostasis. The iconostasis is, of course, the construction of wood and paint that separates the clergy from the laity most of the time. But, like any other saturated phenomenon, it is irreducible to this common experience[26]:

> In actuality, the iconostasis is a boundary between the visible and invisible worlds, and it functions as a boundary by being an obstacle to our seeing the altar, thereby making it

---

[23] Ibid., 215.

[24] Florensky 1996, 46.

[25] Ibid., 59.

[26] Ibid., 63.

accessible to our consciousness by means of its unified row of saints. ... because our sight is weak and our prayers feeble, the Church, in her care for us, gave us visual strength for our spiritual brokenness: the heavenly visions on the iconostasis, vivid, precise, and illuminated, that *articulate*, materially cohere, an image into fixed colors. But this spiritual prop, this material iconostasis, does not conceal from the believer some sharp mystery. ... Destroy the material iconostasis and the altar itself will, as such, wholly vanish from our consciousness.

That is to say, the very stuff of Nature, wood and gold and fire, is taken up in the cult and made into the very possibility of the bracketing of the world. This utterly material, utterly real stuff of the liturgy acts in the liturgy, with and in the place of our earthly inherence, to accomplish this bracketing, so that the spiritual excess of what cannot be simply gazed at instead comes through as it gives itself.[27] That is to say, very much against Lacoste, that the real is not contested in liturgy but is instead included and taken up.

As we can see, the critique of experience, while wholly valid, especially with regard the ordinary *Erleibnis* of walking about and getting things done in a world not filled with the Spirit, still subject to history and worse of this particular history we live within, requires some great deal of nuance. But coming from Lacoste's perspective, a possible critique still stands: fine, one could say: experience can bracket experience. But does not this new focus of attention upon the stuff of the world, all of Nature's beauty, however much it may provide an escape, does that by necessity not assume that the Divine still makes its way through? Could not liturgy and cult, focused upon time-space experience, instead become just as much of an interposition? Who is to say that the Absolute is encountered in this new Natural bracketing?

It is here, it must be admitted, that the going becomes complicated. For here we meet strangely transposed into phenomenology an old debate concerning natural theology. For here the question turns about the simple dispute as to whether phenomenologically reduced Nature speaks of God unambiguously, or not. By way of avoiding too neat a conclusion at the expense of either simply making up stories or giving bad answers, let me instead enumerate some of the points of contention.

It is of course the case that Lacoste is by and large correct about the theological penury of our ordinary experience of the real, but the hope would be that, at the far point of the reduction, perhaps something could be found. The long tradition of Orthodox mystical theology has it, in effect, that part and parcel to the heights of asceticism and sanctification includes the Love of all Nature, simultaneously attending to them with a tender heart and a perfect understanding of the essence of all things.[28]

Florensky and his contemporary Sergei Bulgakov both leapt upon this possibility with their rigorously Orthodox interpretation of Vladimir Solovyev's Sophiology.

---

[27] At this would be unable to be gazed upon simply because it would thus be subject to the myriad psychosocial detritus that Florensky refers to, thus subject to the constitution of the lifeworldly I that Marion critiques, thus subject to the pall of death and the vicissitudes of facticity that Lacoste laments.

[28] Florensky 1997, 207–210, 228–230.

Sophia, God's Creating Wisdom, the dynamic interplay of the second and third persons of the Trinity in their living creation of the World, is thus the all-integral existence of Nature, in its beauty. Sophia is "the Eternal Bride of the Word of God" "existing before the world ... the Church in its Heavenly Aspect ... the True Pole and Incorruptible Aspect of creaturely being" that is revealed to the spiritually cleansed ascetic[29]:

> The primordial root of a person ... is perceived through the heart, and through this root a living link is established with the Mother of the spiritual person, with Sophia, understood as the Guardian Angel of all creation, of all creation consubstantial in love, received through Sophia from the Spirit.

So in the saturated experience of things, reduced beyond horizons to their pure ipseity, God is in fact manifested, and so on Florensky's view the interposition Lacoste fears is truly not a problem. From this theological claim we can at least make the phenomenological suggestion that it is not so much the transcendental horizons of experience that interpose and dismantle the experience of God but instead the fundamental manner of their contingent attunement. The ascetic who sees God in every branch and stone and candle clearly sees these things but is also made privy to the symbolic surplus. That such a visionary is rather rare is a circumstance we shall take up further below.

On this basis, we can return to the questions I mentioned at the beginning: how far the liturgical extends and what place the Natural stuff of life has in the encounter with the Divine. We bring together two considerations already mentioned: first, it seems that any thing, in its ipseity, can accomplish a certain kind of bracketing, but this is specially located in the incorporation of the stuff of Nature into the material elements of the liturgy. But on the far side of this bracketing, at least under the hermeneutic of the legitimating theology Florensky appeals to, the spectacle of all-integral Nature comes through, which thus holds out the possibility, again, of a kind of natural theo-*logy* on the back end of the ascetical endeavor. Since the bracketing that liturgy accomplishes is at least part and parcel with asceticism (it is hard to miss the ascetical dimension in Florensky's insistence on *sobriety* in the liturgy), we seem to be able, perhaps by a leap, to bring together these two into a unified field: if liturgy *is* this bracketing, then there is a general and a special liturgy. The first, the already nascent spiritual quality of Life in Nature, obscure though it may be. The second, the special cultic transformation of the Natural such that the alteration is focused and makes clear this spiritual excess of the bounds of ordinary experience. The big-S Sacraments of the Christian church teach the possibility, and are the training in seeing, the sacramental possibility of all experience. Recall Florensky's image of the iconostasis as a spiritual prop, an aid: it is for the sake of the multitude still in the process of their ascetical work, as it allows the opening onto the general liturgy, which is earthly life itself. The equivocal nature of this appeal to the "general liturgy" should not be passed over too quickly, for it is both the bracketing of horizons (our operating definition so far) and the teaching of the nature of the

---

[29] Ibid., 254.

"work" (the actual meaning of the term "liturgy") of humanity on Earth, which is its sacramental operation.

Let us now turn a critical eye to what seems to be offered here. What is admittedly difficult in this account, and should be mentioned from the start, is that this critique begins with a claim that is already theological and metaphysical to the core: a legitimating hermeneutic is standing and already in place long before any of this can be attained to, which renders as a secondary fact what would hope to be considered primary data. And the scandal here, part and parcel with the whole theological turn anyway, is the claim, at least on Marion's part, to actually be doing phenomenology, which was of course supposed to suspend presuppositions of any sort, at least ideally. And a parallel claim can be seen in Florensky's insistence that what he is attempting to offer is explicitly *not* metaphysical speculation from *a priori* principles but the fruit of *a posteriori* experience.[30] But all seem simply to bite the bullet. Florensky, Marion, and Lacoste all agree on this: God must be named as Creator before we can hear Creation sing His praises.[31] And this should come as little surprise: Lacoste boldly affirms that liturgy suspends experience by means of knowledge; and in Marion's treatment of Revelation as a saturated phenomenon, the eventual farthest edge of the reduction actually collapses into theology. To bracket every name of God is to enter into a new pragmatic relationship with God, which Marion quite boldly describes as an induction into God's horizon: a new hermeneutic is given in this moment of almost wondrous theological empiricism.[32] When our horizons fail, if we persist in the attempt at the encounter, a new horizon is given us. It is appropriate that in Florensky's discussion of the icon, he takes great pains to make clear that the person depicted in the icon is made present: and in the passive reduction before the face of this sanctified Other, the saint *teaches* us.[33]

But what to make of this? At the very least, it seems that this trespassing of the claim of a presuppositionless phenomenology is part and parcel of any attempt at a discussion of religious truth in connection with what appears. A legitimating hermeneutic just *is* what revelation is, at least in part. And so while it is not in any way intellectually honest to *ignore* this trespassing, it seems that the debate that is played out here is hardly decided on its basis: the questions do not even get off the ground in a rigorously atheistic and unknowledgeable phenomenology.[34]

The issue, however, might well be transposed into a considerably more fruitful problematic. Let us grant a unified space of religious knowledge, which is not hard in that all of our disputants actually do operate within traditional, sacramental, liturgically based Christianity. The problematic concerning experience stands. Why? At the naive level of religious experience, Lacoste's critique seems completely justified. And, as we have seen, this critique continues to manifest its legitimacy, if not its complete accuracy, even once we have taken Florensky's thought into account,

---

[30] Ibid., 236.

[31] Lacoste 2004, 102–103; cf. Marion 2013, 411–415.

[32] Marion and Carlson 1994.

[33] Florensky 1996, 165.

[34] As regards the theological knowledge so discussed by Lacoste 2004.

much less that of Marion. This is all because of the very simple fact that the vision of the mystagogical depths of apophatic theology and sophiology are simply not the common stock of Christian worshippers, at least in any conscious way. And it would, of course, seem that this is a deep problem if the claims to a presupposition-less phenomenology remain held as a binding principle. If such were the case, equal access to phenomena seems to be about the only way to legitimate claims about such phenomena.[35] But, as we have seen, the rigorous cataloguing of appearances, in a properly Husserlian fashion, is really not what is at stake here. Instead, the problem becomes a question as to why any sort of equal access is lacking here. And we have a start—and in this paper an altogether too brief start—from Florensky's reminder of the ascetical work that goes hand in hand with the manifestation of God in Nature. As we have said, the contingent attunement of our horizons of experience seems, more than the horizons themselves, to be in some way responsible for their interposition between our awareness and the Absolute.

The possibility of the alterations of such attunement, of course, can be seen in a nascent sense within Marion's discussion of the saturation of horizons, and for our purposes (just as much for Marion's own) his discussion reaches its apogee when aligning his theory of saturated phenomena with the tradition of apophatic theology. Marion's discussion of the tradition of apophatic theology, however, does not make clear the connections to any sort of preparatory or ascetical labor, and he has been criticized for precisely this deficiency.[36] As it stands, we likewise have the difficult that Florensky's own treatment of asceticism, in keeping with his own Eastern Orthodox tradition, is wrapped up within a strongly interpreted theological anthropology, one that makes easy translation into phenomenological investigation difficult. Their shared insistence upon the necessity of the reduction of the spuriously egoistic or worldly horizons of everyday experience do provide a beginning, of course; but to my knowledge, with the partial exceptions of Sartre and Henry, a phenomenological hamartiology has remained a sharp lacuna within phenomenology's theological turn. This problematic, it seems, undergirds the possibility of answering whether or not it is the horizons of experience themselves, or the particular attunement thereof, that limit and play havoc with the possibility of the experience of God; and as such the foregoing debate cannot quite be settled without such a theory. For while Marion and Florensky present a powerful competing vision, it still remains to be clearly proven whether they actually see more than Lacoste, or if they just happen to be "telling stories."[37]

---

[35] This goes doubly for the supposed "phenomenology" of the liturgy: it almost goes without saying that, short of Florensky's discussing the wood-and-paint iconostasis, little of what has come before has much to do with the typical layperson's set of experiences of the liturgy. Cf. Gschwandtner 2014.

[36] Cf. Gschwandtner 2014.

[37] Marion 2002a, 189.

References

Florensky, Pavel. 1996. *Iconostasis*. Trans. Donald Sheehan and Olga Andrejev. Crestwood: St. Vladimir's Seminary Press.
———. 1997. *The Pillar and the Ground of the Truth*. Trans. Boris Jakim. Princeton: Princeton University Press.
Gschwandtner, Christina. 2014. *Degrees of givenness: On saturation in Jean-Luc Marion*. Bloomington: Indiana University Press. [*eBook Collection (EBSCOhost)*, EBSCO*host* (Accessed 15 May 2017).].
Heidegger, Martin. 1993. *What is metaphysics?* In *Basic Writings,* Rev. ed., ed. David Farrell Krell, 89–110. HarperSanFrancisco.
Lacoste, Jean-Yves. 2004. *Experience and the Absolute: Disputed Questions on the Humanity of Man*. Trans. Mark-Raferty-Skehan. Perspectives in Continental Philosophy. New York: Fordham University Press.
Marion, Jean-Luc. 1998. *Reduction and Givenness*. Trans. Thomas A. Carlson. Evanston: Northwestern University Press.
———. 2002a. *Being Given*. Trans. Jeffrey L. Kossky. Stanford: Stanford University Press.
———. 2002b. *In Excess: Studies of Saturated Phenomena. Trans. Robyn Horner and Vincent Berraud*. New York: Fordham University Press.
———. 2013. The banality of saturation. In *Essential writings*, ed. Kevin Hart, 135–155. New York: Fordham University Press.
Marion, Jean-Luc, and Thomas A. Carlson. 1994. Metaphysics and phenomenology: A relief for theology. *Critical Inquiry* 20: 582.
Theophan the Recluse. 2001. *Turning the Heart to God*. Trans. Father Ken Kaisch and Igumen Iana Zhiltsov. Ben Lomond: Conciliar Press.

Christopher Andrew DuPée is an early career independent scholar who studied philosophy at the University College Dublin and theology at the Fuller Theological Seminary in California. DuPée presented his work at the First Conference of the Society for the Phenomenology of Religious Experience, which was hold at the Patriarch Athanagoras Orthodox Institute Graduate and Graduate Theological Union in Berkeley on November 4–5, 2016. His research interests include phenomenology, Russian religious philosophy, Patristics, and the continental philosophy of language.

Chapter 13
Mystical Experience as Existential Knowledge in Raimon Panikkar's *Navasūtrāni*

Leonardo Marcato

Abstract The work of Raimon Panikkar (Barcelona, 1918 – Tavertet, 2010) on mystical experience stands out for its grounding in a dialogical proposal that impacts not only interreligious and intercultural dialogue but also the innermost existential dimension of the believer in particular and the Humankind in general. During his lifetime, he studied Christian, Hindu, and Buddhist spirituality in depth according to his openness to the other and the Other; he developed an original philosophical and theological proposal in which relational ontological pluralism is rooted in the Catholic Trinity. Far from being merely a description of mystical experiences common to various religions, the idea he tries to convey in his *Navasūtrāni* ("Nine Sūtras of Mystical Experience") is theologically and theoretically tied to his Trinitarian and relational (cosmotheandric) ontology and to his pluralist theology of religions at large, where the mystical dimension is grounding for any religious experience.

The first part of this paper will express and summarize these elements of Panikkar's $E = e(l.m.i.r.a)$, his rigorous structure of mystical experience, in the *Navasūtrāni*. In the second part it will be argued not only that Panikkar's *Navasūtrāni* proposal is a phenomenological description of mystical experience regardless of doctrinal and religious differences but further that it crosses over the epistemological and the existential dimension of the Human. In conclusion, it will then be argued that understanding religious experience according to Panikkar can serve as a foundation of how our "being-Human" builds the knowledge of the world.

Keywords Raimon Panikkar studies · Intercultural philosophy of religion · Phenomenology of mystical experience · Gnoseology of mystical experience · Contemporary comparative theology

L. Marcato (✉)
Department of Philosophy and Cultural Heritage, Università Ca' Foscari di Venezia, Venice, Italy

© Springer Nature Switzerland AG 2019
O. Louchakova-Schwartz (ed.), *The Problem of Religious Experience*, Contributions to Phenomenology 103, https://doi.org/10.1007/978-3-030-21575-0_13

Among contemporary works analysing religious experience, that of Raimon Panikkar (Barcelona 1918 – Tavertet 2010) stands out for its grounding on a dialogical proposal. His idea of dialogue impacts deeply not only interreligious and intercultural dialogue proper, but also the innermost existential dimension of the believer (in particular) and Humankind in general. During his lifetime, he studied Christian, Hindu, and Buddhist traditions and wrote profound essays and articles on spirituality. He developed his original philosophical and theological proposal according to his openness to the other and the Other, with a relational (not relativistic) ontological pluralism rooted in the Trinity of his Catholic faith, of which he was a priest, albeit atypical. Far from being merely a description of mystical experiences common to various religions, what he tries to convey in his Navasūtrāni, or "Nine Sūtras of Mystical Experience" (Panikkar 2008a, 169–274), is theologically and theoretically tied to his Trinitarian and relational (cosmotheandric) ontology. He links his argument to how he analyzes the nature of symbol, myth, logos, and pneuma, and to his pluralist theology of religions at large, seeing any religious experience as grounded in the mystical dimension. While focusing on what happens to the Human[1] when a mystical experience takes place, his choice of words and the structure of the argument point to a deeper level of understanding. Panikkar seems to argue that the idea of mystical experience can be traced back to a wider concept of human knowledge of the world and of itself, thus placing mystical experience within a proper theory of knowledge. Such will be the aim of this paper: to introduce Panikkar's theory of mystical experience as a formalized gnoseology by which religious experience, for the very fact of being religious, is linked to the element in the Human that allows them to experience the world and to interrogate it.

The first part of this paper will prepare the ground for understanding the rigorous structure of mystical experience in the *Navasūtrāni* by presenting Panikkar's philosophical theology. Some of his lexicon will be clarified via analysis of the first six *sūtras*. In the second part, thanks to an analysis of the seventh *sūtra*, it will be argued that Panikkar's *Navasūtrāni* proposal not only is a phenomenological description of mystical experience transcending doctrinal and religious differences (or absence thereof) but crosses over to both the epistemological and the existential dimension of the Human. In conclusion, it will be argued that religious experience, in the peculiar sense proposed by Panikkar, not only exists but can be said to be the foundation of how our "being-Human" builds the knowledge of the world.

---

[1] This word, as other in this paper, has been capitalized due to the role that they have in Panikkar's philosophical lexicon. These words include, but are not limited to, Human, God, Divine, Cosmos, Rhythm of Being, Reality. For a comprehensive explanation on Panikkar's lexicon cfr. Pérez Prieto and Meza Rueda 2016.

13.1 The *Navasūtrāni;* or, the Phenomenology of Mystical Experience

During the 2017 Ex Nihilo Zero Conference of the European Academy of Religion, in the panel focused on Panikkar studies, all questions and debates promptly ended up with a question: What is the human being for Panikkar? This cardinal question in the study of this author is not easily answered. He describes the Human as "a Trinitarian mystery" or "the mystery that the man is; being man is the mystery and, for us, the access to mystery" (Panikkar 2010, 141). The Trinitarian dimension is cardinal for Panikkar's philosophy and theology. Reality, he argues, is the dynamic rhythm of the Trinitarian Being, expressed but not divided in its Human, Divine and Cosmic elements. The Cosmic dimension is everything that surrounds us: the physical world, other people, the Earth, the Moon, and the whole universe, from the biggest galaxy to the smallest subatomic particle. The Human dimension is what we are, how we relate to everything, what we think, feel, believe. Divine is the openness to the mystery behind and around us, be it called God, Transcendence, Immanence, the world of ideas, or the world of numbers. These three dimensions are intertwined in a relationship that he calls *ontonomy,* or inter-in-dependence; everything is interconnected without being unified via some kind of pantheism or *panenteism* (Panikkar 2012, 357). This is the reason why Michiko Yusa can say that pebbles speak (Yusa 2012): everything is cosmotheandric; the three dimensions of Reality resonate with one another. When the Human thinks about itself and about the world, there is some part of it that creates a connection with the Divine and the Cosmic alike. Panikkar's main instrument in relating with the world is *logos;* not a mere rational push to analyze and separate one thing from another but that faculty through which the Human is present in the Divine, and the Divine can incarnate in the Human (Panikkar 2012, 433). For this reason, the Human is a mystery: it is, itself, the Human part of the cosmotheandric Rhythm of Being and being it, a part of Reality, which is itself cosmotheandric. The Human is that part of the cosmotheandry that can reflect on itself; with its act of being-in-the-world and knowing-the-world it allows Reality to be known. In this perspective, the very act of thinking, when consciously oriented toward a true understanding of the mystery that it is itself, is deeply mystic.

If thought is a mystical dimension, and if it does not betray its nature by absolutizing itself and becoming simply *ratio,* then Panikkar's mysticism is not what is more commonly pointed at by this term. Usually, Panikkar says mysticism is described as the experience of the *Ultimate Reality* (Panikkar 2008a, 172). Mysticism is thus a supreme experience, spiritual in character, that opens to the absolute Other and is absolutely the transcendence experienced by the subject. This is the reason why mystics are often described as having their heads in the clouds, as shown in the age-old story of Thales and the Thracian maid. They do not look at the reality around them, lost in the ἐκ-στάσις outside themselves and blind to everything that is not the pure experience of God. This is a concept of mysticism that Panikkar rejects. According to him, this is not only a misunderstanding of mysticism by philosophical speculation but also an idea of mysticism still grounded in a dualistic, Cartesian view of reality as divided into immanence and transcendence one. His goal is to define mystical experience from the point of view of the relationship between Human, Cosmos and Divine. In what is apparently a text describing mystical experience, he presents a series of *symbols* and analyses that can be applied not only to the mystical experience per se but also to how the human being experiences the world and itself. *Symbol* here must be understood in two different ways (I'm summarizing here Panikkar's twenty-three lengthy points of *Symbol and symbolization* in Panikkar 2008b, 239–274). First is the traditional idea of *symbol* as one of the possible languages by which mystical experience is transmitted and communicated externally to the subject that experiences it. Second, *symbol* is part of Panikkar's philosophical lexicon: it is the smallest unit in the hermeneutical process, that with which we interpret and analyze and that cannot further be interpreted and analyzed, since to separate its components would mean to destroy both symbol and the meaning that it *speaks about*. Although this may be understood as the impossibility of rationally analyzing a symbol—for if we should try to interpret it, it would crumble in the hands of Human logic—he proposes a philosophical solution to this apparent *aporia*. A symbol speaks about a meaning, and to understand it, it needs to be listened to. A philosophical inquiry that listens, rather than explains, must welcome the idea of a *logos* that accepts languages different from Western formal logic, without refusing or denying it but rather affirming its analytical strength through other languages (Marcato 2017, 136–139). Such a *logos* accepts the idea of early Christian thinkers and philosophers that by opening to the Absolute or, to use Panikkar's words, to the divine element of the cosmotheandric Rhythm of Being, reason can fully understand and, most important, be able clearly to express even what apparently lies outside its boundaries. Panikkar's proposal for a philosophical analysis of mystic experience, then, can be considered as something very akin to Maimonides' approach to Scriptures, or to Dōgen's *Shōbōgenzō*, or to other examples of more mystical approaches to writing: the (assumedly) impossible-to-be-said, formally expressed by *ratio* with full philosophical clarity and systematically presented to the reader.

These elements of his proposal are then condensed and put into practice in the methodology of the nine sūtras in order to express his concept of mysticism. Frequently used in his written production (just to name a few examples: Panikkar 2010, 263–312; 2011a, 192–244; 2011b, 266–270; 2016, 735–784), these sūtras are nine brief sentences followed by lengthy philosophical and hermeneutic digressions not meant to explain directly but to help the understanding of the sūtras themselves and to provide elements for further analyses. Their goal is at the same tame to state a philosophical position and to put forth a starting point of discussion, to engage readers and to invite them in discovering the consequences of a philosophical statement. Thus, as will be argued below, the phenomenology of mystical experience expressed in the Navasūtrāṇi points to something broader, to a properly formalized gnoseology, a theory of how the Human gains knowledge of the world. From mystical experience, then, to a rational expression of how experience happens. But how?

In the first *sūtra,* Panikkar explains how for him *mysticism is the integral experience of Reality* (Panikkar 2008a, 171–179). It is an experience that can approach the "fullness of Reality" immediately, everything that can be bodily, intellectually, or spiritually experienced, or in all these forms, without being modified by a subsequent perspective or logical reelaboration. It is a *pure experience* whereby the subject of it remains indistinguishable from the object of experience—or as long as Reality is perceived in its wholeness and not thanks to some ultimate dimension that "assumes a classification thanks to a pure formal criterion on reality itself" (Panikkar 2008a, 173). Panikkar seems to use the word "reality" with some reluctance. It is a term charged with thousands of years of philosophical conceptualization. He would probably have preferred to use "full experience of Life" instead of "Reality", given the risk of some of the aforementioned conceptualization seeping into his argument, since he is not speaking of a *Dasein,* or *Absolute,* or even God. But in doing so he might have fallen into the opposite, a vitalism devoid of reason, where the only thing that really matters is to possess life. "Life" and "Reality" are homeomorphic equivalents: that is, terms that fulfill the same role in their respective philosophical frameworks, which are vitalism for the former and formalism for the latter. For this reason, a contemplative act, which can experience existence, is the embodiment of intellectual life; and the term "Reality" can be correctly used by Panikkar in this context, given the philosophical dimension of *sūtra* methodology, in order to encompass everything that can be experienced. The dualistic opposition of "being" and "reality" in this first *sūtra* is not only a way for Panikkar to clarify his thought, but it is also an incentive for the reader to think about the differences between the two words and about the experiences that these words refer to. One could summarize a thesis of the first *sūtra* as "mysticism is the awareness of cosmotheandric reality."

Whereas "being Human" means "being the moment in which cosmotheandry is aware of itself," the second *sūtra* says that *experience is the conscious touch of reality* (Panikkar 2008a, 180–187). Cosmotheandric intuition, be it the Trinity or inter-in-dependence (interconnection of everything with everything), before being an intellectual dimension, is an experience lived by the Human (Panikkar 2010, 95). It resides in the Human; it moves its subject toward becoming a part of its relationship with Reality. Rather than "touch," the word "contact" would be better used here. Contact as in *cum-tangere*, "touch together," interpenetration between subject and object so that the distinction loses meaning: "a polarity is because of the other polarity, so that knowledge of one needs also knowledge of the other ... but we cannot rationally and concurrently know the two polarities (A and B—that can't be identified with not-A). The two polarities thus create an a-dual polarization" (Panikkar 2008a, 182). This is the interconnection of everything with everything, or ontonomy: that is, inter-in-dependence. There's absence of object and subject, of terms in a relation, as they are structured by the relation itself; "a-dual polarization" means that what matters in a relation is the polarization itself, which gives meaning to the polarity. Another example: saying that north and south are relative does not mean, in Panikkar's philosophy, that they are north or south according to a point of view, but that there is a *relation* between them. They do not exist *as north and south per se,* but their being north and south is due to how they interact with each other and with east, west, center, travelers, politics, economics, geography, and so on. We can restrict our analysis to details, but they do not lose their relationship with each other and Being itself. Here, Panikkar refers to the theory of *advaita,* or a-dualism, that he derived from his studies of Hindu philosophy and religion. *Advaita* is a fundamental ontological concept for a mystical experience that wants to be properly philosophical, the *opus tripartitum* of body, soul, and spirit; of physicality, language, and feelings, which appear separate only if they are analyzed singly but have no separate givenness if seen with a mystical consciousness of their relationship among themselves—or through the eyes of a poet, as Dante sang when in the Tenth Heaven. Experience, thus, is not and cannot be a purely rational touch or a purely spiritual contact. To open to mystical experience in these terms means to refuse thoughtless vitalism, thoughtful intellectualism, and thought-centred subjectivism. It is to become and to offer a testimony (μαρτύριον) of the ontonomy of reality. "In other words, mystic experience cannot be my (individual) experience without being our (collective) experience" says Panikkar (2008a, 186). Mystical experience happens before any logical reelaboration and allows the subject to *cum-tangere* Reality in a preawareness of the inter-in-dependence; it is at the same time subjective and universal *and none,* taking place and getting validation by an *advaita* moment of mystical relationship. Thus, at the same time is a singular clarity of the subject and the reaffirmation of the connection of everything with everything.

This awareness of mystical experience as at the same time singular and connective extends to the object of experience, too. The third *sūtra* says that *reality is neither subjective nor objective: it is our mythos* (Panikkar 2008a, 188–193). Another term of the philosophical lexicon of Raimon Panikkar, *mythos* is strictly tied to *logos* and *symbol. Mythos* is a word present in his vocabulary from the early stage of his writings (Marcato 2017, 100): it is what we left unsaid in every saying, the framework through which we interpret reality, the glass of the window between us and the world. By expanding on Károly Kerényi's position on mythology (Panikkar 2008b, 266–267), Panikkar sees *mythos* as *what we believe without knowing that we believe it.* It is the left-unsaid behind the *symbol,* what we take for granted when we approach the world, before any logical explanation. More formally, it can be said that the *mythos* is the sum of our presumptions and assumptions, what we never think about when we think. It is the ingrained and undoubted certainty that, for example, lightning is the difference of electric potential between the land and the air. In ancient Greece, during a thunderstorm, it was said that lightnings were thrown by Zeus Νεφεληγερέτα, "Cloud Gatherer." The Father of the Gods, divine symbol of the divine itself in the ancient, patriarchal, Greek society, among his many roles and epithets had that of "Thunderer." Lightning and thunder thus coalesced into the symbolic image of the thunderbolt, which Heraclitus called τὰ ... πάντα οἰακίζει κεραυνός, what puts order in beings. In our contemporary scientific awareness, lightning is a meteorological phenomenon that happens thanks to an exchange of polarities between the atmosphere and Earth's surface. We know that a flux of negatively polarized ions departs from the clouds and makes·contact with the potential difference of the ground, and an electric current is then discharged upwards into the clouds. Zeus and ion particles have the same role in the respective worldviews; it does not matter what science or religion says; we now *know* that there is a discharge of electrical potentials in exactly the same way as the ancient Greek *knew* that it was Zeus exerting dominion on all that is. This is Panikkar's *mythos:* the complex and ever-changing net of unsaid meaning and knowledge from which our worldview is formed.

Saying that reality is our *mythos* means that in the moment of mystical experience our worldview is no longer tied to an ontological and epistemological duality between subject and object, that the act of experiencing reality is no longer tied to such a duality. A mystical experience allows us to build a worldview (and thus, knowledge of the world) from Reality itself, which can be then inflected by subsequent reflection on the experience. "Reality [used here as a homeomorphic equivalent of *mythos*] is what allows us to find a meaning to both subject and predicate" (Panikkar 2008a, 188). Panikkar's argument stems from acknowledging that the expression of *logos* that examines its structure, that wants to comprehend its characteristics, can proceed only from the *mythos* in which it is grounded. The question on reality, looked at from this point of view, cannot be the subject or the predicate of any act of saying, because both reside in its *advaita* harmony, which allows the mystical experience to acknowledge the concrete in the universal and the transcendent in the immanent, resolving both dimensions in the relationship that exists between them and all that is. It allows us to understand that differences are creations of *logos,* of the rational and analytical dimensions of our mind. Panikkar does not say that the differences are unreal—far from it! (Marcato 2015, 198)—they simply come in the wake of this experience, which is the "true epiphany of Everything" (Panikkar 2008a, 193). The Human mind recognizes these analytic distinctions, and from there it can build the scientific process, but their (scientific) reality is in no way challenged by their *reality* (i.e., their *mythos*).

The fourth *sūtra* says *mythos is the last horizon of presence, and the first step of conscience.* When having a mystical experience, the subject is fully aware of its role in the *mythos.* If the subject accepts this role, then accordingly it becomes able to investigate the *mythos.* It is an acceptance in the Augustinian *silentium veritatis,* the *mythos* being a synthesis of assumptions that grounds every step down the logical path. By proceeding from the last Plotinian Ennead (Panikkar 2008a, 199), Panikkar argues that this is a real *Aufhebung* of epistemology: in the traditional understanding of Hegelian dialectics, the second moment, overcome in a final moment of *synthesis* that keeps track of everything behind it, where the earlier steps are considered part of the final whole. Further scientific, psychological, biological analysis usually negates the mythical elements of what they analyze, but Panikkar, son of a chemist and chemist himself before his philosophical and ecclesiastic career, would rather have a more *symbolic* (as in σύν-βάλλω, "cast together") position. In the thunderbolt there are both Zeus and Benjamin Franklin; their value for the knowledge cannot be denied, cannot be refuted, as this would mean to deplete the richness of something. This kind of synthesis that the mystical experience grants does not limit a formal analysis; quite the opposite: it is what gives it value, as it allows consciousness and all its processes (logical, creative, and so on) to be grounded in a worldview stemming from reality itself. This is the turning point of Panikkar's *Navasūtrāni,* as from this *sūtra* forward, while he keeps referring to a mystical experience, his argument gives more and more hints of how this process is a description of gnoseology per se, as I will explain.

This concept of consciousness as grounded in *mythos* is elaborated in the next (fifth) *sūtra,* which says *consciousness is consciousness of beings, of itself, of abstractions or of pure consciousness* (Panikkar 2008a, 201–207). Here, Panikkar further states what he means by "consciousness" and what the content of a consciousness that stems from *mythos* can be. When something is known, the first moment is described as the mystical dimension in which the object is known prior to the genitives that describe it. Through the experience, we know the thunderbolt (and its *mythos*) before we think of all its peculiarities, as when it crashed, who might or might not have been hit, and so on. Consciousness is thus the next step in Panikkar's argument, as it is what transmits knowledge to the experiencing subject:

1. a subject can be conscious of a being when it gains knowledge of it beyond its immediate experience;
2. a subject can be conscious of itself when it gains knowledge of itself, or, in other words, becomes self-conscious;
3. a subject can be conscious of abstract concepts (where "abstract" has to be intended as something that does not have immediate and measurable physicality, like math theorems or ethic predicaments);
4. a subject can be conscious of pure consciousness when it gains knowledge of being part of the act of being conscious. (More on that in a moment.)

The first three points are moments pertaining to the action of the *logos* after the *mythos.* "An epistemology detached by its ontology might be *episteme,* but not *gnosis.* This *gnosis* might be the essence of knowledge, but it is a generic essence, not a specific one" (Panikkar 2008a, 204). And since we must express ourselves with the instruments of language, the only genitive we can give to knowledge in its most pure form is the knowledge of *pisteuma.* This is the fourth moment of consciousness, or consciousness of pure consciousness. *Pisteuma* is another word of Panikkar's lexicon, strictly tied to *mythos* and *logos,* and derived from Husserl's *noematischen Gehalt.* On one side, in Husserl the iletic components of physical perception are given intentionality by the willing act of having an experience, thus translating in a noematic knowledge. On the other, in Panikkar (as previously stated) having an experience means to participate in Reality itself. This kind of *conatus,* act of willing experience, when acted in full consciousness (that is, with full knowledge of it), means to be part of the act, not merely knowing it. It is a moment of faith, of πίστις; thus, *pisteuma* as integration of the merely intellectual nature of the *noēma* (Panikkar 2008a, 269–282). This is the element that more traditionally can be called "spiritual" in Panikkar's take on mystical experience, as the element of faith connects this proposal with the historical and more structured forms of mystic spirituality that the Human created and started to follow in its historical development. Gaining knowledge in a participative way gives further strength to the *advaita* perspective of Panikkar's experience, as there is no subject and object but, again, a joint participation of subject and object in the *mythos*. While it seems that we can't speak of it outside aesthetic language (Taioli 2005), a positive gnoseology that uses the full strength of *ratio*'s approach can be reached through an intermediate step.

This intermediate step is the sixth *sūtra*: *pure knowledge is the experience of a presence full of love* (Panikkar 2008a, 208–219). Traditionally, mysticism is understood as that act of love of a single being toward a (not always personal) transcendent, in a direct relationship that almost leads to identification of the lover with the beloved. Panikkar acknowledges this but interprets these relationships into the cosmotheandric dimension of a mysticism that is a *concrete act of love* toward the Divine and its creation (Panikkar 2008a, 212-–213): that is, an action. Thanks to the experience that Human language calls *amor,* we can see the movement, the *conatus,* of an intellect pushed to know what is other than itself. However, this status also becomes a reason for the heaviest criticism of mysticism and mystics, who according to Panikkar close themselves in a *fuga mundi* where creation is spurned, where the physical and embodied elements of mystical experience are considered as not having the same quality of purely intellectual mystical experience (such as any number of spiritualist movements in every religion have supported). In love, mysticism accepts the intellectual distinction of beings but does not operate upon separation between different beings, instead acknowledging that plurality of beings is the means whereby the subject perceives the a-dualistic relationships that can ground logical thinking, as expressed in the third *sūtra*. Love and knowledge, *conatus* and *ratio,* are present in acknowledging and grounding the existence of a "you" that is not a personified individual but that can be addressed in every aspect of the world. Mystical experience allows the subject to discover otherness as a quality in everything discerned: that is, in everything that following the act of consciousness seems to be separated by the subject. This separation is perceived as every act of experience is *embodied,* as our consciousness is strictly tied to our physical dimension, as the cosmotheandric intuition from which Panikkar moves his argument constantly reminds us. No matter how spiritual and intellectual an experience may be, it is always perceived through and into a body. But the sense of belonging, the act of participation that stems from mystical experience is still present, understood, and kept in the conscious act of knowing. From the experience, we know; from knowledge, we become conscious; from our embodied consciousness, we discover the other. And as every step is kept and grounds the next, otherness is discovered and revealed in and through that love that stems from participation (Panikkar 2008a, 217), in the *embodied* experience of subjectivity.

13.2   Mystical Experience, Epistemology, Existentialism

All the above elements concur toward a systematic definition of mystical experience in the seventh *sūtra*. This is the moment in his writings when Panikkar shows his understanding of mysticism as profoundly and poignantly intellectual. With a rigorous argument, Panikkar exposes how the Human experiences an individual discrimination as separated from *advaita* reality (understood as stated above), identifies this discrimination as an individual being, and from there builds first empirical knowledge and then scientific knowledge. It is neither a scheme nor the separation of a phenomenon in its "parts" but the mediation that allows the description of Panikkar's mysticism. The *sūtra* says that *what we call experience is the result of several factors:* $E = e(l.m.i.r.a)$ (Panikkar 2008a, 221–432; see also Panikkar 2016, 624–626). This formula is the systematic definition of mystical experience and can define this *sūtra* similarly to what happens to the Buddhist *Namu myōhō renge kyō*, where the title of the Lotus sūtra becomes the Lotus sūtra itself. It is the longest and most interesting *sūtra,* providing the aforementioned definition in a heuristic way through the various factors that concur to build the mystical experience. In its analysis, it must be remembered that the framework for the whole argument is the *advaita* perspective stated in the preceding *sūtra*. Each of the factors that builds the formula is not independent but is part of the whole; each one contains the others according to the different facets, and they have to be taken as *symbolic factors* rather than logical factors. $E = e(l.m.i.r.a)$ is like a jewel: with many sides, each one admirable for the quality of the cut or all of them for the light and richness they manifest. How they are formalized and especially the terms that Panikkar uses to define them reveal how this *sūtra* is his gnoseology, his theory of knowledge, formalized and structured.

This *sūtra* begins by stating that "there is no experience E without the equivalent factors, even if our mind can and must think that *there is* (formally) an experience *e* on which it must be grounded" (Panikkar 2008a, 223). E is the experience that the formula refers to: mystical experience, for the time being. On the other hand, *e* is the *pure experience,* the experience of the wholeness of reality expressed in the first *sūtra*—pure in the sense that leaves aside all subsequent distinctions, before any kind of elaboration, qualities, definitions and so on, as will be stated below. The relationship that is created between the two experiences is neither of *deduction* nor of *induction*. To *induce,* according to Panikkar, means to create a formal concept e^{l} that replaces *e* without being *e* but presuming to identify it; it is the action of Western scientism. *Deduction,* on the other hand, cannot describe the relationship between E and *e,* because it will mean to falsify *e* by reducing it to e', a concept no longer formal but created by the reelaboration of E by the subject. In other words, if a relationship stems from deduction, E could be replaced by e', e'', e''', ... e^{n} according to the different subjects of the mystical experience. To apply deduction or induction to analyze the relationship between these two aspects of experience would transform E's *pisteuma,* its preconscious dimension and transcendent validation through participation, into its *noēma,* its rational communicability, depriving it of its proper interdependent nature. Thus, the factors that compose E are *mediators*. This, another term of Panikkar's philosophical lexicon, denotes any element that can create a bridge between subjective and objective, between finite and infinite, between holy and profane; a symbol is a mediator, as is a priest—or even a scientist. It allows the inter-in-dependence to arise and create knowledge. "We are again speaking of the *advaita* consciousness, which is aware of polarity and does not reduce consciousness to intellectual intelligibility" (Panikkar 2008a, 225).

The only way we can speak of *e* as pure experience, as was mentioned, is through three corollaries. The first is the impossibility of isolating it from the experiencing subject and thus defining it as different from or identical with any other experience according to the subject that experiences it. The second corollary strengthens the need to keep *e*'s distance from the other *E*s without pretending that they are aprioristically false and accepting the diversity: a "disagreement is resolved in the dialogical dialogue, where by piercing *logos* (διὰ τὸν λόγον, *dia ton logon*) we might be able to reach the agreement that we are participating of a same *e*" (Panikkar 2008a, 228–229). The third corollary expands the first two by proposing as a value of *e* an apophatic and *advaita* vacuity, which cannot be spoken of and brings *e* outside the analytic power of *ratio:* thus, *e* is open to experience the wholeness of reality. This being "pure" seems to imply, then, that this kind of experience cannot be spoken of in the usual philosophical terms and with an analytical structure, relegating *e* outside logic. What seems to be the capitulation of reason is its victory—albeit under a different light—thanks to the structure of Panikkar's reflection on word and language.

The above happens because while a mystical moment is an apophatic and ineffable experience, we can still talk about it. This is the reason why the second factor is *l*, *language*. A language that must be symbolic, both a-dual expression of word's *sacra quaternitas* (Panikkar 2007) and mediator between consciousness and reality. According to Panikkar's *sacra verbi quaternitas*, one of the most metaphysical elements of his philosophical proposal, the ontological weight of language is on the constituent relationship between *Speaker, Listener, Symbol,* and *Meaning.* It is at the center of this four-point relationship that language emerges, be it verbal or nonverbal ("speaker" and "listener" here have a broad sense: pebbles will speak, and the Stars shall listen), and through it any consciousness builds knowledge (Panikkar 2012, 122). Everything we know, we communicate through language. Through the language, we can know it. "But when we live an experience, it is its enduring in *memory* (*m*) that allows us to talk about it" (Panikkar 2008a, 235): through memory, we keep the recollection of the lived experience. Memory is the mediation between the moment we live the experience and the moment we remember it. But there is more: *memory* brings with it different *memories,* and by our remembering it in different moments, it can change the original experience. If I burn my finger on the stove, I feel pain; but when *memory* comes to the fore, it brings the lesson to avoid what can burn again. If I burn my finger at an early age while someone is barbecuing, I may associate the taste of grilled meat with pain; and if someone offers me grilled meat as an adult, I may reject it because of this association with pain. In this sense, the dimension of memory also shows how the temporal role of experience is not outside experience itself. There is an *ontonomy* that reveals how fixing an experience in a particular time and space is a purely formal construction—that is, the realm of a subsequent reflection of the subject on the experience.

Every time memory raises an experience, the experience *e* is subject to *interpretation* (*i*). Here, interpretation is referred to as a "mediator common to each and every factor of experience" (Panikkar 2008a, 237). If language is the pair of glasses that we use to look at the experience and the ink through which we communicate it, interpretation is the way we comprehend said experience. Through interpretation we make that experience our own, without trying to rationally explain it but by living it. This happens in two moments: in the first moment we interiorize experience, and in the second we recognize that experience is in a relationship with us. Here, we can see the difference between the "hunter's hermeneutic" and the "gatherer hermeneutic" that Panikkar often referred to in his spoken lessons and conferences (Ro 2014): the hunter's hermeneutic brings violence to the experience by dismantling it so that it can understand its parts; the gatherer hermeneutic accepts the fact that to know something, we must wait for it to grow, accept its fruits, listen its *symbol.* In other words, in the first case we take a symbol and analyze its components, an action that, although it allows us to understand what said symbol is "made of," destroys the symbol, which ceases to have its hermeneutic status from that moment forward. In the second case, instead of analyzing the symbol, the methodology expands its knowledge of where the symbol is used, how, when, and so on, akin to an anthropologist who lives in a tribe in order to become part of it, to no longer be an "outsider," and thus come to a lived knowledge of the tribe's practices.

The fifth mediating factor of *E* is *r, reception.* This is a problematic point, as Panikkar is unclear on its definition. He explains it only as "the cultural matrix in which the previous operations take place" (Panikkar 2008a, 239). On one hand, we may understand it as the contingent moment in which *e* happens. Such an interpretation is further corroborated by the fact that Panikkar, in this paragraph, argues that Western science modifies the receptive field of the Human and informs its *framework.* On the other hand, it is highly probable that in this moment Panikkar was thinking about the *mythos* as a precognitive framework in which we live but stylistically decided to keep on in his wordplay on "vision": *lmira* is "el mira," "he looks" in Spanish, and sight is usually the sense through which experience most directly happens. The subject "sees" its experience mediated not only by what it thinks, says, believes, but also by how its *milieu* (the social environment, following Durkheim) reacts and its *mythos* presupposes. An example might be the eminently famous *British humor,* rarely understood by people who do not have the Windsors' vassals' mentality. But it can also mean that while *i*nterpretation refers to *mythos* in its most general sense, Panikkar may have thought of *r*eception as the current *mythos* of a lived experience, of the contemporaneity of the experiencing subject. Nevertheless, this is a point that Panikkar leaves hanging and that will need further in-depth analysis hereafter, as it is not completely developed and seems to be point hastily made in his argument.

The last factor is *a, actualization.* From a gnoseological perspective, it is the cornerstone on which the reception and transmission of experience are grounded. *Actualization* is the "existential factor of every experience: its active translation, its expression in life, its power to transform, its manifestation in the practice" (Panikkar 2008a, 240). Thanks to *actualization*, theoretical knowledge becomes *embodied*, linking the initial moment of experience (burning a finger on the stove) with its persistence (knowing that a hot stove burns) and consequences (not placing a finger on a hot stove) through living the experience in its physical elements. According to Panikkar, it is the existential dimension that turns experience from a mere rational elaboration to a dynamic charge. Embodying a lived experience is what allows the Human to change and modify the world. "Human experience always manifests itself in action. Politics, society, bodies, everything is always an act. If this is not acknowledged, every element of Human thought since the dawn of times is only a sterile lucubration and our interpretation will forever be without grounding" (Panikkar 2008a, 242). Inter-in-dependence of everything with everything cannot forget, in presenting itself as gnoseology, that any deliberation involves and comprehends an element of action.

To summarize, then: the Human *knows* by living an *E*xperience, experience that is the result of diverse factors. The first act, the pure *e*xperience, void of content because content itself, is comprehended through the *l*anguage and stored in *m*emory. This memory can propose the same experience or give birth, in the interrelation with other experiences, to new *e*xperiences. All these are *i*nterpreted based on *r*eception inside the subject's *mythos* and *a*ctualized again, thus expressing *mythos'* fertile and transformative charge in a deep, existential way. If seen according to these elements, and expressed with such a structured definition, it is clear then that $E = e(l.m.i.r.a)$ is not only the formalization of a mystical experience. Any process through which the Human gains knowledge and develops consciousness passes through these steps. If I *e*xperience claps of thunder, I immediately describe them as, indeed, claps of thunder through *l*anguage and create a *m*emory of them, summoning other *m*emories from the past. I then *i*nterpret them according to their *mythos;* they become instruments of Zeus, the sound of Thor's hammer, Raijin's drums, and so on, but I *r*eceive those as the difference of potentiality between the atmosphere and Earth's surface. I then say to whoever is near me, "It is going to rain," thus *a*ctualizing the lived *E*xperience and providing a new *e*xperience to my fellows. It is a full-fledged theory of knowledge, a gnoseology presented as a phenomenology of mystical experience. $E = e(l.m.i.r.a)$: "it looks"; the Human realizes Reality and listens to the wonderful music of the Rhythm of Being. In other words (Panikkar 2008a, 243):

Human experience is the polychrome ray focused in white light that enlightens and dazzles; it is simple because it unites the multiple dimension of humanity in a Human perichoresis; our body, our soul and our spirit take part in it, bringing us in contact with Life, with Reality.

13.3   Conclusion: Religious Mystical Experience and Knowledge of the World

The eight *sūtra* is formulated thus: *we are aware of a triple experience: sensitive, intelligible, and spiritual* (Panikkar 2008a, 244–258). In this *sūtra,* Panikkar seals the gnoseological implication of his theoretical cosmotheandric intuition. Through the opening to the three mental, corporeal, and spiritual senses that mystical experience offers, the Human reaches awareness of the fact that the world inside that it moves is cannot be simplified to a single element of the three stated. Rather, all three interact and intersect in order to allow the self-conscious Human dimension of Cosmotheandry to reach the fourth form of being conscious of pure consciousness and to reveal how everything is connected with everything in an inter-in-dependent relationship, or ontonomy, or *advaita.* According to Panikkar, several ways of thinking, ideologies, and religions during the Human history, which argued that only one of these senses creates knowledge, not only removed part of reality from their frameworks but misinterpreted the very act of knowing. "If sensist (materialistic) reductionism comes from looking only through the first eye, the idealist from the second, pseudo mysticism is the third-eye-only vision. Every monocultural vision lacks perspective" (Panikkar 2008a, 246). If we pretend to know reality via a single means, we fall into monism, the tyranny of one aspect over the other two, no matter if this monism is called "science" or "religion." Seeing reality with only two eyes brings dualism, conflict, the search for a synthesis. A pluralism of different perspectives on the world, when said perspectives acknowledge the need to talk to each other and establish a true dialogue, can lead to true knowledge. This "trueness," though, does not mean that one perspective or the other, or even the fact that there are different perspectives, is true (that would mean to support a naive relativism); on the other hand, it means that Truth can be reached only in the relationship between perspectives, where said relationship is understood as has been expressed above. It is a path to take, a process to unfold, and thus not an object to possess but a task to perform, a responsibility to accept (Calabrese 2012, 49).

This is the reason why the ninth *sūtra* says: *mystic experience has a direct relationship with the wholeness of human condition* (Panikkar 2008a, 259–281). There can be no true mysticism if mysticism cannot and will not speak of its experience. A silent mysticism cannot but gaze at its own navel, as Hegel accused some Eastern traditions of doing. A mystic that refuses to speak, that refuses to express itself and to recognize its own argumentative faculty, inevitably falls into that intimistic solipsism that one of Panikkar's philosophical friends, Enrico Castelli, argued so hard against: "Human communication happens between bread and word. The word needs to be authentic: it must be that Word mediator between Thinking and Being" (Panikkar 2008a, 259). Panikkar's gnoseology is opening to the Human, because in its formal expression it engages every dimension (bodily, mental, spiritual) and is not limited to a solipsism that excludes *aliud;* it opens to a love that accepts *alter.* Philosophy, because it is a victim (unwilling or fully complicit) of one of the most rational perspectives onto which mystical experience opens itself with its ingrained need for rational expressions, for logical formalization, for structured arguments, often forgets to accept Human fullness, reducing itself to a mere *opus rationis*. It risks becoming nothing more than a structure of formal logic, grounded in the relentless power of a *logos* separated from its *mythos*. It is for this reason that Panikkar wanted to ground *logos* in a rational mystic theory, solving this apparent contradiction with the help of *advaita*. This rational mystic theory is not a system to follow, nor a mechanism to be applied, but a useful direction for a new path for Human reason. "*Sūtras* are not harangues; they are a call to meditation, so that Life can be born" (Panikkar 2008a, 273). They do not teach but open themselves to dialogue with the reader. They let those who read them put them into practice, to embody and actualize them, regardless of who their reader is.

Panikkar's deeply philosophical language thus weaves the theoretical and theological into the universal meaning that all intellectuals offer to their Human brothers and sisters. If he did that with a strict logical argument of the Western type, he would betray his intention to speak to everyone. Every *logos,* after all, depends on its *mythos.* Panikkar, with his philosophy wherein the mystical dimension has been recovered and given back its role, proposes to the reader his *mythos,* analyzed with his *logos.* He lets the differences emerge; he offers his philosophy up to be heard, showing the plurality of culture that he experienced himself, and invites the reader to enter a dialogue. "Mystic is, in fact, not a specialization nor a privilege for few; it belongs to the very nature of mankind. Mysticism invites us to participate consciously, that is humanly, to the adventure of reality" (Panikkar 2008a, 247).

References

Calabrese, Alessandro. 2012. *Il paradigma accogliente: La filosofia interculturale in Raimon Panikkar*. Milan: Mimesis.
Marcato, Leonardo. 2015. Il ritmo del Non-Essere: Il negativo nel pensiero di Raimon Panikkar, tra critica a Parmenide e prospettive *Advaita*. In *Forme della negazione*, ed. Leonardo Marcato, 193–210. Milan: Mimesis.
———. 2017. *Le radici del dialogo: Filosofia e teologia nel pensiero di Raimon Panikkar*. Milan: Mimesis.
Pérez Prieto, Victorino, and José Luis Meza Rueda. 2016. *Diccionario Panikkariano*. Barcelona: Herder Editorial.
Panikkar, Raimon. 2007. *Lo spirito della parola*. Turin: Bollati Boringhieri.
———. 2008a. *Opera omnia*, vol. 1, *Mistica e spiritualità*. Tome 1, *Mistica, pienezza di vita*. Milan: Jaca Book.
———. 2008b. *Opera omnia*, vol. 9, *Mistica ed ermeneutica*. Tome 1, *Mito, simbolo, culto*. Milan: Jaca Book.
———. 2010. *Opera omnia*, vol. 8, *Visione trinitaria e cosmoteandrica: Dio—Uomo—Cosmo*. Milan: Jaca Book.
———. 2011a. *Opera omnia*, vol. 1, *Mistica e spiritualità*. Tome 2, *Spiritualità, il cammino della vita*. Milan: Jaca Book.
———. 2011b. *Opera omnia*, vol. 2, *Religione e religioni*. Milan: Jaca Book.

————. 2012. *Opera omnia*, vol. 10, *Filosofia e teologia*. Tome 1, *Il ritmo dell'Essere. Le Gifford lectures*. Milan: Jaca Book.

————. 2016. *Opera Omnia*, vol. 3, *Cristianesimo*. Tome 2, *Una Cristofania (1987–2002)*. Milan: Jaca Book.

Ro, Young-Chan. 2014. *An epistemological foundation of Raimon Panikkar*. Milan: Mimesis.

Taioli, Roberto. 2005. L'estetica come nuova innocenza nel pensiero di Raimon Panikkar. *Città di Vita* 60 (2): 169–178.

Yusa, Michiko. 2012. An Advaitic matter: Pebbles speak. *CIRPIT Review* 3. Kindle edition.

Leonardo Marcato, Ph.D, translator and researcher, has a background in Philosophy of Religion, Religious Studies, and Theoretical Philosophy. The main focus of his work is the thought of Raimon Panikkar, about which he published papers and the monography *Le radici del dialogo. Filosofia e teologia nel pensiero di Raimon Panikkar* [Mimesis, Milan-Udine 2017], and edited *Forme della negazione. Un percorso interculturale tra oriente e occidente* [Mimesis, Milan-Udine 2015]. He also studies the thought of Nishida Kitaro, Digital Philosophy, and Games Philosophy. He is currently Honorary Research Fellow at Ca' Foscari University in Venice (Italy) and member of CESTUDIR (Centre for the Study of Human Rights) at the same University.

Chapter 14
A Kierkegaardian Phenomenology of Divine Presence

Joshua Cockayne

Abstract In this chapter, I argue that two aspects of Kierkegaard's thought can help develop a phenomenology of religious experience. The first of these aspects is the importance Kierkegaard puts on describing God as a subject. Throughout his writings, Kierkegaard emphasizes that God is not primarily an object to be perceived, but rather he is a subject to be interacted with. The second is the concept of "contemporaneity." which plays an important role in much of Kierkegaard's writings. Kierkegaard stresses that Christ is not merely a historical person but, rather, a living person who can be engaged with and experienced as contemporary. I argue that these two aspects of Kierkegaard's writings can inform our phenomenology of religious experience. Building on these two insights, I suggest that the starting point for understanding the nature of religious experiences is to be found not in the writings of the mystics but rather in our everyday experience of personal presence. Following recent work in cognitive psychology, I suggest that being present to a person requires attention shared with that person. Thus, by understanding what it is to experience another person's presence, we can make sense of what it is to experience the divine presence.

Keywords Kierkegaard · Joint attention · Intersubjectivity · Presence

In the Christian tradition, the notion that God is present to and with his followers is of utmost importance. For instance, to take an example from Scripture, the Psalmist asks, "Where can I go from your spirit? Or where can I flee from your presence?" (Psalm 139:7). Another Psalm tells us: "You have made known to me the ways of life; you will make me full of gladness with your presence" (Psalm 16:11).[1] The importance of God's presence is also emphasized in Christian spiritual practice.

---

[1] All Bible references to *New Revised Standard Version.*

J. Cockayne (✉)
University of St Andrews, St Andrews, UK
e-mail: jlc22@st-andrews.ac.uk

© Springer Nature Switzerland AG 2019   231
O. Louchakova-Schwartz (ed.), *The Problem of Religious Experience*,
Contributions to Phenomenology 103,
https://doi.org/10.1007/978-3-030-21575-0_14

Take the Church of England's liturgy of the Eucharist in *Common Worship*, for instance. One option for the president to begin the opening dialogue (the *Sursum Corda, Church of England* 2000) is "The Lord is here," to which the congregation reply, "His Spirit is with us." To take another example from *Common Worship*, in the "Acclamation of Christ at the Dawning of the Day," the congregation are invited to say: "Let us come into his presence with thanksgiving and be glad in Him with psalms." (Church of England 2000)

But what is it to experience God's presence with or to us? And how should we understand the nature of an experience of divine presence? In this chapter, I aim to give an account of the phenomenal nature of divine presence by drawing on the theological writings of Søren Kierkegaard. I will focus on two strands of thought that we find in various places in Kierkegaard's writings. First, for Kierkegaard, God is primarily a subject to be engaged with and not an object to perceive or merely speculate about. I will argue that the intersubjective nature of religious faith has implications for understanding the phenomenology of religious experience. As I will go on to explain, God is not *presented* to a person through religious experience, but rather, God is *present* to that person. Just as another person who is asleep or distracted is not present to me despite being spatiotemporally present, God is not present to a person unless there is some kind of engagement. To explain the nature of this experience of God as a subject, I draw on a second aspect of Kierkegaard's writings, his claim that a Christian believer must become contemporary with the presence of Christ. According to Kierkegaard, a person must not relate to Christ at a distance, as a merely historical figure, but rather she must experience Christ as contemporary to her. To explain what this account of contemporaneity and personal presence amounts to, I offer a model of what it is to be contemporary with Christ that draws on the psychological literature on attention shared between persons. Thus, our starting point for understanding the nature of divine presence, I argue, should be the phenomenology of personal presence more generally.

14.1   Kierkegaard on (Inter)Subjectivity

Before discussing the implications for our phenomenology of religious experience, let us first look at what Kierkegaard writes about the subjective nature of Christian faith. According to the pseudonymous author Johannes Climacus (Kierkegaard 1992, 130–131)[2]:

> Christianity protests against all objectivity, it wants the subject to be infinitely concerned about himself. What it asks about is the subjectivity; the truth of Christianity, if it is at all,

---

[2] Kierkegaard uses pseudonyms throughout his writings, and I follow his wishes not to attribute his pseudonymous writings to him. (See Kierkegaard 1992, 617–630.) The relationship between the historical figure "John of the Ladder" and Kierkegaard's invented pseudonym "Johannes Climacus" is unclear. (See Evans 1992, 8–9.) For the purposes of this discussion, I assume no connection but treat Climacus as a thinker in his own right.

is in this; objectively, it is not at all. … Science and scholarship want to teach that becoming objective is the way, whereas Christianity teaches that the way is to become subjective, that is, truly to become a subject. Lest this seem to be a verbal dispute, let it be said that Christianity explicitly wants to intensify passion to its highest, but passion is subjectivity, and objectively it does not exist at all.

In stating that Christian faith is essentially subjective, Climacus draws attention to the fact that the truth of Christianity cannot be understood "objectively": that is, faith requires more than a commitment to a list of doctrines or to have a set of historical beliefs. In stating that faith is subjective, Climacus is not claiming that faith is irrational or that its truth is relative.[3] But rather, in stating that faith is subjective, Climacus emphasizes the importance of an individual's relationship to the truth of Christianity; faith must be lived out, or actualized, in the life of the individual and not merely understood.[4]

It is important for our purposes here that Climacus's claims concerning subjectivity are not simply about the actualization of certain religious beliefs in the lives of Christian believers. One of the crucial reasons why Christianity must be understood subjectively is that the truth to be learned is not some historical claim, philosophical claim, or even some religious doctrine, but rather it is the revelation of God as a person. As Paul K. Moser and Mark L. McCreary (2010, 132) explain the concern in the broader context of Kierkegaard's writings,

> Kierkegaard does not disapprove of objective knowledge as such … he strongly warns against approaching God as an impersonal object to be studied. In his words "God is not like something one buys in a shop, or like a piece of property" … Instead, God is a personal agent, a subject with definite redemptive purposes for humans. … Merely objective knowledge about God does not entail personally knowing God via a God-relationship.

It is this personal revelation of God that is crucial for Christian faith. Climacus tells us that we must remember that "God is a subject."[5] "Objectively, what is reflected upon," Climacus writes, "is that this is the true God; subjectively, that the individual relates himself to a something in such a way that his relation is in truth a God-relation" (Kierkegaard 1992, 199). What the Christian relates herself to is not an inanimate object; "God is not like something one buys in a shop, or like a piece of property," as Kierkegaard puts it in the *Christian Discourses* (2009, 88). But rather, as Climacus describes (Kierkegaard 1992, 200),

> the existing person who chooses the objective way now enters upon all approximating deliberation intended to bring forth God objectively, which is not achieved in all eternity, because God is a subject and hence only for subjectivity in inwardness. … The objective person is not bothered by dialectical difficulties such as what it means to put a whole

---

[3] See Evans 2006 for a defense of this position.

[4] This intersubjective aspect of Christian faith is explored by Martin Buber (1937) in his discussion of the "I-thou" relationship, which is heavily influenced by Kierkegaard.

[5] Kierkegaard 1992, 200. This has received some attention in the secondary literature, see, for instance, Moser and McCreary 2010; Evans 1992. The theology of God as a subject is explored in Martin Buber's *I and Thou* (1937) and is explored more often in Continental literary approaches to theology. For an example from the analytic tradition, which emphasizes God as a subject, see Moser 2008, 2009, 2013.

research period into finding God, since it is indeed possible that the researcher would die tomorrow, and if he goes on living, he cannot very well regard God as something to be taken along at his convenience, since God is something one takes along à tout prix, which, in passion's understanding, is the true relationship of inwardness with God.

As I will argue, Kierkegaard's emphasis on relating to God as a subject has important implications for our understanding of religious experience. The best way to understand religious experience, if Kierkegaard is right, cannot be through a perceptual model in which a person perceives God as a mere object such as a piece of pottery; but rather a person must approach God as a person to engage with. Before going on to give a more detailed account of religious experience, however, I will consider the other important aspect of Kierkegaard's thought that I think can inform our understanding of religious experience, namely his claims about the Christian believer becoming contemporary with Christ.

14.2   Kierkegaard and Contemporaneity with Christ

What is to relate to God as a subject? At least part of Kierkegaard's response to this question is that a Christian believer must experience Christ as "contemporary" to her. For instance, the pseudonymous author Anti-Climacus begins *Practice in Christianity* by stating that (Kierkegaard 1991, 9):

> it is indeed eighteen hundred years since Jesus Christ walked here on earth, but this is certainly not an event just like other events, which once they are over pass into history and then, as the distant past, pass into oblivion. No, his presence here on earth never becomes a thing of the past. … But as long as there is a believer, this person … must be just as contemporary with Christ's presence as his contemporaries were. This contemporaneity is the condition of faith, and, more sharply defined, it is faith.

In talking of being "contemporary with Christ," what Kierkegaard seeks to stress is that Christ is not merely a historical figure to be speculated about, but rather Christ is a living person, whom we should strive to engage with and imitate today. To stress that Christ is contemporary is to stress that Christian faith is essentially subjective (i.e., it relates essentially to God as a subject) and that the subject of Christ makes God known in a distinct way. We see this line of thought developed in Johannes Climacus's discussion of faith and history in *Philosophical Fragments*. According to Johannes Climacus, both the firsthand witnesses of Christ's life on earth and those from later generations must enter into a relation of contemporaneity with Christ (Kierkegaard 1985, 69). It follows, Climacus thinks, that "there is no follower at second-hand. The first and latest generation are essentially alike" (ibid., 104–105). If a person must relate to Christ as contemporary, then she cannot merely believe that he is the Son of God, or that he existed and walked on the earth—faith requires a person to relate to Christ personally and intimately in her present day. To take this position to its extreme, we see that Climacus thinks even those who existed at the same historical time as Christ might fail to relate to Christ in this way. And thus, "despite his being contemporary, a contemporary can be a non-contemporary" (ibid., 67).

Just as in the discussion of relating to God as a subject, in discussing the notion of contemporaneity Kierkegaard's concern is that God is not merely understood, but rather that he brings about change in the life of the individual. Kierkegaard repeatedly connects being contemporary with Christ with a person's imitating of Christ. Anti-Climacus writes of Christ that (Kierkegaard 1991, 234):

> you yourself were the way and the life—and you have asked only for imitators. If we have dozed off into this infatuation, wake us up, rescue us from this error of wanting to admire or adorningly admire you instead of wanting to follow you and be like you.

We see here that the correct relationship one must take to Christ is one of imitation, and not infatuation or admiration. Furthermore, being contemporary with Christ is importantly connected to the experience of Christ's being present to an individual. Anti-Climacus writes that a believer "must be just as contemporary with Christ's presence as his contemporaries were. This contemporaneity is the condition of faith, and, more sharply defined, it is faith" (ibid., 9). This is not an imagined experience in which an individual relates to Christ from a distance, but an engagement with a living person.[6]

Elsewhere in Kierkegaard's writings, Johannes the Seducer writes that what is lacking from a letter exchange between persons is "the element of contemporaneity" (Kierkegaard 1987, 399), which he defines as being characterized by "the nerve in conversation, the surprise in the outburst, the passionateness, which is the life principle in conversation" (ibid.). The same applies to being contemporary with Christ. Being contemporary with Christ involves some active engagement with the living Christ. Anti-Climacus describes one of the key ways of experiencing Christ's presence as contemporary is through taking communion; he writes that "today he is indeed with you as if he were closer to the earth; he is as if touching the earth; he is present at the altar when you are seeking him; he is present there—but only in order once again from on high to draw you to himself" (Kierkegaard 1991, 156). As George Pattison describes the account of Communion in Kierkegaard's writings, it involves a "concrete encounter … with the person of Jesus Christ" which allows the believer to enter into a "relationship of love with his or her creator" (2012, 160).

What remains to be seen is just how a believer can be contemporary with a figure who existed more than two millennia ago. In the next section, I seek to give an account of experiencing Christ as present to the believer in a manner that is informative to our phenomenology of such an experience.

---

[6] In contrast to my reading of 'contemporaneity', Patrick Stokes (2010, 2015). argues that we should read contemporaneity as 'an *immediately self-reflexive* mode of vision, that is, one in which we apprehend *our relation* to what is imagined *within* the imaginative experience' (2010, 314; emphasis in the original). Elsewhere, I have argued in much more detail that Stokes's reading of contemporaneity is inadequate (Cockayne 2017). I argue that what Stokes's reading fails to acknowledge is that in the Christian tradition, it is commonly accepted that Christ is not a merely historical person, but rather, Christ is a living person (1 John 1:3, Matthew 28:20, Matthew 1:23).

14.3   Divine Presence and the Phenomenology of Religious Experience

In this section, I will apply the two theological observations from Kierkegaard's work to help us think about the nature and phenomenology of religious experience.

Many existing accounts of religious experience in the philosophical literature draw on our experience of ordinary perceptual experience to explain the nature of religious experience. For instance, William Alston, in his influential book, *Perceiving God,* defines a religious experience as a kind of perception in which "something's presenting itself to the subject, S, as so-and-so, as purple, zigzagged, acrid, loud, or whatever" (1991, 38). It is the "phenomenon of apparent presentation of an object" that Alston claims is the distinctive feature of perceptual experience and the feature that differentiates it from other modes of consciousness (1991, 37). Furthermore, since religious experiences are experiences in which an object (God) presents itself to the subject as being "so-and-so," they should be regarded as perceptual experiences.

Now, if we take what Kierkegaard writes about subjectivity and faith seriously, then there is something problematic about the picture of religious experience as perception. As George Pappas highlights, in objecting to Alston's account, it is strange to describe religious experiences as experiences in which something is "presented" (1994, 879–880). He argues that in most reports of religious experience, the subject does not have an object presented to consciousness in the same way as I do when I experience the tree outside my window, for example. Pappas argues that we ought to distinguish between claiming that God is *present* and that God is *presented* (ibid., 880). The latter is a stronger, perceptual claim; the former is just to have an experience in which it seems to the perceiver that God is close by. Pappas argues that it is difficult to see how religious experiences, even those of mystics, are best understood as perceptual experiences at all. Usually religious experiences are described in terms that are in "contrast with perception, rather than as a perception itself or as something closely resembling perception" (ibid.).

I think that Pappas's objection to Alston helps us to see what difference Kierkegaard's discussion of theology makes to our phenomenology. A perceptual or objectual model of religious experience, in which a believer sees God through some mystical qualia, misunderstands the kind of thing God is. Although perception plays some role in experiences of personal presence, it cannot explain entirely what it is for someone to be present—or "contemporary," to use Kierkegaard's terminology. For instance, Johannes the Seducer's exchange with Cordelia requires him to see and hear Cordelia. However, this is not yet to give an account of what it is for a person to be *present.* It is possible to perceive a person as presented without perceiving them as present. When my wife is asleep, I can perceive her as presented (i.e., I can see that there is a body snoring beside me), but I do not perceive her as *present.*

Similarly, if a friend only reads the emails on her mobile phone during our dinner together, I may perceive her as presented, but I do not perceive her as present. What is the key difference between "present" and "presented" in these examples? An apt way of describing the key feature may be that both these persons are physically present but are lacking what Kierkegaard calls "contemporaneity": "the nerve in conversation, the surprise in the outburst, the passionateness, which is the life principle in conversation" (Kierkegaard 1987, 399). If God is a subject and not a mere object, then we surely want to be able to explain how God can be present and not just how God can be presented. In fact, in much of the mystical literature, arguably it is God's presence and not the perception of God as an object that is most prevalent. Let us now consider how this may be put more precisely.

To specify just what a Kierkegaardian phenomenology of religious experience may look like, I will conclude by considering a further criticism of Alston's model of religious experience that I think can explain what it is to be contemporary with Christ.

Following Pappas's objection to Alston, Adam Green (2009) has argued that a perceptual model for understanding religious experiences does not fully account for the interpersonal nature of the Judeo-Christian God very well. Green claims that a perceptual model can only work "if the qualia of the experience are appropriate to an experience of God in the same sense that the qualia of a sense experience of an apple are appropriate for an apple" (ibid., 457). When we experience an apple, we experience it having certain qualities such as its color, size, location, and so forth; the problem comes when we try to understand the nature of mystical experiences in the same way. As Green notes, although spiritual literature often describes feelings such as joy, harmony, and solemnity, "God is not an ineffable joy, a welling harmony, a wafting upwards, or a solemn silence" (ibid.). It is, therefore, difficult to see how these experiences ought to be understood perceptually. Furthermore, a simple perceptual explanation cannot capture the actions that the mystics often describe God as doing. Alston gives examples of God "strengthening," "forgiving," "sympathizing," and "speaking," and he contends that we cannot capture these actions using a simple perceptual model at all. (See Alston 1991, 44.)

When we are aware that a person is sad, we perceive their lowered brow, red eyes, and sluggish demeanor that present themselves to our consciousness, and we then become aware that this person is sad. However, this is not by means of simple perception; the red eyes of this person are not identical with their sadness. Likewise, Green thinks, when we experience God as forgiving it is difficult to construe this in terms of simple perception—What would it be to perceive God as being forgiving? Alston's model fails, thinks Green, because it is difficult to understand religious experience as merely simple perceptual experiences. The disanalogies between religious experience and perceptual experience point to another, better way of understanding religious experiences that more adequately captures the claim that God is a person and not a mere object.

14.4   Joint Attention and Divine Presence

An alternative intersubjective model of religious experience can better capture the phenomenology of religious experience. To see how such an account may proceed, let us consider a concept that psychologists call "joint attention" (or "shared attention"). Simply described, joint attention is a form of social engagement in which we are aware that another person is "in engagement with an object or potential object as a process over time" (Reddy 2012, 137). As Axel Seemen notes in his volume on joint attention, although "the discussion of joint attention is anything but unified" (2012, 1), there is a common position that all discussions of joint attention share. That is, all accounts of joint attention claim "that an adequate understanding of the life of the mind has to pay particular attention to its social dimension" and move from a "solipsistic conception of mind … toward a view of mental phenomena as inherently social" (ibid., 2).

An infant's awareness and engagement with other persons develops over time, and this brings with it a dyadic joint attention—that is, attention that requires only awareness of another person, typically (although not exclusively), through mutual gazing. This basic attention sharing is possible very early on in infants (from zero to two months, according to Vasudevi Reddy: 2012, 145). The ability to jointly attend then develops into triadic joint attention, at around 4–5 months—that is, joint attention in which an infant gains the ability to focus on some independent object while still remaining aware of the other person (Reddy 2005, 85–87). To clarify with an example: when a child looks her mother in the eye, then points toward an object, and then looks back to the eyes of the mother, if the mother follows the direction of her child's gaze, then they had a dyadic joint attention to begin with, followed by a triadic joint attention focusing on the object (Reddy 2012, 145). As the developmental psychopathologist R. Peter Hobson notes (2004, 85–109), joint-attention experiences are essential to the development of an infant's ability for intersubjective engagement and mind reading (i.e. the ability to perceive another's mental states). Hobson cites an experiment conducted in which some infants were shown a monitor with a real-time feed of their mother and others with a delayed feed of their mother. The infants who engaged with the real-time feed responded as if the mother were present in the room, whereas the infants responding to the delayed feed showed signs of distress and looked away (ibid., 38–39). What Hobson takes from this study is that there is a difference between merely responding to certain emotions as they are expressed facially and responding to emotions when we engage in joint attention with the other person.

This work in psychology on the nature of joint attention has been used by a number of philosophers and theologians to help explain how we experience the presence of God.[7] It is important to note at this point, though, that there are some important differences between sharing attention with God and sharing attention with another

---

[7] See, e.g., Stump 2010, chap. 6; Pinsent 2012, chap. 2; Bungum 2013; de Smedt and de Cruz 2013, 2014; Cockayne et al. 2017.

human being. Even though the paradigm examples of joint attention are cases of direct interactive engagement between physically co-present human persons, we need not overly restrict our understanding of joint attention. As Axel Seeman (2012, 1) notes, there is no agreed account or definition of joint attention in the psychological literature; but yet there are at least some psychologists who think that the concept should be extended beyond cases of direct interactive engagement. For instance, Garriy Shteynberg (2015) argues that the concept of joint attention need not be restricted to cases of interactive experience between persons. The rise of online social media provides one example in which joint attention is possible but in which there is no direct interactive experience between individuals (ibid., 587–588). Shteynberg argues that there appear to be other such cases: for instance, he notes, "I can be in a state of shared attention when watching the Olympics with millions of others who do not know me or know that I am watching" (ibid., 581). As Eleonore Stump describes in her discussion of second-person experience (2010, 76), "it is possible for one person to be aware of another as a person without seeing, hearing, smelling, touching, or tasting that other person. For example, if Paula and Jerome are engaged in an animated conversation with one another that they conduct by means of email, Paula is aware of Jerome as a person, even if she does not perceive Jerome."

Drawing from this discussion of joint attention in the psychological literature, we can see how religious experiences may be understood as instances of joint attention with God. For instance, as Johan de Smidt and Helen de Cruz describe in a recent article (2013, 180):

> Theists can … interpret awe as the state of mind in which they can share attention with God over at least some aspects of creation. As in ordinary forms of joint attention, this does not mean they literally can see things the way God does, any more than a toddler joining attention with her father over a horse in a meadow gets access to all her father's knowledge of or earlier experiences with horses. However, by sharing attention she can get a phenomenological sense of joining minds with her father, and becomes aware of the features of the horse that capture his attention. This conceptualization of awe as joint attention over creation provides a new way of interpreting the phenomenological experience of aesthetic nature appreciation, as when we ponder the empty expanse of the prairie or the intricacy of frozen cobwebs.

The most detailed account of how religious experience may be thought of as an instance of sharing attention with God can be found in Green's discussion. He writes that (2009, 462):

> One is engaged in dyadic shared attention with God iff one is aware of God as exhibiting some mental state which is directed towards oneself and the mental state which God exhibits involves an awareness of the co-operative nature of the present attention. This co-operation will be invested with an interactive pattern of affect since to experience God is to experience both the source of all goodness and to experience someone who wants to have the most intimate of relationships with one.

According to Green, this model of religious experience makes sense both of the personal nature of God and of the reports of experiences that we find in accounts of religious experience.

Thinking of religious experience as joint attention offers a way of understanding religious experience that allows for a description of how actions are perceived, as well as emotions and intentions. It also means that God can manipulate the media by which we perceive the world (light, sound, etc.) to reveal his emotions and actions toward us (as in the example cited by de Smedt and de Cruz, for instance). Note that unlike Alston's model, a person does not have to perceive God through any mystical qualia to be sharing attention with God, but rather a person's ordinary perceptual experience can provide the means for experiencing divine personal presence. The individual who experiences God through joint attention does not have to perform an inference to establish that she is experiencing God, but there is an intersubjective relation that occurs between God and her. The individual experiences something of God's emotions or intentions whether that be God's loving, or God's forgiving, or God's imparting mercy.

Although there is clearly a precedent for thinking about religious experience in these terms, an objector may still worry about the application of this literature to the religious case.[8] It should be noted that although the philosophers and theologians cited above do not think of joint attention in merely metaphorical terms, even if one does think that joint attention with God must be conceived of in purely metaphorical terms, this need not undermine its application for my purposes. For even if the best way of understanding the metaphysics of joint attention states does not extend to the case of experiencing God's presence, the phenomenology of such states may still be informative. For the crucial point of the above arguments (at least for this discussion) appears to be this: ordinarily we think of experiences of presence in terms that are phenomenologically different from experiences of perception, and since God is described as being *present to* and with his people in the Christian tradition, we should think of experiencing such presence (in phenomenological terms) as akin to personal presence and not perception. This is helpful even if the sense of joint attention used is metaphorical; looking at related experiences can help us attend to what is distinctive about experiences of presence—it can alert us to the importance of seeing religious experience as an experience in which we attend to God's attention, in which God reveals attitudes and actions to us, and in which God can alert us to features of our ordinary environment. And none of these observations seems to be entirely wedded to a metaphysics of the psychology of joint attention.

Let us now turn to consider this application to the Kierkegaardian account of presence.

14.5   A Kierkegaardian Phenomenology of Divine Presence

A joint attention model of religious experience is much better equipped to capture the phenomenology of being "contemporary with Christ" than a perceptual model, I think. As we have seen, for Kierkegaard, our relation to God is best understood

---

[8] With thanks to an anonymous referee for raising this concern.

not as a relation to an object but rather as a subject to be engaged with and experienced. A Kierkegaardian phenomenology of religious experience needs also to be understood in these terms. The application of the shared attention literature to religious experience gives us a clear account of what Kierkegaard writes about contemporaneity. Just as Kierkegaard is quite happy to use "contemporaneity" to explain lovers' relations to each other as well as a religious believer's relation to Christ, it is important to extend our understanding of personal presence in general to experiencing divine presence. In fact, it is this kind of shared attention that is precisely the experience that Johannes the Seducer cannot have through letter writing to Cordelia but that is essential to his experience of her. If we can extend this account of attention sharing to understand how a person can engage with God's presence (or perhaps Christ's presence, to explain what Kierkegaard writes), then the focus for our understanding of phenomenology and religious experience should first be the phenomenology of interpersonal experience. If we can establish just what it is to experience the presence of another person and to engage with that person, then, I think, we can gain a much richer insight into the experiences that many people claim to have of God.[9]

Finally, it is important to note that, for Kierkegaard, the revelation of God's presence is importantly connected to the work of redemption and sanctification. Unlike ordinary human relationships, in which there can be a kind of mutual understanding and equality of relationship, human beings always relate to God from a position of being sinful (Kierkegaard 1985, 26–30). Thus, for union with God to be possible, some kind of transformation must take place. The experience of God's presence plays an important role in this transformation. For instance, in discussing the awareness of God's presence at the Eucharist, Kierkegaard writes that "it is no doubt a restful position when you kneel at the foot of the altar, but God grant that this indeed may truly be only a faint intimation of your soul's finding rest in God through the consciousness of the forgiveness of sins" (2009, 267). As he puts this point in a journal entry, "by becoming contemporary with Christ (the exemplar), you discover precisely that you don't resemble it at all.. .. From this it follows, then, that you really and truly learn what it is to take refuge in grace" (Cappelørn et al. 2011, 9). The important point for our purposes, then, is that the phenomenology of divine presence is in important ways different from the phenomenology of personal presence in general. The reason for this, as the Eastern Orthodox theologian Anthony Bloom describes, is that "meeting God face to face is always a moment of judgement" (1986, 131).

Thus, although reflecting on the phenomenology of personal presence has its uses for helping us to think about the phenomenology of divine presence, it also has its limits. As Moser and McCreary describe (2010, 131), for Kierkegaard, relating to God

---

[9] I would like to thank David Efird, along with the members of the St. Benedict Society for Philosophy of Religion and Philosophical Theology at the University of York for their helpful comments on an earlier draft of this chapter.

is anything but an object of human speculation. It demands engagement of the human will (and choice), on the basis of a distinctive kind of cognitive "restraining" found in sincere human self-knowledge (before God). One can sincerely inquire about the ingredients of such self-knowledge, including the role of divine intervention, but such inquiry will have to ask about human volition. In particular, is a person sincerely willing to undergo the kind of transformation in question? If not, could this volitional position cloud otherwise available evidence or restraining from God? This question leads to the issue of why God is not more obvious to (all) humans.

This points to one important difference between experiencing God's presence and experiencing personal presence in general. Because of the volitional challenge that experiencing God's presence brings, God is sometimes hidden from us, and we sometimes withdraw from God (even if we are not always aware that we are doing so).[10] And thus, although experiencing God may in many ways be like experiencing any other person, one crucial point of difference is that God may not always be available to us as we would like him to be. There may be times when experiencing God's presence is too painful for us to take and times when we are too busy, distracted, or resistant to attend to God and to face the challenge that accompanies such an experience.

14.6   Conclusion

I have suggested that by building on two theological insights from Kierkegaard's writings (that we relate to God as a subject and not an object, and that we relate to God through becoming contemporary with Christ's presence) we can find a starting point for understanding the phenomenology of religious experience. Moreover, by reflecting on the nature of personal presence and the psychology of relating to another person more generally, we can gain insights into the phenomenology of divine presence. Finally, I've suggested that although such an approach can be useful, we must be aware of the points of difference between relating to persons in general and relating to God. More specifically, if experiencing God's presence provides a volitional and redemptive challenge to us, then we should not be surprised if God's presence is not readily available to us, or if human beings naturally withdraw from experiencing God in this way.[11]

---

[10] See Cockayne 2018 for a more detailed discussion of the issue of God's withdrawing his presence from us.

[11] Many thanks to David Efird and members of the St Benedict Society for Philosophy of Religion at the University of York for comments on an earlier draft of this chapter. I would also like to thank the editor, Olga Louchakova-Schwartz, for her helpful comments and suggestions. Thanks to the Templeton Religion Trust for their generous funding during the writing of this chapter, and to the Society for the Phenomenology of Religious Experience for providing a stipend to cover editing costs.

References

Alston, William. 1991. *Perceiving God: The epistemology of religious experience*. Ithaca: Cornell University Press.

Bloom, Anthony. 1986. *The essence of prayer*. London: Darton, Longman and Todd.

Buber, Martin. 1937. *I and Thou*. Trans. Ronald Gregor Smith. Edinburgh: T. & T. Clark.

Bungum, Donald. 2013. Joint attention, union with God, and the dark night of the soul. *European Journal for the Philosophy of Religion* 5 (4): 187–210.

Cappelørn, Niels Jørgen, et al. [Cappelørn, Niels Jørgen, Alastair Hannay, David Kangas, Bruce H. Kirmmese, George Pattison, Joel D.S. Rasmussen, Vanessa Rumble, and K. Brian Sonderquist.]. 2011. *Kierkegaard's journals and notebooks*, vol. 5, *Journals NB6–NB10*. Princeton: Princeton University Press.

Church of England. 2000. *Common worship: Services and prayers for the Church of England*. London: Church House Publishing.

Cockayne, Joshua. 2017. Contemporaneity and Communion: Kierkegaard on the personal presence of Christ. *British Journal for the History of Philosophy* 25 (1): 41–62.

———. 2018. The dark knight of the soul: Weaning and the problem of divine withdrawal. *Religious Studies* 54 (1): 73–90.

Cockayne, J.L., et al. [Cockayne, J.L., D. Efird, J. Warman, D. Molto, G. Haynes, A. Ludwigs, and R. Tamburro.]. 2017. Experiencing the real presence of Christ in the Eucharist. *Journal of Analytic Theology* 5(1): 175–196.

de Smedt, Johan, and Helen de Cruz. 2013. Delighting in natural beauty: Joint attention and the phenomenology of nature aesthetics. *European Journal for the Philosophy of Religion* 5 (4): 167–186.

———. 2014. The *imago Dei* as a work in progress: A perspective from paleoanthropology. *Zygon* 49 (1): 135–156.

Evans, C. Stephen. 1992. *Passionate reason*. Bloomington: Indiana University Press.

———. 2006. *Kierkegaard on faith and the self: Collected essays*. Waco: Baylor University Press.

Green, Adam. 2009. Reading the mind of God (without Hebrew lessons): Alston, shared attention, and mystical experience. *Religious Studies* 45 (4): 455–470.

Hobson, R. Peter. 2004. *The cradle of thought: Exploring the origins of thinking*. Oxford: Oxford University Press.

Kierkegaard, Søren. 1985. *Philosophical Fragments*. Trans. Howard V. Hong and Edna H. Hong Kierkegaard's Writings, VII. Princeton: Princeton University Press.

———. 1987. *Either/or: Part I*. Trans. Howard V. Hong and Edna H. Hong. Kierkegaard's Writings, IV. Princeton: Princeton University Press.

———. 1991. *Practice in Christianity*. Trans. Howard V. Hong and Edna H. Hong. Kierkegaard's Writings, XX. Princeton: Princeton University Press.

———. 1992. *Concluding Unscientific Postscript to Philosophical Fragments*. Trans. Howard V. Hong and Edna H. Hong. Kierkegaard's Writings, XII.1. Princeton: Princeton University Press.

———. 2009. *Christian Discourses: The Crisis and A Crisis in the Life of an Actress*. Trans. Howard V. Hong and Edna H. Hong. Kierkegaard's Writings, XVII. Princeton: Princeton University Press.

Moser, Paul K. 2008. *The elusive God: Reorientating religious epistemology*. Cambridge: Cambridge University Press.

———. 2009. *The evidence for God: Religious knowledge reexamined*. Cambridge: Cambridge University Press.

———. 2013. *The severity of God: Religion and philosophy reconceived*. Cambridge: Cambridge University Press.

Moser, Paul K., and Mark L. McCreary. 2010. Kierkegaard's conception of God. *Philosophy Compass* 5 (2): 127–135.

Pappas, George. 1994. Perception and mystical experience. *Philosophical and Phenomenological Research* 54 (4): 877–882.

Pattison, George. 2012. *Kierkegaard and the theology of the nineteenth century*. Cambridge: Cambridge University Press.

Pinsent, Andrew. 2012. *The second-person perspective in Aquinas's ethics: Virtues and gifts*. London: Routledge.

Reddy, Vasudevi. 2005. Before the "third element": Understanding attention to self. In *Joint attention: Communication and other minds*, ed. Naomi Eilan et al., 85–110. Oxford: Oxford University Press.

———. 2012. A gaze that grips with me. In *Seemann 2012* (q.v.), 137–158.

Seemann, Axel, ed. 2012. *Joint attention: New developments in psychology, philosophy of mind, and social neuroscience*. Cambridge, MA: MIT Press.

Shteynberg, Garriy. 2015. Shared attention. *Perspectives on Psychological Science* 10 (5): 579–590.

Stokes, Patrick. 2010. "See for your self": Contemporaneity, autopsy and presence in Kierkegaard's moral-religious psychology. *British Journal for the History of Philosophy* 18(2):297–319.

———. 2015. *The naked self: Kierkegaard and personal identity*. Oxford: Oxford University Press.

Stump, Eleonore. 2010. *Wandering in darkness*. Oxford: Oxford University Press.

Joshua Cockayne is a lecturer at the Logos Institute for Analytic and Exegetical Theology at the University of St Andrews. He received his Ph.D. from the University of York for work on Kierkegaard and the philosophy of Christian spirituality. He has published articles on the philosophy of religion, analytic theology, and the theology of Kierkegaard, including topics such as faith, being contemporary with Christ, the imitation of Christ, and Kierkegaard's account of prayer, as well as the communion discourses. Joshua was awarded the Religious Studies postgraduate journal from Cambridge University Press, and the prize is also supported by the British Society for Philosophy of Religion in both 2015 and 2016.

Chapter 15
The Trinitarian Manifestation of God in Jean-Luc Marion's Phenomenology

Adrian Răzvan Șandru

Abstract I shall argue here that Trinity is a leitmotiv in Marion's works and that his latest analysis on said concept can enlighten us on the function of the icon and on the structure of his phenomenology of givenness. As such I will argue for a Trinitarian character of givenness. To prove this, I shall structure this paper as a commentary on *Givenness and Revelation* that will show how this book reveals unclear functions of the Trinity involved in givenness, such as the role of the Holy Spirit, and relate these functions to the strict phenomenological structure of the act of giving. I shall first set the stage for a phenomenological interpretation of Trinity, showing which concepts are at play in Marion's analysis of revelation. This will be followed by the integration of Trinity in the immanent field of phenomenology. Further, I shall show how revelation serves as the model for a new phenomenal logic, and I shall try to explain its manifestation. This will be followed by a presentation of how Marion's new considerations on the topic of revelation can clarify both the role of the given and in addition the role of the subject within Marion's phenomenology of givenness.

Keywords Revelation · Trinity · Immanence · Jean-Luc Marion · Givenness · Saturation · Subject

Trinity has been a recurrent theme of Jean-Luc Marion's works since *God without Being* (hereinafter *GB:* 2012, originally published 1982), where it was mostly

I wish to thank Prof. Dr. Johannes Brachtendorf for his valuable support and recommendations. I wish also to thank Federica María González Luna Ortiz for her helpful feedback. I am also thankful for the support provided by the *Society for the Phenomenology of Religious Experience (SOPHERE)*. This paper is based on a review I wrote on Marion's *Givenness and Revelation.* See Șandru 2016.

A. R. Șandru (✉)
Eberhard-Karls University, Tübingen, Germany
e-mail: adrian-razvan.sandru@uni-tuebingen.de

© Springer Nature Switzerland AG 2019
O. Louchakova-Schwartz (ed.), *The Problem of Religious Experience*,
Contributions to Phenomenology 103,
https://doi.org/10.1007/978-3-030-21575-0_15

analyzed within a theological context. This text does, however, hint at the phenomenological implications of Trinity, which are further developed in Marion's phenomenological works and all the more so in *Being Given* (*BG:* 2002, originally published 1997). Here, Trinity is reduced to an immanence of phenomenological possibility and brought into close connection with what Marion calls a "saturated phenomenon." The phenomenological structure of Trinity is further developed within Marion's works—*In Excess* (*IE:* 2004, originally published 2001a) and *Negative Certainties* (*NC:* 2015, originally published 2010)—and finds a clear formulation in *Givenness and Revelation* (*GR:* 2016a), where Marion argues that the Trinitarian revelation of Christ accomplishes Husserl's principle of principles. Considering this widespread presence of the Trinitarian motif within Marion's investigations upon both theology and phenomenology, the question imposes itself of the continuity of his understanding of the Trinity. I shall therefore set out to investigate the evolution of Trinitarian thought in Marion's works and the consequences it has on the development of his phenomenology of givenness.

Marion bases his earlier understanding of givenness on the concept of distance—in *Idol and Distance* (2001b)—and on the iconic figure in *GB* that allows the full referral to another by confronting the subject with an endless saturation of his intentionality, which in its turn leads to the recognition of the intentionality of the other as love. This opens the ground for a new kind of phenomenological logic, namely that of the gift, which is further developed in *BG*. Here, the icon becomes the standard-bearer of other saturated phenomena: that is, phenomena that give themselves in such a degree that they overwhelm our cognitive capacities. Saturation becomes here the way to givenness, which frees us, according to Marion, from the shackles of metaphysics and of the logic of economic exchange. Saturation is explained by Marion through confrontation of Kant's categories with an excessive intuition.[1] This confrontation leads to the failure of the categories to synthesize and schematize said intuition, which then manifests itself not as an object but as an event, freed from the principles of noncontradiction and of sufficient reason. As this intuition manifests *itself* through the failure of the categories, it is not experienced but received as a counterexperience or counterintentionality. According to Marion, this counterexperience enlarges the phenomenal horizon and opens up onto the possibility of nonobject phenomena. I shall try to show that this road to givenness is opened by the iconic figure, which is itself embedded with Trinitarian motifs. I shall also try to show that not only that Trinity is a continuous presence in Marion's works but that his latest analysis on said concept can enlighten us on the function of the icon and on the structure of his phenomenology of givenness.

In order to prove the Trinitarian character of givenness, I shall structure this paper as a commentary on *GR*, which will show how this book reveals unclear functions of the Trinity involved in givenness, such as the role of the Holy Spirit, and

---

[1] Similar to what Kant calls "the sublime"—i.e., an excessive intuition: "Das Erfahren des Erhabenen ist das Erfahren einer Unangemessenheit zwischen der Auffassung und der Zusammenfassung, das heißt einer Trennung zwischen dem Unendlichen und der Allheit" (Foessel 2008, 110).

relate these functions to the strict phenomenological structure of the act of giving. I shall first (following Marion) set the stage for a phenomenological interpretation of Trinity, showing which concepts are at play in Marion's analysis of revelation. This will be followed by the integration of Trinity in the immanent field of phenomenology. Further on I shall show how revelation serves as the model for a new phenomenal logic and try to explain its manifestation. This will be followed by a presentation of how Marion's new considerations on the topic of revelation can clarify both the role of the given and the role of the subject within Marion's phenomenology of givenness. This last section shall also serve as a conclusion to this paper.

15.1 Receiving by Resisting

The concept of a counterexperience makes an appearance already in the introduction to *GR*, where Marion distinguishes between revealed religion and natural theology, recalling the distinction between *theo*-logy and theo-*logy* made in *GB*. Here he argues that revelation can find its place only within a *theo*-logy that through prayer completely renounces a predicative language. It will instead accept the *logos* of the revelation from elsewhere—that is, from God—and not impose its own logic on the revelatory phenomenon. This view will play a major role in *GR*. Here, revelation is described as being a conflictual experience. Moreover, conflict or resistance is a condition for the reception of revelation, albeit not a sufficient one. Through this conflictual character of revelation, Marion bridges the link between the theological concept of revelation and the phenomenological one of givenness.

In *BG*, givenness is described as a paradox experience that exceeds and thus opposes the Kantian concepts of possible experience as well as going beyond Husserl's *noēsis-noēma* structure—and manifests itself as a saturated phenomenon: that is, a given that gives itself in an excessive degree so that it cannot be brought into a concept-intuition/*noēsis-noēma* adequation. The theme of the saturated phenomenon as a paradox is reiterated in *NC*, a paradox being not a logical contradiction but the inability of logic to ascribe the concepts of possibility or impossibility to what transgresses it. In *GR* the very authenticity of revelation—pure givenness—depends on a *resistance* from the one who witnesses it: if revelation turns out not to be authentic, the resistance and the conflict are resolved within epistemic immanence; if, however, the revelation is authentic, resistance will increase. This can be better explained in connection with Marion's *Banality of Saturation* (2008). Here he describes the steps of saturation, through which one comes to receive a counterexperience: As one is affected by an intuition so powerful that the concept used to intend it cannot conceive of it, she will resist its intensity by trying to find a more adequate concept to accommodate the intuition. This attempt will fail, the intuition being too intense to be grasped through concepts.[2] Such a failure of conceptualizing

---

[2] In opposition to Kant, Marion argues that an excessive intuition—the sublime—does not fall under the ideas of pure reason thus revealing the autonomy of the subject, but shows that noncon-

leads to a disturbance of the subject, who thus experiences resistance coming from elsewhere. Through this resistance coming from elsewhere, but manifesting itself within the immanent resistance of the subject, the counterexperience is received as authentic. This conflictual character is thus inherent to the witnessing of revelation and of saturated phenomena in general, and constitutes what I call a "resistant hermeneutics." (See Şandru 2018.)

This is consistent with both *BG* and (mostly) with *IE*. In *BG* the subject has the possibility of accepting or ignoring the call of the given. This acceptance brings the phenomenality of the given to light. This somewhat active role of the subject is highlighted in *IE*—maybe as a response to the critiques of Marlene Zarader (2003) and others[3]—where the given is phenomenalized through its encounter with the subject. The subject does not constitute the given but acts as its medium, where the given can give itself from itself in order to show itself: "In *In Excess* he [Marion] describes the gifted (l'adonné) as the screen on which givenness is displayed, as in a movie theatre, such that the resistance of the gifted brings the given into visibility" (Harding 2013, 303). What is of importance here is that resistance is ascribed to the subject. This breaks away from Marion's earlier work in *GB*, where resistance is discussed mainly in connection with the imposing power of the iconic figure. In *GB* resistance appears as an obstacle to the infinite expansion of the subject's melancholia—which is a sign of indifference toward Being—and points to the encounter with a counterintentionality that cannot be determined by the subject because it imposes itself on the subject. Even though the concept of resistance implies an activity of both parts, the role of the subject is not made clear here. In opposition to this, *BG* speaks of a more active subject, which becomes even more active—especially hermeneutically—in *IE*. *GR* continues in this line and starts with a talk about resistance as if to highlight that Marion deals with revelation phenomenologically. This understanding of revelation is a somewhat critical one, to be separated from a fanatical, ascetical, or dogmatic one (or all these) but retaining its nonconceptual integrity coming from elsewhere but still manifesting itself within immanence. We thus observe the development of the subject in Marion's works, from mostly passive to a resistant instance that determines the authenticity of revelation but not its mode of givenness, as we shall see further on.

15.2   The Need for a New Logic

The mode of givenness cannot be constituted by the subject, as revelation presents itself in terms that do not accord with our subjective structures. To put this more precisely: revelation or charity presents itself as four-dimensional, and we need to be absorbed within it in order to see it from its own perspective (Marion 2016a, 71). This indicates nothing other than the loss of ipseity or I-intentionality, because our

---

ceptual givens are possible escaping any categorial determination.

[3] For a summary of such critiques, see Westphal (2006). See also Mackinlay (2010).

gaze, which constitutes objects in a three-dimensional space, cannot conceive a four-dimensional phenomenon. Therefore, charity or revelation is to be seen through a gaze that is not finite. The only gaze that is not finite but is still part of the world is that of Christ: "the only infinite phenomenological gaze, yet in our flesh" (Marion 2016a, 72).

This announces the need for a new logic, which would accommodate such a manifestation of revelation. As Marion points out, accepting it by dismissing our reason leads to irrationality or fanaticism. The dismissal of revelation as coming from elsewhere, however, leads to idolatry, the reduction of revelation to our own intentionality as a noematic object. On the other side, trying to maintain the revealed within a rational adaptation of it ends up by limiting revelation to what has not yet been discovered within reason. Thus, concludes Marion, revelation retains its revelatory character only within a phenomenal logic of paradox: "the visibility of the invisible *as such, and which remains so in its very visibility*" (Marion 2016a, 5). This is based on Marion's thesis from *BG*, that something shows itself inasmuch as it gives itself from itself.[4] In this way the paradoxical character of phenomena says nothing more than that they manifest themselves without letting themselves be constituted by a subjective logic. As such, phenomena manifest themselves solely within the parameters of their own character of being given. Thus, the unseen can be made visible within and as its givenness. The fact that phenomena show themselves inasmuch as they give themselves allows Marion to develop a givenness-based hierarchy of phenomena that peaks in the figure of Christ as revelation.[5] Thus, through the analysis of revelation, Marion attempts to uncover the very rule of phenomenality, as will become clear in the following sections.

15.3 An Attempt at a Phenomenal Reappropriation of Revelation

In a historical investigation Marion (2016a) concludes that revelation has been mainly understood from an epistemological perspective, through which revelation is subdued and determined by reason, whether theoretical or practical. According to Marion, the epistemological understanding of revelation subjects *apokalypsis* (revelation) to *alētheia* (truth), which is to be understood in its modern meaning as clear and distinct knowledge. In order to bring revelation to presence as clear and distinct,

---

[4] Marion could not, however, tackle the problem of a theology of revelation in *BG,* as it would have breached the boundaries of immanent phenomenology. See Gschwandtner (2016, 79)

[5] Marion speaks of three kinds of phenomena according to their degree of saturation: weak (where the concept predominates), common-law (which rely on concept-intuition adequation), and saturated phenomena (where the intuition predominates). Saturated phenomena are themselves categorized into four types of givenness: (1) the event; (2) the idol/anamorphosis; (3) flesh; (4) the icon. The icon has the special attribute of incorporating all other types of saturated phenomena and thus exceeds every category of possible experience. The programmatic figure of the icon is described by Marion to be Christ (as phenomenal possibility and not as a historical figure).

it must be subjected to the two principles of contradiction and of sufficient reason, which for Marion are the basic principles of metaphysics.[6]

Against this understanding Marion (2016a) resorts to Pascal in order to show that the will is not preceded by reason, as Descartes argues, but conditions knowing. Marion relates Pascal's statements concerning the priority of the will to Augustine, who stated that only charity, which has been poured into our souls by the Holy Spirit, can lead us to truth. This will be the turning point in reinterpreting revelation, relying on two main arguments as described below.

First, the will to be willingly is conditioned and sparked by revelation as the attraction to see the Father in the Son. This is based on another Augustinian thesis according to which revelation itself is the one that draws us into charity. Thus, the will is itself subordinated to charity. Based on biblical texts, Marion argues that one does not have to will first in order to love, as love itself is what attracts us to will it. Consequently, God's charity is not reduced to a fulfillment of the will. This accordingly goes against both a subjectivistic view of God as well as against a Kantian moral understanding of God and repeats the Logic of the Call developed by Marion in *BG:* the call constitutes the subject and calls him to answer. The call itself becomes manifest only in the answer of the subject. However, because the call called the subject into answering and thus demanded its own manifestation, the call is not constituted by the subject (Marion 2002, 262–270).

Second, the will to be willing consists in faith, which conditions and precedes seeing. Only by accepting Jesus as the Son of the Father can we see the Father in the Son, "as the visibility of the invisibility" (Marion 2002, 41). This seeing of Jesus as the Christ is only possible as we interpret Him in the Holy Spirit.

From these considerations Marion (2016a) draws three conclusions. First, we can see revelation only through faith. Second, in order to believe we need to will it. The will is, however, "put in operation" by the fact of being drawn by and in God's love. And third, we can will something only inasmuch as we love said something. Here the will is equated with love, and revelation becomes possible only inasmuch as it is freed from the logic of natural reason and able to impose its own logic, which must start with the will and end up in love again. Marion thus uncovers a new kind of logic in theology, which is not subdued by the logic of natural reason. In order for philosophical logic to come to terms with the logic of love, it must turn to phenomenology, as Marion argues. Through phenomenology, philosophy can return to the phenomena freed from the conditions of possible experience, through which they can appear only as objects. The main thesis of *BG* is here reiterated in order to show that the logic of the gift is better able to describe phenomena as they give themselves. This implies that the condition for receiving phenomena as they give themselves and not as we conceive of them is that they give themselves from themselves—that is, they give themselves as events and not as objects. This way of self-giving is made apparent in saturated phenomena and all the more so in the

---

[6] This critique is present throughout Marion's works and states that through the principle of contradiction and of sufficient reason philosophy becomes dependent on ipseity, and the entirety of phenomenality is reduced to the constitutive power of the subject. See Gschwandtner (2007).

figure of Christ, who gives himself in an exceptional way. As a saturated phenomenon Christ gives himself as an excess of intuition, which cannot be brought under a concept and is therefore objectively impossible. Because of this lack of signification, the saturated phenomenon requires an endless hermeneutics, as no signification can exhaust its own logic. The saturated phenomenon thus gives itself, against the principles of common logic, as a paradox, which imposes its own hermeneutics. Lacking the necessary concepts, the subject does not see the phenomenon from the perspective of an I, as it cannot synthesize what it sees because of the excess of intuition. Instead it becomes a witness, seeing without knowing, receiving an already synthesized *fait accompli*, seeing what gives itself from itself without being the object of an intentionality or concept. Christ as a saturated phenomenon gives himself from himself and does not abide by the epistemological conditions of experience. He thus contradicts these conditions and is received or seen as nonobjectifiable. He thus gives himself as a paradox that does not exclude logic nor is outside logic but instead extends it to the possibility of describing the impossible as a counterexperience.

This new logic reminds us of *GB,* where the *Eucharistic Hermeneutic* argues for a logic of love, which is not intentional but imposes itself on intentionality to manifest its own way of manifestation. *GR* bridges this view with Marion's later investigations and building on phenomenological considerations *reappropriates* theological concepts. To these means, Marion accentuates the iconic function of the saturated phenomenon—which was already present in *GB* under the banner of a Christological givenness and was further developed under the roof of phenomenological immanence in *BG*—and expands it to a Trinitarian phenomenology.

15.4 Anamorphosis and the Holy Spirit

The above is shown first in the case of a *mysterium* that uncovers itself in the gaze of Christ only insofar as he is the icon of the Father: that is, only insofar as he exhausts the invisibility of the Father and brings it to light in his flesh.[7] The reception of such a phenomenon cannot be known or seen directly. In order to see a *mysterium* the reversal of intentionality is necessary, which implies that the *mysterium* is seen through the gaze of the Father and not transcendentally constituted as an object. The reversal of intentionality is, however, possible only through the Holy Spirit. This is the adaptation of the phenomenon of anamorphosis: a phenomenon becomes visible once we accept its own perspective. Through this acceptance of the

---

[7] This view helps us clarify Marion's understanding of kenosis. What he proposes is not the classical understanding of kenosis—through which the divine is relinquished in Christ's flesh—but an iconic one, which states that Christ acts as an absolute referent to the Father. (See Marion 2016b.) This both continues and clarifies the exposition of the relation between the Son and the Father made in *GB,* which has been understood through the lens of the classical kenotical view. See Specker (2002) and Gschwandtner (2016, 46).

perspective from elsewhere the *mysterium* will not be known or unveiled but rather will show itself from itself in its uncovering. Tobias Specker (2002) already identifies in *GB* three Trinitarian moments of the revelation of God as Son: namely Christ is described first as a gift given absolutely by the Father; second as absolute abandonment (that is, as placing his will at the will of the Father); and last as identity within difference through the agency of the Spirit. Furthermore, the concept of the icon itself is developed in terms of Trinitarian movements: "The icon must always have a trinitarian basis, which alone enables it to maintain the fragile balance between distance and advent, presence and absence, visible and invisible" (Gschwandtner 2016, 46). *GB* speaks, however, mainly about the relation between the Son and the Father and thus neglects the role of the Spirit. In *GR* the Spirit completes the Trinitarian movement by assuming the role of anamorphosis, first described in *BG*. Through this association the Trinitarian aspects of revelation, which are still murky—and mostly just implied—in *GB* are made clear in *GR*.

It is important to note here that in Christ the *mysterium* uncovers itself. This relation between Christ, apokalypsis, and *mysterium* announces a phenomenological principle—"so much mysterion, so much revelation"—which for Marion fulfills the goal of phenomenology: to wit, that something gives itself from itself as itself without a doubled representation. Reinterpreting Husserl's principle of principles, Marion explains this relation as follows: "the phenomenon shows itself in itself and through himself only in as much as it gives itself in and through himself" (Marion 2016a, 76). In short, the mode of appearance coincides with the mode of givenness. The only phenomenon that lives up to this principle and actualizes it is Christ, as he shows himself absolutely, inasmuch as he gives himself absolutely and without condition. The moment of such an absolute manifestation is, however, dependent on the witnesses of such a givenness. More exactly, Christ becomes manifest as the Son of God only as those who witness him choose to answer his call. Answering his call means that the hearers and seers of Christ renounce their own perspective in order to see or hear Christ from the perspective of the Father, namely as the Son of God. In the phenomenological works, the passage from the I to the *adonné* is done prephenomenally by the given that imposes itself and phenomenally through the agency of reduction; consequently, the principle of phenomenology: so much reduction, so much givenness. We can find the same movement in the case of God, too. As one wills to answer the call of charity, one reduces one's I-identity to the state of being a witness. As we have seen, though, the will comes to willing only because it is drawn by the Father toward the Father. This appears to be a hermeneutical circle, which Marion recognizes and embraces as it leads to a Trinitarian manifestation of God: "taking the correct point of view on the phenomenon that God gives us to see (in Jesus Christ) indeed can come only from God himself (the Father), who offers both the phenomenon (what gives itself) and the conditions of its visibility (what shows itself)" (Marion 2016a, 83). This is the turning point toward understanding the Trinitarian manifestation of God, which alone can account for the revelation of the Father in the Son, who acts as the absolute icon. Here two hermeneutical steps are important. First, the Father is the ground and condition for the giving of Jesus as Christ, as the Son of the Father. This because only the Father can give Jesus as his

Son. Second, this implies that Jesus can be seen as the Son of the Father only from the perspective of the Father. This further implies that the perspective of the Father and therefore the Father Himself is constitutive for the phenomenal manifestation of Jesus as Christ. These two steps make way for a conclusion: If we know Jesus as the Son of the Father, we also know the Father, as only from His perspective can Jesus be seen as the Christ. Consequently, and holding true to his status as icon, Jesus never refers to himself but to another, which is also the ground for his revelation. This is a first step in constituting a Trinitarian phenomenality. The second is in tight connection to the characteristic of the icon of letting the gaze of the other target the one who witnesses it. The fact that Jesus is given as the Son of the Father by the Father to human beings implies that humans feel themselves intended by the intentionality of the Father via the agency of the gift: "In this way the putting of Christ into an icon is accomplished, which properly defines the work of the Spirit" (Marion 2016a, 86). The Spirit completes the Trinity by bringing the subject to a Trinitarian perspective, as will be further explained.

15.5   A Logic of Manifestation

In accordance with the iconic function of referring completely to another Marion (2016a) seeks to distance himself from tradition, where substance is of priority and relation is secondary, and accepts the relational shift in the understanding of Trinity led by Karl Barth, Karl Rahner, and Hans Urs von Balthasar.[8] Based on their considerations that Trinity and its revelation constitute the basis of the unity and essence of God, Marion seeks to show how the phenomenological manifestation of God— that is, revelation—argues for the primacy of love or of communion concerning the essence of God. The phenomenological description already made of revelation as a saturated phenomenon would support this shift, as it argues that God is to be seen only as he gives himself. Here, the thesis of *GR* is clearly formulated: "the Trinity offers not only the content of the uncovering, but also its mode of manifestation" (Marion 2016a, 99). Given that God gives himself in a hyperbolic way, saturating and surpassing our conceptual experience, and that such a given can be seen only through its own logic, God should be known only as He gives Himself. Considering that He gives Himself as a Trinity or communion, Trinity has primacy in the phenomenology of religious experience. This is further sustained by Marion's argument that Trinity reveals itself through Christ as an icon, which means that Christ never refers to himself but to another, completely to another. This implies that the more he refers to another—that is, to the Father—the more he appears as an icon and as the Son of God. This further implies that the stronger the communion between Father and Son is, the stronger the unity of God is: "their trinitarian identity [of the Father

---

[8] "The immanent Trinity is the economic Trinity and the economic Trinity is the immanent Trinity" (Rahner 1970: 5). On Rahner, see also Greshake (1997, 143). On Barth, see Hunsinger (2008, 195), and on von Balthasar, see Gorgone (2013, 250).

and the Son] is uncovered in the process of their common manifestation, or rather, in the process of their communion in the manifestation" (Marion 2016a, 103). Within this dynamic the Spirit has the phenomenal function of accomplishing the anamorphosis: that is, of reducing the (Kantian) categorial perspective of the subject to a Trinitarian one: "the Spirit positions the human gaze at the exact place and point of view where the visible face of Christ (Jesus *as* Son) can at once, with a sudden and perfect precision, be uncovered as the very axis where the gaze of the Father on the Son and that of the Son at the Father pass" (Marion 2016a, 108). The Spirit is thus the very act of uncovering. In being such, the Spirit is a unitary part of the uncovering as its act but does not appear, as a visible, within it.

This Trinitarian manifestation accords with the description of the gift described in §§7–12 of *BG contra* Mauss and Derrida. Here Marion argues that the gift can appear as a gift only when it is not inscribed within the economical logic of exchange. This logic can be evaded only as one or all of the constituting/transcendental poles of economic exchange are suspended, namely the giver, the givee, and the gift (or all these). One can assume that in *GR* Marion argues for the suspension of all three transcendental poles: of God as Cause, of humans as reason, and of Christ as historical figure/objective phenomenon. Through this suspension all that manifests itself is givenness as pure act, and the place for givenness is secured.

We can thus conclude that the Trinitarian logic aims at accomplishing the phenomenology of givenness, where the giver and the gift are manifested within the very act of giving as the communion of these three (Marion 2002, 61).[9] Through the fact that the mode of givenness is also implied within givenness itself, the givee is also inscribed within givenness through the reception of its mode of manifestation. Considering this, we can also see what is at stake in *GR*. It seeks not only to explain a possible revelation but to uncover a new logic of phenomenality that argues for a givenness that gives itself inasmuch as it also gives its mode of appearance and thus is not reducible to subjective structures. Given that this mode of givenness appears within a resistance of the subject, Trinity—or at least so Marion argues—remains within immanence as an uncovering of itself in communion with the resistance of the subject.

References

Foessel, Michael. 2008. Die Analytik des Erhabenen. In *Immanuel Kant: Kritik der Urteilskraft*, ed. O. Höffe, 99–121. Berlin: De Gruyter.
Gorgone, Sandro. 2013. Idol und Ikone. In *Jean-Luc Marion: Studien zum Werk,* ed. Hanna-Barbara Gerl-Falkovitz, 237–253. Dresden: Text und Dialog.
Greshake, Gisbert. 1997. *Der dreieine Gott: Eine trinitarische Theologie.* Freiburg: Herder.
Gschwandnter, Christina. 2007. *Reading Jean-Luc Marion: Exceeding metaphysics.* Bloomington: Indiana University Press.
———. 2016. *Marion and theology.* London: Bloomsbury T. & T. Clark.

---

[9] See Marion (2002, 61).

Harding, Brian. 2013. Saturating the phenomenon: Marion and Buber. *Sophia* 52 (2): 295–313.

Hunsinger, G. 2008. Election and the trinity: Twenty-five theses on the theology of Karl Barth. *Modern Theology* 24 (2): 179–198.

Mackinlay, Shane. 2010. *Interpreting excess: Jean-Luc Marion, saturated phenomena, and hermeneutics*. New York: Fordham University Press.

Marion, Jean-Luc. 1982. *Dieu sans l'être*. Paris: Communio Fayard.

———. 1997. *Étant donné: Essai d'une phénoménologie de la donation*. Paris: Presses Universitaires de France.

———. 2001a. *De surcroît*. Paris: Presses Universitaires de France.

———. 2001b. *The idol and distance: Five studies*. New York: Fordham University Press.

———. 2002. *Being given: Toward a phenomenology of givenness*. Stanford: Stanford University Press.

———. 2004. *In excess: Studies of saturated phenomena*. New York: Fordham University Press.

———. 2008. The banality of saturation. In *The visible and the revealed*, ed. Jean-Luc Marion, 119–144. New York: Fordham University Press.

———. 2012. *God without being: Hors-texte*. Chicago: University of Chicago Press.

———. 2015. *Negative certainties*. Chicago: University of Chicago Press.

———. 2016a. *Givenness and revelation*. Oxford: Oxford University Press.

———. 2016b. Kenose und Trinität. *Internationale Katholische Zeitschrift "Communio"* 45: 161–174.

Rahner, Karl. 1970. *The trinity*. New York: Herder and Herder.

Şandru, A.R. 2016. Review of Jean-Luc Marion, *Givenness and revelation*. *Phenomenological Reviews*, September. doi:https://doi.org/10.19079/pr.2016.

———. 2018. Hermeneutics of resistance in Marion's phenomenology of givenness. *Open Theology* 4 (1): 450–470.

Specker, Tobias. 2002. *Einen anderen Gott denken? Zum Verständnis der Alterität Gottes bei Jean-Luc Marion*. Frankfurt a.M.: Josef Knecht.

Westphal, Merold. 2006. Vision and voice: Phenomenology and theology in the work of Jean-Luc Marion. *International Journal for Philosophy of Religion* 60 (1): 117–137.

Zarader, Marlene. 2003. Phenomenality and transcendence. In *Transcendence in philosophy and religion*, ed. James F. Faulconer, 106–120. Bloomington: Indiana University Press.

Adrian Răzvan Şandru is an early career scholar and a tutor at the Eberhard-Karls University (Tübingen), writing his doctoral dissertation under supervision of Prof. Dr. Johannes Brachtendorf. He is specialized in the philosophy of Jean-Luc Marion with a focus on Marion's reading of Immanuel Kant, as well as in theological reading of Marion's own work. Adrian Răzvan Sandru's main interest is in German Idealism – especially Kant's critical thought – and in phenomenology – especially Husserlian tradition – with a special focus in interdisciplinary topics, as reflected in several of his papers and book reviews. Adrian Razvan-Şandru is a research assistant at the Forum Scientiarum (Tübingen). He is also a professional member of the Society for Phenomenology of Religious Experience as well as a CusanusWerk scholar. Before being a CusanusWerk scholar he has also received an Excellence Research Scholarship/Grant from the Babes-Balyai University (01.10.2011 – 31.07.2012 for an interdisciplinary project on Kant and inflationary cosmology) and was a Deutschlandstipendium Scholar (03.2014 – 02.2015).

Chapter 16
Michel Henry as a Philosopher of Religion

Carla Canullo

Abstract Can we count the work of Michel Henry among the philosophies of religion? No doubt, the answer would be negative, because even though this philosopher reflected closely on the subject of religion, especially that of Christianity, he never claimed his reflection to be "the philosophy of religion." However, if we return to the etymology of the word "religion" by recalling that the Latin word *religio* is related to the verbs *relegere* and *religare,* we grasp that in Henry there is this sense of religion as *religare*. Indeed, as well as according to this verb religion is the art of vertically establishing links between humanity and the divine or God, and horizontally between men and women who share the same religious belief, according Henry, religion (*religio*) signifies a bond that binds a human being to God, and this link is that of life in the living. Religion, therefore, is the expression of the "bond" between Life and the living, and perhaps, the understanding of this "bond" is Michel Henry's contribution to the "philosophy of religion"—or even more, his contribution to the explication of what *religio* manifests. The paper will investigate how Henry, in his work, proposes and develops the "religion as link" by placing the emphasis above all on incarnation and flesh, the center of Christianity.

Keywords Kantian criticism · Phenomenology · Life · Incarnation · Truth · Michel Henry

16.1 What Can We Call "Philosophy of Religion"?

Can we count the work of Michel Henry among the philosophies of religion? No doubt, the answer would be negative, because even though this philosopher reflected closely on the subject of religion, especially that of Christianity, he never claimed

C. Canullo (✉)
University of Macerata, Macerata, Italy
e-mail: carla.canullo@unimc.it

© Springer Nature Switzerland AG 2019
O. Louchakova-Schwartz (ed.), *The Problem of Religious Experience*,
Contributions to Phenomenology 103,
https://doi.org/10.1007/978-3-030-21575-0_16

257

his reflection to be "the philosophy of religion." And further, what distinguishes a mere reflection on religion from a "philosophy of religion"? Above all, what should we call "the philosophy of religion"?

In an excellent volume devoted to the philosophy of religion, Jean Grondin, much of whose *pollachōs legetai* in this matter remains unsurpassed, remarks that the task of this discipline is to explain as well as illumine the many instances of indecisiveness in which religion finds itself because of confusion regarding what is called a "religious phenomenon."[1] These are the same confusions that Jean Greisch sought to dispel through his monumental work *Le buisson ardent et les lumières de la raison.*[2] To that end, and prior to proposing the four paradigms of the philosophy of religion and confining Michel Henry to the so-called phenomenological paradigm,[3] Greisch returns to the etymology of the word "religion" by recalling that the Latin word *religio* is related to the verbs *relegere* and *religare.* According to the first verb, "religion connotes the fact of trusting someone, so that 'religion' is fundamentally a 'matter of trust'"; according to the second verb, religion "is the art of vertically establishing links between man and the divine or God, and horizontally between men and women who share the same religious belief."[4] In both cases, and minding the differences, the two verbs indicate that religion represents a "bond"—a fact to which thinking returns in a "philosophy of religion."

Although it is difficult to find the first meaning (*relegere*) in the work of Henry, he does use the word 'religion' in the sense of *religare:* "Religion, *religio,* signifies a bond which binds a man to God,"[5] and "this link is that of life in the living [ones]…. Now, the first and decisive affirmation of Christianity is to set ethics in position of this bond, within the immanence of the living, making Commandment into the Commandment of Life which generates the living, whereby ethics is nothing more than the way in which the living lives his transcendental beginning in such a manner that it can be re-lived."[6] Religion, therefore, is the expression of the "bond" between Life and the living, and perhaps the understanding of this "bond" is Michel Henry's contribution to the "philosophy of religion"—or even more, his contribution to the explication of what *religio* manifests.

Therefore, although Henry never questions historical and theological traits of religion (in particular, of Christianity), a philosophical reflection on the bond/*religio* between Life and the living occupies the central place of his phenomenological path. This is also what our philosopher declared during the meeting (January 19, 2001) at the Catholic Institute of Paris on the occasion of publication of *Incarnation.*[7] In answering Jean Greisch's questions concerning the book, which appeared in 2000, Henry presented the whole body of his work as an interrogation into the foun-

---

[1] Cf. Grondin 2015.

[2] Cf. Greisch 2002–2004.

[3] Cf. Greisch 2002a.

[4] Greisch 2002b, 15.

[5] Henry 2004a, 108, 159.

[6] Ibid., 109.

[7] Cf. Capelle-Dumont 2002.

dation of "his" phenomenology of life as "constituted by what one can call a 'phenomenological dualism' or, a 'double nature of appearance.'"[8] According to this thesis, in the *Incarnation*, the body is conjured up by its double manifestation: as a body appearing among things, and as living flesh revealing itself only "by the immanent and pathetic self-impression of life."[9] Therefore,[10]

> These are just the beginnings of an analysis written for the first time in the years 1946–1950.... Subsequently, these presuppositions of phenomenological dualism have been applied to various problems—Marx and the economy, the unconscious, culture, the work of art, the phenomenological method, and the phenomenology of the twentieth century in general.

Some lines later Henry announces that Christianity has been a special interlocutor in his research. Assuming that "as soon as the phenomenological presuppositions return to their original freshness, they hold truth by themselves,"[11] Truth and Life are identified "in Parousia of the absolute, in which the power of revelation turns out to be nothing other than self-revelation, and thereby, this self-attestation constitutes the essence of all life."[12] Finally, concluding this effective *Selbstdarstellung* Henry states: "In this respect, one can consider the philosophical interpretation of Christianity ... as the meeting of the phenomenology of life and religion, in no way limited—precisely because it is in itself about life in it—which is philosophy."[13] Even if Henry's intention were not at all to formulate a "philosophy of religion," it cannot be doubted that his philosophical interest was directed at the religion in which Life reveals itself. Therefore, as to the question "What shall we call 'philosophy of religion'?" we can answer that, according to Henry, this would be a philosophy of the religion in which life is manifest—namely philosophy of Christianity.

Yet, once this answer has been given, new questions arise: How is it possible to approach Christianity while ignoring doctrinal and dogmatic traits that characterize it as a religion?[14] Further, are we allowed to reflect on Christianity without thinking about the fractures and contradictions that have marked its history? These are questions that Henry will never help us answer, because he does not focus on historically given Christianity. On the contrary, he approaches Christianity through the lenses of the New Testament and of the Church Fathers, including Saint Irenaeus, Tertullian, and Saint Augustine. In the eyes of a more traditional philosopher of religion, such an approach, via a nonhistorical Christianity, would be unsatisfactory and even disappointing. However, by this "phenomenological way" Henry has reached what has evaded any rational and historical approach to religion, precisely because he has deployed his analysis by placing himself in the *Sache selbst* of Christianity and even

---

[8] Ibid., 88–89.

[9] Ibid.

[10] Ibid.

[11] Ibid.

[12] Ibid.

[13] Ibid.

[14] This is the same question that Jean Leclercq addresses in the lecture given in Glasgow as part of a fascinating meditation on the subject of "Christ without Christianity."

in *the essence* of it, as he has done from *L'essence de la manifestation* to the texts dedicated to Christianity itself.[15]

Along with the latter, and according to what the author affirmed during the above-mentioned meeting in Paris in 2001, from the beginning to the end his philosophical path unfolded thanks to Marx, to Freud and the idea of the Unconscious; thanks to Kandinsky, and thanks to literary work.[16] Once this is recognized, two possibilities arise: either religion (that is, Christianity) enters Henry's work toward the end or Henry leads his work in the direction of Christianity because already in *L'essence de la manifestation* (that is, in his early work) he discovers *the possibility of the manifestation* of life that throughout his work plays a decisive and *critical* role. But our hypothesis is that the critical role that Kant ascribes to reason is,[17] in Henry's work, played by life and its manifestation. In other words, *life deploys and develops the criticism of religion.*[18] It was because he envisioned developing this criticism[19] that Henry did not conceive of Christianity in light of its history and chose another path, namely to sift religion through life. Or, and this amounts to the same thing, it is because he wished to display this criticism that he resolved to pass Christianity through the sieve of life, as well as through the Truth that is in Life— through which Christianity becomes manifest in the first place. In our opinion, this is the path that Henry completes so that the unheard-of link that constitutes the soul of religion shines and shows itself, the unheard-of link that the world misunderstood and that Life alone shows.

16.2   Phenomenology of Life and the Criticism of Religion: Michel Henry's Reading of Marx and Feuerbach

We know that Henry's reflection does not begin with a material phenomenology of life. On the contrary, he *first* accomplishes successful reflection on the essence of the manifestation, and *then* shows that this essence is nothing but life. And yet, when in the 1970s he published his monograph on Marx, *life* is *already* the leitmotiv of his interpretation of both Karl Marx's work and Ludwig Feuerbach's *L'essence du christianisme*. In order to show how and to what extent life plays a critical role even in Henry's writing dating back to this period, we must recall the themes that

---

[15] See Henry 1990a, 2002a, b.

[16] Henry 1976a, 1981, 1996b.

[17] Religion must be conceived a new within the delimiters of reason (cf. Kant 1966).

[18] We agree with the reading proposed by Green 2017, 131: "Henry suggests that phenomenology must become 'critical of all revelation.'" Green cites Henry 1990a, 55. Also see Leclercq 2017; Formisano 2017.

[19] Translator's note: the author uses the word "criticism" in a sense of "analysis" or "interrogation."

our philosopher discovers in *L'essence de la manifestation,* which he will never renounce.[20]

In sections 45–51 of this *Hauptwerk,* begun in 1946, Henry engages in analyzing the invisible as the internal structure of immanence. Now, insofar as the invisible is conceived in a positive sense, this analysis is not a "path that leads nowhere," as the above conception of immanence of the invisible is what Henry aims at by laying out phenomenality as both *originelle* and the *originaire* of the invisible. In what is external, in the world, the invisible is elusive, and it appears only thanks to life, in the manifestation given by, and in, the immanence of affectivity—thus evading transcendence and all visibility of the world. This is what Henry explains in his commentary on Novalis's *Hymns to the Night:* "By essence, all life is invisible, the invisible is the essence of life."[21] And again: "The invisible is not beyond the visible, nothing 'transcendent'; it is the original essence of life which, fulfilling itself in a sphere of radical immanence, neither rises in transcendence nor can show itself in it."[22]

A positive definition of the invisible does not mean, first, that we hold the visible and invisible as a juxtaposition; and second, even if we were to do so, a juxtaposition assumes a link that "can be established between the 'opposites.' … The affinity of the opposites, their secret co-belonging to a common essence, not only creates a bond uniting them, but makes the latter effective in the passage of opposites into one other, and as a possibility."[23] Therefore, if the visible and the invisible are released from the resource of the same essence, they are also intended to represent two different modes of manifestation (the manifestation according to the horizon of the world, and the manifestation according to life). These two modalities are what in the 2001 Paris meeting Henry called "phenomenological dualism" and the "duplicity [double nature] of appearance," and what he wished to verify by his phenomenological path, including the reading of Marx— a reading conducted in the light of life.

Life is indeed the leitmotiv of Henry's reading of Marx, because it is only by the measure of life that the main motive of Marx's work—namely the *praxis* on which all social change is based—is enacted. Therefore, in order to be (effective yet also) both effective and real, *praxis* must not be established merely as a theory in a mere mental grasping (as if it were a doctrine). On the contrary, it must be grasped as an action, and as an act whose possibility is situated in life, because being, for an action, means to act, and "to act" exceeds all intuitional knowledge, such as "see" or "regard."

We act without having the intuition of the action that we are carrying out, without being able focus on (observe) our action, and thus without having any objectifying

---

[20] By now, the critical literature devoted to Henry covers all aspects of his work. For Christianity, see David and Greisch 2000; Sansonetti 2006; De Simone 2007; Leclercq and Brohm 2009; Jean et al. 2013; Dufour-Kowalska 2016..

[21] Henry 1990a, 556.

[22] Ibid., 568.

[23] Ibid., 557.

intuition of this very action. All this amounts to saying that in the horizon of the world the action is elusive, because it is given by a phenomenological modality other than that characterizing worldly and visible objects.

Now, since in order to understand human life as such the criticism of all objectivity must be conducted, when, by a reversal of Western philosophy, a new sense of subjectivity is discovered, this criticism is put to the test. Indeed, all of the efforts of Western philosophy have been devoted almost exclusively to subjectivity as "instantiating and receiving the object, 'objectively.'" Consequently, a being has been fashioned "by measure of the object,"[24] and "as the objectivity of being which is established by the sense"; a being has been fashioned as a "sensible object." By contrast, Henry noted, "a being is not something that can be proposed to us as an object, nothing objective or something we can sense or think as such, it is, in a radical and radically new sense, 'subjective.'"[25] In other words, being "is" because life "is" and *praxis* "is," in a manner of lived tension of existence, which is locked in the testing its own acts of pushing, pulling, lifting, or taking.[26] Alienation, capital, history, and the individual are the Marxian themes that Henry sifts through the understanding of *praxis* as living *praxis* (that is, the acting life). That is why, with regard to capitalism, which Marx in *Kapital* likens to a 'vampire,' Henry writes: "The vampire theme is not a metaphor, but the rigorous formulation of the relationship between capital and labor,"[27] because capital does nothing other than to exhaust the worker's life by pulling it down to the level of an object.

During the same period of his analysis of Marx's texts, Henry also addresses the criticism of religion developed by Ludwig Feuerbach in *L'essence du christianisme*. In the article "La critique de la religion et le concept de genre dans *L'essence du christianisme*,"[28] the French philosopher proposes a path that begins with Marx's criticism of Bruno Bauer and ends with Feuerbach's critique of religion—a criticism that Henry will discuss in order to supplant it. It is worth following this path, because it is here that the Henryan conception of religion, as well as his understanding of religion's essence, is declared and manifested. "What is remarkable," writes Henry, "is that Feuerbach's materialism and Bauer's idealism in reference to religion say the same thing, that a single scheme … commands analysis. This is a pattern of consciousness. Criticism of religion is idealistic."[29] In other words, religion is a consequence of a reduction "to a representation, to an object of consciousness posed by it," which "determines the status of the religion, or, better, of the religious, and at the same time contains a principle of its resolution."[30]

Perhaps it may be argued that although this may be true for Bauer, it is not true for Feuerbach, because the latter, by his criticism of religion, envisaged nothing

---

[24] Cf. Henry 1976b and 1976c. For citations, see Henry 1976b, 326.

[25] Ibid.

[26] Ibid., 348.

[27] Henry 1976c, 436.

[28] Henry 2015a.

[29] Ibid., 12.

[30] Ibid.

more than an exit from idealism. However, Henry does not view it this way, because, according to him, Feuerbach fails his intention. Indeed, the criticism of the religion developed by the German philosopher is based on the fact that Christianity has attributed to "God" the infinity of the *Gattung* ("genus") of the "species" to which each individual belongs. But Henry reverses Feuerbach's criticism of Christianity by countering that "the species" is also nothing more than a concept—that is, a representation that consciousness formulates.

Consequently, according to Henry, Feuerbach's criticism of religion remains in the horizon of consciousness, whereby the horizon is the source of all representations of the infinite and therefore the source of the *Gattung* itself. Here are some passages from Feuerbach's work that would confirm Henry's reading of it: "Consciousness in the strict sense, in the proper sense of the term, and the consciousness of the infinite, are inseparable; a limited consciousness is not a consciousness, [because] consciousness is essentially of a universal, infinite nature."[31] And again: "The consciousness [conception] of the infinite is nothing but the consciousness of the infinity of consciousness [itself]." And finally: "In the consciousness of the infinite, the conscious being has as its object the infinity of its own essence."[32] It is thus by distancing himself from Feuerbach's conception of the *Gattung* that Henry asks[33]:

> How can the atheist anthropology be differentiated from the ontology of speculative idealism? How is man's self-awareness different from God's self-consciousness? The God of Hegel is the substance of universality. God's self-consciousness is the self-becoming of this substance, the being for himself of the universal being which belongs to him in principle and defines him. But Feuerbach's "man" is not the individual, he is the genus, the universal. Man's self-consciousness is, therefore, as the self-consciousness of the genus, only the self-consciousness of the universal.

Close to the above, and while still in a direct confrontation with the German philosopher, our author comes to a new expansion of his criticism: if "the man—such is the mystery of religion—objectifies his essence,"[34] "the essence of man is the objectification"[35] that consciousness produces through its representations. According to Henry, Feuerbach's criticism of religion failed because this philosopher fell back into the same system he opposed, namely that idealism according to which all knowledge is based on representations, even the knowledge of being and of God.

Therefore, according to Feuerbach, every essence is represented as well as grasped by consciousness, and among these essences there is also the *anthropological essence of religion*.

It is from his objections to Feuerbach that Henry will begin his journey toward religion and, in particular, to Christianity. He will begin his journey with the aim of seeking an essence of religion whose conception does not stem from consciousness;

---

[31] Ibid., 27. For Henry's citations, see Feuerbach 1968, 118.

[32] Ibid. (Feuerbach 1968, 118).

[33] Ibid., 27–28.

[34] Ibid., 28 (Feuerbach 1968, 347).

[35] Ibid., 28.

in other words, a religion for which consciousness is not the horizon, and, finally, a religion that is conceived by the measure of what makes consciousness itself be what it is—Life.

16.3 Life and Its Truth

Whereas Feuerbach does not overcome the representational horizon of consciousness, Marx understands that the individual does not constitute a type (*Gattung*). It is precisely because the individual lives that he avoids being "the species."[36] This same opinion is found in a passage that most readers of Henry's *Marx* have criticized, where Henry asserts that we fail to understand what "is the idea in the texts he [Marx] has written. What appears in them … is a metaphysics of the individual. Marx is one of the first Christian thinkers of the West."[37] Certainly, Henry is aware that Marx's views on Christianity are both skeptical and ambiguous.[38] Yet, Marx is a "Christian" thinker because his thought is about life and the living: "Whether subjectivity forms the essence of production or whether, in a future socialist world, it withdraws from it [this role]—this in itself is the ground for and the unique theme of conceptual development—Marx's thought confronts us with an abysmal question: What is life?"[39] Both Marx's and Feuerbach's atheisms faced this question: the latter ignores life in favor of *Gattung*—that is, of the "species" conceived by understanding; on the contrary, in Marx all criticism—be it the criticism of history, economy, alienation—never omits life and its link to the living individual. Therefore, life represents the point of departure for any criticism, and the "criticism" of religion in the first place.

In a Kantian sense, life's criticism of religion forces that very religion to discover its most authentic essence, the essence that, from now until *C'est moi la vérité*, Henry will present as the truth according to Christianity, thus completing the arc of his work. In effect, life makes its first appearance in *L'essence de la manifestation* as the "self-testing of the self," whose "condition of possibility" is represented by the *affectivity*,[40] which manifests itself by self-affectivity as "feeling oneself." Therefore, life is the power to "come into itself,"[41] the power to manifest, because

---

[36] Translator's note: Henry's ontological critique underscores Marx's understanding of subjectivity as a living subjectivity, which is something that has sentience, a sensible, conscious experience, and *is in itself a* sensible, sentient, conscious experience. As such, subjectivity cannot be reduced to an idea—neither a regulatory idea, nor, in particular, to a formal idea such as *Gattung* or the type of a species. Although representing the human being, among other beings, as an object of reflection, such objectification of subjectivity has nothing to do with the ontological status of subjectivity per se as it is given.

[37] Henry 1976c, 445.

[38] Cf. note below, n.1, ibid.

[39] Henry 1976c, 484.

[40] Henry 1990a, 596: "Affectivity is the essence of life."

[41] Henry 1985, 384.

of the "original essence of revelation"[42] through which life can self-reveal through the experience it makes of itself. "Life feels, feels itself.", Henry writes. Moreover, it is not something that would have the capacity to feel itself as a quality (property); rather, the capacity to feel itself is life's essence: the pure test of oneself, the feeling of oneself,[43] which causes it to self-affect and become realized. Indeed, "self-affection is not an empty or formal concept, … [but rather] it defines the phenomenological reality of life itself—a reality whose pure substantiality and whose pure phenomenality is the transcendental affectivity."[44] In the final account, life is the power of growth, and "growth is the movement of life that is fulfilled in itself due to what it is, in its subjectivity."[45] And yet, since from *L'essence de la manifestation* life appears through its connection to the affectivity that makes it possible for life to test itself, why is this manifestation not enough for Henry at one point, and why does he turn toward religion, and in particular, toward Christianity?

Perhaps this is so not only because Christianity is the testing ground for the "dualism of the appearance" that Henry mentioned at the 2001 Paris meeting but also because it is, so to speak, "beyond" any rationalization of the *Gattung* that, according to Feuerbach, was the infinite reason for the infinity of being in the individual. It is because of this identification (of life with thought about itself) that Feuerbach has completely missed thinking of the living individual by means of a concept (*Gattung*) that would point to the living individual's essence. According to his thinking, the essence of the living individual would be nothing but a dead concept whose truth is formulated by thought. In other words, *Gattung* causes the individual to be engulfed by the generality of a concept that alienates the self—or better, that conceives this "self" by a concept external to it. It is in order to reverse this conception that Henry searches for truth that comes not from the "outside" but from the "inside," a truth of life. The opening of *C'est moi la vérité* represents a decisive step in this quest, because it affirms and at the same time develops the distinction between the truth of the world and of Christianity. These passages have attracted the attention of many readers of Henry's work. The "outside" of the world represents the horizon of the resource from which all phenomenality is devised. Moreover, the "outside," as such, is the world. We say "the truth of the world," but the expression "the truth of the world" is a tautology.[46] The manifestation is itself the "outside," "the consciousness, the world, the true."[47] By contrast, Life does not manifest itself as a phenomenon or object of the world, nor does it allow itself to be trapped by the light of the world: no one sees Life; only a living being in itself makes a test of it. What makes the living recognize itself as such—*as living?* It cannot be consciousness, because the living lives even when not conscious or when not a theme of rep-

---

[42] Henry 1990a, 565.

[43] Henry 2003, 49.

[44] Henry 1987, 30–31.

[45] Henry 1990b, 55.

[46] Translator's note: tautology in a sense of double meaning: the world is true because it appears as given, but it is not the Truth which is ontologically responsible for this appearance.

[47] Henry, 1996a, 27.

resentations. In contrast to representations that conceive any revelation of the truth by the light of the world, Life reveals itself as stated in Henry's famous passages: "Where does a self-revelation of this kind exist? In Life, as the essence of it. For Life is nothing but a self-revealer—not something that would, moreover, have the property of self-revealing but [something that] is the very act of self-disclosure, self-revelation as such. Wherever something like self-revelation happens, there is life."[48] The essence of life lies in the only Truth that gives itself without becoming a being or an object of the world.

Indeed, "it is only when the truth is understood as that of the world, when it makes all things visible by placing it outside itself, that the division of the concept of Truth, that is, the difference between the Truth itself and what it shows—what it makes true—occurs."[49] Do not separate the truth from the true: this is what Henry intended from the beginning of his work.

We understand why his encounter with Christianity, although late, was not *fortuitous*. In fact, Henry draws from the New Testament a completion of the theses of *L'essence de la manifestation*. In this work "the essence of manifestation" was conceived through the self-revelation of affectivity as the capacity to feel oneself—and in this manner, by the revelation of one's "self." so that the true and truth coincide; but the same coincidence is discovered in the founding texts of Christianity, namely in the texts where truth and the true coincide. and Accordingly, Henry remarks[50]:

> The first decisive feature of the Truth of Christianity is that it does not differ from what it makes true. In it there is no separation between seeing and what is seen, between the light and what it illuminates…. What is a truth that is not different from what is true? If the truth is the manifestation seized in its phenomenological purity, in the phenomenality and not in the phenomenon, then what is phenomenalized is the phenomenality itself. The phenomenalization of phenomenality itself is a pure phenomenological matter, a substance of which all the essence is to appear, phenomenality in its effectuation and by its pure phenomenological effectiveness. What reveals itself is the revelation itself. What is revealed is revelation itself, a revelation of revelation, a self-revelation in its immediate original effulgence.

And a little farther on he adds[51]:

> With this idea of a pure Revelation, of a revelation whose phenomenality is the phenomenalization of phenomenality itself, of an absolute self-revelation that happens without anything that would be other than its own phenomenological substance, we are in the presence of the essence that Christianity maintains as the principle of everything. God is this pure Revelation that reveals nothing but himself. God reveals himself.. .. To tell the truth, Christianity is nothing other that this amazing and rigorous theory of donation sharing with men the self-revelation of God.

With this self-revelation, on one side, one reaches the nonconceptual essence of God (as well as religion), and on the other side, completes the phenomenological arc of Henry's thought from the essence of the manifestation to the essence of

---

[48] Ibid., 39.
[49] Ibid., 35–36.
[50] Ibid.., 36.
[51] Ibid., 36–37.

religion. There is still one final point regarding the bond (*religio*) of Life with every-thing alive. This is what must now be shown in order to grasp the radical difference between the essence of Feuerbach's Christianity and the essence of Henry's Christianity, namely the difference between *the Gattung without man* and *Life giving itself in each of the living.*

16.4 The Essence of Religion and the Essence of Living Beings

The Truth of Life is manifested only from itself and without regard for the represen-tation of consciousness: this is the point where Henry's "criticism of religion" ends. It is a "criticism of religion" because Henry, instead of *presenting* "a philosophy of the Christian religion," takes a different path, whereby *life itself is the criterion by which religion is understood.* Yet, in *L'essence de la manifestation* Henry remarks that no revelation can be given without the "singularization" of an *ipse* that is given. The same motive appears in a text devoted to the commentary on the famous affir-mation "I am the Way, the Truth and the Life": "In so far as the Way consists in the Truth which consists in Life," writes Henry, "it is the elucidation of the relationship established between this Self and Life that matters to us: that I in which Christ is said to be the Word since it is the ego [self] of the absolute Life."[52]

It is because he is Truth and Life that Christ can proclaim himself as the "First Living," where the Truth of Life manifests itself. With respect to *Gattung,* which is nothing more than a representation of consciousness, the Life of the First Living "is repeated in the reciprocal relationship between the phenomenological interiority of the Absolute Life and the man himself, taken for what it is: a living transcendental self."[53] It is thus that the bond of Life and the living is reaffirmed. In an interview with Roland Vaschalde, Henry states: "The central theme of *C'est moi la vérité* [is] the immanence of Life in each one living."[54] It remains to comment on how this is given, and whether religion can cause an understanding of this.

In our opinion, not only does religion make it possible to understand the relation-ship between Life, the First Living, and the living ones, but it also serves as the "evidence" of it. In *L'essence de la manifestation,* Henry introduces the self as the self-revelation of affectivity without explaining its genesis, which is explained later, in *C'est moi la vérité.* In this book, in fact, the "archeology of the Self"[55] is con-ceived in terms of religion—notably Christianity—in dialogue with which Henry's intuition has matured. One of the intuitions that he upholds the most is "the genera-

---

[52] Henry 2015b, 133.

[53] Ibid.

[54] Henry 2007, 19.

[55] Ibid.

tion of a fundamental *Ipseity* in the mutual immanence of Life and a living being."[56]
Christianity triggers this intuition because it does not deliver a representation of
Life (which the consciousness does by the representation of the *Gattung*) but rather
receives the *gift* of Life itself, in the First Life (as Christ), and through that, *in all the
living* who bind themselves to the First Living. And yet, why does it give itself "in
all the living"? What is the conception of Christianity that Henry has in mind?

It is Christianity—or a religion—that is based less on worship and more on the
texts of the New Testament and the Church Fathers; again, it is the Christianity of
the flesh, of the Incarnation. The enduring reflection on the Incarnation would
require that we undertake another Henryan path, that of the flesh and the body, and
that we establish a connection with the work of Henry from another point of view,
as the path we have been discussing does not continue beyond this point.

Consequently, and in conclusion, we turn to another motive that Henry never
ceased to analyze, namely the *unfathomable link* between Life and flesh that belongs
both to the First Living and to everything alive. The link between Life and each living being is given by the flesh that Christ, the First Living, takes on, and that every
living person also assumes.

The flesh is not the visible body, nor is it an object among others: no one sees
any flesh, but nevertheless each one makes the test "in the first person" by the pleasure or the pain that he feels. A flesh—Henry declares it many times—"is only
possible in life, in its self-revelation, as self-impressionality in which each of our
impressions, our joys or our sufferings is originally felt, in such a way that the pure
phenomenological material of this pathetic self-impressionality is nothing but the
flesh itself."[57]

In and through the living flesh and by the grace of Life that sustains it, religion first of all is Life and only after that worship and precept. Therefore religion is
a condition of possibility of the unfathomable link (being such because it escapes
the "outside world") link: the *religio* makes possible the link through which Life
binds to the First Living as well as to each one living. Through the flesh that the First
Living Person and each living person live, Life becomes the essence of a religion;
the flesh is not the cause of human alienation but on the contrary *gives back to each
the authentic self*. It can do so because the manifest "self" is not a "thought" or
"represented" essence. On the contrary, this self comes from a relationship of
descendance ("sonhood," "filiation"), from the fact of being born, because "only the
Sons have a birth, they are born in Life, begotten by it, being alive only as such, as
sons."[58] Perhaps it is understanding of this link—unfathomable in the eyes of the
world—that is Michel Henry's contribution to the philosophy of religion.

---

[56] Ibid.

[57] Henry 2015b, 135.

[58] Henry 2004b, 182.

References

Capelle-Dumont, Ph. (ed.). 2002. *Phénoménologie et incarnation* (Séance Académique autour du Professeur Michel Henry). In *Transversalités*, Revue de L'Institut Catholique de Paris, n° 81, January–March 2002, 5–124.

David, A., and J. Greisch (eds.). 2000. *Michel Henry. L'épreuve de la vie.* Paris: Cerf.

De Simone, G. 2007. *La rivelazione della Vita. Cristianesimo e Filosofia in Michel Henry.* Trapani: Il Pozzo di Giacobbe.

Dufour-Kowalska, G. 2016. *Logos et absolu. Relire la phénoménologie du christianisme de Michel Henry.* Louvain-La-Neuve: Presses Universitaires de Louvain.

Feuerbach, L. 1968. *L'essence du christianisme.* Trans. J.-P. Osier. Paris: Maspero.

Formisano, R. 2017. *Phénoménologie matérielle et philosophie de la religion. Relire Michel Henry à la lumière des inédits.* In *Religion et vérité*, ed. J. Grondin and G. Green, 149–155. Strasbourg: Presses Universitaires de Strasbourg.

Green, G. 2017. *Vérité et non-vérité dans la phénoménologie de la religion de Michel Henry.* In *Religion et vérité*, ed. J. Grondin and G. Green, 129–137. Strasbourg: Presses Universitaires de Strasbourg.

Greisch, J. 2002–2004. *Le Buisson ardent et les lumières de la raison*, 4 vol. Paris: Cerf.

———. 2002a. *Le Buisson ardent et les lumières de la raison, vol. I : Héritages et héritier du XIXe siècle. Introduction générale*, 7–69. Paris: Cerf.

———. 2002b. *Le Buisson ardent et les lumières de la raison*, vol. II: *Les approches phénoménologiques et analytiques*. Ch. V : *La phénoménologie matérielle et la révélation de la Vie absolue (Michel Henry)*, 334–359. Paris: Cerf.

Grondin, J. 2015. *La philosophie de la religion.* Paris: PUF.

Henry, M. 1976a. *L'amour les yeux fermés.* Paris: Gallimard.

———. 1976b. *Marx I. Une philosophie de la réalité.* Paris: Gallimard.

———. 1976c. *Marx II. Une philosophie de l'économie.* Paris: Gallimard.

———. 1981. *Le fils du roi.* Paris: Gallimard.

———. 1985. *Généalogie de la psychanalyse. Le commencement perdu.* Paris: Puf.

———. 1987. *La Barbarie.* Paris: Grasset.

———. 1990a. *L'essence de la manifestation.* Paris: Presses Universitaires de France.

———. 1990b. *Phénoménologie matérielle.* Paris: Puf.

———. 1996a. *C'est moi la vérité. Pour une philosophie du christianisme.* Paris: Seuil.

———. 1996b. *Le cadavre indiscret.* Paris: Albin Michel.

———. 2002a. *Paroles du Christ.* Paris: Seuil.

———. 2002b. *Incarnation. Une philosophie de la chair.* Paris: Seuil.

———. 2003. *Qu'est-ce que cela que nous appelons vie?* In *Phénoménologie de la vie*, I: *De la phénoménologie*, ed. M. Henry, 39–57. Paris: Puf.

———. 2004a. *Le christianisme, une approche phénoménologique ?* In *Sur l'éthique et la religion*, ed. M. Henry, 95–111. Paris: Puf.

———. 2004b. *Parole et religion : la parole de Dieu.* In *Sur l'éthique et la religion. Phenomenologie de la Vie* IV, ed. M. Henry, 177–202. Paris: Puf.

———. 2007. *Entretiens.* Cabris: Sulliver.

———. 2015a. *La critique de la religion et le concept de genre dans* L'essence du christianisme (1972). In *Phénoménologie de la vie* V, ed. Henry, 11–29. Paris: Puf.

———. 2015b. *La vérité selon le christianisme.* In *Phénoménologie de la vie* V, ed. M. Henry, 131–139. Paris: Puf.

Jean, G., J. Leclercq, and N. Monseu (eds.). 2013. *La vie et les vivants. (Re-)lire Michel Henry.* Louvain-La-Neuve: Presses Universitaires de Louvain.

Kant, I. 1966. *Die Religion innerhalb der Grenzen der bloßen Vernunft*. Hamburg: . Meiner. [ed. or.: 1793–1794]).

Leclercq, J. 2017. *Vie et méthode. Le tournant épistémologique de Michel Henry*. In *Religion et vérité*, ed. J. Grondin and G. Green, 139–147. Strasbourg: Presses Universitaires de Strasbourg.

Leclercq, J. and J.-M. Brohm (eds.). 2009. *Michel Henry: Dossier L'Age de L'homme*. Lausanne L'âge de l'homme.

Sansonetti, G. 2006. *Michel Henry: fenomenologia, vita, cristianesimo*. Brescia: Morcelliana.

Carla Canullo teaches Philosophy of Religion and Intercultural Hermeneutics at the University of Macerata (Italy). She is a specialist in contemporary French philosophy and has published many works on Jean Nabert, Emmanuel Levinas, Jean-Luc Marion, Michel Henry, and Jean-Louis Chrétien. Among her books are *La fenomenologia rovesciata: Percorsi tentati in Jean-Luc Marion, Michel Henry, Jean-Louis Chrétien* (Rosenberg and Sellier 2004), (ed.) *Michel Henry: Narrare il pathos* (EUM 2007), *L'estasi della speranza: Ai margini del pensiero di Jean Nabert* (Cittadella 2005). Recently she has published a book on translation as a method for intercultural hermeneutics (*Il chiasmo della traduzione: Metafora e verità* [Mimesis 2017]). She is a member of the board of the Société Francophone de Philosophie de la Religion and was Visiting Professor at Université de Nice Sophia Antipolis and Visiting Scholar at Université Catholique deLouvain-la-Neuve; and she was a member of CREOR Centre for Research on Religion at McGill University.

Chapter 17
Toward a Systematic Phenomenology of the Religious Attitude: Commentary on Part 3

Olga Louchakova-Schwartz

Abstract This is the concluding section to Part 3 of the book *The Problem of Religious Experience*. I discuss a possibility of conducting phenomenological research in the religious attitude and how this attitude can be compatible with phenomenological reduction. Using the findings from Part 3, I examine the isomorphism between perception and the knowledge of God and then revisit the idea of the metaphysical realism of phenomenology in light of Carla Canullo's interpretation of Henry's phenomenology of life as a philosophy of religion.

Keywords Phenomenological theology · Phenomenological method · The natural attitude · Religious experience · Michel Henry · Phenomenological reduction

Phenomenological investigations are conducted under the attitude of metaphysical neutrality (Zahavi 2017, 30). However, the presuppositionlessness of phenomenology is subtler than an unequivocal elimination of all metaphysical assumptions. For example, the genetic analysis of meaning brings in assumptions of its own (see Sarna 1989; Zahavi 2017, 63), and, even though such assumptions do not turn phenomenology into a realist metaphysical project, they do imply a concept of "origin." Further, in French phenomenology, consistent interest in appearances led to metaphysics in its own right, with a comparison of theological monisms (Marrès 2017) and absorption of the concepts of Trinitarian theology (Marion 2002a, b), Christology (Henry 2003), and some aspects of Talmudic Judaism (Levinas 1969). In 2015, working on the interpretive commentaries to Michel Henry, Joseph Rivera (2015) introduced the term "phenomenological theology." In a parallel process, in theology

O. Louchakova-Schwartz (✉)
Jesuit School of Theology of Santa Clara University, Graduate Theological Union, Berkeley, CA, USA

University of California, Davis, CA, USA

© Springer Nature Switzerland AG 2019
O. Louchakova-Schwartz (ed.), *The Problem of Religious Experience*,
Contributions to Phenomenology 103,
https://doi.org/10.1007/978-3-030-21575-0_17

itself, the "convincingness deficit" of reasoning asks for solutions from phenomenology (Ben Simpson 2014; Kirkpatrick 2016). The theme of Part 3 evolves around
this problematic, leading one to ask on what terms God can be admitted into phenomenological investigations. In the porousness of anatheism (Kearney 2011), is it
permissible for phenomenology to be doxastic, and what would phenomenological
research of religious experience look like in this context? Using the findings in Part
3, I offer some modest reflections on this subject.

17.1 Conditions of Possibility for Doxastic Phenomenological Research

Under the term "doxastic," I understand a research situation in which a researcher's
belief in the Absolute is not suspended for the sake of "scientific" performance but
participates in the researcher's conclusions regarding the truth. (Cf. Turri 2010.)
Religious experience presents a special situation in such an inquiry. In *The Varieties
of Religious Experience*, James (2017, Lecture III; also paragraphs *103, 109),* noted
that religious experience has a sense of immediate reality to it. Augmented by a
motivational force of feeling, this sense is not less (and is perhaps more) than the
sense of reality in the everyday. The God of experience feels real. Phenomenology
suggests that the everyday sense of reality is aprioristic: in the natural attitude, the
world is real because it is shared with others and because of the tangibility of our
lived bodies. In the religious attitude, the sense of reality is equally attributed to the
space of liturgy (cf. DuPée in this volume), to the presence of the Other (as in
Cockayne's paper in this volume, and cf. Norenberg 2017), and can be found in
denuded phenomenological materiality of the "nondual" religious experience
(Louchakova-Schwartz, Chap. 5 in this volume; Louchakova-Schwartz 2017; or cf.
Louchakova-Schwartz 2013). Motivated by affect, mediated by intentional excess
(cf. Marion 2002b), conversion is not an intellectual event but a full-bodied lived
experience, *Erlebnis.* Religious experience has a "convincingness surplus." (Cf.
Davis 1989.) Nonetheless, its relationship with both traditional theology and theological phenomenology has been complicated. Though integrating individual subjective experience with theological dogma would seem a natural fit for Tillich's
method of correlation (cf. Hammond 1964; Bowker 2000, 594–595), in theology
the historicized thematization of the idea of the Holy refers to experience as experience of a community relating to the transcendent by means of various religious
practices (Olson 2014; similar concepts are found in the writings of von Balthasar,
Rahner, and Barth). Such treatment of experience is different from the understanding of experience in phenomenology, as a subjectively appropriated *Erlebnis.* On
the other hand, at least within the systematic theology, theology is understood as an
exercise in reasoning that aims at explaining doctrinal positions. The notion of
experience of God is left to mystics and ecstatics, whereas common sense believers
have "faith," which is understood as a commitment to beliefs that they can

reasonably explain. Thus, apart from the mystical theology of monasticism and the mystagogy of the Eastern Orthodox Church (e.g., Louchakova-Schwartz 2016; Roy 2001, 2003), religious experience has not been a major focus of theological reflection.[1]

There appear to be too many questions with regard to whose textual accounts of experience and in which theological context should be "canonical," whose authority, if anyone's, can validate experiences, and so on, for experience to be taken seriously as theological evidence. Further, even though theological phenomenology does not at all need religious experience as such for evidence (see Janicaud et al. 2000) and, on the contrary, discusses appearances as such, its eidetic findings have not yet been worked into a descriptive phenomenology. Theological phenomenology cannot answer questions such as, for example, whether there is any difference between a scientific *Eureka!* and a revelation. Part 3 presents a modest step in this direction, toward *the systematic descriptive phenomenology of the religious attitude,* with "attitude" understood here, in the phenomenological manner, as a disposition of consciousness defining one's sense of reality.

With the religious attitude as both the focus of and container for investigations, can such doxastic phenomenology stand as a phenomenology proper? Can it deliver "research-grade" findings, or would there be, as noted by DuPée (in this volume) quoting Marion, just "telling stories"? Several considerations apply. First, a switch of research attitude from presuppositionless to religious would mean thinking of "God in experience" not just constitutively or even ontologically but realistically. Such thinking would ascribe the Absolute a real participation in experience (cf. Seifert 2009; Mezei 2017), or, as one finds in some idealistic monisms, the Absolute must be immanent, or experience must be a field of the Absolute, or the like. DuPée, Marcato, and Canullo in the present volume discuss the options for such an immanent God-horizon, as does Dahl (2010) also in discussing the locations of mystery, and Șandru and Mezzanzanica (in the present book) in addressing the invisible. This suggests a very difficult question: Are there aspects of first-person consciousness that can be co-shared between the human being and the Absolute, as properties or essences and not just in eidetic thinking?[2] In Indian monisms, or some forms of Islam, in Sufism, such a question is answered affirmatively, but such an affirmative answer presents a big problem for doctrinal theology.

---

[1] Special thanks to Alison Benders and Adrian Răzvan Sandru for attracting my attention to these distinctions. Alison Benders (personal communication July 3, 2018) also indicated that among the practicing American clergy, there is a resurgence of interest in the empirical dimension of contemplative prayer (prayer as "a long hard look at the real"; prayer as stillness in the presence of the divine, being with God), which arguably is what Christianity is and should be about, but which was derailed by Constantine in 323.

[2] This appears to be the case for the chapters by Cockayne or Canullo; cf. the Monophysitism-Nestorianism controversy, or the logic of Vedanta, or Islamic knowledge-by-presence (Yazdī 1992). Șandru commented that this sounds a bit like an Augustinian thesis in which consciousness is regarded as an *imago dei,* by means of which human beings share certain divine structures of thinking; in Marion's case the subject does not share aspects of the divine consciousness but is forced to accept a logic different from its own.

Examining such aspects presupposes not only *locating* the sphere of religious experience but *characterizing* such a sphere with regard to its situated conditions of truth and its origination. (See Șandru and Canullo in this volume.) Just these few initial concerns show that the doxastic approach shifts the paradigm of phenomenological investigations from a focus on egological consciousness to consciousness shared with the invisible Other who participates, either remotely or closely, in the constitution of the former. Building such a phenomenology needs the foundation of a mature phenomenology of consciousness, and is, as shown by Canullo in this volume, in itself a matter of research.

As *Wissenschaft* (cf. Pannenberg 1973; Westphal 2013; Zachhuber 2013), phenomenology operates by submitting empirical data to the verdict of reason. Westphal (2013, 523) calls phenomenology a descriptive form of empiricism. However, "descriptive" represents an important difference: empiricism and phenomenology exercise radically different approaches to experience—which of course is the subject of extensive analyses in Husserl's *Ideas I* and *II,* in Merleau-Ponty's *Phenomenology of Perception,* and more recently, in Luft's *Subjectivity and Lifeworld in Transcendental Phenomenology* (2011). In order to describe experience, one exits the natural attitude and enters the attitude of phenomenological reduction, in this manner gaining access both to a rigorous, scientific treatment of subjectivity and to a fresh outlook on something very familiar—namely one's own consciousness. One of arguments against an "overconfident" admission of religious experience into theological nomenclature (in an "experiential-expressive" mode) is that it tends to romanticize experience in the absence of due reflection (Biernot and Lombaard 2017). But, as noted by Leonard (2013), theology's interest in experience changes over time, and so we ask not whether experience can be a source of theology but how we can "accurately and critically" approach religious experience as such (Cooke 1980, 72, quoted in Leonard 2013, 44; also see Gunter's 1966 defense of Bergson against accusations of anti-intellectualism).

In the doxastic approach to phenomenology, reduction is two-sided: on one side, it prepares messy experience for "critical and accurate" reflection of reason; at the same time reduction keeps analysis "data-driven." However, the analytic suspension of the idea of God could mean throwing the baby away with the bath: that is, losing the very core of experience. The methodological "storehouse of phenomenology—*epoché,* bracketing, reduction, transcendental subjectivity" (Natanson 1998, 4)—is always modified according to the need of the phenomenon under investigation, which in the case of a theologically minded phenomenology would be God's presence in the given and the ego's engagement with it. This suggests including the noneidetic forms of intuition—for instance, imagination (in the work of Raimon Panikkar: see Marcato in the present volume) or the intuition of life (e.g., Canullo in the present volume or Louchakova-Schwartz 2013). In this manner, theological tradition receives its "greening"[3] by the phenomenological infusion of essential revelation.

---

[3] For the use of "green" or "blue-green" as "youthful," see De Blois 2007; Schwartz 2013.

17.2   The Religious Attitude

Whether "the Absolute should fall under the knife of phenomenological reduction" (Farley 2016, 2) is, of course, not a new question. Thinkers such as Levinas, Marion, and Lacoste outlined this theorem, agreeing essentially on its negative solution. However, their eidetic view of the problem often leaves out concerns which rise in the concreteness of case studies. I shall revisit this question in the context of concrete phenomenological research.

The idea of God enters doxastic phenomenology in two ways: in the worldview and in the final reflection. However, phenomenologically, religious experience has been defined in consideration not of the worldview but of the lifeworld. Lifeworld is not a worldview: the former is lived and shared by many (Yu 1999), and the latter is a representation, a thought that may or may not be shared. (Cf. Carr 1987.) A religious or scientific worldview may pertain to the same lifeworld of the everyday; apologetics may pertain to this lifeworld as an interpretive frame for ordinary experience; and religious experience can be a disruption—all in the same lifeworld.

In the past, the scientific worldview has been thought of as exclusively reason-based, but this does not hold true any more: atheism has long been acknowledged as a form of belief. On the other hand, the religious worldview is also grounded in logical reasoning; the difference between the two worldviews is not in how reasonable they are but in their explanatory schemata for reality, which lately display mutual interpenetration or even complementarity (Harrison 2006; Kontala 2016).[4] Consequently, whether we conduct phenomenological analyses nontheistically (as, e.g., in Husserl or Merleau-Ponty) or theistically (as, e.g., in Marion's Trinitarian theological view discussed by Şandru in this volume, or according to Henry's latest works as discussed in Canullo's chapter), these phenomenological analyses would be rational.

As already mentioned, the scientific and religious worldviews interpenetrate each other. The like can be observed in relation to the attitudes: religious ascetic and meditative practices modify the sense of reality, of internal and external, and other ontological presuppositions of the natural attitude (cf. Louchakova-Schwartz 2012, 2017). The attitude, as a category important in phenomenological analysis, and the worldview are closely connected categories, as "views pertaining to the world" (Bartlett 1969). Insofar as the natural attitude serves as a foundation for the scientific attitude (Gurwitsch and Embree 1978), so it does for the religious attitude (Kuhar 2005). If, in the transition to phenomenological attitude, the natural attitude is subject to bracketing, the question will be which assumptions pertaining to religious attitude within the natural attitude can be admitted into the phenomenological attitude instead of being bracketed out with the assumptions of the natural attitude. I suggest that such an enduring assumption will be the one that serves as a condition of possibility for conscious experience per se.

---

[4] Buckareff and Nagasawa (2016) showed that the scientific discoveries of the past century both influenced the worldviews and created the alternative ideas of the Deity.

By a logic similar to what Henry applied to the role of life in his analysis of manifestation, and (in my opnion) by the similar logic that Marion applied in his approach to givenness, the Absolute—God—would be the assumption that cannot be bracketed out. The religious attitude suggests that God not only is real (although not in the same mode of givenness as the universe) but is an irreducible condition of the possibility of consciousness (or, if one prefers, of appearances). One can argue that even though phenomenological reduction must suspend the ontological assumptions of the natural attitude, it cannot end up with an analysis of appearances devoid of their own conditions of possibility. Similarly, *in the religious attitude,* the Absolute is a condition of possibility for all consciousness, and therefore cannot be touched by reduction.[5] Notably, this condition of possibility operates only under the religious attitude—much as the scientific attitude has its own host of *a prioris.* In the case of the religious attitude, God would be thought of not just as an idea of God but as a participant in *Erlebnis* and in the acts of consciousness—or the mind can be thought of as a part of God. (Cf. Buckareff and Nagasawa 2016.) Even though transcendental reduction under such an attitude becomes problematic, such doxastic phenomenology carries its own reductions, which aim for logical congruence and fidelity to experience: that is, for valid findings. (For examples, see the Kantian criticism in Canullo's chapter in this book or the analysis of Trinitarian perception in Sandru's.)

By doing phenomenology doxastically in the first-person approach, I mean explication of both experience and of supramundane reality as it bears upon the structure of experience. In such an attitude one does not suspend the idea of God in the same manner as one suspends the concepts pertaining to the natural attitude. This idea of the Absolute remains in the background, temporally out of use, from the initial phenomenological reduction on, until the final reflection, in which this idea is again hermeneutically reengaged. Bringing in God as a referent for reflective reasoning on the descriptive datum of experience does not diminish the rationality of the phenomenological approach, nor does the intuitionism of the phenomenological approach diminish the strength of theological reasoning: the two appear complementary. Focusing on God within the phenomenological findings would be similar to thematic reduction in the transcendental horizons, not making the findings less true but rather expanding the scope of their validity. For example, in the present volume, after describing phenomenological givenness of presence, Cockayne expands his findings to include the proposition of how presence can become a divine counterpart of one's attentional processes.

The next consideration is, perhaps, a more substantial one. The situation with the phenomenological analysis of religious attitude is similar to the subject of the 1989 debate between Gurwitsch and Schutz (Natanson 1998). Gurwitsch objected to Schutz's phenomenological treatment of the social world (in what was termed "the phenomenology of the natural attitude"—i.e., phenomenology without the full ontological bracketing) as incompatible with transcendental reduction. However,

---

[5] As A.-R. Şandru pointed out to me, this requires further analysis with regard to Marion's view because of Marion's reduction of the horizons of being and life to givenness.

Schutz was not using the transcendental reduction; he limited his phenomenology to description, and this move yielded valuable findings that continue fertilizing contemporary social science. As we saw in Parts 1 and 2 above, even in analysis of religious experience along traditional phenomenological lines—that is, as consciousness and without concern for the efficient cause of such experience (i.e., God)—the full bracketing out of ontological claims is not always possible. For example, Laude or Costello (both chapters in Volume 1) keep ontological claims in their phenomenology. At some point in his book *Anonymity,* Natanson remarks that phenomenology (i.e., any phenomenology) *is* metaphysics: that is, "a discipline of origin" (Natanson 1998, 4). Similarly, a doxastic analysis of religious experience in Part 3 of this book eventually turns into genetic phenomenology within the essential horizon of religious attitude. The mode of existence of this horizon needs still to be clarified—which would be a phenomenological problem separate from the theological problem of God's availability in the human condition.

17.3 The Situated God

Volume 1 of the present book demonstrated that God's participation in experience can be associated with several phenomenological locales, such as self-awareness, embodied subjectivity, intersubjectivity, the invisible, and affective feeling. Volume 2 adds the "presence" and the phenomenological space opened by liturgy, at the least. Each time, the structure of experience corresponds to a set of theological concepts. For example, Panikkar's view of a cosmotheandric universe (a God who shares the essence with the human person and also has a cosmic form, resonant with Indian Vedanta) corresponds with religious experience as knowledge involving all possible cognitive faculties, including imagination. The structured character of the Trinity corresponds with the structures of perception. In another example, the idea of God's energies, uncreated and therefore God himself (cf. Lossky 1976) according to cataphatic mystical theology of the Orthodox Church, corresponds to this statement of Theophan the Recluse (1991, 8): "While your eyes see a tangible object, your mind will be contemplating a spiritual one." In this manner, ideas become associated with the structure of experience. In the religious attitude, such structures are ontologically and constitutively decentered. For example, it is God in its locale, and not the ego in its response to the Word, that is the originator of intentionality—for instance in Marion's notion of the call.

Springing forth from the understanding of the natural world (cf. Allston 1992), the modern-day religious attitude is hybridized. For example, in Forrest's pantheism (2016), God, who is correlated with physical processes in the universe in the manner of universal mental states, has its unity underwritten by networks of relationships. On one hand, this idea bears a strong resemblance to complexity theory, and on the other, to the Absolute of the Church of Religious Science (Holmes 1926) and other variations on the theme of Vedanta such as *The Self-Aware Universe* (Goswami 1995). The modal pantheism of Nagasawa (2016) suggests a God who is a totality of all possible worlds (with a realistically thought logical space that is the core of God), reminding one of the Islamic hadith "Heaven and earth cannot contain Me, but the Heart of My faithful servant containeth Me" (Ibn Arabī 1981, 16, 42). An emergent God who is less than the physical world from which it emerges like a property of a complex system (Thomas 2016) is similar both to the Divinity of Kundalini theology in Hinduism and to Life in Christian metaphysics of life. This hybridization shows up in research: for example, Cockayne's phenomenological metaphysics of presence (in this volume) incorporates God into cognitively understood attentional processes as an agent who sets up cognition.

The protean God of experience reveals itself and hides within degrees of self-disclosure afforded by the ethics of the ego's attitude. For example, DuPée (in the present volume) shows that whereas liturgy, in Lacoste's view, subverts the natural horizons of experience to show God, the *eschaton* is not revealed. The availability of *theōsis* (in Eastern Orthodox terms) depends on the ethics of relationship with God: if, out of its own vanity or pride, the ego appropriates the Divine, this means a cessation of authentic experience. The ego is also "weak," and in facing the invisible it needs a prop, a supporting image, an iconostasis, a representation of beauty that simultaneously brackets out the usual perception and becomes a gateway into the invisible. As DuPée puts it in his chapter in this volume:

> we can at least make the phenomenological suggestion that it is not so much the transcendental horizons of experience that interpose and dismantle the experience of God but instead the fundamental manner of their contingent attunement.

In this manner, the phenomenology of religious experience turns into an ascetic and ethical enterprise: the experience of God shows up within the conditions of possibility afforded by ethical and ascetic attunement of the ego, and the decentered constitution from the locations of the Absolute appears to be in reciprocal relationship with the ego-centered constitutive processes, or even works against its resistance (as in Şandru; Louchakova-Schwartz, Concluding Reflections to Part 1).

The first three chapters of Part 3, by DuPée, Marcato, and Cockayne, are variations on the theme of the ego's relationship with God. In Şandru's explication of the Trinitarian phenomenological theology of Marion, it becomes clear that even though God's availability in experience is optional, it follows a certain intelligible regularity. For example, the Trinity serves as a phenomenological principle of principles, as the structure of presentive intuition. The structures of meaning in the Trinitarian theology of Marion appear "isomorphic" to the structures of intentionality initiated by the call, and so forth. A theological difficulty with such isomorphism is in reconciling the measure of God's participation in experience and the finitude of human existence (i.e., the limited horizon of *Dasein:* Farley 2016 in the introduction to Falque 2016; cf. Kivistö and Pihlström 2017). Clearly, the search for answers emerges out of the given, *not in generalizable reflection but in concrete situatedness,* with philosophical clarifications tied to such individual manifestations of experience in *correlational* analysis with the theology of God's engagement in these forms of experience. As Bloechl (2014, 13) says in his commentary on Lacoste:

On the one hand, Lacoste rejects the modern habit of grounding religious thought in the category of experience (e.g., Schleiermacher) and in its place proposes an account of our "liturgical" relation with God. On the other hand, he also rejects any attempt to submit the meaning of that relation to the self-authenticating reason of a system (e.g., Hegel). These two efforts are of a single piece. To exist *coram Deo* is not to feel the constant presence of the divine but on the contrary to sometimes, perhaps often, suffer precisely the failure or lack of such a presence—and of course as the failure or lack of what one genuinely wants most.

In other words, it depends. When in *Confessions* Augustine, a former Manichean contemplative turned Christian, contrasts the affective God of Christianity with the cold God-being of Greek philosophy, he does so by juxtaposing two forms of religious experience. We have to admit that the differences that such contrasting reveals—that is, differences between the different kinds of religious experience described and understood in the context of faith—remain puzzling. Augustine himself does not explain the difference in experience. It appears that he uses the difference to make the observation that one has a choice which God to believe. As Bloechl (2003, 9) says: "The Wholly Transcendent occasionally breaks into the immanence that is otherwise severed from it." A dialogical structure (Peperzak 2003) of this situation requires two participants, and so the spectacle of religious experience becomes an interface, a lens that, by means of the presence of the Other, highlights and magnifies one's own human makeup. Hence here are different "experiences" versus an "experience" of singularity— for example, for Niketas Stethatos (1995, 148) "God is dispassionate intellect"; for Saint Hesychios the Priest (1979), it is the God of Prayer; for Suhrawardī (1999), experience of thought is religious experience, and so on. In other words, religious experience becomes configured according to the particular habitualities of the self.

17.4 Religious Experience and Metaphysical Realism

I argued that if one suspends the ontological assumptions pertaining to the natural attitude but retains ontological assumptions pertaining to the religious attitude, the descriptive part of the phenomenological approach can be still carried through. I also suggested that in the religious attitude, religious experiences can be understood as forms of the interface between the human self and the invisible reality of the Wholly Transcendent, whereby the constitution of the interface at least partly depends on the habitualities of the ego. Such understanding presents only a beginning of analysis, with a multitude of issues that need to be worked out, including the relationship of the descriptive phenomenological research of religious experience to nuanced problems in the dialogue between theology and philosophy as these are outlined in recent publications (e.g., Falque et al. 2018). Among such issues will be yet another problem resulting from the ontological engagement of descriptive phenomenology conducted in the religious attitude, specifically: What verification criteria can one use for the situation in which not only does the analysis of experience reference the structure of one's theological ideas but the form of experience itself is configured by the habitualities of one's ego? What would be the first-person authority of a researcher in such a situation, and how can it play itself out in the case of a second-person approach?

There are resources available in descriptive analysis per se, such as for example the eidetic identification of essences pertaining to experience. In the absence of the world object (or world objects), one can refer to group memory: that is, compare the findings obtained in first-person research or on live informants (or both), via textual and other forms of traditional accounts, on a case-by-case basis. (See, e.g., Steinbock 2007; Louchakova-Schwartz 2016; Trajtelová in Part 4 of this book.) However, there may be other possibilities on the cusp of different disciplinary approaches. For example, the phenomenology of life has been termed "metaphysical realism" because of its fidelity to the givenness of life that it shares with the natural sciences (e.g., Thompson 2010).

Such "realistication" of phenomenology is not a "naturalization" of it (which was objected to by Husserl) but an effort to include into analysis the aspects of the invisible skimmed over by the transcendental reduction. Canullo, in this volume, shows how such an approach in the phenomenological philosophy of Michel Henry leads to an understanding of a very practical and real situation in which the invisible tethers between life and labor and production define subjectively lived experiences. Another related example is in the work of Bozga (2009), who takes up the singularity of life (which is unveiled within the sameness of subjectivity) as a hidden third participant in the analysis of the relationship between sense and signification. In such approaches, the "realistication" and "theologization" of phenomenology go hand in hand; but of course to bring the point fully home, further research and criticism are necessary.

References

Allston, William P. 1992. Religious experience and religious belief. In *Contemporary perspectives on religious epistemology*, ed. R. Douglas Geivett and Brendan Sweetman, 295–303. Oxford: Oxford University Press.
Bartlett, S.J. 1969. *The worldview of phenomenology*. High Table Address given before the students and faculty of Raymond College, University of the Pacific, Stockton, California, 10 December 1969. https://philarchive.org/archive/BARTWO-24. Accessed 23 June 2018.
Ben Simpson, C. 2014. *Merleau-Ponty and theology*. London: Bloomsbury.
Biernot, D., and C. Lombaard. 2017. Religious experience in the current theological discussion and in the church pew. *HTS Teologiese Studies/Theological Studies* 73(3), a4347: 1–12. https://doi.org/10.4102/hts.v73i3.4347. Accessed 22 June 2018.
Bloechl, Jefferey, ed. 2003. *Religious experience and the end of metaphysics*. Bloomington: Indiana University Press.
———, (ed.). 2014. Introduction. In *From theology to theological thinking*, ed. Jean-Yves Lacoste. Trans. W.C. Hackett, 1–19. Charlottesville: University of Virginia Press.
Bowker, John, (ed.). 2000. The Concise Oxford dictionary of world religions. Oxford: Oxford University Press.

Bozga, Adina. 2009. *The exasperating gift of singularity: Husserl, Levinas, Henry.* Bucharest: Zeta Books.

Buckareff, Andrei A., and Yujin Nagasawa, eds. 2016. *Alternative concepts of God.* Oxford: Oxford University Press.

Carr, D. 1987. World, world-view, lifeworld: Husserl and conceptual relativists. In *Interpreting Husserl,* ed. D. Carr, 213–225. Dordrecht: Springer.

Cooke, Bernard J. 1980. The experiential "Word of God." In *Consensus in Theology? A Dialogue with Hans Küng and Edward Schillebeeckx,* ed. Leonard Swidler, 58–62. Philadelphia: Westminster Press.

Davis, C.F. 1989. *The evidential force of religious experience.* Oxford: Clarendon Press.

De Blois, François Clément. 2007. The Name of the Black Sea. In *Iranian languages and texts from Iran and Turan: Ronald E. Emmerick memorial volume,* ed. Maria Macuch et al. Iranica 13:1–8. Wiesbaden: Harrassowitz.

Falque, E., et al. [Falque, E., B.B. Onishi, and L. McCracken], (eds.). 2018. *The loving struggle.* London: Rowman and Littlefield.

Farley, Mathew. 2016. Introduction. In *Crossing the rubicon,* ed. E. Falque, 1–14. New York: Fordham University Press.

Forrest, P. 2016. The personal pantheist conception of god. In *Alternative concepts of God,* ed. Andrei A. Buckareff and Yujin Nagasawa, 21–40. Oxford: Oxford University Press.

Goswami, Amit. 1995. *The self-aware universe.* New York: Tarcher.

Gunter, Peter Addison Yancey. 1966. Bergson's reflective anti-intellectualism. *Personalist* 47 (1): 43–60.

Gurwitsch, Aron, and Lester E. Embree. 1978. *Phenomenology and the theory of science.* Ann Arbor: Reprinted for Northwestern University Press by University Microfilms International.

Hammond, G.B. 1964. An examination of Tillich's method of correlation, Journal of the American Academy of Religion 32(3):248–251. https://doi.org/10.1093/jaarel/XXXII.3.248. Accessed 19 July 2018.

Harrison, V. 2006. Scientific and religious worldview: Antagonism, non-antagonistic incommensurability and complementarity. *The Heythrop Journal* 47: 349–366.

Henry, Michel. 2003. *I am the truth: Toward a philosophy of Christianity.* Stanford: Stanford University Press.

Hesychios the Priest. 1979. On watchfulness and holiness: Written for Theodulos. In *The Philokalia,* vol. 1. Eds. and Trans. G.E.H. Palmer, P. Sherrard, and K. Ware, 161–198. Boston: Faber and Faber.

Ibn Arabī, Muhyi-d-Din. 1981. *Kernel of the kernel.* Trans. Bulent Rauf. Roxburgh, Rox: Beshara Publications. [Translation of *Lubb al-lubab* with commentary by Ismail Hakki Bursevi.]

James, William. 2017. The varieties of religious experience. New York: Longmanns, Green and Co. Retrieved from https://www.gutenberg.org/files/621/621-pdf.pdf, January 28 2019.

Janicaud, Dominique, et al. . 2000. *Phenomenology and the "theological turn": The French debate.* [Janicaud, Dominque, Jean-François Courtine, Jean-Louis Chrétien, Jean-Luc Marion, Michel Henry, and Paul Ricœur.]. New York: Fordham University Press.

Kearney, Richard. 2011. *Anatheism.* New York: Columbia University Press.

Kirkpatrick, Kate. 2016. Analytic theology and the phenomenology of faith. *Journal of Analytic Theology* 4: 222–233. https://doi.org/10.12978/jat.2016-4.100004100810a. Accessed 10 Apr 2018.

Kivistö, Sari, and Sami Pihlström. 2017. Theodicies as the failure of recognition. *Religions* 8: 242–260. https://doi.org/10.3390/rel8110242. Accessed 23 June 2018.

Kontala, Janne. 2016. Emerging non-religious world-view prototypes: A faith Q-sort study on Finnish group-affiliates. Åbo: Åbo Akademi University Press. https://www.doria.fi/bitstream/handle/10024/125841/kontala_janne.pdf?sequence=2. Accessed 18 June 2018.

Kuhar, R.M. 2005. *An exploration of the impact of education and engagement in science on scientists' metaphysical beliefs and spirituality.* PhD dissertation, Institute of Transpersonal Psychology. ProQuest Dissertations & Theses 305376149.

Leonard, Ellen. 2013. Experience as a source for theology: A Canadian and feminist perspective. *Studies in Religion/Sciences Religieuses* 19 (2): 143–162.

Levinas, Emmanuel. 1969. *Totality and infinity: An essay on exteriority*. Pittsburgh: Duquesne University Press.

Lossky, Vladimir. 1976. *The mystical theology of the Eastern Church*. Crestwood: St. Vladimir's Seminary Press.

Louchakova-Schwartz, O. 2012. *Phenomenological method in the study of esotericism, Part 1: Lebenswelt*. Paper presented at "Esotericism, religion, and culture," the fourth international conference of the Association for the Study of Esotericism, held at the University of California, Davis, June 14–17, 2012.

———. 2013. Direct intuition: Strategies of knowledge in the phenomenology of life, with reference to the philosophy of illumination. In *Phenomenology and the human positioning in the cosmos, Book 1*, ed. A.-T. Tymieniecka. Analecta Husserliana: The yearbook of phenomenological research, 113: 291–315. Dordrecht: Springer.

———. 2016. Theophanis the Monk and Monoimus the Arab in a phenomenological-cognitive perspective. *Cognitive Science of Religion, Open Access: Open Theology* 2 (1): 53–78. https://doi.org/10.1515/opth-2016-0005. Accessed 22 June 2018.

———. 2017. Qualia of God: Phenomenological materiality in introspection, with reference to Advaita Vedanta. Phenomenology of Religious Experience, Open Access: Open Theology 3(1):257–273. Published Online: 2017-05-18 | doi:https://doi.org/10.1515/opth-2017-0021. Accessed 23 June 2018.

Luft, Sebastian. 2011. *Subjectivity and lifeworld in transcendental phenomenology*. Evanston: Northwestern University Press.

Marion, Jean-Luc. 2002a. *Being given: Toward a phenomenology of givenness*. Stanford: Stanford University Press.

———. 2002b. *In excess: Studies of saturated phenomena*. New York: Fordham University Press.

Marrès, Thierry, (ed.). 2017. *Idéalismes d'Orient et d'Occident: Exercices d'inter-fécondation*. Louvain-la-Neuve: Academia-L'Harmattan.

Mezei, M.B. 2017. Realist phenomenology and philosophy of religion: A critical reflection. *Logos i Ethos* 1(44): 47–70. https://doi.org/10.15633/lie.2121. Accessed 26 June 2018.

Nagasawa, Y. 2016. Modal pantheism. In *Alternative concepts of God*, ed. Andrei A. Buckareff and Yujin Nagasawa, 91–105. Oxford: Oxford University Press.

Natanson, M. 1998. Alfred Schutz: Philosopher and social scientist. Human Studies 21:1–12. https://doi.org/10.1023/A:1005381432621. Accessed 18 June 2018.

Niketas Stethatos. 1995. On spiritual knowledge, love and perfection of living: One hundred texts. In *The Philokalia*, vol. 4, ed. Eds. and Trans. G.E.H. Palmer, P. Sherrard, and K. Ware, 139–176. London: Faber and Faber.

Nörenberg, Henning. 2017. The numinous, the ethical, and the body: Rudolf Otto's "The idea of the holy" revisited. *Open Theology* 3 (1): 546–564. Retrieved 24 June 2018 from. https://doi.org/10.1515/opth-2017-0042.

Olson, R.E. 2014. Thoughts about the role of experience in theology: Part 1. *Patheos*, November 18, 2014. http://www.patheos.com/blogs/rogereolson/2014/11/thoughts-about-the-role-of-experience-in-theology-part-one/. Accessed 26 June 2018.

Pannenberg, Wolfhart. 1973. *Wissenschaftstheorie und Theologie. Frankfurt a.M.*: Suhrkamp.

Rivera, Joseph. 2015. *The contemplative self after Michel Henry: A phenomenological theology*. Notre Dame: University of Notre Dame Press.

Roy, Louis. 2001. *Transcendent experiences: Phenomenology and critique*. Toronto: University of Toronto Press.

———. 2003. *Mystical consciousness: Western perspectives and dialogue with Japanese thinkers*. Albany: SUNY Press.

Sarna, J.W. 1989. On some presuppositions of Husserl's "presuppositionless" philosophy. In *Man within his life-world*, ed. A.T. Tymieniecka. Analecta Husserliana: The yearbook of phenomenological research, 27: 643–670. Dordrecht: Springer.

Schwartz, M. 2013. Buddhist Sogdian (')xs'yn prtw: A "firmament" not firmly founded. In *Commentationes Iranicae, Vladimiro f. Aaron Livschits nonagenario donum natalicum*, ed. S.R. Tokhtasev and P.B. Lurje. St. Petersburg: Nestor-Istorija.

Seifert, Josef. 2009. *Discours de méthodes: The methods of philosophy and realist phenomenology*. Heusenstamm: Ontos Verlag.

Suhrawardī, Shihāb al-Dīn Yahyá ibn Habash. 1999. The philosophy of illumination = Hikmat al-ishrāq: A New Critical Edition of the Text of Hikmat al-ishrāq. Trans. John Walbridge and Hossein Ziai. Provo: Brigham Young University Press.

Theophan the Recluse. 1991. *The heart of salvation*. Newbury: Praxis Press.

Thomas, Emily. 2016. Samuel Alexander's space-time God: A naturalist rival to current emergentist theologies. In *Alternative concepts of God*, ed. Andrei A. Buckareff and Yujin Nagasawa, 225–273. Oxford: Oxford University Press.

Thompson, E. 2010. *Mind in life*. Cambridge: Belknap Press.

Turri, J. 2010. On the relationship between propositional and doxastic justification. *Philosophy and Phenomenological Research* 80 (2): 312–326.

Westphal, Merold. 2013. Phenomenology. In *The Oxford handbook of theology and modern European thought*, ed. N. Adams, G. Pattison, and G. Ward, 523–542. Oxford: Oxford University Press.

Yazdī, Mahdī Hā'irī. 1992. *The principles of epistemology in Islamic philosophy: Knowledge by presence*. New York: SUNY Press.

Yu, C.C. 1999. Schutz on lifeworld and cultural difference. In *Schutzian social science*, ed. L. Embree, 159–172. Dordrecht: Springer.

Zachhuber, Johannes. 2013. Wissenschaft. In *The Oxford handbook of theology and modern European thought*, ed. N. Adams, G. Pattison, and G. Ward, 479–498. Oxford: Oxford University Press.

Zahavi, Dan. 2017. Ownership, memory, attention: Commentary on Ganeri. Australasian Philosophical Review 1(4):406–415.

Olga Louchakova-Schwartz, M.D. Ph.D. (the editor) is a comparative religionist, philosopher, and interdisciplinary researcher. She holds the titles Professor of Philosophy of Religion, Spirituality, and Human Development at the Hult International Business School, and Clinical Professor at the UC Davis School of Medicine, Department of Public Health Sciences. She is also a Visiting Scholar at the Graduate Theological Union in Berkeley, Adjunct Lecturer in Spirituality and Phenomenology of Religion at the Jesuit School of Theology, and a Founding President of the Society for the Phenomenology of Religions Experience. Prior to her work in philosophy, she was a senior scientist at the Pavlov Institute of the Academy of Sciences in Russia, and after that, Director of Research and the Founding Director of the Neurophenomenology Center at the former Institute of Transpersonal Psychology, from which she holds the title Professor Emerita of Psychology and Comparative Religion. She studied phenomenology with Amedeo and Barbro Giorgi and with Anna-Teresa Tymieniecka, Her chief research interests are in religious subjectivity and religious experience in contemporary and historical contexts. She has published on fifteenth century and contemporary Kundalini Tantra, eighth century Advaita Vedanta and Neo-Vedanta, early Christianity, seventh–tenth century Hesychasm, contemporary Turkish and American Sufism, the Soviet spiritual underground, and the Islamic Philosophy of Illumination. Her cognitive phenomenological research of Tibetan Tantric meditation was featured on BBC, Science Daily, and other important forums. She has published more than 200 papers and book chapters, and is an Associate Editor of the Journal of Theoretical and Philosophical Psychology, and guest editor for Open Theology, De Gruyter (2017; 2018, 2019, 2020 to appear).

Part IV. Theistic Approaches to the Psychological Horizons in Religious Experiencing

Chapter 18
Religious Experience as Experience of Repentance: How Phenomenology Increases Our Knowledge of Religious Experiences

Bianca Bellini

Abstract What are the essential traits of religious experiences? Should we account for them, or could we confine such experiences to a merely subjective dimension, which does not call for justification before others? This paper relies on descriptive phenomenology to argue that the dimension of religious experiences is not immune from justification. Indeed, it is the effort of justification that spurs us to identify the essential traits of religious experiences. An appeal to descriptive phenomenology will enable us to regard repentance as the core of such experiences and to grasp other phenomena essentially related to it. So, this paper intends to appeal to phenomenology as a descriptive philosophical method and tries to relate it to the dimension of religious experiences. This means that we will delve into the nature of phenomenology itself so as to understand what our main goal entails: Are there specific phenomenological issues that we should appeal to in our effort of accounting for religious experiences from a phenomenological perspective? Our phenomenological reflections upon repentance will show how its role exceeds the religious dimension, since it will turn out to be an essential keystone of the process of self-shaping too.

Keywords Repentance · self-reorchestration · conversion · self-shaping · individual destiny · justification

The topic of religion is often tackled from a philosophical or theological standpoint; nonetheless, at first blush, religion seems to be a quite unapproachable topic: religious experiences seem to be too subjective or even too intimate to call for research focusing on their inherent trademarks. Should we account for this kind of experience, or could we confine such experiences to a merely subjective dimension, which does not call for justification before others? This paper argues that we have

B. Bellini (✉)
Vita-Salute San Raffaele University, Milan, Italy

© Springer Nature Switzerland AG 2019
O. Louchakova-Schwartz (ed.), *The Problem of Religious Experience*,
Contributions to Phenomenology 103,
https://doi.org/10.1007/978-3-030-21575-0_18

to account for this kind of experience and that such an attempt flows into the identification of the essential traits of religious experience. Within this framework, we will bring to light the contribution of descriptive phenomenology that spurs us to account for religious experiences and, in so doing, fosters the identification of religious experiences' essential traits. Phenomenological contributions to every kind of topic—from religion to aesthetics, from psychopathology to history—clarify the innermost essence of the experiences in question. Giving rise to phenomenological reflections means focusing on the nature of our experiences as double-sided, simultaneously subjective and intersubjective. On the one hand, our experiences are marked by traits that proceed solely from the subject of the experience itself; on the other hand, our experiences are marked by traits that also characterize other subjects' kindred experiences. This means that every single experience is neither solipsistic nor completely sharable. Phenomenological analyses come to grips with these two sides of the coin and, in so doing, clarify obfuscated features of the kind of experience at issue. It is worth noticing that our effort of giving rise to phenomenological reflections concerning religious experiences does not imply that we will appeal to phenomenologists who have already tackled this topic, like Hering (1925) or Scheler (2000). Indeed, this paper intends to appeal to phenomenology as a descriptive philosophical method while relating it to religious experiences.

The paper consists of four parts. In the first, we will delve into the nature of phenomenology itself so as to understand what our main goal (the phenomenological reflections concerning religious experiences) entails: Are there specific phenomenological issues that we should address in our effort of accounting for religious experiences? Far from borrowing the concepts from Hering's or Scheler's phenomenological philosophy to explain this kind of experience, we will illumine the issues typical of descriptive phenomenology. Furthermore, the second part will argue for *repentance* as an availability to personal reorchestration at the core of religious experiences: its innermost nature in its essential links with other phenomena will be investigated. This analysis will make us realize that the impact of repentance is not confined to the religious dimension: indeed, repentance plays a key role in the formation of individuality as well, and the third part will bring into visibility this unexpected involvement typical of repentance. Finally, the fourth part will clarify the reasons why we should keep on investigating the nature of religious experiences.

18.1 Descriptive Phenomenology and Religious Experience: How to Set the Stage for a Phenomenological Analysis of Religious Experience

How to begin a theoretical (philosophical) research of religion? What could we deem as a valuable starting point or just as a meaningful landmark? It seems that the unavoidable condition we should first rest upon is *experience*. Let us ascertain whether this proposal is well founded. First of all, we have to distinguish religion as a social system from religion as one's own religion: the former refers to religious faith in general, whereas the latter refers to *my* personal enterprise in faith; the former is linked to theology, whereas the latter is linked to *my* religion. This paper will delve into the first-person perspective of religious experience: this means that we will neither investigate the theological bedrocks of religious faith, nor will we investigate religious faith from a sociological or psychological perspective. Indeed, this is the question that constitutes the silver thread running through our analysis: What are the essential traits of religious experience as *my* experience of religious faith? What are the forces that nourish this specific kind of experience? So, we are going to broach the overall issue of religion by investigating the forces underpinning religious experience—that is, the forces that nourish how I experience *my* religious faith. Such a choice implies two doubts: First, why do we lean on experience? Second, why do we lean on first-person perspective experience? We are going to answer these questions by appeal to a few aspects typical of the philosophical method of inquiry that is phenomenology. This first paragraph purports to argue for a twofold thesis: descriptive phenomenology spurs us to mark the beginning of our analysis by appeal to experience itself, and phenomenology regarded as *a descriptive method of philosophical investigation* is a valuable means to identify the essential traits typical of religious experiences. Within this framework, phenomenology will turn out to be a method radically increasing our knowledge of religious experiences.

There are theoretical analyses that regard etymological remarks, literary exemplifications, or philosophical standpoints as apt springboards: it seems that these starting frames are not suitable for the topic of religion. The reason for such inadequacy follows from what everyone would at first blush ascribe to religious experience as its hallmark: it is something pretty personal. Because of this trait, it could seem quite a hazard to put a lot of effort into research focused on such a theme. Surely, every experience stemming from the first-person perspective is "pretty personal," but religious experiences seem to be so personal that they do not even call for philosophical research. They seem not to call for theoretical study, since it appears that every analysis focused on this matter may end up warping it, without accounting for it appropriately. It is as if we had to treat the issue of love: What should we begin with? Well, on a closer look, the topic of religion is even more complicated than love. On the one hand, we would agree on the following claim: everyone loves. Surely, very different objects of love exist (love for a friend, love for a partner, love for a pet, love for one's job, and so on, and so forth); anyway, it seems unlikely that none of these is the one that matters in one's personal life. On the other hand, we would not agree on the claim that everyone faces religious experiences. So, although both the dimension of love and the scope of religious feelings and understanding are experiences so strictly personal that they seem to be barely examinable from a standpoint overcoming the first-person perspective, this imbalance stands out.

Why is an analysis focused on religion in such a plight? In order to untangle this, the notion of *experience* comes in handy: we cannot give rise to a study on religion outside the frame of experience. The experience at stake is exactly of the first-person perspective. This first paragraph intends to examine the issues typical of descriptive phenomenology so as understand why descriptive phenomenology spurs us to focus on experience of the first-person perspective and, in so doing, on why it is a valuable means to broach the issue of religious experience.

At first blush, the field of religious experience is an issue that theology or philosophy of religion broach. In spite of the radical differences between these two approaches, both of them aim at grasping specifics of religious experience: which spiritual and historical roots it relies on, what it strives for, how religious texts contribute to religious faith, how saintly lives could contribute to the probability of it, what ties human nature to divine nature and vice versa, and so on. Within this framework, the philosophical and theological remarks we could appeal to are surely countless. So, the point is: How could a phenomenological approach enrich our comprehension of religious experiences? Why should we appeal to phenomenology?

The answer to these questions lies in comprehending what characterizes phenomenology as a philosophical method of description and what makes possible different scopes of its application, specifically, the religious one: far from being confined to a method we could simply follow, phenomenology seems to be a matter of a *triple commitment:* that is, a theoretical, applicative, and performative commitment. What does that mean? When we *apply* phenomenology to those phenomena that concern us (applicative commitment), we strive to comprehend their intrinsic *essence* (theoretical commitment). If we relate phenomenology (as *a descriptive method of philosophical investigation*) to the range of phenomena inhabiting the *Lebenswelt*, to the scope of our own personal experiences, then we reach a high degree of *clarification* and *comprehension* regarding them and their *essence*. In so doing, we disclose ways of phenomenological reflection and application: for example, it is possible to give rise to a phenomenology of politics (starting from Spiegelberg 1986), of religion (starting from Scheler 2000), of fantasy (starting from Husserl 1980), of ethics (starting from Hartmann 1962), of aesthetics (starting from Dufrenne 1953), and so forth. Phenomenology's nature consists in the disclosure of phenomenological ways of application. This means that it is possible for us to disclose new ways of phenomenological applications, new ways of relating phenomenology to different kinds of experiences, scopes, phenomena, and so on, and so forth. Applying phenomenology means relating it to "something"— for example, the topic of affectivity, of emotions, of religious experience, the phenomenon of habit, and anything whatever—and combing through its essence. So, on the one hand, this applicative nature of phenomenology allows us to relate it to the scope of religious experiences. On the other hand, the theoretical nature of phenomenology allows us to identify the essential traits typical of religious experiences. However, in order for this disclosure of phenomenological ways of application to play out, a *performative* commitment is necessary: in order to carry out phenomenological reflections, we need to act, to do something. Phenomenology does not merely call for a theoretical and applicative commitment. It entails a strong *performative* commitment: we have to bracket the natural attitude, to carry out a phenomenological reduction, to vary the phenomena in their essential traits—

according to the eidetic variation—to let the phenomenon catch our attention, and so on. (Cf. Husserl 1913, §§1–46.)

This triple commitment flows into the possibility of giving rise to phenomenological analyses: nothing prevents us from grappling with it from a phenomenological standpoint. Theoretical, applicative, and performative facets of phenomenology constitute the forces we rely on during the effort of bringing to light the essential traits of the phenomena surrounding us. For example, the applicative nature of phenomenology pointedly stands out in Scheler's thought, since he relates phenomenology to different phenomena and, in so doing, discloses new phenomenological ways of reflection: phenomenology and individuality (Scheler 2014), phenomenology and religion (Scheler 2000), phenomenology and exemplars (Scheler 1911–21), and so on. Such an applicative phenomenological nature, which spurs us to relate phenomenology to various phenomena—so as to reach a higher degree of comprehension regarding them—is unavoidably linked with a performative phenomenological nature: in order to undertake phenomenological reflections, to disclose new phenomenological ways, we are supposed to be *active* thinkers.

Once phenomenology is chosen as a way of inquiry, the latter entails a double dynamic: if we appeal to phenomenology, we have to be aware of this double dynamic that such an appeal implies. On the one hand, phenomenology demands to be applied to that phenomenon or those phenomena that we wish to comprehend with regard to their intrinsic *essence*: thanks to this performative commitment we disclose ways of phenomenological reflection and application. On the other hand, we are supposed to examine better and in great detail the theoretical commitment that lays the foundation for such a disclosure.

Phenomenology *inherently* strives to be related to the scope of our own personal *experiences*. Such an application is not for its own sake but rather for an overarching comprehension of our being in the world—the theoretical commitment of phenomenology. Otherwise, if phenomenology were conceived of as a philosophical field that is supposed to be merely studied and not applied, then it would cease to be what its founder devised it to be and it would be forced to be less than it is actually capable of being. Phenomenology is a philosophical method we should appeal to if we aim at gaining *evidence* and *clarification* with regard to the phenomena surrounding us in the world-of-life. According to Husserl, phenomenological philosophy is not to be conceived of as "a mere life occupation in the ordinary sense" ("ein bloß schönen Lebensberuf im gewöhnlichen Wortsinne"). Indeed, it appeals to and affects the innermost folds of life. For this reason, Husserl is proud of the kind of philosophy Ingarden's stance exemplifies. He writes: "I am sure about your future, since you belong to that narrow group of my students who do not deem philosophy as a mere life occupation [*Lebensberuf*] in the ordinary sense; indeed, they think that philosophy is an occupation [*Beruf*] in the highest sense, because it points to the unique vocation [*Ruf*] that pertains to the individual core of the person herself."[1]

---

[1] Ingarden 1968, 34: "Ihrer Zukunft bin ich sicher. Sie gehören zu den ganz weniger meiner

Phenomenological philosophy calls for an *adherence to life:* that is, to those experiences that characterize our daily being in the world-of-life. Otherwise, the philosophical root of phenomenology itself would be definitively undermined and downplayed. This is the reason why first-person perspective experience represents an unavoidable landmark for a phenomenological analysis.

This methodological point—the first-person perspective—goes along with three other key points that seem to constitute the core of phenomenology regarded as *a descriptive method of philosophical investigation:* (1) identifying the *essential traits* of the phenomenon at stake (objectivity), and such traits should account for my own experience as well as for others' experiences (intersubjectivity); (2) the effort at shedding light on the nature of the phenomena surrounding us in the world-of-life, that is to say, the effort at bringing to light the structure of the world-of-life and, in so doing, "phenomenalizing" what we talk about; (3) the task of justification, that is to say, the endeavor to "account for." So, we will appeal to experiences of the first-person perspective to identify the essential traits of religious experiences: this identification enables us to phenomenalize what we talk about when talking about religious experiences and, subsequently, to account for them. These four methodological points constitute the landmarks that will guide us through a phenomenological study on religion.

Nonetheless, one could surmise that experiences of the first-person perspective lead to merely subjective outcomes, which have no grip on the intersubjective sphere. Indeed, an analysis proceeding from the first-person perspective should strive to achieve theoretical goals that go beyond a personal horizon. And it is exactly the appeal to phenomenology (regarded as *a descriptive method of philosophical investigation*) that enables us to attain outcomes on both sides—that is to say, on a strictly subjective level (i.e., first-person perspective) and on an intersubjective level (i.e., the aspect my first-person perspective shares with others' first-person perspectives). The condition of possibility for such a twofold outcome consists in the nature of phenomenological method itself: from a phenomenological perspective, the issue of knowledge ("what is such-and-such": de Warren 2009, 12) flows into the issue of givenness ("how, and under what conditions, objects with a determinate sense of being so-and-so are at all given to consciousness": de Warren 2009, 12). This means that taking stock of the ways of givenness is the jumping-off point for any analysis that aims at broaching any epistemological issue.

So, phenomenology spurs us to conceive of experience as the inescapable starting and arrival point. Now, what does this priority of experience entail? And so, how does this link between phenomenology and experience play out? As Jaspers (1965) clearly pointed out, philosophy is in our world and has to refer to it: surely, it points toward and turns to horizons that overcome worldliness in order to experience the present in the light of eternity. Anyway, Jaspers claims that even the sharpest

---

Schüler, denen die Philosophie nicht ein bloß schönen Lebensberuf im gewöhnlichen Wortsinne ist, sondern Beruf im höchsten Sinne, der auf einen über persönlichen, den Herzpunkt der Persönlichkeit treffenden Ruf hindeutet." All translations are my own unless noted otherwise.

reflection acquires its actual meaning only when it points back to human existence here and now. This means that human experience is the boundary that philosophy could dare to overcome only in the light of the effort of comprehending human experience itself. With this purpose, it is useful to hark back to Husserl's remarks focusing on experience's weight, and specifically on first-person perspective experiences:

> *immediate "seeing,"* not merely sensuous, experiential seeing, but *seeing in the universal sense as an originally presentive consciousness of any kind whatever,* is the ultimate legitimizing source of all rational assertions. This source has its legitimizing function only because, and to the extent that, it is an originally presentive source. If we see an object with full clarity, if we have effected an explication and a conceptual apprehension purely on the basis of the seeing and within the limits of what is actually seized upon in seeing, if we then see (this being a new mode of "seeing") how the object is, the faithful expressive statement has, as a consequence, its legitimacy. Not to assign any value to "I see it" as an answer to the question, "Why?" would be a countersense—as, yet again, we see. Moreover, as may be added here to prevent possible misinterpretations, that does not exclude the possibility that, under some circumstances, one seeing conflicts with another and likewise that one *legitimate* assertion conflicts with another.[2]

In order to grasp the importance ascribed by Husserl to experience, we could hark back to a passage from Husserl's lectures on Fichte at the University of Freiburg. In the second lecture, Husserl quotes Fichte as highlighting the unquestioning value of life. According to Fichte, every kind of reflection, despite its abstractness, has to refer to and hold sway over life: every thought or theory stems from life and has to refer to it again. As Husserl himself maintains, Fichte's approach toward philosophy mirrors the unavoidability of experience as the frame into which every sort of reflection needs to be set. Fichte maintains that only life has an unconditional and unrestricted meaning, and so the value of every reflection strictly depends upon its reference to life itself: every thought has to stem from it and then return back to it. Husserl directly quotes Fichte ("nothing has unconditional value and meaning except life") and emphasizes that, for him, every theoretical interpretation aims for inner transformations of human beings, through a manifestation of the ends to which humanity itself is devoted.[3]

---

[2] Husserl 1913, 36–37 (translation: Husserl 1983, 36–37): "Das unmittelbare 'Sehen,' nicht bloß das sinnliche, erfahrende Sehen, sondern das sehen überhaupt als originär gebendes Bewusstsein welcher Art immer, ist die letzte Rechtsquelle aller vernünftigen Behauptungen. Rechtgebende Funktion hat sie nur, weil und soweit sie originär gebende ist. Sehen wir einen Gegenstand in voller Klarheit, haben wir rein auf Grund des Sehens und im Rahmen des wirklich sehend Erfaßten Explikation und begriffliche Fassung vollzogen, sehen wir dann (als eine neue Weise des 'Sehens'), wie beschaffen der Gegenstand ist, dann hat die getreue ausdrückende Aussage ihr Recht. Für die Frage nach ihrem Warum dem 'ich sehe es' keinen Wert beimessen, wäre Widersinn—wie wir abermals einsehen. Das schließt übrigens nicht aus, wie hier, um mögliche Mißdeutungen vorzubeugen, beigefügt sei, daß unter Umständen doch ein Sehe mit einem anderen Sehen streiten kann und ebenso eine rechtmäßige Behauptung mit einer anderen."

[3] Husserl 1987, 278: "Fichte gleicht Platon auch darin, daß für ihn, der, wie wir früher ausgeführt, durchaus idealistischer Praktiker ist, die theoretische Weltinterpretation als Fundament gilt für eine praktische Menschheitserhöhung und -erlösung, für eine innere Umschaffung des Menschen durch Aufweisung der sich aus ihr ergebenden Menschheitsziele. 'Nichts hat,' sagt Fichte einmal,

Hence, we could surmise that Jaspers, Husserl, and Fichte meaningfully highlight that the compass and value of every kind of theoretical and philosophical research strongly depend upon the degree of reference to experience. Such a methodological input brings out the nature of the outcomes that we will achieve through this research: they have to be relevant to experience: that it to say, to first-person perspective religious experiences. They should provide an insightful view on this type of experience, and such a clarifying portrait is supposed to stem from this type of experience itself: experience is to be conceived of as the unavoidable starting and arrival point.

Therefore, we can apply phenomenology to religious issues and develop a phenomenology of religious experience. The fruitfulness of the link between phenomenology and religious experiences strictly stands out through the striking outcomes we can achieve by virtue of this nexus. In fact, tackling religious experiences from a phenomenological viewpoint will enable us to argue for these three key theses: first, repentance as availability to self-reorchestration is the hallmark of religious experience; second, the role of repentance as availability to self-reorchestration is not confined to religious experiences, since it plays a pivotal role in the process of self-shaping too; third, these outcomes bring to light the purposes typical of phenomenological analyses focused on religious experience.

18.2   The Phenomenological Charge to Provide and Demand Reasons: The Essential Traits of Religious Experience and Repentance as Availability to Self-Reorchestration

According to our methodological choice (i.e., descriptive phenomenology), experience is the springboard to start with and, in so doing, we should grasp the traits distinguishing religious experiences. This means that we should be able to account for certain experiences as *religious* experiences, no matter whether these are my experiences or the experiences of others. This double issue is of paramount concern, since it highlights the *objectivity* of the traits this research searches for. Undertaking a phenomenological study of religion implies striving for the identification of traits whose validity is objective: such traits make a certain experience a *religious* experience before *me* and before *others*. This objectivity does not undermine the strictly personal side of the experience itself. Indeed, it enhances and improves this side, since it is recognized as such before others too. Furthermore, it is worth noticing that such an objectivity is what collective religious practices rest upon: they mirror the existence of common underlying traits that make my personal religious experiences not incomprehensible in others' eyes and that lay the foundation for collective

---

'unbedingten Wert und Bedeutung als das Leben, alles übrige Denken, Dichten, Wissen hat nur Wert, insofern es auf irgendeine Weise sich auf das Leben bezieht, von ihm ausgeht und auf dasselbe zurückzulaufen beabsichtigt.'"

religious experiences. Tracking down these twofold traits[4] and accounting for them stem right from the innermost nature of phenomenology. In fact, at phenomenology's core is the Socratic charge to provide and demand justifications in order to ground beliefs, actions, judgments, and mutual interaction in *evidence* and *accessibility* (Husserl 1956, 9). Insofar as phenomenology is a philosophical method that aims for clarification and evidence, an enduring attempt to answer the question that bases every belief, action, and judgment is at stake: "Why?"—that is to say, "Why do you believe X?" "Why do I act in this way?" "Why is this experience to be conceived of as a religious one?" "Why is this other experience not to be conceived of as a religious one?" and so on, and so forth. (Cf. Husserl 2004, §7.)

Following Husserl, the active effort of justifying and showing reasons for our beliefs, judgments, and actions characterizes the effort of reaching clarification and evidence. Husserl's theses would be misunderstood if clarification and evidence were confined to a merely subjective sphere. Indeed, the reasons we offer and demand have to comply with a standard of *common accessibility and comprehension.* Even if they count only for me, they have to be acceptable for others too. We should offer *and* demand reasons that justify beliefs, judgments, and actions in order for us to base our *subjective* and *intersubjective* life on evidence and clarification and, consequently, on mutual accessibility. We have to justify ourselves to others as well as others have to justify themselves to us: this mutual link cannot be split. Husserl himself suggests what we should rely on to answer this fundamental question ("Why?"): by appeal to our first-person perspective experiences (Husserl 1983, 36):

> immediate *"seeing,"* not merely sensuous, experiential seeing, but *seeing in the universal sense as an originally presentive consciousness of any kind whatever,* is the ultimate legitimizing source of all rational assertions. This source has its legitimizing function only because, and to the extent that, it is an originally presentive source. ... Not to assign any value to "I see it" as an answer to the question "Why?" would be a countersense.

So, Husserl spurs us to undertake the Socratic charge to provide and demand justification in order for us to ground beliefs, actions, judgments, and mutual interaction in evidence. This *practice of justification* occurs in light of accessibility: the reasons we offer and demand mark the social space we live in. This phenomenological stance is here remarkable since it becomes really challenging with regard to the religious sphere: we are called to *account for* our religious experiences, which are not to be confined to a solipsistic or incommunicable area. Our right and duty to offer and demand reasons is again at stake, and it plays a crucial role in religious experiences: they do not have to be confined to a merely subjective sphere. They have to be comprehensible for others too: *phenomenology spurs us to account for religious experiences.* In the wake of this urge to offer and demand reasons, the phenomenological attempt of this research concerns the identification of the traits underlying religious experiences: if we identify these essential traits, then we will be able to *account for* such experiences. The task of justification (why is this experience religious?) and the phenomenological theoretical commitment (what are the

---

[4] Traits that account for my personal religious experiences as well for others' religious experiences.

essential traits of a religious experience?) are inherently interwoven. If we relate *our duty and right to justification* to the scope of religious experiences, how could we justify ourselves before others? Which traits do we lean on to *account for* religious experiences? What are the distinguishing features of religious experiences?

Since we possibly deal with *religious experiences* rather than *experience of religion*, this research has to be hedged in by a *specific* religious experience: for example, Catholic Christian experience. Descriptive phenomenology urges us to (1) focus our attention on first-person perspective experience; (2) identify the essential traits of religious experiences, and such traits should account for my experience as well as for others' experiences; (3) shed light on the nature of the religious experiences and, in so doing, "phenomenalize" what we talk about when talking about religious experiences; (4) account for religious experiences. We will argue that it is *repentance* that distinguishes religious experiences from other kinds of experiences: the core of Catholic Christian religious experience is repentance as *the sole force that we rely on to endlessly renew ourselves in the light of God's endless openness to our availability to personal reorchestration*. It is enough that God is the core of such an endless renewal to deem a certain experience as a religious experience. So, why should we regard repentance as the hallmark of religious experience?

If we appeal to first-person perspective experience and consider this experience as infused with a few traits that characterize others' experiences too, we could endorse this claim: my faith in God is such that the doorway to God is always open. Is there something that prevents me from returning to God? The sole obstacle to God is me. What does this mean? According to Christian religious experience, the relation that God established with human beings is based on two keystones: mercy and forgiveness. These two are the threads that tie us to God. Through mercy and forgiveness we are given the *unconditional* opportunity to endlessly experience the relation with God (Pope Francis 2016):

> God, as soon as we give him the chance, he remembers us. He is ready to completely and forever cancel our sin, because his memory—unlike our own—does not record evil that has been done or keep score of injustices experienced. God has no memory of sin, but only of us, of each of us, who are his beloved children. And he believes that it is always possible to start anew, to raise ourselves up. Let us also ask for the gift of this open and living memory. Let us ask for the grace of never closing the doors of reconciliation and forgiveness, but rather of knowing how to go beyond evil and differences, opening every possible pathway of hope. As God believes in us, infinitely beyond any merits we have, so too we are called to instill hope and provide opportunities to others. Because even if the Holy Door closes, the true door of mercy, which is the heart of Christ, always remains open wide for us. From the lacerated side of the Risen One until the very end of time flow mercy, consolation, and hope.

If mercy and forgiveness of God give us the *unconditional* opportunity to endlessly experience the relation with God, what prevents us from returning to God whenever we strayed from Him? If the possibility to return to God is always open, what could prevent us from experiencing, again and again, His mercy and forgiveness? Or, if we put it in first-person perspective, what enables *me* to experience God's mercy and forgiveness whenever *I* strayed from Him? Since God is willing to forgive me, then it is up to me whether to return to Him or not; but what allows me to give rise to such a return whenever I strayed from Him? It seems that *repentance* makes room for this unremitting return to God whenever I strayed from Him. Therefore, we have to identify the essential traits of repentance so as to comprehend its role in religious experience.

18.2.1   The Possibility of an Endless Rebirth and Renewal: The Essence of Repentance

What ties repentance to religious experiences? Why should we regard repentance as the core of religious experiences? Scheler's stance on the matter turns out to be notable, since he aims at disclosing a new way of philosophical investigation that relates phenomenology to religion by means of the features of repentance itself that he highlights.

At the beginning of his essay on repentance, Scheler (2010) clearly distinguishes a religious meaning from a nonreligious meaning of this term: repentance "is a form of self-healing of the soul, is in fact its only way of regaining its lost powers. And in religion it is something yet more: it is the natural function with which God endowed the soul, in order that the soul might return to him whenever it strayed from him." (Scheler 2010, 39). Repentance is a force we rely on for a new start. If such a force is related to the religious field, then its compass is even broader: it is not us who give rise to this newness; it is God who enables us to give rise to this newness. Without this possibility, when we distance ourselves from God, we are detached from Him once and for all. But repentance is not confined to the religious experience only: in religion it is something yet more. Scheler fosters us to distinguish a *basic* nonreligious meaning of repentance ("a form of self-healing of the soul, [the] only way of regaining its lost powers") from an *additional* religious meaning of repentance ("the natural function with which God endowed the soul, in order that the soul might return to him whenever it strayed from him"). This means that we have to comprehend the essence of repentance so as to comprehend its role in religious experiences.

How to tackle the topic of repentance independently of any religious reference? Could we consider repentance as a trait of personal individuality, devoid of any religious implication? If we succeed in answering such questions, then we will comprehend the role of repentance in religious experiences.

In order to grasp this nonreligious meaning of repentance, we have to consider another passage from Scheler (2010, 40):

> we are not the disposers merely of our future; there is also no part of our past life which ... might not still be genuinely altered in its meaning and worth, through entering our life's total significance as a constituent of the self-revision which is always possible. ... It is not repented but only unrepented guilt that holds the power to bind and determine the future. Repentance kills the life-nerve of guilt's action and continuance. It drives motive and deed ... out of the living centre of the Self, and thereby enables life to begin, with a spontaneous,

virginal beginning, a new course springing forth from the centre of the personality which, by virtue of the act of repentance, is no longer in bonds.

Scheler is describing how we *experience* our past, and, in so doing, he describes repentance as a force that allows us to see the past in a new light and ascribe to it a new meaning. Without the possibilities yielded by repentance, we would be inescapably sucked into our past, hedged in by it. Repentance turns to the possibilities that nourish a person's individuality and carries out a *rebirth* that *frees* the person from her past, since it frees her from the type of individual she thought to be. The possibility of rebirth and change repentance brims with brings out our inmost ability to hold sway over the past as well as over the future. Naturally, we cannot alter the contents of our past. Indeed, we can hold sway over the meaning and sense of our past, and consequently such a power has a crashing impact on how we live our present and future.

Repentance is a force that makes room for an actual personal upheaval that brings about an overarching self-revision. Repentance sets the stage for an endless rebirth *before myself,* since it enables me to reorchestrate myself in a new but coherent way. Thanks to repentance my personal upheavals do not flow into a random and incoherent series of changes. Repentance enables us to tether personal upheavals to a new meaning that we ascribe to our past. In so doing, personal upheavals stem from a reorchestration of the meaning that we ascribe to our past. In fact Scheler specifies that "we are not the disposers merely of our future; there is also no part of our past life which … might not still be genuinely altered in its meaning and worth, through entering our life's total significance as a constituent of the self-revision which is always possible."

These remarks help us to better understand the role up to repentance in the formation of individuality. We are arguing that repentance sets the stage for an endless rebirth *before myself* since it enables me to reorchestrate myself in a coherent way. Such a coherence depends upon the fact that repentance enables me to give rise to a connection between the type of individual I think to be now and the type of individual I thought to be in the past. When I discover something disruptively new about myself, I experience a breaking point in my process of self-shaping: I am no longer the individual I thought to be. I discovered that *that individual* is not me any more. I am a new individual. How could such a personal change coexist with the past version of myself? Repentance is the trait of my individuality that allows me to ascribe a new meaning to my past so as to see my past in the light of my new self-awareness.

And in religion repentance is something yet more: repentance sets the stage for an endless rebirth *before God,* since it enables me to return to Him whenever I strayed from Him. What underlies this rebirth is the possibility of change: thanks to this possibility, the doorway to God is always open; it depends only upon our choice. Without the possibility of a limitless *rebirth* and *renewal*—which repentance makes possible—this chance would be shut off. This possibility of an endless personal rebirth nourishes the relationship with God. As Scheler points out, repentance enables the soul to "regain its lost powers," to "return to God whenever it strayed from him": it is "a form of self-healing of the soul." God gives us the opportunity to endlessly reorchestrate ourselves by changing the meaning and worth of our past actions and returning to Him as renewed persons. Repentance is the sole *way back* to God, and the sole rebirth we could appeal to in order to *endlessly* experience the mercy and forgiveness of God. Repentance depends upon us. It is *I* who endlessly has the chance to renew myself, experiences repentance with regard to that type of individual whom I thought to be. Repentance triggers a personal change that makes me a new individual before God (Buber 2015, 8):

> turning is capable of renewing a man from within and changing his position in God's world, so that he who turns is seen standing above the perfect *zaddik,* who does not know the abyss of sin. But turning means here something much greater than repentance and acts of penance; it means that by a reversal of his whole being, a man who had been lost in the maze of selfishness, where he had always set himself as his goal, finds a way to God, that is, a way to the fulfillment of the particular task for which he, this particular man, has been destined by God. Repentance can only be an incentive to such active reversal; he who goes on fretting himself with repentance, he who tortures himself with the idea that his acts of penance are not sufficient, withholds his best energies from the work of reversal.

Repentance, rebirth, forgiveness, and mercy are the traits characterizing the relationship that God decided—and endlessly wants—to establish with human beings, who endlessly have the chance to renew themselves, experience repentance with regard to those persons that they were or those actions that they did, and cross the threshold into God's mercy and forgiveness.

Now, it seems that a doubt arises: if repentance actually gives me the opportunity to endlessly alter myself in light of God, then how is coherence preserved? That is to say, provided that repentance is the availability to reorchestrate oneself, is coherence of the self a goal to bear in mind? It does not seem so. God exemplifies the *maximum* case of incoherence: He made Himself human; and what can be farther away than flesh from God's nature? This means that what matters is openness to God and availability to reorchestrate oneself accordingly, rather than one's personal coherence.

So, repentance turned out to be a radical *availability to personal reorchestration*: the openness to reorchestrate oneself *before God* and also *before oneself.*[5] Repentance plays this key role in a twofold manner: on the one hand, it is the linchpin that nourishes the relation with God, and on the other hand, it is the linchpin that nourishes the process of self-shaping. This double role is due to the inner nature of repentance, whose meaning *exceeds* the religious scope. Regardless of its involvement in the sphere of religious experiences, repentance is a force we appeal to in the process of shaping ourselves. This means that repentance plays a role in such a process *independently of* any religious meaning. However, if such a religious meaning were present, then its role would be even broader, as Scheler himself stresses. So, we could claim that its involvement in religious experiences brings to

---

[5] See also Gabriel Marcel, who develops explicitly the notion of "availability" (disponibilité) especially in Être et avoir, Homo viator, and his essay Appartenance et disponibilité. (Cf. Sweetman 2002.)

the verge repentance in its role and the meaning related to the process of self-shaping. This remark is very important, since religious repentance and nonreligious repentance do not differ completely. Indeed, regardless of the frame in which repentance is set (religious or not), there is a common trait that defines repentance: *conversion*. What does this mean? Conversion is the *core of repentance;* it is the upheaval that repentance triggers. And this is the ground against which other distinguishing features of repentance stand out. Nonetheless, it seems that the modification of the frame of repentance brings about a radical modification of the role that *conversion* plays in being the essence of repentance.

To understand this, etymological pointers come in handy: from Old French *convertir*, from Vulgar Latin *convertire*, from Latin *convertere* "turn around; transform," from *cum-* "with; together; thoroughly" + *vertere* "to turn." Generally, conversion refers to a radical change specific in each case: for example, the act of exchanging one type of money for another; with regard to the military or other scope, a change of front while troops attack the flank, or a change in the units or form of an expression (for instance, "conversion from Fahrenheit to Centigrade"), and so on. The change may also imply a turning toward "something," in light of which the change plays out. Religious experiences of repentance mean a *turning toward* God, and a personal change ensues from such a movement accordingly. The role ascribed to conversion in nonreligious experiences of repentance still concerns a *turning toward*, but this movement solely regards a new self-awareness and a personal change that ensues from such a movement accordingly. Conversion in nonreligious experiences of repentance pertains to a personal reorchestration that does not take place *before God*, which is no more the mainspring and landmark of this self-change.

So, repentance is defined as *availability of the self to personal reorchestration*, either before oneself or before God. Within this framework, religious repentance allows me to reorchestrate the sense and meaning of myself *before* God, and to continue endlessly reorchestrating my relation with God. Repentance sets the stage for rebirth and renewal that, along with mercy and forgiveness, nourish one's relation with God.[6]

---

[6] It is worth noticing that such a role ascribed to repentance is related solely to *Catholic Christian* religious experiences. Among different religious contexts, only Catholicism entails repentance as an inherent hallmark. Catholic Christianity is the sole religion in which God made Himself human: Jesus Christ is God. He Himself experienced human life and, consequently, human fallibility. For this reason, God's mercy is endlessly open to human beings. Such a mercy has value only insofar as humans are faced with the experience of repentance. This thrust—hinged upon mercy, repentance, and the full humanity of Jesus Christ—is a trait typical only of Catholic Christianity. This role ascribed to repentance does not work with regard to the other main forms of Christianity, namely Orthodox Christianity and Protestant Christianity. This occurs for two main reasons. First, according to Orthodox Christianity, man was born pure, whereas according to Catholic Christianity man was born in sin. Second, according to Protestant Christianity, salvation occurs by faith alone, whereas according to Catholic Christianity salvation occurs by faith and works. These two hallmarks typical of Orthodox Christianity and Protestant Christianity prevent repentance from playing a key role in the corresponding religious experiences.

18.2.2 How Repentance Implies Self-Revision, Rebirth, and Pledge

Scheler's pointers turned out to be useful for bringing into sharp profile a few distinguishing features of the phenomenon of repentance and the pivotal role it plays in the *possibility* of *experiencing* the relationship with God. This starting comprehension of repentance makes us wonder which other phenomena—besides mercy, forgiveness, and rebirth—repentance is inherently tied to. Which other phenomena could help us to comprehend the nature of repentance? Far from being a detached or even isolated phenomenon, repentance stands out as an *overarching* experience stemming from a personal conversion and striving for an endless rebirth. If we try to better understand the inherent nature of repentance—or, as Scheler aspires to do, to carry out a phenomenology of repentance (Scheler 2010)—it seems that repentance, regardless of the religious or nonreligious frame in which it is set, turns to the past in the form of self-revision, to the present in the form of rebirth, and to the future in the form of pledge. This means simply that repentance makes possible a freedom to bring up consequences on three temporal planes. First, with regard to the past, repentance is tied to self-revision, since it is by self-revision that I reorchestrate myself, ascribing to my past a new and different meaning. Second, with regard to the present, repentance is tied to rebirth, since it essentially consists in yielding new possibilities and so in restoring our capacity to give rise to newness. The way we are appealing to the concept of "rebirth" is clearly related to Arendt's perspective on "natality," a term Arendt herself used (Arendt 1958, 246):

> the life span of man running toward death would inevitably carry everything human to ruin and destruction if it were not for the faculty of interrupting it and beginning something new, a faculty which is inherent in action like an ever-present reminder that men, though they must die, are not born in order to die but in order to begin.

Third, with regard to the future, repentance entails a pledge insofar as it implies an effort of change pointed toward the future: the personal change must persist in the future. This issue is very close to Arendt's stance on the act of promising, which she regards as the counterpart of forgiveness.[7] According to her, the ability to forgive is the sole ability that enables us to release ourselves from the consequences of what we have done, and the ability to promise is the sole ability that enables us to bind ourselves to the future. Let us take a closer look at her position (Arendt 1958, 237):

> the possible redemption from the predicament of irreversibility—of being unable to undo what one has done though one did not know, and could not have known, what he was doing—is the faculty of forgiving. The remedy for unpredictability, for the chaotic

---

[7] The link between repentance and forgiveness represents an interesting follow-up of this paper and should be investigated: how are they intertwined? Could repentance be considered as a sort of forgiveness of oneself? Is repentance the necessary condition of forgiveness? It is worth noticing that religious repentance seems to imply two different kinds of forgiveness: the first proceeds from God and turns to those who experienced repentance, whereas the second proceeds from those who experienced repentance and turns to themselves or to others. It is a matter of two planes: the former is vertical and the latter is horizontal.

uncertainty of the future, is contained in the faculty to make and keep promises. The two faculties belong together in so far as one of them, forgiving, serves to undo the deeds of the past, whose "sins" hang like Damocles' sword over every new generation; and the other, binding oneself through promises, serves to set up in the ocean of uncertainty, which the future is by definition, islands of security without which not even continuity, let alone durability of any kind, would be possible in the relationships between men. Without being forgiven, released from the consequences of what we have done, our capacity to act would, as it were, be confined to one single deed from which we could never recover; we would remain the victims of its consequences forever. ... Without being bound to the fulfilment of promises, we would never be able to keep our identities. ... Both faculties, therefore, depend on plurality, on the presence and acting of others, for no one can forgive himself and no one can feel bound by a promise made only to himself; forgiving and promising enacted in solitude or isolation remain without reality and can signify no more than a role played before one's self.

Since Arendt's stance leads to thorough comprehension of repentance, her thesis enriches our account of repentance. In light of her insights, we argue that repentance turns to the present in the form of rebirth (cf. Arendt 2000), to the future in the form of pledge, and—we add—to the past in the form of self-revision. This thesis leads to two conclusions.

First, the fact that self-revision, rebirth, and pledge pertain to the essence of repentance implies that these three phenomena pertain to the essence of religious experiences as well. The core of religious experience consists in repentance, which is inherently tethered to self-revision, rebirth, and pledge. Moreover, this clarifies both the *essence* of repentance and the essence of religious experiences.

Second, it is worth pondering the following statement by Arendt: "without being bound to the fulfillment of promises, we would never be able to keep our identities" (Arendt 1958, 237). Arendt insightfully links the act of promising with the issue of personal identity. This reference is of paramount concern, since repentance itself turned out to be inherently linked with the act of promising, and the above means that repentance is somehow tied to the issue of personal identity. How does this link play out? If repentance is to be determined as *availability to personal reorchestration*—namely an inherent endless openness to reorchestrate oneself before God and in relation with Him—how could we better describe repentance as availability to personal reorchestration, before oneself, and with regard to the formation of personal individuality?

18.3   Repentance as an Overall Condition of the Self

If we consider the whole of our past, we could surely notice how our individuality changed over time. How is it possible that my own individuality could radically change? How is it possible that what I deemed as the core of my individuality could suddenly turn out to be nothing more than a veil overshadowing other deeper layers of my individuality? Such questions flow into a more specific and crucial issue: Is individuality endowed with a trait that renders it open to any kind of personal reorchestration? Repentance appeared to be this trait. If we put into brackets the religious wake of such a phenomenon, we come to realize that repentance is what sets the stage for any possible upheaval of my own individuality, since it enables me, as a person, to become a new individual, specifically, *that* individual I discovered myself to be. It enables me to distance myself from the individual I thought to be, and so it allows me to lay the foundation for a radical personal change. It enables me to be the same person even if I become an individual different from the one I was before.

We came to realize that repentance plays a role in the process of self-shaping, and now we are realizing that its role holds sway over our conception of individuality: if we admit that it plays a role as availability to self-reorchestration, we are forced to endorse a view of the self that ascribes a key role to personal upheavals. This point entails that we should clarify the pattern of individuality we are referring to: Scheler's stance on the core of personal individuality is here at stake. Specifically, we are referring to the innermost core of individuality that pertains to what Scheler names "individual destiny." An overview on this notion will bring to light a view on the self that ascribes to upheavals a key role in the formation of individuality, as our account of repentance implies.

The expression "individual destiny" refers to the unique destiny everyone is called upon to unveil in her life. Scheler refers to it also as my *Ruf,* "das Bewusstsein des individuellen Sollens," my "persönliches Heil," my "individuelle Bestimmung," "individual-persönliches Wertwesen" (Scheler 1973a, 489–494). All these terms refer to a common point: my own personal vocation, my own individual destiny, which gradually becomes clear to me through my capacity to *fühlen,* my capacity to let me be affected by my emotional responses to the axiological richness of the world I live in.[8] My own individual destiny is what Scheler names "An-sich-Gutes für *mich*" ("good-in-itself for *me*"). What does it mean to say that my own destiny is a good "in itself" as well as a good "for me"?

Scheler describes this individual destiny as subjective and objective at the same time. It is "in itself" as well as "for me." It is neither a relativistic nor a dogmatic rift: "für jede Person [gibt es] noch ein *individualgültiges,* aber nicht minder objektives und prinzipiell einsichtiges Gute" (Scheler 2014, 621). Individual destiny is characterized by a specific objectivity that makes it understandable by other persons too. Scheler emphasizes how the comprehension of my own individual destiny is

---

[8] The axiological and emotional dimensions are two keystones of Scheler's thought. Unfortunately we do not have enough space to delve into Scheler's account of them. However, we must notice that Scheler is a pivotal harbinger of an overarching reappraisal of the role up to the emotional dimension and, especially, to love. A reappraisal of this sphere entails a deep comprehension of the link that ties our heart ("Gemüt") to the axiological dimension that reality brims with. According to Scheler, the emotional sphere is infused with a strict lawfulness, and the axiological lawfulness of my emotional life (i.e., "ordo amoris") resembles an axiological lawfulness of reality. Within this framework, emotions are not mere reactions to stimuli. (Cf. De Monticelli 2003.) Indeed, they are a specific form of openness toward the world: Scheler reappraises emotional life as the key to the perception of the axiological substratum of reality. For this issue, see Scheler 1915, 1973a, and 1973b.

not confined to myself: it is something that others could recognize too. I am not locked in my individuality as if in a prison closed off to anybody else. (Cf. Scheler 1973b, 104.) Therefore, just as others could find a way toward my innermost personal core, so could I help others in their effort at finding the way toward themselves: just as others could be the key to myself, so could I be the key to the personal core of another person. If we rely on this Schelerian remark and the previous pointers, we have reasons for arguing that other persons could play a pivotal role in the process I undertake in order to know and shape myself, since the core of my individuality—my individual destiny—is *in itself* in addition to being *for me*. Others could radically aid me in shedding light on my individual destiny, which (Scheler 1973a, 490):

> is good precisely in the sense of being "independent of my knowledge." For this includes the "good-in-itself." Yet it is the "good-in-itself" for "me" in the sense that there is an experienced reference to me which is contained (descriptively put) in the special non-formal content of this good-in-itself, something that comes from this content and points to "me," something that whispers, "For you." And precisely this content places me in a unique position in the moral cosmos and obliges me with respect to actions, deeds, and works, etc., which, when I represent them, all call, "I am for you and you are for me."

The core of my individuality is my unique individual destiny, and I can strive to *gradually unveil* it. In fact, following Scheler, we realize that individual destiny calls for recognition rather than a sort of creation: the individual destiny "is not something we have to posit, but something we have to recognize" (Scheler 1973b, 103). We are called to *recognize* our own individual destiny: this act of recognition is to be regarded as a gradual *process,* since it relies upon a gradual effort of discovering and unveiling. And in this process other persons could play a key role, since they could help me to understand myself—that is, my individual destiny and its deepest facets. But it is always a matter of an effort of self-knowledge, a continuous striving for a deeper self-knowledge (Scheler 1973b, 108):

> it goes without saying that what is always present to us and is secretly at work in us, what always directs and leads us without forcing us, cannot be perceived as a separate and distinct content of consciousness—which is always only a "process" which stops, then starts again. Obviously the eternal wisdom which speaks in us and guides us is not loud and commanding, but a still and merely monitory wisdom. However, it speaks all the louder, the more we act against it.

It follows that presumably we cannot identify a final stage of this process of self-knowledge: my individual destiny is not an X I can immediately grasp through self-interpretation. The individual essence of my individual destiny comes to light through an unremitting process of self-knowledge that aims to unveil the deepest layers of my individual destiny (Scheler 1973b, 106):

> *individual destiny* is a *timeless and essential value-essence* [*Wertwesenheit*] in the form of *individuality*. And, since it is not formed or posited by the spirit in man but is only recognized, since its fullness is only successively unveiled, as it were, in the course of our experiences of life and action, it exists only for the spiritual individuality in us. Individual destiny is, therefore, a matter of *insight*, while fate is only something to be confirmed, a fact which in itself is *value-blind*.

Scheler does not go any further, but we could surmise that this account implies that I should be always willing to question myself, my certainties about my individuality, my beliefs about my individual destiny. I could always discover new and unexpected facets of my individual destiny. Therefore if I am not always willing to *reorchestrate* myself in the light of possible new self-awareness, then I end up being stuck. If I cannot presume to be able to immediately grasp the core of my individuality, I must be willing to continuously revise and question myself, since the essence of myself is not fixed once and for all.

As the individual destiny comes to light through a gradual recognition, delusions as well as errors are surely possible: "the subject can deceive himself about this [the individual destiny], he can (freely) fail to achieve it, or he can recognize and actualize it" (Scheler 1973b, 104). We can err in reckoning our individual destiny; we can be deluded into thinking that we have finally grasped the core of our individual destiny. This process of self-knowledge is as knotty as cloudy, since there is no positive image of our individual destiny (Scheler 1973b, 107):

> the mode of givenness of the particular material, the unique content of individual destiny ... is peculiar to each man alone. There is no positive, circumscribed image of it, still less a formulatable law. The image of our destiny is thrown in relief only in the recurrent traces left when we turn away from it, when we follow "false tendencies."

There is always something new to be discovered about my individuality and its destiny, and so I am always given the opportunity to reshape myself in light of the new awareness I gain. This is the reason why self-revision and self-reorchestration—implied by repentance—play a key role. The perfection that pertains to personal individuality is that it is an "unfinished totality" (Cusinato 2014, 195): far from being only ontologically *new* beings, as individual persons we are also—and first of all—ontologically *innovative* beings. My individuality does not take shape by being coherent: what defines my individuality is my ability to fail and to arise again as a new individual, since I have discovered something new about my individual destiny. Repentance is a force I rely on for this new start. Repentance is the *sole* force that allows me to see the past in a new light and to become someone else without turning into someone else. It is the sole force that warrants change and identity at the same time. The possibility of rebirth and change that repentance brims with brings out our inmost ability to hold sway over the sense and meaning of the past. As an unfinished totality, I could always come to know something unexpected about my individuality, and every step of my self-knowledge might require me to reorchestrate myself, to re-shape myself accordingly.

Self-shaping is an enduring process, radically open to change and grounded in repentance as the force that individuality draws upon to avoid finality of self-knowledge. A person couldn't claim: "I am what I now am." Since individual destiny calls for an endless task of self-discovery, there are always new layers that I could discover, and there are possibilities of an upheaval for me. However, in order for these upheavals to actually unfold, I must be equipped with an ability that allows me to free myself from my past self-knowledge: repentance lays the foundation for an endless availability to self-reorchestration and self-revision. In the effort of knowing myself I come to know new facets of my individuality, and I try to shape myself accordingly.

For instance, if I realize that my individual destiny has nothing to do with my actual career (self-knowledge), then I may try to shape myself accordingly (self-shaping) by wondering which new career could better resemble my "good-in-itself for *me*." So I could decide to take a leave of absence in order to take into account new job offers. This new self-awareness makes me regard my past career in a completely different manner, but this new view would not be possible if I kept on thinking that my past career is square with my individuality. We cannot understand the role that repentance is playing here if we do not distance ourselves from its widespread religious meaning. Repentance sets the stage for a self-revision: I come to realize that those past moments of my life were necessary for me to be what I am, but I come to realize that I am not any more that past variant of myself, since I have discovered deeper layers of my individuality. And this new self-awareness is such that I experience repentance toward that past variant of myself. This experience of repentance frees myself from that past variant of myself.[9] Repentance is the overall condition of the self (Cusinato 2014, 320–321):

> il pentimento propriamente non riguarda le conseguenze infelici di un mio atto: verso di essere non si prova pentimento, ma piuttosto senso di colpa. Che cosa ferisce nel pentimento? Quello che fa star male, è l'essere responsabili di un certo atto che non ci corrisponde più. ... Il nucleo più autentico della mia singolarità, che nel frattempo si è trasformato, continua a essere "oggettivamente" responsabile di un giudizio o di un atto che ora contraddice esplicitamente l'ordine del mio sentire attuale.

Cusinato is a contemporary philosopher and, in this quotation, specifies that repentance does not turn to the consequences of my past actions. Indeed, repentance turns to the responsibility of a certain act that does not resemble my individuality any more, since my individuality itself has altered in the meanwhile. It follows that repentance is inherently tethered to a deep personal upheaval: I discovered something new with regard to my individual destiny, and so my past belief related to the essence of my individual destiny that spurred me to act in a certain way does not resemble my current awareness of my individual destiny. Repentance regards what I am not any more ("ci si pente infatti solo verso ciò che non si è più," Cusinato 2014, 321). Repentance is the sign of a deep personal transformation and the outcome of a personal rebirth. Repentance is the sign of a *breaking point* in my process of self-shaping: I am aware of a breaking point between my past and my current awareness of my individual destiny. Repentance enables me to give rise to a personal rebirth that definitively distances myself from that past, which does not resemble my individuality any more. I can alter the sense of my past in light of my new self-awareness and by virtue of the dynamic essence of my individual destiny, which

---

[9] Naturally, it would be empirically false to claim that repentance plays such a role in *any* self-variation; it would be empirically false to claim that *every time* we experience a self-change we feel repentance toward our past variants of ourselves. Indeed, what we are arguing refers only to *upheavals*, namely radical self-changes that turn completely upside down our certainties about our individuality.

is not predetermined as fate is ("nel pentimento si esprime la dinamica di un vivente che non ha un destino, prigioniero del proprio passato, ma una destinazione aperta al futuro," Cusinato 2014, 322). Cusinato is stressing that repentance emphasizes the pliable nature of individuality, which is not hedged in by fate: individuality is tied to an individual destiny, which is absolutely open to endless reorchestrations.

Before we conclude this analysis, it is worth noticing that the term "reorchestration" intends to emphasize that we do not "create" anything new with regard to our individuality. We discover something new, and this discovery may spur us to reorchestrate and reshape ourselves. Sure, there are circumstances that do not depend upon my will or choice and influence my knowledge of my individual destiny (like the historical context I find myself in), but there is a deep core that inherently characterizes the individuality of each person independently of such circumstances. I do not create my individual destiny. I discover it, and, especially, I continuously discover newer and newer facets of it. And when I realize that the awareness of the essence of my individual destiny is different from my past awareness about it, then repentance enables me to give rise to a personal rebirth: repentance turns to what I am not any more. By ascribing to my past a new meaning, I am given the opportunity to reshape myself and shape the future: insofar as I can reorchestrate the meaning of my past, I can shape the meaning of my future ("il futuro si schiude solo nella misura in cui il senso del passato si riapre. ... Il futuro rimane aperto solo se il senso del passato rimane aperto." Cusinato 2014, 323). I can shape my future only on condition that I may change the meaning of my past. Repentance as availability to self-reorchestration is the outcome of an effort at taking care of oneself: this means that if I nourish my process of self-knowledge and self-shaping, then I am able to give rise to a personal rebirth when I am faced with a breaking point in the formation of my individuality.

18.4 What Does Phenomenological Philosophy of Religious Experience Aim for?

From a religious standpoint, repentance could be deemed as *availability to personal re-orchestration before God*: it mirrors my own availability to *re-orchestrate* myself in light of God's openness to my own repentance. Such an awareness seems to bring about that "fear and trembling" described by Kierkegaard (1986). This crippling and numbing feeling accompanies faith in a paradox that no words can explain. I can always reorchestrate my individuality in light of my repentance before God. I can always undo myself from what I did or who I was. I can always ascribe a new sense and meaning to the past and to myself. The innermost core of repentance is something really astounding: when we fully become aware of it, we are caught by fear and trembling, since a horizon of an endless range of personal conversions and upheavals stands out.

For this reason, the inner essence of religious experience goes beyond the calmness we are prone to confining it to. (Cf. Kierkegaard 1986.) We have to face the angst that religious experience arouses. This kind of experiences spurs us to cope with endless possibilities of self-reorchestration *before God*. Religious experiences should not be confined to a mere habit or ritual. They urge us to be completely aware of the mystery we are faced with. According to Kierkegaard, if we listen to the life of Abraham in the wake of this mood, then such a story will unavoidably paralyze and blind us. Without repeating Kierkegaard, it seems we should underscore the wordless shock resulting from experiences of faith. And Martin Buber (1948) highlights the role of this angst by maintaining that Christian faith is a vital relation with the content of the underlying belief, and it is a relation encompassing every side of life; otherwise faith itself would be untrue and misleading. Christian faith demands an overarching feeling, not just a matter of a façade.

So, the phenomenological philosophy of Christian religious experience aims at understanding repentance together with self-shaping, mercy, rebirth, forgiveness, self-revision, and pledge. Examining repentance means examining those phenomena that revolve around it and that, consequently, define religious experiences themselves. This last paragraph enables us to pinpoint the last phenomenon entailed by repentance—self-choice. The process of choosing oneself has a pivotal role through repentance. In fact, repentance itself seems to imply an endless *self-choice*: every time I give rise to a new self—that is, every time I discover new layers of my individual destiny—I (can) choose that self. Within this frame, it is worth referring to Kierkegaard (1992), who maintains that the deepest personality who does not choose itself is nothing in comparison with the most wretched one who chose itself: what matters most is to be that person one chooses to be rather than just being this or that. According to Kierkegaard, everyone can achieve such a goal if she strives and aims for it. On purpose, Kierkegaard avails himself of the expression "choosing oneself" instead of "knowing oneself": the former brings to light a feature that the latter overshadows. The process Kierkegaard is referring to entails a continuously active role of the subject: it is a goal that cannot be achieved once and for all—and Scheler would surely agree with this thesis. Self-knowledge here is both the starting and the arrival point, not a mere contemplation, but a reflection upon oneself and also an action towards oneself.

18.4.1   The Effort of Accounting for Religious Experiences Is a Dignifying Affair

It is worth concluding this analysis with a reference to Rainer Forst's (2014) notable stance on the innermost nature of persons as *justifying* beings. This paper identified the essential traits of religious experiences: since phenomenology's pivotal concern is to account for every aspect of experience in question, the task of justification of discovered essential traits is remarkable especially in the religious dimension, which is highly personal, and therefore the task of justification before others may lose its grip. Subsequently, this last paragraph intends to bring to light the link that tethers the "phenomenological task of justification" to the notion of human dignity. Forst (2014) deals with the concept of dignity and accounts for it by appeal to the notion of person as a *justifying* being. So, Forst's viewpoint is now taken into account, since it enables us to better understand the nexus between phenomenology and religious experiences in light of the pivotal role he ascribes to the practice of justification that everyone should carry out.

"Human beings are supposed to be 'inviolable' in their dignity. But what does this mean and where does this special status come from?" (Forst 2014, 96). The notion of dignity is often mentioned, and moreover it often ends up playing a crucial role in defending rights and claims, even if its meaning is not so clear as such a frequent appeal demands. For this reason, Forst's theoretical endeavor consists in grasping the nature of dignity in order to clearly account for its meaning. In this view, each person is to be conceived of as a justifying being: that is to say, as "a being who uses and 'needs' justifications in order to lead a life 'fit for human beings' among her fellows" (Forst 2014, 96). Consequently, persons themselves are to be regarded as beings who have an unconditional right to *justification* (*die Rechtfertigung*), which is a basic right that acts as foundation for all other rights. Thereby, Forst identifies a valuable link between human dignity and the Socratic charge, which is to provide and demand justification in order to ground beliefs, actions, judgments, and mutual interaction in evidence and accessibility for others. He ties the concept of dignity to the practice of justification that defines our intrinsic nature as persons. Moreover, he specifies the criteria that one should appeal to in order to offer and demand justification. These criteria clearly evoke the phenomenological issue of shared evidence and accessibility (Forst 2014, 101–102).

> when it comes to justifying morally relevant actions in a social context, the decisive criteria are reciprocity and generality, since such actions must be justified by appeal to norms which can claim to hold in a reciprocal and general fashion. ... It follows that, in justifying or challenging a moral norm ... no one can make specific claims that he denies to others ... no one can simply assume that others share his own perspective, evaluations, convictions, interests, or needs. ... And, finally, it follows that no affected person may be prevented from raising objections, and that the reasons that are supposed to legitimize a norm must be such that they can be shared by all persons (generality).

So, defining persons as justifying beings, along with these two criteria (generality and reciprocity), Forst (2014, 101) reaches a high level of clarification concerning the phenomenon of dignity: "to *act* with dignity means being able to justify oneself to others" (ibid., 101). This practice of justification takes place in the *social space* ("die soziale Raum"), which he defines (ibid., 95–96) as a space of reasons ("Raum von Gründen"). This means that the social space primarily consists of the reasons that we offer and demand in order to justify beliefs, actions, and judgments. On the one hand, *offering justifications* means appealing to reciprocity and generality: actions, beliefs, and judgments have to be justified through statements that can claim to hold reciprocally and generally. On the other hand, *demanding justifica-*

tions means carrying out *the critique of relations of justification* ("Kritik der Rechtfertigungsverhältnisse")—the critical analysis of political, historical, economical, and social relations that are not justified or that are not justifiable.

This idea is close to the Socratic and Husserlian idea that every *awakened* life carries out and implies activity, responsibility, critique, and efforts of clarification and comprehension. Further, according to Forst, Reason (*Vernunft*) is immanently linked to reasons (*Gründe*), which have to be reasonable and universally justifiable (Forst 2002, 197). Moreover, the practice of justification strongly entails responsibility and autonomy as a person's distinguishing features. According to Forst, persons are autonomous and responsible insofar as they act—besides with consciousness—with *justification*: so long as they offer and demand reasons, they are responsible for their actions, beliefs, and judgments (Forst 2002, 256):

> as *responsible* persons they are *responding* persons, and we expect of them that they have considered their reasons for action and can justify them. In this sense, autonomous persons are reasonable in terms of practical reason: they have reasons for their actions that they can justify to themselves and can communicate and justify to others, so that these reasons … can be shared.

As *responsible* persons we must be willing to offer and demand reasons in order to justify beliefs, actions, and judgments: and the religious dimension is not immune from this moral practice.

18.5 Concluding Remarks

This paper aimed at treating the question of the hallmarks of religious experiences. A methodological part justified the use of phenomenology as the theoretical foundation for such analysis. The paper identified the core of religious experiences as repentance, focusing afterwards on the role that repentance plays in the formation of individuality: this view appeals to Scheler's notion of "individual destiny" to account for a pattern of individuality that ascribes a key role to personal upheavals.

The phenomenological approach examines repentance not as an isolated phenomenon but rather in its intertwining with rebirth, forgiveness, mercy, pledge, self-revision, self-shaping, and self-choice. Repentance as *availability to personal reorchestration before God* is the core of religious experiences, and repentance as *availability to personal reorchestration before oneself* is the unavoidable keystone of the process of self-shaping. This means that the phenomenology of religious experiences should also treat the question of the linkage between personal individuality and religious experiences, between oneself and God, and between oneself and others.

References

Arendt, H. 1958. *The Human Condition*. Chicago: University of Chicago Press.
———. 2000. Truth and politics. In *The portable Hannah Arendt*, ed. P. Baehr, 545–575. New York: Penguin Books.
Buber, M. 1948. *Das Problem des Menschen*. Heidelberg: Lambert Schneider.
———. 2015. *The Way of Man According to the Teachings of Hasidism*. Trans. M. Friedman. Available via OGF 5/2015. https://combonianum.org. Accessed 15 May 2017.
Cusinato, G. 2014. *Periagoge: Teoria della singolarità e filosofia come cura del desiderio*. Verona: QuiEdit.
De Monticelli, R. 2003. *L'ordine del cuore: Etica e teoria del sentire*. Milan: Garzanti.
de Warren, N. 2009. *Husserl and the Promise of Time. Subjectivity in Transcendental Phenomenology*. Cambridge: Cambridge University Press.
Dufrenne, M. 1953. *Phénoménologie de l'expérience esthétique*. Paris: Presses Universitaires de France.
Forst, R. 2002. *Contexts of Justice: Political Philosophy Beyond Liberalism and Communitarianism*. Trans. John M. Farrell. Berkeley: University of California Press.
———. 2014. The grounds of critique: On the concept of human dignity in social orders of justification. In *Justification and Critique: Towards a Critical Theory of Politics*, ed. R. Forst, 95–108. Trans. C. Cronin. Cambridge: Polity Press. German edition: Forst, R. 2011. Der Grund der Kritik: Zum Begriff der Menschenwürde in sozialen Rechtfertigungsordnungen. In R. Forst, *Kritik der Rechtfertigungsverhältnisse: Perspektiven einer kritischen Theorie der Politik*. 119–133. Berlin: Suhrkamp Verlag.
Hartmann, N. 1962. *Ethik: Die Struktur des ethischen Phänomens (Phänomenologie der Sitten)*. Berlin: De Gruyter.
Hering, J. 1925. *Phénoménologie et philosophie religieuse: Étude sur la théorie de la connaissance religieuse*. Strasbourg: Imprimerie Alsacienne.
Husserl, E. 1913. *Ideen zu einer reinen Phänomenologie und phänomenologischen Philosophie. Erstes Buch: Allgemeine Einführung in die reine Phänomenologie*. Halle: Verlag von Max Niemeyer.
———. 1956. *Erste Philosophie (1923–24). Erster Teil: Kritische Ideengeschichte*. Dordrecht: Springer.
———. 1980. Phantasie, Bildbewusstsein, Erinnerung: Zur Phänomenologie der anschaulichen Vergegenwärtigungen. In *Texte aus dem Nachlass, 1898–1925*. Dordrecht: Springer.
———. 1983. *Ideas pertaining to a pure phenomenology and to a phenomenological philosophy. First Book: General Introduction to a Pure Phenomenology*. Trans. F. Kersten. The Hague: Martinus Nijhoff Publishers.
———. 1987. Fichtes Menschheitsideal: Drei Vorlesungen, 1917. In *Aufsätze und Vorträge (1911–1921)*, ed. E. Husserl, 1987, 267–292. Dordrecht: Springer.
———. 2004. *Einleitung in die Ethik: Vorlesungen, Sommersemester 1920–1924*. Dordrecht: Springer.
Ingarden, R., ed. 1968. *Briefe an Roman Ingarden: Mit Erläuterungen und Erinnerungen an Husserl*. The Hague: Martinus Nijhoff Publishers.
Jaspers, K. 1965. *Kleine Schule des philosophischen Denkens*. Munich: Piper Verlag.
Kierkegaard, S. 1986. *Fear and Trembling*. Trans. A. Hannay. London: Penguin Classics.
———. 1992. *Either/or: A Fragment of Life*. Trans. A. Hannay. London: Penguin Classics.
Pope Francis. 2016. *Holy mass for the closing of the jubilee of mercy*. Papal mass. Homily of His Holiness Pope Francis. Solemnity of Our Lord Jesus Christ, King of the Universe. St. Peter's Square, Sunday, 20 November 2016. Available via https://w2.vatican.va. Accessed 25 May 2017.
Scheler, M. 1911–1921. Vorbilder und Führer. In *Schriften aus dem Nachlaß, Bd. 1: Zur Ethik und Erkenntnislehre*, Gesammelte Werke 10, ed. M. Scheler 1957, 255–344. Bern: Francke Verlag.

———. 1915. Liebe und Erkenntnis. In *Schriften zur Soziologie und Weltanschauungslehre,* Gesammelte Werke 6, ed. M. Scheler 1963, 77–98. Bern: Francke Verlag.

———. 1973a. *Formalism in Ethics and Non-Formal Ethics of Values: A New Attempt Toward the Foundation of an Ethical Personalism.* Trans. Manfred S. Frings and Roger L. Funk. Evanston: Northwestern University Press.

———. 1973b. Ordo amoris. In *Selected Philosophical Essays,* ed. M. Scheler, 98–135. Trans. D. Lachterman. Evanston: Northwestern University Press.

———. 2000. *Vom Ewigen im Menschen.* Gesammelte Werke 5. Bonn: Bouvier Verlag.

———. 2010. Repentance and rebirth. In *The Eternal in Man,* ed. M. Scheler, 35–65. Trans. B. Noble. New Brunswick: Transaction Publishers.

———. 2014. *Der Formalismus in der Ethik und die materiale Wertethik: Neuer Versuch der Grundlegung eines ethischen Personalismus.* Hamburg: Felix Meiner Verlag.

Spiegelberg, H. 1986. *Steppingstones: Toward an ethics for fellow existers; Essays,* 1944–1983. Dordrecht: Martinus Nijhoff Publishers.

Sweetman, B. 2002. Gabriel Marcel: Ethics within a Christian existentialism. In *Phenomenological approaches to moral philosophy,* ed. John J. Drummond and L. Embree, 269–288. Dordrecht: Kluwer Academic Publishers.

Bianca Bellini obtained her Ph.D. in 2018 fromVita-Salute San Raffaele University (Milan), where she graduated with a bachelor's degree focused on the link between phenomenology and self-knowledge and a master's degree focused on the link between phenomenology and literature. During her Ph.D. study, her interest in literature has led her to approach the topic of imagination, whereas her interest in individuality has led her to approach the topic of self-shaping: these interests flow together into a project that intends to argue for the role of imaginative experiences in the process of self-shaping. Her research purports to argue that fantasy is a fundamental force that nourishes self-shaping along with two other forces that constitute pivotal keystones of the same process, namely exemplariness and repentance. This research project relies on Max Scheler's stance on personal individuality and Edmund Husserl's stance on fantasy. Her participation in international conferences has enabled her to develop the main theses underlying this project, and a research period at the Husserl Archives in Leuven (2016) enabled her to improve her knowledge of Husserl's texts and manuscripts. In Leuven she met the co-tutor of her Ph.D. thesis, Nicolas de Warren, who, along with Roberta De Monticelli as tutor, guides her through her Ph.D. thesis.

Chapter 19
On Vocation and Identity in Western Mysticism

Jana Trajtelová

Abstract This chapter concerns the meaning of identity and vocation in the experience of mystical and contemplative life. It employs various perspectives (biblical, mystical, existential, and psychological) to elucidate the investigated phenomena in their essential structures. First, we are led toward the deepest structures and constitutive movements of a human person as they are found in mysticism of Saint John of the Cross. The meaning of idolatry and possessive ways of self-appropriation are discussed. Later on, peering into the biblical experience of vocation, vocation as *telos* and orientation is demonstrated. In the process of uncovering the authentic identity, the crucial role of the mechanism of dispossession and the presence of the elusive "primordial call" is revealed. Keeping the principle of "precedence of being," personal narratives and accepted roles and functions of an individual need to remain nourished by Being in order for them to stay vocationally significant and efficient. "Vocational identity" is defined as the identity discovered, appropriated, and sustained in and through the experience of the primordial call. Mystical elusiveness proves to be the only firm standpoint for the appropriation of one's own true "self," for approaching the sense of one's true personal identity, and for discovering and developing his or her vocational dimension.

Keywords Western mysticism · Dispossession · Gift · Identity · Vocation · Idolatry · Primordial call

In my chapter, I explore the meaning of vocation and identity in religious experience, more concretely in the experience of genuine mystical and contemplative life.[1] I focus on a theistic type of mysticism or the so-called Abrahamic tradition (even

---

[1] The two coincide in essential structures and movements. Genuine mysticism leads into and involves contemplative life (contemplative consciousness); genuine contemplation leads into and uncovers the depths of mystical life. The two corroborate each other.

J. Trajtelová (✉)
Trnava University in Trnava, Trnava, Slovakia

© Springer Nature Switzerland AG 2019
O. Louchakova-Schwartz (ed.), *The Problem of Religious Experience*,
Contributions to Phenomenology 103,
https://doi.org/10.1007/978-3-030-21575-0_19

though my main mystical authors here are specific—Saint John of the Cross, Meister Eckhart). While searching for the most profound sense of personal identity, first I qualify which self-identifying experiences cannot stand as a solid base for approaching the problem of personal identity and individuation. Second, I then uncover the meaning and main constitutive aspects of vocational experience. To embrace this overly complex issue, I present several complementary perspectives that elucidate each other (like employing existential and psychological observations); however, the main experiential field is the descriptions of the mystics themselves.

19.1   Toward the Deepest Structures and Constitutive Movements of the Human Person: Experience of Mystical Life

19.1.1   Mystical Dispossession: How to Get "Everything" from "Nothing"

First of all, a genuine mystical life is a challenging existential process of profound personal *transformation.* Saint John of the Cross, a Spanish mystic of the sixteenth century, refers to this as the "dark night." Nowadays, theologians, philosophers, spiritual teachers and seekers, psychologists, and psychotherapists are rediscovering its essential and universal anthropological significance. Let me use the mystic's own terms to explain this experience (or these experiences).

Saint John of the Cross distinguishes between the active part of the night (the "night of the senses," like active asceticism) and the passive night of the spirit (mystical affliction). He understands active asceticism (the sensual night) as the preparatory stage for a truly decisive event of the dark night of the spirit, which brings the essential transformation such as a profound renewal of the personal core and a radical existential refocusing of the whole personal orientation.

Following systematically a transformative process in this mystic's writings,[2] we witness how each *relation of possession,* even the most subtle form of it, is negated (e.g., taken away): no more of *my* sensual delights, *my* good deeds and virtues, *my* intellectual abilities, *my* knowledge and judgments, *my* prayers and piety, *my* friends or enemies, *my* meaning of life, even *my* identity and *my* God. Obviously, it is not the goods themselves that are at stake here but the *mineness* in them all. As Meister Eckhart teaches, it is not things in themselves that are obstacles on the way to unity but the *me* in all these things—hence the sense of his famous "detachment"

---

[2] Saint John of the Cross has dedicated two of his major treatises to the systematic explanation of the experiences of the so-called dark night (*Ascent of Mount Carmel* and *The Dark Night*) and the other two to the mystical experiences of divine intimacy and union (*Spiritual Canticle* and *The Living Flame of Love*). The Spanish *nada* ("nothing," experienced as dispossession, distance, and affliction) and *todo* ("everything," experienced as loving, nearness, and bliss) are two complementary (rather than strictly sequential) aspects of the same mystical path.

(*Abgeschiedenheit*) (Cf. Eckhart 2016). This *dispossessive mechanism* is quite simple and reveals the existential meaning of passivity: passivity in the etymological sense of *pathos;* it has the sense of the passivity of the patient, which also means complete existential powerlessness and poverty. An unwelcome superfluity of inapprehensible meaning paralyzes the self-supporting activities of the ego. But in the affliction of the dark night, there is no enhancing self-supporting activity possible, no expectation of the redemptive meaning or relief. The mystic is left with the paralyzing, painful "nothing" (*nada*), which means a sheer dispossession, disability, and controllessness; and precisely at this point, it is hard, if not impossible, to find any mineness in the overabundance of *pathos,* of the receptive passivity of mystical affliction. Through rather a violent manner, the natural egoic activities seem to resign and are put out of play. However, the following effect is amazing: the radical experience of dispossession, for a mystic, can turn into a significant means of self-transcendence and transformation, pointing beyond, far beyond the limits of mineness set by the possessive tendencies of the untransformed self.

The essential meaning of the whole mystical process lies in the possibility to empty, to open, and to dispose a mystic for the *new way* of receptivity. Meister Eckhart presents this as a simple "mystical" principle: the more emptying, the more fulfilling. What is to be received, we can call the "gift." The gift (as opposed to "possession") is given beyond the realm of possessiveness and controllability; mystics and contemplatives insist on its principally *ungraspable* and *elusive* character.

19.2   The Meaning of the Gift

Saint John of the Cross teaches that radical dispossession radically disposes oneself for the radical gift, which is the mystical union. He says that if "the soul" were perfectly dispossessed of itself, it would "possess" "the Beloved" (God); even more, it would *be* Him as fully indrawn into loving divine communion. This is why he praises a painful process of transformation in his famous poem[3]:

> "O guiding night!
> O night more lovely than the dawn!
> O night that has united.
> the Lover with his beloved,
> transformed the beloved in her Lover.

It is important to emphasize that the transformative meaning of the mystical *nada* can emerge only within the overall perspective of loving. I showed elsewhere that precisely loving sustains the possibility of transformation through affliction.[4] Otherwise we would be dealing with a mere personal destruction and disintegration through suffering.

---

[3] John of the Cross 1991, 51.
[4] Trajtelová 2011.

Christian mystics often suggest that all the gifts that God has ever given to anyone have been given as a preparation (or disposition) for the one and only Gift—God Himself. The mystical unity is overly dynamic and creative: it is a perfect mutual giving of gifts, where the gift, the gifted, and the gift-giver coincide; where the Lover, Beloved, and Loving are almost indiscernible, and still not totalizing or being reduced to one another.

Saint John of the Cross, for example, in *The Living Flame of Love,* describes the *immediate* sharing of the Divine Life in the deepest "center" of the "soul," "touching of the bare cores."[5] Loving as "mutual substantial sharing" brings the bliss and sweetness that the mystic is trying to depict by various images, none of which is static. For John of the Cross, the perfection of divine union lies in the perfection of mutual self-offering and receiving in loving. The extent of mystical likeness and unity is the extent of the perfection of loving[6]:

> The Beloved lives in the lover and the lover in the Beloved. Love produces such likeness in this transformation of lovers that one can say each is the other and both are one. The reason is that in the union and transformation of love each gives possession of self to the other and each leaves and exchanges self for the other. Thus each one lives in the other and is the other, and both are one in the transformation of love.

Saint John of the Cross explains *divinization* (*endiosamiento*—such a brainteaser for philosophers and theologians!) with breathtaking simplicity as the perfect "passing out of self to the Beloved."[7] The meaning of this mystical *transformation* (*transformación*) is nothing other than the perfect existential conversion of the fundamental personal orientation: from the self to the Beloved, from the "possession" to the gift, from individual egoic isolation and limitations to co-creative participation in the profound interconnectedness of all created beings in and through its mysterious Divine Source.

At this point, we do not need to go into more detail with the descriptions of the highest apices of the mystical life. What I have described here is sufficient for exposing the main mechanisms that will remain in play while thinking of the problem of identity. Still, let me sketch the philosophical-anthropological basis for further considerations about the human person as opened up in the mystical life.

19.2.1 Question of the Ground

I will try to sketch briefly the mystic's description of the most intimate sphere of a human person. Perhaps needless to say, every mystic struggles with describing or conceptualizing the experience of "something" that is beyond words and concepts, even beyond any suitable image and metaphor (however helpful and necessary they

---

[5] "Toque de sustancias desnudas." Cf. San Juan de la Cruz 1993, 817.

[6] John of the Cross 1991, 518.

[7] Ibid., 578.

are for us!). By using various images and metaphors and paradoxical or contradictory expressions, they attempt to speak about the "unspeakable" and uncover what can be structurally referred to as the deepest "essential core" or "center" of a person.

Mystics claim that entering that boundless immanence (and transcendence—at the same time!) means entering the mystery of God *and* one's own true self. This deepest "ground" seems to have no "bottom" or boundaries and in no way can be understood in static terms. Let me offer few examples:

Saint John of the Cross, using traditional Christian concepts, writes: "It should be known that the Word, the Son of God, together with the Father and the Holy Spirit, is hidden by essence and his presence [*esencial y presencialmente*] in the innermost being of the soul."[8] The whole creative loving divine community (the Trinity) is essentially present in the deepest center of a human person. Elsewhere he speaks more loosely about the "most hidden dwelling" where the Beloved hides and where He wants to be found and encountered. He speaks of the "center" (*centro*), "substance" (*sustancia*), the"bottom" or "the ground of the soul" (*el fondo del alma*), "the infinite center of the substance of the soul" (*el infinito centro de la sustancia del alma*), "the living point" (*el vivo punto*) where the "living divine flame" burns, or the "center of love" (*centro del amor*). Saint John of the Cross in a very dynamic way describes the *immediate sharing of the divine life:* that is, "essential sharing," as the "touching of the bare cores" (*toque de sustancias desnudas*) in this "center of love." "Here" the lovers play "the tender games of love"; here "the divine fire sweetly burns"; here one comes to the "mutual co-breathing" where the Breath is the divine Loving itself. All the mystic's descriptions are strikingly dynamic, and they all are expressing something of the ever-creative movement of the lifegiving divine life within the person's most intimate "core."[9]

In her study on the mysticism of Saint John of the Cross, Edith Stein comments on the mystic's "center of the soul" in traditional terms as the sheer dimension of spirit that is beyond any form, image, or concept, freed from any determinations of the natural psychophysical life, and that must be the very source of all unique personal life and freedom. She continues by saying that only from this deepest interiority we can truly comprehend and justly evaluate our own being and understand or appropriate the uniqueness of our personal vocation.[10] Similarly, Thomas Merton often emphasizes that entering into unity with God means entering one's own identity in the sense of his or her vocation. He adds that this "vocational identity" (my

---

[8] Ibid., 480.

[9] Cf. Meister Eckhart using the famous image of eternally bearing God's own Son in the center of one's soul and the eternal bearing of "myself" as God's own Son. Johannes Tauler speaks of the divine ground in the depths of the soul and employs the compelling metaphor of the abyss— "Abyssus abyssum invocat" ("Der Abgrund ruft dem Abgrund," "Abyss calls out to abyss," Ps 41:8)—to express the intimate union of the created and uncreated "longing" and their intimate mutual communication and loving interchange. He speaks similarly of the Eckhartian "sparking" (*funken*) that is bursting into a fire of longing for God and is the creative divine Longing itself.

[10] Cf. Stein 2003.

term) seems to be unique but is never a private matter and always has much broader impact (Merton 1972, 65–66):

> One of the paradoxes of the mystical life is this: that a man cannot enter into the deepest center of himself and pass through that center into God, unless he is able to pass entirely out of himself and empty himself and give himself to other people in the purity of a selfless love. ... The more we are one with God, the more we are united with one another.

My point in recounting all these experiential insights is to show that the most intimate immanence of a person cannot be at all qualified as ontological stillness or isolation; rather, it can be qualified as having *transsubjective, dynamic, creative,* and *elusive* character and efficacy. The deepest sense of personal identity must be sought here.

19.2.2 The Meaning of Idolatry

To proceed further with the identity issue, let me link the previous exposition with the theological and philosophical question of idolatry. In what follows, I will sketch four interrelated perspectives.

1. Going back to biblical experience, idolatry refers to worshipping false gods or gods made up for the sake of worship ("make us a god who would walk before us" Ex 32:1). The idol is a man-made construct, *maase jad haádám* ("work of the hands of man"), representing certain supernatural powers and services. Prophets constantly warn of serving idols—false gods, man-made illusions of the real. The French theologian and philosopher Tresmontant suitably defines idolatry as the "ontological fallacy," "ontological mistake," or "ontological deceit"[11]—as the misunderstanding and misuse of the beings in their proper identity and order. However, idols are easy to be reached for and possessed, easily visible, well-defined, exclusively and exhaustibly given: they have their names, characters, stories, and functions (unlike *Yahve*, The One Who *Is*, whose name is so sacred that it cannot even be uttered and whose image cannot be made).

2. This mechanism is brought into view in the mystical experience of *dispossession* (above). The mystic is led to abandon every subtle mineness, every subtle subjective construction that he tended to impose on the meaning of things and events and thus contaminate and obscure the reality as it is in itself. The simple mystical imperative of dispossession speaks of the biblical destruction of idols, including the images of God or oneself. In this sense Eckhart speaks provocatively of abandoning God for the sake of God. *Stagnation, fixation, mortification* of meanings or attachment to an *exclusive* meaning are all signs of idolatrous possessive grasp, ontological perversion, counteracting the free-flowing character of the gift. The unbound, creative, all-permeating "flowing" of the divine mystery, according to mystics, is principally elusive—when it comes to a possessive

---

[11] Cf. Tresmontant 1953.

grasp, it is experienced as an *elusiveness* itself. This is what I try to allude to with the term "elusiveness."[12]

3. In terms of intentionality, the idolatrous possessive movement is principally self-referential. That is why by the *ego* we can understand primarily the centered accumulation or density of self-concerned and self-absorbed intentionality that, given the sustaining aspect of psychological time (personal narrative), creates the isolated, self-oriented illusion of personal identity. On the contrary, genuinely *transcending intentionality* aims always at otherness, outside or *beyond* the isolated self-referential circle in which untransformed consciousness usually gets trapped, and thus opens and liberates it. That is why Frankl recognizes every truly transpersonal mode of attention or any other-than-myself directedness of intentionality as the basic human mode of transcendence.[13]

4. Philosophically, the simple mechanism of idolatry can be found arising with objectifying thinking, "reflexive ego-awareness."[14] The "Cartesian" thought reaches for God, for the other or oneself as for an "object," and so *loses immediate connection* with Being, and all that it gets are its own conceptual constructs deepening the separation from the real: thinking mirrors only itself. That is why "Cartesian" consciousness remains imprisoned in itself: there can be no real transcendence.[15] This is the main point that Jaspers, Marcel, Levinas, or Marion articulated in their several ways with philosophical mastery. That is why Merton claims that in order to liberate (transform) our consciousness, we need to lose our cultural and religious identities, all our "untrue" selves.[16] "The tragedy is that our consciousness is totally alienated from this inmost ground of our identity."[17]

---

[12] Mystics and contemplatives are able to execute radically a type of "egoic reduction"—the reduction of mineness normally imposed on phenomena. This is the meaning of all meditative and contemplative praxis, too: to learn to see the "things themselves." There is no imposition of the possessive self on the phenomena, no arbitrary restriction of their sense to my sense: hence the meaning of Eckhart's *Abgeschiedenheit* ("detachment") or of the way of *nada* ("nothing") advised by John of the Cross: that is, the sense of self-abandonment as the most well-known religious imperative. That is why the contemplative consciousness is alert, open, and integrated; subjective constructions set upon reality are recognized and abandoned.

[13] These observations are based loosely on Frankl's pondering on intentionality and transcendence; for an example, see Frankl and Lapide 2005.

[14] Cf. Merton 1968, 27.

[15] Ibid,. 23.

[16] Thomas Merton speaks about contemplative consciousness, which goes beyond the "social and cultural self" and which is the "ground of openness" (ibid., 25). That is why Zen, for Merton, is only the radical consequence of the spiritual claim of dispossession. "Zen is consciousness unstructured by particular form or particular system, a trans-cultural, trans-religious, trans-formed consciousness. It is therefore in a sense ´void.´ But it can shine through this or that system, religious or irreligious, just as light can shine through glass that is blue, or green, or red, or yellow" (ibid., 4). For Sufis, *fana* demands also such "extinction of social and cultural self, which would be determined by the structural form of religious customs" (ibid., 5).

[17] Ibid., 12. Christian tradition speaks here in terms of "original sin" or "fall."

19.2.3   Possessive Ways of Self-Appropriation

It is clear now that the same claim of breaking off with idols applies for the issue of self-identification and personal identity. Let me develop the theme further with several useful concretizations; these should highlight the "commonality" and great practicality of mystical insights in our everyday lives.

At this juncture I will mention observations of the psychiatrist Gerald G. May, who was trying to set the foundations for what he called "contemplative psychology."[18] I find his observations relevant and useful for understanding the close connection between the timeless teaching of mystics and psychology's search for the "key" to mental health and personal wholeness, which philosophically points to (ontologically relevant) constitutive structures of a human person.

May explains that the way of appropriating one's individual identity possessively is at the basis of the "natural" mechanism of addiction.[19] In the new light that modern psychology and neurology have shed on attachments and addictions, given his own therapeutic experiences with addicts, he recognizes striking similarities between addictive comportment (and its treatment) and the teaching of the dark night by Saint John of the Cross (May 2004). The sixteenth-century mystic revealed and described roots and structures of the enslavements of the addicted mind and offered the way of "healing," which he himself went through.[20]

For us, the most interesting of May's recognitions is that one of the strongest attachments containing a heavy addiction mechanism is an attachment to mental images that we sustain about ourselves in our search for self-definition and self-assertion. May recognizes various forms of self-identification and describes their

---

[18] May (1982, 27; also chap. 2) reconnects the science of "psyche" and traditional wisdom, and applies the research in therapeutic praxis: "A contemplative psychology is an approach to human experience that maintains that wisdom depends upon a full cooperation of all ways of knowing: Observation, logical inference, behavioral learning, and intuition. It acknowledges that the purest form of knowing is intuition and it seeks to expand the innate human capacity for intuitive perception. The goal of a contemplative psychology is not the separate autonomy of the individual but the realization of tone's essential rootedness in God and relatedness in creation. Its means are not willful mastery but willing surrender. Its resources lie in the comparison of spiritual traditions of both East and West. And its laboratory is the stillness of the human mind in silence." May himself experienced much suffering and was traumatized by his service during the war in Vietnam. He was known for his gentle spirit and his own inexhaustible spiritual search and yearning. For most of his life, he was working as a therapist of the worst kinds of addictions.

[19] The complex mechanisms of addiction he observes closely in his book *Addiction and Grace* (2007) from psychological, neurological, and theological points of view. These mechanisms, biologically necessary and good, become problematic when it comes to specifically human personal growth (May 2007).

[20] The liberating aspect of suffering through acceptance and loving was pointed out also in the writings of the Austrian psychiatrist V. E. Frankl or of the theologian P. Tillich (1952). Speaking about compulsory thinking and behavior, about compulsory emotional responses, is only another way of expressing the same addictive mechanism of mind processes and patterns (which can grow pathologically into neurosis or other psychic disorders, especially when it regards self-definition and self-assertion).

inherent mechanism and persistence. He defines an "idol" as a mental image taken exhaustively *as* reality and not only as image (normally because it is psychologically safer, because our representations of reality are relatively controllable). May (1982, 111) says: "If we are relatively free from mistaking image for reality in other areas, we at least idolize our self-images. When I speak of myself I am almost always referring to the image I have of myself, and I habitually assume that I am talking about something solid and objectifiable."[21] Self-image, May reminds us, is a product of the "dualistic," objectifying mind. It is constructed by the reflective act of self-definition, which is a "specific mental process that occurs whenever one does, thinks, or senses something that differentiates oneself from the rest of the world."[22] Experiences opposed to this would be unifying contemplative awareness and, in the extreme, the mystical states of nonduality.

"Self-image is the product of a complex process of self-definition associated with one's sense of body, of will, of relationship with others, and of desire or aspiration. It includes intricate combinations of memories and behavior patterns, habits and needs—everything that one could use to describe or characterize oneself."[23] Self-image is always connected with the image of the world that the person appropriates, including the highest personal ideals and values. When an essential part of a self-image is threatened, all the habitual (addicted) ways in which one views and comports oneself are endangered. Loosely in Frankl's (1950) words: when a relative meaning that was absolutized in person's life is perishing or lost, it is usually personally and psychologically devastating—for instance, the absolutized meaning made a great part of one's identity.

Indeed, May's therapeutic praxis and his own experiences taught him that breaking off from this attachment is most painful; the egoic mind cannot bear facing the "nothing" of what is left of oneself, of one's putative identity (literally no-thing: e.g., beyond the reach of objectification). Let us recall how Saint John of the Cross

---

[21] May 1982, 111.

[22] He goes on to clarify that "self-image is an ongoing composite of conscious and unconscious conceptions and feeling-tones that are identified as the sense of 'me.' Self-definition can occur without bringing self-image into awareness, but reflection on self-image always involves self-definition" (ibid., 334).

[23] Ibid., 101:
The act of self-definition constantly creates self-image, which has four fundamental components:

- Body: the image we have of our physiques, combined with the sense of being "in" our bodies and the perception of our geographical location in relation to "other" people and things.
- Will: the sense of volition, how we manage ourselves and our lives; our perceptions of what we can and cannot control in ourselves and in the environment.
- Desire: what characteristically attracts and repels us; the things we hope for and the things we fear; what gives us pleasure and pain.
- Relationship: our basic sense of alone-ness or together-ness; our confidence and fear with others; our sense of relatedness to other people, society, and the world and cosmos around us.

These four components, with various refinements and elaborations, make up that complicated and intricate mental production called self-image (ibid., 104).

writes about the worst point of the "night," "mystical death": the terrible undoing (*deshacimiento*)[24] "in its [the soul's [very substance" and the purification of the very "roots of the soul."[25] May uncovers the deeply rooted fear of the loss of self-definition. For the naturally self-centered self, every collapse of self-image is a real, painful death (comparable to, for example, ending up with a serious life-endangering addiction such as on drugs or in an emotionally abusive relationship). However, for the deeper, vocational sense of self, true self, it is the most liberating movement.

Of course, we normally approach ourselves through self-images, and in everyday life it is quite effective and necessary; it is the practical way we are in the world and the main way for coping with it. One can define oneself as a good citizen, faithful believer, good teacher, or successful writer, devoted lover, caring partner, loving father or mother, or even as a zealous or detached spiritual seeker. And he or she, in a certain sense, really "is" all this. The problem arises when the image, which plays an essential part in self-identification (given aspirations, desires, or values of a person), is threatened, since the complete identification with the role, with one's own conceptual image of oneself, was made; when the psychological (individual and cultural) conditioning, which we normally use for coping in our habitual or obsessive ways of behaving and thinking, becomes questioned, ineffective, or out of play. And it is precisely the point of all contemplative praxis: to learn to let them go, to "see" the *real* beyond the mental constructions, to hear the stillness beyond the mental noise, to transcend one's own mind's conditionings, within which the self-definitions are created.[26]

After reducing all the conditioned forms of self-identification, is there anything left of a "person"? May says yes, and "if one could but give up the struggle for self-definition, being would spring forth in fullness and truth."[27] Mystical and contemplative experience suggests that precisely through this loss of self-definition one can glimpse the unconditioned, most profound sense of his or her identity. There seems to be *something* more permanent and truly essential, whence a true identity of a person may arise (if identity is a proper word at all)—unlike everything that social and relational constellations can provide.[28]

---

[24] John of the Cross 1993, 532.

[25] "When this purgative contemplation oppresses a soul, it feels very vividly indeed the shadow of death, the sighs of death, and the sorrows of hell, all of which reflect the feeling of God's absence, of being chastised and rejected by him, and of being unworthy of him, as well as the object of his anger. The soul experiences all this and even more, for now it seems that this affliction will last forever" (John of the Cross 1991, 404).

[26] "Contemplation is the highest expression of man's intellectual and spiritual life. It is that life itself, fully awake, fully active, fully aware that it is alive.. .. It is a vivid realization of the fact that life and being in us proceed from an invisible, transcendent and infinitely abundant Source. Contemplation is, above all, awareness of the reality of that Source" (Merton 1972, 1).

[27] May 1977, 11.

[28] Zen tradition speaks about an emptiness and a "mirror." "The trouble is that as long as you are given to distinguishing, judging, categorizing and classifying—or even contemplating—you are superimposing something else on the pure mirror" (Merton 1968, 7). Merton discusses here Daisetz T. Suzuki's view on Meister Eckhart: "In any case this passage reflects Eckhart's Zen-like

19.3 Experience of Vocation

Until this point, it has seemed easier to approach the deepest meaning of identity of a person in a negative way: what it is *not*, what does *not* essentially constitute it. Self-images and related personal narratives dependent on external circumstances, according to mystics, are not who one most deeply *is*.

And still, even the self-appropriations via our personal narratives cannot claim to be completely irrelevant, which is more obvious (or emphasized) in the Western tradition. Again, the situation seems much more complex and needs to employ another significant religious experience, the experience of *vocation*. Taking into account the experience of the *call* in the following, I will try to elucidate the complexity of dynamics of personal identity in mystical and contemplative experience.

19.3.1 Vocation as Telos and Orientation

Steinbock in his article "Phenomenology of Vocations" (2016) rightly notes that the question of personal identity is rooted in vocational experience.[29] Without it, the philosophical account of the problem remains incomplete or necessarily stays at the surface of our experience of ourselves (I as a construct of a mere narration, no-self doctrines, for example). To open a complex meaning of this experience, let us turn first again to traditional biblical expressions of it, following its philosophical implications. The English word "call," or "calling," serves as the eloquent equivalent of the term "vocation." The Latin *vox* ("voice"), *vocare* ("to call"), *vocatus* ("called") stand at the root of the English word. From the early fifteenth century it was intended to express a "spiritual calling," "consecration" (in the sense of a divine call to a religious life). Only later did it appear in its secularized form to express a personal devotion to a certain occupation or profession.

Within this tradition, we can recall the theological and philosophical meaning of well-known biblical stories like the call of Abraham, Samuel, and other prophets. Here we would need to speak at great length about the philosophical significance of the *call-response structure*, and we would need to consider the philosophical

---

equation of God as infinite abyss and ground (cf. Sunyata), with the true being of the self grounded in Him; hence it is that Eckhart believes: only when there is no self left as a 'place' in which God acts, only when God acts purely in himself, do we at last recover our 'true self' (in terms of Zen, 'no-self')" Cf. ibid., 10.

[29] Anthony Steinbock's phenomenological investigation into the meaning of vocational experience (Cf. Steinbock 2016) carefully maps the broad problem field. He recognizes the specific experiential structures and essential distinctions among various phenomena that—in common experience and common language—are commonly (and rather misleadingly) aligned with the phenomenon of vocation itself. These distinctions are essential for the recognition of the genuine meaning and constitutive aspects of this specific human experience.

meaning of a personal name /and the divine Name Yahve / ("I have called you by name; you are mine" Is 43:1). I only briefly recall the most relevant implications.

It is important to note that the Abrahamic religious experience includes uniqueness and diversity in its specific sense of identity and vocation (as is obvious even in such doctrinally unbounded authors as Thomas Merton).[30] Inspired by Tresmontant (1953), we can loosely interpret the call of Abraham as the call to genuine and creative (self)-transcendence of a person. The call represents here an *invitation to transcend,* first of all *oneself:* to step out of an anonymity without name, home, meaning of life, identity; to step out of individual and cultural predeterminations; to step out of the "mythical" and its determining pregiven meaning; to abandon all the self-constructed idols. The call includes the constant invitation to self-transcendence and transformation (dispossession).

The call gives the called a proper name and points toward the peculiar, *unique* meaning of an individual existence, always in interconnectedness with a broader interpersonal community. The call moves him or her forward throughout the individual and collective historicity toward the open future. (*History* is not a mere arbitrary *narration* any more but discovers its *telos,* its essential orientation and deeper meaning.)

The significance of the "name" embraces both the following attributes. First, the *perfection (wholeness) of individual uniqueness and concreteness of the person* (in flesh and blood, not as a mere mysterious or vague "spiritual substance") in his or her fullest possible actualization or realization; it is being actualized in and as a free co-creation within the dynamic relation with God and in unity with Him. Second, his or her *unique external narrative* or "mission" (and its unique *telos*), which bears a deeper *transformative* meaning for the person *and* for wider community (see the story of Jonah), and which is to be accomplished in a way that only she or he can accomplish. In this way, the individual uniqueness enters history and co-creates the broader generative context.

Vocational experience is never aimless or inert. It has its *telos,* sets the unique personal orientation, and bears a great creative potential. The very notion of the "call" refers to a movement, event, dynamism, teleology; it is quite the opposite of emptiness, inertia, or dissolving stillness. For the mystics, the call emerges from the deepest "center," which is qualified rather with ceaseless though peaceful dynamics of the overflowing creative emergence of Divine Being (as Loving).

---

[30] "A tree gives glory to God by being a tree," writes Thomas Merton, claiming that the perfection of creation lies precisely in the uniqueness of the individual identity of each particular created being. "This leaf has its own texture and its own pattern of veins and its own holy shape, and the bass and trout hiding in the deep pools of the river are canonized by their beauty and their strength. …The great, gashed, half-naked mountain is another of God's saints. There is no other like him" (Merton 1972, 29–30).

19.3.2   Vocation as the Primordial Call and the Precedence of Being

It seems that there is an even deeper, *foundational* "layer" of the meaning of the vocation than the one that is expressed in an experience of being called to action, or even in discovering one's own unique life orientation, appropriating the personal life-meaning and *telos*. Let us try to look closer at how these, including the individual narratives or the external roles, relate to the bare, imageless sense of the self that I have previously emphasized.

When we commonly speak about "vocation," we usually think about a certain specific life task, deed, or work for the goodness of oneself or the community, or some specific way of life (e.g., being a monk or eremite). But this is precisely the point, in my view, that can be misleading, obscuring the real meaning of vocation and the relation between our external identities and the deepest self.

If we turn our attention to the mystics again, we will find that the profound *call* they experienced within all their lives was first of all *not* a call to *do* something but a call to *be* (using more Eckhartian terminology). In other words, it is not what one does that is so important but *how* one *is*. The individual search for vocation is a search not for the *what of doing* but for the *how of being*.[31]

Mentioning the "call to be," or the "call to love," we hit a whole new, broad area essentially relevant for our problematics, reaching to the profound dimensions of a *divine calling:* the phenomenon of *desire* and what I term *primordial call* or *primordial vocation*. All the actions God takes in a person's life story are taken only for the one and only Act—God's own loving self-offering and self-surrendering. For the mystics, this is the definite *telos* of desire and the whole transformational process. Everything else seems to be just additional. *The deepest unity with the Source of Being is the "foundational center" of any unique personal vocational experience.*

I showed before that *Being* here must be understood in a very dynamic, creative, and transpersonal way: *being* as *becoming*, as a creation and co-creation constantly

---

[31] From the perspective of phenomena, the "how of being" implies also the "how of seeing." Living out of the deepest vocational dimension brings one liberation for the world and the things themselves in their peculiar identities (contemplative consciousness). By contrast, living out of one's restricted possessive self means not only to blur or obstruct one's own vocational possibilities but also to restrict the identity of things to one's own possessive demands, mirroring mineness in and through them. Only the free, open, inclusive contemplative view can really "see" and appreciate the things *as what they are themselves* and *as they are meant to be;* in this sense it is also legitimate to speak about a unique *vocational identity* of each finite being. Everything has its unique place in the order of being; everything in its own unique peculiar way radiates the "breath of its Creator."

Thinking over and explaining Anthony Steinbock's notion of de-limitation (cf. Trajtelová 2014, 131–159), I showed elsewhere how the subjective impositions of sense "limit" phenomena so that they are disabled, unable to reveal themselves in their original *specificity* as what they are themselves *and* as they are originally *more* than themselves (*as de-limited*) while they point iconically beyond themselves precisely *through being what they are*. Contemplative consciousness is always opened for "more" of phenomena and refers to their original *polysemy* (e.g., phenomena as having open "iconic" character with possibly inexhaustible creative emergence of sense emerging precisely through their specificity, distinctiveness, and uniqueness).

bursting forth. It seems to coincidence. The Sacred Name in Hebrew also refers to this unceasing creative dynamics of the divine life itself (*Ehyeh Asher Ehyeh,* Ex 3:14—from the verb *hayah,* usually translated "to be" but more properly "to be becoming"). The turn toward the *precedence of being*, the turn toward the ground of loving, is itself recognized by mystics as the *primordial call*.

Being a teacher, a philosopher, a painter, or a mother can in itself remain peripheral to who we really are (independently of the inherent interpersonal value these have in themselves), and it does, unless these roles are freely lived out of the Source of all being, doing, and goodness. Every life-enhancing, truly creative *doing bursts out of being*, not the other way round. Only such doing bears the genuine vocational impact and becomes generatively relevant, like standing up for justice (for example, as Martin Luther King, Jr.) or serving the poorest (for example, as Mother Teresa).[32] Even more, anything that a person would do out of her or his vocational dimension has itself vocational significance and weight (even the "pots and pans" for Saint Teresa of Avila may become the vocation for that particular present moment). Every single life event, however ordinary, can become vocationally relevant.

Then, the meaning of the personal vocation points to the *primordial call,* which is to be, as the *infinite claim,* creatively realized within the finite, restricted life conditions of an individual. The primordial call is the heart of all creative vocational potential; it shapes and guides the unique personal *telos* and orientation. Primordial calling is realized within the concrete individual, cultural, and historical conditions, realized *in* and *through* and *as* the complete uniqueness of an individual person (e.g., the complete individual incarnation of the divine perfection).

The deeper the union, the more external contexts, roles, or narratives become the *essential* means of and for the realization of the infinite claim. The life paths we choose, the functions we accept, and the roles we appropriate bear the real vocational significance—without ever being identified (attached) to them (and precisely because of not being idolatrously identified with them). In this way, the roles become not limiting and restricting any longer but instead enabling, opening, enhancing, nourishing the vocational experience; they become irreplaceable means for authentic social communication and interpersonal loving. Only thus (as we see in the lives of mystics, contemplatives, artists, true reformers, or genuine lovers) is the infinite claim realized within the finite restrictions in an infinitely creative and unbounding way.

---

[32] However, even deeds, styles, or comportment can, in turn, sustain the vocational orientation. For someone, going to a monastery or developing painting techniques can provide nourishing conditions for evolving her or his vocational identity. Nevertheless, living in a monastery or being a painter would be a matter not of mere doing but of a peculiar and integrated way of being, and is still expressive of who the person is (not what the person does). Being a painter, then, points not to doing but toward a personally unique kind of relating to and expressing of reality—in a way that no one else does or can express—which also means a unique revelation of the Divine: hence the unique co-creation. (This was depicted with mastery in Tarkovsky's film character Andrei Rublev, and in a "negative way" in his counterfeit, prideful Kirill, who stressed "doing," external identity, self-image, and self-importance (Cf. Trajtelová and Steinbock 2016).

According to the mystics, this is the universal meaning of vocation for each human person—to *be* freely (consciously) an essential constituent of co-creation in an absolutely unique, profoundly personal way, reconnecting the others and the world with the unifying Divine Source.

19.4   Conclusion

Below I summarize ten essential points related to the authentic process of appropriating personal identity according to examples found in the contemplative and mystical life.

1. The deepest sense of who one is cannot be derived from externally played roles, and it has nothing to do with self-images and self-definitions. In order to reach the deepest sense of identity, one has to lose and transcend all these.
2. The general mechanism of mystical dispossession must be applied to how a person relates to herself or himself. The rule of idollessness first of all holds for our self-images and arbitrary "identities" (e.g., attachments to our personal situational roles, social statuses, professions, religious or political beliefs, ideologies, and so on).
3. A genuine personal identity, its most profound sense, is revealed "from inside out" (and not the reverse): that is, out of the "deepest core" of the personal life.
4. In the deepest dimensions of a person there is nothing to grasp onto: only creative transsubjective dynamics of the ever-elusive emergence of Divine Being (Loving), which is the source of the most profound vocational experience, of the primordial call.
5. Vocational identity is the identity discovered, appropriated, and sustained in and through the experience of the primordial call.
6. The primordial call is foundational for all the other external vocational "specifications."
7. Vocational experience implies a unique personal orientation and bears a great creative potential, which is realized "from inside out" (radiating from the Source) as a free co-creation in an absolutely unique, profoundly personal way. The infinite claim is creatively realized within the finite, restricted cultural and historical conditions of an individual (via his or her personal narrative).
8. Keeping the principle of "precedence of being over doing," personal narratives and accepted roles and functions must be nourished by and rooted in Being in order for them to stay vocationally significant and efficient. Cut from the Source, they fall back to *mere* narratives and roles.
9. Experienced as the gift, arising out of the ungraspable free dynamics of the most intimate immanence of the person, vocational identity can never be closely defined, limited, or restricted in any arbitrary subjective manner. Similarly, vocation can never be exhaustibly apprehended or accomplished. The slightest arbitrary fixation of sense, holding on to self-made self-images or

accomplishments, would already mean withdrawing from or missing one's vocational orientation. It remains ever open and elusive.

10. Mystical elusiveness is paradoxically the only genuine and firm standpoint for the appropriation of one's own true "self," for approaching the sense of one's true personal identity, and for discovering and developing his or her vocational dimension (vocational identity).[33]

References

Frankl, V.E. 1950. *Homo patiens: Versuch einer Pathodizee*. Vienna: Deuticke.
Frankl, V.E., and P. Lapide. 2005. *Gottsuche und Sinnfrage: Ein Gespräch*. Munich: Gütersloher Verlagshaus.
John of the Cross. 1991. *The collected works of St. John of the Cross*. ed. K. Kavanaugh and O. Rodríguez. Washington, DC: Institute of Carmelite Studies.
———. [Juan de la Cruz.]. 1993. *Obras completas*. Burgos: Editorial Monte Carmelo.
May, G.G. 1977. *The open way*. New York: Paulist Press.
———. 1982. *Will and spirit: A contemplative psychology*. New York: HarperCollins.
———. 2004. *The dark night of the soul: A psychiatrist explores the connection between darkness and spiritual growth*. New York: HarperCollins.
———. 2007. *Addiction and grace: Love and spirituality in the healing of addictions*. New York: HarperCollins.
Meister Eckhart. 2016. Reden der Unterscheidunge. In *Meister Eckharts Reden der Unterscheidung*, ed. Ernst Diederichs. Berlin: De Gruyter.
Merton, T. 1968. *Zen and the birds of appetite*. New York: New Directions.
———. 1972. *New seeds of contemplation*. New York: New Directions.
Stein, E. 2003. The science of the Cross, vol. 6 of L. Gelber, ed. The collected works of Edith *Stein*. Washington, DC: ICS Publications.
Steinbock, A.J. 2016. Phenomenology of vocations. In *The yearbook on history and interpretation of phenomenology, 2016: Vocations, social identities, spirituality; phenomenological perspectives*, ed. J. Trajtelová, 17–46. Frankfurt a.M.: Peter Lang.
Tillich, P. 1952. *The courage to be*. New Haven: Yale University Press.
Trajtelová, J. 2011. *Vzdialenosť a blízkosť mystiky: Fenomenologická štúdia fundamentálnych pohybov v mystike západnej tradície* [The distance and proximity of mysticism: A phenomenological study of fundamental movements in the mysticism of Western tradition.]. Trnava: Filozofická Fakulta Trnavskej Univerzity.
———. 2014. On verticality and de-limitation. In *The yearbook on history and interpretation of phenomenology, 2014: Normativity and typification,* ed. J. Trajtelová, 131–159. Frankfurt a.M: Peter Lang.
Trajtelová, J., and A.J. Steinbock. 2016. Transcendence as creativity: Vocation in Andrei Tarkovsky. In *The yearbook on history and interpretation of phenomenology, 2016: Vocations, social identities, spirituality; phenomenological perspectives,* ed. J. Trajtelová, 125–159. Frankfurt a.M.: Peter Lang.
Tresmontant, C. 1953. *Essai sur la pensée hébraique*. Paris: Ed. du Cerf.

[33] I would like to thank to The Society for the Phenomenology of Religious Experience (SOPHERE) for their kind financial support for the publication of this chapter.

Jana Trajtelová, PhD., works as a Scholarly Assistant at the Department of Philosophy, Faculty of Philosophy and Arts at Trnava University in Trnava, Slovakia. Her main area of specialization is Phenomenology, Philosophical Antropology and Philosophy of Religion. She is a member of the Center for Phenomenological Studies at the Department of Philosophy, Trnava University and the main editor of *The Yearbook on History and Interpretation of Phenomenology*. In 2011 she has published a book on the phenomenology of mysticism, more concretely of the mystical experience of John of the Cross and Meister Eckhart (*Distance and Proximity of Mysticism: Phenomenological Study of Fundamental Movements in Traditional Western Mysticism,* 2011). She has written on "*Ways of intersubjectivity and interpersonality in A. J. Steinbock*" as a part of the book *From Intersubjectivity to Interpersonality* (2014). She is the co-translator of Anthony Steinbock's book *Home and Beyond: Generative Phenomenology after Husserl* into Slovak (Domáce a cudzie: Generatívna fenomenológia a Husserl, 2013).

Chapter 20
Religious Experience and the Practice of Psychology: Commentary on Part 4

Olga Louchakova-Schwartz

Abstract This concluding section to Part 4 of the book *The Problem of Religious Experience: Case Studies in Phenomenology* discusses the relationship between the descriptive phenomenological research of the meaning of religious experience and the practice of psychotherapy. It is shown that phenomenological findings present the essential meaning-structure of religious experience in a holistic matter: that is, in irreducible lived connections with other aspects of the mind, as well as in the transformative impact of experience on the self. Bellini's research of repentance, and Trajtelová's research of mystical identity in Part 4 are juxtaposed with psychology's attitudes to phenomenology and religious experience, suggesting that psychology represents its own finite province of meaning, which in its highly pragmatic orientation is distinct from the emancipatory finite province of meaning that is religion. Nevertheless, opening the boundaries and admitting the phenomenological clarifications of religious experience into psychology would enhance the latter's diagnostic and healing potential.

Keywords Religious experience · Psychology · Descriptive phenomenology · Repentance · Vocation · Personal growth

Two papers in Part 4, by Bellini and Trajtelová, resonate with Steinbock's (2007) phenomenological mapping of the complex architectonics of meaning associated with religious experience in Islamic, Christian, and Jewish mysticism. Many theoretical contributions of Steinbock's approach are well described (see Trajtelová 2011, 2014; Davis 2012; Alvis 2017), and so I'd like to focus on the pragmatic

O. Louchakova-Schwartz (✉)
Jesuit School of Theology of Santa Clara University, Graduate Theological Union, Berkeley, CA, USA

University of California, Davis, CA, USA

© Springer Nature Switzerland AG 2019
O. Louchakova-Schwartz (ed.), *The Problem of Religious Experience*,
Contributions to Phenomenology 103,
https://doi.org/10.1007/978-3-030-21575-0_20

aspect of the findings by Bellini and Trajtelová, as to whether they can be used in the clinical practice of psychology. This appears to be a natural fit: written in the classical phenomenological manner, both papers outline the structures of meaning in the psychological immanent sphere. However, both authors are very clear that they study specific forms of religious experiencing. Accordingly their investigations do not remain limited to the psychological immanent sphere but also reach into another of sphere of inner life, namely the religious sphere of transimmanence. Bellini's description of the "turning to God" and "turning to oneself" (cf. "the self-interiorizing of subjectivity," which I discussed above in Chap. 6, the Commentary on Part 1) and Trajtelová's examinations of the self both refer to processes in this transimmanent sphere. As is expected on the basis of researches done by Dahl (2010) and Barber (2017, also in Part 2 of this book), the two spheres of experience overlap and are transparent to each other. Both chapters utilize a descriptive phenomenological method, at times reaching into the genetic (temporal) and passive dimensions of constitutive analyses when the nature of their investigations requires it. Bellini uncovers the essential generalizable structure of repentance in the traditional philosophical first-person approach. By contrast, Trajtelová uses meta-analyses of the textual evidence that reference first-person experiences. A resonance between their findings shows that the two approaches are basically compatible. Finding that repentance exists in a temporally extended constitutive connection with mercy and forgiveness, Bellini opens the door for future investigations of emotions in the context of temporal psychological transitions of subjectivity. (Cf. de Warren 2009.) All such findings and many others in these richly innovative papers would be of use both to psychotherapists in clinical practice (cf. Properzi 2012) and to theoretical and philosophical psychologists interested in the development of theories of psychological subjectivity.

However, constraints arise. Drawing on the evidential force of experience, both chapters are phenomenological in their theoretical orientation. For example, Bellini anchors her thoroughly designed justifications (i.e., claims to truth) in the work of Scheller, De Monticelli, Ingarden, Hartman's analysis of ethics, de Warren's analyses of Husserl's theory of time, and other theorists central to the tradition of phenomenological philosophy. By contrast, and as is well known, psychology and psychotherapy ground themselves in empiricism. The evidence-based model, a magical mantra of clinical psychology for the last two decades, requires that "the practices of scientific psychology … [should] assume that objectivity is desirable, even if not completely possible, and that subjectivity is a source of bias that must be minimized or eliminated" (Gough and Madill 2012).

This suggests two things. First, it means that a scholar-practitioner in psychology should rely on evidence obtained in theory-laden, mostly experimental research designs centered around aprioristically identified variables—an approach that seems very rational but is de facto in hidden ways doxastic. (Cf. Goldman and Blanchard 2018; Jones 2003.) Doxastic aspects implicit in the reduction of psychology to natural science have been critiqued many times (e.g., in positive psychology, Peterson 2009; by Brentano, Feest 2014) as follows (Fuller 2013, 433):

...[they] lack the auxiliary assumptions that would warrant making a generalization about the clinical effectiveness...[and the] use of simple induction, while ignoring important inferential gaps. Future... [research] should aspire to be well-reasoned rather than simply evidence-based; argue from a plurality of evidence; be wary of hasty inductions; appropriately limit the scope of their recommendations; and avoid making law-like, prescriptive generalizations.

Second, in the statement quoted above from Gough and Madill (2012, who are actually critical of the position cited), "objectivity" is used in place of "epistemic validity," and "subjectivity" is used in place of "bad research." Correctly stated, this should say: "the practices of scientific psychology ... [should] assume that epistemic validity is desirable, even if not completely possible, and that bad research must be minimized or eliminated." But confusion reigns, and the call to eliminate bad research becomes a call to eliminate subjective perspectives, whereby in the next step "subjective perspectives" become "subjectivity," which should also be eliminated. This rebounds as elimination of *the living subjectivity of the subject* from most of psychological thinking and practice (with the exclusion of existential-humanistic psychology and related perspectives).

Of course, descriptive phenomenology exercised its modest but tangible influence on practices of mental health.[1] But the translation of phenomenology's findings into common sense, ordinary language has been a problem early on (Osborn 1934), and so psychology developed a "phenomophobia" (Smith 2012). Phenomenology has been accused of arrogance (Flakne 2017), idealism (Hösle 2017), excessive theorizing (Gasché 2017), of being devoid of foundation (Migasiński 2003), of solipsism (Hutcheson 1981), of Cartesian dualism (Jopling 1996), and of other sins, possibly mortal. Philosophers fired back with criticism (e.g., famously, Wittgenstein) of the "conceptual confusion and barrenness" (García-Prada 1990) of psychology that sacrificed essential philosophical agendas to the need to be institutionalized and more and more hounded by growing efforts of self-definition.

My sincere hope is that the value of the findings in Part 4, and in the present book overall, outweighs interdisciplinary tensions. A holistic picture of the mind delivered by phenomenological research is not reachable by methods that reduce cognition to a registry of variables. For example, Bellini shows repentance as an overall condition of the self, in irreducible interrelationship with mercy, forgiveness, and psychological growth, and as a condition of the possibility for ongoing personal transformation. By contrast, exclusively psychological studies of an isolated faculty of forgiveness (e.g., Worthington and Sandage 2016) cannot illumine changes in the whole self. By the same token, psychological studies of psychospiritual transformation do not account for the central role of the active ego in this process (e.g., Hefner 2006; contrasted here with the approach taken by Bellini), what creates this impres-

---

[1] For a review of phenomenological approaches to subjectivity in psychology, see Zippel 2010. For an example of the adaptation of phenomenological method in qualitative psychological research, see Giorgi 1997. For the practical uses of phenomenology in psychology, see DeRobertis 1996, 2017; Schneider 2010; in psychiatry, see Fuchs and Pallagrosi 2018.

sion of transformation being a "beyond meaning" (Leffel 2011) event of mystical collaboration with the holy spirit (e.g., Bratcher 2018)—that is, an event beyond the scope of psychology—which are classic examples of obfuscated forms of experience in need of phenomenological research.

The subtleties of compound, multifarious organization of meaning in religious experience in its distinction from other forms of experience, including ordinary experience, psychosis, and altered perception—for instance, in hypnosis or under psychedelic therapy—have not been integrated into clinical practice (for examples, see Cottam et al. 2011; DeHoff 2015; and Marriott et al. 2018). Meanwhile, such distinctions are foundational in consideration of normality, normativity, and differential diagnoses. Religious experience has been confused with transference (Sieve 1999), experiences of homogamy (Jackson et al. 2015), epilepsy (Devinsky and Lai 2008), social cognition in group ritual (Barsalou et al. 2005), and otherwise treated reductively. "Reduction" is meant here in a negative sense, such as substituting something that is not for something that is, for example taking an experience of conversion to be a psychotic episode (cf. Kingdon et al. 2010; Alminhana and Moreira-Almeida 2014; Kéri 2017), sending the subject into a psychiatric emergency room and on medications. Other examples of reduction in this sense include the psychoanalytic (e.g., Freudian) reading of religious experience (e.g., Holliman 2002) or reduction to the state of altered perception (e.g., Valla and Prince 1989) and a matter of personal interpretation that is not generalizable and therefore not valid (cf. Spilka and McIntosh 1995). A few decades ago, psychotherapy would simply divest itself of concerns for religious experience by such formulae as "refer spiritual problems outside the domain of psychotherapy to the client's minister" (Sacks 1985, 26). In the last two decades, the interest of psychologists in religious experience grew exponentially, toward more exploratory and less reductionist attitudes (e.g., Lindholm 2014; McNamara 2016; Greene 2017) and sufficiently for therapists to discuss spiritual and religious issues with their clients (e.g., Brown et al. 2013), but a confusion between religious experience and psychosis still remains unresolved (e.g., Huguelet et al. 2010; Hanevik et al. 2017, and many more).

Are these problems with understanding religious experience a confusion, or is something else involved? As Barber (2017) has shown, religion is an emancipating province of meaning. The everyday lifeworld is open to religious sense, but within this world psychology has its own boundaries. Psychology is difficult to categorize as science, but it has been characterized as ideology (Parker 2007); I would like to suggest that on the whole, with its focus on the mind and behavior, practices, institutions, hierarchical relevances, social typification, relationship between people, organization of its professional and clinical communities, codes of ethics, and so on, it is certainly a province of meaning in its own right. (Cf. Ayaß 2017.) Stepping into a therapy office means crossing a boundary from the reality of the everyday life into a virtual space in which one's life conventions will be overturned. In Schutz's view (explicated by Barber in Chap. 8 above), the boundaries between the religious province of meaning and the everyday are permeable and updated on a regular basis. Although the concept of the everyday serves as a gateway into analyses of the social world, the place of psychology in this scheme of things has not been examined. This missing reflection is part of a more general picture: despite ongoing discussions on the email lists of the American Psychological Association, systematic sociological reflections on psychotherapy have been perilously absent after the work of Foucault and Laing: "The relative neglect of psychotherapy, by contrast with the attention historians have paid to other professions, particularly psychiatry, has also under-played its societal impact" (Marks 2017). But even in the absence of such systematic reflection, it has been shown that the orientation of psychology, and of psychotherapy in particular, is pragmatic. (Cf. Cushman 1996) The intentional world of psychology definitely has a boundary (Gelfand et al. 2006). I wish to suggest that psychology occupies its own finite province of meaning. (Cf. Slife and Reber forthcoming.) If this is so, the transactions of meaning between the two provinces—one being the emancipatory province of religion (Barber 2017a, b) and the other being the pragmatic province of psychology—may be quite limited if not strained. (Cf. Renn 2006.)

For example, both Bellini and Trajtelová show not only that the meaning of religious experiences has temporally extended, generalizable structures, but also that such structures exercise a profound constitutive influence on personal consciousness. Both researchers interpret the structures they describe as a necessary condition of possibility for positive transformation and adult development, but such an ontological connection is invisible in the horizon of psychology. (Cf. Dawkins 2016; Greene 2017.) Bellini writes about repentance, which is a topic expelled from psychology: when Leonard Cohen—who, as a poet, "didn't have any confidence in the therapeutic model" and preferred Zen (Bernhard 2001)—sings, "When they said repent, I wonder what they meant" ("The Future"), he means it.

Outside Catholic religious communities, repentance is rarely considered. (Cf. Exline et al. 2017.) Bellini proposes a model according to which the religious experience of repentance destabilizes the self so that the self can both face the deity and find in itself the sources of change. By contrast, in a psychological view, ego destabilization is what we want to avoid: yes, there is posttraumatic growth, but why self-inflict yet another trauma by repentance? But no pain, no gain: one struggles to change, but change does not come. What Bellini demonstrates is that the mind has a natural mechanism that is not optional but constitutive for personal transformation, and if one wants a change, that natural mechanism has to be engaged. Trajtelová shows that natural possibilities of self-reconstitution have been used for centuries by many mystics. In my view, and despite her building parallels with seemingly analogous claims in the existential-humanistic tradition, her findings de facto present a challenge to usual psychotherapeutic practices. Her vision is an ontopoietic one (cf. Louchakova 2005): new identity grows ontologically, from the ground of being, after the ego is effaced. But no therapeutic means can attain the depth of mystical self-effacement or decloaking of passivity to the degree passivity makes itself available in the dark night of the soul. These are deeply theistic states of mind: such experiences are both metaphysical and relational, and Christological, and therefore hard to get to within a nontheistic approach to the mind, which is what psychology predominantly is. (Cf. Slife and Reber forthcoming.) In the psychological sphere, the ego is in control of the relationship it posits with the imaginal other (e.g., in psychological techniques such as the "empty chair" in gestalt therapy, or in creating transferences and projections), but the religious experience of the Other is "in excess," by the invisible law of ethical bonds (as I described in Chap. 11, Part 2), not imaginary but real intimacy. As Trajtelová shows, this intimacy takes place when all the psychological habitualities are suspended, as a process I described earlier in Chap. 6: the self-internalization of subjectivity in the religious sphere.

References

Alminhana, Letícia Oliveira, and Alexander Moreira-Almeida. 2014. Anomalous experiences and schizotypy: A necessary distinction between pathological and non-pathological psychotic experiences. *Psyche en Geloof* 25 (2): 127–134.

Alvis, J.W. 2017. Review of *Phenomenology & mysticism: The verticality of religious experience*, by Anthony Steinbock. *Human Studies* 40(4): 589–598. https://doi.org/10.1007/s10746-016-9412-6. Accessed 30 June 2018.

Ayaß, Ruth. 2017. Life-world, sub-worlds, after-worlds: The various "realnesses" of multiple realities. *Human Studies* 40 (4): 519–542.

Barber, Michael. 2017a. *Religion and humor as emancipating provinces of meaning*. New York: Springer.

———. 2017b. Religion and the appresentative mindset. *Open Theology* 3(1): 397–407. Retrieved 2 July 2018 from doi: https://doi.org/10.1515/opth-2017-0031. Accessed 25 June 2018.

Barsalou, L.W., et al. [Barsalou, L.W., A.K. Barbey, W.K. Simmons, and A. Santos.]. 2005. Embodiment in religious knowledge. *Journal of Cognition and Culture* 5(1–2): 14–57. https://doi.org/10.1163/1568537054068624. Accessed 30 June 2018.

Bernhard, Brendan. 2001. Angst and aquavit. *LA Weekly,* 26 September. http://www.laweekly.com/news/angst-and-aquavit-2133857. Accessed 30 June 2018.

Bratcher, Jeremy K. 2018. *Restor(y)ing discipleship: Using the transformative character arc as a pathway for cooperation with the holy spirit in Christian spiritual formation*. PhD dissertation, Biola University. ProQuest Information & Learning. AAI10682536.

Brown, Ottilia, et al. [Brown, Ottilia, Diane Elkonin, and Samantha Naicker.]. 2013. The use of religion and spirituality in psychotherapy: Enablers and barriers. *Journal of Religion and Health* 52(4): 1131–1146. http://www.jstor.org/stable/24485123. Accessed 30 June 2018.

Cottam, S., et al. [Cottam, S., S.N. Paul, O.J. Doughty, L. Carpenter, D.J. Done, A. Al-Mousawi, and S. Karvounis.]. 2011. Does religious belief enable positive interpretation of auditory hallucinations? A comparison of religious voice hearers with and without psychosis. *Cognitive Neuropsychiatry* 16(5): 403–421.

Cushman, Philip. 1996. *Constructing the self, constructing America*. Lebanon: Da Capo Press.

Davis, Jennifer. 2012. Review of *Phenomenology and mysticism: The verticality of religious experience,* by Anthony J. Steinbock. *Philosophy in Review* 32 (4): 335–336.

Dawkins, III John A. 2016. *Transformed to be transformed: Developing teen missional leaders*. PhD dissertation, Eastern University, ProQuest Dissertations Publishing. 10105461.

de Warren, Nicolas. 2009. Husserl and the promise of time. In *Subjectivity in transcendental phenomenology*. Cambridge: Cambridge University Press.

DeHoff, S.L. 2015. Distinguishing mystical religious experience and psychotic experience: A qualitative study interviewing Presbyterian Church (U.S.A.) professionals. *Pastoral Psychology* 64(1):21–39. doi:https://doi.org/10.1007/s11089-013-0584-y. Accessed 30 June 2018.

DeRobertis, Eugene. 1996. *Phenomenological psychology*. Lanham: University Press of America.

———. 2017. *The phenomenology of learning and becoming*. New York: Palgrave.

Devinsky, O., and G. Lai. 2008. Spirituality and religion in epilepsy. *Epilepsy & Behavior* 12(4): 636–643. doi:https://doi.org/10.1016/j.yebeh.2007.11.011. Accessed 28 June 2018.

Exline, J.J., et al. [Exline, J.J., J.A. Wilt, N. Stauner, V.A. Harriott, and S.N. Saritoprak.]. 2017. Self-forgiveness and religious/spiritual struggles. In *Handbook of the psychology of self-forgiveness,* ed. L. Woodyat et al, 131–145. Cham: Springer. https://doi.org/10.1007/978-3-319-60573-9_10. Accessed 28 June 2018.

Feest, Uljana. 2014. The continuing relevance of nineteenth-century philosophy of psychology: Brentano and the autonomy of psychological methods. In *New directions in the philosophy of science,* ed. M.C. Galavotti and F. Stadler, 693–709. Dordrecht: Springer.

Flakne, April N. 2017. Is direct perception arrogant perception? Toward a critical, playful intercorporeity. In Helen Fielding and Dorothea E. Olkowski, eds., Feminist phenomenology futures, 277–298. Bloomington: Indiana University Press. http://www.jstor.org/stable/j.ctt2005vm7.19. Accessed 28 June 2018.

Fuchs, Thomas, and Mauro Pallagrosi. 2018. Phenomenology of temporality and dimensional psychopathology. In *Dimensional psychopathology*, ed. Massimo Biondi et al., 287–300. Cham: Springer.

Fuller, Jonathan. 2013. Rhetoric and argumentation: How clinical practice guidelines think. *Journal of Evaluation in Clinical Practice* 19 (3): 433–441.

García-Prada, J.M. 1990. The "life-world" and the crisis of psychology. In *Man's self-interpretation-in-existence,* ed. A.T. Tymieniecka. Analecta Husserliana: The yearbook of phenomenological research 29: 285–297. Dordrecht: Springer.

Gasché, Rodolphe. 2017. Breaking with the primacy of the theoretical. In *Persuasion, reflection, judgment: Ancillae vitae,* Rodolphe Gasché 73–87. Bloomington: Indiana University Press. http://www.jstor.org/stable/j.ctt2005wvb.10. Accessed 28 June 2018.

Gelfand, Michele J., et al. [Gelfand, Michele J., Lisa H. Nishii, and Jana L. Raver.]. 2006. On the nature and importance of cultural tightness-looseness. *Journal of Applied Psychology* 91(6): 1225–1244.

Giorgi, A. 1997. The theory, practice, and evaluation of the phenomenological method as a qualitative research procedure. *Journal of Phenomenological Psychology* 28 (2): 235–260.

Goldman, Alvin, and Thomas Blanchard. 2018. Social epistemology. In *The Stanford encyclopedia of philosophy* (summer edition), ed. Edward N. Zalta.. https://plato.stanford.edu/archives/sum2018/entries/epistemology-social/.

Gough, B., and A. Madill. 2012. Subjectivity in psychological science: From problem to prospect. *Psychololgical Methods* 17 (3): 374–384. https://doi.org/10.1037/a0029313. Accessed 28 June 2018.

Greene, R. 2017. *The religious and spiritual healing capacity of the transcendent function and its application in clinical treatment.* PhD dissertation, William James College. ProQuest Information & Learning. AAI10186350.

Hanevik, Hilde, et al. [Hanevik, Hilde, Knut A. Hestad, Lars Lien, Inge Joa, Tor Ketil Larsen, and Lars Johan Danbolt.]. 2017. Religiousness in first-episode psychosis. *Archiv für Religionspsychologie/Archive for the Psychology of Religions* 39(1): 1–26.

Hefner, Philip. 2006. Spiritual transformation and healing: An encounter with the sacred. In *Spiritual transformation and healing: Anthropological, theological, neuroscientific, and clinical perspectives*, ed. Joan D. Koss-Chioino and Philip Hefner, 119–133. Walnut Creek: AltaMira Press.

Holliman, P.J. 2002. Religious experience as selfobject experience. In A. Goldberg, ed., Postmodern self psychology, 193–205. New York: The Analytic Press. https://search.proquest.com/docvie w/620015726?accountid=14505. Accessed 30 June 2018.

Hösle, Vittorio. 2017. The search for a foundation of the human sciences and the social sciences in neo-Kantianism and Dilthey, and Husserl's exploration of consciousness. In *A Short History of German Philosophy,* ed. V. Hösle. Trans. Steven Rendall, 193–216. Princeton: Princeton University press. http://www.jstor.org/stable/j.ctt1q1xqxv.16. Accessed 30 June 2018.

Huguelet, P., et al. [Huguelet, P., S. Mohr, C. Gilliéron, P.-Y. Brandt, and L. Borras.]. 2010. Religious explanatory models in patients with psychosis: A three-year follow-up study. *Psychopathology* 43(4): 230–239.

Hutcheson, Peter. 1981. Solipsistic and intersubjective phenomenology. *Human Studies* 4(2): 165–178. http://www.jstor.org/stable/20008799. Accessed 27 June 2018.

Jackson, J., et al. [Jackson, J., J. Halberstadt, J. Jong, and H. Felman.]. 2015. Perceived openness to experience accounts for religious homogamy. *Social Psychological and Personality Science* 6(6): 630–638. doi:https://doi.org/10.1177/1948550615574302. Accessed 30 June 2018.

Jones, Ward E. 2003. Is scientific theory-commitment doxastic or practical? Synthese 137(3):325–344. http://www.jstor.org/stable/20118366. Accessed 28 June 2018.

Jopling, David A. 1996. Sub-phenomenology. Human Studies 19(2):153–173. http://www.jstor.org/stable/20011102. Accessed 28 June 2018.

Kéri, Szabolcs. 2017. Self-transformation at the boundary of religious conversion and psychosis. *Journal of Religion and Health* (September 15). https://doi.org/10.1007/s10943-017-0496-8. Accessed 30 June 2018.

Kingdon, D., et al. [Kingdon, D., R. Siddle, F. Naeem, and S. Rathod.]. 2010. Spirituality, psychosis, and the development of 'normalizing rationales.' In *Psychosis and spirituality—Consolidating the new paradigm,* ed. I. Clarke, 239–248. Chichester: Wiley.

Leffel, G. Michael. 2011. Beyond meaning: Spiritual transformation in the paradigm of moral intuitionism; A new direction for the psychology of spiritual transformation—Introduction. In Ralph L. Piedmont and Andrew Village, eds. *Research in the Social Scientific Study of Religion* 22: 25–28. http://booksandjournals.brillonline.com/content/books/10.1163/ej.9789004207271.i-360.14. Accessed 28 June 2018.

Lindholm, J.A. 2014. The quest for meaning and wholeness: Spiritual and religious connections in the lives of college faculty San Francisco: Jossey-Bass. https://search.proquest.com/docview/1653147653?accountid=14505. Accessed 28 June 2018.

Louchakova, O. 2005. Ontopoiesis and union in the prayer of the heart: Contributions to psychotherapy and learning. In *Logos of phenomenology and phenomenology of the logos. Book four: The logos of scientific interrogation; Participating in nature–life–sharing in life,* ed. A.-T. Tymieniecka. Analecta Husserliana: The yearbook of phenomenological research 91: 289–311. Dordrecht: Kluwer.

Marks, S. 2017. Psychotherapy in historical perspective. *History of the Human Sciences* 30(2): 3–16. https://doi.org/10.1177/0952695117703243. Accessed 18 June 2018.

Marriott, Michael R., et al. [Marriott, Michael R., Andrew R. Thompson, Graham Cockshutt, and Georgina Rowse.]. 2018. Narrative insight in psychosis: The relationship with spiritual and religious explanatory frameworks. *Psychology and Psychotherapy: Theory, Research and Practice* (March 25): https://doi.org/10.1111/papt.12178. Accessed 25 June 2018.

McNamara, P. 2016. *Dreams and visions: How religious ideas emerge in sleep and dreams.* Santa Barbara: Praeger/ABC-CLIO. https://search.proquest.com/docview/1890138732?accountid=14505. Accessed 28 June 2018.

Migasiński, Jacek. 2003. Rozumność i philoosphia. *Roczniki Filozoficzne /Annales de Philosophie / Annals of Philosophy* 51(1): 209–217. http://www.jstor.org/stable/43408472. Accessed 28 June 2018.

Osborn, Andrew D. 1934. Some recent German critics of phenomenology. *The Journal of Philosophy* 31 (14): 377–382. https://doi.org/10.2307/2015614. Accessed 25 June 2018.

Parker, Ian. 2007. Psychology as ideology: Individualism explained. In *Revolution in psychology: Alienation to emancipation,* ed. Ian Parker, 33–54. London: Pluto Press. https://doi.org/10.2307/j.ctt18dztgn.6. Accessed January 6, 2018.

Peterson, C. 2009. *Subjective and objective research in positive psychology.* Posted 23 May 2009. https://www.psychologytoday.com/us/blog/the-good-life/200905/subjective-and-objective-research-in-positive-psychology. Accessed 29 June 2018.

Properzi, Mauro. 2012. Exploring psychology and religious rxperience: Relevant issues and core questions. *Issues in Religion and Psychotherapy* 34(1): article 9.. https://scholarsarchive.byu.edu/irp/vol34/iss1/9. Accessed 30 June 2018.

Renn, Joachim. 2006. Appresentation and simultaneity: Alfred Schutz on communication between phenomenology and pragmatics. *Human Studies* 29(1): 1–19. http://www.jstor.org/stable/27642733. Accessed 28 June 2018.

Sacks, Joseph M. 1985. Religious issues in psychotherapy. *Journal of Religion and Health* 24(1): 26–30. http://www.jstor.org/stable/27505803. Accessed 28 June 2018.

Schneider, Kirk. 2010. Existential psychotherapy. In *Corsini encyclopedia of philosophy*. Wiley online library. https://doi.org/10.1002/9780470479216.corpsy2005. Accessed 28 June 2018.

Sieve, C.B. 1999. *Countertransference experiences in the analysis of religious material in psychoanalytic psychotherapy: An intersubjective analysis*. PhD dissertation, Massachusetts School of Professional Psychology. ProQuest Information & Learning. AEH9930451.

Slife, B.D., and J.S. Reber. Forthcoming. Against methodological confinement. *Psychology of Religion and Spirituality*.

Smith, Bruce R. 2012. Afterword: Phenomophobia; or, who is afraid of Merleau-Ponty? *Criticism* 54(3): 479–483. http://www.jstor.org/stable/23267676. Accessed 28 June 2018.

Spilka, B., and D.N. McIntosh. 1995. Attribution theory and religious experience. In *Handbook of religious experience*, ed. R.W. Hood, Jr., 421–445. Birmingham: Religious Education Press. https://search.proquest.com/docview/618772904?accountid=14505. Accessed 28 June 2018.

Valla, J., and R.H. Prince. 1989. Religious experiences as self-healing mechanisms. In *Altered states of consciousness and mental health*, ed. C.A. Ward, 149–166. Thousand Oaks: Sage.

Worthington, Everett L., Jr., and Steven J. Sandage. 2016. *Forgiveness and spirituality in psychotherapy: A relational approach*. Washington, DC: American Psychological Association. doi:https://doi.org/10.1037/14712-000. Accessed 28 June 2018.

Zippel, Nicola. 2010. The way to the subject between phenomenology and psychology. *Philosophy Today* 54 (Suppl): 128–134.

Olga Louchakova-Schwartz, M.D. Ph.D. (the editor) is a comparative religionist, philosopher, and interdisciplinary researcher. She holds the titles Professor of Philosophy of Religion, Spirituality, and Human Development at the Hult International Business School, and Clinical Professor at the UC Davis School of Medicine, Department of Public Health Sciences. She is also a Visiting Scholar at the Graduate Theological Union in Berkeley, Adjunct Lecturer in Spirituality and Phenomenology of Religion at the Jesuit School of Theology, and a Founding President of the Society for the Phenomenology of Religions Experience. Prior to her work in philosophy, she was a senior scientist at the Pavlov Institute of the Academy of Sciences in Russia, and after that, Director of Research and the Founding Director of the Neurophenomenology Center at the former Institute of Transpersonal Psychology, from which she holds the title Professor Emerita of Psychology and Comparative Religion. She studied phenomenology with Amedeo and Barbro Giorgi and with Anna-Teresa Tymieniecka, Her chief research interests are in religious subjectivity and religious experience in contemporary and historical contexts. She has published on fifteenth century and contemporary Kundalini Tantra, eighth century Advaita Vedanta and Neo-Vedanta, early Christianity, seventh–tenth century Hesychasm, contemporary Turkish and American Sufism, the Soviet spiritual underground, and the Islamic Philosophy of Illumination. Her cognitive phenomenological research of Tibetan Tantric meditation was featured on BBC, Science Daily, and other important forums. She has published more than 200 papers and book chapters, and is an Associate Editor of the Journal of Theoretical and Philosophical Psychology, and guest editor for Open Theology, De Gruyter (2017; 2018, 2019, 2020 to appear).

Printed by Books on Demand, Germany